iOS Programming
THE BIG NERD RANCH GUIDE

JOE CONWAY & AARON HILLEGASS

BiG
nerD
ranch

iOS Programming: The Big Nerd Ranch Guide

by Joe Conway and Aaron Hillegass

Big Nerd Ranch, Inc.
1989 College Ave.
Atlanta, GA 30317
(404) 478-9005
http://www.bignerdranch.com/
book-comments@bignerdranch.com

The 10-gallon hat with propeller logo is a trademark of Big Nerd Ranch, Inc.

Exclusive worldwide distribution of the English edition of this book by

Pearson Technology Group
800 East 96th Street
Indianapolis, IN 46240 USA
http://www.informit.com

ISBN-10 0321821521
ISBN-13 978-0321821522

Third edition, second printing, August 2012

Acknowledgments

While our names appear on the cover, many people helped make this book a reality. We would like to take this chance to thank them.

- The other instructors who teach the iOS Bootcamp fed us with a never-ending stream of suggestions and corrections. They are Scott Ritchie, Brian Hardy, Mikey Ward, Christian Keur, Alex Silverman, Owen Matthews, Brian Turner, Juan Pablo Claude, and Bolot Kerimbaev.

- Our tireless editor, Susan Loper, took our distracted mumblings and made them into readable prose.

- Our technical reviewers, Bill Monk and Jawwad Ahmad, helped us find and fix flaws.

- Ellie Volckhausen designed the cover. (The photo is of the bottom bracket of a bicycle frame.)

- Chris Loper at IntelligentEnglish.com designed and produced the print book and the EPUB and Kindle versions.

- The amazing team at Pearson Technology Group patiently guided us through the business end of book publishing.

The final and most important thanks goes to our students whose questions inspired us to write this book and whose frustrations inspired us to make it clear and comprehensible.

Table of Contents

Introduction

An aspiring iOS developer faces three basic hurdles:

- *You must learn the Objective-C language.* Objective-C is a small and simple extension to the C language. After the first four chapters of this book, you will have a working knowledge of Objective-C.

- *You must master the big ideas.* These include things like memory management techniques, delegation, archiving, and the proper use of view controllers. The big ideas take a few days to understand. When you reach the halfway point of this book, you will understand these big ideas.

- *You must master the frameworks.* The eventual goal is to know how to use every method of every class in every framework in iOS. This is a project for a lifetime: there are over 3000 methods and more than 200 classes available in iOS. To make things even worse, Apple adds new classes and new methods with every release of iOS. In this book, you will be introduced to each of the subsystems that make up the iOS SDK, but we will not study each one deeply. Instead, our goal is get you to the point where you can search and understand Apple's reference documentation.

We have used this material many times at our iOS Development Bootcamp at Big Nerd Ranch. It is well-tested and has helped hundreds of people become iOS application developers. We sincerely hope that it proves useful to you.

Prerequisites

This book assumes that you are already motivated to learn to write iOS apps. We won't spend any time convincing you that the iPhone, the iPad, and the iPod touch are compelling pieces of technology.

We also assume that you know the C programming language and something about object-oriented programming. If this is not true, you should probably start with an introductory book on C and Objective-C, such as *Objective-C Programming: The Big Nerd Ranch Guide*.

What's Changed in the Third Edition?

This edition assumes that the reader is using Xcode 4.3 and running applications on an iOS 5 device or simulator.

With iOS 5, automatic reference counting (ARC) is the default memory management for iOS. We've redone the memory management chapter to address ARC, and we use ARC throughout the book.

You'll find new chapters on using gesture recognizers, storyboards, **NSRegularExpression**, and iCloud. We've also added two chapters dedicated to the the Model-View-Controller-Store design pattern, which we use at Big Nerd Ranch and believe is well-suited for many iOS applications.

Besides these obvious changes, we made thousands of tiny improvements that were inspired by questions from our readers and our students. Every page of this book is just a little better than the corresponding page from the second edition.

Our Teaching Philosophy

This book will teach you the essential concepts of iOS programming. At the same time, you'll type in a lot of code and build a bunch of applications. By the end of the book, you'll have knowledge *and* experience. However, all the knowledge shouldn't (and, in this book, won't) come first. That's sort of the traditional way we've all come to know and hate. Instead, we take a learn-while-doing approach. Development concepts and actual coding go together.

Here's what we've learned over the years of teaching iOS programming:

- We've learned what ideas people must have to get started programming, and we focus on that subset.

- We've learned that people learn best when these concepts are introduced *as they are needed*.

- We've learned that programming knowledge and experience grow best when they grow together.

- We've learned that "going through the motions" is much more important than it sounds. Many times we'll ask you to start typing in code before you understand it. We get that you may feel like a trained monkey typing in a bunch of code that you don't fully grasp. But the best way to learn coding is to find and fix your typos. Far from being a drag, this basic debugging is where you really learn the ins and outs of the code. That's why we encourage you to type in the code yourself. You could just download it, but copying and pasting is not programming. We want better for you and your skills.

What does this mean for you, the reader? To learn this way takes some trust. And we appreciate yours. It also takes patience. As we lead you through these chapters, we will try to keep you comfortable and tell you what's happening. However, there will be times when you'll have to take our word for it. (If you think this will bug you, keep reading – we've got some ideas that might help.) Don't get discouraged if you run across a concept that you don't understand right away. Remember that we're intentionally *not* providing all the knowledge you will ever need all at once. If a concept seems unclear, we will likely discuss it in more detail later when it becomes necessary. And some things that aren't clear at the beginning will suddenly make sense when you implement them the first (or the twelfth) time.

People learn differently. It's possible that you will love how we hand out concepts on an as-needed basis. It's also possible that you'll find it frustrating. In case of the latter, here are some options:

- Take a deep breath and wait it out. We'll get there, and so will you.

- Check the index. We'll let it slide if you look ahead and read through a more advanced discussion that occurs later in the book.

- Check the online Apple documentation. This is an essential developer tool, and you'll want plenty of practice using it. Consult it early and often.

- If it's Objective-C or object-oriented programming concepts that are giving you a hard time (or if you think they will), you might consider backing up and reading our *Objective-C Programming: The Big Nerd Ranch Guide*.

How To Use This Book

This book is based on the class we teach at Big Nerd Ranch. As such, it was designed to be consumed in a certain manner.

Set yourself a reasonable goal, like "I will do one chapter every day." When you sit down to attack a chapter, find a quiet place where you won't be interrupted for at least an hour. Shut down your email, your Twitter client, and your chat program. This is not a time for multi-tasking; you will need to concentrate.

Do the actual programming. You can read through a chapter first, if you'd like. But the real learning comes when you sit down and code as you go. You will not really understand the idea until you have written a program that uses it and, perhaps more importantly, debugged that program.

A couple of the exercises require supporting files. For example, in the first chapter you will need an icon for your Quiz application, and we have one for you. You can download the resources and solutions to the exercises from `http://www.bignerdranch.com/solutions/iOSProgramming3ed.zip`.

There are two types of learning. When you learn about the Civil War, you are simply adding details to a scaffolding of ideas that you already understand. This is what we will call "Easy Learning". Yes, learning about the Civil War can take a long time, but you are seldom flummoxed by it. Learning iOS programming, on the other hand, is "Hard Learning," and you may find yourself quite baffled at times, especially in the first few days. In writing this book, we have tried to create an experience that will ease you over the bumps in the learning curve. Here are two things you can do to make the journey easier:

- Find someone who already knows how to write iOS applications and will answer your questions. In particular, getting your application onto the device the first time is usually very frustrating if you are doing it without the help of an experienced developer.

- Get enough sleep. Sleepy people don't remember what they have learned.

How This Book Is Organized

In this book, each chapter addresses one or more ideas of iOS development followed by hands-on practice. For more coding practice, we issue challenges towards the end of each chapter. We encourage you to take on at least some of these. They are excellent for firming up the concepts introduced in the chapter and making you a more confident iOS programmer. Finally, most chapters conclude with one or two "For the More Curious" sections that explain certain consequences of the concepts that were introduced earlier.

Chapter 1 introduces you to iOS programming as you build and deploy a tiny application. You'll get your feet wet with Xcode and the iOS simulator along with all the steps for creating projects and files. The chapter includes a discussion of Model-View-Controller and how it relates to iOS development.

Chapters 2 and 3 provide an overview of Objective-C and memory management. Although you won't create an iOS application in these two chapters, you will build and debug a tool called RandomPossessions to ground you in these concepts.

In Chapters 4 and 5, you will learn about the Core Location and MapKit frameworks and create a mapping application called Whereami. You will also get plenty of experience with the important design pattern of delegation as well as working with protocols, frameworks, object diagrams, the debugger, and the Apple documentation.

Chapters 6 and 7 focus on the iOS user interface with the Hypnosister and HypnoTime applications. You will get lots of practice working with views and view controllers as well as implementing panning, zooming, and navigating between screens using a tab bar.

In Chapter 8, you will create a smaller application named HeavyRotation while learning about notifications and how to implement autorotation in an application. You will also use autoresizing to make HeavyRotation iPad-friendly.

Chapter 9 introduces the largest application in the book – Homepwner. (By the way, "Homepwner" is not a typo; you can find the definition of "pwn" at www.urbandictionary.com.) This application keeps a record of your possessions in case of fire or other catastrophe. Homepwner will take nine chapters total to complete.

In Chapters 9, 10, and 15, you will build experience with tables. You will learn about table views, their view controllers, and their data sources. You will learn how to display data in a table, how to allow the user to edit the table, and how to improve the interface.

Chapter 11 builds on the navigation experience gained in Chapter 7. You will learn how to use **UINavigationController**, and you will give Homepwner a drill-down interface and a navigation bar.

In Chapter 12, you'll learn how to take pictures with the camera and how to display and store images in Homepwner. You'll use **NSDictionary** and **UIImagePickerController**.

In Chapter 13, you'll learn about **UIPopoverController** for the iPad and modal view controllers. In addition, you will make Homepwner a universal application – an application that runs natively on both the iPhone and the iPad.

Chapter 14 delves into ways to save and load data. In particular, you will archive data in the Homepwner application using the **NSCoding** protocol. The chapter also explains the transitions between application states, such as active, background, and suspended.

Chapter 16 is an introduction to Core Data. You will change the Homepwner application to store and load its data using an **NSManagedObjectContext**.

Chapter 17 introduces the concepts and techniques of internationalization and localization. You will learn about **NSLocale**, strings tables, and **NSBundle** as you localize parts of Homepwner. This chapter will complete the Homepwner application.

In Chapter 18, you will use **NSUserDefaults** to save user preferences in a persistent manner.

In Chapters 19 and 20, you'll create a drawing application named TouchTracker to learn about touch events. You'll see how to add multi-touch capability and how to use **UIGestureRecognizer** to respond to particular gestures. You'll also get experience with the first responder and responder chain concepts and more practice with **NSDictionary**.

In Chapter 21, you'll learn how to use Instruments to optimize the performance of your applications. This chapter also includes explanations of Xcode schemes and the static analyzer.

Chapters 22 and 23 introduce layers and the Core Animation framework with a brief return to the HypnoTime application to implement animations. You will learn about implicit animations and animation objects, like **CABasicAnimation** and **CAKeyframeAnimation**.

Chapter 24 covers a new feature of iOS for building applications called storyboards. You'll piece together an application using **UIStoryboard** and learn more about the pros and cons of using storyboards to construct your applications.

Chapter 25 ventures into the wide world of web services as you create the Nerdfeed application. This application fetches and parses an RSS feed from a server using **NSURLConnection** and **NSXMLParser**. Nerdfeed will also display a web page in a **UIWebView**.

In Chapter 26, you will learn about **UISplitViewController** and add a split view user interface to Nerdfeed to take advantage of the iPad's larger screen size.

Chapter 27 will teach you about the how and why of blocks – an increasingly important feature of the iOS SDK. You'll create a simple application to prepare for using blocks in Nerdfeed in the next chapter.

In Chapters 28 and 29, you will change the architecture of the Nerdfeed application so that it uses the Model-View-Controller-Store design pattern. You'll learn about request logic and how to best design an application that communicates with external sources of data.

In Chapter 30, you'll learn how to enable an application to use iCloud to synchronize and back up data across a user's iOS devices.

Style Choices

This book contains a lot of code. We have attempted to make that code and the designs behind it exemplary. We have done our best to follow the idioms of the community, but at times we have wandered from what you might see in Apple's sample code or code you might find in other books. You may not understand these points now, but it is best that we spell them out before you commit to reading this book:

• There is an alternative syntax for calling accessor methods known as *dot-notation*. In this book, we will explain dot-notation, but we will not use it. For us and for most beginners, dot-notation tends to obfuscate what is really happening.

• In our subclasses of **UIViewController**, we always change the designated initializer to **init**. It is our opinion that the creator of the instance should not need to know the name of the XIB file that the view controller uses, or even if it has a XIB file at all.

• We will always create view controllers programmatically. Some programmers will instantiate view controllers inside XIB files. We've found this practice leads to projects that are difficult to comprehend and debug.

• We will nearly always start a project with the simplest template project: the empty application. The boilerplate code in the other template projects doesn't follow the rules that precede this one, so we think they make a poor basis upon which to build.

We believe that following these rules makes our code easier to understand and easier to maintain. After you have worked through this book (where you *will* do it our way), you should try breaking the rules to see if we're wrong.

Typographical Conventions

To make this book easier to read, certain items appear in certain fonts. Class names, method names, and function names appear in a bold, fixed-width font. Class names start with capital letters, and method names start with lowercase letters. In this book, method and function names will be formatted the same for simplicity's sake. For example, "In the **loadView** method of the **RexViewController** class, use the **NSLog** function to print the value to the console."

Variables, constants, and types appear in a fixed-width font but are not bold. So you'll see, "The variable fido will be of type float. Initialize it to M_PI."

Applications and menu choices appear in the Mac system font. For example, "Open Xcode and select New Project... from the File menu."

All code blocks will be in a fixed-width font. Code that you need to type in is always bold. For example, in the following code, you would type in everything but the first and last lines. (Those lines are already in the code and appear here to let you know where to add the new stuff.)

```
@interface QuizAppDelegate : NSObject <UIApplicationDelegate> {
    int currentQuestionIndex;

    // The model objects
    NSMutableArray *questions;
    NSMutableArray *answers;

    // The view objects
    IBOutlet UILabel *questionField;
    IBOutlet UILabel *answerField;
    UIWindow *window;
}
```

Necessary Hardware and Software

You can only develop iOS apps on an Intel Mac. You will need to download Apple's iOS SDK, which includes Xcode (Apple's Integrated Development Environment), the iOS simulator, and other development tools.

You should join Apple's iOS Developer Program, which costs $99/year, for three reasons:

- Downloading the latest developer tools is free for members.

- Only signed apps will run on a device, and only members can sign apps. If you want to test your app on your device, you will need to join.

- You can't put an app in the store until you are a member.

If you are going to take the time to work through this entire book, membership in the iOS Developer Program is, without question, worth the cost. Go to http://developer.apple.com/programs/ios/ to join.

What about iOS devices? Most of the applications you will develop in the first half of the book are for the iPhone, but you will be able to run them on an iPad. On the iPad screen, iPhone applications appear in an iPhone-sized window. Not a compelling use of the iPad, but that's okay when you're starting with iOS. In these first chapters, you'll be focused on learning the fundamentals of the iOS SDK, and these are the same across iOS devices. Later in the book, we'll look at some iPad-only options and how to make applications run natively on both iOS device families.

Excited yet? Good. Let's get started.

1

A Simple iOS Application

In this chapter, you are going to write your first iOS application. You probably won't understand everything that you are doing, and you may feel stupid just going through the motions. But going through the motions is enough for now. Mimicry is a powerful form of learning; it is how you learned to speak, and it is how you'll start iOS programming. As you become more capable, you can experiment and challenge yourself to do creative things on the platform. For now, just do what we show you. The details will be explained in later chapters.

When you are writing an iOS application, you must answer two basic questions:

- How do I get my objects created and configured properly? (Example: "I want a button here entitled Show Estimate.")

- How do I deal with user interaction? (Example: "When the user presses the button, I want this piece of code to be executed.")

Most of this book is dedicated to answering these questions.

When an iOS application starts, it puts a *view* on the screen. You can think of this view as the background on which everything else appears: buttons, labels, etc. Buttons and labels are also views. In fact, anything that can appear to the user is a view.

The iOS SDK is an object-oriented library, and views are represented by objects. Each view is an instance of one of several subclasses of the **UIView** class. For example, a button is an instance of **UIButton**, which is a subclass of **UIView**. (We will discuss objects, instances, and classes in detail in Chapter 2.)

For your first iOS application, you will visually create and configure your view objects. This application, called Quiz, will show a user a question and then reveal the answer when the user presses a button. Pressing another button will show a new question (Figure 1.1).

Figure 1.1   Your first application: Quiz

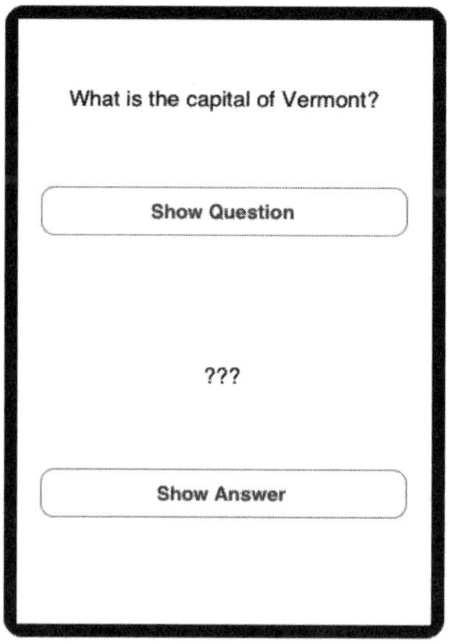

Creating an Xcode Project

Open Xcode and, from the File menu, select New and then New Project....

A new workspace window will appear, and a sheet will slide from its toolbar with several application templates to choose from. On the lefthand side, select Application from the iOS section. From the choices that appear, select Single View Application and press the Next button (Figure 1.2). (Apple changes these templates and their names often. If you do not see the same options for selecting a template, either now or later in the book, check our forums at http://forums.bignerdranch.com for instructions on how to proceed.)

Figure 1.2   Creating a new project

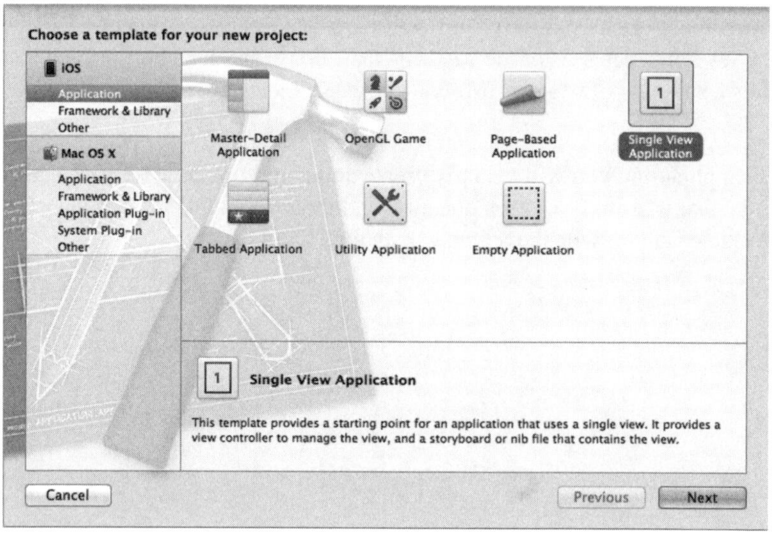

On the next pane, enter Quiz for the Product Name and com.bignerdranch as the Company Identifier. (Or replace bignerdranch with your company name). Enter Quiz in the Class Prefix field, and from the pop-up menu labeled Device Family, select iPhone. We only want the box labeled Use Automatic Reference Counting checked, so uncheck the others. Once your screen looks like Figure 1.3, press Next.

Figure 1.3   Naming a new project

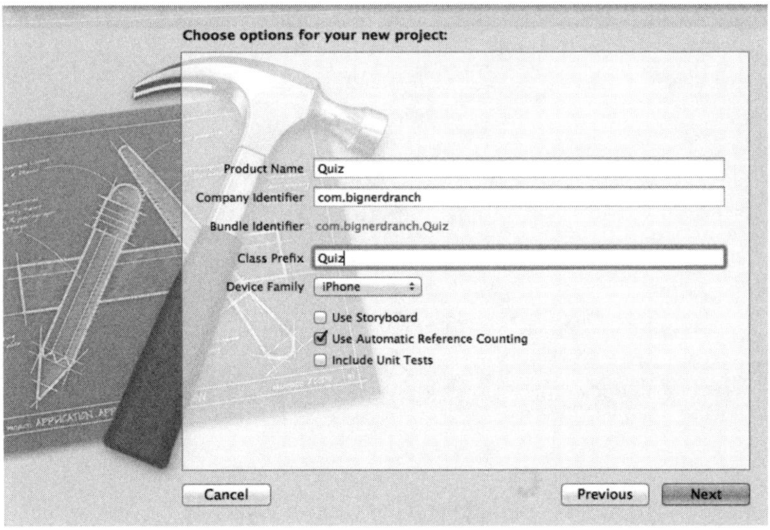

We chose iPhone for this application's device family, but Quiz will run on the iPad, too. It will run in an iPhone-sized window that does not make the most of the iPad screen, but that's okay for now. For the applications in the first part of this book, we will stick with the iPhone device family template. In these chapters, you'll be focused on learning the fundamentals of the iOS SDK, and these are the same across devices. Later, we will look at some iPad-only options and how to make applications run natively on both iOS device families.

Now another sheet will appear asking you to save the project. Save the project in the directory where you plan to store all of the exercises in this book. You can uncheck the box that creates a local git repository, but keeping it checked doesn't hurt anything.

Once the project is created, it will open in the Xcode workspace window (Figure 1.4).

Figure 1.4   Xcode workspace window

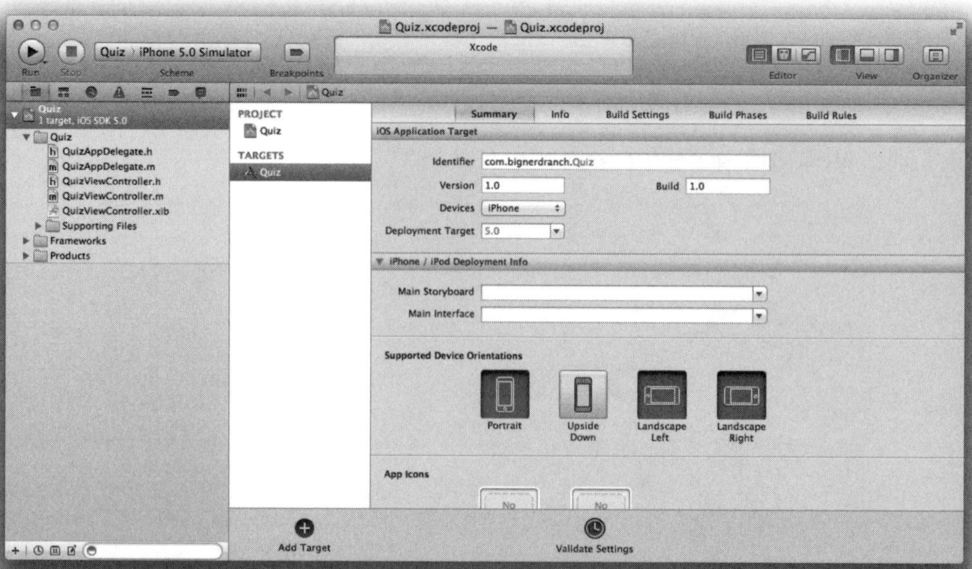

(Feeling overwhelmed by the number of buttons, views, and gadgets in the workspace? Don't worry – in this chapter, we'll cover a few in detail, and we'll cover others later as they are needed. In the meantime, you can mouse over any of the buttons for a brief description of what it does.)

Take a look at the lefthand side of the workspace window. This area is called the navigator area, and it displays different *navigators* – tools that show you different pieces of your project. You can choose which navigator to use by selecting one of the icons in the navigator selector, which is the bar just above the navigator area.

The navigator currently open is the *project navigator*. (If the project navigator is not visible, click the ▄ icon in the navigator selector.) The project navigator shows you the files that make up your project (Figure 1.5). These files can be grouped into folders to help you organize your project. A few groups have been created by the template for you; you can rename them whatever you want or add new ones. The groups are purely for the organization of files and do not correlate to the filesystem in any way.

Figure 1.5   Quiz application's files in the project navigator

Building Interfaces

Now you're going to create the user interface for Quiz using Xcode's visual tool for building interfaces. In many GUI builders on other platforms, you describe what you want an application to look like and then press a button to generate a bunch of code. Xcode's interface builder is different. It is an object editor: you create and configure view objects and then save them into an archive. The archive is a XIB (pronounced "zib") file.

A XIB file is an XML representation of the archived objects. When you build a project, the XIB file is compiled into a NIB file. Developers work with XIB files (they're easier to edit), and applications use NIB files (they're smaller and easier to parse). However, most iOS developers use the words XIB and NIB interchangeably.

When you build an application, the compiled NIB file is copied into the application's *bundle*. The bundle is a directory containing the application's executable and any resources the executable uses.

When your application reads in, or loads, the NIB file from the bundle at runtime, the objects in the archive are brought to life. Your first application will have only one NIB file, and it will be loaded when the application first launches. A complex application, however, can have many NIB files that are loaded as they are needed.

In the project navigator, find and select the file named `QuizViewController.xib`. When you open this (or any) XIB file from the project navigator, the editor area displays a dock view and a canvas. The dock view is on the lefthand side of the editor area, and it shows the objects in the XIB file. You can expand the dock view into an outline by clicking the disclosure button in the bottom left corner of the canvas (Figure 1.6). The dock shows fewer details and is useful when screen real estate is running low. However, for learning purposes, it is easier to see what is going on in the outline view.

Figure 1.6   Editing a XIB file in Xcode

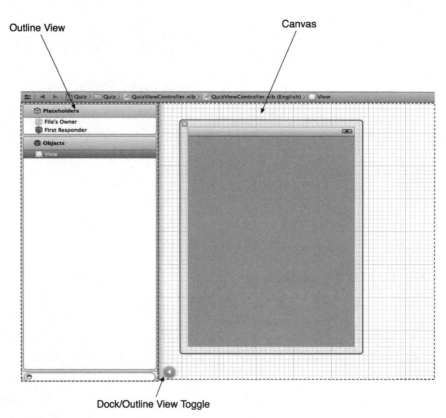

Right now, the outline view shows that QuizViewController.xib contains three objects:

File's Owner
: This is the object that will have access to the objects archived in the XIB file. It will be an instance of **QuizViewController**, which is the object responsible for managing events that occur on this interface.

First Responder
: This object doesn't have much use in iOS right now; it is a relic from Desktop Cocoa. You can ignore it.

View
: An instance of **UIView** that represents the application interface.

The canvas portion of the editor area is for viewing and manipulating the layout of your interface. Click on the View object in the outline view to display it on the canvas. You can move the view by dragging in the blue-shaded area around it. Note that moving the view doesn't change anything about the actual object; it just re-organizes the canvas. You can also close the view by clicking on the x in its top left corner. Again, this doesn't delete the view; it just removes it from the canvas. You can get it back by selecting it again in the outline view.

The view object in Figure 1.6 is the foundation of your user interface and appears exactly as it will in your application. Flip back to Figure 1.1, and you'll see that Quiz needs four additional interface elements: two text labels and two buttons.

To add these elements, you need to get to the *utilities area*. In the top-right corner of Xcode's toolbar, find the ▣▣▣ buttons labeled View. These buttons toggle the navigator, debug area, and utilities area. Click the right button to reveal the utilities area (Figure 1.4).

The utilities area appears to the right of the editor area and has two sections: the *inspector* and the *library*. The top section is the inspector, which contains settings for the file that is currently displayed in the editor area. The bottom section is the library, which lists items you can add to a file or project. You can change the relative sizes of these sections by dragging the line between them.

At the top of each section is a selector for different types of inspectors and libraries (Figure 1.7). From the library selector, select the ❀ icon to reveal the *object library*. This library contains the objects you can add to a XIB file.

Figure 1.7   Xcode utilities area

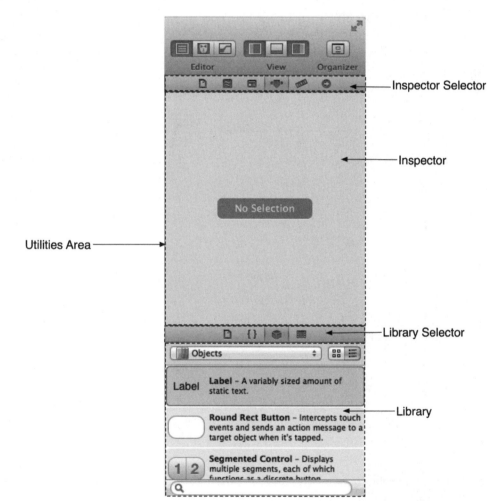

In the library, find the Label object. (It may be right at the top; if not, scroll down the list or use the search bar at the bottom of the library.) Then select the label in the library and drag it onto the view object that is already on the canvas. Position this label in the center of the view, near the top. Your interface now includes a label, and in the outline view, notice that there is now a Label underneath the View.

Next, drag another label onto the view and position it in the center closer to the bottom. Then, find Round Rect Button in the library and drag two buttons onto the view. Position one below each label. You can resize an object by selecting it and then dragging its corners and edges. Make all four objects wide enough that they span most of the window.

Now let's give the buttons helpful titles. You can edit the title of a button simply by double-clicking it. Change the top button to Show Question and the bottom button to Show Answer. You can edit the text of a label the same way; delete the text in the top label so that it is blank and have the bottom label display ???. Your interface should look like the one in Figure 1.8.

Figure 1.8   Adding buttons and labels to the view

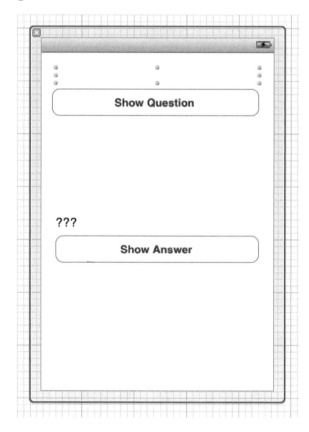

The labels and buttons are objects (of type **UILabel** and **UIButton**), and objects have instance variables that specify their behavior and appearance. For example, when you entered a title for the top button, you set that button's title instance variable. You can edit a few of these instance variables directly on the canvas, but most must be edited in the *attributes inspector*. Select the bottom label and then click the ☜ icon in the inspector selector to reveal the attributes inspector.

In the attributes inspector, you can set the instance variables of the selected object. For example, labels have a `textAlignment` instance variable. The default is left-aligned, but we want this text to be centered. Near the top of this inspector, find the segmented control for alignment. Select the centered text option, as shown in Figure 1.9.

Figure 1.9   Centering the label text

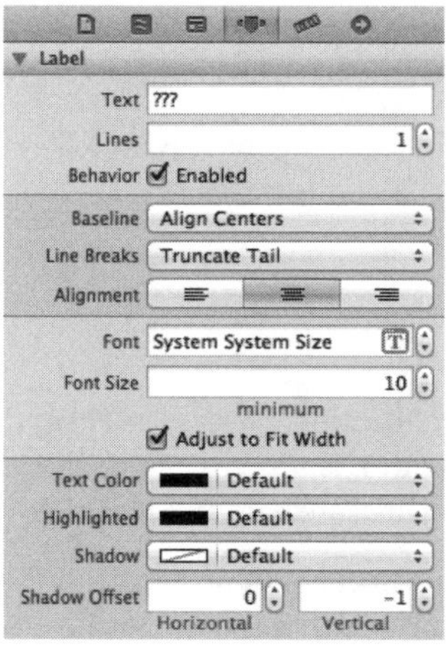

Notice the ??? is now centered in the bottom label. Now center the text in the top label. (There's no text now, but there will be in the running application.)

Your application's interface now looks like it should, but before we start writing code, let's dive into some programming theory.

Model-View-Controller

You may hear iOS programmers mention the Model-View-Controller pattern. What this means is every object you create is exactly one of the following: a model object, a view object, or a controller object.

View objects are visible to the user. In Quiz, the buttons, labels, and the view they are placed on top of are all view objects. Views are usually standard **UIView** subclasses (**UIButton**, **UISlider**), but you will sometimes write custom view classes. These typically have names like **DangerMeterView** or **IncomeGraphView**.

Model objects hold data and know nothing about the user interface. In this application, the model objects will be two lists of strings: the `questions` array and the `answers` array. Figure 1.10 displays the object diagram of the Quiz application's model objects.

Figure 1.10   Diagram of model objects in Quiz

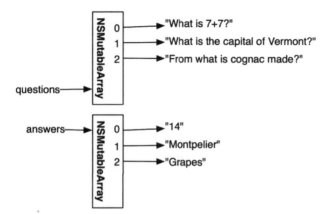

Model objects typically use standard collection classes (**NSArray**, **NSDictionary**, **NSSet**) and standard value types (**NSString**, **NSDate**, **NSNumber**). But there can be custom classes, which typically have names that sound like data-bearing objects, such as **InsurancePolicy** or **PlayerHistory**.

View and model objects are the factory workers of an application – they focus tightly on specific tasks. For example, an instance of **UILabel** (a view object) knows how to display text in a given font within a given rectangle. An **NSString** instance (a model object) knows how to store a character string. But the label doesn't know *what* text it should display, and the string doesn't know *what* characters it should store.

This is where *controller objects* come in. Controllers are the managers in an application. They keep the view and model objects in sync, control the "flow" of the application, and save the model objects out to the filesystem (Figure 1.11). Controllers are the least reusable classes that you will write, and they tend to have names like **ScheduleController** and **ScoreViewController**.

Figure 1.11   MVC pattern

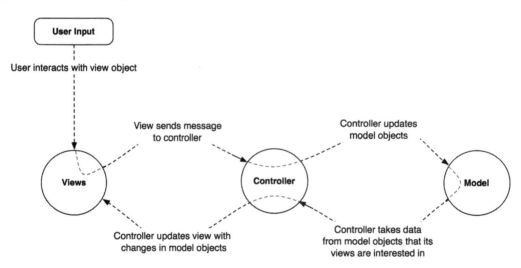

When you create a new iOS project from a template, the template automatically makes a controller object for you. For Quiz, this controller is the **QuizViewController**. Most applications have more than one controller object, but a simple application like Quiz only needs one. (Actually, the template creates another controller for Quiz – the **QuizAppDelegate**. Every iOS application has an "app delegate" object, and it is the primary controller of the application. However, to keep things simple, we won't use the app delegate until Chapter 6.)

One of the **QuizViewController**'s tasks will be showing the user a new question when the Show Question button is tapped. Tapping this button will trigger a method in the **QuizViewController**. This method will retrieve a new question from an array of questions and place that question in the top label. These interactions are laid out in the object diagram for Quiz shown in Figure 1.12.

Figure 1.12   Object diagram for Quiz

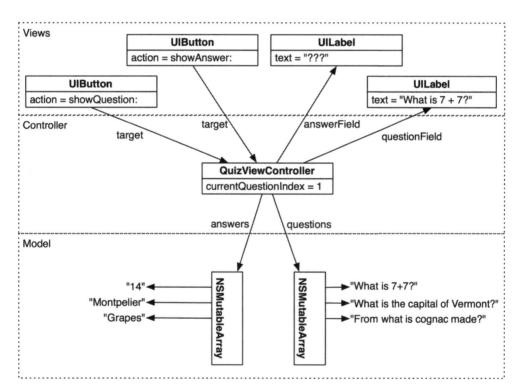

This diagram is the big picture of Quiz. It's okay if it doesn't make perfect sense yet; it will make more by the end of the chapter.

Declarations

To manage its relationships and responsibilities, the **QuizViewController** object needs five instance variables and two methods. In this section, you will declare these in the **QuizViewController** header file, QuizViewController.h.

Declaring instance variables

Here are the five instance variables **QuizViewController** needs:

questions	a pointer to an **NSMutableArray** containing instances of **NSString**
answers	a pointer to another **NSMutableArray** containing instances of **NSString**
currentQuestionIndex	an int that holds the index of the current question in the questions array
questionField	a pointer to the **UILabel** object where the current question will be displayed
answerField	a pointer to the **UILabel** object where the current answer will be displayed

In the project navigator, select QuizViewController.h to open the file in the editor. Add the following code: a set of curly brackets and, inside the brackets, the declarations for the five instance variables. Notice the bold type? In this book, code that you need to add is always bold; the code that's not bold is there to tell you where to type in the new stuff.

```
@interface QuizViewController : UIViewController
{
    int currentQuestionIndex;

    // The model objects
    NSMutableArray *questions;
    NSMutableArray *answers;

    // The view objects - don't worry about IBOutlet -
    // we'll talk about it shortly
    IBOutlet UILabel *questionField;
    IBOutlet UILabel *answerField;
}

@end
```

(Scary syntax? Feelings of dismay? Don't panic – you will learn more about the Objective-C language in the next chapter. For now, just keep going.)

Declaring methods

Each of the buttons needs to trigger a method in the **QuizViewController**. A method is a lot like a function – a list of instructions to be executed. Declare two methods in QuizViewController.h. Add this code after the curly brackets and before the @end.

```
@interface QuizViewController : UIViewController
{
    int currentQuestionIndex;

    // The model objects
    NSMutableArray *questions;
```

```
    NSMutableArray *answers;

    // The view objects
    IBOutlet UILabel *questionField;
    IBOutlet UILabel *answerField;
}

- (IBAction)showQuestion:(id)sender;
- (IBAction)showAnswer:(id)sender;

@end
```

Save `QuizViewController.h`.

What do `IBOutlet` and `IBAction` do in the declarations you just entered? They allow you to connect your controller and your view objects in the XIB file.

Making Connections

A *connection* lets one object know where another object is in memory so that the two objects can work together. When the Quiz application loads `QuizViewController.xib`, the view objects that make up the interface and the **QuizViewController** have no idea how to reach each other. The **QuizViewController** needs to know where the labels are in memory so that it can tell them what to display. The buttons need to know where the **QuizViewController** is so that they can report when they are tapped. Your objects need *connections*.

Figure 1.13 shows the connections for Quiz. Some have already been made by the template (between the `view` outlet of **QuizViewController** and the **UIView** instance, for example), and some were made implicitly (dragging objects onto the view object in the XIB file set up connections between the view and the buttons and labels). However, you still have a few more connections to make to get your objects communicating properly.

Figure 1.13   Current connections and needed connections

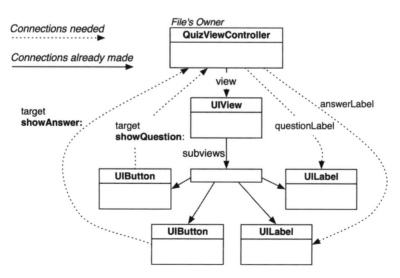

Here are the missing connections:

- **QuizViewController**, the controller object, must have pointers to the **UILabel** instances so it can tell them what to display.

- The **UIButton** instances must have pointers to the **QuizViewController** so they can send messages to the controller when tapped.

Setting pointers

Let's start with the connections to the **UILabel** instances. The instance of **QuizViewController** has a pointer called questionField. You want questionField to point to the instance of **UILabel** at the top of the view.

Select QuizViewController.xib in the project navigator to reopen it. In the outline view, find the File's Owner object (which is standing in for the **QuizViewController**). Right-click or Control-click on the File's Owner to bring up the connections panel (Figure 1.14). Then drag from the circle beside questionField to the **UILabel**.

Figure 1.14 Setting questionField

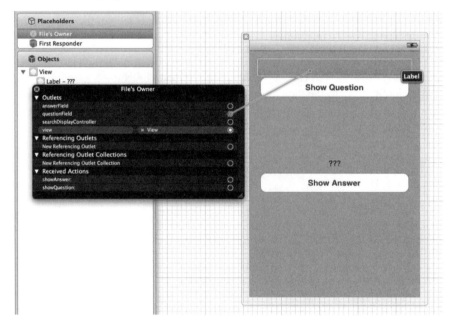

(If you do not see questionField here, double-check your QuizViewController.h file for typos. Did you end each line with a semicolon? Have you saved the file since you added questionField?)

Now when this XIB file is loaded when the application launches, the **QuizViewController**'s questionField pointer will automatically point to this instance of **UILabel**. This will allow the **QuizViewController** to talk to the label it calls questionField. This is the label on top of the screen.

Next, drag from the circle beside answerField to the other **UILabel** (Figure 1.15).

Figure 1.15 Setting answerField

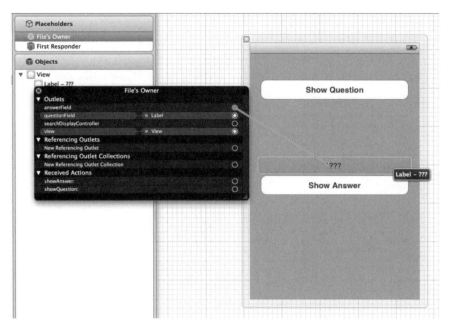

Notice that you drag *from* the object with the pointer *to* the object that you want that pointer to point at. Also, notice that the pointers that appear in the connections panel are the ones that you decorated with IBOutlet in QuizViewController.h.

Setting targets and actions

When a **UIButton** is tapped, it sends a message to another object. The object that is sent the message is called the *target*. The message is called the *action*, and it is the name of the method that tapping the button should trigger. So the button needs answers to two questions: "Who's the target?" and "What's the action?" For the Show Question button, we want the target to be **QuizViewController** and the action to be **showQuestion:**.

To set an object's target and action, you Control-drag *from* the object *to* its target. When you release the mouse, the target is set, and a pop-up menu appears that lets you choose the action. Select the Show Question button and Control-drag (or right-drag) to the File's Owner (**QuizViewController**). Once File's Owner is highlighted, release the mouse button and choose **showQuestion:** from the pop-up menu, as shown in Figure 1.16. Notice that the choices in this menu are the methods you decorated with IBAction in QuizViewController.h.

Figure 1.16   Setting Show Question target/action

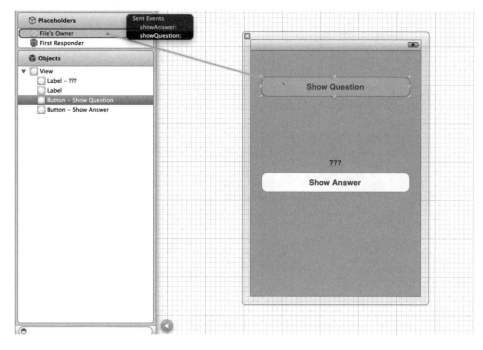

Now set the target and action of the Show Answer button. Select the button and Control-drag *from* the button *to* the File's Owner. Then choose **showAnswer:** from the pop-up menu (Figure 1.17).

Figure 1.17   Setting Show Answer target/action

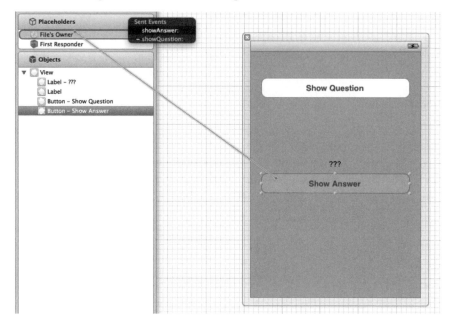

Summary of connections

There are now five connections between your **QuizViewController** and other objects. You've set the pointers answerField and questionField to point at the labels. That's two. The **QuizViewController** is the target for both buttons. That's four. The project's template made one additional connection: the view outlet of **QuizViewController** is connected to the View object that represents the background of the application. That makes five.

You can check these connections in the *connections inspector*. Select the File's Owner in the outline view and then click the ❂ icon in the inspector selector to reveal the connections inspector in the utilities area. (Figure 1.18).

Figure 1.18 Checking connections in the Inspector

Your XIB file is complete. The view objects have been created and configured, and all the necessary connections have been made to the controller object. Save your XIB file, and let's move on to writing methods.

Implementing Methods

Methods and instance variables are declared in the header file (in this case, QuizViewController.h), but the actual code for the methods is placed in the implementation file (in this case, QuizViewController.m). Select QuizViewController.m in the project navigator.

When you create a new application in Xcode, the template fills in a lot of boiler-plate code. This code may be useful for you later on, but for now, it is distracting. So we're going to remove it. In QuizViewController.m, delete everything between the @implementation and @end directives so that QuizViewController.m looks like this:

```
@implementation QuizViewController

@end
```

When the application launches, the **QuizViewController** will be sent the message **initWithNibName:bundle:**. In QuizViewController.m, implement the **initWithNibName:bundle:** method by adding the following code that creates two arrays and fills them with questions and answers.

```
@implementation QuizViewController

- (id)initWithNibName:(NSString *)nibNameOrNil bundle:(NSBundle *)nibBundleOrNil
{
    // Call the init method implemented by the superclass
    self = [super initWithNibName:nibNameOrNil bundle:nibBundleOrNil];
    if (self) {
        // Create two arrays and make the pointers point to them
        questions = [[NSMutableArray alloc] init];
        answers = [[NSMutableArray alloc] init];

        // Add questions and answers to the arrays
        [questions addObject:@"What is 7 + 7?"];
        [answers addObject:@"14"];

        [questions addObject:@"What is the capital of Vermont?"];
        [answers addObject:@"Montpelier"];

        [questions addObject:@"From what is cognac made?"];
        [answers addObject:@"Grapes"];
    }

    // Return the address of the new object
    return self;
}

@end
```

As you work through this book, you will type a lot of code. Notice that as you were typing this code, Xcode was ready to fill in parts of it for you. For example, when you started typing **initWithNibName:bundle:**, it suggested this method before you could finish. You can hit the Return key to accept Xcode's suggestion or select another suggestion from the pop-up box that appears.

However, there are two things to watch out for when using code-completion. First, when you accept a code-completion suggestion for a method that takes arguments, Xcode puts *placeholders* in the areas for the arguments.

Placeholders are not valid code, and you have to replace them to build the application. This can be confusing because placeholders often have the same names that you want your arguments to have. So the text of the code looks completely correct, but you get an error.

Figure 1.19 shows two placeholders you might have seen when typing in the previous code.

Figure 1.19   Example of code-completion placeholder and errors

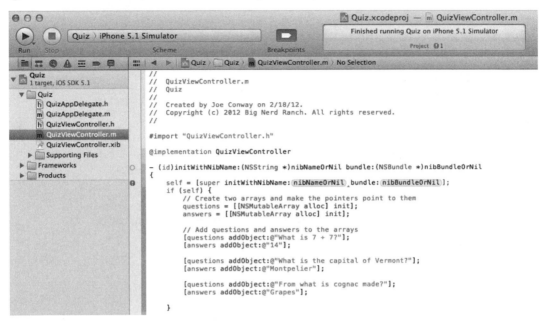

See the `nibNameOrNil` and `nibBundleOrNil` in the first line of the implementation of
`initWithNibName:bundle:`? Those are placeholders. You can tell because they are inside slightly-
shaded, rounded rectangles. The fix is to delete the placeholders and type in arguments of your own
(with the same names). The rounded rectangles will go away, and your code will be correct and valid.

Second, don't blindly accept the first suggestion **Xcode** gives you without verifying it. Cocoa Touch
uses naming conventions, which often cause distinct methods, types, and variables to have very similar
names. Many times, the code-completion will suggest something that looks an awful lot like what you
want, but it is not the code you are looking for. Always double-check.

Now back to your code. In the declarations in `QuizViewController.h`, neither `questions` or `answers`
is labeled `IBOutlet`. This is because the objects that `questions` and `answers` point to are created and
configured programmatically in the code above instead of in the XIB file. This is a standard practice:
view objects are typically created in XIB files, and model objects are always created programmatically.

In addition to the **`initWithNibName:bundle:`** method, we need two action methods for when the
buttons are tapped. In `QuizViewController.m`, add the following code after the implementation of
`initWithNibName:bundle:`. Make sure this code is before the @end directive but not inside the curly
brackets of the **`initWithNibName:bundle:`** implementation.

```
    ...
    // Return the address of the new object
    return self;
}

- (IBAction)showQuestion:(id)sender
{
    // Step to the next question
    currentQuestionIndex++;

    // Am I past the last question?
    if (currentQuestionIndex == [questions count]) {

        // Go back to the first question
        currentQuestionIndex = 0;
    }

    // Get the string at that index in the questions array
    NSString *question = [questions objectAtIndex:currentQuestionIndex];

    // Log the string to the console
    NSLog(@"displaying question: %@", question);

    // Display the string in the question field
    [questionField setText:question];

    // Clear the answer field
    [answerField setText:@"???"];
}

- (IBAction)showAnswer:(id)sender
{
    // What is the answer to the current question?
    NSString *answer = [answers objectAtIndex:currentQuestionIndex];

    // Display it in the answer field
    [answerField setText:answer];
}

@end
```

Flip back to Figure 1.12. This diagram should make a bit more sense now that you have all of the objects and the connections shown.

Build and Run on the Simulator

Now you are ready to build the application and run it on the simulator. You can click the iTunes-esque play button in the top left corner of the workspace, but you'll be doing this often enough that it's easier to remember and use the keyboard shortcut Command-R. Either way, make sure that the Simulator option is selected in the pop-up menu next to the play button (Figure 1.20).

Figure 1.20   Running the application

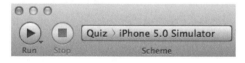

If there are any errors or warnings, you can view them in the *issue navigator* by selecting the ▲ icon in the navigator selector (Figure 1.21). The keyboard shortcut for the issue navigator is Command-4. In fact, the shortcut for any navigator is Command plus the navigator's position in the selector. For example, the project navigator is Command-1.

Figure 1.21 Issue navigator with errors and warnings

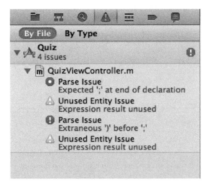

You can click on any issue in the issue navigator, and it will take you to the source file and the line of code where the issue occurred. Find and fix any issues you have (i.e., code typos!) by comparing your code with the book's and then build the application again. Repeat this process until your application compiles.

Once your application has compiled, it will launch in the iOS simulator. But before you play with it, you'll want the console visible so that you can see the output of the log statements. To see the console, reveal the *debug area* by clicking the middle button in the ▣▣▣ group at the top right of the workspace window.

The console is on the righthand side of the debug area, and the variables view is on the left. You can toggle these panels with the ▣▣▣ control in the top-right corner of the debug area Figure 1.22. You can also resize the debug area and its panels by dragging their frames. (In fact, you can resize any area in the workspace window this way.)

Figure 1.22   Debug area expanded

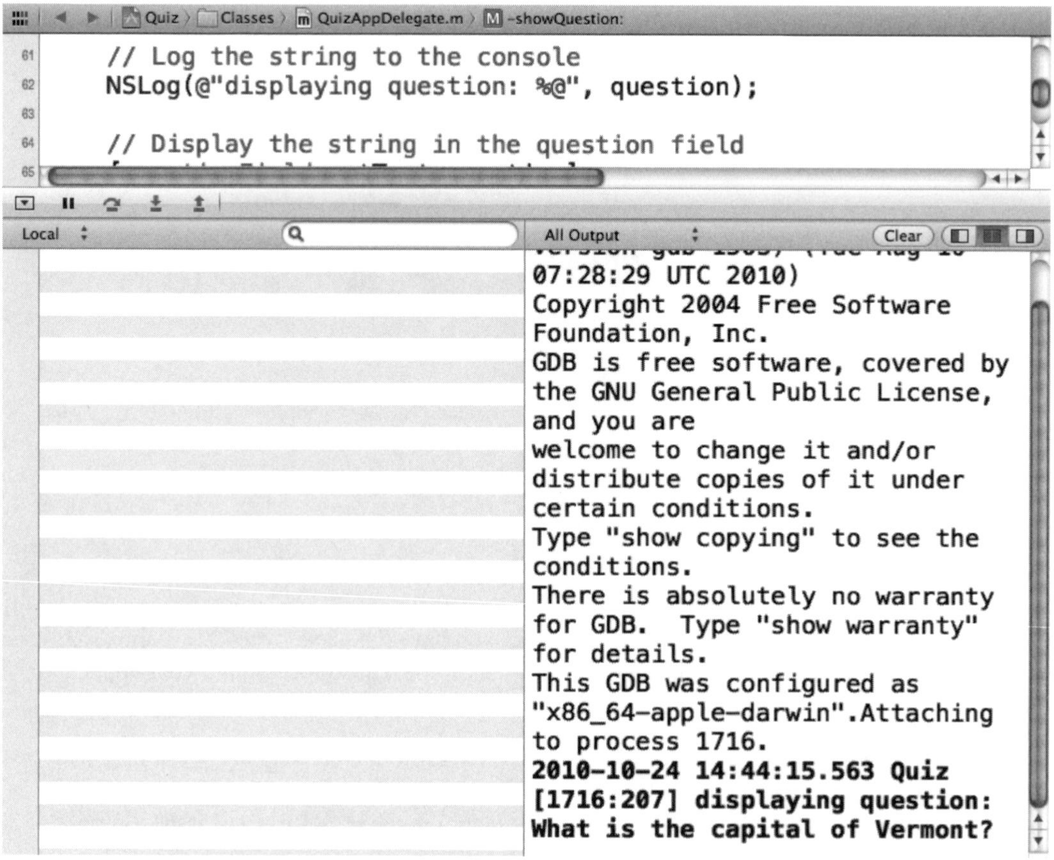

Play around with the Quiz application. You should be able to tap the Show Question button and see a new question in the top label; tapping Show Answer should show the right answer. If your application isn't working as expected, double-check your connections in QuizViewController.xib and check the console output when you tap the buttons.

Deploying an Application

Now that you've written your first iOS application and run it on the simulator, it's time to deploy it to a device.

To install an application on your development device, you need a developer certificate from Apple. Developer certificates are issued to registered iOS Developers who have paid the developer fee. This certificate grants you the ability to sign your code, which allows it to run on a device. Without a valid certificate, devices will not run your application.

Apple's Developer Program Portal (http://developer.apple.com) contains all the instructions and resources to get a valid certificate. The interface for the set-up process is continually being updated by Apple, so it is fruitless to describe it in detail. Instead, use the Development Provisioning Assistant, a step-by-step guide available on the program portal.

Work through the Development Provisioning Assistant, *paying careful attention to each screen.* At the end, you will have added the required certificates to Keychain Access and the provisioning profile to Xcode.

If you're curious about what exactly is going on here, there are four important items in the provisioning process:

Developer Certificate

This certificate file is added to your Mac's keychain using Keychain Access. It is used to digitally sign your code.

App ID

The application identifier is a string that uniquely identifies your application on the App Store. Application identifiers typically look like this: `com.bignerdranch.AwesomeApp`, where the name of the application follows the name of your company.

The App ID in your provisioning profile must match the *bundle identifier* of your application. A development profile, like you just created, will have a wildcard character (*) for its App ID and therefore will match any bundle identifier. To see the bundle identifier for the Quiz application, select the project in the project navigator. Then select the Quiz target and the Summary pane.

Device ID (UDID)

This identifier is unique for each iOS device.

Provisioning Profile

This is a file that lives on your development device and on your computer. It references a Developer Certificate, a single App ID, and a list of the device IDs for the devices that the application can be installed on. This file is suffixed with `.mobileprovision`.

When an application is deployed to a device, Xcode uses a provisioning profile on your computer to access the appropriate certificate. This certificate is used to sign the application binary. Then, the development device's UDID is matched to one of the UDIDs contained within the provisioning profile, and the App ID is matched to the bundle identifier. The signed binary is then sent to your development device where it is confirmed by the same provisioning profile on the device and, finally, launched.

Open Xcode and plug your development device (iPhone, iPod touch, or iPad) into your computer. This will automatically open the Organizer window, which you can re-open by clicking the 🔲 button from the top right corner of the workspace. You can select Devices from the top of the Organizer window to view all of the provisioning information.

To run the Quiz application on your device, you must tell Xcode to deploy to the device instead of the simulator. Locate the pop-up button named Scheme in the top left of the workspace window. Choose iOS Device from the right portion of the list, as shown in Figure 1.23. (If iOS Device is not an option, find the choice that reads something like Joe Conway's iPhone.) Build and run your application (Command-R), and it will appear on your device.

Figure 1.23   Choosing the device

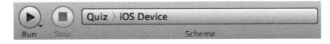

Application Icons

Once the Quiz application is installed on your development device, return to the device's Home screen. You'll see that its icon is a plain white tile. Let's give Quiz a better icon.

An *application icon* is a simple image that represents the application on the iOS desktop. Different devices require different sized icons, and these requirements are shown in Table 1.1.

Table 1.1   Application icon sizes by device

Device	Application icon size
iPhone/iPod touch without Retina display	57x57 pixels
iPhone/iPod touch with Retina display	114x114 pixels
iPad	72x72 pixels

If you supply a single application icon image at 57x57 pixels, that image will be scaled up on devices where a larger icon is required. This is never good. A scaled-up icon will be pixellated and scream, "We're amateurs!" to your customers. Therefore, any application you deploy to the App Store should have an icon for every device class on which it can run.

We have prepared two icon image files (sizes 57x57 and 114x114) for the Quiz application. You can download these icons (along with resources for other chapters) from `http://www.bignerdranch.com/solutions/iOSProgramming3ed.zip`. Unzip `iOSProgramming3ed.zip` and find the `Icon.png` and the `Icon@2x.png` files in the `Resources` directory of the unzipped folder. (If you open these images, you'll see that they aren't glossy and don't have rounded corners like other application icons. These effects are applied for you by the OS.)

Now you're going to add these icons to your application bundle as *resources*. In general, there are two kinds of files in an application: code and resources. Code (like `QuizViewController.h` and `QuizViewController.m`) is used to create the application itself. Resources are things like images and sounds that are used by the application at runtime. XIB files, which are read in at runtime, are also resources.

In the project navigator, select the `Quiz` project, which is at the top of the list and slightly shaded. Then, in the editor area, select Quiz from under the Targets heading. Finally, select Summary from the top of the editor area (Figure 1.24).

Figure 1.24   Adding the smaller icon in the Summary panel

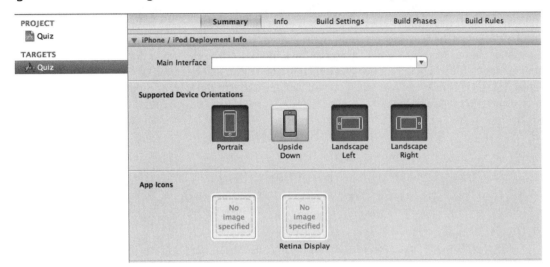

This panel is where you can set a number of options for the application, including its icon. Drag the Icon.png file from Finder onto the tile in the App Icons section. This will copy the Icon.png file into your project's directory on the filesystem and add a reference to that file in the project navigator. (You can Control-click on a file in the project navigator and select the option to Show in Finder to confirm this.)

Next, drag the Icon@2x.png file from Finder onto the tile labeled Retina Display. (Note that there isn't a tile here for the iPad because Quiz is an iPhone application.)

Build and run the application again. After you exit the application, you should see the Quiz application with the BNR logo.

When you dragged the image files onto the icon tiles, two things happened. First, the image files were added to your project. (You can verify this by returning to the project navigator, where you'll find Icon.png and Icon@2x.png in the list of files.) Second, two entries were made in the Quiz-Info.plist file. When you add an icon, the Icon files value is updated with the names of the files you added. You can verify this by selecting Quiz-Info.plist and viewing it in the editor area. You can also select the Info item next to Summary to see the same information.

Launch Images

Another item you can set for an application in the Summary panel is the *launch image*, which appears while an application is loading. (If you don't supply a launch image, the user will see a black screen during this period.) The launch image has a specific role on iOS: it conveys to the user that the application is indeed launching and depicts the user interface that the user will interact with once the application has finished launching. Therefore, a good launch image is a content-less screenshot of the application. For example, the Weather application's interface is a rounded square with the name of a city and its current temperature; Weather's launch image is just that rounded square. (Keep in mind that the launch image is replaced after the application has launched; it does not become the background image of the application.)

Xcode can grab a screenshot from your device, and you can use this screenshot as the launch image for Quiz. To get a screenshot, build and run Quiz on a device. Open the Organizer window in Xcode and locate your device from the device list. (It will be the one with a green dot next to it.) Underneath your device, select the Screenshots item. In the bottom righthand corner of the editor area, click New Screenshot, and the screenshot will appear in the editor area. You can either drag this image onto the Launch Images tile or click the Save as Launch Image button at the bottom of the Organizer window (Figure 1.25). (For most applications, you will first have to edit the screenshot in an image-editing application to get the right look.)

Figure 1.25   Taking a screenshot with Xcode

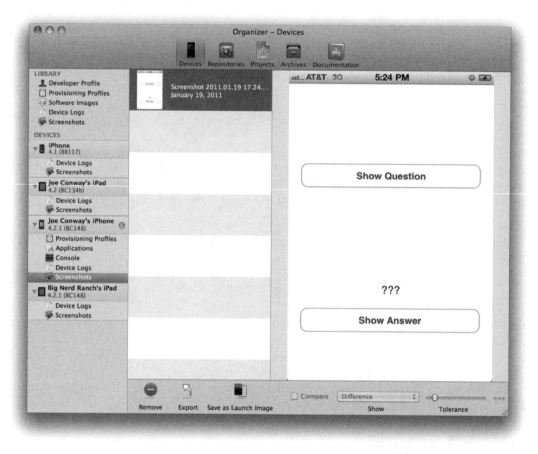

Build and run the application. As the application launches, you will briefly see the launch image.

A launch image must fit the screen of the device it is being launched on. Table 1.2 shows the different size images you will need for each type of device.

Table 1.2 Launch image sizes by device

Device	Launch image size
iPhone/iPod touch without Retina display	320x480 pixels
iPhone/iPod touch with Retina display	640x960 pixels
iPad	1024x768 pixels

(Note that Table 1.2 lists the screen resolutions of the devices; the real status bar is overlaid on top of the status bar in the launch image.)

Just like with application icons, there are tiles for different-sized images for each supported device. And, just like with icons, if you provide only one image, that image will be scaled to fit the device's screen. So provide an image for every possible device.

One thing the launch image should *not* do is display a splash screen for your company or application. While many applications (especially games) use splash screens as launch images, here is the argument against it: The amount of time it takes to load any application depends on the hardware it is running on. Right now, iOS devices aren't very powerful, and a large application may take a few seconds to load. This gives the user ample time to ingest a launch image. However, as iOS devices become more powerful, that launch image may only appear for a fraction of a second. This would appear as a disconcerting flash to users, who would wonder, "Have I pressed something wrong? How do I go back to that screen?" There are infinite ways of expressing your creativity on the platform from within an application – the launch image isn't one of them.

Congratulations! You have written your first application and installed it on your device. Now it is time to dive into the big ideas that make it work.

2

Objective-C

iOS applications are written in the Objective-C language using the Cocoa Touch library. Objective-C is a simple extension of the C language, and Cocoa Touch is a collection of Objective-C classes. This book assumes you know some C and understand the ideas of object-oriented programming. If C or object-oriented programming makes you feel uneasy, we recommend starting with *Objective-C Programming: The Big Nerd Ranch Guide*.

In this chapter, you will learn the basics of Objective-C and create an application called RandomPossessions. Even if you are familiar with Objective-C, you should still go through this chapter to create the **BNRItem** class that you will use later in this book.

Objects

Let's say you need a way to represent a party. Your party has a few attributes that are unique to it, like a name, a date, and a list of invitees. You can also ask the party to do things, like send an email reminder to all the invitees, print name tags, or cancel the party altogether.

In C, you would define a *structure* to hold the data that describes a party. The structure would have data members – one for each of the party's attributes. Each data member would have a name and a type.

To create an individual party, you would use the function **malloc** to allocate a chunk of memory large enough to hold the structure. You would write C functions to set the value of its attributes and have it perform actions.

In Objective-C, instead of using a structure to represent a party, you use a *class*. A class is like a cookie-cutter that produces objects. The **Party** class creates objects, and these objects are instances of the **Party** class. Each instance of the **Party** class can hold the data for a single party (Figure 2.1).

Figure 2.1   A class and its instances

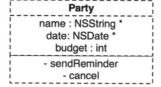

The class acts as a factory

Party
name : NSString *
date: NSDate *
budget : int
- sendReminder
- cancel

that creates instances of that class

Party
name = @"Lenny's Birthday"
date = 4/12/2015
budget = 200
- sendReminder
- cancel

Party
name = @"Prom"
date = 5/14/2013
budget = 10000
- sendReminder
- cancel

An instance of **Party**, like all objects, is a chunk of data stored in memory, and it stores the values for its attributes in *instance variables*. So an instance of **Party** might have the instance variables name, date, and budget.

A C structure is a chunk of memory, and an object is a chunk of memory. A C structure has data members, each with a name and a type. Similarly, an object has instance variables, each with a name and a type.

But there is an important difference between a structure in C and a class in Objective-C: a class has *methods*. A method is similar to a function: it has a name, a return type, and a list of parameters that it expects. A method also has access to an object's instance variables. If you want an object to run the code in one of its methods, you send that object a *message*.

Using Instances

In order to use an instance of a class (an object), you must have a variable that points to the object. A pointer variable stores the location of an object in memory, not the object itself. (It "points to" the object.) A variable that points to an object is declared like so:

```
Party *partyInstance;
```

This variable is named partyInstance. It is meant to be a pointer to an instance of the class **Party**. However, this does not create a **Party** instance – only a variable that can point to a **Party** object.

Creating objects

An object has a life span: it is created, sent messages, and then destroyed when it is no longer needed.

To create an object, you send an **alloc** message to a class. In response, the class creates an object in memory and gives you a pointer to it, and then you store that pointer in a variable:

```
Party *partyInstance = [Party alloc];
```

Here an instance of type **Party** is created, and you are returned a pointer to it in the variable partyInstance. When you have a pointer to an instance, you can send messages to it. The first message you *always* send to a newly allocated instance is an initialization message. Although sending an **alloc** message to a class creates an instance, the instance isn't valid until it has been initialized.

```
[partyInstance init];
```

Because an object must be allocated *and* initialized before it can be used, we always combine these two messages in one line.

```
Party *partyInstance = [[Party alloc] init];
```

The code to the right of the assignment operator (=) says, "Create an instance of **Party** and send it the message **init**." Both **alloc** and **init** return a pointer to the newly created object so that you have a reference to it.

Combining two messages in a single line of code is called a *nested message send*. The innermost brackets are evaluated first, so the message **alloc** is sent to the class **Party** first. This returns a new, uninitialized instance of **Party** that is then sent the message **init**.

Sending messages

What do you do with an instance that has been initialized? You send it more messages.

Let's take a closer look at message anatomy. First of all, a message is always contained in square brackets. Within a pair of square brackets, a message has three parts:

receiver   a pointer to the object being asked to execute a method

selector   the name of the method to be executed

arguments   the values to be supplied as the parameters to the method

A party might have a list of attendees that you can add to by sending the party the message **addAttendee:**.

```
[partyInstance addAttendee:somePerson];
```

Sending the **addAttendee:** message to partyInstance (the receiver) triggers the **addAttendee:** method (named by the selector) and passes in somePerson (an argument).

The **addAttendee:** message has only one argument, but Objective-C methods can take a number of arguments or none at all. The message **init**, for instance, has no arguments.

An attendee to a party might RSVP with an edible item. Thus, a party may have another method named **addAttendee:withDish:**. This message takes two arguments: the attendee and the dish the attendee plans to bring. Each argument is paired with a label in the selector, and each label ends with a colon. The selector is all of the labels taken together (Figure 2.2).

Figure 2.2   Parts of a message send

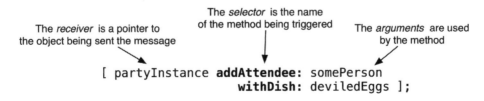

This pairing of labels and arguments is an important feature of Objective-C. In other languages, this method would look like this:

```
partyInstance.addAttendeeWithDish(somePerson, deviledEggs);
```

In these languages, it isn't completely obvious what each of the arguments sent to this function are. In Objective-C, however, each argument is paired with the appropriate label.

```
[partyInstance addAttendee:somePerson withDish:deviledEggs];
```

It takes some getting used to, but eventually, Objective-C programmers appreciate the clarity of arguments being interposed into the selector. The trick is to remember that for every pair of square brackets, there is only one message being sent. Even though **addAttendee:withDish:** has two labels, it is still only one message, and sending that message results in only one method being executed.

In Objective-C, the name of a method is what makes it unique. Therefore, a class cannot have two methods with the same name. However, two methods can have the same individual label, as long as the name of each method differs when taken as a whole. For example, our **Party** class has two methods, **addAttendee:** and **addAttendee:withDish:**. These are two distinct methods and do not share any code.

Also, notice the distinction being made between a *message* and a *method*: a method is a chunk of code that can be executed, and a message is the act of asking a class or object to execute a method. The name of a message always matches the name of the method to be executed.

Destroying objects

To destroy an object, you set the variable that points at it to nil.

```
partyInstance = nil;
```

This line of code destroys the object pointed to by the partyInstance variable and sets the value of the partyInstance variable to nil. (It's actually a bit more complicated than that, and you'll learn about the details of memory management in the next chapter.)

The value nil is the zero pointer. (C programmers know it as NULL. Java programmers know it as null.) A pointer that has a value of nil is typically used to represent the absence of an object. For example, a party could have a venue. While the organizer of the party is still determining where to host the party, venue would point to nil. This allows us to do things like so:

```
if (venue == nil) {
    [organizer remindToFindVenueForParty];
}
```

Objective-C programmers typically use the shorthand form of determining if a pointer is nil:

```
if (!venue) {
    [organizer remindToFindVenueForParty];
}
```

Since the ! operator means "not," this reads as "if there is not a venue" and will evaluate to true if venue is nil.

If you send a message to a variable that is nil, nothing happens. In other languages, sending a message to the zero pointer is illegal, so you see this sort of thing a lot:

```
// Is venue non-nil?
if (venue) {
    [venue sendConfirmation];
}
```

In Objective-C, this check is unnecessary because a message sent to `nil` is ignored. Therefore, you can simply send a message without a `nil`-check:

```
[venue sendConfirmation];
```

If the venue hasn't been chosen yet, you won't send a confirmation anywhere. (A corollary: if your program isn't doing anything when you think it should be doing something, an unexpected `nil` pointer is often the culprit.)

Beginning RandomPossessions

Before you dive into the UIKit, the set of libraries for creating iOS applications, you're going to write an application that will let you focus on the Objective-C language. Open Xcode and select File → New → New Project.... In the lefthand table in the Mac OS X section, click Application and then select Command Line Tool from the upper panel, as shown in Figure 2.3. Click the Next button.

Figure 2.3   Creating a command line tool

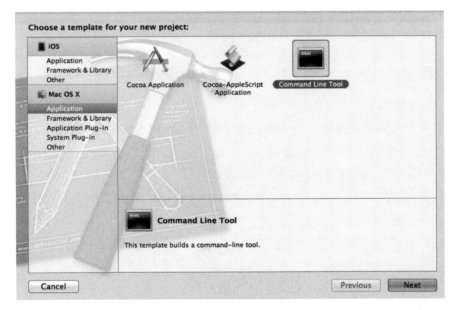

(If there is no Command Line Tool choice, first make sure that you have selected Application from underneath the Mac OS X header. If Command Line Tool is still is not an option, visit our forums at `http://forums.bignerdranch.com`. Apple frequently changes the names and style of these templates. We'll keep you updated as the templates change.)

On the next panel, name the product RandomPossessions, choose Foundation as its type, and make sure the box labeled Use Automatic Reference Counting is checked (Figure 2.4). Click Next, and you will be prompted to save the project. Save it some place safe – you will be reusing parts of this code in future projects.

Figure 2.4   Naming the project

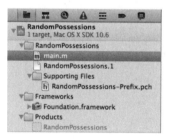

One source file (main.m) has been created for you in the RandomPossessions group of the project navigator (Figure 2.5).

Figure 2.5   Project navigator for command line tool template

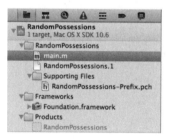

Click on main.m to open it in the editor area, and you'll see that some code has been written for you – most notably, a **main** function that is the entry point of any C or Objective-C application.

Time to put your knowledge of Objective-C basics to the test. Delete the line of code that **NSLog**s "Hello, World!" and replace it with lines that create and destroy an instance of the Objective-C class **NSMutableArray**.

```
#import <Foundation/Foundation.h>
```

```
int main (int argc, const char * argv[])
{
    @autoreleasepool {

        // insert code here...
        NSLog(@"Hello, World!");

        // Create a mutable array object, store its address in items variable
        NSMutableArray *items = [[NSMutableArray alloc] init];

        // Destroy the array pointed to by items
        items = nil;
    }
    return 0;
}
```

Once you have an instance of **NSMutableArray**, you can send it messages, like **addObject:** and **insertObject:atIndex:**. In this code, the receiver is the items variable that points at the newly instantiated **NSMutableArray**. Add a few strings to the array instance.

```
int main (int argc, const char * argv[])
{
    @autoreleasepool {

        // Create a mutable array object, store its address in items variable
        NSMutableArray *items = [[NSMutableArray alloc] init];

        // Send the message addObject: to the NSMutableArray pointed to
        // by the variable items, passing a string each time.
        [items addObject:@"One"];
        [items addObject:@"Two"];
        [items addObject:@"Three"];

        // Send another message, insertObject:atIndex:, to that same array object
        [items insertObject:@"Zero" atIndex:0];

        items = nil;
    }
    return 0;
}
```

When this application executes, it creates an **NSMutableArray** and fills it with four instances of **NSString** (another Objective-C class). Let's confirm that these strings were added to the array. In main.m, after adding the final object to the array, loop through every item in the array and print each one to the console.

```
int main (int argc, const char * argv[])
{
    @autoreleasepool {

        // Create a mutable array object, store its address in items variable
        NSMutableArray *items = [[NSMutableArray alloc] init];

        // Send the message addObject: to the NSMutableArray pointed to
        // by the variable items, passing a string each time.
        [items addObject:@"One"];
        [items addObject:@"Two"];
        [items addObject:@"Three"];
```

```
        // Send another message, insertObject:atIndex:, to that same array object
        [items insertObject:@"Zero" atIndex:0];

        // For every item in the array as determined by sending count to items
        for (int i = 0; i < [items count]; i++) {
            // We get the ith object from the array and pass it as an argument to
            // NSLog, which implicitly sends the description message to that object
            NSLog(@"%@", [items objectAtIndex:i]);
        }

        items = nil;
    }
    return 0;
}
```

There is some interesting syntax in this code that we'll get to in a second. But for now, go ahead and click the Run button. It may seem like nothing has happened because the program exits right away, but the *log navigator* tells another story.

To reveal the log navigator, select the 📭 icon or use the keyboard shortcut Command-7. The log navigator stores the build results and console output from each build of your application. Select Debug RandomPossessions at the top of the log navigator to see your console output in the editor area (Figure 2.6).

Figure 2.6   Console output

Now let's go back and take a closer look at the code in your **main** function.

Creating strings

First, notice the @"One" argument in the first **addObject:** message sent to items.

```
[items addObject:@"One"];
```

In Objective-C, when you want a hard-coded string, you prefix a character string with an @ symbol. This creates an instance of **NSString** that holds the character string.

But, wait – aren't instances created by sending **alloc** to a class? Yes, but the @ prefix is a special case just for the **NSString** class. It is convenient shorthand for creating strings.

The following code shows three such uses, and each is completely valid Objective-C, where **length** is a message you can send to an instance of **NSString**:

```
NSString *myString = @"Hello, World!";
int len = [myString length];

len = [@"Hello, World!" length];

myString = [[NSString alloc] initWithString:@"Hello, World!"];
len = [myString length];
```

Format strings

Next, let's look at the **NSLog** function we used to print to the console. **NSLog** takes a variable number of arguments and prints a string to the console. The first argument is required and must be an **NSString** instance. This instance is called the *format string*, and it contains text and a number of tokens. The tokens (also called format specifications) are prefixed with a percent symbol (%), and each additional argument passed to the function replaces a token in the format string. Tokens also specify the type of the argument they correspond to. Here's an example:

```
int a = 1;
float b = 2.5;
char c = 'A';
NSLog(@"Integer: %d Float: %f Char: %c", a, b, c);
```

The order of the arguments matters: the first token is replaced with the second argument (the format string is always the first argument), the second token is replaced with the third argument, and so on. The console output would be

```
Integer: 1 Float: 2.5 Char: A
```

In C, there is a function called **printf** that does the same thing. However, **NSLog** adds one more token to the available list: %@. The type of the argument this token responds to is "any object." When %@ is encountered in the format string, instead of the token being replaced by the corresponding argument, that argument is sent the message **description**. The **description** method returns an **NSString** that replaces the token. Because the argument is sent a message, that argument must be an object. As we'll see shortly, every object implements the method **description**, so any object will work.

NSArray and NSMutableArray

What exactly is this **NSMutableArray** object you're using? An array is a collection object (also called a container). The Cocoa Touch frameworks provide a handful of collection objects, including **NSDictionary** and **NSSet**, and each has a slightly different use. An array is an ordered list of objects, and these objects can be accessed by an index. Other languages might call it a list or a vector. An **NSArray** is immutable, which means you cannot add or remove objects after the array is instantiated. You can, however, retrieve objects from the array. **NSArray**'s mutable subclass, **NSMutableArray**, lets you add and remove objects dynamically.

In Objective-C, an array does not actually *contain* the objects that belong to it; instead it holds a pointer to each object. When an object is added to an array,

```
[array addObject:object];
```

the address of that object in memory is stored inside the array.

So, to recap, in your command line tool, you created an instance of **NSMutableArray** and added four instances of **NSString** to it, as shown in Figure 2.7.

Figure 2.7   NSMutableArray instance

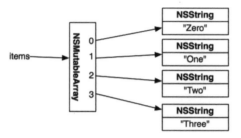

Arrays can only hold references to Objective-C objects. This means primitives and C structures cannot be added to an array. For example, you cannot have an array of ints. Also, because arrays hold pointers to objects, *a single array can contain objects of different types.* This is different from most strongly-typed languages where an array can only hold objects of its declared type.

You can ask an array how many objects it is currently storing by sending it the message **count**.

```
int numberOfObjects = [array count];
```

This information is important because if you ask for an object from an array at an index that is greater than the number of objects in the array, an exception will be thrown. (Exceptions are very bad; they will most likely cause your application to crash. We'll talk more about exceptions at the end of this chapter.)

When an object is added to an array with the message **addObject:**, it is added at the end of the array. You can also insert objects at a specific index – as long as that index is less than or equal to the current number of objects in the array.

```
int numberOfObjects = [array count];
[array insertObject:object
          atIndex:numberOfObjects];
```

Note that you cannot add nil to an array. If you need to add "holes" to an array, you must use **NSNull**. **NSNull** is an object that represents nil and is used specifically for this task.

```
[array addObject:[NSNull null]];
```

To retrieve the pointer to an object later, you send the message **objectAtIndex:** to the array.

```
NSString *object = [array objectAtIndex:0];
```

Subclassing an Objective-C Class

Classes, like **NSMutableArray**, exist in a hierarchy, and every class has exactly one superclass – except for the root class of the entire hierarchy: **NSObject** (Figure 2.8). A class inherits the behavior of its superclass, which means, at a minimum, every class inherits the methods and instance variables defined in **NSObject**.

As the top superclass, **NSObject**'s role is to implement the basic behavior of every object in Cocoa Touch. Three of the methods **NSObject** implements are **alloc**, **init**, and **description**. (We sometimes say "**description** is a method *on* **NSObject**" and mean the same thing.)

Figure 2.8   Class hierarchy

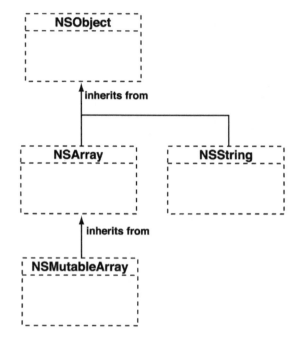

A subclass adds methods and instance variables to extend the behavior of its superclass. For example, **NSMutableArray** extends **NSArray**'s ability to hold pointers to objects by adding the ability to dynamically add and remove objects.

A subclass can also override methods of its superclass. For example, sending the **description** message to an **NSObject** returns the object's class and its address in memory, like this: <QuizViewController: 0x4b222a0>.

A subclass of **NSObject** can override this method to return something that better describes an instance of that subclass. For example, **NSString** overrides **description** to return the string itself. **NSArray** overrides **description** to return the description of every object in the array.

Creating an NSObject subclass

In this section, you're going to create a subclass of **NSObject** named **BNRItem**. An instance of the **BNRItem** class will represent an item that a person owns in the real world. To create a new class in Xcode, choose File → New → New File.... In the lefthand table of the panel that appears, select Cocoa from the Mac OS X section. Then select Objective-C class from the upper panel and hit Next (Figure 2.9).

Figure 2.9   Creating a class

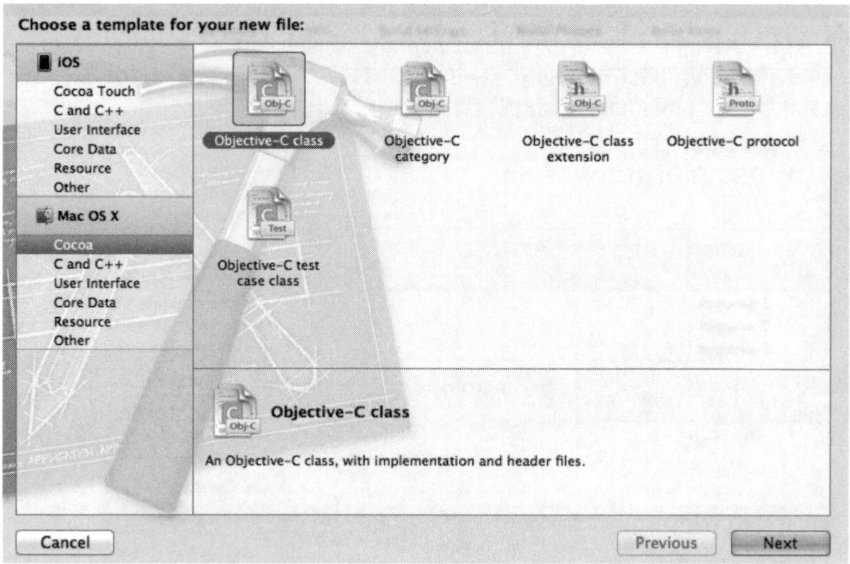

Choose a template for your new file:

iOS
- Cocoa Touch
- C and C++
- User Interface
- Core Data
- Resource
- Other

Mac OS X
- Cocoa
- C and C++
- User Interface
- Core Data
- Resource
- Other

Objective-C class   Objective-C category   Objective-C class extension   Objective-C protocol

Objective-C test case class

Objective-C class

An Objective-C class, with implementation and header files.

Cancel   Previous   Next

On the next panel, name this new class **BNRItem**. Select NSObject as the superclass and click Next, as shown in Figure 2.10.

Figure 2.10   Choosing a superclass

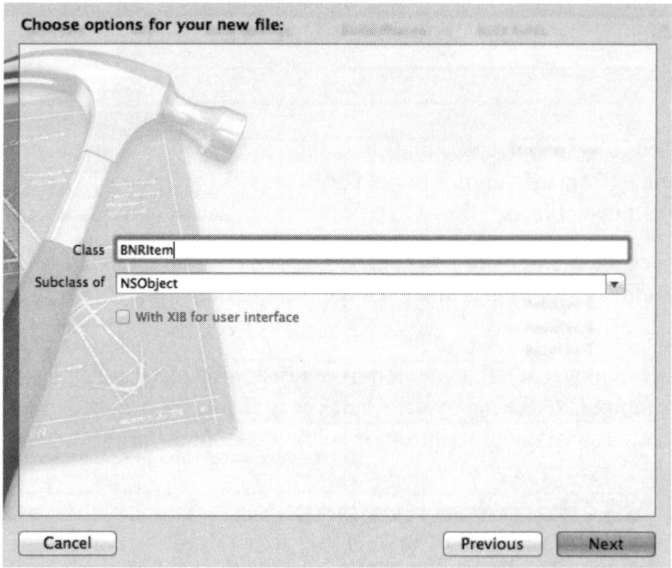

Choose options for your new file:

Class   BNRItem

Subclass of NSObject

☐ With XIB for user interface

Cancel   Previous   Next

A panel will drop down that prompts you to create the files for this new class (Figure 2.11). When creating a new class for a project, you want to save the files that describe it inside the project's source directory on the filesystem. By default, the current project directory is already selected for you. You can also choose the group in the project navigator that these files will be added to. Because these groups are simply for organizing and because this project is very small, just stick with the default. Make sure the checkbox is selected for the RandomPossessions target. This ensures that this class will be compiled when the RandomPossessions project is built. Click Create.

Figure 2.11   Saving class files

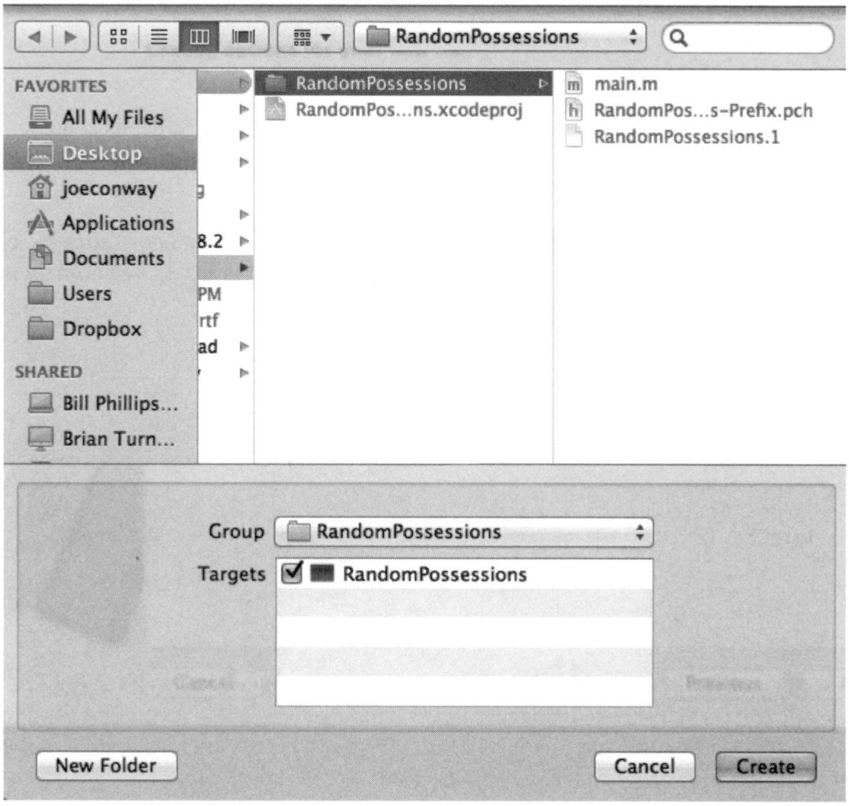

Creating the **BNRItem** class generated two files: BNRItem.h and BNRItem.m. Locate those files in the project navigator. BNRItem.h is the *header file* (also called an interface file). This file declares the name of the new class, its superclass, the instance variables that each instance of this class has, and any methods this class implements. BNRItem.m is the implementation file, and it contains the code for the methods that the class implements. Every Objective-C class has these two files. You can think of the header file as a user manual for an instance of a class and the implementation file as the engineering details that define how it really works.

Open BNRItem.h in the editor area by clicking on it in the project navigator. The file currently looks like this:

```
#import <Foundation/Foundation.h>

@interface BNRItem : NSObject

@end
```

Objective-C retains the keywords of the C language, and additional keywords specific to Objective-C are distinguishable by the @ prefix. To declare a class in Objective-C, you use the keyword @interface followed by the name of this new class. After a colon comes the name of the superclass. Objective-C only allows single inheritance, so you will only ever see the following pattern:

```
@interface ClassName : SuperclassName
```

The @end directive indicates that the class has been fully declared.

Instance variables

So far, the **BNRItem** class doesn't add anything to its superclass **NSObject**. It needs some item-like instance variables. An item, in our world, is going to have a name, a serial number, a value, and a date of creation.

Instance variables for a class are declared in between curly brackets immediately after the class declaration. In BNRItem.h, add four instance variables (and the curly brackets that contain them) to the **BNRItem** class:

```
#import <Foundation/Foundation.h>

@interface BNRItem : NSObject
{
    NSString *itemName;
    NSString *serialNumber;
    int valueInDollars;
    NSDate *dateCreated;
}

@end
```

Now every instance of **BNRItem** has one spot for a simple integer and three spots to hold references to objects, specifically two **NSString** instances and one **NSDate** instance. (A reference is another word for pointer; the * denotes that the variable is a pointer.) Figure 2.12 shows an example of a **BNRItem** instance after its instance variables have been given values.

Figure 2.12   A BNRItem instance

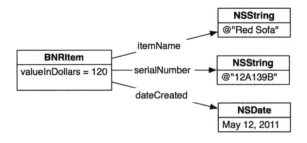

Notice that Figure 2.12 shows a total of four objects: the **BNRItem**, two **NSString**s, and the **NSDate**. Each of these objects is its own object and exists independently of the others. The **BNRItem** only has pointers to the three other objects. These pointers are the instance variables of **BNRItem**.

For example, every **BNRItem** has a pointer instance variable named itemName. The itemName of the
BNRItem shown in Figure 2.12 points to an **NSString** instance whose contents are "Red Sofa." The
"Red Sofa" string does not live inside the **BNRItem**, though. The **BNRItem** instance knows where
the "Red Sofa" string lives in memory and stores its address as itemName. One way to think of this
relationship is "the **BNRItem** calls this string its itemName. "

The story is different for the instance variable valueInDollars. This instance variable is *not* a pointer
to another object; it is just an int. Non-pointer instance variables are stored inside the object itself. The
idea of pointers is not easy to understand at first. In the next chapter, you'll learn more about objects,
pointers, and instance variables, and, throughout this book, we will make use of object diagrams like
Figure 2.12 to drive home the difference between an object and a pointer to an object.

Accessor methods

Now that you have instance variables, you need a way to get and set their values. In object-oriented
languages, we call methods that get and set instance variables *accessors*. Individually, we call them
getters and *setters*. Without these methods, an object cannot access the instance variables of another
object.

Accessor methods look like this:

```
// a getter method
- (NSString *)itemName
{
    // Return a pointer to the object this BNRItem calls its itemName
    return itemName;
}

// a setter method
- (void)setItemName:(NSString *)newItemName
{
    // Change the instance variable to point at another string,
    // this BNRItem will now call this new string its itemName
    itemName = newItemName;
}
```

Then, if you wanted to access (set or get) a **BNRItem**'s itemName, you would send the **BNRItem** one of
these messages:

```
// Create a new BNRItem instance
BNRItem *p = [[BNRItem alloc] init];

// Set itemName to a new NSString
[p setItemName:@"Red Sofa"];

// Get the pointer of the BNRItem's itemName
NSString *str = [p itemName];

// Print that object
NSLog(@"%@", str); // This would print "Red Sofa"
```

In Objective-C, the name of a setter method is **set** plus the name of the instance variable it is changing
– in this case, **setItemName:**. In other languages, the name of the getter method would likely be
getItemName. However, in Objective-C, the name of the getter method is just the name of the instance
variable. Some of the cooler parts of the Cocoa Touch library make the assumption that your classes
follow this convention; therefore, stylish Cocoa Touch programmers always do so.

In BNRItem.h, declare accessor methods for the instance variables of **BNRItem**. You will need getters and setters for valueInDollars, itemName, and serialNumber. For dateCreated, you only need a getter method.

```
#import <Foundation/Foundation.h>

@interface BNRItem : NSObject
{
    NSString *itemName;
    NSString *serialNumber;
    int valueInDollars;
    NSDate *dateCreated;
}
- (void)setItemName:(NSString *)str;
- (NSString *)itemName;

- (void)setSerialNumber:(NSString *)str;
- (NSString *)serialNumber;

- (void)setValueInDollars:(int)i;
- (int)valueInDollars;

- (NSDate *)dateCreated;
@end
```

(For those of you with some experience in Objective-C, we'll talk about properties in the next chapter.)

Now that these accessors have been declared, they need to be defined in the implementation file. Select BNRItem.m in the project navigator to open it in the editor area.

At the top of any implementation file, you must import the header file of that class. The implementation of a class needs to know how it has been declared. (Importing a file is the same as including a file in the C language except you are ensured that the file will only be included once.)

After the import statement is the implementation block that begins with the @implementation keyword followed by the name of the class that is being implemented. All of the method definitions in the implementation file are inside this implementation block. Methods are defined until you close out the block with the @end keyword.

When you created this class, the template you used may have inserted methods for you. However, we want to start from scratch. Using boilerplate methods before you understand what they do keeps you from learning how things actually work. In BNRItem.m, delete everything that the template may have added between @implementation and @end. Your file should look like this:

```
#import "BNRItem.h"

@implementation BNRItem

@end
```

Now we can define some methods of our own – starting with the accessor methods for the variables you declared in BNRItem.h. We're going to skip memory management until the next chapter, so the accessor methods for **BNRItem** are very simple. In BNRItem.m, add the following code.

```
#import "BNRItem.h"
```

```
@implementation BNRItem

- (void)setItemName:(NSString *)str
{
    itemName = str;
}
- (NSString *)itemName
{
    return itemName;
}

- (void)setSerialNumber:(NSString *)str
{
    serialNumber = str;
}

- (NSString *)serialNumber
{
    return serialNumber;
}

- (void)setValueInDollars:(int)i
{
    valueInDollars = i;
}

- (int)valueInDollars
{
    return valueInDollars;
}

- (NSDate *)dateCreated
{
    return dateCreated;
}

@end
```

Notice that the setter methods assign the appropriate instance variable to point at the incoming object, and the getter methods return a pointer to the object the instance variable points at. (For valueInDollars, the setter just assigns the passed-in value to the instance variable, and the getter just returns the instance variable's value.)

Build your application (without running) to ensure that there are no compiler errors or warnings. To build only, select Product → Build or use the shortcut Command-B.

Now that your accessors have been declared and defined, you can send messages to **BNRItem** instances to get and set their instance variables. Let's test this out. In main.m, import the header file for **BNRItem** and create a new **BNRItem** instance. After it is created, log its instance variables to the console.

```
#import "BNRItem.h"

int main (int argc, const char * argv[])
{
    @autoreleasepool {

        NSMutableArray *items = [[NSMutableArray alloc] init];
        [items addObject:@"One"];
```

```
    [items addObject:@"Two"];
    [items addObject:@"Three"];
    [items insertObject:@"Zero" atIndex:0];

    for (int i = 0; i < [items count]; i++) {
        NSLog(@"%@", [items objectAtIndex:i]);
    }

    BNRItem *p = [[BNRItem alloc] init];
    NSLog(@"%@ %@ %@ %d", [p itemName], [p dateCreated],
                         [p serialNumber], [p valueInDollars]);


    items = nil;
    }

    return 0;
}
```

Build and run the application. Check the console by selecting the entry at the top of the log navigator. At the end of the console output, you should see a line that has three "(null)" strings and a 0. When an object is created, all of its instance variables are set to 0. For pointers to objects, that pointer points to nil; for primitives like int, the value is 0.

To give this **BNRItem** some substance, you need to create new objects and pass them as arguments to the setter methods for this instance. In main.m, type in the following code:

```
// Notice we omitted some of the surrounding code. The bold code is the code to add,
// the non-bold code is existing code that shows you where to type in the new stuff.

BNRItem *p = [[BNRItem alloc] init];

// This creates a new NSString, "Red Sofa" and gives it to the BNRItem
[p setItemName:@"Red Sofa"];

// This creates a new NSString, "A1B2C" and gives it to the BNRItem
[p setSerialNumber:@"A1B2C"];

// We send the value 100 to be used as the valueInDollars of this BNRItem
[p setValueInDollars:100];

NSLog(@"%@ %@ %@ %d", [p itemName], [p dateCreated],
                     [p serialNumber], [p valueInDollars]);
```

Build and run the application. Now you should see values for everything but the dateCreated, which we'll take care of shortly.

Instance methods

Not all instance methods are accessors. You will regularly find yourself wanting to send messages to instances that perform other tasks. One such message is **description**. You can implement this method in **BNRItem** to return a string that describes a **BNRItem** instance. Because **BNRItem** is a subclass of **NSObject** (the class that originally declares the **description** method), when you re-implement **description** in the **BNRItem** class, you are *overriding* it. When overriding a method, all you need to do is define it in the implementation file; you do not need to declare it in the header file because it has already been declared by the superclass.

In BNRItem.m, override the **description** method. This new code can go anywhere between @implementation and @end, as long as it is not inside the curly brackets of an existing method.

```
- (NSString *)description
{
    NSString *descriptionString =
        [[NSString alloc] initWithFormat:@"%@ (%@): Worth $%d, recorded on %@",
                          itemName,
                          serialNumber,
                          valueInDollars,
                          dateCreated];

    return descriptionString;

}
```

Now whenever you send the message **description** to an instance of **BNRItem**, it will return an **NSString** that describes that instance. In main.m, substitute this new method into the **NSLog** that prints out the instance variables of the **BNRItem**.

```
[p setValueInDollars:100];

NSLog(@"%@ %@ %@ %d", [p itemName], [p dateCreated],
                      [p serialNumber], [p valueInDollars]);

// Remember, an NSLog with %@ as the token will print the
// description of the corresponding argument
NSLog(@"%@", p);

items = nil;
```

Build and run the application and check your results in the log navigator. You should see a log statement that looks like this:

```
Red Sofa (A1B2C): Worth $100, recorded on (null)
```

What if you want to create an entirely new instance method, one that you are not overriding from the superclass? You declare the new method in the header file and define it in the implementation file. A good method to begin with is an object's initializer.

Initializers

At the beginning of this chapter, we discussed how an instance is created: its class is sent the message **alloc**, which creates an instance of that class and returns a pointer to it, and then that instance is sent the message **init**, which gives its instance variables initial values. As you start to write more complicated classes, you will want to create initialization methods, or *initializers*, that are like **init** but take arguments that the object can use to initialize itself. For example, the **BNRItem** class would be much cleaner if we could pass one or more of its instance variables as part of the initialization process.

To cover the different possible initialization scenarios, many classes have more than one initializer. Each initializer begins with the word **init**. Naming initializers this way doesn't make these methods different from other instance methods; it is only a naming convention. However, the Objective-C community is all about naming conventions, which you should strictly adhere to. (Seriously. Disregarding naming conventions in Objective-C results in problems that are worse than most beginners would imagine.)

For each class, regardless of how many initialization methods there are, one method is chosen as the *designated initializer*. The designated initializer makes sure that every instance variable of an object is valid. ("Valid" has different meanings, but in this context it means "when you send messages to this object after initializing it, you can predict the outcome and nothing bad will happen.")

Typically, the designated initializer has parameters for the most important and frequently used instance variables of an object. The **BNRItem** class has four instance variables, but only three are writeable. Therefore, **BNRItem**'s designated initializer should accept three arguments. In BNRItem.h, declare the designated initializer:

```
    NSDate *dateCreated;
}

- (id)initWithItemName:(NSString *)name
      valueInDollars:(int)value
        serialNumber:(NSString *)sNumber;

- (void)setItemName:(NSString *)str;
```

This method's name, or selector, is **initWithItemName:valueInDollars:serialNumber:**. This selector has three labels (**initWithItemName:**, **valueInDollars:**, and **serialNumber:**), which tells you that the method accepts three arguments.

These arguments each have a type and a parameter name. In the declaration, the type follows the label in parentheses. The parameter name then follows the type. So the label **initWithItemName:** is expecting a pointer to an instance of type **NSString**. Within the body of this method, you can use name to reference the **NSString** object pointed to.

id

Take another look at the initializer's declaration; its return type is id (pronounced "eye-dee"). This type is defined as "a pointer to any object." (id is a lot like void * in C.) **init** methods are always declared to return id.

Why not make the return type BNRItem *? After all, that is the type of object that is returned from this method. A problem will arise, however, if **BNRItem** is ever subclassed. The subclass would inherit all of the methods from **BNRItem**, including this initializer and its return type. An instance of the subclass could then be sent this initializer message, but what would be returned? Not a **BNRItem**, but an instance of the subclass. You might think, "No problem. Override the initializer in the subclass to change the return type." But in Objective-C, you cannot have two methods with the same selector and different return types (or arguments). By specifying that an initialization method returns "any object," we never have to worry what happens with a subclass.

isa

As programmers, we always know the type of the object that is returned from an initializer. (How do we know this? It is an instance of the class we sent **alloc** to.) The object itself also knows its type – thanks to its isa pointer.

Every object has an instance variable called isa. When an instance is created by sending **alloc** to a class, that class sets the isa instance variable of the returned object to point back at the class that created it (Figure 2.13). We call it the isa pointer because an object "is a" instance of that class.

Figure 2.13   The isa pointer

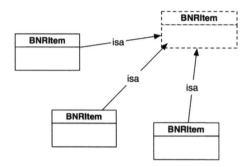

The isa pointer is where Objective-C gets much of its power. At runtime, when a message is sent to an object, that object goes to the class named in its isa pointer and says, "I was sent this message. Run the code for the matching method." This is different than most compiled languages, where the method to be executed is determined at compile time.

Implementing the designated initializer

Now that you have declared the designated initializer in BNRItem.h, you need to implement it. Open BNRItem.m. Recall that the definitions for methods go within the implementation block in the implementation file, so add the designated initializer there.

```
@implementation BNRItem

- (id)initWithItemName:(NSString *)name
        valueInDollars:(int)value
          serialNumber:(NSString *)sNumber
{
    // Call the superclass's designated initializer
    self = [super init];

    // Give the instance variables initial values
    [self setItemName:name];
    [self setSerialNumber:sNumber];
    [self setValueInDollars:value];
    dateCreated = [[NSDate alloc] init];

    // Return the address of the newly initialized object
    return self;
}
```

In the designated initializer, the first thing you always do is call the superclass's designated initializer using super. The last thing you do is return a pointer to the successfully initialized object using self. So to understand what's going on in an initializer, you will need to know about self and super.

self

Inside a method, self is an implicit local variable. There is no need to declare it, and it is automatically set to point to the object that was sent the message. (Most object-oriented languages have this concept, but some call it this instead of self.) Typically, self is used so that an object can send a message to itself:

```
- (void)chickenDance
{
    [self pretendHandsAreBeaks];
    [self flapWings];
    [self shakeTailFeathers];
}
```

In the last line of an **init** method, you always return the newly initialized object so that the caller can assign it to a variable:

```
return self;
```

super

Often when you are overriding a method, you want to keep what the method of the superclass is doing and have your subclass add something new on top of it. To make this easier, there is a compiler directive in Objective-C called super:

```
- (void)someMethod
{
    [self doMoreStuff];
    [super someMethod];
}
```

How does super work? Usually when you send a message to an object, the search for a method of that name starts in the object's class. If there is no such method, the search continues in the superclass of the object. The search will continue up the inheritance hierarchy until a suitable method is found. (If it gets to the top of the hierarchy and no method is found, an exception is thrown.)

When you send a message to super, you are sending a message to self, but the search for the method skips the object's class and starts at the superclass. In the case of **BNRItem**'s designated initializer, we send the **init** message to super. This calls **NSObject**'s implementation of **init**.

If an initializer message fails, it will return nil. Therefore, it is a good idea to save the return value of the superclass's initializer into the self variable and confirm that it is not nil before doing any further initialization. In BNRItem.m, edit your designated initializer to confirm the initialization of the superclass.

```
- (id)initWithItemName:(NSString *)name
        valueInDollars:(int)value
          serialNumber:(NSString *)sNumber
{
    // Call the superclass's designated initializer
    self = [super init];

    // Did the superclass's designated initializer succeed?
    if (self) {
        // Give the instance variables initial values
        [self setItemName:name];
        [self setSerialNumber:sNumber];
        [self setValueInDollars:value];
        dateCreated = [[NSDate alloc] init];
    }

    // Return the address of the newly initialized object
    return self;
}
```

Other initializers and the initializer chain

A class can have more than one initializer. First, let's consider a hypothetical example. **BNRItem** could have an initializer that takes only an **NSString** for the itemName. Its declaration would look like this:

```
- (id)initWithItemName:(NSString *)name;
```

In this initializer's definition, you wouldn't replicate the code in the designated initializer. Instead, this initializer would simply call the designated initializer, pass the information it was given as the itemName, and pass default values for the other arguments.

```
- (id)initWithItemName:(NSString *)name
{
    return [self initWithItemName:name
                    valueInDollars:0
                      serialNumber:@""];
}
```

Using initializers as a chain like this reduces the chance for error and makes maintaining code easier. For classes that have more than one initializer, the programmer who created the class chooses which initializer is designated. You only write the core of the initializer once in the designated initializer, and other initialization methods simply call that core with default values.

Now let's look at a real example. **BNRItem** actually has another initializer, **init**, which it inherits from its superclass **NSObject**. If **init** is sent to an instance of **BNRItem**, none of the stuff you put in the designated initializer will be called. Therefore, you must link **BNRItem**'s implementation of **init** to its designated initializer.

In BNRItem.m, override the **init** method to call the designated initializer with default values for all of the arguments.

```
- (id)init
{
    return [self initWithItemName:@"Item"
                    valueInDollars:0
                      serialNumber:@""];
}
```

The relationships between **BNRItem**'s initializers (real and hypothetical) are shown in Figure 2.14; the designated initializers are white, and the additional initializer is gray.

Figure 2.14   Initializer chain

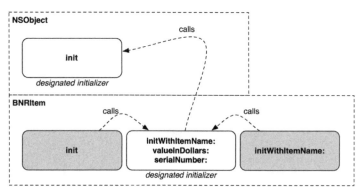

Let's form some simple rules for initializers from these ideas.

- A class inherits all initializers from its superclass and can add as many as it wants for its own purposes.

- Each class picks one initializer as its *designated initializer*.

- The designated initializer calls the superclass's designated initializer.

- Any other initializer a class has calls the class's designated initializer.

- If a class declares a designated initializer that is different from its superclass, the superclass's designated initializer must be overridden to call the new designated initializer.

Using Initializers

Currently, the code in main.m sends the message **init** to the new instance of **BNRItem**. With these new initializer methods, this message will run the **init** method you just implemented in **BNRItem**, which calls the designated initializer (**initWithItemName:valueInDollars:serialNumber:**) and passes default values. Let's make sure this works as intended.

In main.m, log the **BNRItem** to the console after it is initialized but before the setter messages are sent.

```
BNRItem *p = [[BNRItem alloc] init];

NSLog(@"%@", p);

// This creates a new NSString, "Red Sofa", and gives it to the BNRItem
[p setItemName:@"Red Sofa"];
```

Build and run the application. Notice that the console spits out the following messages:

```
Item (): Worth $0, recorded on 2011-07-19 18:56:42 +0000
Red Sofa (A1B2C): Worth $100, recorded on 2011-07-19 18:56:42 +0000
```

Now replace the code that initializes the **BNRItem** and the code sets its instance variables with a single message send using the designated initializer. Also, get rid of the code that populates the **NSMutableArray** with strings and prints them to the console. In main.m, make the following changes:

```
#import <Foundation/Foundation.h>
#import "BNRItem.h"

int main (int argc, const char * argv[])
{
    @autoreleasepool {

        NSMutableArray *items = [[NSMutableArray alloc] init];
        [items addObject:@"One"];
        [items addObject:@"Two"];
        [items addObject:@"Three"];
        [items insertObject:@"Zero" atIndex:0];

        for (int i = 0; i < [items count]; i++) {
            NSLog(@"%@", [items objectAtIndex:i]);
        }
```

```
        BNRItem *p = [[BNRItem alloc] init];
        NSLog(@"%@ %@ %@ %d", [p itemName], [p dateCreated],
                              [p serialNumber], [p valueInDollars]);

        BNRItem *p = [[BNRItem alloc] initWithItemName:@"Red Sofa"
                                         valueInDollars:100
                                           serialNumber:@"A1B2C"];

        NSLog(@"%@", p);

        items = nil;
    }
    return 0;
}
```

Build and run the application. Notice that the console now prints a single **BNRItem** that was instantiated with the values passed to **BNRItem**'s designated initializer.

Class methods

Methods come in two flavors: instance methods and class methods. *Instance methods* (like **init**) are sent to instances of the class, and *class methods* (like **alloc**) are sent to the class itself. Class methods typically either create new instances of the class or retrieve some global property of the class. Class methods do not operate on an instance or have any access to instance variables.

Syntactically, class methods differ from instance methods by the first character in their declaration. An instance method uses the - character just before the return type, and a class method uses the + character.

One common use for class methods is to provide convenient ways to create instances of that class. For the **BNRItem** class, it would be nice if you could create a random item so that you could test your class without having to think up a bunch of clever names. In BNRItem.h, declare a class method that will create a random item.

```
@interface BNRItem : NSObject
{
    NSString *itemName;
    NSString *serialNumber;
    int valueInDollars;
    NSDate *dateCreated;
}

+ (id)randomItem;

- (id)initWithItemName:(NSString *)name
        valueInDollars:(int)value
          serialNumber:(NSString *)sNumber;
```

Notice the order of the declarations for the methods. Class methods come first, followed by initializers, followed by any other methods. This is a convention that makes your header files easier to read.

In BNRItem.m, implement **randomItem** to create, configure, and return a **BNRItem** instance. (Again, make sure this method is between the @implementation and @end.)

```
+ (id)randomItem
{
    // Create an array of three adjectives
```

```
NSArray *randomAdjectiveList = [NSArray arrayWithObjects:@"Fluffy",
                                                         @"Rusty",
                                                         @"Shiny", nil];

// Create an array of three nouns
NSArray *randomNounList = [NSArray arrayWithObjects:@"Bear",
                                                   @"Spork",
                                                   @"Mac", nil];

// Get the index of a random adjective/noun from the lists
// Note: The % operator, called the modulo operator, gives
// you the remainder. So adjectiveIndex is a random number
// from 0 to 2 inclusive.
NSInteger adjectiveIndex = rand() % [randomAdjectiveList count];
NSInteger nounIndex = rand() % [randomNounList count];

// Note that NSInteger is not an object, but a type definition
// for "unsigned long"

NSString *randomName = [NSString stringWithFormat:@"%@ %@",
            [randomAdjectiveList objectAtIndex:adjectiveIndex],
            [randomNounList objectAtIndex:nounIndex]];

int randomValue = rand() % 100;

NSString *randomSerialNumber = [NSString stringWithFormat:@"%c%c%c%c%c",
                                '0' + rand() % 10,
                                'A' + rand() % 26,
                                '0' + rand() % 10,
                                'A' + rand() % 26,
                                '0' + rand() % 10];


BNRItem *newItem =
    [[self alloc] initWithItemName:randomName
                     valueInDollars:randomValue
                       serialNumber:randomSerialNumber];
    return newItem;
}
```

This method creates two arrays using the method **arrayWithObjects:**. This method takes a list of objects terminated by nil. nil is not added to the array; it just indicates the end of the argument list.

Then **randomItem** creates a string from a random adjective and noun, a random integer value, and another string from random numbers and letters. It then creates an instance of **BNRItem** and sends it the designated initializer message with these randomly-created objects and int as parameters.

In this method, you also used **stringWithFormat:**, which is a class method of **NSString**. This message is sent directly to **NSString**, and the method returns an **NSString** instance with the passed-in parameters. In Objective-C, class methods that return an object of their type (like **stringWithFormat:** and **randomItem**) are called *convenience methods*.

Notice the use of self in **randomItem**. Because **randomItem** is a class method, self refers to the **BNRItem** class itself instead of an instance. Class methods should use self in convenience methods instead of their class name so that a subclass can be sent the same message. In this case, if you create a subclass of **BNRItem**, you can send that subclass the message **randomItem**. Using self (instead of **BNRItem**) will allocate an instance of the class that was sent the message and set the instance's isa pointer to that class.

Testing your subclass

Open main.m. Delete the code that previously created and logged a single **BNRItem**. Then add **BNRItem** instances to the array and log them instead. Change your **main** function to look just like this:

```
#import <Foundation/Foundation.h>
#import "BNRItem.h"

int main (int argc, const char * argv[])
{
    @autoreleasepool {
        NSMutableArray *items = [[NSMutableArray alloc] init];

        BNRItem *p = [[BNRItem alloc] initWithItemName:@"Red Sofa"
                                        valueInDollars:100
                                          serialNumber:@"A1B2C"];

        NSLog(@"%@", p);


        for (int i = 0; i < 10; i++) {
            BNRItem *p = [BNRItem randomItem];
            [items addObject:p];
        }

        for (int i = 0; i < [items count]; i++) {
            NSLog(@"%@", [items objectAtIndex:i]);
        }


        items = nil;
    }
    return 0;
}
```

Build and run your application and then check the output in the log navigator. All you did was replace what objects you added to the array, and the code runs perfectly fine with a different output (Figure 2.15). Creating this class was a success.

Figure 2.15   Application result

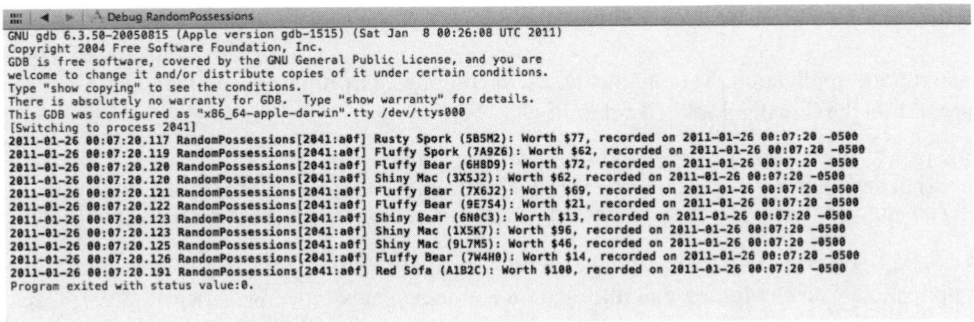

```
▦ ◀ ▶ ⅄ Debug RandomPossessions
GNU gdb 6.3.50-20050815 (Apple version gdb-1515) (Sat Jan  8 00:26:08 UTC 2011)
Copyright 2004 Free Software Foundation, Inc.
GDB is free software, covered by the GNU General Public License, and you are
welcome to change it and/or distribute copies of it under certain conditions.
Type "show copying" to see the conditions.
There is absolutely no warranty for GDB.  Type "show warranty" for details.
This GDB was configured as "x86_64-apple-darwin".tty /dev/ttys000
[Switching to process 2041]
2011-01-26 00:07:20.117 RandomPossessions[2041:a0f] Rusty Spork (5B5M2): Worth $77, recorded on 2011-01-26 00:07:20 -0500
2011-01-26 00:07:20.119 RandomPossessions[2041:a0f] Fluffy Spork (7A9Z6): Worth $62, recorded on 2011-01-26 00:07:20 -0500
2011-01-26 00:07:20.120 RandomPossessions[2041:a0f] Fluffy Bear (6H8D9): Worth $72, recorded on 2011-01-26 00:07:20 -0500
2011-01-26 00:07:20.120 RandomPossessions[2041:a0f] Shiny Mac (3X5J2): Worth $62, recorded on 2011-01-26 00:07:20 -0500
2011-01-26 00:07:20.121 RandomPossessions[2041:a0f] Fluffy Bear (7X6J2): Worth $69, recorded on 2011-01-26 00:07:20 -0500
2011-01-26 00:07:20.122 RandomPossessions[2041:a0f] Fluffy Bear (9E7S4): Worth $21, recorded on 2011-01-26 00:07:20 -0500
2011-01-26 00:07:20.123 RandomPossessions[2041:a0f] Shiny Bear (6N0C3): Worth $13, recorded on 2011-01-26 00:07:20 -0500
2011-01-26 00:07:20.123 RandomPossessions[2041:a0f] Shiny Mac (1X5K7): Worth $96, recorded on 2011-01-26 00:07:20 -0500
2011-01-26 00:07:20.125 RandomPossessions[2041:a0f] Shiny Mac (9L7M5): Worth $46, recorded on 2011-01-26 00:07:20 -0500
2011-01-26 00:07:20.126 RandomPossessions[2041:a0f] Fluffy Bear (7W4H0): Worth $14, recorded on 2011-01-26 00:07:20 -0500
2011-01-26 00:07:20.191 RandomPossessions[2041:a0f] Red Sofa (A1B2C): Worth $100, recorded on 2011-01-26 00:07:20 -0500
Program exited with status value:0.
```

Check out the #import statements at the top of main.m. Why did you have to import the class header BNRItem.h when you didn't you have to import, say, NSMutableArray.h? **NSMutableArray** comes from the Foundation framework, so it is included when you import Foundation/Foundation.h. On the other hand, your class exists in its own file, so you have to explicitly import it into `main.m`. Otherwise, the compiler won't know it exists and will complain loudly.

Exceptions and Unrecognized Selectors

An object only responds to a message if its class implements the associated method. Objective-C is a dynamically-typed language, so it can't always figure out at compile time (when the application is built) whether an object will respond to a message. Xcode will give you an error if it thinks you are sending a message to an object that won't respond, but if it isn't sure, it will let the application build.

If, for some reason (and there are many), you end up sending a message to an object that doesn't respond, your application will throw an *exception*. Exceptions are also known as *run-time errors* because they occur once your application is running as opposed to *compile-time errors* that show up when your application is being built, or compiled. (We'll come back to compile-time errors in Chapter 4.)

To practice dealing with exceptions, we're going to cause one in RandomPossessions. In `BNRItem.h`, declare a new method:

```
@interface BNRItem : NSObject
{
    NSString *itemName;
    NSString *serialNumber;
    int valueInDollars;
    NSDate *dateCreated;
}
- (void)doSomethingWeird;

+ (id)randomItem;
```

You are going to send the message **doSomethingWeird** to an instance of **BNRItem**. The problem? You didn't implement **doSomethingWeird** in BNRItem.m – you only declared it in BNRItem.h. Therefore, **BNRItem** does not implement **doSomethingWeird**, and an exception will be thrown. In `main.m`, send this message to a **BNRItem**.

```
for (int i = 0; i < 10; i++) {
    BNRItem *p = [BNRItem randomItem];
    [p doSomethingWeird];
    [items addObject:p];
}
```

Build and run the application. Your application will compile, start running, and then halt. Check your console and find the line that looks like this:

```
2011-11-14 12:23:47.990 RandomPossessions[10288:707] ***
Terminating app due to uncaught exception 'NSInvalidArgumentException', reason:
'-[BNRItem doSomethingWeird]: unrecognized selector sent to instance 0x100117280'
```

This is what an exception looks like. What exactly is it saying? First it tells us the date, time, and name of the application. You can ignore that information and focus on what comes after the "***." That line tells us that an exception occurred and the reason.

The reason is the most important piece of information an exception gives you. Here the reason tells us that an *unrecognized selector* was sent to an instance. You know that selector means message. You sent a message to an object, and the object does not implement that method.

The type of the receiver and the name of the message are also in this output, which makes it easier to debug. An instance of **BNRItem** was sent the message **doSomethingWeird**. The - at the beginning tells you the receiver was an instance of **BNRItem**. A + would mean the class itself was the receiver.

Xcode did try to warn us that something bad might happen: check the issue navigator to see the warning from the compiler that **BNRItem** has an incomplete implementation.

There are two important lessons to take away from this. First, always check the console if your application halts or crashes; errors that occur at runtime (exceptions) are just as important as those that occur during compiling. Second, remember that *unrecognized selector* means the message you are sending isn't implemented by the receiver. And by remember, I mean write it down somewhere. You will make this mistake more than once, and you'll want to be able to diagnose it quickly.

Some languages use try and catch blocks to handle exceptions. While Objective-C has this ability, we don't use it very often in application code. Typically, an exception is a programmer error and should be fixed in the code instead of handled at runtime.

Before continuing, remove the exception-causing code: first from main.m...

```
for (int i = 0; i < 10; i++) {
    BNRItem *p = [BNRItem randomItem];
    [p doSomethingWeird];
    [items addObject:p];
}
```

and then from BNRItem.h...

```
- (void)doSomethingWeird;
```

Fast Enumeration

Before Objective-C 2.0, we iterated through arrays the way you did in your **main** function:

```
for (int i = 0; i < [items count]; i++) {
    BNRItem *item = [items objectAtIndex:i];
    NSLog(@"%@", item);
}
```

Objective-C 2.0 introduced *fast enumeration*. With fast enumeration, you can write that code segment much more succinctly. Make the following change in main.m:

```
for (int i = 0; i < [items count]; i++) {
    BNRItem *item = [items objectAtIndex:i];
    NSLog(@"%@", item);
}

for (BNRItem *item in items) {
    NSLog(@"%@", item);
}

items = nil;
```

In this chapter, we have covered the basics of Objective-C. In the next chapter, we will discuss memory management in Cocoa Touch.

Challenges

Most chapters in this book will finish with at least one challenge that encourages you to take your work in the chapter one step further and prove to yourself what you've learned. We suggest that you tackle as many of these challenges as you can to cement your knowledge and move from *learning* iOS development from us to *doing* iOS development on your own.

Challenges come in three levels of difficulty:

- Bronze challenges typically ask you to do something very similar to what you did in the chapter. These challenges reinforce what you learned in the chapter and force you to type in similar code without having it laid out in front of you. Practice makes perfect.

- Silver-level challenges require you to do more digging and more thinking. You will need to use methods, classes, and properties that you haven't seen before. But the tasks are still similar to what you did in the chapter.

- Gold challenges are difficult and can take hours to complete. They require you to understand the concepts from the chapter and then do some quality thinking and problem-solving on your own. Tackling these challenges will prepare you for the real-world work of iOS development.

Before beginning any challenge: *always make a copy of your project directory in Finder and attack the challenge in that copy.* Many chapters build on previous chapters, and working on challenges in a copy of the project assures you will be able to progress through the book.

Bronze Challenge: Bug Finding

Create a bug in your program by asking for the eleventh item in the array. Run it and note the exception that gets thrown.

Silver Challenge: Another initializer

Create another initializer method for **BNRItem**. This initializer is *not* the designated initializer of **BNRItem**. It takes an **NSString** that identifies the itemName of the item and an **NSString** that identifies the serialNumber.

Gold Challenge: Another Class

Create a subclass of **BNRItem** named **BNRContainer**. A **BNRContainer** should have an array of subitems that contains instances of **BNRItem**. Printing the description of a **BNRContainer** should show you the name of the container, its value in dollars (a sum of all items in the container plus the value of the container itself), and a list of every **BNRItem** it contains. A properly-written **BNRContainer** can contain instances of **BNRContainer**. It can also report back its full value and every contained item properly.

Are You More Curious?

In addition to Challenges, many chapters will conclude with one or more "For the More Curious" sections. These sections offer deeper explanations of or additional information about the topics presented in the chapter. The knowledge in these sections is not absolutely essential to get you where you're going, but we hope you'll find it interesting and useful.

For the More Curious: Class Names

In simple applications like RandomPossessions, we only use a handful of classes. However, as applications grow larger and more complex, the number of classes grows. At some point, you will run into a situation where you have two classes that could easily be named the same thing. This is bad news. If two classes have the same name, it is impossible for your program to figure out which one it should use. This is known as a *namespace collision*.

Other languages solve this problem by declaring classes inside a *namespace*. You can think of a namespace as a group, to which classes belong. To use a class in these languages, you have to specify both the class name and the namespace.

Objective-C has no notion of namespaces. Instead, we prefix class names with two or three letters to keep them distinct. For example, in this exercise, the class was named **BNRItem** instead of **Item**.

Stylish Objective-C programmers always prefix their model and view classes. The prefix is typically related to the name of the application you are developing or the library it belongs to. For example, if I were writing an application named "MovieViewer," I would prefix all classes with **MV**. Classes that you will use across multiple projects typically bear a prefix that is related to your name (**JC**), your company's name (**BNR**), or a portable library (a library for dealing with maps might use **MAP**).

Controller objects, on the other hand, are typically only used in a single application and do not need a prefix. This isn't a rule – you can prefix your controller objects if you like, and you definitely should if they will be used in other applications.

Notice that Apple's classes have prefixes, too. Apple's classes are organized into frameworks (which we'll talk about in Chapter 4), and each framework has its own prefix. For instance, the **UILabel** class belongs to the UIKit framework. The classes **NSArray** and **NSString** belong to the Foundation framework. (The **NS** stands for NeXTSTEP, the platform for which these classes were originally designed.)

3

Managing Memory with ARC

In this chapter, you'll learn how memory is managed in iOS and the concepts that underlie *automatic reference counting*, or ARC. We'll start with some basics of application memory.

The Heap

All Objective-C objects are stored in a part of memory called *the heap*. When we send an **alloc** message to a class, a chunk of memory is allocated from the heap. This chunk includes space for the object's instance variables.

For example, consider an instance of **NSDate**, which represents a specific point in time. An **NSDate** has two instance variables: a double that stores the number of seconds since a fixed reference point in time and the isa pointer, which every object inherits from **NSObject**. A double is eight bytes, and a pointer is 4 bytes, so each time **alloc** is sent to the **NSDate** class, 12 bytes is allocated from the heap for a new **NSDate** object.

Consider another example: **BNRItem**. A **BNRItem** has five instance variables: four pointers (isa, itemName, serialNumber, and dateCreated) and an int (valueInDollars). The amount of memory needed for an int is four bytes, so the total size of a **BNRItem** is 20 bytes (Figure 3.1).

Figure 3.1   Byte count of BNRItem and NSDate instances

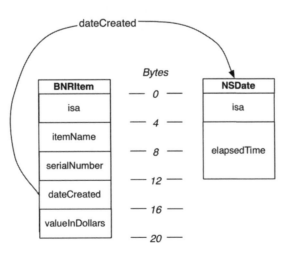

Notice in Figure 3.1 that the **NSDate** object does not live inside the **BNRItem**. Objects never live inside one another; they exist separately on the heap. Instead, objects keep references to other objects as needed. These references are the pointer instance variables of an object. Thus, when a **BNRItem**'s dateCreated instance variable is set, the *address* of the **NSDate** instance is stored in the **BNRItem**, not the **NSDate** itself. So, if the **NSDate** was 10, 20, or even 1000 bytes, it wouldn't affect the size of the **BNRItem**.)

The Stack

There is another part of memory called the *stack* that is separate from the heap. The reason for the names heap and stack has to do with how we visualize them. The heap is a giant heaping mess of objects, and we use pointers to remember where those objects are stored within the heap. The stack, on the other hand, can be visualized as a physical stack of *frames*.

When a method (or function) is executed, it allocates a chunk of memory from the stack. This chunk of memory is called a frame, and it stores the values for variables declared inside the method. A variable declared inside a method is called a *local variable*.

When an application launches and runs the **main** function, the frame for **main** is put at the bottom of the stack. When **main** calls another method (or function), the frame for that method is added to the top of the stack. Of course, that method could call another method, and so on, until we have a towering stack of frames. Then, as each method or function finishes, its frame is "popped off" the stack and destroyed. If the method is called again, a brand new frame will be allocated and put on the stack.

For example, in your RandomPossessions application, the **main** function runs **BNRItem**'s **randomItem** method, which in turn runs **BNRItem**'s **alloc** method. The stack would look like Figure 3.2. Notice that **main**'s frame stays alive while the other methods are executing because it has not yet finished executing.

Figure 3.2   Stack growing and shrinking

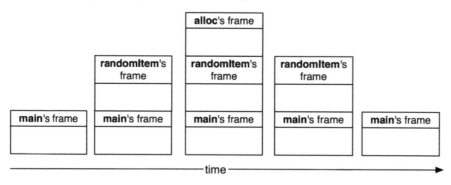

Recall that the **randomItem** method runs inside of a loop in the **main** function. So with every iteration, the stack grows and shrinks as frames are pushed on and popped off the stack.

Pointer Variables and Object Ownership

Pointer variables convey *ownership* of the objects that they point to.

- When a method (or function) has a local variable that points to an object, that method is said to *own* the object being pointed to.

- When an object has an instance variable that points to another object, the object with the pointer is said to *own* the object being pointed to.

Think back to your RandomPossessions application as a whole. Or, better yet, reopen RandomPossessions.xcodeproj and have another look at the code in main.m. In this application, an instance of **NSMutableArray** is created in the **main** function, and then 10 **BNRItem** instances are added to the array.

Figure 3.3 shows the objects in RandomPossessions and the pointers that reference them.

Figure 3.3   Objects and pointers in RandomPossessions

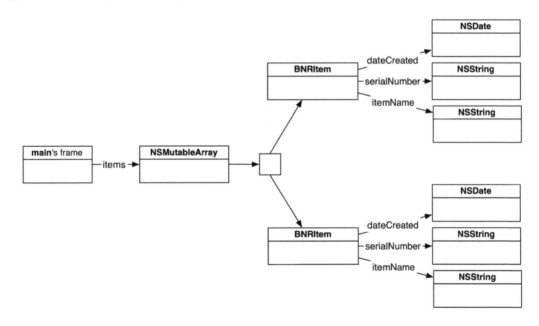

The **NSMutableArray** is pointed to by the local variable items within the **main** function, so the **main** function owns the **NSMutableArray**. Each **BNRItem** instance owns the objects pointed to by its instance variables.

In addition, the **NSMutableArray** owns the **BNRItems**. Recall that a collection object, like an **NSMutableArray**, holds pointers to objects instead of actually containing them. These pointers convey ownership: an array owns the objects it points to.

The relationship between pointers and object ownership is important for understanding memory management in iOS.

Memory Management

If heap memory were infinite, we could create all the objects we needed and have them exist for the entire run of the application. But an application gets only so much heap memory, and memory on an iOS device is especially limited. So it is important to destroy objects that are no longer needed to free up and reuse heap memory. On the other hand, it is critical *not* to destroy objects that *are* still needed.

The idea of object ownership helps us determine whether an object should be destroyed.

- *An object with no owners should be destroyed.* An ownerless object cannot be sent messages and is isolated and useless to the application. Keeping it around wastes precious memory. This is called a *memory leak.*

- *An object with at least one owner must not be destroyed.* If an object is destroyed but another object or method still has a pointer to it (or, more accurately, a pointer to where it used to live), then you have a very dangerous situation: sending a message to an object that no longer exists will crash your application. This is called *premature deallocation.*

Using ARC for memory management

The good news is that you don't need to keep track of who owns whom and what pointers still exist. Instead, your application's memory management is handled for you by *automatic reference counting*, or ARC.

In both projects you've built in Xcode so far, you've made sure to Use Automatic Reference Counting when creating the project (Figure 3.4). This won't change; all of your projects in this book will use ARC for managing your application's memory.

Figure 3.4   Naming a new project

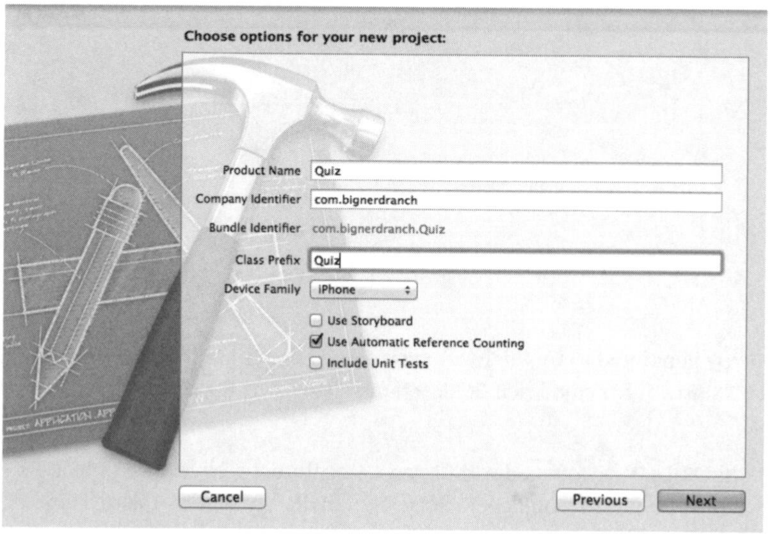

(If the Use Automatic Reference Counting box in Figure 3.4 was unchecked, the application would use *manual reference counting* instead, which was the only type of memory management available before iOS 5. For more information about manual reference counting and **retain** and **release** messages, see the For the More Curious section at the end of this chapter.)

ARC can be relied on to manage your application's memory automatically for the most part, but it's important to understand the concepts behind it to know how to step in when you need to. So let's return to the idea of object ownership.

How objects lose owners

We know that an object is safe to destroy – and should be destroyed – when it no longer has any owners. So how does an object lose an owner?

- A variable that points to the object is changed to point to another object.

- A variable that points to the object is set to `nil`.

- A variable that points to the object is itself destroyed.

Let's take a look at each of these situations.

Why might a pointer change the object it points to? Imagine a **BNRItem**. The **NSString** that its `itemName` instance variable points to reads "Rusty Spork." If we polished the rust off of that spork, it would become a shiny spork, and we'd want to change the `itemName` to point at a different **NSString** (Figure 3.5).

Figure 3.5   Changing a pointer

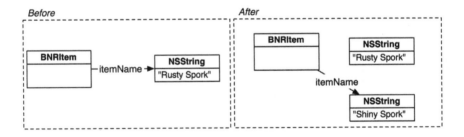

When the value of `itemName` changes from the address of the "Rusty Spork" string to the address of the "Shiny Spork" string, the "Rusty Spork" string loses an owner.

Why would you set a pointer to `nil`? Remember that setting a pointer to `nil` represents the absence of an object. For example, say you have a **BNRItem** that represents a television. Then, someone scratches off the television's serial number. You would then set its `serialNumber` instance variable to `nil`. The **NSString** that `serialNumber` used to point to loses an owner.

When a pointer variable itself is destroyed, the object that the variable was pointing at loses an owner. At what point a pointer variable will get destroyed depends on whether it is a local variable or an instance variable.

Recall that instance variables live in the heap as part of an object. When an object gets destroyed, its instance variables are also destroyed, and any object that was pointed to by one of those instance variables loses an owner.

Local variables live in the method's frame. When a method finishes executing and its frame is popped off the stack, any object that was pointed to by one of these local variables loses an owner.

There is one more important way an object can lose an owner. Recall that an object in a collection object, like an array, is owned by the collection object. When you remove an object from a mutable collection object, like an **NSMutableArray**, the removed object loses an owner.

```
[items removeObject:p];     // object pointed to by p loses an owner
```

Keep in mind that losing an owner doesn't necessarily mean that the object gets destroyed; if there is still another pointer to the object somewhere, then that object will continue to exist. However, when an object loses its last owner, it means certain and appropriate death.

Because objects own other objects, which can own other objects, the destruction of a single object can set off a chain reaction of loss of ownership, object destruction, and freeing up of memory.

We have an example of this in RandomPossessions. Take another look at the object diagram of this application.

Figure 3.6   Objects and pointers in RandomPossessions

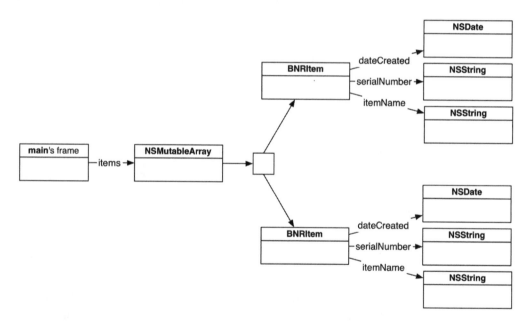

In main.m, after you finish printing out the array of **BNRItem**s, you set the items variable to nil. Setting items to nil causes the array to lose its only owner, so that array is destroyed.

But it doesn't stop there. When the **NSMutableArray** is destroyed, all of its pointers to **BNRItem**s are destroyed. Once these variables are gone, no one owns any of the **BNRItem**s, so they are all destroyed.

Destroying a **BNRItem** destroys its instance variables, which leaves the objects pointed to by those variables unowned. So they get destroyed, too.

Let's add some code so that we can see this destruction as it happens. **NSObject** implements a **dealloc** method, which is sent to an object when it is about to be destroyed. We can override this method in **BNRItem** to print something to the console when a **BNRItem** is destroyed. In RandomPossessions.xcodeproj, open BNRItem.m and override **dealloc**.

```
- (void)dealloc
{
    NSLog(@"Destroyed: %@", self);
}
```

In main.m, add the following line of code.

```
NSLog(@"Setting items to nil...");
items = nil;
```

Build and run the application. After the **BNRItem**s print out, you will see the message announcing that items is being set to nil. Then, you will see the destruction of each **BNRItem** logged to the console.

At the end, there are no more objects taking up memory, and only the **main** function remains. All this automatic clean-up and memory recycling occurs simply by setting items to nil. That's the power of ARC.

Strong and Weak References

So far, we've said that anytime a pointer variable stores the address of an object, that object has an owner and will stay alive. This is known as a *strong reference*. However, a variable can optionally *not* take ownership of an object it points to. A variable that does not take ownership of an object is known as a *weak reference*.

A weak reference is useful for an unusual situation called a *retain cycle*. A retain cycle occurs when two or more objects have strong references to each other. This is bad news. When two objects own each other, they will never be destroyed by ARC. Even if every other object in the application releases ownership of these objects, these objects (and any objects that they own) will continue to exist by virtue of those two strong references.

Thus, a retain cycle is a memory leak that ARC needs your help to fix. You fix it by making one of the references weak. Let's introduce a retain cycle in RandomPossessions to see how this works. First, we'll give **BNRItem** instances the ability to hold another **BNRItem** (so we can represent things like backpacks and purses). In addition, a **BNRItem** will know which **BNRItem** holds it. In BNRItem.h, add two instance variables and accessors

```
@interface BNRItem : NSObject
{
    NSString *itemName;
    NSString *serialNumber;
    int valueInDollars;
    NSDate *dateCreated;
```

```
    BNRItem *containedItem;
    BNRItem *container;
}

+ (id)randomItem;

- (id)initWithItemName:(NSString *)name
        valueInDollars:(int)value
          serialNumber:(NSString *)sNumber;

- (void)setContainedItem:(BNRItem *)i;
- (BNRItem *)containedItem;

- (void)setContainer:(BNRItem *)i;
- (BNRItem *)container;
```

Implement the accessors in BNRItem.m.

```
- (void)setContainedItem:(BNRItem *)i
{
    containedItem = i;

    // When given an item to contain, the contained
    // item will be given a pointer to its container
    [i setContainer:self];
}

- (BNRItem *)containedItem
{
    return containedItem;
}

- (void)setContainer:(BNRItem *)i
{
    container = i;
}

- (BNRItem *)container
{
    return container;
}
```

In main.m, remove the code that populated the array with random items. Then create two new items, add them to the array, and make them point at each other.

```
#import <Foundation/Foundation.h>
#import "BNRItem.h"

int main (int argc, const char * argv[])
{
    @autoreleasepool {
        NSMutableArray *items = [[NSMutableArray alloc] init];

        for (int i = 0; i < 10; i++) {
            BNRItem *p = [BNRItem randomItem];
            [items addObject:p];
        }

        for (BNRItem *item in items)
            NSLog(@"%@", item);
```

```
        BNRItem *backpack = [[BNRItem alloc] init];
        [backpack setItemName:@"Backpack"];
        [items addObject:backpack];

        BNRItem *calculator = [[BNRItem alloc] init];
        [calculator setItemName:@"Calculator"];
        [items addObject:calculator];

        [backpack setContainedItem:calculator];

        NSLog(@"Setting items to nil...");
        items = nil;
    }
    return 0;
}
```

Here's what the application looks like now:

Figure 3.7   RandomPossessions with retain cycle

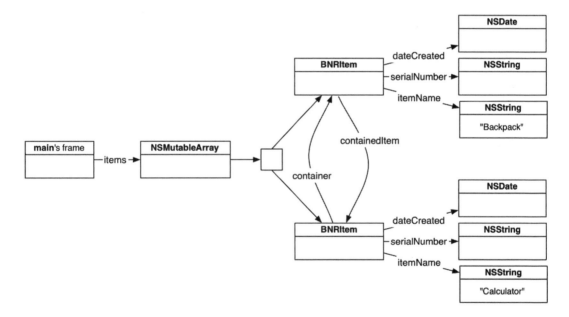

Per our understanding of memory management so far, both **BNRItem**s should be destroyed along with their instance variables when items is set to nil. Build and run the application. Notice that the console does not report that these objects have been destroyed.

This is a retain cycle: the backpack and the calculator have strong references to one another, so there is no way to destroy these objects. Figure 3.8 shows the objects in the application that are still taking up memory once items has been set to nil.

Figure 3.8   A retain cycle!

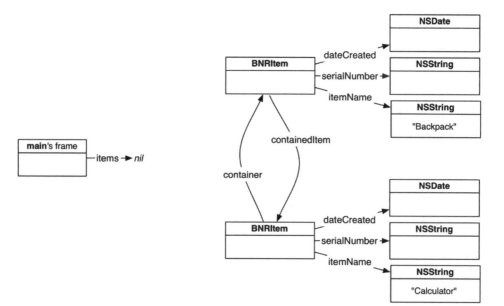

The two **BNRItem**s cannot be accessed by any other part of the application (in this case, the **main** function), yet they still exist in their own little world doing nothing useful. Moreover, because they cannot be destroyed, neither can the other objects that their instance variables point to.

To fix this problem, one of the pointers between the **BNRItem**s needs to be a weak reference. To decide which one should be weak, think of the objects in the cycle as being in a parent-child relationship. In this relationship, the parent can own its child, but a child should never its parent. In our retain cycle, the backpack is the parent, and the calculator is the child. Thus, the backpack can keep its strong reference to the calculator (`containedItem`), but the calculator's reference to the backpack (`container`) should be weak.

To declare a variable as a weak reference, we use the __weak attribute. In BNRItem.h, change the `container` instance variable to be a weak reference.

```
__weak BNRItem *container;
```

Build and run the application again. This time, the objects are destroyed properly.

Every retain cycle can be broken down into a parent-child relationship. A parent typically keeps a strong reference to its child, so if a child needs a pointer to its parent, that pointer must be a weak reference to avoid a retain cycle.

A child holding a strong reference to its *parent's* parent also causes a retain cycle. So the same rule applies in this situation: if a child needs a pointer to its parent's parent (or its parent's parent's parent, etc.), then that pointer must be a weak reference.

It's good to understand and look out for retain cycles, but keep in mind that they are quite rare. Also, Xcode has a Leaks tool to help you find them. We'll see how to use this tool in Chapter 21.

An interesting property of weak references is that they know when the object they reference is destroyed. Thus, if the backpack is destroyed, the calculator automatically sets its `container` instance variable to `nil`. In `main.m`, make the following changes to see this happen.

```
NSMutableArray *items = [[NSMutableArray alloc] init];

BNRItem *backpack = [[BNRItem alloc] init];
[backpack setItemName:@"Backpack"];
[items addObject:backpack];

BNRItem *calculator = [[BNRItem alloc] init];
[calculator setItemName:@"Calculator"];
[items addObject:calculator];

[backpack setContainedItem:calculator];

NSLog(@"Setting items to nil...");
items = nil;

backpack = nil;

NSLog(@"Container: %@", [calculator container]);

calculator = nil;
```

Build and run the application. Notice that after the backpack is destroyed, the calculator reports that it has no container without any additional work on our part.

A variable can also be declared using the __unsafe_unretained attribute. Like a weak reference, an unsafe unretained reference does not take ownership of the object it points to. Unlike a weak reference, an unsafe unretained reference is not automatically set to `nil` when the object it points to is destroyed. This makes unsafe unretained variables, well, unsafe. To see an example, change `container` to be unsafe unretained in `BNRItem.h`.

```
__unsafe_unretained BNRItem *container;
```

Build and run the application. It will most likely crash. The reason? When the calculator was asked for its container within the **NSLog** function call, it obligingly returned its value – the address in memory where the non-existent backpack used to live. Sending a message to a non-existent object resulted in a crash. Oops.

As a novice iOS programmer, you won't use __unsafe_unretained. As an experienced programmer, you probably won't use it, either. It exists primarily for backwards compatibility: applications prior to iOS 5 could not use weak references, so to have similar behavior, they must use __unsafe_unretained.

Be safe. Change this variable back to __weak.

```
__weak BNRItem *container;
```

Here's the current diagram of RandomPossessions. Notice that the arrow representing the `container` pointer variable is now a dotted line. A dotted line denotes a weak (or unsafe unretained reference). Strong references are always solid lines.

Figure 3.9   RandomPossessions with retain cycle avoided

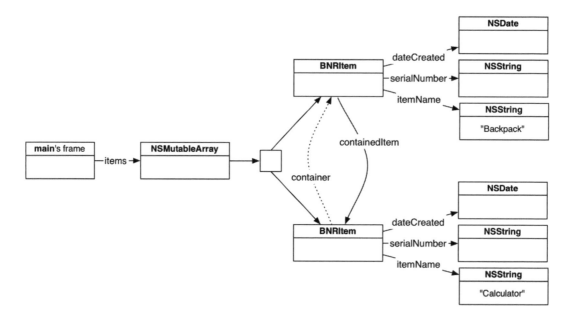

Properties

Each time we've added an instance variable to **BNRItem**, we've declared and implemented a pair of accessor methods. Now we're going to see how to use *properties* instead. Properties are a convenient alternative to writing out accessors for instance variables – one that saves a lot of typing and makes your class files much clearer to read.

Declaring properties

A property is declared in the interface of a class where methods are declared. A property declaration has the following form:

```
@property NSString *itemName;
```

When you declare a property, you are implicitly declaring a setter and a getter for the instance variable of the same name. So the above line of code is equivalent to the following:

```
- (void)setItemName:(NSString *)str;
- (NSString *)itemName;
```

Each property has a set of attributes that describe the behavior of the accessor methods. The attributes are declared in parentheses after the @property directive. Here is an example:

```
@property (nonatomic, readwrite, strong) NSString *itemName;
```

There are three property attributes. Each attribute has two or three options, one of which is the default and does not have to explicitly declared.

The first attribute of a property has two options: nonatomic or atomic. This attribute has to do with multi-threaded applications and is outside the scope of this book. Most Objective-C programmers typically use nonatomic: we do at Big Nerd Ranch, and so does Apple. In this book, we'll use nonatomic for all properties.

Let's change **BNRItem** to use properties instead of accessor methods. In BNRItem.h, replace all of your accessor methods with properties that are nonatomic.

```
- (id)initWithItemName:(NSString *)name
        valueInDollars:(int)value
          serialNumber:(NSString *)sNumber;

- (void)setItemName:(NSString *)str;
- (NSString *)itemName;

- (void)setSerialNumber:(NSString *)str;
- (NSString *)serialNumber;

- (void)setValueInDollars:(int)i;
- (int)valueInDollars;

- (NSDate *)dateCreated;

- (void)setContainedItem:(BNRItem *)i;
- (BNRItem *)containedItem;

- (void)setContainer:(BNRItem *)i;
- (BNRItem *)container;

@property (nonatomic) BNRItem *containedItem;
@property (nonatomic) BNRItem *container;

@property (nonatomic) NSString *itemName;
@property (nonatomic) NSString *serialNumber;
@property (nonatomic) int valueInDollars;
@property (nonatomic) NSDate *dateCreated;

@end
```

Unfortunately, nonatomic is not the default option, so you will always need to explicitly declare your properties to be nonatomic.

The second attribute of a property is either readwrite or readonly. A readwrite property declares both a setter and getter, and a readonly property just declares a getter. The default option for this attribute is readwrite. This is what we want for all of **BNRItem**'s properties with the exception of dateCreated, which should be readonly. In BNRItem.h, declare dateCreated as a readonly property so that no setter method is declared for this instance variable.

```
@property (nonatomic, readonly) NSDate *dateCreated;
```

The final attribute of a property describes its memory management. The default option depends on the type of the property. A property whose type is not a pointer to an object, like int, does not need memory management and thus defaults to assign. **BNRItem** only has one property that is not a pointer to an object, valueInDollars. For pointers to objects, like **NSString ***, this attribute defaults to strong. **BNRItem** has five object pointer properties: four of these will use strong, and the container property will use weak to avoid a retain cycle. With pointers to objects, it is good to be explicit and use the strong property to avoid confusion. In BNRItem.h, update the property declarations as shown.

```
@property (nonatomic, strong) BNRItem *containedItem;
@property (nonatomic, weak) BNRItem *container;

@property (nonatomic, strong) NSString *itemName;
@property (nonatomic, strong) NSString *serialNumber;
@property (nonatomic) int valueInDollars;
@property (nonatomic, readonly, strong) NSDate *dateCreated;
```

Build and run the application. You should see the exact same behavior as the last time you ran it. The only difference is that BNRItem.h is much cleaner.

Synthesizing properties

In addition to using a property to declare accessor methods, you can *synthesize* a property to generate the code for the accessor methods in the implementation file. Right now, BNRItem.m defines the accessor methods declared by each property. For example, the property itemName declares two accessor methods, **itemName** and **setItemName:**, and these are defined in BNRItem.m like so:

```
- (void)setItemName:(NSString *)str
{
    itemName = str;
}

- (NSString *)itemName
{
    return itemName;
}
```

When you synthesize a property, you don't have to type out the accessor definitions. You can synthesize a property by using the @synthesize directive in the implementation file. In BNRItem.m, add a synthesize statement for itemName and delete the implementations of **setItemName:** and **itemName**.

```
@implementation BNRItem
@synthesize itemName;

- (void)setItemName:(NSString *)str
{
    itemName = str;
}
- (NSString *)itemName
{
    return itemName;
}
```

You can synthesize properties in the same synthesize statement or split them up into multiple statements. In BNRItem.m, synthesize the rest of the instance variables and delete the rest of the accessor implementations.

```
@implementation
@synthesize itemName;
@synthesize containedItem, container, serialNumber, valueInDollars,
    dateCreated;

- (void)setSerialNumber:(NSString *)str
{
    serialNumber = str;
}
- (NSString *)serialNumber
```

```
{
    return serialNumber;
}
- (void)setValueInDollars:(int)i
{
    valueInDollars = i;
}
- (int)valueInDollars
{
    return valueInDollars;
}

- (NSDate *)dateCreated
{
    return dateCreated;
}

- (void)setContainedItem:(BNRItem *)i
{
    containedItem = i;

    // When given an item to contain, the contained
    // item will be given a pointer to its container
    [i setContainer:self];
}
- (BNRItem *)containedItem
{
    return containedItem;
}

- (void)setContainer:(BNRItem *)i
{
    container = i;
}
- (BNRItem *)container
{
    return container;
}
```

Usually, synthesized accessors work fine, but sometimes you need an accessor method to do some additional work. This is the case for **setContainedItem:**. Here is our original implementation:

```
- (void)setContainedItem:(BNRItem *)i
{
    containedItem = i;
    [i setContainer:self];
}
```

The synthesized setter won't include the second line establishing the reciprocal relationship between the container and the containedItem. Its implementation just looks like this:

```
- (void)setContainedItem:(BNRItem *)i
{
    containedItem = i;
}
```

Because we need this setter to do additional work, we cannot rely on the synthesized method and must write the implementation ourselves. Fortunately, writing our own implementation does not conflict with synthesizing the property. Any implementation we add will override the synthesized version. In BNRItem.m, add back the implementation of **setContainedItem:**.

```
- (void)setContainedItem:(BNRItem *)i
{
    containedItem = i;
    [i setContainer:self];
}
```

Build and run the application again. It should work the same as always, but your code is much cleaner.

Synthesizing a property that you declared in the header file is optional, but typical. The only reason not to synthesize a property is if both the getter and the setter methods have additional behavior you need to implement.

Instance variables and properties

With properties, we can go even one step further in code clarity. By default, a synthesized property will access the instance variable of the same name. For example, the itemName property accesses the itemName instance variable: the **itemName** method returns the value of the itemName instance variable, and the **setItemName:** method changes the itemName instance variable.

If there is no instance variable that matches the name of a synthesized property, one is automatically created. So declaring an instance variable *and* synthesizing a property is redundant. In BNRItem.h, remove all of the instance variables as well as the curly brackets.

```
@interface BNRItem : NSObject
{
    NSString *itemName;
    NSString *serialNumber;
    int valueInDollars;
    NSDate *dateCreated;

    BNRItem *containedItem;
    __weak BNRItem *container;
}
```

Build and run the application. Notice there are no errors and everything works fine. All of the instance variables (like itemName and dateCreated) still exist even though we no longer explicitly declare them.

Copying

There is one more change we need to make to our properties – specifically, the two properties that point to instances of **NSString**.

In general, when you have a property that points to an instance of a class that has a mutable subclass (like **NSString** or **NSArray**), it is safer to make a copy of the object to point to rather than pointing to an existing object that could have other owners.

For instance, imagine if a **BNRItem** was initialized so that its itemName pointed to an instance of **NSMutableString**.

```
NSMutableString *mutableString = [[NSMutableString alloc] init];

BNRItem *item = [[BNRItem alloc] initWithItemName:mutableString
                                    valueInDollars:5
                                      serialNumber:@"4F2W7"]];
```

This code is valid because an **NSMutableString** is also an instance of its superclass, **NSString**. The problem is that the string pointed to by mutableString can be changed without the knowledge of the **BNRItem** that also points to it.

You may be wondering why this is a real problem. In your application, you're not going to change this string unless you mean to. However, when you write classes for others to use, you can't be sure how they will use your classes, and you have to program defensively.

In this case, the defense is to declare this property using the memory management attribute copy instead of strong. In BNRItem.h, change the itemName and serialNumber properties to copy.

```
@property (nonatomic, copy) NSString *itemName;
@property (nonatomic, copy) NSString *serialNumber;
```

Now the generated setter method for the synthesized itemName property looks like this:

```
- (void)setItemName:(NSString *)str
{
    itemName = [str copy];
}
```

Instead of setting itemName to point to the **NSString** object pointed to by str, this setter sends the message **copy** to that **NSString**. The **copy** method returns a new **NSString** object (not an **NSMutableString**) that has the same values as the original string, and itemName is set to point at the new string. In terms of ownership, copy gives you a strong reference to the object pointed to. The original string is not modified in any way: it doesn't gain or lose an owner, and none of its data changes.

Dot Syntax

We should mention an alternative syntax for sending accessor messages to an object called dot syntax:

```
// Following two lines are exactly equivalent
int value = [item valueInDollars];
int value = item.valueInDollars;

// Following two lines are exactly equivalent
[item setValueInDollars:5];
item.valueInDollars = 5;
```

We have reservations about Objective-C newcomers using dot syntax. We think it hides the fact that you are actually sending a message and can be confusing. Once you are comfortable with Objective-C, it is totally okay to use dot syntax. But while you are learning, it's better to use square brackets to make sure you understand what is really going on.

This book will always use square brackets for sending accessor messages.

For the More Curious: Autorelease Pool and ARC History

Before automatic reference counting (ARC) was added to Objective-C, we had *manual reference counting*. With manual reference counting, ownership changes only happened when you sent an explicit message to an object.

```
[anObject release]; // anObject loses an owner

[anObject retain]; // anObject gains an owner
```

This was a bummer: Forgetting to send **release** to an object before setting a pointer to point at something else was a guaranteed memory leak. Sending **release** to an object if you had not previously sent **retain** to the object was a premature deallocation. A lot of time was spent debugging these problems, which could become very complex in large projects.

During the dark days of manual reference counting, Apple was contributing to an open source project known as the Clang static analyzer and integrating it into Xcode. You'll see more about the static analyzer in Chapter 21, but the basic gist is that it could analyze code and tell you if you were doing something silly. Two of the silly things it could detect were memory leaks and premature deallocations. Smart programmers would run their code through the static analyzer to detect these problems and then write the necessary code to fix them.

Eventually, the static analyzer got so good that Apple thought, "Why not just let the static analyzer insert all of the retain and release messages?" Thus, ARC was born. People rejoiced in the streets, and memory management problems became a thing of the past.

(Some people have an irrational fear of letting the compiler do their work for them and say they prefer manual memory management for this reason. If someone says something like that to you, open up one of their .m files, go to the Product menu, and select Generate Assembly File from the Generate Output menu item. Tell them if they don't trust the compiler, then they should be writing the assembly code they see in front of them.)

Another thing programmers had to understand in the days of manual reference counting was the *autorelease pool*. When an object was sent the message **autorelease**, the autorelease pool would take ownership of an object temporarily so that it could be returned from the method that created it without burdening the creator or the receiver with ownership responsibilities. This was crucial for convenience methods that created a new instance of some object and returned it:

```
- (BNRItem *)someItem
{
    BNRItem *item = [[[BNRItem alloc] init] autorelease];

    return item;
}
```

Because you had to send the **release** message to an object to relinquish ownership, the caller of this method had to understand its its ownership responsibilities. But it was easy to get confused.

```
BNRItem *item = [BNRItem someItem]; // I guess I own this now?

NSString *string = [item itemName]; // Well if I own that, do I own this?
```

Thus, objects created by methods other than **alloc** and **copy** would be sent **autorelease** before being returned, and the receiver of the object would take ownership as needed or just let it be destroyed after using it within the method in which it was returned.

With ARC, this is done automatically (and sometimes optimized out completely). An autorelease pool is created by the @autoreleasepool directive followed by curly brackets. Inside those curly brackets, any newly instantiated object returned from a method that doesn't have **alloc** or **copy** in its name is placed in that autorelease pool. When the curly bracket closes, any object in the pool loses an owner.

```
@autoreleasepool {
    // Get a BNRItem back from a method that created it, method doesn't say alloc/copy
    BNRItem *item = [BNRItem someItem];
} // item loses an owner and is destroyed because nothing else took ownership of it
```

iOS applications automatically create an autorelease pool for you, and you really don't have to concern yourself with it. But isn't it nice to know what that @autoreleasepool is for?

4

Delegation and Core Location

In this chapter, we will introduce delegation, a recurring design pattern of Cocoa Touch development, and the Core Location framework, which provides the location-finding features of iOS. In addition, we will see how to use the debugger that Xcode provides to find and fix problems in your code.

Also, in this chapter and the next, you will write an application called Whereami. This application will find the geographical location of the device, display it on an interactive map, and allow the user to tag the current location with a pin and a title.

From the File menu, select New and then New Project.... On the next window, select Application from the iOS section and create a Single View Application. Configure this project as shown in Figure 4.1.

Figure 4.1 Configuring the Whereami project

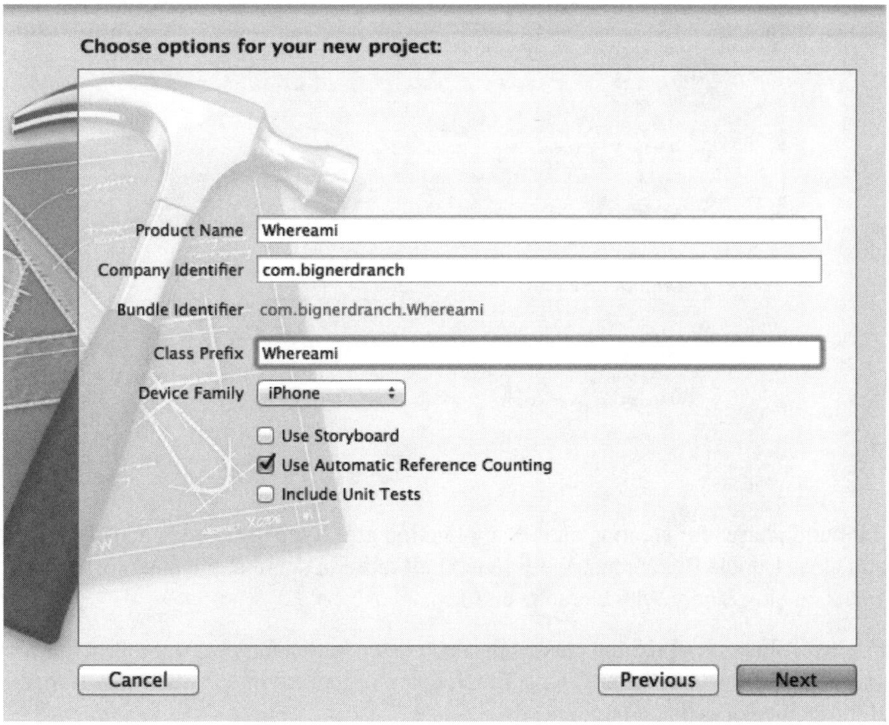

81

Projects, Targets, and Frameworks

Let's look more closely at the what this new project actually is. A *project* is a file that contains a list of references to other files (source code, resources, frameworks, and libraries) as well as a number of settings that lay out the rules for items within the project. Projects end in .xcodeproj, as in Whereami.xcodeproj.

A project always has at least one target. A *target* uses the files in the project to build a particular product. When you build and run, you build and run the target, not the project. The *product* the target builds is typically an application, although it can be a compiled library or a unit test bundle.

When you create a new project and choose a template, Xcode automatically creates a target for you. When you created the Whereami project, you selected an iOS application template, so Xcode created an iOS application target and named it Whereami.

In the project navigator, select the Whereami project (the item at the very top). Notice that the Whereami project and the Whereami target are listed in the editor area. Select the Whereami target to see the details and settings that define this target. We won't discuss all of these now, but we'll come back to different ones throughout the book as we need them. From the choices at the top of the editor area, select Build Phases (Figure 4.2). The target's build phases are a series of steps, and these steps lead, in this case, to an iOS application.

Figure 4.2   Build phases of the Whereami target

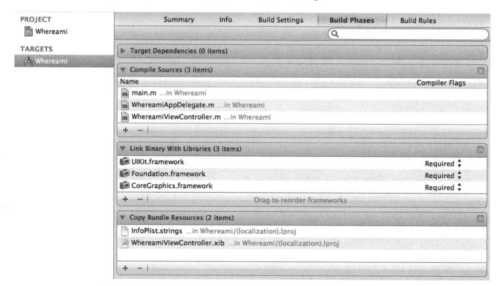

The essential build phases for creating an iOS application are Compile Sources, Link Binary With Libraries, and Copy Bundle Resources. We'll look at all three in detail at the end of the chapter. For now, let's focus on Link Binary With Libraries and *frameworks*.

A framework is a collection of related classes that you can add to a target. Cocoa Touch is a collection of frameworks. One of the benefits of Cocoa Touch being organized into frameworks is that you only have to add the frameworks that a target needs.

To see what frameworks are already linked to your target, click the disclosure button next to Link Binary With Libraries. Right now, there are three: the UIKit framework contains classes that make up the iOS user interface, the Foundation framework includes classes like **NSString** and **NSArray**, and Core Graphics enables the graphics library that we will dig into starting in Chapter 6.

Whereami also needs the Core Location framework, which includes the classes related to finding a device's location. To add this framework to your target, click the plus (+) button in the bottom left corner of the Link Binary With Libraries section. A sheet that displays the available frameworks will appear (Figure 4.3). Select CoreLocation.framework from this list and click Add.

Figure 4.3   Adding the Core Location framework

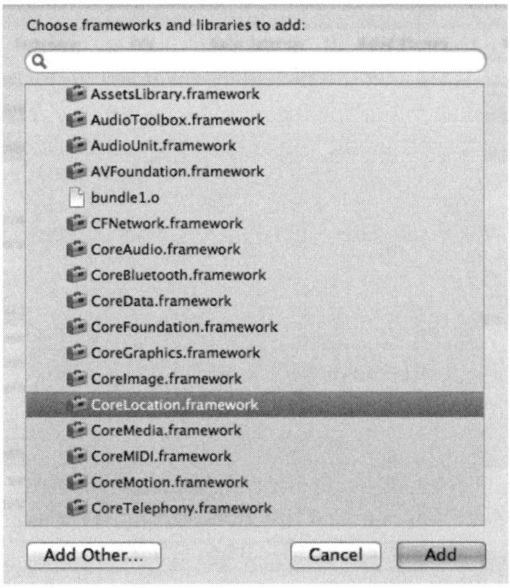

CoreLocation.framework will now appear in the Link Binary With Libraries phase and in the project navigator. In the project navigator, you can move the framework to the Frameworks group to keep your project tidy, but you don't have to.

Make sure you remember how to add a framework to a project – you will be doing it often!

Core Location

The Core Location framework contains the classes that enable applications to determine the device's geographical location. No matter what type of iOS device is being used, the Core Location code you write does not change.

In addition to adding the Core Location framework to your target, you also have to import the framework's header file into files that need to know about Core Location classes. Every framework has a header file that imports the header file of every class in that framework. This file is always the name of the framework suffixed with .h.

Open WhereamiViewController.h and import the Core Location header file at the top. Also, add an instance variable to hold a pointer to an instance of **CLLocationManager** – one of the classes in the Core Location framework.

```
#import <UIKit/UIKit.h>
#import <CoreLocation/CoreLocation.h>

@interface WhereamiViewController : UIViewController
{
    CLLocationManager *locationManager;
}

@end
```

CLLocationManager is the class that interfaces with the location hardware of the device. An instance of **CLLocationManager** has a number of properties that specify its behavior. We're going to set one of them: desiredAccuracy.

The desiredAccuracy property tells the location manager how accurate the location-finding should be. This is important because there is a tradeoff between the accuracy of the location and the amount of time and battery life required to determine the location. Moreover, the accuracy ultimately depends on the type of device the user has, the availability of cellular towers and satellites, and the availability of known wireless access points.

Open WhereamiViewController.m and delete all of the code between @implementation and @end. The file should now look like this:

```
#import "WhereamiViewController.h"

@implementation WhereamiViewController

@end
```

Now in WhereamiViewController.m, override **initWithNibName:bundle:** to instantiate a **CLLocationManager**, set the desiredAccuracy to request the most accurate location data as often as possible, and then tell the **CLLocationManager** to start working.

```
- (id)initWithNibName:(NSString *)nibNameOrNil bundle:(NSBundle *)nibBundleOrNil
{
    self = [super initWithNibName:nibNameOrNil bundle:nibBundleOrNil];

    if (self) {
        // Create location manager object
        locationManager = [[CLLocationManager alloc] init];

        // And we want it to be as accurate as possible
        // regardless of how much time/power it takes
        [locationManager setDesiredAccuracy:kCLLocationAccuracyBest];

        // Tell our manager to start looking for its location immediately
        [locationManager startUpdatingLocation];
    }

    return self;
}
```

Once you tell the **CLLocationManager** to start working, it does its thing while the rest of the application continues with other tasks – like accepting user input or updating the interface.

Receiving updates from CLLocationManager

If you build and run this code right now, the location manager will get your current location, but you won't see this information anywhere. Your application has to retrieve the location from the location manager. You might guess that there is a property on **CLLocationManager** called currentLocation that we can access to retrieve the location. It's a good guess, but there isn't.

Instead, whenever the location manager finds the current location, it sends the message **locationManager:didUpdateToLocation:fromLocation:** to its *delegate*. What object is the location manager's delegate? We get to decide.

Every **CLLocationManager** has a delegate property, and we can set this property to point to the object that we want to receive the "location found" message. For Whereami, this object is the **WhereamiViewController** (Figure 4.4).

Figure 4.4 Whereami object diagram

In WhereamiViewController.m, update the **initWithNibName:bundle:** method to set the delegate property of the location manager to be the instance of **WhereamiViewController**.

```
locationManager = [[CLLocationManager alloc] init];

// There will be a warning from this line of code; ignore it for now
[locationManager setDelegate:self];

[locationManager setDesiredAccuracy:kCLLocationAccuracyBest];
```

Two of the arguments of **locationManager:didUpdateToLocation:fromLocation:** are instances of a class named **CLLocation**. (All of the classes in the Core Location framework are prefixed with **CL**.) When a **CLLocationManager** has enough data to produce a new location, it creates an instance of **CLLocation**, which contains the latitude and longitude of the device (Figure 4.5). It also contains the accuracy of its reading and, depending on the device, the elevation above sea level.

Figure 4.5   A CLLocation object

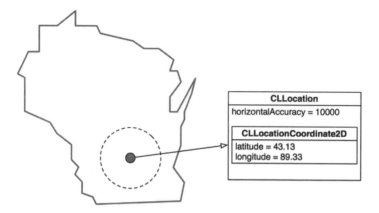

Because the **CLLocationManager** sends the **locationManager:didUpdateToLocation:fromLocation:** message to its delegate, you must implement this method in WhereamiViewController.m. For now, just have this method print the device's location to the console. (Be very careful that there are no typos or capitalization errors, or the method won't be called. The selector of the message the location manager sends must exactly match the selector of the method implemented.)

```
- (void)locationManager:(CLLocationManager *)manager
      didUpdateToLocation:(CLLocation *)newLocation
             fromLocation:(CLLocation *)oldLocation
{
    NSLog(@"%@", newLocation);
}
```

You also need to know if the **CLLocationManager** fails to find its location and why. If it fails, **CLLocationManager** sends a different message to its delegate – **locationManager:didFailWithError:**. In WhereamiViewController.m, implement this method.

```
- (void)locationManager:(CLLocationManager *)manager
        didFailWithError:(NSError *)error
{
    NSLog(@"Could not find location: %@", error);
}
```

Build and run the application. You can build to the simulator or to a device by selecting the appropriate item from the Scheme pop-up button next to the Run and Stop buttons.

If you are running Whereami on the simulator, you'll have to simulate its location once Whereami is running. When you run an application from Xcode, a bar appears at the bottom of the editor area with several icons. Click the ⊿ icon in this bar and then select a location from the drop-down list (Figure 4.6).

Figure 4.6   Simulating a location

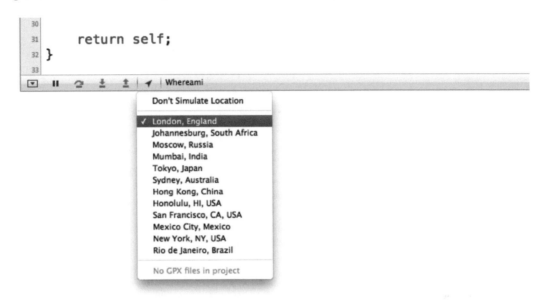

After giving permission for the application to use location services on the device and waiting a few seconds while the location is found (or simulated), your console will display the description of the location object, which will look something like this:

```
<+37.33168900, -122.03073100> +/- 100.00m (speed -1.00 mps / course -1.00)
```

Delegation

When you set the `delegate` property of the **CLLocationManager** and implemented the two location-finding methods in **WhereamiViewController**, you were using a design pattern called *delegation*. This is a very common pattern in Cocoa Touch, and many classes have a `delegate` property.

Delegation is an object-oriented approach to *callbacks*. A callback is a function that is supplied in advance of an event and is called every time the event occurs. Some objects need to make a callback for more than one event. For instance, the location manager wants to "callback" when it finds a new location and when it encounters an error.

However, there is no built-in way for two (or more) callback functions to coordinate and share information. This is the problem addressed by delegation – we supply a single delegate to receive all of the event messages for a particular object. This delegate object can then store, manipulate, act on, and relay the related information as it sees fit.

Let's compare delegation with another object-oriented approach to callbacks: target-action pairs. You used target-action pairs with the **UIButton**s in your Quiz application from Chapter 1. In a target-action pair, you have a target object that you send an action message when a particular event occurs (like a button tap). A new target-action pair must be created for each distinct event (like a tap, a double tap, or a long press). With delegation, you set the delegate once and then can send it messages for many different events. The delegate will implement the methods that correspond to the events it wants to hear about (Figure 4.7).

Figure 4.7   Target-action vs. delegation

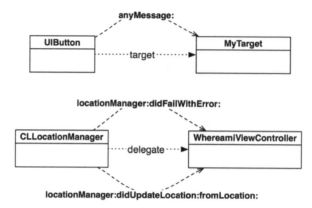

Also, with a target-action pair, the action message can be any message. In delegation, an object can only send its delegate messages from a specific set listed in a *protocol*.

Protocols

For every object that can have a delegate, there is a corresponding *protocol* that declares the messages that the object can send its delegate. The delegate implements methods from the protocol for events it is interested in. When a class implements methods from a protocol, it is said to *conform to* the protocol.

The protocol for **CLLocationManager**'s delegate looks like this:

```
// Note that we omitted a few methods from
// the real declaration of this protocol
// for brevity's sake
@protocol CLLocationManagerDelegate <NSObject>

@optional

- (void)locationManager:(CLLocationManager *)manager
    didUpdateToLocation:(CLLocation *)newLocation
          fromLocation:(CLLocation *)oldLocation;

- (void)locationManager:(CLLocationManager *)manager
      didUpdateHeading:(CLHeading *)newHeading;

- (BOOL)locationManagerShouldDisplayHeadingCalibration:(CLLocationManager *)manager;

- (void)locationManager:(CLLocationManager *)manager
        didEnterRegion:(CLRegion *)region;

- (void)locationManager:(CLLocationManager *)manager
      didFailWithError:(NSError *)error;
@end
```

This protocol, like all protocols, is declared with the directive @protocol followed by its name, CLLocationManagerDelegate. The NSObject in angled brackets refers to the NSObject protocol and tells us that CLLocationManagerDelegate includes all of the methods in the NSObject protocol. The methods specific to CLLocationManagerDelegate are declared next, and the protocol is closed with an @end directive.

Note that a protocol is not a class; it is simply a list of methods. You cannot create instances of a protocol, it cannot have instance variables, and these methods are not implemented anywhere in the protocol. Instead, implementation is left to each class that conforms to the protocol.

We call protocols used for delegation *delegate protocols*, and the naming convention for a delegate protocol is the name of the delegating class plus the word Delegate. Not all protocols are delegate protocols, however, and we will see an example of a different kind of protocol in the next chapter.

The protocols we've mentioned so far are part of the iOS SDK, but you can also write your own protocols. We'll do that later in Chapter 13 and Chapter 26.

Protocol methods

In the CLLocationManagerDelegate protocol, we see two kinds of methods: methods that handle information updates and methods that handle requests for input. For example, the location manager's delegate implements the **locationManager:didEnterRegion:** method if it wants to hear from the location manager that the device has entered a particular region. This is an information update.

On the other hand, **locationManagerShouldDisplayHeadingCalibration:** is a request for input. A location manager sends its delegate this message to ask if it should display the heading calibration. The method returns a Boolean value, which is the delegate's answer.

Methods declared in a protocol can be required or optional. By default, protocol methods are required. If a protocol has optional methods, these are preceded by the directive @optional. Looking back at the CLLocationManagerDelegate protocol, you can see that all of its methods are optional. This is typically true of delegate protocols.

Before sending an optional message, the object first asks its delegate if it is okay to send that message by sending another message, **respondsToSelector:**. Every object implements this method, which checks at runtime whether an object implements a given method. You can turn a method selector into a value that you can pass as an argument with the @selector() directive. For example, **CLLocationManager** could implement a method that looks like this:

```
- (void)finishedFindingLocation:(CLLocation *)newLocation
{
    // locationManager:didUpdateToLocation:fromLocation:
    // is an optional method, so we check first.
    SEL updateMethod = @selector(locationManager:didUpdateToLocation:fromLocation:);

    if ([[self delegate] respondsToSelector:updateMethod]) {
        // If the method is implemented, then we send the message.
        [[self delegate] locationManager:self
                    didUpdateToLocation:newLocation
                          fromLocation:oldLocation];
    }
}
```

If a method in a protocol is required, then the message will be sent without checking first. This means that if the delegate does not implement that method, an unrecognized selector exception will be thrown, and the application will crash.

To prevent this from happening, the compiler will insist that a class implement the required methods in a protocol. But, for the compiler to know to check for implementations of a protocol's required methods, the class must explicitly state that it conforms to a protocol. This is done in the class header file: the protocols that a class conforms to are added to a comma-delimited list inside angled brackets in the interface declaration following the superclass.

In WhereamiViewController.h, declare that **WhereamiViewController** conforms to the CLLocationManagerDelegate protocol.

```
@interface WhereamiViewController : UIViewController <CLLocationManagerDelegate>
```

Build the application again. Now that you've declared that **WhereamiViewController** conforms to the CLLocationManagerDelegate protocol, the warning from the line of code where you set the delegate of the locationManager disappears. Furthermore, if you want to implement additional methods from the CLLocationManagerDelegate protocol in **WhereamiViewController**, those methods will now be auto-completed by Xcode.

Delegation, controllers, and memory management

From the perspective of the model-view-controller pattern, **WhereamiViewController** is a controller object. It is typically the case that delegates are controller objects. In addition, a controller object typically owns the objects that are delegating to it. For example, **WhereamiViewController** owns the **CLLocationManager**, and the **CLLocationManager**'s delegate is the **WhereamiViewController**.

Figure 4.8   Controllers own objects, objects delegate to controllers

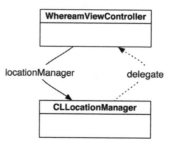

From our discussion in Chapter 3, recall that this reciprocal relationship would create a retain cycle if both objects held strong references to each other. To avoid such a cycle, the **CLLocationManager**'s delegate property is not a strong reference. But it is not a weak reference, either. To maintain backwards-compatibility with non-ARC versions of iOS, delegate properties are __unsafe_unretained.

Because delegate is unsafe unretained instead of weak, it is not automatically set to nil when the object it points to is destroyed. You have to do that yourself in the delegate object's **dealloc** method.

In WhereamiViewController.m, override **dealloc**.

```
- (void)dealloc
{
    // Tell the location manager to stop sending us messages
    [locationManager setDelegate:nil];
}
```

It is a little deceptive on our part to have you implement **dealloc** for **WhereamiViewController**. Why? Because the **WhereamiViewController** will never be destroyed in this application – the

dealloc method you just implemented will never be called. The Whereami application needs the **WhereamiViewController** from beginning to end, so the **WhereamiViewController** always has an owner.

However, many controller objects in your applications will get destroyed, and some of these will be delegates of other objects. As you go through this book, you'll start to see which controllers in an application get destroyed and which stick around for the life of the application. For now, it is best to be safe, learn the ropes, and implement **dealloc** for **WhereamiViewController** to set the locationManager's delegate to nil.

In the next chapter, we'll give Whereami a user interface. Right now, let's take a look at how to work with the debugger that comes with Xcode.

Using the Debugger

When an application is launched from Xcode, the debugger is attached to it. The debugger monitors the current state of the application, like what method it is currently executing and the values of the variables that are accessible from that method. Using the debugger can help you understand what an application is actually doing, which, in turn, helps you find and fix bugs.

Using breakpoints

One way to use the debugger is to set a *breakpoint*. Setting a breakpoint on a line of code pauses the execution of the application at that line (before it executes). Then you can execute the subsequent code line by line. This is useful when your application is not doing what you expected and you need to isolate the problem.

In WhereamiViewController.m, find the line of code in **initWithNibName:bundle:** where you instantiate the **CLLocationManager**. Set a breakpoint by clicking the gutter (the lightly shaded bar on the left side of the editor area) next to that line of code (Figure 4.9). The blue indicator shows you where the application will "break" the next time you run it.

Figure 4.9   A breakpoint

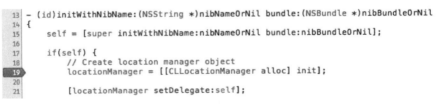

```
13   - (id)initWithNibName:(NSString *)nibNameOrNil bundle:(NSBundle *)nibBundleOrNil
14   {
15       self = [super initWithNibName:nibNameOrNil bundle:nibBundleOrNil];
16
17       if(self) {
18           // Create location manager object
19           locationManager = [[CLLocationManager alloc] init];
20
21           [locationManager setDelegate:self];
```

Build and run the application. The application will start and then halt before the line of code where you put the breakpoint. Notice the green indicator that appears on the same line as the breakpoint. This indicator shows you the current point of execution.

Now our application is temporarily frozen in time, and we can examine it more closely. In the navigator area, click the ☰ icon to open the *debug navigator*. This navigator shows a *stack trace* of where the breakpoint stopped execution. A stack trace shows you the methods and functions whose frames were in the stack when the application broke. The slider at the bottom of the debug navigator expands and collapses the stack. Drag it to the right to see all of the methods in the stack trace. (Figure 4.10).

Figure 4.10   The debug navigator

The method where the break occurred is at the top of the stack trace. It was called by the method just below it, which was called by the method just below it, and so on. This chain of method calls continues all the way back to **main**. Notice that the two methods that you implemented are in black text and the methods belonging to Apple are in gray.

Select the method at the top of the stack. This will display the implementation of **initWithNibName:bundle:** in the editor area. Below the editor area, check out the variables view to the left of the console. This area shows the variables within the scope of this method along with their current values (Figure 4.11).

Figure 4.11   Debug area with variables view

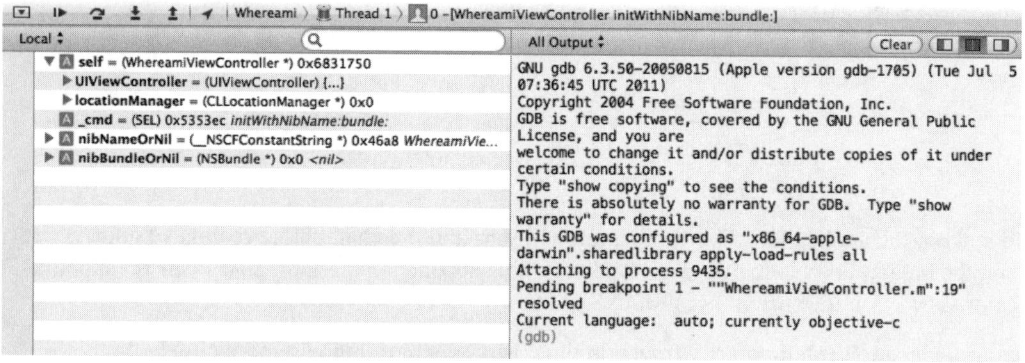

(If you don't see the variables view, find the  ⬛⬛⬛ control above the console. Click the center button to see both the console and the variables view.)

In the variables view, a pointer variable shows the object's address in memory. (There are some exceptions; for an **NSString**, the actual string is shown instead.) A variable that is not a pointer, like int, just shows its value.

Click the disclosure button next to self. The first item under self is its superclass. In the context of this method, self is a pointer to the instance of **WhereamiViewController**, so its superclass is **UIViewController**. Clicking the disclosure button next to **UIViewController** will show the variables self inherits from its superclass.

After the superclass, the object's instance variables are listed, which for **WhereamiViewController** is just locationManager. The breakpoint is set to the line that creates the instance of **CLLocationManager** and assigns it to locationManager. That line of code has yet to be executed, so locationManager is still set to nil (0x0).

Stepping through code

In addition to giving you a snapshot of the application at a given point, the debugger also allows you to *step through* your code line by line and see what your application does as each line executes. The buttons that control the execution are on the *debugger bar* that sits between the editor area and the debug area (Figure 4.12).

Figure 4.12   Debugger bar

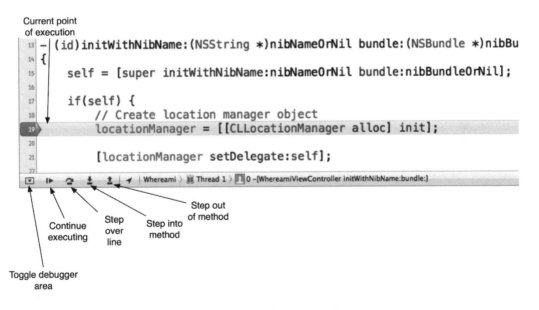

Click the button that steps over a line. This will execute just the current line of code, which instantiates the **CLLocationManager**. Notice that the green execution indicator moves to the next line. Even more interesting, the variables view shows that the value of locationManager has changed to a valid address in memory – this object is now alive and well.

At this point, you could continue stepping through the code to see what happens. Or you could click the button to continue executing your code normally. Or you could step into a method. Stepping into a method takes you to the method that is called by the line of code that currently has the green execution indicator. Once you're in the method, you have the chance to step through its code in the same way.

Let's add a method that we can step into and out of. Declare the following method in WhereamiViewController.h.

```
#import <UIKit/UIKit.h>
#import <CoreLocation/CoreLocation.h>

@interface WhereamiViewController : UIViewController <CLLocationManagerDelegate>
{
    CLLocationManager *locationManager;
}

- (void)doSomethingWeird;

@end
```

In WhereamiViewController.m, implement this method to log some stuff to the console.

```
- (void)doSomethingWeird
{
    NSLog(@"Line 1");
    NSLog(@"Line 2");
    NSLog(@"Line 3");
}
```

Next in WhereamiViewController.m, send this message to the instance of **WhereamiViewController** in **initWithNibName:bundle:**.

```
- (id)initWithNibName:(NSString *)nibNameOrNil bundle:(NSBundle *)nibBundleOrNil
{
    self = [super initWithNibName:nibNameOrNil bundle:nibBundleOrNil];

    if (self) {
        // Create location manager object
        locationManager = [[CLLocationManager alloc] init];

        [self doSomethingWeird];
```

Finally, drag your breakpoint to this newly-implemented line. Build and run the application.

When the execution halts, click the button on the debugger bar to step into this method. The execution indicator will jump *inside* the **doSomethingWeird** method to the first line of its implementation. Now click the button to step over a line. The line of code that logs Line 1 will execute, and you will see its text in the console.

The execution indicator is now at the statement that logs Line 2. If you've decided that you've seen enough of this fascinating method, you can click the button to step out of it. Notice that the rest of the log statements appear in the console, and the execution indicator is now back in **initWithNibName:bundle:** – right after the call to **doSomethingWeird**. This behavior is important to understand: when you step out of a method, you don't cancel its execution; the method finishes normally and returns to the code that called it.

To remove the breakpoint, simply drag it off the gutter. Or click the ➥ icon in the navigator selector to reveal the breakpoint navigator and see all the breakpoints in your project. From there, you can select a breakpoint and hit the delete key.

Sometimes, a new developer will set a breakpoint and forget about it. Then, when the application is run, execution stops, and it looks like the application has crashed. If an application of yours unexpectedly halts, make sure you aren't stopped on a forgotten breakpoint.

Diagnosing crashes and exceptions

While you can set breakpoints yourself to break on a particular line, it would be nice if the debugger would automatically set a breakpoint on any line that causes your application to crash or that causes an exception to be thrown.

To get the debugger to do this, we need to add a breakpoint for all exceptions. Select the breakpoint navigator. Then, at the bottom of the navigator area, click the + icon and select Add Exception Breakpoint.... Then, click the Done button on the panel that pops up (Figure 4.13).

Figure 4.13   Turning on exception breakpoints

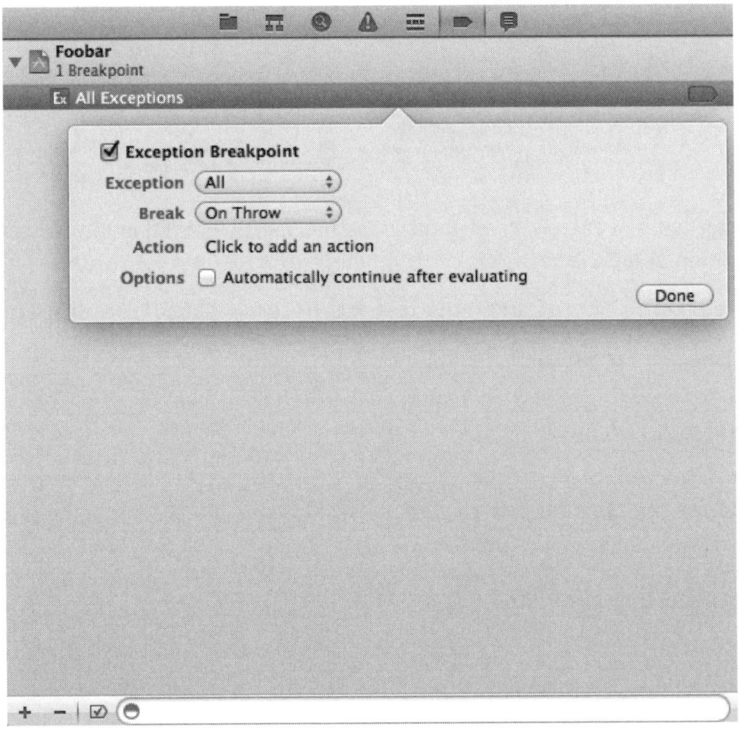

Now let's introduce an exception in Whereami. In `WhereamiViewController.m`, delete the entire implementation of **doSomethingWeird**:

```
- (void)doSomethingWeird
{
    NSLog(@"Line 1");
    NSLog(@"Line 2");
    NSLog(@"Line 3");
}
```

But don't delete the line in **initWithNibName:bundle:** that sends the **doSomethingWeird** message.

Now **WhereamiViewController** no longer implements **doSomethingWeird**, so when it sends this message to `self`, an unrecognized selector exception will be thrown. Build and run the application.

Immediately after launch, the application will blow up. The debugger will show you where (look for the green execution indicator), and the console will show you why. Notice that the stack trace is a bit longer this time, and the method that caused the exception is not at the top of the stack trace. This will sometimes be the case: your code supplies bad data (like an unrecognized selector) to a method, and then somewhere within that method's implementation, the application crashes. To find the source of the error, look for the methods you implemented in the stack trace. The culprit may not be at the top, but it will certainly be one of yours.

Also notice that the compiler warned you that the method definition was not found for **doSomethingWeird** (Figure 4.14).

Figure 4.14   Unimplemented method warning

This warning means that you declared a method in the header file but did not implement it. Now remove the declaration of **doSomethingWeird** from WhereamiViewController.h.

```
@interface WhereamiViewController : UIViewController <CLLocationManagerDelegate>
{
    CLLocationManager *locationManager;
}

- (void)doSomethingWeird;
@end
```

Build the application again. This time, instead of a warning, you get an error at the point where **doSomethingWeird** is sent to self (Figure 4.15).

Figure 4.15   Missing method error

WhereamiViewController.m
Automatic Reference Counting Issue
Receiver type 'WhereamiViewController' for instance message does not declare a method with selector 'doSomethingWeird'

Now the compiler is telling you that this method doesn't exist at all. (If you defined **doSomethingWeird** in WhereamiViewController.m above where you called it, the compiler won't complain. As long as the compiler has seen a declaration or a definition of the method before it is used, the compiler won't care. However, you should always declare your methods in the class header file so you don't have to worry about the order of your methods in the implementation file.)

It is important that you can interpret error and warning messages to understand what needs to be fixed. These messages may seem arcane, but it is only because they use terminology that you are still becoming familiar with. A suggestion: Whenever you see a warning or error, write it down somewhere. When you fix it, write down what you did to fix it.

Remove the line of code that sends **doSomethingWeird** to self in WhereamiViewController.m.

```
- (id)initWithNibName:(NSString *)nibNameOrNil bundle:(NSBundle *)nibBundleOrNil
{
    self = [super initWithNibName:nibNameOrNil bundle:nibBundleOrNil];
```

```
if (self) {
    // Create location manager object
    locationManager = [[CLLocationManager alloc] init];

    [self doSomethingWeird];
```

Your application should run correctly again. Build and run to make sure before heading to the next chapter.

Bronze Challenge: Distance Filter

Change the **CLLocationManager** so that it only updates its delegate with a new location if the device has moved more than 50 meters.

To complete this challenge, you'll need to search in the iOS SDK documentation to find out more about **CLLocationManager**. This is a little ahead of schedule. The next chapter is where you will learn how to use the documentation. In the meantime, here are some some brief instructions: From the Help menu in Xcode, select the Documentation and API Reference item. Then search for CLLocationManager.

Silver Challenge: Heading

Using delegation, retrieve the heading information from the **CLLocationManager** and print it to the console. (Hint: You need to implement at least one more delegate method and send another message to the location manager; you must also have a device that has a compass on it. Try searching the documentation for both **CLLocationManager** and CLLocationManagerDelegate.)

For the More Curious: Build Phases, Compiler Errors, and Linker Errors

Building an application in Xcode takes several steps. We call these steps *build phases*, and you saw them earlier in this chapter when you added the Core Location framework to the Whereami target (Figure 4.2). Here is what each build phase does:

Compile Sources	This build phase contains the source code files that are compiled when this target is built. By default, any time you add a source code file to a project, it is added to this build phase.
Link Binary With Libraries	After your source code has been compiled, it is linked with the frameworks (libraries). This allows your code to use classes from these frameworks.
Copy Bundle Resources	After your code is compiled and linked, an executable is created and placed inside an application bundle, which is really just a folder. Then the resources listed in this phase are added to the bundle alongside the executable. These resources are the data files that your application uses at runtime, like XIB files and any images or sounds that are part of the application. By default, when you add a file to a project that is not source code, it is added to this build phase.

We usually see errors during the Compile Sources phase, but sometimes we get errors during the Link Binary With Libraries phase. Errors generated during these phases are easier to diagnose and correct if you understand them in more detail.

Preprocessing

The Compile Sources build phase can be broken into two steps: preprocessing and compiling. The goal of the preprocessing phase is to create an *intermediate file* for each implementation file (.m). The intermediate file is still Objective-C code like the implementation file, but, as we will see, the intermediate file can get very large.

To create an intermediate file, the preprocessor resolves all the preprocessor directives in the implementation file. Preprocessor directives are statements prefixed with the pound symbol (#), like #import. The resolution of a #import statement replaces the import statement with the contents of the imported file. (You can view the contents of an imported file by Command-clicking the import statement.)

For example, consider WhereamiViewController.m, which imports WhereamiViewController.h. The intermediate file created for WhereamiViewController.m contains all the code from WhereamiViewController.h and WhereamiViewController.m. But, it doesn't stop there. WhereamiViewController.h imports two files, UIKit.h and CoreLocation.h. These two files import more header files, which import more header files, and so on. The intermediate file for WhereamiViewController.m is all of the code in all of these files (Figure 4.16).

Figure 4.16   Preprocessor creates intermediate files

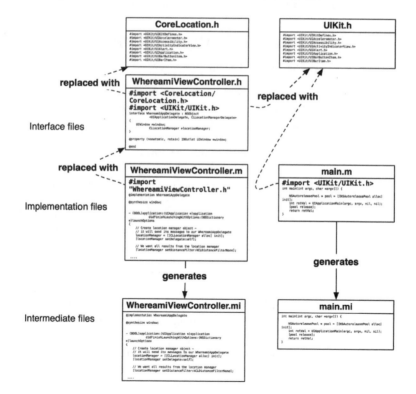

Compiling

Once the preprocessor has finished, the generated intermediate files are compiled. Compiling an intermediate file takes the Objective-C code and turns it into machine code. This machine code is stored in an *object file*, one for each intermediate file.

The compiling phase – the transition to machine code – is where we see most of our errors as programmers. When the compiler doesn't understand our code, it generates an error. We call errors generated during this phase *compile-time errors* or *syntax errors*. Compile-time errors are typically misplaced semicolons, unbalanced square brackets ([]) or curly ones ({}), spelling or capitalization errors.

These types of errors also occur when you use a class that hasn't been declared. To see an example of a compile-time error, comment out the following line in WhereamiViewController.h:

```
// #import <CoreLocation/CoreLocation.h>
```

Build the application again, and the compile phase will fail. To see the problem up close, click the ▲ icon to open the issue navigator or hit Command-4. This navigator shows you any errors or warnings in your code (Figure 4.17). You can click on an individual error to see the line of code that generated the error.

Figure 4.17   Build results with compile-time error

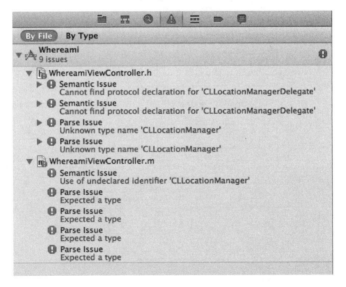

Before you removed the import statement, the intermediate file created from WhereamiViewController.m contained the code from CoreLocation.h, which contained the interface declaration for **CLLocationManager** and the protocol declaration for CLLocationManagerDelegate. Without the import statement, these files do not become part of the generated intermediate file, and the compiler has no idea what to do with these lines of code. Note that the compiler can only read one intermediate file at a time, so even though the class and protocol are in other intermediate files, the compiler still generates an error when they are not declared for WhereamiViewController.m.

Uncomment the import statement. You should be able to build again with no errors.

Linking

An object file contains the machine code for the methods implemented in the implementation file. However, within an implementation file, you use code from other implementation files. For example, WhereamiViewController.m uses the **startUpdatingLocation** method, and the machine code for that method is in the object file generated from CLLocationManager.m.

Instead of copying the code for this method into the object file for WhereamiViewController.m, the compiler leaves a link to the object file for CLLocationManager.m. The Link Binary With Libraries phase is where these links are resolved. For short, we just call it the *linking phase*.

Recall earlier in the chapter that you *linked* the Core Location framework to your target. A framework is a collection of classes, and a class is defined by two files: a header file and an implementation file. A framework, however, has pre-compiled its implementation files and shoved the resulting object files into one or more *library* files. (That's why in Objective-C you can't see the implementation files in a framework – they are already machine code.) Where you used code from the classes in the Core Location framework in your own classes, the compiler put a link in your object files to the Core Location library (Figure 4.18).

Figure 4.18   Compiler creates object files; linker resolves links

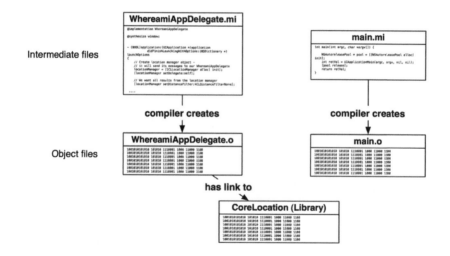

If a link cannot be resolved (because the object file that contains the code cannot be found or because the object file doesn't contain the referenced code), you get a *linker error*. Linker errors are more difficult for new developers to understand because they use unfamiliar terms and because there isn't one line of code that generated the error. So let's cause a linker error just for practice. Select CoreLocation.framework from the project navigator and hit the Delete key. On the window that appears, choose Remove Reference Only. Build the application again, and you will see new errors (Figure 4.19).

Figure 4.19 Build results with linker error

You can select an error in the issue navigator to see a more detailed description of what is going on. (You can also go to the log navigator and select the most recent Build Whereami item and see the same information.) Notice that the errors generated are underneath the item named Link. When you see linker errors, it is typically because you did not add the appropriate framework to your target. Add the `CoreLocation.framework` file back to the target in the Link Binary With Libraries build phase and build again to confirm that you have fixed the error.

5

MapKit and Text Input

In this chapter, you will finish the Whereami application using the MapKit framework, the **UITextField** class, and more delegation. We will also dive into the Apple documentation.

Right now, your Whereami application finds the location and prints it to the console. At the end of this chapter, the application will show a map of the current location instead. In addition, the user will have the option to tag and name the current location with a MapKit *annotation*. The default MapKit annotation appears as a red pin on the map (Figure 5.1).

Figure 5.1   Completed Whereami application

Object Diagrams

iOS applications can get very large and use many classes and methods. One way to keep your head wrapped around a project is to draw an *object diagram*. Object diagrams show the major objects in an application and any objects they have as instance variables. (At Big Nerd Ranch, we use a program called OmniGraffle to draw our object diagrams.) Most exercises in this book will show you an object diagram to give you the big picture of the application you are developing. Figure 5.2 shows the object diagram for the complete Whereami application.

Figure 5.2   Whereami object diagram

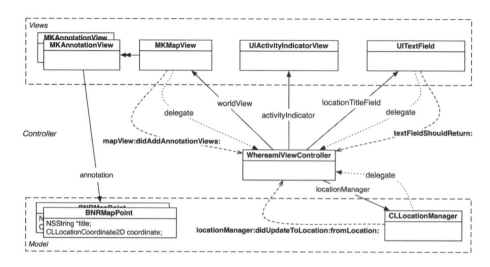

Let's go through this diagram. At the top are the view objects:

• Several instances of **MKAnnotationView** appear as icons on the **MKMapView**.

• An **MKMapView** displays the map and the labels for the recorded locations.

• A **UIActivityIndicatorView** indicates that the device is working and not stalled.

• A **UITextField** allows the user to input text to label the current location on the map.

The model objects are on the bottom. One is an instance of **CLLocationManager**, which interacts with the device's hardware to determine the user's location. The other model objects are instances of a class called **BNRMapPoint**, which you will create later in this chapter.

In the middle of everything is the controller object, **WhereamiViewController**.
WhereamiViewController is responsible for processing updates and requests from objects and for updating the user interface. It is the delegate for the **MKMapView**, the **UITextField**, and the **CLLocationManager**.

Take a look at the messages these objects send to their delegate, the **WhereamiViewController**.
MKMapView sends **mapView:didAddAnnotationViews:** when a view (or views) is added. **UITextField** sends **textFieldShouldReturn:** when the user has finished entering text. **CLLocationManager** sends **locationManager:didUpdateToLocation:fromLocation:** to inform **WhereamiViewController** of a location update.

MapKit Framework

The Core Location framework tells us where we are in the world; the MapKit framework shows us that world. Most of MapKit's work is done by the class **MKMapView**. Instances of this type display a map, track touches, and display annotations. (They can do more, but that's all you will need for this application.)

First, add the MapKit framework to your project. (If you've forgotten how, flip back to the beginning of Chapter 4 to refresh your memory.)

You must also import the MapKit header file into files that will use MapKit classes. At the top of WhereamiViewController.h, import the MapKit header.

```
#import <UIKit/UIKit.h>
#import <CoreLocation/CoreLocation.h>
#import <MapKit/MapKit.h>
```

To determine the necessary instance variables for the **WhereamiViewController**, review the object diagram in Figure 5.2. You'll need an **MKMapView**, a **UITextField**, and a **UIActivityIndicatorView**. (We'll handle the **MKAnnotationView**s in a later section.) Declare these instance variables in WhereamiViewController.h.

```
@interface WhereamiViewController : UIViewController
    <CLLocationManagerDelegate>
{
    CLLocationManager *locationManager;

    IBOutlet MKMapView *worldView;
    IBOutlet UIActivityIndicatorView *activityIndicator;
    IBOutlet UITextField *locationTitleField;
}

@end
```

Recall that IBOutlet means you will create objects in a XIB file. In the project navigator, select WhereamiViewController.xib to open it in the editor area. Then select the View object in the outline view to show the **UIView** instance on the canvas, and we can begin building the user interface.

Interface Properties

In the object library, use the search box at the bottom of the library pane to find an **MKMapView** (Figure 5.3). Then drag the map view onto the **UIView**. (Remember – the object library is at the bottom of the utilities area. To show the utilities area, click the right button in the View segmented control in the top right corner of the workspace. The keyboard shortcut is Command-Option-0. Then, select the ⬢ icon from the library selector.)

Figure 5.3   Dropping MKMapView

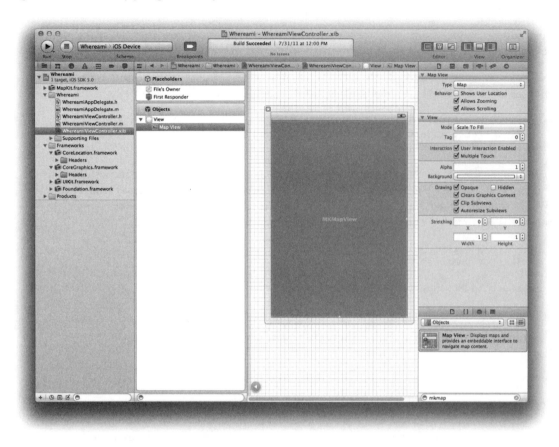

Now drag a **UITextField** and a **UIActivityIndicatorView** onto the **MKMapView**. Resize, position, and set their connections, as shown in Figure 5.4. To make a connection, first right-click (or Control-click) on the object with the instance variable to bring up its connection panel. Then drag from the circle by the instance variable to the object you want it to point to. The arrows in Figure 5.4 show the direction to drag when making connections.

Figure 5.4 Whereami XIB layout

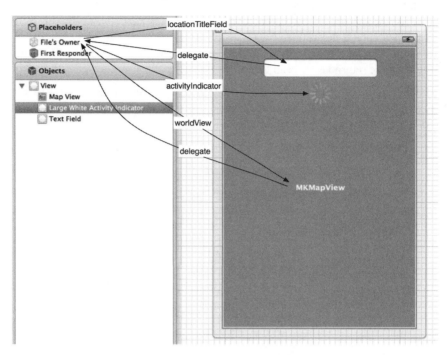

Notice that you made five connections. Three of those connections are from the File's Owner to the **UIActivityIndicatorView**, **MKMapView** and **UITextField**. The other two connections are from the **UITextField** and **MKMapView** to the File's Owner.

The direction of the connection is the same as the direction in which messages are sent. Therefore, these connections allow the **WhereamiViewController** to send messages to the activity indicator, the map view, and the text field and allow the text field and the map view to send messages back to the **WhereamiViewController**.

After making the five connections, select the File's Owner and check the connections inspector. (Click the ⊙ icon in the inspector selector.) Your connections should look like Figure 5.5. (The view connection was established by the template.)

Figure 5.5 Finished connections

Now let's adjust the properties of the **UITextField**. First, we want the **UITextField** to have helpful placeholder text, like Enter Location Name. Next, consider the keyboard. When a **UITextField** is activated, a keyboard appears on the screen. (We'll see why this happens later in this chapter.) The keyboard's appearance is determined by a set of the **UITextField**'s properties called UITextInputTraits. One of these properties is the type of the keyboard's return key. For this application, we want the return key to read Done.

Make these changes in the attributes inspector of the utilities area. Select the **UITextField** and then, from the inspector selector, select the 🔻 icon to reveal the attributes inspector. Change the values for Placeholder and Return Key to match what is shown in Figure 5.6.

Figure 5.6   UITextField attributes

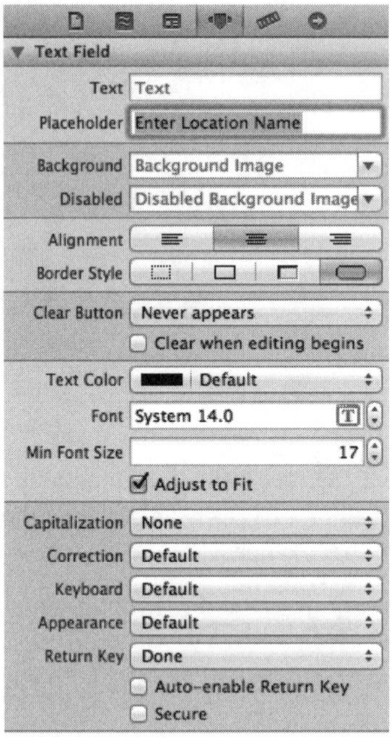

While we're here, let's change an attribute for the **UIActivityIndicatorView**. Wouldn't it be nice if the activity indicator hid itself when it is not spinning? Select the **UIActivityIndicatorView** to reveal its attributes in the attribute inspector. Then check the box labeled Hides When Stopped, as shown in Figure 5.7.

Figure 5.7   UIActivityIndicator attributes

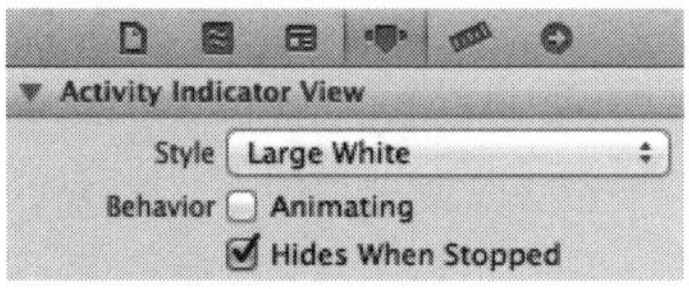

Being a MapView Delegate

When Whereami launches, we want it to find the current location and display it on a map. In the last chapter, you worked directly with Core Location to find the user's location. Now this won't be necessary because an instance of **MKMapView** knows how to use Core Location to find the user's location. All you have to do is set the showsUserLocation property of an **MKMapView** to YES, and it will find and show the user's location on the map.

After the interface loads, the **WhereamiViewController** is sent the message **viewDidLoad**. This is when you will tell the **MKMapView** to update its location. (We'll talk about **viewDidLoad** in detail in Chapter 7.) Implement this method in WhereamiViewController.m.

```
- (void)viewDidLoad
{
    [worldView setShowsUserLocation:YES];
}
```

Now that we have the **MKMapView** to determine the location, we don't need the locationManager to do it. Remove the line of code that tells the locationManager to start updating in WhereamiViewController.m. Leave the rest of the setup code for the location manager in place.

```
- (id)initWithNibName:(NSString *)nibNameOrNil bundle:(NSBundle *)nibBundleOrNil
{
    self = [super initWithNibName:nibNameOrNil bundle:nibBundleOrNil];
    if (self) {
        locationManager = [[CLLocationManager alloc] init];
        [locationManager setDelegate:self];
        [locationManager setDesiredAccuracy:kCLLocationAccuracyBest];

        [locationManager startUpdatingLocation];
    }
    return self;
}
```

Build and run the application. Once the application launches, the map will display a blue annotation dot on your current location. If you are using the simulator, choose a location to simulate by clicking the ◀ icon in the debugger bar and selecting an option.)

Unfortunately, you are looking at a map of the entire world, so the blue dot that identifies your location is the size of Brazil. The application clearly needs to zoom in on the current location to be useful. Let's figure out when and how we can make it do this.

For now, assume there is a "zoom-in-on-location" message you can send to an instance of **MKMapView**. The question is *when* would you send that message? When the application starts, it takes time for the device to determine the location. So you can't send it in **initWithNibName:bundle:** because you don't yet know the location to zoom in on. Nor do you want to continually tell the **MKMapView** to zoom its map; that would be inefficient.

Instead, how about delegation? **MKMapView** has a delegate property that you set to be the instance of **WhereamiViewController**. In WhereamiViewController.h, declare that **WhereamiViewController** conforms to the MKMapViewDelegate protocol.

```
@interface WhereamiViewController : UIViewController
    <CLLocationManagerDelegate, MKMapViewDelegate>
{
```

The map view will send messages to its delegate when interesting events happen. Perhaps there is a message in the MKMapViewDelegate protocol for when the map view finds the user's location. Finding the location is an interesting event, and it would be the perfect time to "do the zoom." We can find out if the protocol declares such a message in the Apple documentation.

Using the documentation

There's nothing more important we can teach you than how to use the Apple documentation. So hang on as we tackle – step-by-step – the questions of when and how to display a zoomed-in map of the current location.

The documentation is divided into four parts: API Reference, System Guides, Tools Guides, and Sample Code. The API Reference shows you every class, protocol, function, structure, method, and anything else you may use from Cocoa Touch. The System Guides give you high-level overviews and discussion about concepts in Cocoa Touch. The Tools Guide is the manual for Xcode and the rest of the developer tools suite.

While all four parts are useful, the API Reference is absolutely essential to everyday programming. There are so many classes and methods built into Cocoa Touch that it is impossible for a developer to remember them all. At no point in your iOS developer career will you outgrow the API Reference.

From the Help menu, choose Documentation and API Reference. The organizer window will appear with the Documentation item selected (Figure 5.8). In the lefthand panel, find the search box at the top. Click the magnifying glass icon in the search box and choose Show Find Options to show the Find Options panel, which allows you to tailor your search. In the search box, enter MKMapViewDelegate.

Figure 5.8   Documentation Window

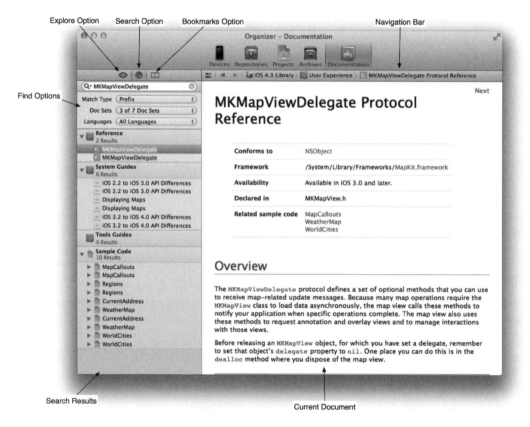

When you search for a term, the results from each part of the documentation are listed in the table on the left side of the window. The top section titled Reference is the API Reference.

Search results from the API Reference are contained in nested categories. Each result has an icon that indicates whether it is a class, a method, a protocol, or something else. Collectively, we call these items *symbols*, and their mappings are shown in Figure 5.9.

Figure 5.9   Documentation symbol guide

C Objective-C Class	f C Function
Pr Objective-C Protocol	T C Typedef
C Objective-C Category	E C Enumeration
M Objective-C Method	# C Macro
P Objective-C Property	V Constant variable

In your search results, look under the Reference heading for an item titled MKMapViewDelegate and labeled with a Pr icon. Select that item to see the reference page for the MKMapViewDelegate protocol (Figure 5.10). Then scroll down to the Tasks section, which groups the protocol's methods by their use.

Figure 5.10   MKMapViewDelegate protocol reference

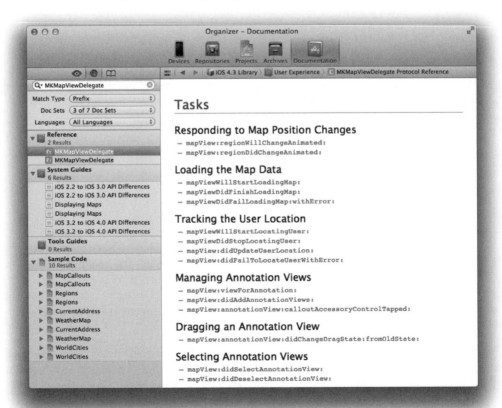

Recall that we're looking for a method that the **MKMapView** will send its delegate when it has found the user's location. See anything interesting? How about **mapView:didUpdateUserLocation:**? Blue text in the documentation indicates hyperlinks, so you can click on this method name to get more details (Figure 5.11).

Figure 5.11   A method in the API Reference

Within the figure:

mapView:didUpdateUserLocation:

Tells the delegate that the location of the user was updated.

```
- (void)mapView:(MKMapView *)mapView didUpdateUserLocation:(MKUserLocation
*)userLocation
```

Parameters
mapView
  The map view that is tracking the user's location.
userLocation
  The location object representing the user's latest location.

Discussion
While the showsUserLocation property is set to YES, this method is called whenever a new location update is received by the map view.

This method is not called if the application is currently running in the background. If you want to receive location updates while running in the background, you must use the Core Location framework.

Availability
Available in iOS 4.0 and later.

Declared In
MKMapView.h

The documentation confirms that this is the method we need, so go ahead and implement a stub for it in WhereamiViewController.m. The code completion should kick in after a few keystrokes; make sure you choose the right method from the choices offered.

```
- (void)mapView:(MKMapView *)mapView
    didUpdateUserLocation:(MKUserLocation *)userLocation
{

// Here we are...  but how do we actually zoom?

}
```

Now that we know when to zoom, we can turn our attention to the problem of how. To problem-solve in programming, it's best to start with the goal and what we already know. The goal is to display a map that is zoomed in on the user's current location. We know that when the **MKMapView** finds the user's location, it sends the message **mapView:didUpdateUserLocation:** to its delegate. We also know that, in the **mapView:didUpdateUserLocation:** method, a pointer to an **MKUserLocation** instance will be available.

In addition, we know from experience that the **MKMapView** does not automatically zoom in when it finds the user's location, so it must be told to do so. This, of course, means that **MKMapView** must implement a method that zooms in on a location. Let's track down this method in the API Reference.

Search for the **MKMapView** class. In the class reference page, look for Manipulating the Visible Portion of the Map in the Tasks section. There are a handful of methods and properties in this section; we'll start at the top with the `region` property. The details for `region` tell us that this property is of type `MKCoordinateRegion` and that it provides an implicit zoom. Sounds perfect. But to set this property, we need to know more about `MKCoordinateRegion`.

Search for `MKCoordinateRegion`. Its details are in the Map Kit Data Types Reference. `MKCoordinateRegion` has two members of types `CLLocationCoordinate2D` and `MKCoordinateSpan`. The `CLLocationCoordinate2D` is the center of the map and the `MKCoordinateSpan` determines the level of zoom (Figure 5.12).

Figure 5.12   Parts of an MKCoordinateRegion

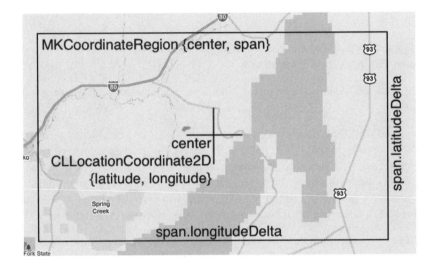

To set the `region` property of the map view, we'll need to package up one of these instances, so let's find out how we can do this. Search again for `MKCoordinateRegion` and this time select the Map Kit Functions Reference. One of these functions, **MKCoordinateRegionMakeWithDistance**, allows you to specify a region with a `CLLocationCoordinate2D` and the north-south and east-west limits of the zoom in meters. For the limits, we'll use 250 by 250 meters. For the coordinate, we need the user's location. Where can we get that?

How about the **MKUserLocation** object that the **MKMapView** sends its delegate in the **mapView:didUpdateUserLocation:** message? Search the documentation for **MKUserLocation**, and you'll find it has a property called `location` that holds the current location of the device. Keep drilling down, and you'll find that `location` points to a **CLLocation** object, which has a `coordinate` property of type `CLLocationCoordinate2D`. Success! We can use information in the **MKUserLocation** to prepare an `MKCoordinateRegion`, which we then can use to set the `region` property of the map view.

From what we know now, getting the information from the **MKUserLocation** takes two steps: we would send **MKUserLocation** the message **location** and then send the returned **CLLocation** object the message **coordinate**. The data returned from **coordinate** then would become the `MKCoordinateRegion`'s center.

But nosing around the API Reference has its rewards. Before we add this code to `WhereamiViewController.m`, take another look at the **MKUserLocation** reference. At the top, it tells us that **MKUserLocation** conforms to the protocol MKAnnotation. Click on the link for that protocol, and you'll see that classes conforming to it are required to have a property named coordinate of type CLLocationCoordinate2D. So we can simplify the process and send the message **coordinate** directly to the **MKUserLocation**.

In WhereamiViewController.m, add the new code to **mapView:didUpdateUserLocation:**.

```
- (void)mapView:(MKMapView *)mapView
     didUpdateUserLocation:(MKUserLocation *)userLocation
{
    CLLocationCoordinate2D loc = [userLocation coordinate];
    MKCoordinateRegion region = MKCoordinateRegionMakeWithDistance(loc, 250, 250);
    [worldView setRegion:region animated:YES];
}
```

Notice that the **MKMapView** is sent the message **setRegion:animated:** instead of simply **setRegion:**. What's the difference? Check the documentation.

Build and run the application again. Select a location from the debugger bar. The map will then zoom in on this location.

This is pretty standard workflow for iOS programming: you want an object to do something and you follow the bread crumbs in the API Reference. There will be dead ends and wild goose chases, but eventually you'll find what you need. As you go through this book, don't hesitate to look up the classes, protocols, and methods we use to see what else they can do. You want to become as comfortable as possible with the API Reference. The more you use it, the easier it will be to progress as an iOS developer. *You cannot be an iOS developer without using the API Reference.*

Apple will continue to update the iOS SDK and introduce iOS devices with new features and capabilities. If you are comfortable using Apple's documentation, you will be ready for whatever Apple dreams up in the future.

Your own MKAnnotation

Now that Whereami displays a nicely-zoomed map of the current location, we can turn to adding annotations. Let's start with an introduction to the MKAnnotation protocol.

MKAnnotation is not a delegate protocol. Instead, it declares a set of methods that are useful to any class that wants to display instances of itself on a map view. Imagine an application that maps everything in a neighborhood, including restaurants, factories, and train stations. These classes could be very different and hierarchically unrelated in the application, but if they conform to MKAnnotation, they all can be added to an **MKMapView**.

When an object conforming to MKAnnotation is added to an **MKMapView**, an instance of **MKAnnotationView** (or one of its subclasses) is created and added to the map view. The **MKAnnotationView** keeps a pointer to the MKAnnotation-conforming object that it represents so it can ask it for data as needed. The relationships between these objects are shown in Figure 5.13.

Figure 5.13   MKMapView and its annotations

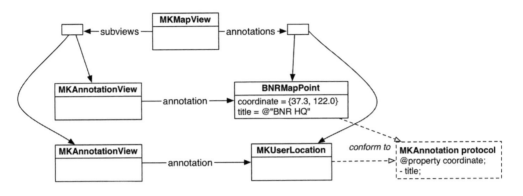

Now you're going to write a new class called **BNRMapPoint** that will conform to MKAnnotation. When the user tags a location, an instance of **BNRMapPoint** will be created and represented on the map.

From the File menu, select New and then New File.... Then from the iOS section, choose Cocoa Touch, select Objective-C class, and click Next (Figure 5.14).

Figure 5.14   Creating an NSObject subclass

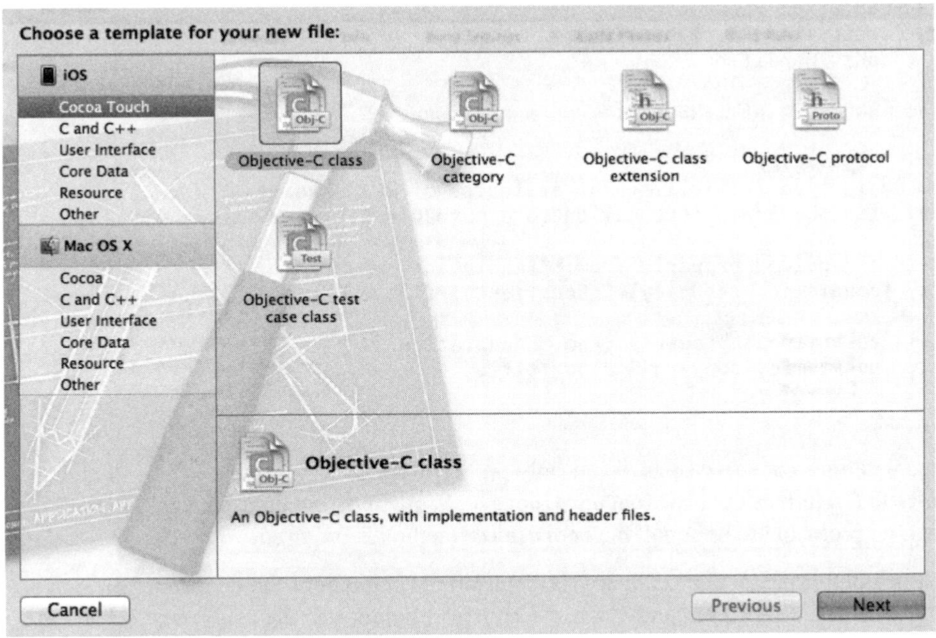

On the next pane, enter **BNRMapPoint**, select **NSObject** from the superclass list, and hit Next.

Figure 5.15   Naming the subclass

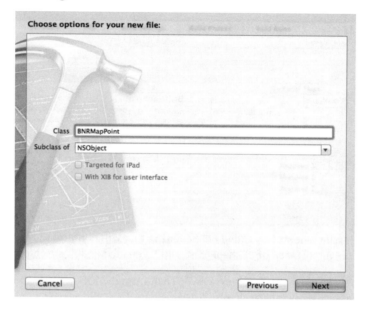

In BNRMapPoint.h, declare that **BNRMapPoint** conforms to MKAnnotation. Also declare two properties and an initializer.

```
#import <Foundation/Foundation.h>
#import <CoreLocation/CoreLocation.h>
#import <MapKit/MapKit.h>

@interface BNRMapPoint : NSObject <MKAnnotation>
{
}
// A new designated initializer for instances of BNRMapPoint
- (id)initWithCoordinate:(CLLocationCoordinate2D)c title:(NSString *)t;

// This is a required property from MKAnnotation
@property (nonatomic, readonly) CLLocationCoordinate2D coordinate;

// This is an optional property from MKAnnotation
@property (nonatomic, copy) NSString *title;

@end
```

The protocol defines coordinate as a read-only property, which means there is a method named **coordinate** that returns a CLLocationCoordinate2D. While most methods declared in the MKAnnotation protocol are optional, the **coordinate** method is required.

Switch to BNRMapPoint.m. (The keyboard shortcut for switching between the header file and the implementation file is Command-Control-Up arrow.) Synthesize the properties and add the implementation for the initializer.

```
#import "BNRMapPoint.h"

@implementation BNRMapPoint
```

```
@synthesize coordinate, title;

- (id)initWithCoordinate:(CLLocationCoordinate2D)c title:(NSString *)t
{
    self = [super init];
    if (self) {
        coordinate = c;
        [self setTitle:t];
    }
    return self;
}

@end
```

Per our initializer rules from Chapter 2, override **init** in BNRMapPoint.m to call the new designated initializer. (This method may already be implemented by the template, so make sure to replace its contents if that is the case.)

```
- (id)init
{
    return [self initWithCoordinate:CLLocationCoordinate2DMake(43.07, -89.32)
                             title:@"Hometown"];
}
```

In our code, we declared coordinate as a readonly property just like the protocol does. But we didn't have to. We could have just implemented a **coordinate** method that returns a CLLocationCoordinate2D. The MKAnnotation protocol, like all protocols, only dictates method signatures. As long as the signatures match exactly, the conforming class can implement them however it wants.

As implemented, **BNRMapPoint** will return the values of its instance variables (coordinate and title) when sent the messages **coordinate** and **title** from the MKAnnotation protocol. However, those methods could return a constant value or perform some logic, as in the following implementation:

```
- (NSString *)title
{
    if ([self isEastOfTheMississippi])
        return @"Buying supplies"

    return @"On the Oregon Trail, uncharted territory";
}
```

We can think of a protocol as a contract, whereby the conforming class says, "I promise to give you my interpretation of this contract when asked." The objects that speak to the conforming class through the protocol honor this contract by saying, "I promise to only ask you things in this contract." For example, **MKAnnotationView** has an annotation property declared as

```
@property (nonatomic, retain) id <MKAnnotation> annotation;
```

This declaration says that the annotation can be of any type (id), as long as it conforms to the MKAnnotation protocol (<MKAnnotation>). Therefore, the **MKAnnotationView** will only send messages from the MKAnnotation protocol to its annotation; it won't make any assumptions about the other messages that object might respond to.

You've added a lot of code, so you may want to build the application (Command-B) to check for syntax errors before you continue. There's no need to run it, though, because the application's behavior hasn't changed.

Tagging locations

Now that you have a class that conforms to MKAnnotation, you can display instances of it on the map. The user will enter the location's name in the **UITextField** and then tap the Done button on the keyboard. The tapping of the Done button is the signal to add an annotation. How will we know this event has occurred? Delegation, again.

In the XIB file, you set the text field's delegate to be the instance of **WhereamiViewController**. This means you can send **WhereamiViewController** messages in the UITextFieldDelegate protocol. One of these methods is **textFieldShouldReturn:**. When the keyboard's return key is tapped, the **UITextField** sends this message to its delegate and asks if it really should return. In this method, the delegate has the opportunity to perform tasks that should coincide with the returning of the text field.

In WhereamiViewController.h, declare that **WhereamiViewController** conforms to the UITextFieldDelegate protocol.

```
@interface WhereamiViewController : UIViewController
    <CLLocationManagerDelegate, MKMapViewDelegate,
    UITextFieldDelegate>
{
```

In WhereamiViewController.m, implement **textFieldShouldReturn:**.

```
- (BOOL)textFieldShouldReturn:(UITextField *)textField
{
    // This method isn't implemented yet - but will be soon.
    [self findLocation];

    [textField resignFirstResponder];

    return YES;
}
```

For now, ignore **findLocation**. You will write the implementation for that in a moment. First, let's talk about text editing and the *first responder*. **UIResponder** is a class in the UIKit framework. A responder is responsible for receiving and handling events that are associated with it. **UIView** is a subclass of **UIResponder**. Therefore, **UIView** objects can receive events. A button is a responder that handles touch events, like a tap. Shaking a device and tapping a key on the keyboard also generate events.

One of the responders is the *first responder*. Only one responder can be the first responder at a time. The first responder handles events that aren't associated with a position on the screen. For instance, a tap is sent to the view object that was tapped, but shaking the device has no position on the screen, so that event is sent to the first responder instead. We'll talk more about the first responder and event-handling in Chapter 6 and Chapter 19.

For now, let's focus on **UITextField**. A **UITextField** is also a responder: it is a direct subclass of **UIControl**, which is a subclass of **UIView**, which is a subclass of **UIResponder**. When a **UITextField** is tapped, it handles this event by becoming the first responder.

When a **UITextField** becomes the first responder, a keyboard automatically appears on the screen. To remove the keyboard from the screen, you tell the **UITextField** to give up its first responder status by sending it the message **resignFirstResponder**. Once the first responder is no longer a **UITextField**, the keyboard will disappear.

(Everything about **UITextField** holds true for the class **UITextView**, too. The difference between **UITextView** and **UITextField** is that **UITextView** allows for multi-line editing: a text view's return

key enters the newline character whereas a text field's return key dispatches the delegate method
textFieldShouldReturn:.)

Putting the pieces together

To finish your Whereami application, you just need to add two final methods: **findLocation**,
which is sent in **textFieldShouldReturn:**, and **foundLocation:**, which will be sent in
locationManager:didUpdateToLocation:fromLocation:. In WhereamiViewController.h, declare
these two methods.

```
@interface WhereamiViewController : UIViewController
    <CLLocationManagerDelegate, MKMapViewDelegate,
     UITextFieldDelegate>
{
    CLLocationManager *locationManager;

    IBOutlet MKMapView *worldView;
    IBOutlet UIActivityIndicatorView *activityIndicator;
    IBOutlet UITextField *locationTitleField;
}

- (void)findLocation;
- (void)foundLocation:(CLLocation *)loc;

@end
```

The **findLocation** method will tell the locationManager to start looking for the current location. It
will also update the user interface so that the user can't re-enter text into the text field and will start the
activity indicator spinning. The **foundLocation:** method will create an instance of **BNRMapPoint** and
add it to the worldView. It will also handle the map's zoom and reset the states of the UI elements and
the locationManager.

In WhereamiViewController.m, import BNRMapPoint.h and implement the two methods.

```
#import "WhereamiViewController.h"
#import "BNRMapPoint.h"

@implementation WhereamiViewController

- (void)findLocation
{
    [locationManager startUpdatingLocation];
    [activityIndicator startAnimating];
    [locationTitleField setHidden:YES];
}

- (void)foundLocation:(CLLocation *)loc
{
    CLLocationCoordinate2D coord = [loc coordinate];

    // Create an instance of BNRMapPoint with the current data
    BNRMapPoint *mp = [[BNRMapPoint alloc] initWithCoordinate:coord
                                                        title:[locationTitleField text]];
    // Add it to the map view
    [worldView addAnnotation:mp];

    // Zoom the region to this location
```

```
    MKCoordinateRegion region = MKCoordinateRegionMakeWithDistance(coord, 250, 250);
    [worldView setRegion:region animated:YES];

    // Reset the UI
    [locationTitleField setText:@""];
    [activityIndicator stopAnimating];
    [locationTitleField setHidden:NO];
    [locationManager stopUpdatingLocation];
}
```

Note that when importing files, you put quotation marks around header files you create and angled brackets around header files from frameworks. Angled brackets tell the compiler, "Only look in the system libraries for this file." Quotation marks say, "Look in the directory for this project first, and if you don't find something, then look in the system libraries." Finally, send the message **foundLocation:** when a new location is found by the **CLLocationManager**. Update the delegate method **locationManager:didUpdateToLocation:fromLocation:** in WhereamiViewController.m:

```
- (void)locationManager:(CLLocationManager *)manager
    didUpdateToLocation:(CLLocation *)newLocation
           fromLocation:(CLLocation *)oldLocation
{
    NSLog(@"%@", newLocation);

    // How many seconds ago was this new location created?
    NSTimeInterval t = [[newLocation timestamp] timeIntervalSinceNow];

    // CLLocationManagers will return the last found location of the
    // device first, you don't want that data in this case.
    // If this location was made more than 3 minutes ago, ignore it.
    if (t < -180) {
        // This is cached data, you don't want it, keep looking
        return;
    }

    [self foundLocation:newLocation];
}
```

Build and run the application. Simulate the location, and then enter a title into the text field. An annotation will appear on the map at your current location. Tap the pin to show the title.

Bronze Challenge: Map Type

Have the map display satellite imagery instead of a street map. (Hint: **MKMapView** has a mapType property.)

Silver Challenge: Changing the Map Type

Add a **UISegmentedControl** to the interface. It should have three items – one for each mapType of **MKMapView**. Changing the segmented control should change the map type.

Gold Challenge: Annotation Extras

Using the **NSDate** and **NSDateFormatter** classes, have your tagged annotations show the dates they were tagged.

6

Subclassing UIView and UIScrollView

In previous chapters, you've created several views: a **UIButton**, a **UILabel**, etc. But what exactly is a view?

- A view is an instance of **UIView** or one of its subclasses.

- A view knows how to draw itself on the application's window, an instance of **UIWindow**.

- A view exists within a hierarchy of views. The root of this hierarchy is the application's window.

- A view handles events, like touches.

In this chapter, you are going to create your own **UIView** subclass that fills the screen with concentric circles, as shown in Figure 6.1. You will also learn how to draw text and enable scrolling and zooming.

Figure 6.1 View that draws concentric circles

In Xcode, select File → New → New Project.... From the iOS section, select Application and choose the Empty Application template for this project (Figure 6.2).

Figure 6.2   Empty Application template

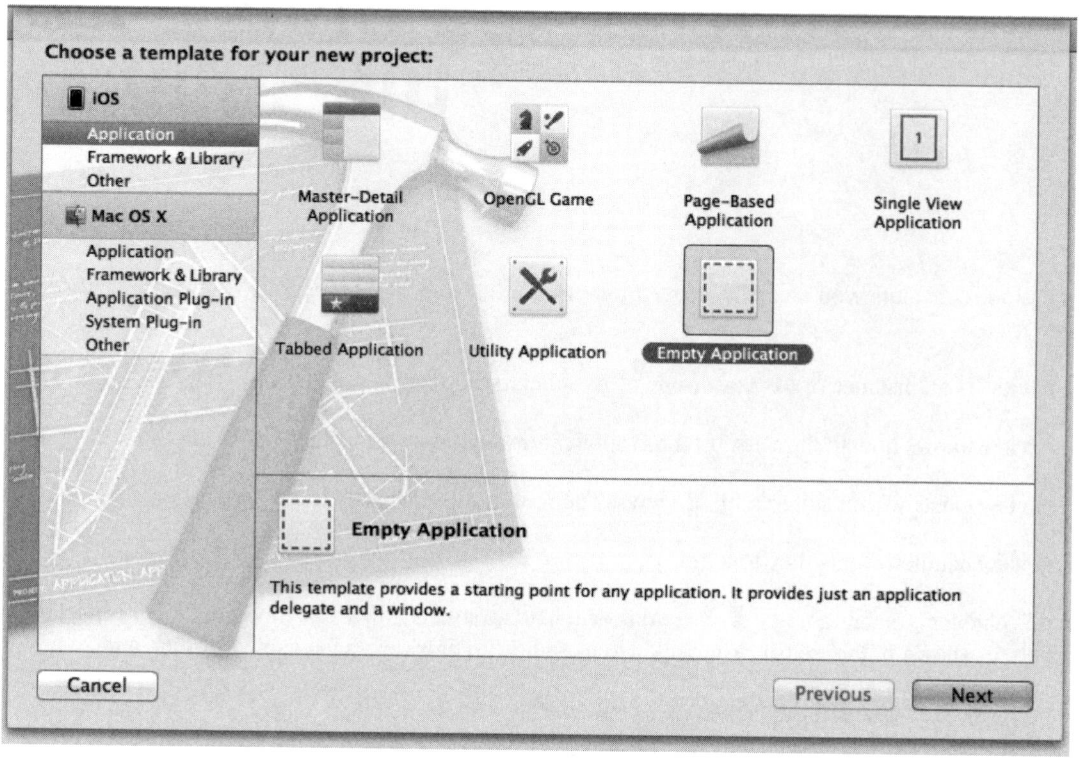

After clicking Next, enter Hypnosister for the product name and class prefix. Make the device family iPhone and make sure the Use Automatic Reference Counting box is checked (Figure 6.3).

Figure 6.3   Configuring Hypnosister

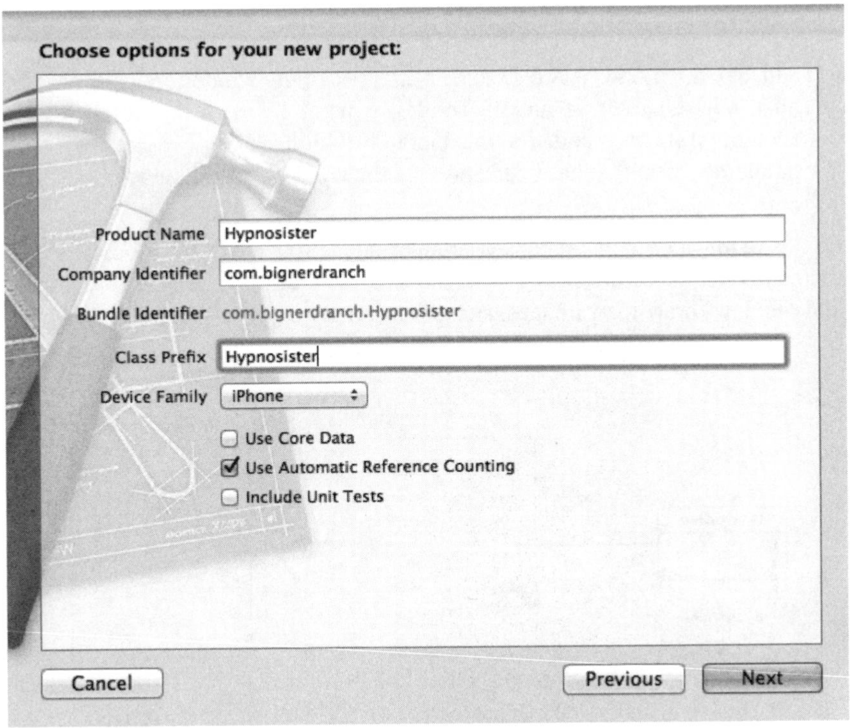

Views and the View Hierarchy

Views make up the user interface of an application. Each view maintains an image that represents it. For example, a **UIButton**'s image is a rounded rectangle with a title in the center. A **UILabel**'s image is just text. When something about a view changes, like a **UILabel**'s text property or a **UIButton**'s title, the view's image is redrawn so that these changes become visible on screen.

Another subclass of **UIView** is **UIWindow**. Every application has exactly one instance of **UIWindow** that serves as the container for all the views in the application. The window is created when the application launches. Open HypnosisterAppDelegate.m and find the **application:didFinishLaunchingWithOptions:** method.

```
- (BOOL)application:(UIApplication *)application
    didFinishLaunchingWithOptions:(NSDictionary *)launchOptions
{
    self.window = [[UIWindow alloc] initWithFrame:[[UIScreen mainScreen] bounds]];
    // Override point for customization after application launch.

    self.window.backgroundColor = [UIColor whiteColor];
    [self.window makeKeyAndVisible];
    return YES;
}
```

In **application:didFinishLaunchingWithOptions:**, the template added code that creates a **UIWindow** object and sends it the message **makeKeyAndVisible**. This puts the window on the screen, and once a window is on the screen, you can add other views to it.

(Note that every iOS application template adds this code. It is not specific to the Empty Application template. You can see the same code in your `QuizAppDelegate.m` and `WhereamiAppDelegate.m` files, which were created by the Single View Application template.)

When a view is added to a window, it is said to be a *subview* of the window. Views that are subviews of the window can also have subviews, and the result is a hierarchy of view objects. A view will appear on the screen if and only if its been added to this hierarchy – either directly as a subview of the window or as a subview of another view that has been added to the window. Thus, the window is the root of the view hierarchy.

When the screen is redrawn (which happens after an event is processed), the window's image is drawn to the screen. Then, all of the subviews of the window draw their images to the screen, then the subviews of the subviews draw their images, and so on (Figure 6.4).

Figure 6.4   Drawing a view hierarchy to the screen

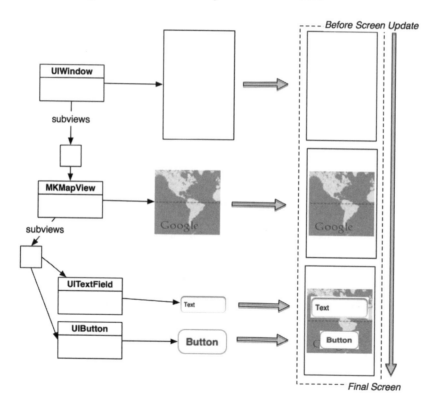

Creating a user interface boils down to this: create each view's image and add each view to the view hierarchy. Classes like **UIButton**, **MKMapView** and **UITextField** already know what their images look like. Sometimes, however, you want to create views that draw something not supplied by Apple. In that case, you need to create a custom view object and write the code to create its image.

Creating a Custom View

To create a custom view, you subclass **UIView** and customize that subclass's image. Create a new iOS Objective-C class (Figure 6.5).

Figure 6.5 Creating a new class

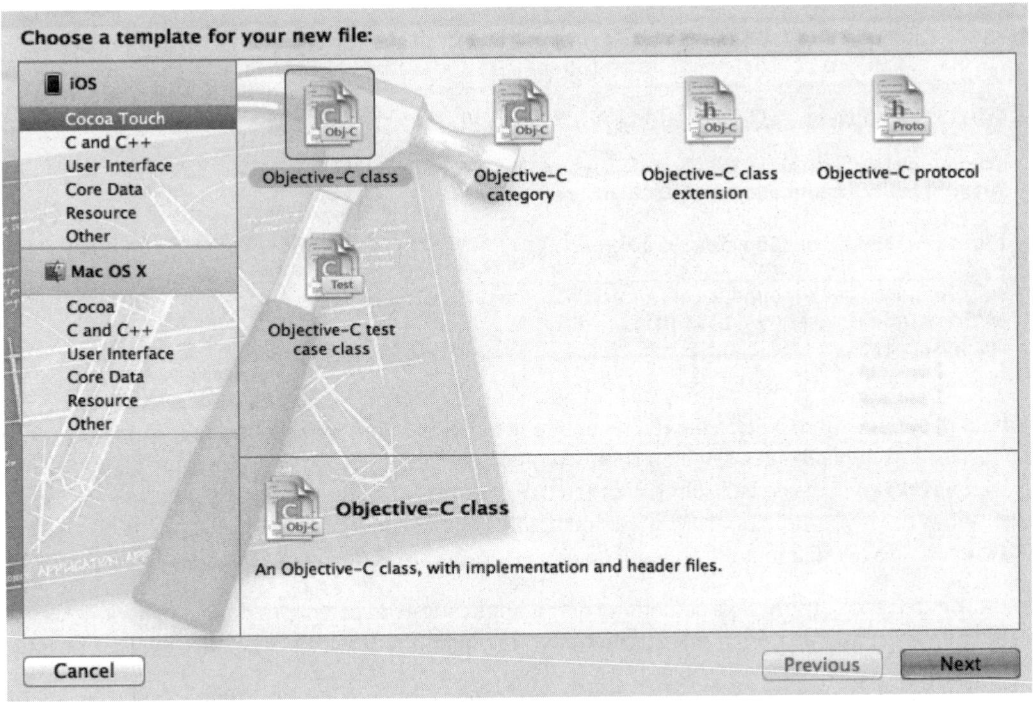

On the second pane of the assistant, choose **NSObject** as a superclass and name the class **HypnosisView**. Click Create on the sheet that drops down. Then, open HypnosisView.h in the editor area. Change **HypnosisView**'s superclass from **NSObject** to **UIView**.

```
@interface HypnosisView : NSObject
@interface HypnosisView : UIView
```

You now have a **UIView** subclass.

(Why didn't we select **UIView** as the superclass in the assistant? When you're learning, it is important to start with the simplest template available in Xcode. Most classes and projects in this book will do so. Templates are great for speeding up development, but they get in the way when you're learning. Typing in each line of code instead of relying on the "magic" of a template will make you more comfortable when you're writing iOS applications on your own.)

Let's create an instance of **HypnosisView**, set its backgroundColor (a property inherited from **UIView**), and add the **HypnosisView** to the view hierarchy.

Open HypnosisterAppDelegate.m. At the top of this file, import the header file for **HypnosisView**.

```
#import "HypnosisterAppDelegate.h"
#import "HypnosisView.h"

@implementation HypnosisterAppDelegate
```

Locate the method **application:didFinishLaunchingWithOptions:** near the top of HypnosisterAppDelegate.m. In this method, create an instance of **HypnosisView** and add it as a subview of the window.

```
- (BOOL)application:(UIApplication *)application
    didFinishLaunchingWithOptions:(NSDictionary *)launchOptions
{
    self.window = [[UIWindow alloc] initWithFrame:[[UIScreen mainScreen] bounds]];
    // Override point for customization after application launch.

    CGRect viewFrame = CGRectMake(160, 240, 100, 150);

    HypnosisView *view = [[HypnosisView alloc] initWithFrame:viewFrame];
    [view setBackgroundColor:[UIColor redColor]];

    [[self window] addSubview:view];

    self.window.backgroundColor = [UIColor whiteColor];
    [self.window makeKeyAndVisible];
    return YES;
}
```

Build run the application. Notice the red rectangle towards the bottom right corner of the screen: this is the instance of **HypnosisView**, which is drawn on top of the **UIWindow** (the white background). This **HypnosisView** instance is a subview of the **UIWindow**. When you add a view as a subview of another view, the inverse relationship is automatically established: the **HypnosisView**'s superview is the **UIWindow**. (To avoid a retain cycle, the superview property is declared as __unsafe_unretained.)

Also, notice that the console says something about applications expecting to have a root view controller. You can ignore this. It doesn't hurt anything, and it will make sense after the next chapter.

This is your first time programmatically creating an instance of a view and adding it as a subview of another view, but you have been doing the same thing all along in XIB files. In your XIB files, when you dragged a view from the library onto the canvas, you created the view instance. When you dragged that view on top of another view, you established a subview/superview relationship between those two views. A view created programmatically and a view created by loading a XIB file are no different once the application is executing.

When creating a view programmatically, you use **alloc** and an initializer message like you would for any other object. The designated initializer of **UIView**, and thus **HypnosisView**, is **initWithFrame:**. This method takes a CGRect structure as an argument. This CGRect is the view's *frame*.

Every view instance has a frame rectangle. A view's frame specifies the view's size and position relative to its superview. A frame is represented by a CGRect structure and contains the members origin and size (Figure 6.6). These members are also structures. The origin is of type CGPoint and contains two float members: x and y. The size is of type CGSize and has two float members: width and height. (A structure is not an Objective-C object, so you can't send it messages, and you don't declare it as a pointer.)

Figure 6.6   CGRect

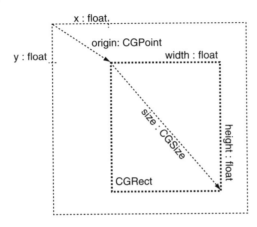

Thus, a view is always a rectangle. Because the **HypnosisView**'s origin is (160, 240), its top left corner is 160 points to the right and 240 points down from the top-left corner of the window (its superview). This places the top-left corner of the **HypnosisView** in the middle of the screen. Also, the **HypnosisView** stretches 100 points to the right and 150 points down due to its size.

Create another instance of **HypnosisView** in HypnosisterAppDelegate.m and add it to the window in a different position and with a different size and background color.

```
[[self window] addSubview:view];

CGRect anotherFrame = CGRectMake(20, 30, 50, 50);

HypnosisView *anotherView = [[HypnosisView alloc] initWithFrame:anotherFrame];
[anotherView setBackgroundColor:[UIColor blueColor]];

[[self window] addSubview:anotherView];

self.window.backgroundColor = [UIColor whiteColor];
```

Build and run again. Notice that there are now two rectangles; these are the two instances of **HypnosisView**. Figure 6.7 shows the view hierarchy.

Figure 6.7   View hierarchy with both HypnosisViews as subviews of the window

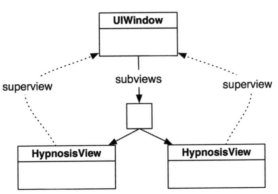

A view hierarchy can be deeper than two levels. In HypnosisterAppDelegate.m, insert anotherView as a subview of the first view instead of as a subview of the window.

```
HypnosisView *anotherView = [[HypnosisView alloc] initWithFrame:anotherFrame];
[anotherView setBackgroundColor:[UIColor blueColor]];

[[self window] addSubview:anotherView];
[view addSubview:anotherView];
```

Build and run the application. Notice that even though anotherView's frame did not change, its position on the screen did. A view's frame is relative to its superview, not the window, so the top-left corner of anotherView is now inset (20, 30) points from the top-left corner of view. Figure 6.8 shows the new view hierarchy.

Figure 6.8   View hierarchy with one HypnosisView as a subview of the other

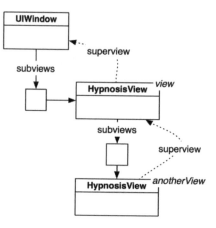

The drawRect: Method

So far, you have created a **UIView** subclass, created two instances of it, and inserted them into the view hierarchy.

We gave these two views instances distinguishable backgroundColors so that we can see their position and size on the screen. But views comprise all iOS interfaces, so clearly there must be a way to draw more than just colored rectangles. The drawing that makes a view interesting happens in the **UIView** method **drawRect:**. By default, **drawRect:** does nothing, but **UIView** subclasses override this method to perform custom drawing.

When you override **drawRect:**, you issue drawing instructions that create the image for instances of your **UIView** subclass. These drawing instructions come from the Core Graphics framework, which is automatically added to an application target when you create a new project.

Let's override **drawRect:** in **HypnosisView**. The first thing we need to do in **drawRect:** is grab a pointer to a *drawing context*. A drawing context maintains the state of drawing (like the current drawing color and thickness of the pen) and performs drawing operations. A drawing operation draws shapes using the current drawing state. At the end of **drawRect:**, the image produced by the context becomes that view's image.

Before a view is sent the message **drawRect:**, a drawing context is automatically created and set as the "current context." In HypnosisView.m, enter the following code to grab a pointer to that context in **drawRect:**.

```
- (void)drawRect:(CGRect)dirtyRect
{
    CGContextRef ctx = UIGraphicsGetCurrentContext();
}
```

The type CGContextRef is defined as CGContext * – a pointer to a CGContext. CGContext is a structure that represents a drawing context. (The suffix Ref makes it easy to distinguish between pointers to C structures and pointers to Objective-C objects.) Here, ctx points to the current drawing context.

A view's image is the same size as it appears on the screen, i.e., the same size as the view's frame. The frame describes the view's size relative to the view's superview. However, the view shouldn't have to know about its superview until it gets to compositing its image to the screen. So, there is a separate CGRect property of **UIView** named bounds that gives the view its size independent of its superview. In HypnosisView.m, get the bounds rectangle in **drawRect:** after you get a pointer to the drawing context.

```
- (void)drawRect:(CGRect)dirtyRect
{
    CGContextRef ctx = UIGraphicsGetCurrentContext();
    CGRect bounds = [self bounds];
}
```

The drawing operations you perform on the **CGContextRef** must fall within the bounds rectangle; otherwise, they will be clipped to that rectangle. Let's draw a circle in the center of the bounds rectangle. Add the following code to **drawRect:**.

```
- (void)drawRect:(CGRect)dirtyRect
{
    CGContextRef ctx = UIGraphicsGetCurrentContext();
    CGRect bounds = [self bounds];

    // Figure out the center of the bounds rectangle
    CGPoint center;
    center.x = bounds.origin.x + bounds.size.width / 2.0;
    center.y = bounds.origin.y + bounds.size.height / 2.0;

    // The radius of the circle should be nearly as big as the view
    float maxRadius = hypot(bounds.size.width, bounds.size.height) / 4.0;

    // The thickness of the line should be 10 points wide
    CGContextSetLineWidth(ctx, 10);

    // The color of the line should be gray (red/green/blue = 0.6, alpha = 1.0);
    CGContextSetRGBStrokeColor(ctx, 0.6, 0.6, 0.6, 1.0);

    // Add a shape to the context - this does not draw the shape
    CGContextAddArc(ctx, center.x, center.y, maxRadius, 0.0, M_PI * 2.0, YES);

    // Perform a drawing instruction; draw current shape with current state
    CGContextStrokePath(ctx);
}
```

Build and run the application. The same blue and red squares are there, but now each square has a gray circle within it. These gray circles are the result of the **drawRect:** method for instances of **HypnosisView**.

Notice that a view's backgroundColor is always drawn regardless of what **drawRect:** does. Typically, you set the backgroundColor of a view to clear so that only **drawRect:**'s results show. In HypnosisterAppDelegate.m, remove the code that sets the background color of each of these views.

```
HypnosisView *view = [[HypnosisView alloc] initWithFrame:viewFrame];
[view setBackgroundColor:[UIColor redColor]];

[[self window] addSubview:view];

CGRect anotherFrame = CGRectMake(20, 30, 50, 50);

HypnosisView *anotherView = [[HypnosisView alloc] initWithFrame:anotherFrame];
[anotherView setBackgroundColor:[UIColor blueColor]];
```

Then, in HypnosisView.m, override **initWithFrame:** to set the background color of every **HypnosisView** to clear.

```
- (id)initWithFrame:(CGRect)frame
{
    self = [super initWithFrame:frame];
    if (self) {
        // All HypnosisViews start with a clear background color
        [self setBackgroundColor:[UIColor clearColor]];
    }
    return self;
}
```

Build and run the application. Figure 6.9 shows the clear backgrounds and the resulting circles that look a little like an olive.

Figure 6.9   Current results

Remember that you are looking at two view instances that are stacked on top of each other. The circles are different sizes because the frame of each view (and, thus, the bounds and the image that represents the view) are different sizes.

While the bounds origin is typically (0, 0) and the size is typically equal to the frame's size, this is sometimes not the case. Thus, when drawing, you should never use constant numbers. Instead, use a combination of the origin and size of the bounds to specify the coordinates that you draw to.

Core Graphics

The functions and types that begin with CG come from the Core Graphics framework, a C language API for 2D drawing. The hub of the Core Graphics framework is CGContextRef: all other Core Graphics functions and types interact with a drawing context in some way, and then the context creates an image.

Let's look at the Core Graphics functions you used in the implementation of **HypnosisView**'s **drawRect:** method. You set up the drawing state with **CGContextSetLineWidth** and then set its color using **CGContextSetRGBStrokeColor**.

Next, you added a *path* to the context using **CGContextAddArc**. A path is a collection of points that forms a shape and can form anything from a square to a circle to a human outline. There are a number of Core Graphics functions like **CGContextAddArc** that you can use to add a path to a context. (Search the documentation for CGContextRef to find them.)

After a path has been added to a context, you can perform a drawing operation. There are three drawing operations:

- **CGContextStrokePath** will draw a line along the path.

- **CGContextFillPath** will fill the shape made by the path.

- **CGContextClip** will limit future drawing operations to the area defined by the path. For example, drawing a square to a context that has been clipped to a circle of the same size will result in drawing a circle.

After a drawing operation, the current path is removed from the context. Thus, to draw more than one circle, you have to add a path to the context for each circle. In HypnosisView.m, modify **drawRect:** to draw a number of concentric circles.

```
- (void)drawRect:(CGRect)dirtyRect
{
    CGContextRef ctx = UIGraphicsGetCurrentContext();
    CGRect bounds = [self bounds];

    CGPoint center;
    center.x = bounds.origin.x + bounds.size.width / 2.0;
    center.y = bounds.origin.y + bounds.size.height / 2.0;

    float maxRadius = hypot(bounds.size.width, bounds.size.height) / 4.0;
    float maxRadius = hypot(bounds.size.width, bounds.size.height) / 2.0;

    CGContextSetLineWidth(ctx, 10);

    CGContextSetRGBStrokeColor(ctx, 0.6, 0.6, 0.6, 1.0);
```

```
CGContextAddArc(ctx, center.x, center.y, maxRadius, 0.0, M_PI * 2.0, YES);

CGContextStrokePath(ctx);

// Draw concentric circles from the outside in
for (float currentRadius = maxRadius; currentRadius > 0; currentRadius -= 20) {
    // Add a path to the context
    CGContextAddArc(ctx, center.x, center.y,
                    currentRadius, 0.0, M_PI * 2.0, YES);

    // Perform drawing instruction; removes path
    CGContextStrokePath(ctx);
}
}
```

Build and run the application again. This time, each **HypnosisView** draws a number of circles.

That is one ugly screen; let's get rid of one of the instances of **HypnosisView** and make the remaining one the size of the screen. In HypnosisterAppDelegate.m, modify **application:didFinishLaunchingWithOptions:**.

```
CGRect viewFrame = CGRectMake(160, 240, 100, 150);

HypnosisView *view = [[HypnosisView alloc] initWithFrame:viewFrame];

HypnosisView *view = [[HypnosisView alloc] initWithFrame:[[self window] bounds]];
[[self window] addSubview:view];

CGRect anotherFrame = CGRectMake(20, 30, 50, 50);

HypnosisView *anotherView = [[HypnosisView alloc] initWithFrame:anotherFrame];

[view addSubview:anotherView];
```

Build and run the application. Now you have a single instance of **HypnosisView** that fills the entire screen. Much better.

There are Core Graphics functions to draw most anything you like. Check the documentation for functions and types beginning with CG.

UIKit Drawing Additions

There are a number of Foundation and UIKit classes that can work with a CGContextRef. One such class is **UIColor**. An instance of **UIColor** represents a color and can be used to set the current drawing color of the context. In HypnosisView.m, replace the line of code that changes the stroke color with one that uses **UIColor**'s **colorWithRed:green:blue:alpha:** method.

```
CGContextSetLineWidth(ctx, 10);

CGContextSetRGBStrokeColor(ctx, 0.6, 0.6, 0.6, 1.0);
[[UIColor colorWithRed:0.6 green:0.6 blue:0.6 alpha:1] setStroke];
```

Build and run the application again. The **HypnosisView** will look the same as before.

There are a number of prepared **UIColor** instances you can use for common colors. Change this line of code again:

```
[[UIColor colorWithRed:0.6 green:0.6 blue:0.6 alpha:1] setStroke];
[[UIColor lightGrayColor] setStroke];
```

Build and run again. The color of the circles should be about the same, but the code is much simpler.

NSString has the ability to draw to a `CGContextRef`. Sending the message **drawInRect:withFont:** to an **NSString** will draw that string in the given rectangle with the given font to the current context. In `HypnosisView.m`, add the following code to the end of **drawRect:**.

```
    for (float currentRadius = maxRadius; currentRadius > 0; currentRadius -= 20) {
        CGContextAddArc(ctx, center.x, center.y,
                        currentRadius, 0, M_PI * 2.0, YES);

        CGContextStrokePath(ctx);
    }

    // Create a string
    NSString *text = @"You are getting sleepy.";

    // Get a font to draw it in
    UIFont *font = [UIFont boldSystemFontOfSize:28];

    CGRect textRect;

    // How big is this string when drawn in this font?
    textRect.size = [text sizeWithFont:font];

    // Let's put that string in the center of the view
    textRect.origin.x = center.x - textRect.size.width / 2.0;
    textRect.origin.y = center.y - textRect.size.height / 2.0;

    // Set the fill color of the current context to black
    [[UIColor blackColor] setFill];

    // Draw the string
    [text drawInRect:textRect
            withFont:font];
}
```

Let's spice it up with a shadow. Add the following code in `HypnosisView.m`.

```
[[UIColor blackColor] setFill];

// The shadow will move 4 points to the right and 3 points down from the text
CGSize offset = CGSizeMake(4, 3);

// The shadow will be dark gray in color
CGColorRef color = [[UIColor darkGrayColor] CGColor];

// Set the shadow of the context with these parameters,
// all subsequent drawing will be shadowed
CGContextSetShadowWithColor(ctx, offset, 2.0, color);


// Draw the string
[text drawInRect:textRect
        withFont:font];
```

Build and run the application. You now have shadow.

UIColor's **setStroke** method replaces **CGContextSetRGBStrokeColor**, but it is a one-to-one line replacement, so it doesn't save that much work. **NSString**'s **drawInRect:withFont:**, on the other hand, buys you a lot of convenience. **UIImage** has a similar useful method, **drawInRect:**, for drawing an image object to a context.

Redrawing Views

When a **UIView** instance receives the message **setNeedsDisplay**, it will redraw its image. View subclasses send themselves **setNeedsDisplay** when their drawable content changes. For example, a **UILabel** will mark itself for re-display if it is sent the message **setText:**. (It has to redraw its image if the text it displays changes.)

The redrawing of a view's image is not immediate; instead, it is added to a list of views that need updating. To understand when views actually get redrawn, we need to talk about the *run loop* – the infinite loop that comprises an iOS application. The run loop's job is to listen for input (a touch, Core Location updates, data coming in through a network interface, etc.) and then find the appropriate handlers for that event (like an action or a delegate method for an object). Those handler methods call other methods, which call more methods, and so on. Once all the methods have completed, control returns to the run loop. At this point, the views are redrawn. Figure 6.10 shows where redrawing views happens in the run loop.

Figure 6.10   Redrawing views with the run loop

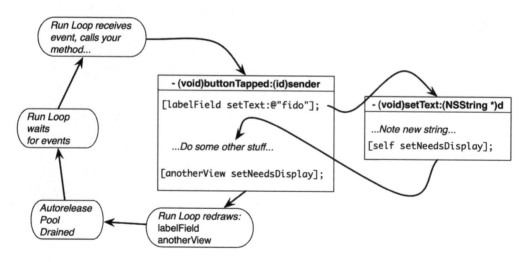

When control returns to the run loop, it says, "Well, a bunch of code was just executed. I'm going to check if any views need to be redrawn." Then the run loop prepares the necessary drawing contexts and sends the message **drawRect:** to all of the views that have been sent **setNeedsDisplay** in this iteration of the loop.

If one view redraws its image, the other views on the screen are not required to redraw theirs. Instead, their existing images will just be composited on the screen again. This optimization is why drawing and animation on iOS feels so responsive.

To see the effect of redrawing a view's image, let's give **HypnosisView** a circleColor property. Each circle that the **HypnosisView** draws will be the color pointed to by this property. In HypnosisView.h, declare this property.

```
@interface HypnosisView : UIView
{

}
@property (nonatomic, strong) UIColor *circleColor;
@end
```

In HypnosisView.m, synthesize this property to automatically create the instance variable, setter, and getter.

```
@implementation HypnosisView
@synthesize circleColor;
```

Now, in HypnosisView.m, update the **initWithFrame:** method to create a default circleColor.

```
- (id)initWithFrame:(CGRect)frame
{
    self = [super initWithFrame:frame];
    if (self) {
        [self setBackgroundColor:[UIColor clearColor]];
        [self setCircleColor:[UIColor lightGrayColor]];
    }
    return self;
}
```

Then, in **drawRect:**, modify the message that sets the context's stroke color to use the circleColor instead of light gray.

```
CGContextSetLineWidth(ctx, 10);

[[self circleColor] setStroke];

for (float currentRadius = maxRadius; currentRadius > 0; currentRadius -= 20) {
    CGContextAddArc(ctx, center.x, center.y, currentRadius, 0.0, M_PI * 2.0, YES);

    CGContextStrokePath(ctx);
}
```

Build and run the application. The circles are the same color because we don't have a way to change circleColor from the default once the application is running. Let's make the circle color change when the user shakes the device. To find out how to respond to a shake, we need to see how motion events are handled.

Motion Events

In Chapter 5, we briefly talked about **UIView**'s superclass, **UIResponder**. Instances of **UIResponder** can become the first responder of the window and will receive events when the device is shaken or a key is pressed on the keyboard. You will make the instance of **HypnosisView** the first responder of Hypnosister's window. Shaking the device will send a message to the **HypnosisView**, and that method will change its circleColor.

To give a **UIResponder** first responder status, you send it the message **becomeFirstResponder**. In HypnosisterAppDelegate.m, tell the **HypnosisView** instance to become the first responder. The

becomeFirstResponder method returns a Boolean value indicating whether the receiving object successfully became the first responder of the window.

```
[[self window] addSubview:view];

BOOL success = [view becomeFirstResponder];
if (success) {
    NSLog(@"HypnosisView became the first responder");
} else {
    NSLog(@"Could not become first responder");
}

self.window.backgroundColor = [UIColor whiteColor];
```

Build and run the application. Notice that the console tells you that the **HypnosisView** failed to become the first responder. Most **UIResponder** objects return NO in **becomeFirstResponder**. This is because most views, by default, only care about events connected with themselves, and they (almost) always get a chance to handle these events. For example, a tapped **UIButton** gets sent a message regardless of who the first responder is. So, a responder object must explicitly state that it is willing to become the first responder. In HypnosisView.m, override the **UIResponder** method **canBecomeFirstResponder** to return YES.

```
- (BOOL)canBecomeFirstResponder
{
    return YES;
}
```

Build and run the application again. The console will report that the **HypnosisView** is now the first responder.

The methods for receiving events are also implemented in **UIResponder**, and they must be overridden in subclasses of **UIResponder** for instances to respond to events. For handling shakes, the methods you override in a **UIResponder** subclass are known as the motion event methods. They are declared like so:

```
// Send to the first responder when the user starts shaking the device
- (void)motionBegan:(UIEventSubtype)motion withEvent:(UIEvent *)event;

// Sent to the first responder when the user stops shaking the device
- (void)motionEnded:(UIEventSubtype)motion withEvent:(UIEvent *)event;

// Sent to the first responder if the motion event is interrupted, like when
// a phone call or SMS message occurs while shaking
- (void)motionCancelled:(UIEventSubtype)motion withEvent:(UIEvent *)event;
```

Thus, for **HypnosisView** to know and take action when a shake starts, it must implement the method **motionBegan:withEvent:**. Override this method in HypnosisView.m so that the start of a shake changes the circleColor.

```
- (void)motionBegan:(UIEventSubtype)motion withEvent:(UIEvent *)event
{
    NSLog(@"Device started shaking!");
    [self setCircleColor:[UIColor redColor]];
}
```

Build and run the application. Give the device a shake. (If you are using the simulator, simulate a shake by selecting Shake Gesture from the Hardware menu in the simulator application.) The console reports that the device has started shaking. But no matter how vigorously you shake the device, the circle color will not change. What gives?

When the circleColor of a **HypnosisView** changes, the instance variable circleColor is set to point at a new **UIColor** instance. However, we didn't tell the **HypnosisView** that it needs to redraw its image when this happens. We have to send the message **setNeedsDisplay** to the **HypnosisView** after it changes its circleColor.

In HypnosisView.m, implement **setCircleColor:** to send this message after it changes its circleColor instance variable.

```
- (void)setCircleColor:(UIColor *)clr
{
    circleColor = clr;
    [self setNeedsDisplay];
}
```

Build and run the application again. Shake the device, and the circles will change to red.

Notice that **motionBegan:withEvent:** has a UIEventSubtype argument. This argument holds the type of motion event that triggered this method. Right now, there is only one type of motion event: a shake. In the future, there may be more. You should maintain future compatibility by making sure that only shake events change the color of the **HypnosisView**. In HypnosisView.m, add the following code to **motionBegan:withEvent:**.

```
- (void)motionBegan:(UIEventSubtype)motion withEvent:(UIEvent *)event
{
    if (motion == UIEventSubtypeMotionShake) {
        NSLog(@"Device started shaking!")
        [self setCircleColor:[UIColor redColor]];
    }
}
```

Using UIScrollView

When you want to let the user scroll around your view, you typically make your view the subview of a **UIScrollView**, as shown in Figure 6.11.

Figure 6.11   Object diagram

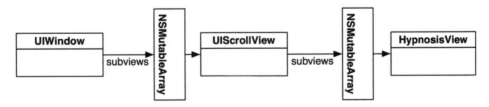

Scroll views are typically used for views that are larger than the screen. A scroll view draws a rectangular portion of its subview, and moving your finger, or *panning*, on the scroll view changes the position of that rectangle on the subview. Thus, you can think of the scroll view as a viewing port that you move around a virtual world (Figure 6.12). The size of the scroll view is the size of this viewing port. The size of the area it can view is the **UIScrollView**'s contentSize, which is typically the size of the **UIScrollView**'s subview.

Figure 6.12   UIScrollView and its content area

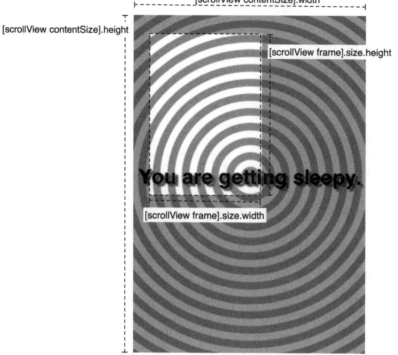

In HypnosisterAppDelegate.m, put a super-sized version of **HypnosisView** inside a scroll view and add that scroll view to the window:

```
- (BOOL)application:(UIApplication *)application
    didFinishLaunchingWithOptions:(NSDictionary *)launchOptions
{
    self.window = [[UIWindow alloc] initWithFrame:[[UIScreen mainScreen] bounds]];
    // Override point for customization after application launch.

    CGRect screenRect = [[self window] bounds];

    // Create the UIScrollView to have the size of the window, matching its size
    UIScrollView *scrollView = [[UIScrollView alloc] initWithFrame:screenRect];
    [[self window] addSubview:scrollView];

    HypnosisView *view =
        [[HypnosisView alloc] initWithFrame:[[self window] bounds]];

    // Create the HypnosisView with a frame that is twice the size of the screen
    CGRect bigRect = screenRect;
    bigRect.size.width *= 2.0;
    bigRect.size.height *= 2.0;
    HypnosisView *view = [[HypnosisView alloc] initWithFrame:bigRect];

    [[self window] addSubview:view];
```

```
// Add the HypnosisView as a subview of the scrollView instead of the window
[scrollView addSubview:view];

// Tell the scrollView how big its virtual world is
[scrollView setContentSize:bigRect.size];

BOOL success = [view becomeFirstResponder];
```

Build and run your application. You can pan your view up and down, left and right.

Panning and paging

In the last example, a scroll view was used to move around a much larger view. A scroll view can pan between a number of different view instances. For example, if there are two screen-sized views, a user could pan between them. In HypnosisterAppDelegate.m, shrink the **HypnosisView** back to the size of the screen and add another screen-sized **HypnosisView** as a subview of the **UIScrollView**. Also, make the contentSize twice as wide as the screen, but the same height.

```
CGRect bigRect = screenRect;
bigRect.size.width *= 2.0;
bigRect.size.height *= 2.0;

HypnosisView *view = [[HypnosisView alloc] initWithFrame:bigRect];

HypnosisView *view = [[HypnosisView alloc] initWithFrame:screenRect];

[scrollView addSubview:view];

// Move the rectangle for the other HypnosisView to the right, just off
// the screen
screenRect.origin.x = screenRect.size.width;
HypnosisView *anotherView = [[HypnosisView alloc] initWithFrame:screenRect];
[scrollView addSubview:anotherView];

// Tell the scrollView how big its virtual world is
[scrollView setContentSize:bigRect.size];
```

Build and run the application. Pan from left to right to see each instance of **HypnosisView**.

Notice that you can stop in between the two **HypnosisView**s. Sometimes you want this, but other times, you do not. To force the scroll view to snap its viewing port to one of the views, turn on paging for the scroll view in HypnosisterAppDelegate.m.

```
UIScrollView *scrollView = [[UIScrollView alloc] initWithFrame:screenRect];
[scrollView setPagingEnabled:YES];
[[self window] addSubview:scrollView];
```

Build and run the application. Pan to the middle of two **HypnosisView**s and see how it automatically scrolls to one of the views. Paging works by taking the size of the scroll view's bounds and dividing up the contentSize it displays into sections of the same size. After the user pans, the view port will scroll to show only one of these sections.

Zooming

A **UIScrollView** can also zoom in and out on its content. To zoom, a scroll view needs to know the minimum and maximum zoom levels, and it needs to know the view to zoom in on.

A **UIScrollView** can technically only zoom in on one view. So remove the code that creates another **HypnosisView** in HypnosisterAppDelegate.m and change the contentSize of the **UIScrollView** back to the size of the screen.

```
CGRect bigRect = screenRect;
bigRect.size.width *= 2.0;
HypnosisView *view = [[HypnosisView alloc] initWithFrame:screenRect];

[scrollView addSubview:view];


screenRect.origin.x = screenRect.size.width;
HypnosisView *anotherView = [[HypnosisView alloc] initWithFrame:screenRect];
[scrollView addSubview:anotherView];

[scrollView setContentSize:bigRect.size];
```

Then, in HypnosisterAppDelegate.m, disable paging and set the zoom properties and delegate of the **UIScrollView**.

```
UIScrollView *scrollView = [[UIScrollView alloc] initWithFrame:screenRect];
[scrollView setPagingEnabled:YES];

[scrollView setMinimumZoomScale:1.0];
[scrollView setMaximumZoomScale:5.0];

// You will get a warning here, ignore it for now
[scrollView setDelegate:self];

[[self window] addSubview:scrollView];
```

Build and run the application. You should see one **HypnosisView**, which you cannot pan or zoom.

To zoom, you must implement the method **viewForZoomingInScrollView:** in the **UIScrollView**'s delegate. This method returns the instance of the view to zoom in on. The view will be the instance of **HypnosisView**, and the **UIScrollView**'s delegate will be the **HypnosisterAppDelegate**.

Currently, **HypnosisterAppDelegate** has a pointer to **HypnosisView** in a local variable in **application:didFinishLaunchingWithOptions:**. However, to zoom, **HypnosisterAppDelegate** will need access to that view in another method – **viewForZoomingInScrollView:**. This means **HypnosisterAppDelegate** needs an instance variable that points to a **HypnosisView** instead of a local variable. In HypnosisterAppDelegate.h, declare that **HypnosisterAppDelegate** conforms to UIScrollViewDelegate and declare an instance variable to hold the **HypnosisView**.

```
#import <UIKit/UIKit.h>

// Don't forget this import statement!
#import "HypnosisView.h"

@interface HypnosisterAppDelegate : UIResponder
    <UIApplicationDelegate, UIScrollViewDelegate>
{
    HypnosisView *view;
}
@property (strong, nonatomic) UIWindow *window;

@end
```

Now, in `HypnosisterAppDelegate.m`, put the **HypnosisView** into the instance variable instead of a local variable.

```
HypnosisView *view = [[HypnosisView alloc] initWithFrame:screenRect];
view = [[HypnosisView alloc] initWithFrame:screenRect];

[scrollView addSubview:view];
```

Finally, implement **viewForZoomingInScrollView:** in `HypnosisterAppDelegate.m` to return this view.

```
- (UIView *)viewForZoomingInScrollView:(UIScrollView *)scrollView
{
    return view;
}
```

Build and run the application. Pinch and pull with two fingers to zoom in and out. (On the simulator, you can simulate two fingers by holding down the Option key, clicking, and then moving the mouse.) Pan with one finger to scroll once you have zoomed in.

Hiding the Status Bar

When you're being hypnotized, you probably don't want to see the time or your remaining battery charge – these things cause anxiety. So, you're going to hide the status bar before you make the window visible. In `HypnosisterAppDelegate.m`, add a line near the top of **application:didFinishLaunchingWithOptions:**.

```
- (BOOL)application:(UIApplication *)application
    didFinishLaunchingWithOptions:(NSDictionary *)launchOptions
{
    self.window = [[UIWindow alloc] initWithFrame:[[UIScreen mainScreen] bounds]];

    [[UIApplication sharedApplication] setStatusBarHidden:YES
                            withAnimation:UIStatusBarAnimationFade];
```

Build and run the application again. Notice the status bar fading out after the application launches. You can also hide the status bar before your application appears on the screen by adding a new key-value pair to the application's info property list. To do this, select the project from the project navigator. Then select the Hypnosister target and the Info pane in the editor area (Figure 6.13). This pane is an editor for the `Info.plist` file that is a part of every iOS application. (You could select the Hypnosister-Info.plist file from the project navigator, but this interface shows the key-value pairs more clearly.)

Figure 6.13   Info property list with hidden status bar

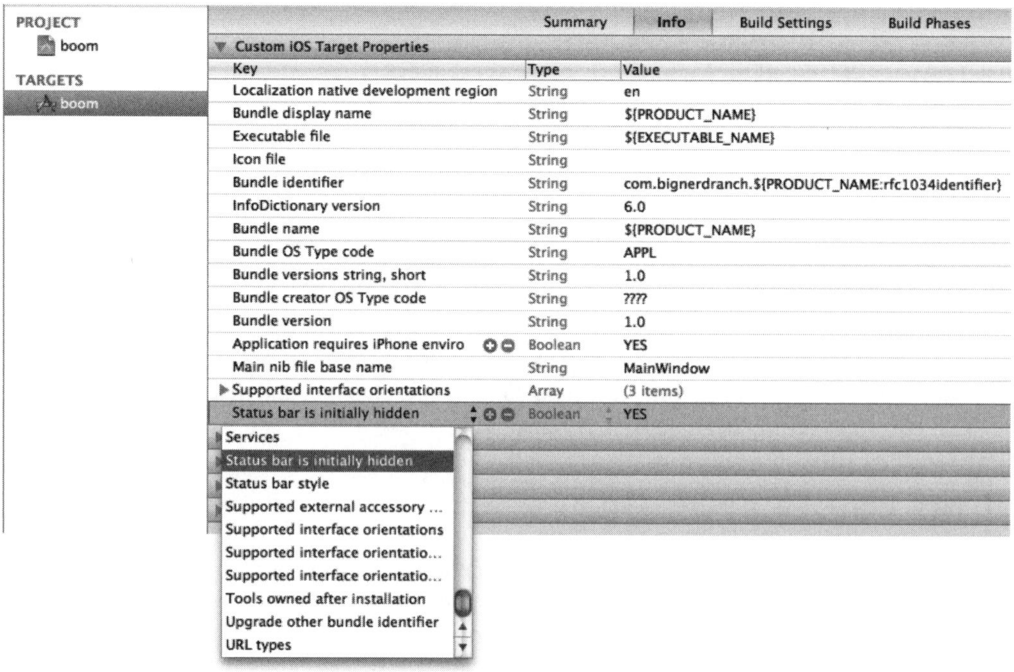

Select the last row and click the + icon next to the key name to add another key-value pair. A new row will appear, and a pop-up menu will open in the Key column. Choose Status bar is initially hidden from this list and hit return. In the Value column, change the value to YES. Now the status bar will be hidden as soon as you launch the application.

Bronze Challenge: Colors

Make the circles appear in assorted colors. (Remember to make a copy of your project to work on challenges.)

Silver Challenge: Shapes

Make it so every **HypnosisView** instance has a green crosshair in the middle. This crosshair should not have a shadow, but it should be drawn on top of the text. (Hint: you will need to use the functions **CGContextMoveToPoint**, **CGContextAddLineToPoint**, **CGContextSaveGState**, **CGContextRestoreGState**.)

Gold Challenge: Another View and Curves

Make another **UIView** subclass. This subclass should draw the Big Nerd Ranch logo. (For the logo, use the file that you used for the application icon of the Quiz application.)

The logo should be clipped to a circle that contains just the hat. The logo should have a black outline with a shadow underneath it. Also, the circle should have a slightly blue gradient coming from the top of the circle to the center of it. This view instance should be a subview of the **HypnosisView**. (Hint: you will need to use **UIImage**, CGColorSpaceRef, CGGradientRef, **CGContextClip** and a few other functions and types you have seen in previous challenges and this chapter.)

Figure 6.14   Finished gold challenge

7

View Controllers

In the Quiz application, you wrote all of your code in a `QuizViewController` class. An instance of this class was the controller for the Quiz application: It had pointers to the labels on the screen, and the buttons sent messages to it when they were tapped. It also had pointers to model objects that made up the data of the application.

The Quiz application had only one screen, so it was sufficient to have only one controller object for that application. However, most applications have more than one screen. Having one controller and many screens is messy because the controller has too many objects to manage. When designing iOS applications, it is best to have a controller for every screen.

UIViewController

A `UIViewController` instance specializes in controlling a single screen within an application. Every `UIViewController` has a `view` property that points to an instance of `UIView` or one of its subclasses, and this view is its screen. Typically, this `view` is a fullscreen view. More often than not, the `view` also has subviews. Thus, a view controller controls a view hierarchy. Because the `view` is the root of this hierarchy, when the `view` of a view controller is added as a subview of the window, the entire view hierarchy is added.

Creating HypnoTime

Create a new iOS project from the Empty Application template. Name this project HypnoTime and configure the project as shown in Figure 7.1.

Figure 7.1   Creating a new project

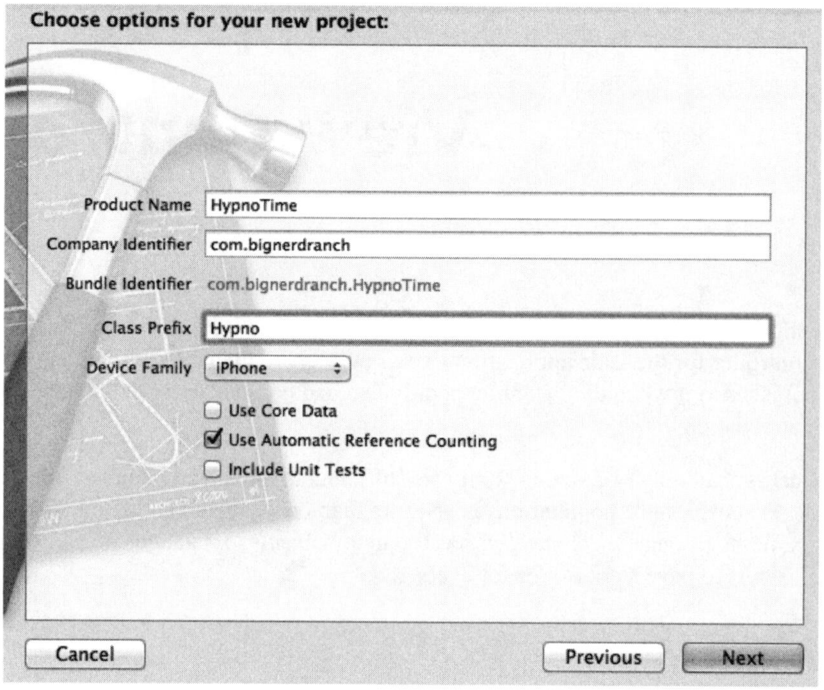

Unlike Quiz and Whereami, this application will have two subclasses of **UIViewController** – one called **HypnosisViewController** and another called **TimeViewController**. Each view controller will control a view, and users will be able to swap between the views depending on whether they want to be hypnotized or just want to see what time it is. The swapping will be handled by another class, **UITabBarController**. We'll get to tab bar controllers in the second part of this chapter after we create the two view controllers.

Subclassing UIViewController

You never create instances of **UIViewController** directly; instead, you create subclasses of **UIViewController** to instantiate. From the File menu, select New File... from the New menu item.

From the iOS section, select Cocoa Touch and then choose Objective-C class. Hit Next.

On the next pane, name this class **HypnosisViewController**, choose **NSObject** as the superclass, and hit Next (Figure 7.2). Save the files when prompted to do so.

Figure 7.2   Creating HypnosisViewController

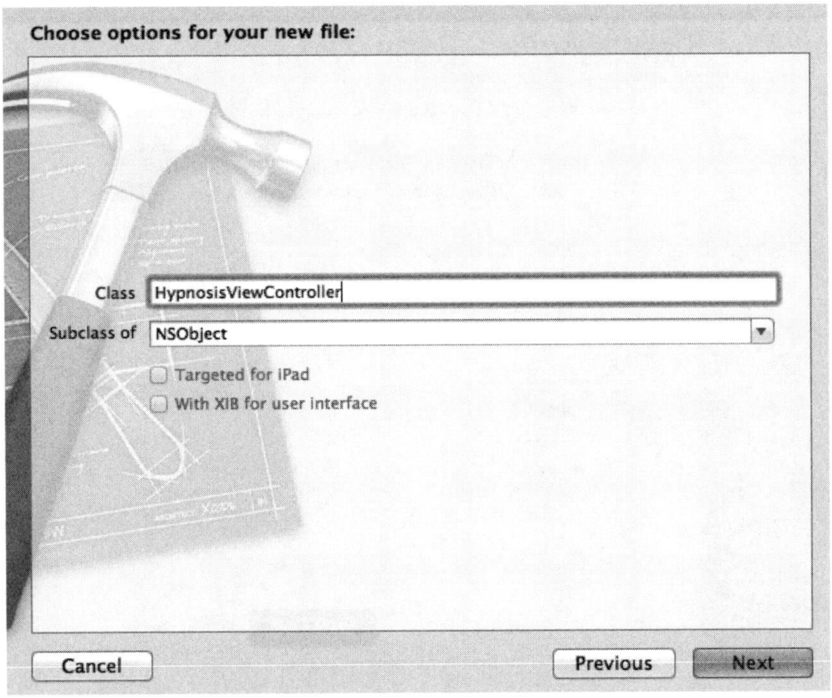

Open HypnosisViewController.h and change the superclass to **UIViewController**.

```
@interface HypnosisViewController : NSObject
@interface HypnosisViewController : UIViewController
```

@end

A view controller is responsible for creating its view hierarchy. **HypnosisViewController**'s view hierarchy will be made up of only one view, an instance of **HypnosisView** – the **UIView** subclass you created in Chapter 6. Locate HypnosisView.h and HypnosisView.m in Finder and drag them into HypnoTime's project navigator.

In the sheet that appears, check the box to Copy items into destination group's folder and the box to add these files to the target that is HypnoTime (Figure 7.3). Then click Finish. This will create a copy of the two files, add those files to HypnoTime's directory on the filesystem, and then add them to the HypnoTime project.

Figure 7.3   Adding HypnosisView to HypnoTime

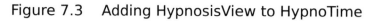

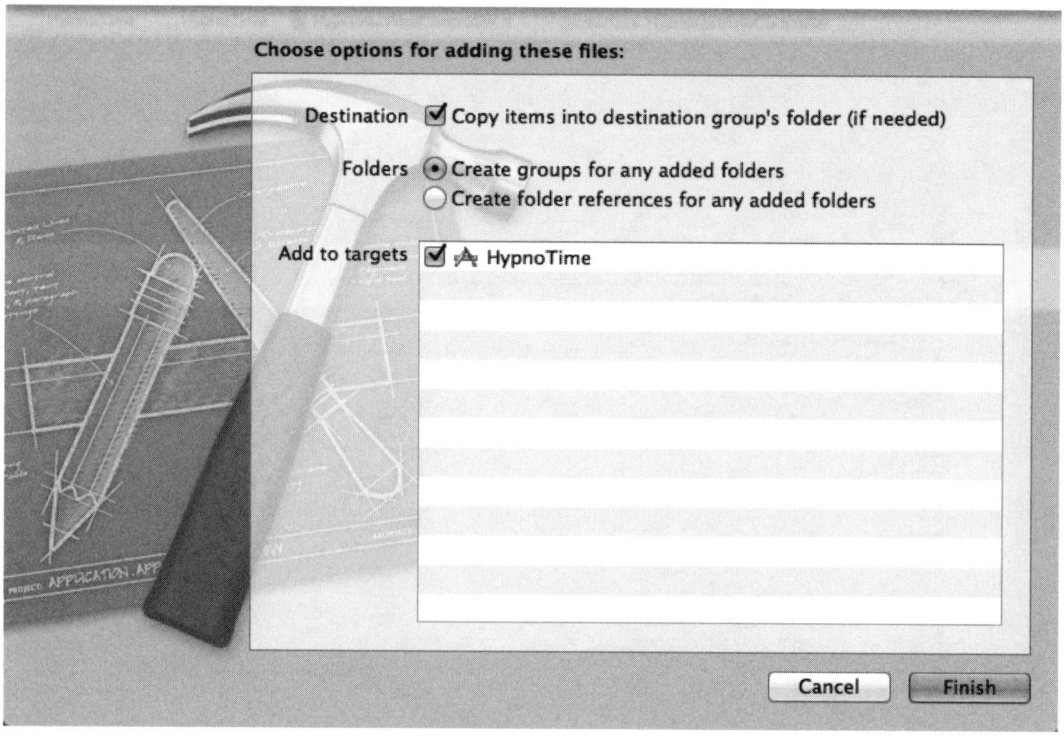

A **UIViewController** subclass creates its view hierarchy by overriding the method **loadView**. This method creates a view instance and sets it as the view of the view controller. In HypnosisViewController.m, override **loadView**, making sure to import the header file for **HypnosisView** at the top of this file.

```
#import "HypnosisViewController.h"
#import "HypnosisView.h"

@implementation HypnosisViewController

- (void)loadView
{
    // Create a view
    CGRect frame = [[UIScreen mainScreen] bounds];
    HypnosisView *v = [[HypnosisView alloc] initWithFrame:frame];

    // Set it as *the* view of this view controller
    [self setView:v];
}
@end
```

In HypnoAppDelegate.m, create an instance of **HypnosisViewController** and set it as the rootViewController of the **UIWindow**. Make sure to import HypnosisViewController.h at the top of this file.

```
#import "HypnoAppDelegate.h"
#import "HypnosisViewController.h"

@implementation HypnoAppDelegate

@synthesize window = _window;

- (BOOL)application:(UIApplication *)application
    didFinishLaunchingWithOptions:(NSDictionary *)launchOptions
{
    self.window = [[UIWindow alloc] initWithFrame:[[UIScreen mainScreen] bounds]];
    // Override point for customization after application launch.

    HypnosisViewController *hvc = [[HypnosisViewController alloc] init];

    [[self window] setRootViewController:hvc];

    self.window.backgroundColor = [UIColor whiteColor];
    [self.window makeKeyAndVisible];
    return YES;
}
```

Build and run the application. You will see an instance of **HypnosisView** grace the screen; this is **HypnosisViewController**'s view.

Figure 7.4   Application diagram

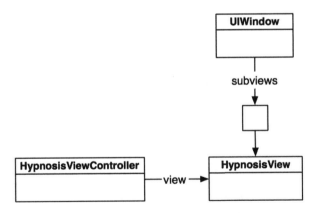

Setting a view controller as the rootViewController of a window adds that view controller's view as a subview of the window (Figure 7.4). It also automatically resizes the view to be the same size as the window. Given what you learned in Chapter 6, you could write **setRootViewController:** yourself:

```
- (void)setRootViewController:(UIViewController *)vc
{
    // Get the view of the root view controller
    UIView *rootView = [vc view];

    // Make a frame that fits the window's bounds
    CGRect viewFrame = [self bounds];
    [rootView setFrame:viewFrame];
```

```
    // Insert this view as window's subview
    [self addSubview:rootView];
}
```

(This method does are a few more things, but this is what we are interested in right now).

Another UIViewController

Now let's turn to HypnoTime's second **UIViewController** subclass. Create a new **NSObject** subclass and name it **TimeViewController**.

In TimeViewController.h, change the superclass to **UIViewController**.

```
@interface TimeViewController : NSObject
@interface TimeViewController : UIViewController
```

A **TimeViewController**'s screen will show a **UILabel** and a **UIButton** that updates that label to the current time. Thus, the **TimeViewController**'s view will be a blank, full-screen **UIView** that has two subviews – the button and label (Figure 7.5).

Figure 7.5   TimeViewController's view hierarchy

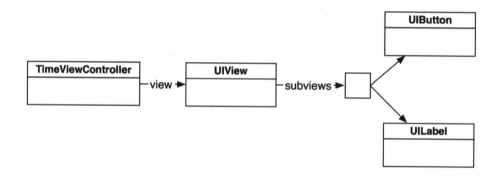

When creating **HypnosisViewController**'s view hierarchy, you did so programmatically: in **loadView**, you instantiated **HypnosisView** and set it as the view. This view did not have any subviews.

TimeViewController's view will have two subviews. When a view controller's view has subviews, it is best to create and load its view hierarchy in a XIB file instead of overriding **loadView**. Creating a view programmatically or from a XIB doesn't make any difference once the application is running; a XIB file is just easier when you need to lay out multiple view objects.

Create a new XIB file by selecting File+New+New File.... From the iOS section, select User Interface and then choose the Empty XIB template (Figure 7.6). On the next pane, select iPhone from the pop-up menu.

Figure 7.6   Creating an empty XIB

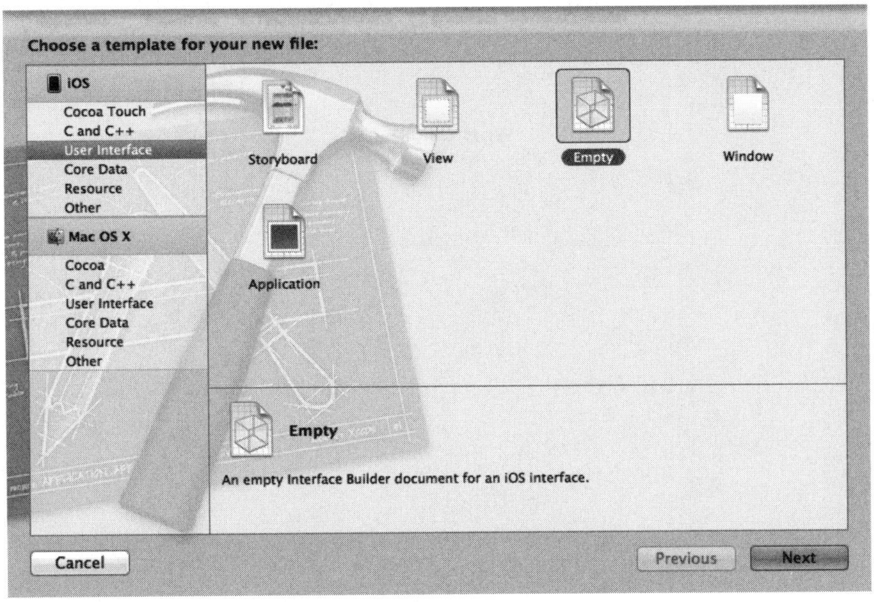

Name this file `TimeViewController.xib` and save it. Then select it in the project navigator to show it the editor area. (It is important to name files as we tell you. Sometimes, people like to name files differently as they are working through this book. This is not a good idea; many of the names are intentional because of assumptions built into the iOS SDK. We'll talk more about these assumptions later, and you can experiment then.)

Demystifying the XIB: File's Owner

In previous chapters, you have been editing XIB files and seeing interfaces in your application without much explanation of how they got there. Now it's time to learn how XIB files work.

XIB files contains objects: dragging an object onto the canvas saves that object into the XIB file. When the XIB file is loaded, those objects are loaded back into memory.

In `TimeViewController.xib`, drag a **UIView** onto the canvas and then drag a **UIButton** and a **UILabel** onto the view. Give the button a title that reads What time is it?. Give the label text that reads ??? and center it (Figure 7.7).

Figure 7.7   TimeViewController's XIB file

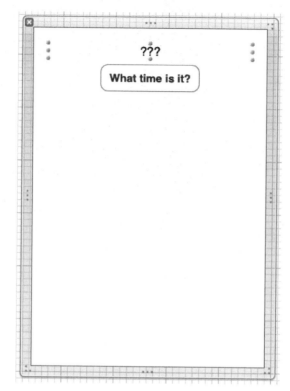

Notice that these objects appear under the Objects section in the outline view (Figure 7.8). Objects that appear in this section are the objects that are saved in this XIB file. We have a special term for this type of saving called archiving. Thus, the objects in this section are known as *archived objects*.

Figure 7.8   Objects in TimeViewController.xib

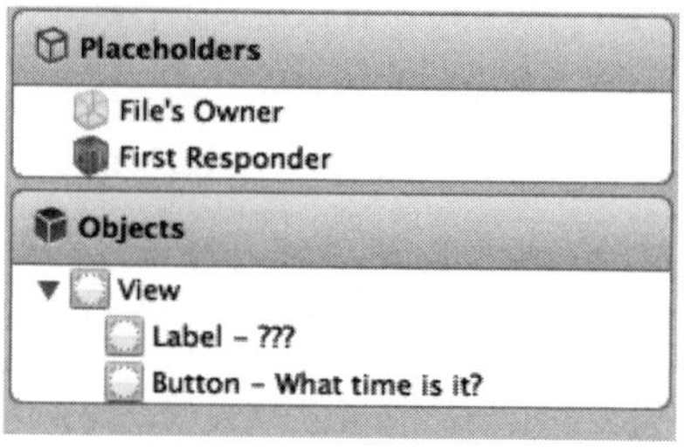

There is another type of object in a XIB file: *placeholder objects*. There are two objects in this XIB file in the Placeholder section: File's Owner and First Responder. You can safely ignore the First Responder, but the File's Owner is very important.

To understand the File's Owner, you must first understand the need for it. When a view controller loads its view, it sets its `view` property so that it knows what its view is and can put it on the screen. For the **HypnosisViewController**, we did this programmatically, so it was done in **loadView** and all set at compile time.

Not so with **TimeViewController**. When an instance of **TimeViewController** needs to load its view, it will load the XIB file. When this happens, all of the archived objects in the XIB will be created, and **TimeViewController** can't know which of those objects is its view.

Here's where the File's Owner comes in: the File's Owner is a hole in the XIB file. You make connections between objects in the XIB and File's Owner when configuring the interface. When the XIB file is loaded, the **TimeViewController** drops itself in the File's Owner hole, and all the connections between the File's Owner and the archived objects will be made to the **TimeViewController**.

To be able to set the connections that a **TimeViewController** needs, we have to tell Xcode that **TimeViewController** is the class of the object that will drop itself into the hole. Select the File's Owner object on the outline view and click the ▣ icon in the inspector area to show the identity inspector. Change the Class to **TimeViewController** (Figure 7.9).

Figure 7.9 Identity inspector for File's Owner

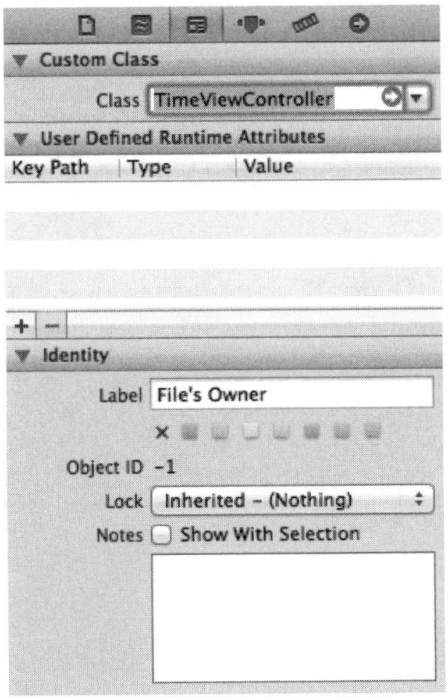

Control-click on the File's Owner object to bring up the panel of available connections. Now that we've specified the class as a **UIViewController** subclass, you are offered the view outlet. Connect this outlet to the **UIView** object in the XIB file. Now when the **TimeViewController** loads the XIB file, it will have the appropriate connections and will be able to load its view.

Figure 7.10   File's Owner

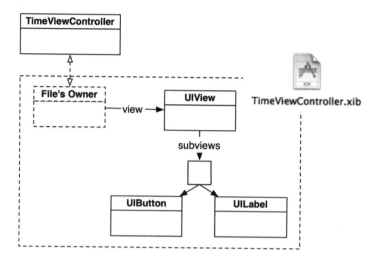

Thus, an outlet connection in a XIB file is equivalent to sending the object with the outlet a setter message based on the name of the outlet. For example, setting the `view` outlet of an object will send the message **setView:** to that object when the XIB file is loaded. The argument to this method is the object on other end of the connection.

Let's test this out. Open `HypnoAppDelegate.m`, create an instance of **TimeViewController**, and set it as the `rootViewController` of the window. Make sure to import `TimeViewController.h`.

```
#import "HypnoAppDelegate.h"
#import "HypnosisViewController.h"
#import "TimeViewController.h"

@implementation HypnoAppDelegate

@synthesize window = _window;

- (BOOL)application:(UIApplication *)application
    didFinishLaunchingWithOptions:(NSDictionary *)launchOptions
{
    self.window = [[UIWindow alloc] initWithFrame:[[UIScreen mainScreen] bounds]];
    // Override point for customization after application launch.

    // Now that we aren't using hvc, this line will generate a warning - ignore it
    HypnosisViewController *hvc = [[HypnosisViewController alloc] init];

    TimeViewController *tvc = [[TimeViewController alloc] init];

    [[self window] setRootViewController:hvc];
    [[self window] setRootViewController:tvc];

    self.window.backgroundColor = [UIColor whiteColor];
    [self.window makeKeyAndVisible];
    return YES;
}
```

Build and run the application. As you might expect, you see the **TimeViewController**'s view that you created in TimeViewController.xib. Now we need to connect up the subviews.

Since **TimeViewController** is controlling this view hierarchy, it is responsible for updating the label when the button is tapped. Thus, **TimeViewController** must be the target of the **UIButton** and have a pointer to the **UILabel**. In TimeViewController.h, declare an outlet and a method.

```
@interface TimeViewController : UIViewController
{
    IBOutlet UILabel *timeLabel;
}
- (IBAction)showCurrentTime:(id)sender;
@end
```

Open TimeViewController.xib and connect the timeLabel outlet of File's Owner (which we now know is the **TimeViewController**) to the **UILabel**. Then connect the **UIButton** to the File's Owner and select **showCurrentTime:**. These connections are shown in Figure 7.11.

Figure 7.11   TimeViewController XIB connections

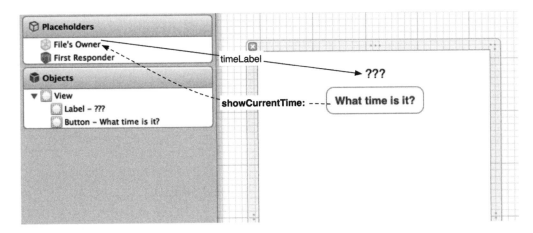

In TimeViewController.m, implement the action method:

```
- (IBAction)showCurrentTime:(id)sender
{
    NSDate *now = [NSDate date];

    NSDateFormatter *formatter = [[NSDateFormatter alloc] init];
    [formatter setTimeStyle:NSDateFormatterMediumStyle];

    [timeLabel setText:[formatter stringFromDate:now]];
}
```

Build and run the application. Tap the What time is it? button, and you will see the current time on the **UILabel**. Figure 7.12 is the object diagram for the application as it currently stands.

Figure 7.12   TimeViewController's view on the window

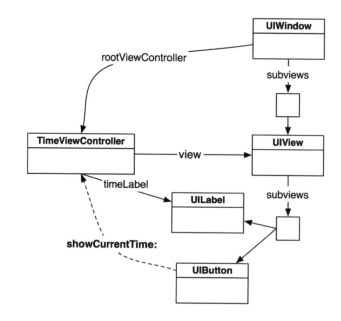

Let's recap what you know so far about view controllers and loading views. A view controller controls a screen, which is a view. The view controller's view, in turn, has subviews, which make up a view hierarchy. A view controller can get its view two different ways:

- A view controller whose view doesn't have any subviews will override **loadView** to create a view instance and send the message **setView:** to itself.

- A view controller with a more complex view hierarchy will load its view from a XIB file by connecting its view outlet to the top-level view archived in the XIB.

UITabBarController

View controllers become more interesting when the user's actions can cause another view controller to be presented. In this book, we will show you a number of ways to present view controllers. We'll start with a **UITabBarController** to swap between instances of **HypnosisViewController** and **TimeViewController**.

UITabBarController keeps an array of **UIViewController**s. It also maintains a tab bar at the bottom of the screen with a tab for each view controller in this array. Tapping on a tab results in the presentation of the view of the view controller associated with that tab.

In HypnoAppDelegate.m, create an instance of **UITabBarController**, give it both view controllers, and install it as the rootViewController of the window.

```
- (BOOL)application:(UIApplication *)application
    didFinishLaunchingWithOptions:(NSDictionary *)launchOptions
{
    self.window = [[UIWindow alloc] initWithFrame:[[UIScreen mainScreen] bounds]];
    // Override point for customization after application launch.

    HypnosisViewController *hvc = [[HypnosisViewController alloc] init];

    TimeViewController *tvc = [[TimeViewController alloc] init];

    UITabBarController *tabBarController = [[UITabBarController alloc] init];

    NSArray *viewControllers = [NSArray arrayWithObjects:hvc, tvc, nil];
    [tabBarController setViewControllers:viewControllers];

    [[self window] setRootViewController:tvc];
    [[self window] setRootViewController:tabBarController];

    self.window.backgroundColor = [UIColor whiteColor];
    [self.window makeKeyAndVisible];
    return YES;
}
```

Build and run the application. Tap on the black tabs at the bottom of the screen to swap between the two view controllers.

Notice that the **UITabBarController** is the rootViewController of the window. This means that **UITabBarController** is itself a subclass of **UIViewController**. A **UITabBarController**, then, has a view property. Its view is a blank **UIView** with two subviews: the tab bar and the view of the selected view controller (Figure 7.13).

Figure 7.13   UITabBarController diagram

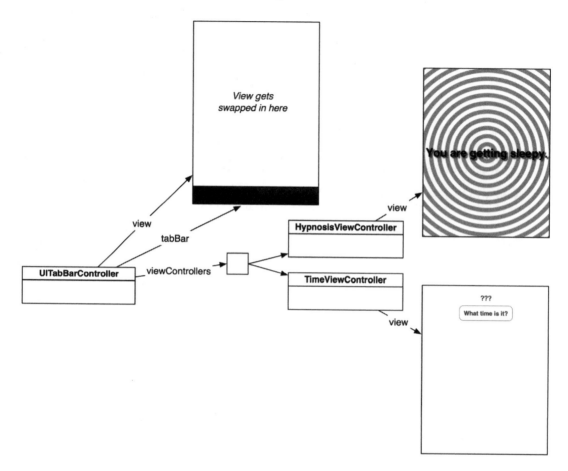

Each tab on the tab bar can display a title and an image. Each view controller maintains a `tabBarItem` property for this purpose. When a view controller is contained by a **UITabBarController**, its tab bar item appears in the tab bar. Figure 7.14 shows an example of this relationship in the iPhone's Phone application.

Figure 7.14   UITabBarItem example

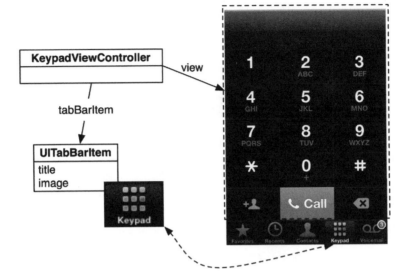

Let's start by putting titles on our tab bar items. Open HypnosisViewController.m. Override **UIViewController**'s designated initializer, **initWithNibName:bundle:**, to get and set a tab bar item for **HypnosisViewController**.

```
- (id)initWithNibName:(NSString *)nibName bundle:(NSBundle *)bundle
{
    // Call the superclass's designated initializer
    self = [super initWithNibName:nil
                           bundle:nil];
    if (self) {
        // Get the tab bar item
        UITabBarItem *tbi = [self tabBarItem];

        // Give it a label
        [tbi setTitle:@"Hypnosis"];
    }

    return self;
}
```

Then open TimeViewController.m and do the same thing.

```
- (id)initWithNibName:(NSString *)nibName bundle:(NSBundle *)bundle
{
    // Call the superclass's designated initializer
    self = [super initWithNibName:nil
                           bundle:nil];
    if (self) {
        // Get the tab bar item
        UITabBarItem *tbi = [self tabBarItem];

        // Give it a label
        [tbi setTitle:@"Time"];
    }
```

```
        return self;
}
```

Build and run the application. Two labeled tab bar items will appear on the tab bar (Figure 7.15).

Figure 7.15   Tab bar items with labels

Now let's add an image for each tab bar. Locate the image files Hypno.png, Time.png, Hypno@2x.png, and Time@2x.png in the Resources directory you downloaded from http://www.bignerdranch.com/solutions/iOSProgramming3ed.zip. Drag these files into HypnoTime's project navigator and check the box to copy the files into the project directory. Then, in HypnosisViewController.m, edit **initWithNibName:bundle::**

```
- (id)initWithNibName:(NSString *)nibName bundle:(NSBundle *)bundle
{
    self = [super initWithNibName:nil
                           bundle:nil];

    if (self) {
        UITabBarItem *tbi = [self tabBarItem];
        [tbi setTitle:@"Hypnosis"];

        // Create a UIImage from a file
        // This will use Hypno@2x.png on retina display devices
        UIImage *i = [UIImage imageNamed:@"Hypno.png"];

        // Put that image on the tab bar item
        [tbi setImage:i];
    }

    return self;
}
```

Open TimeViewController.m and do the same thing:

```
- (id)initWithNibName:(NSString *)nibName bundle:(NSBundle *)bundle
{
    self = [super initWithNibName:nil
                           bundle:nil];

    if (self) {
        UITabBarItem *tbi = [self tabBarItem];
        [tbi setTitle:@"Time"];

        UIImage *i = [UIImage imageNamed:@"Time.png"];
        [tbi setImage:i];
    }

    return self;
}
```

Now when you build and run the application, you will also see helpful images in the tab bar to help users understand their options. (Figure 7.16).

Figure 7.16   Tab bar items with labels and icons

View Controller Lifecycle

A **UIViewController** begins its life when it is allocated and sent an initializer message. A view controller will see its view created, moved on screen, moved off screen, destroyed, and created again – perhaps many times over. These events make up the view controller lifecycle.

Initializing view controllers

The designated initializer of **UIViewController** is **initWithNibName:bundle:**. This method takes two arguments that specify the name of the view controller's XIB file inside a bundle. (Remember that building a target in Xcode creates an application bundle; this is the same kind of bundle we're talking about here.)

Passing nil for both arguments says, "When you load your view, search for a XIB file whose name is the same as your class and search inside the application bundle." For example, **TimeViewController** will load the TimeViewController.xib file. You can be more explicit about it; add the following code to TimeViewController.m.

```
- (id)initWithNibName:(NSString *)nibName bundle:(NSBundle *)bundle
{
    self = [super initWithNibName:nil
                           bundle:nil];

    // Get a pointer to the application bundle object
    NSBundle *appBundle = [NSBundle mainBundle];

    self = [super initWithNibName:@"TimeViewController"
                           bundle:appBundle];

    if (self) {
        UITabBarItem *tbi = [self tabBarItem];
        [tbi setTitle:@"Time"];

        UIImage *i = [UIImage imageNamed:@"Time.png"];
        [tbi setImage:i];
    }

    return self;
}
```

In practice, iOS programmers use the name of the **UIViewController** subclass as the name of the XIB file. Thus, when creating view controllers, you need only send **init**. This is equivalent to passing nil for both arguments of **initWithNibName:bundle:**.

```
TimeViewController *tvc = [[TimeViewController alloc] init];
// same as:
TimeViewController *tvc = [[TimeViewController alloc] initWithNibName:nil
                                                              bundle:nil];
```

You can override **initWithNibName:bundle:** to perform some extra initialization steps if you need them.

Note that the view controller's view does not appear anywhere in the view controller's initializer. Nothing that has to do with the view happens here. We'll see why in the next section.

UIViewController and lazy loading

When a **UIViewController** is instantiated, it doesn't create or load its view right away. Only when the view is moving to the screen will a view controller bother to create its view. By loading views only when needed, the application doesn't take up memory that it doesn't need to.

Every **UIViewController** implements the method **viewDidLoad** that gets executed right after it loads its view. In HypnosisViewController.m, override this method to log a message to the console.

```
- (void)viewDidLoad
{
    // Always call the super implementation of viewDidLoad
    [super viewDidLoad];

    NSLog(@"HypnosisViewController loaded its view.");
}
```

Then, in TimeViewController.m, override the same method.

```
- (void)viewDidLoad
{
    [super viewDidLoad];

    NSLog(@"TimeViewController loaded its view.");
}
```

Build and run the application. Notice that the console reports that **HypnosisViewController** loaded its view right away. Tap on **TimeViewController**'s tab – the console will report that its view is now loaded. At this point, both views have been loaded, so switching between the tabs now will no longer trigger the **viewDidLoad** method. (Try it and see.)

A view controller will destroy its view if the system is running low on memory and if its view isn't currently on the screen. Run HypnoTime in the simulator. Select the Time tab so that both views are loaded.

Now, in the simulator, select Simulate Memory Warning from the Hardware menu. This simulates what happens when the operating system is running low on memory and tells your application to clean up stuff it isn't using.

Switch back to the Hypnosis tab; notice that the console reports that **HypnosisViewController** loaded its view again. Now switch to the Time tab and notice that **TimeViewController** did *not* reload its view.

TimeViewController's view was on the screen when the memory warning occurred, so its view was not destroyed. (Destroying a view that is on the screen would result in a miserable user experience.) **HypnosisViewController**'s view, on the other hand, was *not* on the screen during the memory warning, so it was destroyed. When you returned to that view, it was recreated and reloaded.

When the Hypnosis tab bar item was tapped, the **UITabBarController** asked the **HypnosisViewController** for its view so it could add it as a subview of its own view. **HypnosisViewController**, like all view controllers, automatically calls **loadView** if it is sent the message **view** and does not yet have its view. The implementation of **UIViewController**'s **view** method looks something like this:

```
- (UIView *)view
{
    if ([self isViewLoaded] == NO)
    {
        // If I don't currently have a view, then create it
        [self loadView];
        [self viewDidLoad];
    }

    // The view is definitely going to exist here, so return it
    return view;
}
```

UIViewControllers that load their view from a XIB file follow the same behavior. In fact, the default implementation of **loadView** loads the XIB file specified by **initWithNibName:bundle:**. So when view controllers that load their views programmatically override **loadView**, they intentionally don't call the superclass's implementation. If they did, it would kick off a search for a XIB file.

Because a view controller's view can be destroyed and reloaded, you need to take some precautions when writing code that initializes a view controller. Let's do something wrong to see the potential problem.

In TimeViewController.m, set the background color of **TimeViewController**'s view in **initWithNibName:bundle:**.

```
- (id)initWithNibName:(NSString *)nibName bundle:(NSBundle *)bundle
{
    self = [super initWithNibName:@"TimeViewController"
                           bundle:[NSBundle mainBundle]];

    if (self) {
        UITabBarItem *tbi = [self tabBarItem];
        [tbi setTitle:@"Time"];

        UIImage *i = [UIImage imageNamed:@"Time.png"];
        [tbi setImage:i];

        [[self view] setBackgroundColor:[UIColor greenColor]];
    }

    return self;
}
```

Build and run the application. The first thing you will notice is that the console reports that **HypnosisViewController** immediately loads its view. Switch to the Time tab, and note that the background color is green. Then switch back to the Hypnosis tab and simulate a memory warning.

Now switch back to the Time tab, and you'll see that the background color is no longer green. The view controller reloaded its view, but the view controller's initializer was not called again. So, the line of code that set the background color of its view to green was not executed, and the view in question was not configured correctly when the view was reloaded.

This is an important lesson: while you can do initial set-up for a view controller in `initWithNibName:bundle:`, you should never access a view controller's view or any view in its view hierarchy in that method. Instead, **viewDidLoad** is where you should put any extra set-up messages you wish to send to a view controller's view or any of its subviews.

In `TimeViewController.m`, move the line of code that changes the background color from `initWithNibName:bundle:` to `viewDidLoad`.

```
- (id)initWithNibName:(NSString *)nibName bundle:(NSBundle *)bundle
{
    self = [super initWithNibName:@"TimeViewController"
                           bundle:[NSBundle mainBundle]];

    if (self) {
        UITabBarItem *tbi = [self tabBarItem];
        [tbi setTitle:@"Time"];

        UIImage *i = [UIImage imageNamed:@"Time.png"];
        [tbi setImage:i];

        [[self view] setBackgroundColor:[UIColor greenColor]];
    }

    return self;
}

- (void)viewDidLoad
{
    [super viewDidLoad];

    NSLog(@"TimeViewController loaded its view.");

    [[self view] setBackgroundColor:[UIColor greenColor]];
}
```

Build and run the application. Switch between tabs and simulate memory warnings. No matter what you do, the background color of **TimeViewController**'s view will be green.

Unloading views

If **TimeViewController** destroys its view during a memory warning, the view's subviews will no longer be able to appear on screen and should be destroyed, too. This is what will happen with the **UIButton**; it is only owned by the view, so when the view is destroyed, the button is destroyed. However, the **UILabel** will continue to exist because it is still pointed to by the timeLabel instance variable of **TimeViewController**. (Figure 7.17).

Figure 7.17 TimeViewController before and after memory warning

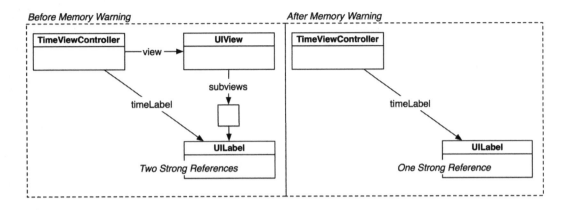

When **TimeViewController** recreates its view, it will create a new instance of **UILabel** and set its timeLabel instance variable to point to it. At this point, the old label will be destroyed. But we shouldn't wait on **TimeViewController** to reload its view to fix this memory leak. We can't be sure when or even if that will happen.

After a view controller's view is unloaded during a memory warning, the view controller is sent the message **viewDidUnload**. You override this method to get rid of any strong references to subviews of the view controller's view. In TimeViewController.m, override **viewDidUnload**.

```
- (void)viewDidUnload
{
    [super viewDidUnload];
    NSLog(@"Unloading TimeViewController's subviews");
    timeLabel = nil;
}
```

Build and run this application. Tap on the Time tab and then go back to the Hypnosis tab. Simulate a memory warning and note the log message in the console. Notice that if you simulate a memory warning while **TimeViewController**'s view is visible, you will not see this message – a view is only unloaded if it is not on the screen.

Overriding **viewDidUnload** is one way to fix this problem, but we can solve it more simply with weak references. If you specify that timeLabel is a weak reference, then the view would keep the only strong reference to the **UILabel**, and when the view was destroyed, the **UILabel** would be destroyed, and timeLabel would automatically be set to nil.

Figure 7.18 TimeViewController before and after memory warning (with weak reference)

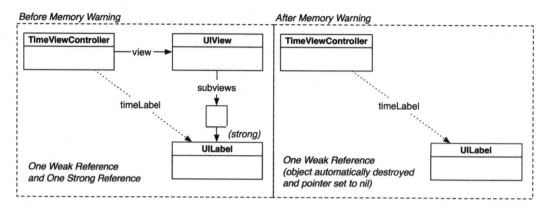

In `TimeViewController.h`, declare that `timeLabel` is a weak reference.

```
@interface TimeViewController : UIViewController
{
    __weak IBOutlet UILabel *timeLabel;
}
```

Then, change **viewDidUnload** in `TimeViewController.m` so that it confirms that `timeLabel` is nil as soon as the view is unloaded.

```
- (void)viewDidUnload
{
    [super viewDidUnload];

    NSLog(@"Unloading TimeViewController's subviews");
    timeLabel = nil;

    NSLog(@"timeLabel = %@", timeLabel);
}
```

Build and run the application. Make **TimeViewController** unload its view by simulating a memory warning while its view is not visible. Notice that `timeLabel` is nil by the time **viewDidUnload** runs.

The situation of a view controller having two references to a view is common. To avoid memory leaks, the convention for `IBOutlets` is to declare them as weak references. There is one exception to this rule: you must keep a strong reference to top-level objects in a XIB file. A top-level object in a XIB file sits in the top-level of the of the Objects section in the outline view; you don't have to click the disclosure tab next to another object to see it. For example, a view controller's view is a top-level object, but its subviews are not (Figure 7.19).

Figure 7.19 XIB top level objects

The view controller, then, has ownership of its view, which owns all of its subviews. All of the objects continue to exist as long as you need them to. Therefore, you do not need to implement viewDidUnload to release subviews of a view controller's view. In TimeViewController.m, you can delete the implementation of this method.

```
- (void)viewDidUnload
{
    [super viewDidUnload];

    NSLog(@"timeLabel = %@", timeLabel);
}
```

Appearing and disappearing views

In addition to loading and unloading, the view of a view controller also appears and disappears at certain times. **UIViewController** has several methods that get called at these points in the lifecycle:

viewWillAppear:	when its view is about to be added to the window
viewDidAppear:	when its view has been added to the window
viewWillDisappear:	when its view is about to be dismissed, covered, or otherwise hidden from view
viewDidDisappear:	when its view has been dismissed, covered, or otherwise hidden from view

These methods are useful because a view controller is only created once, but its view usually gets displayed (and dismissed or hidden) several times. You often need a way to override the default behavior at these times in the life of view controller. For example, you may want to do some sort of initialization each time the view is moved on screen, like displaying the most current time in **TimeViewController**'s view. Here you would use **viewWillAppear:** or **viewDidAppear:**.

Similarly, if you had a large data structure that you only needed while the view controller was being displayed, you might want to do some clean-up each time the view controller was moved off screen. Then you would use **viewWillDisappear:** or **viewDidDisappear:**. Note that these methods, as defined in **UIViewController**, do nothing. They are there so that your subclasses can override them.

```
- (void)viewWillAppear:(BOOL)animated;
- (void)viewDidAppear:(BOOL)animated;
- (void)viewWillDisappear:(BOOL)animated;
- (void)viewDidDisappear:(BOOL)animated;
```

Now let's override **viewWillAppear:** to initialize the time label of the **TimeViewController** to the current time and to log to the console. While we're at it, let's override **viewWillDisappear:** to log to the console, too. In TimeViewController.m, make the following changes:

```
- (void)viewWillAppear:(BOOL)animated
{
    NSLog(@"CurrentTimeViewController will appear");
    [super viewWillAppear:animated];
    [self showCurrentTime:nil];
}
```

```
- (void)viewWillDisappear:(BOOL)animated
{
    NSLog(@"CurrentTimeViewController will DISappear");
    [super viewWillDisappear:animated];
}
```

Build and run the application. Note that each time you return to the Time tab, the time label is updated and a log statement appears in the console. And each time you leave that screen, you see another log statement in the console.

The most important thing to keep in mind is that the view and its view controller are separate objects. You can think of the view as a renewable resource that the view controller uses to communicate with the user. Figure 7.20 shows the life cycle of a view controller's view in full.

Figure 7.20   Lifecycle of a view controller's view

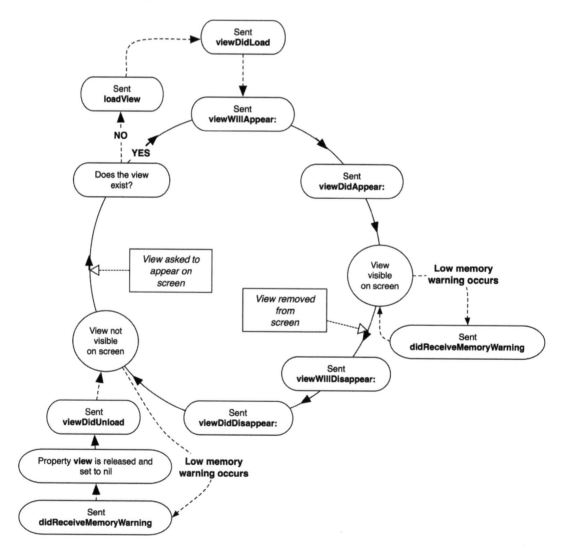

View Controller Subclasses and Templates

In this exercise, you created a **UIViewController** subclass using the **NSObject** template and an empty XIB file. This is useful for learning how the XIB file works. However, in practice, you typically let Xcode do the grunt work and use the **UIViewController** subclass template.

Over the course of this book, you will create a lot of view controllers. To save on time and potential errors, you'll use the **UIViewController** template when a view controller will have a XIB file. When you create a view controller subclass with a XIB template, the XIB's File's Owner is already set to the class of that view controller. It also has an instance of **UIView** already hooked up to the File's Owner's view outlet.

There is a drawback, however, to using the view controller template: there is a lot of code written in the implementation file. It becomes difficult to see what's going on with all of this extra junk in the file. Therefore, whenever you create a view controller using this template, the first thing we'll ask you to do is delete all of the code in the implementation file between the @implementation and @end directives.

Bronze Challenge: Another Tab

Create a new **UIViewController** subclass. Its view should be an instance of **MKMapView**. Make this view controller the third view controller in the **UITabBarController**.

Silver Challenge: Controller Logic

Add a **UISegmentedControl** to **HypnosisViewController**'s view with segments for Red, Green, and Blue. When the user taps the segmented control, change the color of the circles in **HypnosisView**. Be sure to create a copy of the project and work from that copy while attempting this challenge.

For the More Curious: The main Function and UIApplication

A C application begins by executing a **main** function. An Objective-C application is no different, but we haven't seen **main** in any of our iOS applications. Let's take a look now.

Open main.m in the HypnoTime project navigator. It looks like this:

```
int main(int argc, char *argv[])
{
    @autoreleasepool {
        return UIApplicationMain(argc, argv,
                            nil, NSStringFromClass([HypnoAppDelegate class]));
    }
}
```

The function **UIApplicationMain** creates an instance of a class called **UIApplication**. For every application, there is a single **UIApplication** instance. This object is responsible for maintaining the run loop. Once the application object is created, its run loop essentially becomes an infinite loop: the executing thread will never return to **main**.

Another thing the function **UIApplicationMain** does is create an instance of the class that will serve as the **UIApplication**'s delegate. Notice that the final argument to the **UIApplicationMain** function is an **NSString** that is the name of the delegate's class. So, this function will create an instance of **HypnoAppDelegate** and set it as the delegate of the **UIApplication** object. (Where does the **Hypno** in **HypnoAppDelegate** come from? It's what you entered for the class prefix when creating this project.)

Right before the run loop begins accepting events, the application sends a message to its delegate saying, "Get ready because here we go!" This message is **application:didFinishLaunchingWithOptions:**. You implemented this method in HypnoAppDelegate.m to create the window and the controller objects used in this application.

Every iOS application follows this pattern. If you're still curious, go back and check the main.m files in the Quiz and Whereami applications you wrote earlier.

For the More Curious: Retina Display

With the release of iPhone 4, Apple introduced the Retina display for the iPhone and iPod touch. The Retina display has much higher resolution – 640x960 pixels compared to 320x480 pixels on earlier devices. Let's look at what you should do to make graphics look their best on both displays.

For vector graphics, like **HypnosisView**'s **drawRect:** method and drawn text, you don't need to do anything; the same code will render as crisply as the device allows. However, if you draw using Core Graphics functions, these graphics will appear differently on different devices. In Core Graphics, also called Quartz, we describe lines, curves, text, etc. in terms of *points*. On a non-Retina display, a point is 1x1 pixel. On a Retina display, a point is 2x2 pixels (Figure 7.21).

Figure 7.21   Rendering to different resolutions

As described to Core Graphics (vector graphics)

As rendered to 3GS (1 point = 1 pixel)

As rendered to Retina Display (1 point = 2 pixels)

Given these differences, bitmap images (like JPEG or PNG files) will be unattractive if the image isn't tailored to the device's screen type. Say your application includes a small image of 25x25 pixels. If this image is displayed on a Retina display, then the image must be stretched to cover an area of 50x50 pixels. At this point, the system does a type of averaging called anti-aliasing to keep the image from looking jagged. The result is an image that isn't jagged – but it is fuzzy (Figure 7.22).

Figure 7.22 Fuzziness from stretching an image

You could use a larger file instead, but the averaging would then cause problems in the other direction when the image is shrunk for a non-Retina display. The only solution is to bundle two image files with your application: one at a pixel resolution equal to the number of points on the screen for non-Retina displays and one twice that size in pixels for Retina displays.

Fortunately, you do not have to write any extra code to handle which image gets loaded on which device. All you have to do is suffix the higher-resolution image with @2x. Then, when you use **UIImage**'s **imageNamed:** method to load the image, this method looks in the bundle and gets the file that is appropriate for the particular device.

Once the simulator application is running, you can change which display is being simulated. To see HypnoTime in a Retina display, go to the Hardware menu, select Device, and then choose iPhone (Retina). Notice that the tab bar items are crisp on both types of displays. (If you're even more curious, you can remove the @2x files from your project and build and run again to see the difference.)

8

Notification and Rotation

Objective-C code is all about objects sending messages to other objects. This communication usually occurs between two objects, but sometimes a bunch of objects are concerned with one object. They all want to know when this object does something interesting, and it's not feasible for that object to send messages to every interested object.

Instead, an object can post notifications about what it is doing to a centralized notification center. Interested objects register to receive a message when a particular notification is posted or when a particular object posts. In this chapter, you will learn how to use a notification center to handle notifications. You'll also learn about the autorotation behavior of **UIViewController**.

Notification Center

Every application has an instance of **NSNotificationCenter**, which works like a smart bulletin board. An object can register as an observer ("Send me 'lost dog' notifications"). When another object posts a notification ("I lost my dog"), the notification center forwards the notification to the registered observers (Figure 8.1).

Figure 8.1   NSNotificationCenter

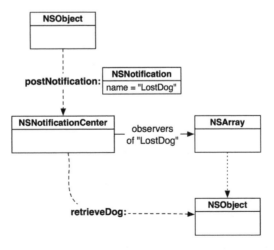

Notifications are instances of **NSNotification**. Every **NSNotification** object has a name and a pointer back to the object that posted it. When you register as an observer, you can specify a notification name, a posting object, and the message you want sent to you when a qualifying notification is posted.

The following snippet of code registers you for notifications named `LostDog` that have been posted by any object. When an object posts a `LostDog` notification, you'll be sent the message **retrieveDog:**.

```
NSNotificationCenter *nc = [NSNotificationCenter defaultCenter];
[nc addObserver:self                    // The object self will be sent
    selector:@selector(retrieveDog:)    // retrieveDog:
        name:@"LostDog"                 // when @"LostDog" is posted
      object:nil];                      // by any object.
```

Note that `nil` works as a wildcard in the notification center world. You can pass `nil` as the `name` argument, which will give you every notification regardless of its name. If you pass `nil` for the notification name and the posting object, you will get every notification.

The method that is triggered when the notification arrives takes an **NSNotification** object as the argument:

```
- (void)retrieveDog:(NSNotification *)note
{
    id poster = [note object];
    NSString *name = [note name];
    NSDictionary *extraInformation = [note userInfo];
}
```

Notice that the notification object may have a `userInfo` dictionary attached to it. This dictionary is used to pass additional information, like a description of the dog that was found. Here's an example of an object posting a notification with a `userInfo` dictionary attached:

```
NSDictionary *extraInfo = [NSDictionary dictionaryWithObject:@"Fido" forKey:@"Name"];
NSNotification *note = [NSNotification notificationWithName:@"LostDog"
                                                    object:self
                                                  userInfo:extraInfo];
[[NSNotificationCenter defaultCenter] postNotification:note];
```

For a (real-world) example, when a keyboard is coming onto the screen, it posts a `UIKeyboardDidShowNotification` that has a `userInfo` dictionary. This dictionary contains the on-screen region that the newly visible keyboard occupies.

This is important: the notification center does not keep strong references to its observers. If the object doesn't remove itself as an observer before it is destroyed, then the next time a notification that the object registered for is posted, the center will try to send the object a message. Since that object no longer exists, your application will crash. Thus, if an object registers with the notification center, that object must unregister in its **dealloc** method.

```
- (void)dealloc
{
    [[NSNotificationCenter defaultCenter] removeObserver:self];
}
```

It's important to understand that **NSNotification**s and the **NSNotificationCenter** are not associated with visual "notifications,", like push and local notifications that the user sees when an alarm goes off or a text message is received. **NSNotification**s and the **NSNotificationCenter** comprise a design pattern, like target-action pairs or delegation.

UIDevice Notifications

One object that regularly posts notifications is **UIDevice**. Here are the constants that serve as names of the notifications that a **UIDevice** posts:

```
UIDeviceOrientationDidChangeNotification
UIDeviceBatteryStateDidChangeNotification
UIDeviceBatteryLevelDidChangeNotification
UIDeviceProximityStateDidChangeNotification
```

Wouldn't it be cool to get a message when the device rotates? Or when the phone is placed next to the user's face? These notifications do just that.

Create a new Empty Application project and name it HeavyRotation. Enter Rotation into the Class Prefix field, enter iPhone for the device family, and only check the box for Use Automatic Reference Counting.

In RotationAppDelegate.m, register to receive notifications when the orientation of the device changes:

```
- (BOOL)application:(UIApplication *)application
    didFinishLaunchingWithOptions:(NSDictionary *)launchOptions
{
    self.window = [[UIWindow alloc] initWithFrame:[[UIScreen mainScreen] bounds]];
    // Override point for customization after application launch.

    // Get the device object
    UIDevice *device = [UIDevice currentDevice];

    // Tell it to start monitoring the accelerometer for orientation
    [device beginGeneratingDeviceOrientationNotifications];

    // Get the notification center for the app
    NSNotificationCenter *nc = [NSNotificationCenter defaultCenter];

    // Add yourself as an observer
    [nc addObserver:self
          selector:@selector(orientationChanged:)
              name:UIDeviceOrientationDidChangeNotification
            object:device];

    self.window.backgroundColor = [UIColor whiteColor];
    [self.window makeKeyAndVisible];

    return YES;
}
```

Now, whenever the device's orientation changes, the message **orientationChanged:** will be sent to the instance of **RotationAppDelegate**. In the same file, add an **orientationChanged:** method:

```
- (void)orientationChanged:(NSNotification *)note
{
    // Log the constant that represents the current orientation
    NSLog(@"orientationChanged: %d", [[note object] orientation]);
}
```

Build and run the application. (This is best run on the device because the simulator won't let you achieve some orientations. If you must use the simulator, you can change the orientation by choosing Rotate Left or Rotate Right from the Hardware menu.)

Take another look at the @selector directive you used when you added an observer to the notification center. This directive takes the name of a method and wraps it up in a SEL data type. Doing so allows method names to be passed as arguments to methods. But the method name must be exact. Here, the name of the method is **orientationChanged:** including the colon. If you omit the colon from the @selector directive like this,

```
@selector(orientationChanged)
```

then the application will crash when the device rotates and for good reason: The notification center will send the message **orientationChanged** to the **RotationAppDelegate**. **RotationAppDelegate** does not implement to a method named **orientationChanged**. It implements a method named **orientationChanged:**. The colon is an essential part of the method name.

Many classes post notifications including **UIApplication**, **NSManagedObjectContext**, **MPMoviePlayerController**, **NSFileHandle**, **UIWindow**, **UITextField**, and **UITextView**. See their class reference pages in the documentation for details.

Autorotation

Many applications rotate and resize all of their views when the user rotates the device. You could implement this using **UIDevice** notifications, but it would be a lot of work. Fortunately, you can use *autorotation* to simplify the process.

If the view on screen is controlled by a view controller, when the device is rotated, the view controller is asked if it is okay to rotate the view. If the view controller agrees, the view is resized and rotated. Its subviews are also resized and rotated.

You will need a **UIViewController** subclass to get this autorotating behavior. This view controller's view will have subviews, so we will use the **UIViewController** template with a XIB file to create this class.

Select File → New → New File.... From the iOS section, select Cocoa Touch, choose the Objective-C class template, and click Next.

Figure 8.2   UIViewController template

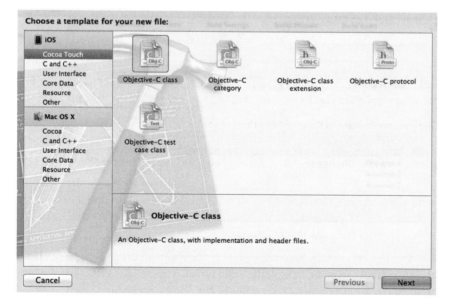

On the next pane, name this new subclass **HeavyViewController**, select UIViewController as the superclass, uncheck Targeted for iPad, and check With XIB for user interface. Then click Next (Figure 8.3).

Figure 8.3   UIViewController template options

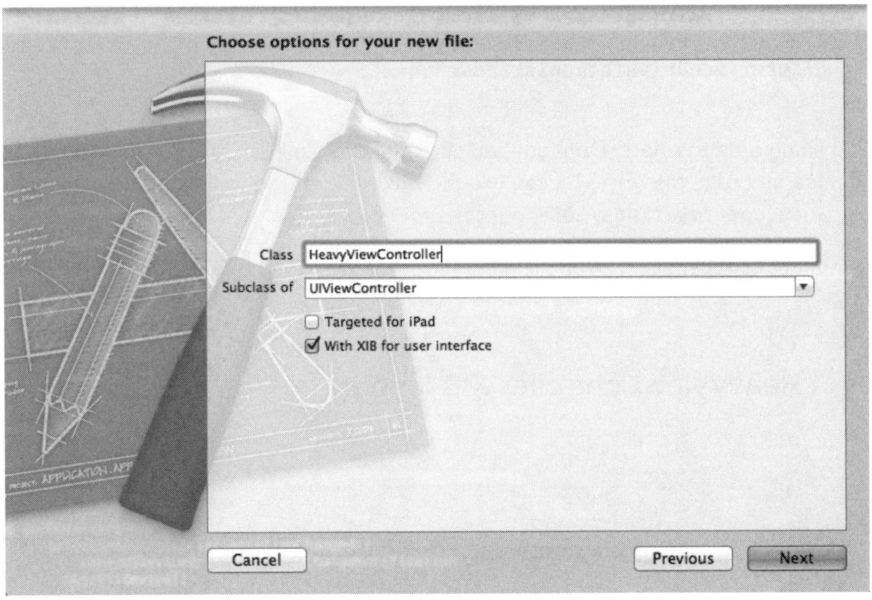

Save these new files when the sheet appears. Then, open HeavyViewController.m and delete everything between @implementation and @end. The file should look like this:

```
#import "HeavyViewController.h"

@implementation HeavyViewController

@end
```

Using this template gives you a subclass of **UIViewController** named **HeavyViewController**. You also get a XIB file named HeavyViewController.xib. This XIB file has a File's Owner of type **HeavyViewController**, whose view outlet is connected to a 320x460 point sized view object.

To implement autorotation in HeavyRotation, you need to do two things:

- Override **shouldAutorotateToInterfaceOrientation:** in **HeavyViewController** to allow autorotation.

- Carefully set the autoresize mask on each subview so that it acts reasonably when the superview is resized to fill the rotated window.

When the device rotates, view controllers whose views are currently on the screen will be sent the message **shouldAutorotateToInterfaceOrientation:**. This method returns a BOOL that indicates whether it is okay to autorotate the view controller's view.

For iPhone applications, you typically allow right-side up, landscape left, and landscape right. On the iPad, you typically allow all orientations, including upside-down. In HeavyViewController.m, implement this method to return YES for the three typical iPhone orientations.

```
- (BOOL)shouldAutorotateToInterfaceOrientation:(UIInterfaceOrientation)x
{
    // Return YES if incoming orientation is Portrait
    // or either of the Landscapes, otherwise, return NO
    return (x == UIInterfaceOrientationPortrait)
        || UIInterfaceOrientationIsLandscape(x);
}
```

Now let's find something to rotate. Drag any image (smaller than 1024x1024) from Finder into the project navigator. (Alternatively, you can use the file joeeye.jpg in the solutions at http://www.bignerdranch.com/solutions/iOSProgramming3ed.zip.)

Open HeavyViewController.xib. Drop a slider, an image view, and two buttons on the view (Figure 8.4).

Figure 8.4   HeavyViewController XIB layout

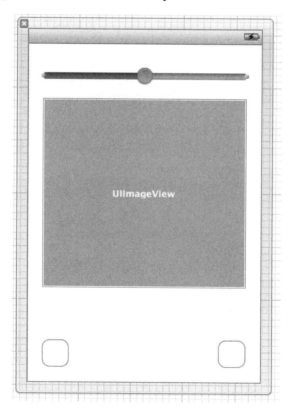

Then select the **UIImageView** and show the attributes inspector. Set the Image property to your image file, set the Mode to Aspect Fit, and set the background color to gray, as shown in Figure 8.5.

Figure 8.5   UIImageView attributes

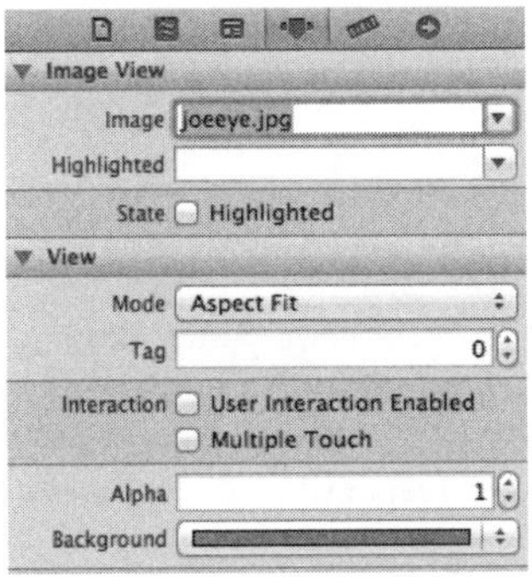

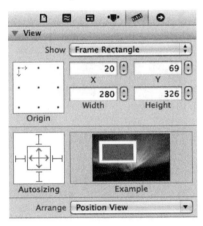

When the device rotates, two things happen. First, the view is rotated to be aligned with the device orientation. Second, the view is resized to fit the screen. For example, a view that is 320 points wide and 480 points tall in portrait mode will be 480 points wide and 320 points tall in landscape mode. When a view is resized, it will *autoresize* all of its subviews. Each subview is resized according to its *autoresizing mask* property. You can modify the autoresizing mask of a view by selecting the view in the XIB file and then clicking the ✍ icon to reveal the *size inspector* (Figure 8.6).

Figure 8.6   Autosizing in size inspector

Check out the box labeled Autosizing in Figure 8.6. You can click this control in six different places: on the four sides outside the inner box and along the vertical and horizontal axes inside the inner box. We call the outside four *struts*, and the inside two *springs*. Clicking on one of these areas toggles an autoresizing mask option. A solid red line means the option is on, and a dim red dotted line means the option is off.

A spring that is turned on tells the view to change size when its superview changes size. For example, if you turn on the horizontal spring, the view will change its width at the same rate that its superview changes its width.

A strut tells the view to keep the margin between the view and its superview constant. For example, if you turn on the left strut, the view will maintain the distance from the left side of its superview when the superview changes its width.

You can toggle the springs and struts and watch the animated example next to the Autosizing area to see what happens.

In your HeavyRotation application, you have four views. Here's how you want them to handle autorotation:

- The image view should stay centered and resize with its superview.

- The slider should get wider but not taller. It should stay fixed at the top of the superview and keep the same distance from the left and right edges.

- The two buttons should stay with their respective corners and *not* resize.

Now select each view and set the autoresize mask appropriately. Figure 8.7 shows the correct arrangement of struts and springs for each view.

Figure 8.7   Autoresizing mask for views

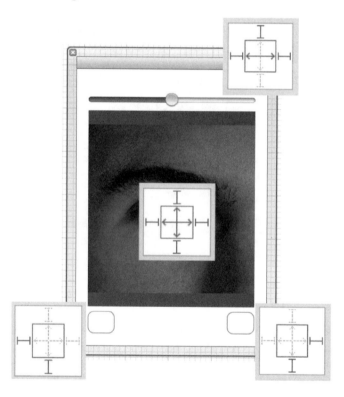

Finally, to finish this application, you need to create an instance of **HeavyViewController** and set it as the rootViewController of the window. In RotationAppDelegate.m, add the following lines of code to **application:didFinishLaunchingWithOptions:**. Make sure to include the import statement at the top of the file.

```
#import "RotationAppDelegate.h"

#import "HeavyViewController.h"
```

```
@implementation RotationAppDelegate
- (BOOL)application:(UIApplication *)application
    didFinishLaunchingWithOptions:(NSDictionary *)launchOptions
{
    self.window = [[UIWindow alloc] initWithFrame:[[UIScreen mainScreen] bounds]];
    // Override point for customization after application launch.

    // Get the device object
    UIDevice *device = [UIDevice currentDevice];

    // Tell it to start monitoring the accelerometer for orientation
    [device beginGeneratingDeviceOrientationNotifications];

    // Get the notification center for the app
    NSNotificationCenter *nc = [NSNotificationCenter defaultCenter];

    // Add yourself as an observer
    [nc addObserver:self
          selector:@selector(orientationChanged:)
              name:UIDeviceOrientationDidChangeNotification
            object:device];


    HeavyViewController *hvc = [[HeavyViewController alloc] init];
    [[self window] setRootViewController:hvc];

    self.window.backgroundColor = [UIColor whiteColor];
    [self.window makeKeyAndVisible];

    return YES;
}
```

Build and run the application. It should autorotate when you rotate the device, as shown in Figure 8.8. (You can also run the application in the simulator and rotate it from the Hardware menu or use the keyboard shortcuts Command-Right Arrow and Command-Left Arrow.)

Figure 8.8   Running rotated

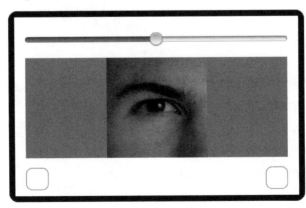

When a view is autorotated, it changes its size (the width becomes the height and vice versa). This is why the mask is called an auto*resizing* mask. Another time a view's size must change is when the size of the device does. For instance, if HeavyRotation was a *universal application* (that runs on both the iPad and iPhone device families), then the interface for the iPad version would have to fit the larger screen size.

When a universal application launches on the iPad, the window is resized to fit the larger screen. Thus, the subview of the window (the view controller's view) and its subviews are also resized. The autoresizing masks will do the same job here as they do when rotating the device to preserve the interface of the application.

Let's make HeavyRotation a universal application to see this happen. Select the project from the project navigator. Then, select the HeavyRotation target from the editor area. Select Universal from the Device Family pop-up menu, as shown in Figure 8.9.

Figure 8.9   Universalizing HeavyRotation

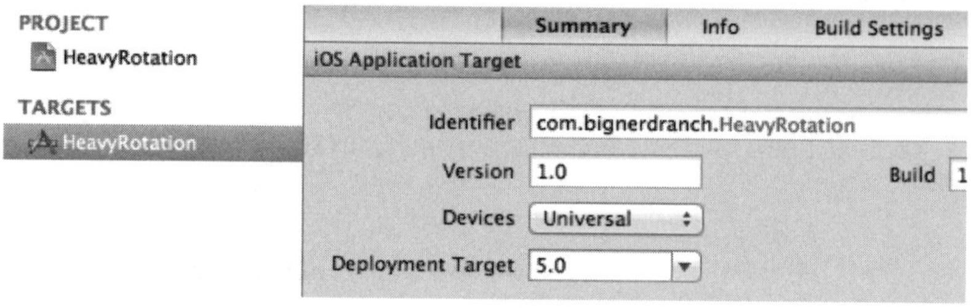

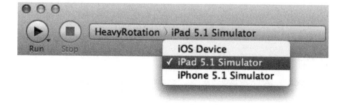

From the Scheme menu next to the Run button, choose either the iPad simulator or an iPad device if you've got one plugged in (Figure 8.10). Then build and run. Notice that the interface automatically resizes itself appropriately for the larger window.

Figure 8.10   Changing simulator

From the Scheme menu next to the Run button, choose either the iPad simulator or an iPad device if you've got one plugged in (Figure 8.10). Then build and run. Notice that the interface automatically resizes itself appropriately for the larger window.

Setting autoresizing masks programmatically and bitwise operations

The autoresizing mask can also be set programmatically by sending the message setAutoresizingMask: to a view.

```
[view setAutoresizingMask:UIViewAutoresizingFlexibleLeftMargin |
                    UIViewAutoresizingFlexibleHeight];
```

This says that the view will resize its height when its superview's height changes; this is the same as checking the vertical spring in a XIB file. It also says that the left margin is flexible – which is the same as *un*-checking the left strut. In a XIB file, this autoresizing mask would match the one shown in Figure 8.11.

Figure 8.11   Autoresizing mask with flexible left margin and flexible height

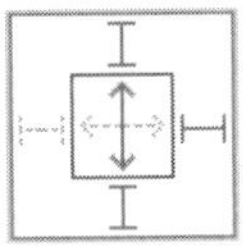

Back in the code, notice the | operator in the argument of **setAutoresizingMask:**. That is the bitwise-OR operator. Each autoresizing constant is equal to a power of two. (You can find all the UIViewAutoresizing constants in the **UIView** class reference page in the documentation.) For example, the flexible left margin constant is 1 (2^0), and the flexible height constant is 16 (2^4). The property autoresizingMask is just an int and, like all values on a computer, is represented in binary. Binary numbers are a string of 1s and 0s. Here are a few examples of numbers in base 10 (decimal; the way we think about numbers) and base 2 (binary; the way a computer thinks about numbers):

1_{10} = 00000001_2
2_{10} = 00000010_2
16_{10} = 00010000_2
27_{10} = 00011011_2
34_{10} = 00100010_2

In decimal representation, we have 10 different digits: 0 - 9. When we count past 9, we run out of symbols to represent the number, so we add a new digit column. A digit in the second column is worth 10 times more than a digit in the first column; a digit in the third column is worth 10 times more than the second column and so on. The same general idea is true for binary numbers, except we only have two digits (0 and 1), so we must add a new digit column each time we would normally use a 2. Because of this, each digit in binary is only worth two times more than the digit to the right of it. The rightmost digit is multiplied by 1, the one to the left of that is multiplied by 2, then 4, 8, and so on.

When talking about binary numbers, we call each digit a *bit*. We can think of each bit as an on-off switch, where 1 is "on" and 0 is "off." When thinking in these terms, we can use an int (which has space for at least 32 bits) as a set of on-off switches. Each position in the number represents one switch – a value of 1 means true, 0 means false. Essentially, we are shoving a ton of BOOLs into a single value. We call numbers used in this way *bitmasks*, and that's why the autoresize settings of a view are called the autoresizing mask.

A number that only has one bit set to 1 (the rest are 0) is a power of two. Therefore, we can use numbers that are powers of two to represent a single switch in a bitmask – each autoresizing constant is a single switch. We can turn on a switch in a bitmask using the bitwise-OR operation. This operation takes two numbers and produces a number where a bit is set to 1 if either of the original numbers had a 1 in the same position. When you bitwise-OR a number with 2^n, it flips on the switch at the nth position. For example, if you bitwise-OR 1 and 16, you get the following:

```
  00000001 ( 1₁₀, UIViewAutoresizingFlexibleLeftMargin)
| 00010000 (16₁₀, UIViewAutoresizingFlexibleHeight)
----------
  00010001 (17₁₀, both UIViewAutoresizingFlexibleHeight
              and UIViewAutoresizingFlexibleLeftMargin)
```

The complement to the bitwise-OR operator is the bitwise-AND (&) operator. When you bitwise-AND two numbers, the result is a number that has a 1 in each bit where there is a 1 in the same position as *both* of the original numbers.

```
  00010001 (17₁₀, FlexibleHeight and FlexibleLeftMargin)
& 00010000 (16₁₀, FlexibleHeight)
----------
  00010000 (16₁₀, YES)

  00010001 (17₁₀, FlexibleHeight and FlexibleLeftMargin)
& 00000010 ( 2₁₀, FlexibleWidth)
----------
  00000000 ( 0₁₀, NO)
```

Since any non-zero number means YES (and zero is NO), we use the bitwise-AND operator to check whether a switch is on or not. Thus, when a view's autoresizing mask is checked, the code looks like this:

```
if ([self autoresizingMask] & UIViewAutoresizingFlexibleHeight)
{
    // Resize the height
}
```

Forcing Landscape Mode

If your application only makes sense in landscape mode, you can force it to run that way. First, in your view controller implement **shouldAutorotateToInterfaceOrientation:** to only return YES for landscape orientations.

```
- (BOOL)shouldAutorotateToInterfaceOrientation:(UIInterfaceOrientation)x
{
    return UIInterfaceOrientationIsLandscape(x);
}
```

An application's Info.plist contains a key-value pair that specifies the valid initial orientations of the application. Select the project from the project navigator, then the HeavyRotation target from the editor area, and finally the Summary pane.

Figure 8.12   Choosing the initial orientations

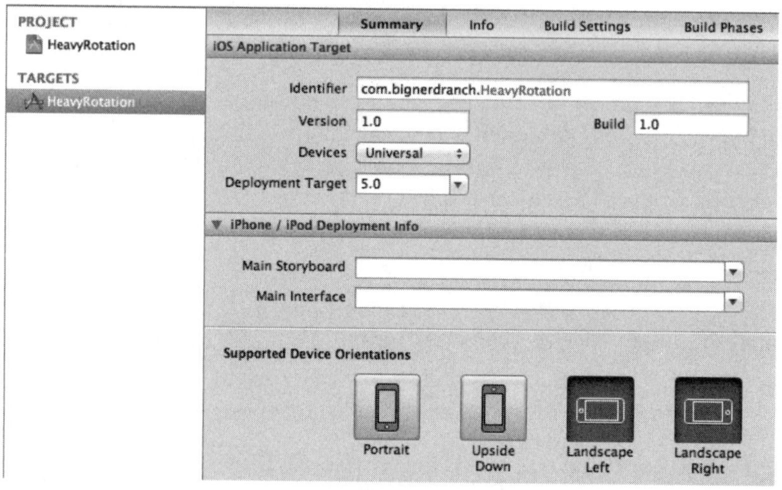

Find a section in the target's summary called Supported Device Orientations. This section contains four toggle buttons that specify which orientations are allowed. Buttons that are pushed in are valid.

Note that selecting orientations here only applies to orientation when the application launches; it does not control orientation once the application is running. You still have to tell your view controller to allow autorotation only to landscape orientations in **shouldAutorotateToInterfaceOrientation:**.

Bronze Challenge: Proximity Notifications

Register for proximity notifications. Proximity refers to the nearness of the device to the user. It is typically used to tell whether the iPhone is next to the user's face (as in talking on the phone). When this notification is posted, change the background color of **HeavyViewController**'s view to dark gray. You will need to turn on proximity monitoring, which is only available on the iPhone:

```
[device setProximityMonitoringEnabled:YES];
```

Silver Challenge: Programmatically Setting Autoresizing Masks

For every subview of **HeavyViewController**'s view, set the autoresizing mask programmatically. The behavior of the application should remain the same. (Hint: to programmatically change the autoresizing mask of a view, you must have a pointer to it in **HeavyViewController**.)

Gold Challenge: Overriding Autorotation

After reading the section called "For the More Curious: Overriding Autorotation", place another **UIButton** on the lefthand side of the **HeavyViewController**'s view. When the device rotates to landscape, this button should appear centered on the righthand side of the view. (And when the device rotates back to portrait, the button should appear on the lefthand side again.)

For the More Curious: Overriding Autorotation

In most cases, autorotation does the right thing if the autoresizing masks are properly set. However, you might want to take additional action on an autorotation or override the autorotation process altogether to change the way the view looks when it rotates. You can do this by overriding **willAnimateRotationToInterfaceOrientation:duration:** in a view controller subclass.

When a view controller is about to autorotate its view, it checks to see if you have implemented this method. If you have, then this method is invoked during the animation block of the rotation code. Therefore, all changes to subviews in this method will be animated as well. You can also perform some custom code within this method. Here is an example that will reposition a button and change the background color on autorotation:

```
- (void)willAnimateRotationToInterfaceOrientation:(UIInterfaceOrientation)x
                                         duration:(NSTimeInterval)duration
{
    // Assume "button" is a subview of this view controller's view

    UIColor *color = nil;
    CGRect bounds = [[self view] bounds];
    // If the orientation is rotating to Portrait mode...
    if (UIInterfaceOrientationIsPortrait(x)) {
```

```
        // Put the button in the top right corner
        [button setCenter:CGPointMake(bounds.size.width - 30,
                                      20)];

        // the background color of the view will be red
        color = [UIColor redColor];
    } else {  // If the orientation is rotating to Landscape mode

        // Put the button in the bottom right corner
        [button setCenter:CGPointMake(bounds.size.width - 30,
                                      bounds.size.height - 20)];

        // the background color of the view will be blue
        color = [UIColor blueColor];
    }
    [[self view] setBackgroundColor:color];
}
```

Overriding this method is useful when you want to update your user interface for a different orientation. For example, you could change the zoom or position of a scroll view or even swap in an entirely different view. Make sure, however, that you do not replace the view of the view controller in this method. If you wish to swap in another view, you must swap a subview of the view controller's view.

9

UITableView and UITableViewController

Many iOS applications show the user a list of items and allow the user to select, delete, or reorder items on the list. Whether an application displays a list of people in the user's address book or a list of items on the App Store, it's a **UITableView** doing the work.

A **UITableView** displays a single column of data with a variable number of rows. Figure 9.1 shows some examples of **UITableView**.

Figure 9.1 Examples of UITableView

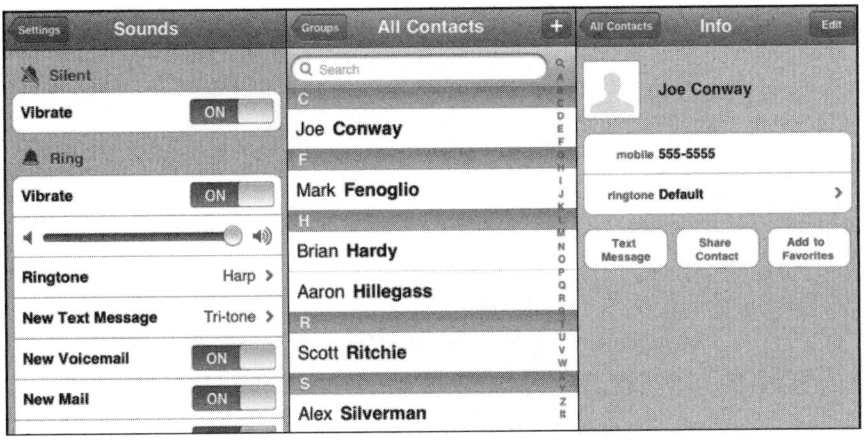

Beginning the Homepwner Application

In this chapter, you are going to start an application called Homepwner that keeps an inventory of all your possessions. In the case of a fire or other catastrophe, you'll have a record for your insurance company. ("Homepwner," by the way, is not a typo. If you need a definition for the word "pwn," please visit www.urbandictionary.com.)

So far, your iOS projects have been small, but Homepwner will grow into a realistically complex application over the course of nine chapters. By the end of this chapter, Homepwner will present a list of **BNRItem** objects in a **UITableView**, as shown in Figure 9.2.

Figure 9.2   Homepwner: phase 1

Create a new iOS Empty Application project and configure it as shown in Figure 9.3.

Figure 9.3   Configuring Homepwner

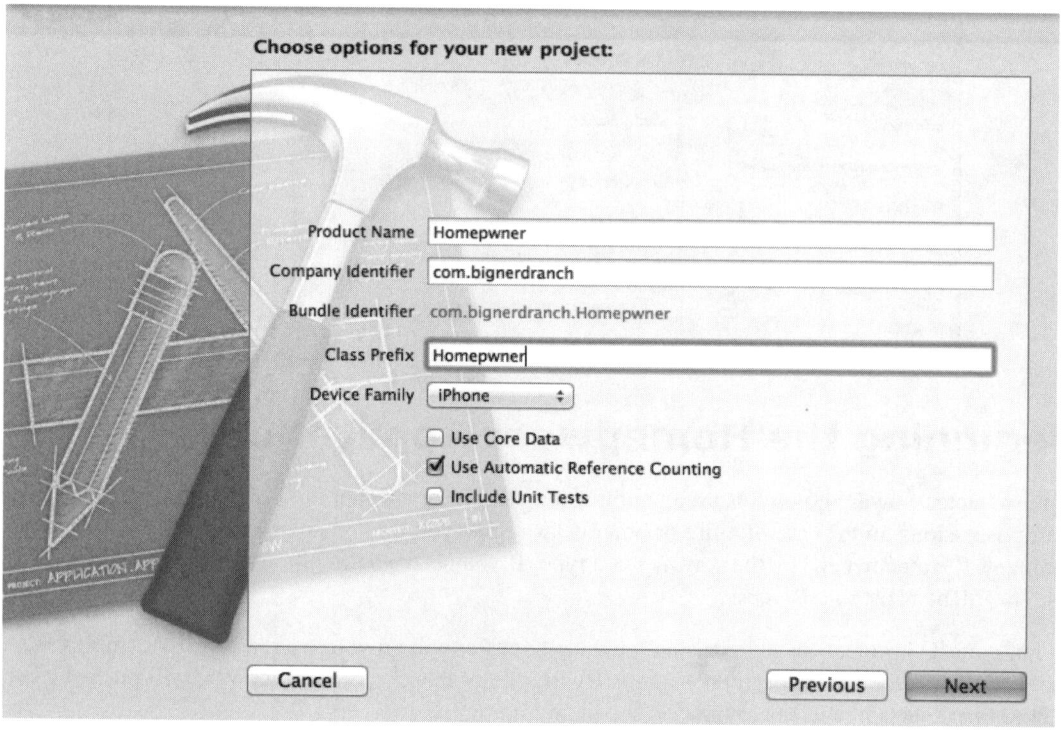

UITableViewController

UITableView is a view object, so, according to Model-View-Controller, it knows how to draw itself, but that's it. It doesn't handle application logic or data. Thus, when using a **UITableView**, you must consider what else is necessary to get the table working in your application

- A **UITableView** typically needs a view controller to handle its appearance on the screen.

- A **UITableView** needs a *data source*. A **UITableView** asks its data source for the number of rows to display, the data to be shown in those rows, and other tidbits that make a **UITableView** a useful user interface. Without a data source, a table view is just an empty container. The dataSource for a **UITableView** can be any type of Objective-C object as long as it conforms to the UITableViewDataSource protocol.

- A **UITableView** typically needs a *delegate* that can inform other objects of events involving the **UITableView**. The delegate can be any object as long as (you guessed it!) it conforms to the UITableViewDelegate protocol.

An instance of the class **UITableViewController** can fill all three roles: view controller, data source, and delegate.

UITableViewController is a subclass of **UIViewController**, so a **UITableViewController** has a view. A **UITableViewController**'s view is always an instance of **UITableView**, and the **UITableViewController** handles the preparation and presentation of the **UITableView**. When a **UITableViewController** creates its view, the dataSource and delegate instance variables of the **UITableView** are automatically set to point at the **UITableViewController** (Figure 9.4).

Figure 9.4   UITableViewController-UITableView relationship

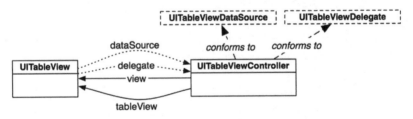

Subclassing UITableViewController

Now you're going to write a subclass of **UITableViewController** for Homepwner. For this view controller, we'll use the **NSObject** template. From the File menu, select New and then New File.... From the iOS section, select Cocoa Touch, choose Objective-C class, and hit Next. Then, select NSObject from the pop-up menu and enter **ItemsViewController** as the name of the new class. Click Next and then click Create on the next sheet to save your class.

Open ItemsViewController.h and change its superclass:

~~@interface ItemsViewController : NSObject~~

@interface ItemsViewController : UITableViewController

The designated initializer of **UITableViewController** is **initWithStyle:**, which takes a constant that determines the style of the table view. There are two options: UITableViewStylePlain, where each row is a rectangle, and UITableViewStyleGrouped, where the top and bottom rows have rounded corners. In ItemsViewController.m, implement the following initializers.

```
#import "ItemsViewController.h"

@implementation ItemsViewController

- (id)init
{
    // Call the superclass's designated initializer
    self = [super initWithStyle:UITableViewStyleGrouped];
    if (self) {

    }
    return self;
}

- (id)initWithStyle:(UITableViewStyle)style
{
    return [self init];
}
```

This will ensure that all instances of **ItemsViewController** use the UITableViewStyleGrouped style, no matter what initialization message is sent to it.

Open HomepwnerAppDelegate.m. In **application:didFinishLaunchingWithOptions:**, create an instance of **ItemsViewController** and set it as the rootViewController of the window. Make sure to import the header file for **ItemsViewController** at the top of this file.

```
#import "ItemsViewController.h"

@implementation HomepwnerAppDelegate

- (BOOL)application:(UIApplication *)application
    didFinishLaunchingWithOptions:(NSDictionary *)launchOptions
{
    self.window = [[UIWindow alloc] initWithFrame:[[UIScreen mainScreen] bounds]];
    // Override point for customization after application launch.

    // Create a ItemsViewController
    ItemsViewController *itemsViewController = [[ItemsViewController alloc] init];

    // Place ItemsViewController's table view in the window hierarchy
    [[self window] setRootViewController:itemsViewController];

    self.window.backgroundColor = [UIColor whiteColor];
    [self.window makeKeyAndVisible];
    return YES;
}
```

190

Build and run your application. You will see the default appearance of a plain **UITableView** with no content, as shown in Figure 9.5. How did you get a table view? As a subclass of **UIViewController**, a **UITableViewController** inherits the **view** method. This method calls **loadView**, which creates and loads an empty view object if none exists. A **UITableViewController**'s view is always an instance of **UITableView**, so sending **view** to the **UITableViewController** gets you a bright, shiny, and empty table view.

Figure 9.5   Empty UITableView

An empty table view is a sad table view. You should give it some rows to display. Remember the **BNRItem** class you wrote in Chapter 3? Now you're going to use that class again: each row of the table view will display an instance of **BNRItem**. Locate the header and implementation files for **BNRItem** (BNRItem.h and BNRItem.m) in Finder and drag them onto Homepwner's project navigator. Make sure you use the files from Chapter 3, not the unfinished files from Chapter 2.

When dragging these files onto your project window, select the checkbox labeled Copy items into destination group's folder when prompted. This will copy the files from their current directory to your project's directory on the filesystem and add them to your project.

UITableView's Data Source

The process of providing a **UITableView** with rows in Cocoa Touch is different from the typical procedural programming task. In a procedural design, you tell the table view what it should display. In Cocoa Touch, the table view asks another object – its dataSource – what it should display. In our case, the **ItemsViewController** is the data source, so it needs a way to store item data.

In Chapter 2, you used an **NSMutableArray** to store **BNRItem** instances. You will do the same thing in this chapter, but with a little twist. The **NSMutableArray** that holds the **BNRItem** instances will be abstracted into another object – a **BNRItemStore** (Figure 9.6).

Figure 9.6   Homepwner object diagram

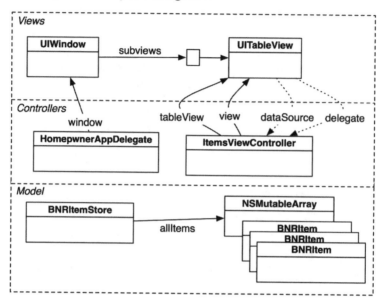

If an object wants to see all of the items, it will ask the **BNRItemStore** for the array that contains them. In future chapters, you'll make the store responsible for performing operations on the array, like reordering, adding, and removing **BNRItem**s. It will also be responsible for saving and loading the **BNRItem**s from disk.

Creating BNRItemStore

From the File menu, select New and then New File.... Create a new **NSObject** subclass and name it **BNRItemStore**.

BNRItemStore will be a singleton. This means there will only be one instance of this type in the application; if you try to create another instance, the class will quietly return the existing instance instead. A singleton is useful when you have an object that many objects will talk to. Those objects can ask the singleton class for its one instance, which is better than passing that instance as an argument to every method that will use it.

To get the (single instance of) **BNRItemStore**, you will send the **BNRItemStore** class the message **sharedStore**. Declare this class method in BNRItemStore.h.

```
#import <Foundation/Foundation.h>

@interface BNRItemStore : NSObject
{

}
// Notice that this is a class method and prefixed with a + instead of a -
```

```
+ (BNRItemStore *)sharedStore;
```

@end

When this message is sent to the **BNRItemStore** class, the class will check to see if the single instance of **BNRItemStore** has already been created. If it has, the class will return the instance. If not, it will create the instance and return it. In BNRItemStore.m, implement **sharedStore**.

```
+ (BNRItemStore *)sharedStore
{
    static BNRItemStore *sharedStore = nil;
    if (!sharedStore)
        sharedStore = [[super allocWithZone:nil] init];

    return sharedStore;
}
```

Notice that the variable sharedStore is declared as static. Unlike a local variable, a *static variable* does not live on the stack and is not destroyed when the method returns. Instead, a static variable is only declared once (when the application is loaded into memory), and it is never destroyed. A *static variable* is like a local variable in that you can only access this variable in the method in which it is declared. Therefore, no other object or method can use the **BNRItemStore** pointed to by this variable except via the **sharedStore** method.

The initial value of sharedStore is nil. The first time this method runs, an instance of **BNRItemStore** will be created, and sharedStore will be set to point to it. In subsequent calls to this method, sharedStore will still point at that instance of **BNRItemStore**. This variable has a strong reference to the **BNRItemStore** and, since this variable will never be destroyed, the object it points to will never be destroyed either.

To enforce the singleton status of **BNRItemStore**, you must ensure that another instance of **BNRItemStore** cannot be allocated. One approach would be to override **alloc** in **BNRItemStore** so that it does not create a new instance but returns the existing instance instead.

However, there is a problem with this approach: **alloc** is a dummy method. It just calls **allocWithZone:**, which then calls the C function **NSAllocateObject**, which does the actual memory allocation (Figure 9.7).

Figure 9.7   Default allocation chain

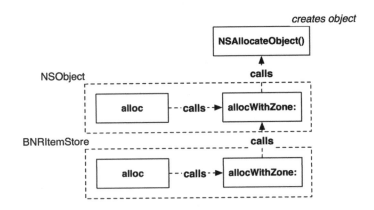

Thus, a knowledgeable programmer could still create an instance of **BNRItemStore** via **allocWithZone:**, which would bypass our sneaky **alloc** trap. To prevent this possibility, override **allocWithZone:** in BNRItemStore.m to return the single **BNRItemStore** instance.

```
+ (id)allocWithZone:(NSZone *)zone
{
    return [self sharedStore];
}
```

Now if **sharedStore** were to send **alloc** or **allocWithZone:** to **BNRItemStore**, then the method would call **BNRItemStore**'s implementation of **allocWithZone:**. That implementation just calls **sharedStore**, which would then call **BNRItemStore**'s **allocWithZone:** again, which would then call **sharedStore**, which would... well, you get the picture.

Figure 9.8   Not sending allocWithZone: to NSObject causes loop

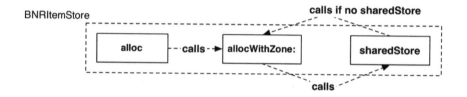

This is why we had **sharedStore** call **NSObject**'s implementation of **allocWithZone:**.

```
sharedStore = [[super allocWithZone:nil] init];
```

By sending **allocWithZone:** to super, we skip over our trap and get an instance of **BNRItemStore** when we need it (Figure 9.9).

Figure 9.9   BNRItemStore and NSObject allocation methods

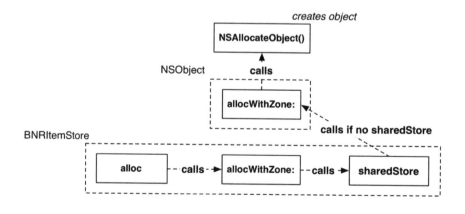

We can only skip over our **alloc** trap within the implementation of **BNRItemStore** because the super keyword is only relevant to the class in which the method is implemented.

Now we have ensured that multiple instances of **BNRItemStore** cannot be created. We have also ensured that once the instance of **BNRItemStore** is created, it is never destroyed because a static variable (that never gets destroyed) always maintains ownership of it.

In BNRItemStore.h, give **BNRItemStore** an instance variable to hold an array of **BNRItem** instances and declare two more methods:

```
#import <Foundation/Foundation.h>

@class BNRItem;

@interface BNRItemStore : NSObject
{
    NSMutableArray *allItems;
}
+ (BNRItemStore *)sharedStore;

- (NSArray *)allItems;
- (BNRItem *)createItem;

@end
```

See the @class directive? That tells the compiler that there is a **BNRItem** class and that it doesn't need to know this class's details in the current file. This allows us to use the **BNRItem** symbol in the declaration of **createItem** without importing BNRItem.h. Using the @class directive can speed up compile times considerably because fewer files have to be recompiled when one file changes. (Wonder why? Flip back and read the section called "For the More Curious: Build Phases, Compiler Errors, and Linker Errors".)

In files that actually send messages to the **BNRItem** class or instances of it, you must import the file it was declared in so that the compiler will have all of its details. At the top of BNRItemStore.m, import BNRItem.h.

```
#import "BNRItemStore.h"
#import "BNRItem.h"
```

In BNRItemStore.m, override **init** to create an instance of **NSMutableArray** and assign it to the instance variable.

```
- (id)init
{
    self = [super init];
    if (self) {
        allItems = [[NSMutableArray alloc] init];
    }

    return self;
}
```

Now implement the two methods in BNRItemStore.m.

```
- (NSArray *)allItems
{
    return allItems;
}
```

```
- (BNRItem *)createItem
{
    BNRItem *p = [BNRItem randomItem];

    [allItems addObject:p];

    return p;
}
```

Implementing data source methods

In ItemsViewController.m, import BNRItemStore.h and BNRItem.h and update the designated initializer to add 5 random items to the **BNRItemStore**.

```
#import "ItemsViewController.h"
#import "BNRItemStore.h"
#import "BNRItem.h"

@implementation ItemsViewController

- (id)init
{
    // Call the superclass's designated initializer
    self = [super initWithStyle:UITableViewStyleGrouped];
    if (self) {
        for (int i = 0; i < 5; i++) {
            [[BNRItemStore sharedStore] createItem];
        }
    }
    return self;
}
```

Now that there are some items in the store, you need to teach **ItemsViewController** how to turn those items into rows that its **UITableView** can display. When a **UITableView** wants to know what to display, it sends messages from the set of messages declared in the UITableViewDataSource protocol.

From the Help menu, choose Documentation and API Reference to open the iOS SDK documentation. Find the UITableViewDataSource protocol documentation (Figure 9.10).

Figure 9.10   UITableViewDataSource protocol documentation

There are many methods here, but notice the two marked *required method*. For **ItemsViewController** to conform to UITableViewDataSource, it must implement **tableView:numberOfRowsInSection:** and **tableView:cellForRowAtIndexPath:**. These methods tell the table view how many rows it should display and what content to display in each row.

Whenever a **UITableView** needs to display itself, it sends a series of messages (the required methods plus any optional ones that have been implemented) to its dataSource. The required method **tableView:numberOfRowsInSection:** returns an integer value for the number of rows that the **UITableView** should display. In the table view for Homepwner, there should be a row for each entry in the store (Figure 9.11).

Figure 9.11   Obtaining the number of rows

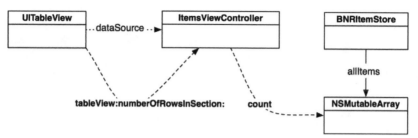

In `ItemsViewController.m`, implement `tableView:numberOfRowsInSection:`. This method returns the number of rows to display as an `NSInteger`, which is just another name for `int`.

```
- (NSInteger)tableView:(UITableView *)tableView
 numberOfRowsInSection:(NSInteger)section
{
    return [[[BNRItemStore sharedStore] allItems] count];
}
```

Wondering about the section that this method refers to? Table views can be broken up into sections, and each section has its own set of rows. For example, in the address book, all names beginning with "D" are grouped together in a section. By default, a table view has one section, and in this chapter, we will work with only one. Once you understand how a table view works, it is not hard to use multiple sections. In fact, using sections is the first challenge at the end of this chapter.

The second required method in the `UITableViewDataSource` protocol is `tableView:cellForRowAtIndexPath:`. To implement this method, we'll need to learn about another class – `UITableViewCell`.

UITableViewCells

A `UITableViewCell` is a subclass of `UIView`, and each row in a `UITableView` is a `UITableViewCell`. (Recall that a table in iOS can only have one column, so a row only has one cell.) The `UITableViewCell`s are subviews of the `UITableView`.

A cell itself has one subview – its `contentView` (Figure 9.12). The `contentView` is the superview for the content of the cell. It also can draw an accessory indicator. The accessory indicator shows an action-oriented icon, such as a checkmark, a disclosure icon, or a fancy blue dot with a chevron inside. These icons are accessed through pre-defined constants for the appearance of the accessory indicator. The default is `UITableViewCellAccessoryNone`, and that's what we'll use in this chapter. But you'll see the accessory indicator again in Chapter 15. (Curious now? See the reference page for `UITableViewCell` for more details.)

Figure 9.12   UITableViewCell layout

The real meat of a **UITableViewCell** is the three subviews of the contentView. Two of those subviews are **UILabel** instances that are properties of **UITableViewCell** named textLabel and detailTextLabel. The third subview is a **UIImageView** called imageView (Figure 9.13). In this chapter, we'll only use textLabel.

Figure 9.13 UITableViewCell hierarchy

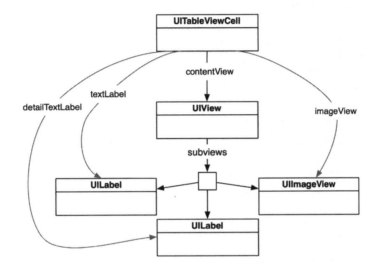

Each cell also has a UITableViewCellStyle that determines which subviews are used and their position within the contentView. Examples of these styles and their constants are shown in Figure 9.14.

Figure 9.14 UITableViewCellStyles

Creating and retrieving UITableViewCells

In this chapter, each cell will display the **description** of a **BNRItem** as its textLabel. To make this happen, you need to implement the second required method from the UITableViewDataSource protocol, **tableView:cellForRowAtIndexPath:**. This method will create a cell, set its textLabel to the **description** of the corresponding **BNRItem**, and return it to the **UITableView** (Figure 9.15).

Figure 9.15   UITableViewCell retrieval

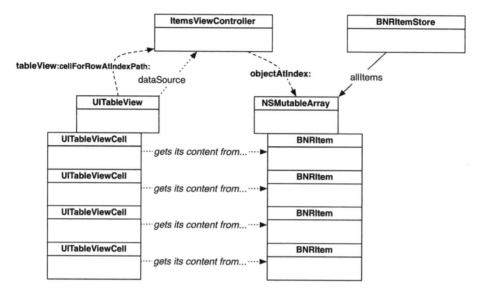

How do you decide which cell a **BNRItem** corresponds to? One of the parameters sent to **tableView:cellForRowAtIndexPath:** is an **NSIndexPath**, which has two properties: section and row. When this message is sent to a data source, the table view is asking, "Can I have a cell to display in section X, row Y?" Because there is only one section in this exercise, the table view only needs to know the row. In ItemsViewController.m, implement **tableView:cellForRowAtIndexPath:** so that the *n*th row displays the *n*th entry in the allItems array.

```
- (UITableViewCell *)tableView:(UITableView *)tableView
        cellForRowAtIndexPath:(NSIndexPath *)indexPath
{
    // Create an instance of UITableViewCell, with default appearance
    UITableViewCell *cell =
        [[UITableViewCell alloc] initWithStyle:UITableViewCellStyleDefault
                            reuseIdentifier:@"UITableViewCell"];

    // Set the text on the cell with the description of the item
    // that is at the nth index of items, where n = row this cell
    // will appear in on the tableview
    BNRItem *p = [[[BNRItemStore sharedStore] allItems]
                                objectAtIndex:[indexPath row]];

    [[cell textLabel] setText:[p description]];

    return cell;
}
```

Build and run the application now, and you'll see a **UITableView** populated with a list of random **BNRItem**s. Yep, it was that easy. You didn't have to change anything about **BNRItem** – you simply changed the controller object and let the controller interface with a different view. This is why

Model-View-Controller is such a powerful concept. With a minimal amount of code, you were able to show the same data in an entirely different way.

Reusing UITableViewCells

iOS devices have a limited amount of memory. If we were displaying a list with thousands of entries in a **UITableView**, we would have thousands of instances of **UITableViewCell**. And your long-suffering iPhone would sputter and die. In its dying breath, it would say "You only needed enough cells to fill the screen... arrrghhh!" It would be right.

To preserve the lives of iOS devices everywhere, you can reuse table view cells. When the user scrolls the table, some cells move offscreen. Offscreen cells are put into a pool of cells available for reuse. Then, instead of creating a brand new cell for every request, the data source first checks the pool. If there is an unused cell, the data source configures it with new data and returns it to the table view.

Figure 9.16   Reusable UITableViewCells

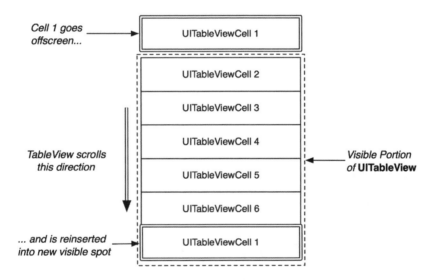

There is one problem: sometimes a **UITableView** has different types of cells. Occasionally, you have to subclass **UITableViewCell** to create a special look or behavior. However, different subclasses floating around the pool of reusable cells create the possibility of getting back a cell of the wrong type. You must be sure of the type of the cell returned to you so that you can be sure of what properties and methods it has.

Note that you don't care about getting any specific cell out of the pool because you're going to change the cell content anyway. What you need is a cell of a specific type. The good news is every cell has a reuseIdentifier property of type **NSString**. When a data source asks the table view for a reusable cell, it passes a string and says, "I need a cell with this reuse identifier." By convention, the reuse identifier is simply the name of the cell class.

In ItemsViewController.m, update **tableView:cellForRowAtIndexPath:** to reuse cells:

```
- (UITableViewCell *)tableView:(UITableView *)tableView
        cellForRowAtIndexPath:(NSIndexPath *)indexPath
{
    UITableViewCell *cell =
        [[UITableViewCell alloc] initWithStyle:UITableViewCellStyleDefault
                            reuseIdentifier:@"UITableViewCell"];

    // Check for a reusable cell first, use that if it exists
    UITableViewCell *cell =
        [tableView dequeueReusableCellWithIdentifier:@"UITableViewCell"];

    // If there is no reusable cell of this type, create a new one
    if (!cell) {
        cell = [[UITableViewCell alloc]
                    initWithStyle:UITableViewCellStyleDefault
                reuseIdentifier:@"UITableViewCell"];
    }

    BNRItem *p = [[[BNRItemStore sharedStore] allItems]
                                objectAtIndex:[indexPath row]];


    [[cell textLabel] setText:[p description]];

    return cell;
}
```

(If you have a table view that uses multiple styles of the same type of cell, you can suffix the reuse identifier with the name of that style, e.g. UITableViewCell-Default.)

Reusing cells means that you only have to create a handful of cells, which puts fewer demands on memory. Your application's users (and their devices) will thank you. Build and run the application. The behavior of the application should remain the same.

Code Snippet Library

You may have noticed that when you start typing the method definition for init in an implementation file, Xcode will automatically add an **init** implementation in your source file. If you haven't noticed this, go ahead and type init in an implementation file and wait for the code-completion to kick in.

The freebie code comes from the *code snippet library*. You can see the code snippet library by opening the utilities area and selecting the {} icon in the library selector (Figure 9.17). Alternatively, you can use the shortcut Command-Control-Option-2, which reveals the utilities area and the Code Snippet Library. Substituting another number in the shortcut selects the corresponding library.

Figure 9.17 Code snippet library

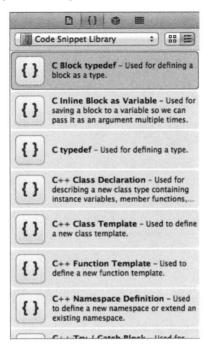

Notice that there are a number of code snippets available (Figure 9.17). Click on one, and in a moment, a window will appear with the details for that snippet. Click the Edit button on the code snippet detail window (Figure 9.18).

Figure 9.18 Snippet editing window

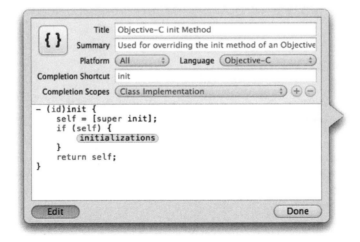

The Completion Shortcut field in the edit window shows you what to type in a source file to have Xcode add the snippet. This window also tells you that this snippet can be used in an Objective-C file as long as you are in the scope of a class implementation.

You can't edit any of the pre-defined code snippets, but you can create your own. In ItemsViewController.m, locate the implementation of **tableView:numberOfRowsInSection:**. Highlight the entire method:

```
- (NSInteger)tableView:(UITableView *)tableView
 numberOfRowsInSection:(NSInteger)section
{
    return [[[BNRItemStore sharedStore] allItems] count];
}
```

Drag this highlighted code into the code snippet library. The edit window will appear again, allowing you to fill out the details for this snippet.

One issue with this snippet is that the return statement is really specific to this application – it would be much more useful if the value returned was a code completion placeholder that you could fill in easily. In the edit window, modify the code snippet so it looks like this:

```
- (NSInteger)tableView:(UITableView *)tableView
 numberOfRowsInSection:(NSInteger)section
{
    return <#number of rows#>;
}
```

Then fill out the rest of the fields in the edit window as shown in Figure 9.19 and click Done.

Figure 9.19   Creating a new snippet

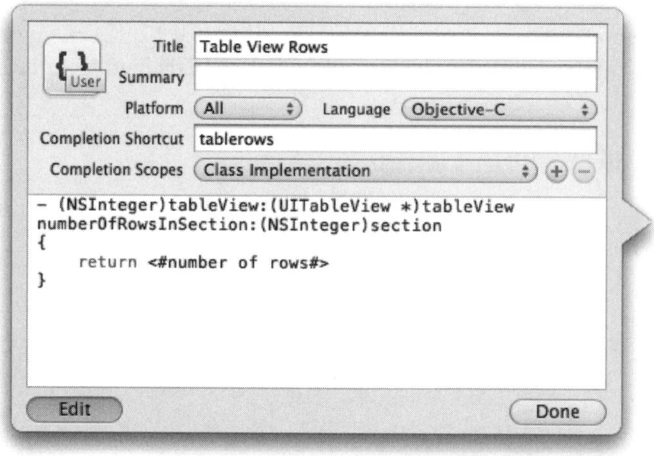

Back in ItemsViewController.m, start typing tablerows. Xcode will recommend this code snippet and pressing the return key will automatically complete it for you – and the number of rows placeholder will be selected. You'll have to type in the code to get the number of rows yourself. Snippets aren't magical – just handy.

Before continuing, make sure to remove the code entered by the snippet because you have already defined **tableView:numberOfRowsInSection:** in ItemsViewController.m.

Bronze Challenge: Sections

Have the **UITableView** display two sections – one for items worth more than $50 and one for the rest. Before you start this challenge, copy the folder containing the project and all of its source files in Finder. Then tackle the challenge in the copied project; you'll need the original to build on in the coming chapters.

Silver Challenge: Constant Rows

Make it so the last row of the **UITableView** always has the text No more items!. Make sure this row appears regardless of the number of items in the store (including 0 items).

Gold Challenge: Customizing the Table

Make each row's height 60 points except for the last row from the medium challenge, which should remain 44 points. Then, change the font size of every row except the last to 20 points. Finally, make the background of the **UITableView** display an image. (This image should be 460x320 pixels or 920x640 pixels depending on whether your device supports retina display. Bonus points for appropriately handling both retina display and non-retina display devices correctly with the same application.)

10

Editing UITableView

In the last chapter, you created an application that displays a list of **BNRItem** instances in a **UITableView**. The next step for Homepwner is allowing the user to interact with the table – to add, delete, and move rows. Figure 10.1 shows what Homepwner will look like by the end of this chapter.

Figure 10.1 Homepwner in editing mode

Editing Mode

UITableView has an editing property, and when this property is set to YES, the **UITableView** enters editing mode. Once the table view is in editing mode, the rows of the table can be manipulated by the user. The user can change the order of the rows, add rows, or remove rows. Editing mode does not allow the user to edit the *content* of a row.

But first, the user needs a way to put the **UITableView** in editing mode. For now, you're going to include a button that toggles editing mode in the *header view* of the table. A header view appears at the top of a section of a table and is useful for adding section-wide or table-wide titles and controls. It can be any **UIView** instance. There's also a footer view for the bottom of a section that works the same way. Figure 10.2 shows a table with two sections. Each section has a **UISlider** for a header view and a **UILabel** for a footer view.

Figure 10.2   UITableView header and footer views

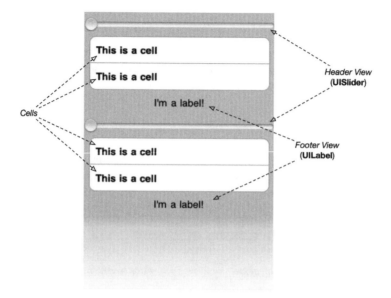

The header view will appear at the top of the list of **BNRItem**s. It will have two subviews that are instances of **UIButton**: one to toggle editing mode and the other to add a new **BNRItem** to the table. You will create this view and its subviews in a XIB file, and **ItemsViewController** will unarchive that XIB file when it needs to display the header view.

First, let's set up the necessary code. Reopen Homepwner.xcodeproj. In ItemsViewController.h, declare an instance variable of type **UIView** for your header view and three new methods.

```
@interface ItemsViewController : UITableViewController
{
    IBOutlet UIView *headerView;
}

- (UIView *)headerView;
- (IBAction)addNewItem:(id)sender;
- (IBAction)toggleEditingMode:(id)sender;

@end
```

Notice that headerView is a strong reference. This is because it will be a top-level object in the XIB file.

Now we need to create the new XIB file. Unlike the previous XIB files you created, this XIB file won't deal at all with the view controller's view. (As a subclass of **UITableViewController**, **ItemsViewController** already knows how to create its view.) XIB files are typically used to create the view for a view controller, but they can also be used any time you want to layout view objects, archive them, and have them loaded at runtime.

From the File menu, select New and then New File.... From the iOS section, select User Interface, choose the Empty template, and hit Next (Figure 10.3). On the next pane, select iPhone. Save this file as HeaderView.

Figure 10.3   Creating a new XIB file

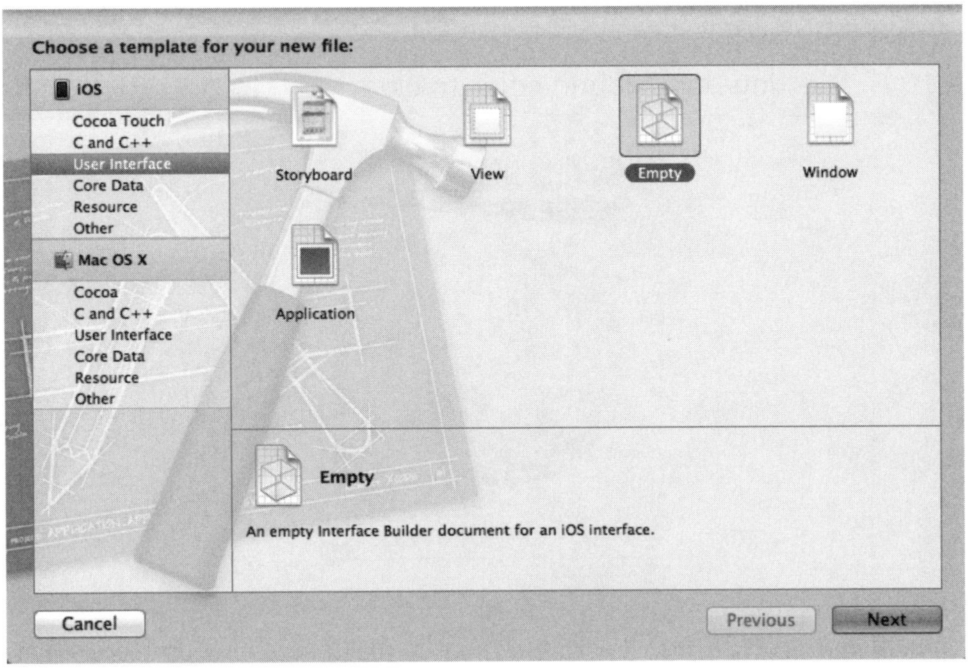

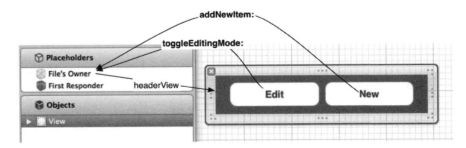

In HeaderView.xib, select the File's Owner object and change its Class to **ItemsViewController** in the identity inspector (Figure 10.4).

Figure 10.4   Changing the File's Owner

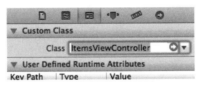

Drag a **UIView** onto the canvas. Then drag two instances of **UIButton** onto that view. Resize the **UIView** and make the connections shown in Figure 10.5.

Figure 10.5   HeaderView XIB layout

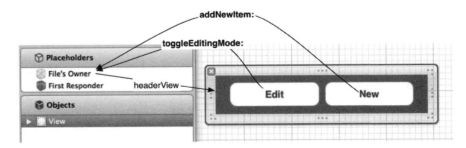

Also, change the background color of the **UIView** instance to be completely transparent. To do this, select the view and show the attributes inspector. Click the color picker labeled Background to show the color wheel and then drag the Opacity slider to 0 (Figure 10.6).

Figure 10.6   Setting background color to clear

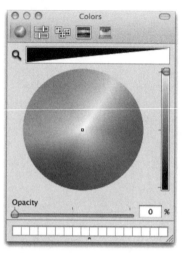

So far, your XIB files have been loaded automatically by the implementation of **UIViewController**. For example, **TimeViewController** in Chapter 7 knew how to load TimeViewController.xib because of code written in its superclass, **UIViewController**. For HeaderView.xib, you're going to write the code to have the **ItemsViewController** load this XIB file manually.

To load a XIB file manually, you use **NSBundle**. This class is the interface between an application and the application bundle it lives in. When you want to access a file in the application bundle, you ask **NSBundle** for it. An instance of **NSBundle** is created when your application launches, and you can get a pointer to this instance by sending the message **mainBundle** to **NSBundle**.

Once you have a pointer to the main bundle object, you can ask it to load a XIB file. In ItemsViewController.m, implement **headerView**.

```
- (UIView *)headerView
{
    // If we haven't loaded the headerView yet...
    if (!headerView) {
        // Load HeaderView.xib
        [[NSBundle mainBundle] loadNibNamed:@"HeaderView" owner:self options:nil];
    }

    return headerView;
}
```

You don't have to specify the suffix of the file name; **NSBundle** will figure it out. Also, notice that you passed self as the owner of the XIB file. This places the instance of **ItemsViewController** in the File's Owner hole of the XIB file.

The first time the **headerView** message is sent to the **ItemsViewController**, it will load HeaderView.xib and keep a pointer to the view object in the instance variable headerView. The buttons in this view will send messages to the **ItemsViewController** when tapped.

Now that you've created headerView, you need to make it the header view of the table. This requires implementing two methods from the UITableViewDelegate protocol in ItemsViewController.m.

```
- (UIView *)tableView:(UITableView *)tv viewForHeaderInSection:(NSInteger)sec
{
    return [self headerView];
}

- (CGFloat)tableView:(UITableView *)tv heightForHeaderInSection:(NSInteger)sec
{
    // The height of the header view should be determined from the height of the
    // view in the XIB file
    return [[self headerView] bounds].size.height;
}
```

These two methods are listed as optional in the protocol, but if you want a header view, you must implement both.

Now that these methods are implemented, the **UITableView** will send these messages to its delegate, the **ItemsViewController**, when it needs to show the header view. The first time **tableView:heightForHeaderInSection:** is sent to **ItemsViewController**, it will send itself the message **headerView**. At this time, headerView will be nil, which will cause **headerView** to be loaded from the XIB file.

Build and run the application to see the interface. Ignore the incomplete implementation warnings; you'll implement **toggleEditingMode:** and **addNewItem:** shortly. Until you do, tapping a button will generate an exception because the action methods of the buttons are not implemented.

While XIB files are typically used to create the view for a view controller (for example, TimeViewController.xib), you've now seen that a XIB file can be used any time you wish to archive view objects. In addition, any object can load a XIB file manually by sending the message **loadNibNamed:owner:options:** to the application bundle.

UIViewController's default XIB loading behavior uses the same code. The only difference is that it connects its view outlet to the view object in the XIB file. Imagine what the default implementation of **loadView** for **UIViewController** probably looks like:

```
- (void)loadView
{
    // If a nibName was passed to initWithNibName:bundle:
    if ([self nibName]) {
        // Load that nib file, with ourselves as the file's owner, thus connecting
        // the view outlet to the view in the nib
        [[NSBundle mainBundle] loadNibNamed:[self nibName] owner:self options:nil];
    }
    else {
        // What is the name of this class?
        NSString *className = NSStringFromClass([self class]);

        // What's the full path of the nib file?
        NSString *nibPath = [[NSBundle mainBundle] pathForResource:className
                                                            ofType:@"nib"];

        // If there really is a nib file at that path, load it
        if ([[NSFileManager defaultManager] fileExistsAtPath:nibPath]) {
            [[NSBundle mainBundle] loadNibNamed:className owner:self options:nil];
        }
        else {
```

```
        // If there is no nib, just create a blank UIView
        UIView *view = [[UIView alloc] initWithFrame:CGRectZero];
        [self setView:view];
    }
  }
}
```

Now let's implement the **toggleEditingMode:** method. We could toggle the editing property of **UITableView** directly. However, **UITableViewController** also has an editing property. A **UITableViewController** instance automatically sets the editing property of its table view to match its own editing property. Which one should we set? Follow the Model-View-Controller pattern: talk to the controller and let the controller talk to the view.

To set the editing property for a view controller, you send it the message **setEditing:animated:**. In ItemsViewController.m, implement **toggleEditingMode:**.

```
- (IBAction)toggleEditingMode:(id)sender
{
    // If we are currently in editing mode...
    if ([self isEditing]) {
        // Change text of button to inform user of state
        [sender setTitle:@"Edit" forState:UIControlStateNormal];
        // Turn off editing mode
        [self setEditing:NO animated:YES];
    } else {
        // Change text of button to inform user of state
        [sender setTitle:@"Done" forState:UIControlStateNormal];
        // Enter editing mode
        [self setEditing:YES animated:YES];
    }
}
```

Build and run your application, tap the Edit button, and the **UITableView** will enter editing mode (Figure 10.7).

Figure 10.7   UITableView in editing mode

Adding Rows

There are a number of ways to add rows to a table view at runtime. The built-in behavior for adding a row is to display a new row with a green plus sign icon. However, this technique has fallen out of favor because it's cumbersome to enter editing mode and then find the row with the plus sign icon – especially in large tables.

So we're going to use the New button in the header view instead. When this button is tapped, a new row will be added to the **UITableView**. In ItemsViewController.m, implement **addNewItem:**.

```
- (IBAction)addNewItem:(id)sender
{
    // Make a new index path for the 0th section, last row
    int lastRow = [[self tableView] numberOfRowsInSection:0];
    NSIndexPath *ip = [NSIndexPath indexPathForRow:lastRow inSection:0];

    // Insert this new row into the table.
    [[self tableView] insertRowsAtIndexPaths:[NSArray arrayWithObject:ip]
                            withRowAnimation:UITableViewRowAnimationTop];
}
```

Build and run the application. Tap the New button and... the application crashes. The console tells us that the table view has an internal inconsistency exception.

Remember that, ultimately, it is the dataSource of the **UITableView** that determines the number of rows the table view should display. After inserting a new row, the table view has six rows (the original five plus the new one). Then, it runs back to its dataSource and asks it for the number of rows it should be displaying. **ItemsViewController** consults the store and returns that there should be five rows. The **UITableView** then says, "Hey, that's not right!" and throws an exception.

You must make sure that the **UITableView** and its dataSource agree on the number of rows. Thus, you must also add a new **BNRItem** to the **BNRItemStore** before you insert the new row. Update **addNewItem:** in ItemsViewController.m.

```
- (IBAction)addNewItem:(id)sender
{
    int lastRow = [[self tableView] numberOfRowsInSection:0];

    // Create a new BNRItem and add it to the store
    BNRItem *newItem = [[BNRItemStore sharedStore] createItem];

    // Figure out where that item is in the array
    int lastRow = [[[BNRItemStore sharedStore] allItems] indexOfObject:newItem];

    NSIndexPath *ip = [NSIndexPath indexPathForRow:lastRow inSection:0];

    // Insert this new row into the table.
    [[self tableView] insertRowsAtIndexPaths:[NSArray arrayWithObject:ip]
                            withRowAnimation:UITableViewRowAnimationTop];
}
```

Build and run the application. Tap the New button and watch the new row slide into the bottom position of the table. Remember that the role of a view object is to communicate model objects to the user; updating views without updating the model objects isn't very useful.

Also, notice that you are sending the message **tableView** to the **ItemsViewController** to get at the table view. This method is inherited from **UITableViewController**, and it returns the controller's table view. While you can send the message **view** to an instance of **UITableViewController** and get a pointer to the same object, using **tableView** tells the compiler that the object returned will be an instance of class **UITableView**. Thus, sending a message that is specific to **UITableView**, like **insertRowsAtIndexPaths:withRowAnimation:**, won't generate a warning.

Now that you have the ability to add rows and items, remove the code in the **init** method in ItemsViewController.m that puts 5 random items into the store.

```
- (id)init
{
    // Call the superclass's designated initializer
    self = [super initWithStyle:UITableViewStyleGrouped];
    if (self) {
        for (int i = 0; i < 5; i++) {
            [[BNRItemStore sharedStore] createItem];
        }
    }
    return self;
}
```

Build and run the application. There won't be any rows when you first fire up the application, but you can add some by tapping the New button.

Deleting Rows

In editing mode, the red circles with the dash (shown in Figure 10.7) are deletion controls, and touching one should delete that row. However, at this point, touching a deletion control doesn't do anything. (Try it and see.) Before the table view will delete a row, it sends its data source a message about the proposed deletion and waits for a confirmation message before pulling the trigger.

When deleting a cell, you must do two things: remove the row from the **UITableView** and remove the **BNRItem** associated with it from the **BNRItemStore**. To pull this off, the **BNRItemStore** must know how to remove objects from itself. In BNRItemStore.h, declare a new method.

```
@interface BNRItemStore : NSObject
{
    NSMutableArray *allItems;
}
+ (BNRItemStore *)sharedStore;

- (void)removeItem:(BNRItem *)p;
```

In BNRItemStore.m, implement **removeItem:**.

```
- (void)removeItem:(BNRItem *)p
{
    [allItems removeObjectIdenticalTo:p];
}
```

You could use **NSMutableArray**'s **removeObject:** method here instead of **removeObjectIdenticalTo:**, but consider the difference: **removeObject:** goes to each object in the array and sends it the message **isEqual:**. A class can implement this method to return YES or NO based on its own determination. For example, two **BNRItem**s could be considered equal if they had the same valueInDollars.

The method **removeObjectIdenticalTo:**, on the other hand, removes an object if and only if it is the exact same object as the one passed in this message. While **BNRItem** does not currently override **isEqual:** to do special checking, it could in the future. Therefore, you should use **removeObjectIdenticalTo:** when you are specifying a particular instance.

Now you will implement **tableView:commitEditingStyle:forRowAtIndexPath:**, a method from the UITableViewDataSource protocol. (This message is sent to the **ItemsViewController**. Keep in mind that while the **BNRItemStore** is the where the data is kept, the **ItemsViewController** is the table view's "data source.")

When **tableView:commitEditingStyle:forRowAtIndexPath:** is sent to the data source, two extra arguments are passed along with it. The first is the **UITableViewCellEditingStyle**, which, in this case, is UITableViewCellEditingStyleDelete. The other argument is the **NSIndexPath** of the row in the table.

In ItemsViewController.m, implement this method to have the **BNRItemStore** remove the right object and to confirm the row deletion by sending the message **deleteRowsAtIndexPaths:withRowAnimation:** back to the table view.

```
- (void)tableView:(UITableView *)tableView
    commitEditingStyle:(UITableViewCellEditingStyle)editingStyle
     forRowAtIndexPath:(NSIndexPath *)indexPath
{
    // If the table view is asking to commit a delete command...
    if (editingStyle == UITableViewCellEditingStyleDelete)
    {
        BNRItemStore *ps = [BNRItemStore sharedStore];
        NSArray *items = [ps allItems];
        BNRItem *p = [items objectAtIndex:[indexPath row]];
        [ps removeItem:p];

        // We also remove that row from the table view with an animation
        [tableView deleteRowsAtIndexPaths:[NSArray arrayWithObject:indexPath]
                        withRowAnimation:UITableViewRowAnimationFade];
    }
}
```

Build and run your application, create some rows, and then delete a row. It will disappear. Try out some of the different row animations!

Moving Rows

To change the order of rows in a **UITableView**, you will use another method from the UITableViewDataSource protocol – **tableView:moveRowAtIndexPath:toIndexPath:**.

To delete a row, you had to send the message **deleteRowsAtIndexPaths:withRowAnimation:** to the **UITableView** to confirm the deletion. Moving a row, however, doesn't require confirmation; the table view moves the row on its own authority and reports the move to its the data source by sending the message **tableView:moveRowAtIndexPath:toIndexPath:**. You just have to catch this message to update your data source to match the new order.

But before we can implement the data source method, we need to give the **BNRItemStore** a method to change the order of **BNRItem**s in its allItems array. In BNRItemStore.h, declare this method.

```
- (void)moveItemAtIndex:(int)from
                toIndex:(int)to;
```

Implement this method in BNRItemStore.m.

```
- (void)moveItemAtIndex:(int)from
              toIndex:(int)to
{
    if (from == to) {
        return;
    }
    // Get pointer to object being moved so we can re-insert it
    BNRItem *p = [allItems objectAtIndex:from];

    // Remove p from array
    [allItems removeObjectAtIndex:from];

    // Insert p in array at new location
    [allItems insertObject:p atIndex:to];
}
```

In ItemsViewController.m, implement **tableView:moveRowAtIndexPath:toIndexPath:** to update the store.

```
- (void)tableView:(UITableView *)tableView
  moveRowAtIndexPath:(NSIndexPath *)sourceIndexPath
        toIndexPath:(NSIndexPath *)destinationIndexPath
{
    [[BNRItemStore sharedStore] moveItemAtIndex:[sourceIndexPath row]
                                        toIndex:[destinationIndexPath row]];
}
```

Build and run your application. Check out the new reordering controls (the three horizontal lines) on the side of each row. Touch and hold a reordering control and move the row to a new position (Figure 10.8).

Figure 10.8   Moving a row

Note that simply implementing **tableView:moveRowAtIndexPath:toIndexPath:** caused the reordering controls to appear. This is because Objective-C is a very smart language. The **UITableView** can ask its data source at runtime whether it implements `tableView:moveRowAtIndexPath:toIndexPath:`. If it does, the table view says, "Good, you can handle moving rows. I'll add the re-ordering controls." If not, it says, "You bum. If you are too lazy to implement that method, I'm not putting controls there."

Bronze Challenge: Renaming the Delete Button

When deleting a row, a confirmation button appears labeled Delete. Change the label of this button to Remove.

Silver Challenge: Preventing Reordering

Make it so the table view always shows a final row that says No more items!. (This part is the same as a challenge from the last chapter. If you've already done it, great!) Then make it so that this row can't be moved.

Gold Challenge: Really Preventing Reordering

After completing the silver challenge, you may notice that even though you can't move the No more items! row itself, you can still drag other rows underneath it. Make it so that no matter what, the No more items! row can never be knocked out of the last position.

UINavigationController

In Chapter 7, you learned about **UITabBarController** and how it allows a user to access different screens. A tab bar controller is great when you have screens that don't rely on each other, but what if you want to move between related screens?

For example, the Settings application has multiple related screens of information: a list of settings (like Sounds), a detailed page for each setting, and a selection page for each detail. This type of interface is called a *drill-down interface*.

In this chapter, you will use **UINavigationController** to add a drill-down interface to Homepwner that lets the user view and edit the details of a **BNRItem**. (Figure 11.1).

Figure 11.1 Homepwner with UINavigationController

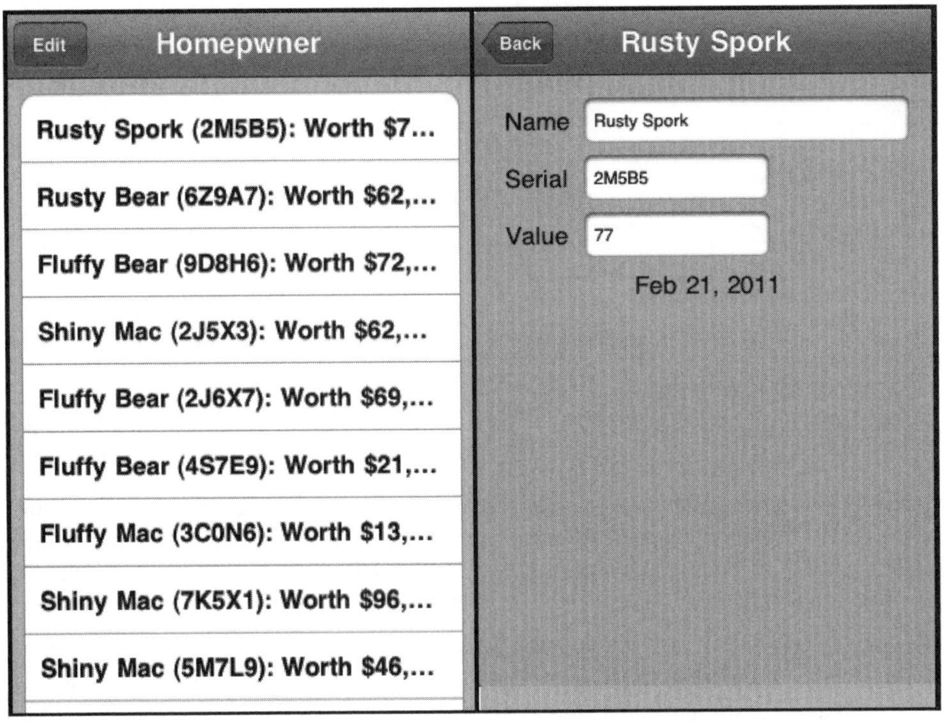

UINavigationController

When your application presents multiple screens of information, **UINavigationController** maintains a stack of those screens. Each screen is the view of a **UIViewController**, and the stack is an array of view controllers. When a **UIViewController** is on top of the stack, its view is visible.

When you initialize an instance of **UINavigationController**, you give it one **UIViewController**. This **UIViewController** is the navigation controller's *root view controller*. The root view controller is always on the bottom of the stack. More view controllers can be pushed on top of the **UINavigationController**'s stack while the application is running. This ability to add to the stack at runtime is missing from **UITabBarController**, which gets all of its view controllers when it is initialized. With a navigation controller, only the root view controller is guaranteed to always be in the stack.

When a **UIViewController** is pushed onto the stack, its view slides onto the screen from the right. When the stack is popped, the top view controller is removed from the stack, and the view of the one below it slides onto the screen from the left.

Figure 11.2 shows a navigation controller with two view controllers: a root view controller and an additional view controller above it at the top of the stack. The view of the additional view controller is what the user sees because that view controller is at the top of the stack.

Figure 11.2   UINavigationController's stack

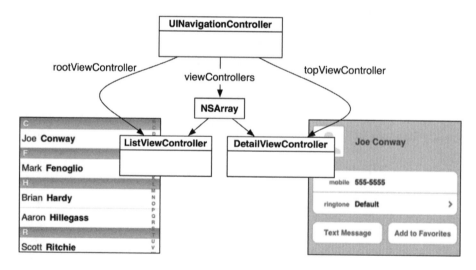

Like **UITabBarController**, **UINavigationController** has a viewControllers array. The root view controller is the first object in the array. As more view controllers are pushed onto the stack, they are added to the end of this array. Thus, the last view controller in the array is the top of the stack. **UINavigationController**'s topViewController property keeps a pointer to the top of the stack.

UINavigationController is a subclass of **UIViewController**, so it has a view of its own. Its view always has two subviews: a **UINavigationBar** and the view of topViewController (Figure 11.3). You can install a navigation controller as the rootViewController controller of the window to insert its view as a subview of the window.

Figure 11.3   A UINavigationController's view

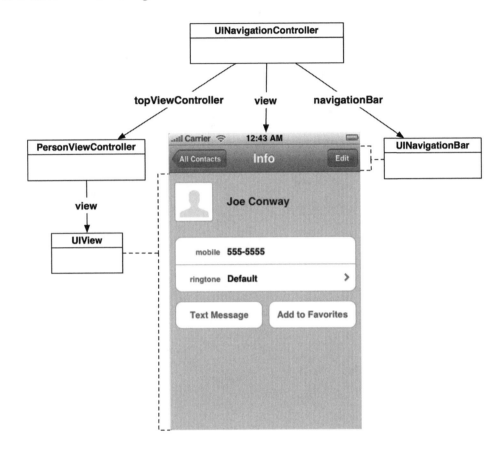

In this chapter, you will add a **UINavigationController** to the Homepwner application and make the **ItemsViewController** the **UINavigationController**'s rootViewController. Then, you will create another subclass of **UIViewController** that can be pushed onto the **UINavigationController**'s stack. When a user selects one of the rows, the new **UIViewController**'s view will slide onto the screen. This view controller will allow the user to view and edit the properties of the selected **BNRItem**. The object diagram for the updated Homepwner application is shown in Figure 11.4.

Figure 11.4   Homepwner object diagram

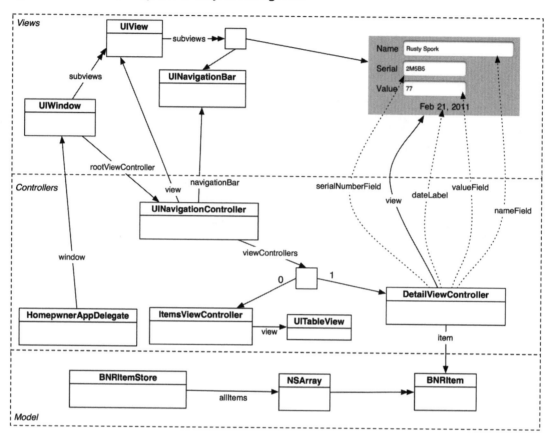

This application is getting fairly large, as you can see in the massive object diagram. Fortunately, view controllers and **UINavigationController** know how to deal with this type of complicated object diagram. When writing iOS applications, it is important to treat each **UIViewController** as its own little world. The stuff that has already been implemented in Cocoa Touch will do the heavy lifting.

Now let's give Homepwner a navigation controller. Reopen the Homepwner project and then open HomepwnerAppDelegate.m. The only requirements for using a **UINavigationController** are that you give it a root view controller and add its view to the window.

In **application:didFinishLaunchingWithOptions:**, create the **UINavigationController**, give it a root view controller of its own, and set the **UINavigationController** as the root view controller of the window.

```
- (BOOL)application:(UIApplication *)application
    didFinishLaunchingWithOptions:(NSDictionary *)launchOptions
{
    self.window = [[UIWindow alloc] initWithFrame:[[UIScreen mainScreen] bounds]];
    // Override point for customization after application launch.

    ItemsViewController *itemsViewController = [[ItemsViewController alloc] init];
```

```
    // Create an instance of a UINavigationController
    // its stack contains only itemsViewController
    UINavigationController *navController = [[UINavigationController alloc]
            initWithRootViewController:itemsViewController];

    [[self window] setRootViewController:itemsViewController];
    // Place navigation controller's view in the window hierarchy
    [[self window] setRootViewController:navController];

    self.window.backgroundColor = [UIColor whiteColor];
    [self.window makeKeyAndVisible];
    return YES;
}
```

Build and run the application. Homepwner will look the same as it did before – except now it has a **UINavigationBar** at the top of the screen (Figure 11.5). Notice how **ItemsViewController**'s view was resized to fit the screen with a navigation bar. **UINavigationController** did this for you.

Figure 11.5   Homepwner with an empty navigation bar

An Additional UIViewController

To see the real power of **UINavigationController**, you need another **UIViewController** to put on the navigation controller's stack. Create a new Objective-C class (File → New → New File...). Name this class **DetailViewController** and choose UIViewController as the superclass. Check the box With XIB for user interface (Figure 11.6).

Figure 11.6   View controller with XIB subclass

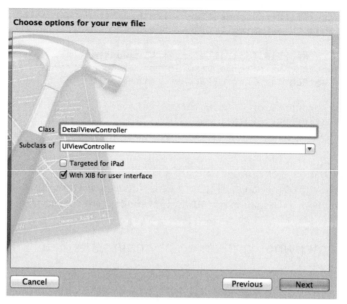

In DetailViewController.m, delete all of the code between the @implementation and @end directives so that the file looks like this:

```
#import "DetailViewController.h"

@implementation DetailViewController

@end
```

In Homepwner, we want the user to be able to tap an item to get another screen with editable text fields for each property of that **BNRItem**. This view will be controlled by an instance of **DetailViewController**.

The detail view needs four subviews – one for each instance variable of a **BNRItem** instance. And because you need to be able to access these subviews during runtime, **DetailViewController** needs outlets for these subviews. Therefore, you need to add four new outlets to **DetailViewController**, drag the subviews onto the view in the XIB file, and then make the connections.

In previous exercises, these were three distinct steps: you added the outlets in the interface file, then you configured the interface in the XIB file, and then you made connections. We can combine these steps using a shortcut in Xcode. First, open DetailViewController.xib by selecting it in the project navigator.

Now, Option-click on DetailViewController.h in the project navigator. This shortcut opens the file in the *assistant editor*, right next to DetailViewController.xib. (You can toggle the assistant editor by clicking the middle button from the Editor control at the top of the workspace; the shortcut to display the assistant editor is Command-Option-Return; to return to the standard editor, use Command-Return.)

You will also need the object library available so that you can drag the subviews onto the view. Show the utilities area by clicking the right button in the View control at the top of the workspace (or Command-Option-0).

Your window is now sufficiently cluttered. Let's make some temporary space. Hide the navigator area by clicking the left button in the View control at the top of the workspace (the shortcut for this is Command-0). Then, change the outline view in the XIB file to the dock view by clicking the toggle button in the lower left corner of the outline view. Your workspace should now look like Figure 11.7.

Figure 11.7   Laying out the workspace

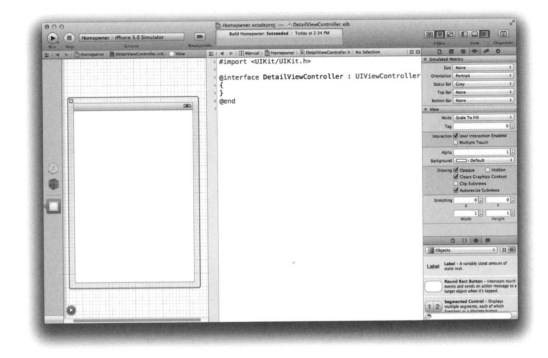

Now, drag four **UILabel**s and three **UITextField**s onto the view in the canvas area and configure them to look like Figure 11.8.

Figure 11.8   Configured DetailViewController XIB

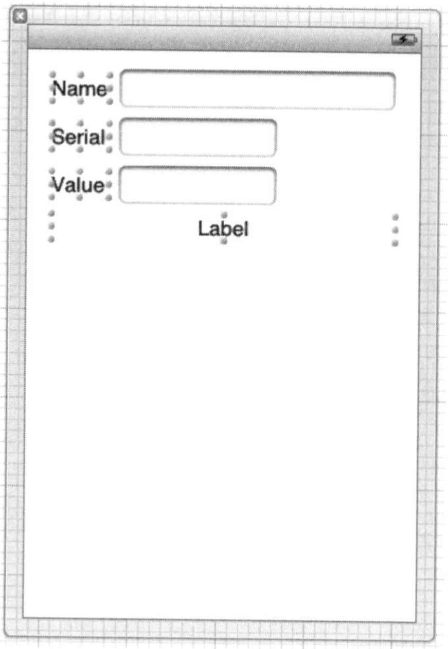

The three **UITextField**s and bottom **UILabel** will be outlets in **DetailViewController**. Here comes the exciting part. First, in DetailViewController.h, add the instance variable curly brackets.

```
@interface DetailViewController : UIViewController
{

}
@end
```

Next, back in the XIB file, Control-drag from the **UITextField** next to the Name label to the instance variable area (inside the curly brackets) in DetailViewController.h, as shown in Figure 11.9.

Figure 11.9 Dragging from XIB to source file

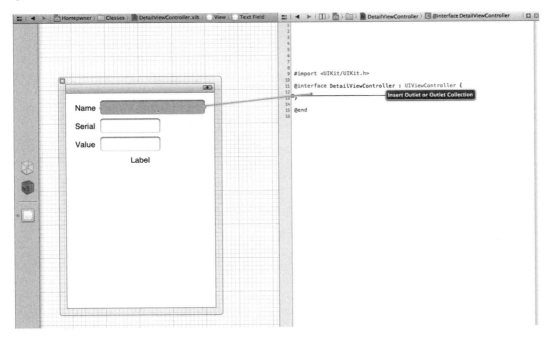

Let go while still inside the instance variable area, and a pop-up window will appear. Enter nameField into this field, select Weak from the Storage pop-up menu, and click Connect (Figure 11.10).

Figure 11.10 Auto-generating an outlet and making a connection

This will create an IBOutlet instance variable of type **UITextField** named nameField in **DetailViewController**. You chose Weak storage for this instance variable because the object it will point to is not a top-level object in the XIB file.

In addition, this **UITextField** is now connected to the nameField outlet of the File's Owner in the XIB file. You can verify this by Control-clicking on the File's Owner to see the connections. Also notice that hovering your mouse above the nameField connection in the panel that appears will reveal the **UITextField** that you connected. Two birds, one stone.

Create the other three outlets the same way and name them as shown in Figure 11.11.

Figure 11.11   Connection diagram

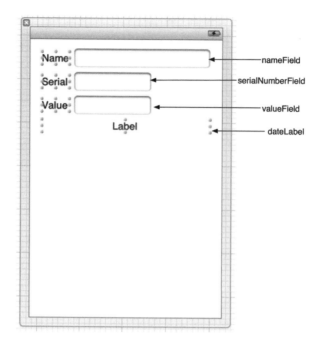

After making the connections, `DetailViewController.h` should look like this:

```
#import <UIKit/UIKit.h>

@interface DetailViewController : UIViewController
{
    __weak IBOutlet UITextField *nameField;
    __weak IBOutlet UITextField *serialNumberField;
    __weak IBOutlet UITextField *valueField;
    __weak IBOutlet UILabel *dateLabel;
}
@end
```

If your file looks different, then your outlets aren't connected right. For instance, if you see property declarations instead of instance variable declarations, then you let go of the Control-drag outside of the instance variable area.

Fix any disparities between your file and the code shown above in three steps: First, go through the Control-drag process and make connections again until you have the four lines shown above in your `DetailViewController.h`. Second, remove any wrong code (like property declarations) that got created. Finally, check for any bad connections in the XIB file. In `DetailViewController.xib`, Control-click on the File's Owner. If there are yellow warning signs next to any connection, click the x icon next to those connections to disconnect them.

It's important to ensure there are no bad connections in a XIB file. A bad connection typically happens when you change the name of an instance variable but do not update the connection in the XIB file. Or, you completely remove an instance variable but do not remove it from the XIB file. Either way, a bad connection will cause your application to crash when the XIB file is loaded.

When you make a connection, the XIB file is supplying data at runtime to a view controller. The view controller then uses this data in its existing methods to form the connection. For example, the nameField connection is set with the following code:

```
[self setValue:recordedObject forKey:@"nameField"];
```

The **setValue:forKey:** method will search the receiver (self) for an instance variable named nameField. If it can't find such a variable, an unknown key exception is thrown.

To see the runtime error generated by a bad connection, create a new temporary outlet for **DetailViewController** and connect it. Then, delete the instance variable but do not disconnect that outlet in DetailViewController.xib. Build and run, create and tap on a row, and then check the console as your application crashes and burns. The exception will look something like this:

```
'NSUnknownKeyException', reason: '
[<DetailViewController 0x68c0740> setValue:forUndefinedKey:]:
this class is not key value coding-compliant for the key nameField.'
```

Return to the XIB and disconnect the bad outlet.

Now let's make more connections. For each of the **UITextField**s in the XIB file, connect the delegate property to the File's Owner. (Remember, Control-drag from the **UITextField** to the File's Owner and select delegate from the list.)

Next, let's consider the **DetailViewController**'s view. Right now, it has a plain white background. Let's give it the same background as the **UITableView**. Recall that a view controller's view is not created until the view controller loads it the first time, so the code to perform extra setup on the view should be in **viewDidLoad**. Override this method in DetailViewController.m.

```
- (void)viewDidLoad
{
    [super viewDidLoad];
    [[self view] setBackgroundColor:[UIColor groupTableViewBackgroundColor]];
}
```

Now that this project has a good number of source files, you will be switching between them fairly regularly. One way to speed up switching between commonly accessed files is to use Xcode tabs. If you double-click on a file in the project navigator, the file will open in a new tab. You can also open up a blank tab with the shortcut Command-T. The keyboard shortcuts for cycling through tabs are Command-Shift-} and Command-Shift-{. (You can see the other shortcuts for project organization by selecting the General tab from Xcode's preferences.)

Navigating with UINavigationController

Now you have a navigation controller and two view controller subclasses. Time to put the pieces together. The user should be able to tap a row in **ItemsViewController**'s table view and have the **DetailViewController**'s view slide onto the screen and display the properties of the selected **BNRItem** instance.

Pushing view controllers

Of course, you need to create an instance of **DetailViewController**. Where should this object be created? Think back to previous exercises where you instantiated all of your controllers in the method

application:didFinishLaunchingWithOptions:. For example, in the Chapter 7 chapter, you created both view controllers and immediately added them to tab bar controller's `viewControllers` array.

However, when using a **UINavigationController**, you cannot simply store all of the possible view controllers in its stack. The `viewControllers` array of a navigation controller is dynamic – you start with a root view controller and add view controllers depending on user input. Therefore, some object other than the navigation controller needs to create the instance of **DetailViewController** and be responsible for adding it to the stack.

This object must meet two requirements: it needs to know when to push **DetailViewController** onto the stack, and it needs a pointer to the navigation controller to send the navigation controller messages, namely, **pushViewController:animated:**.

ItemsViewController fills both requirements. First, it knows when a row is tapped in a table view because, as the table view's delegate, it receives the message **tableView:didSelectRowAtIndexPath:** when this event occurs. Second, any view controller in a navigation controller's stack can get a pointer to that navigation controller by sending itself the message **navigationController** (Figure 11.12). As the root view controller, **ItemsViewController** is always in the navigation controller's stack and thus can always access it.

Figure 11.12   navigationController property

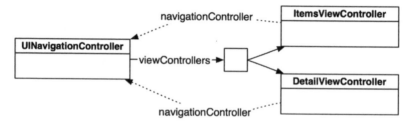

Therefore, **ItemsViewController** will be responsible for creating the instance of **DetailViewController** and adding it to the stack. At the top of ItemsViewController.h, import the header file for **DetailViewController**.

#import "DetailViewController.h"

@interface ItemsViewController : UITableViewController

When a row is tapped, its delegate is sent **tableView:didSelectRowAtIndexPath:**, which contains the index path of the selected row. In ItemsViewController.m, implement this method to create a **DetailViewController** and then push it on top of the navigation controller's stack.

@implementation ItemsViewController

```
- (void)tableView:(UITableView *)aTableView
    didSelectRowAtIndexPath:(NSIndexPath *)indexPath
{
    DetailViewController *detailViewController = [[DetailViewController alloc] init];

    // Push it onto the top of the navigation controller's stack
    [[self navigationController] pushViewController:detailViewController
                                    animated:YES];
}
```

Build and run the application. Create a new item and select that row from the **UITableView**. Not only are you taken to **DetailViewController**'s view, but you also get a free animation and a button in the **UINavigationBar** titled Back. Tap this button to get back to **ItemsViewController**.

Since the **UINavigationController**'s stack is an array, it will take ownership of any view controller added to it. Thus, the **DetailViewController** is owned only by the **UINavigationController** after **tableView:didSelectRowAtIndexPath:** finishes. When the stack is popped, the **DetailViewController** is destroyed. The next time a row is tapped, a new instance of **DetailViewController** is created.

Having a view controller push the next view controller is a common pattern. The root view controller typically creates the next view controller, and the next view controller creates the one after that, and so on. Some applications may have view controllers that can push different view controllers depending on user input. For example, the Photos pushes a video view controller or an image view controller onto the navigation stack depending on what type of media was selected.

(The iPad-only class **UISplitViewController** calls for a different pattern. The iPad's larger screen size allows two view controllers in a drill-down interface to appear on screen simultaneously instead of being pushed onto the same stack. You'll learn more about **UISplitViewController** in Chapter 26.)

Passing data between view controllers

Of course, the **UITextField**s on the screen are currently empty. To fill these fields, you need a way to pass the selected **BNRItem** from the **ItemsViewController** to the **DetailViewController**.

To pull this off, you will give **DetailViewController** a property to hold a **BNRItem**. When a row is tapped, **ItemsViewController** will give the corresponding **BNRItem** to the instance of **DetailViewController** that is being pushed onto the stack. The **DetailViewController** will populate its text fields with the properties of that **BNRItem**. Editing the text in the **UITextField**s on **DetailViewController**'s view will change the properties of that **BNRItem**.

In DetailViewController.h, add this property. Also, at the top of this file, forward declare **BNRItem**.

```
#import <UIKit/UIKit.h>

@class BNRItem;

@interface DetailViewController : UIViewController
{
    __weak IBOutlet UITextField *nameField;
    __weak IBOutlet UITextField *serialNumberField;
    __weak IBOutlet UITextField *valueField;
    __weak IBOutlet UILabel *dateLabel;
}
@property (nonatomic, strong) BNRItem *item;
@end
```

In DetailViewController.m, synthesize the accessors for item and import **BNRItem**'s header file.

```
#import "BNRItem.h"

@implementation DetailViewController

@synthesize item;
```

When the **DetailViewController**'s view appears on the screen, it needs to setup its subviews to show the properties of the item. In DetailViewController.m, override **viewWillAppear:** to transfer the item's properties to the various **UITextField**s.

```
- (void)viewWillAppear:(BOOL)animated
{
    [super viewWillAppear:animated];

    [nameField setText:[item itemName]];
    [serialNumberField setText:[item serialNumber]];
    [valueField setText:[NSString stringWithFormat:@"%d", [item valueInDollars]]];

    // Create a NSDateFormatter that will turn a date into a simple date string
    NSDateFormatter *dateFormatter = [[NSDateFormatter alloc] init];
    [dateFormatter setDateStyle:NSDateFormatterMediumStyle];
    [dateFormatter setTimeStyle:NSDateFormatterNoStyle];

    // Use filtered NSDate object to set dateLabel contents
    [dateLabel setText:[dateFormatter stringFromDate:[item dateCreated]]];
}
```

In ItemsViewController.m, add the following code to **tableView:didSelectRowAtIndexPath:** so that **DetailViewController** has its item before **viewWillAppear:** gets called.

```
- (void)tableView:(UITableView *)aTableView
    didSelectRowAtIndexPath:(NSIndexPath *)indexPath
{
    DetailViewController *detailViewController = [[DetailViewController alloc] init];

    NSArray *items = [[BNRItemStore sharedStore] allItems];
    BNRItem *selectedItem = [items objectAtIndex:[indexPath row]];

    // Give detail view controller a pointer to the item object in row
    [detailViewController setItem:selectedItem];

    [[self navigationController] pushViewController:detailViewController
                                          animated:YES];
}
```

Many programmers new to iOS struggle with how data is passed between **UIViewController**s. Having all of the data in the root view controller and passing subsets of that data to the next **UIViewController** (like you just did) is a clean and efficient way of performing this task.

Build and run your application. Create a new item and select that row in the **UITableView**. The view that appears will contain the information for the selected **BNRItem**. While you can edit this data, the **UITableView** won't reflect those changes when you return to it. To fix this problem, you need to implement code to update the properties of the **BNRItem** being edited. In the next section, we'll see when to do this.

Appearing and disappearing views

Whenever a **UINavigationController** is about to swap views, it sends out two messages: **viewWillDisappear:** and **viewWillAppear:**. The **UIViewController** that is about to be popped off the stack is sent the message **viewWillDisappear:**. The **UIViewController** that will then be on top of the stack is sent **viewWillAppear:**.

When a **DetailViewController** is popped off the stack, you will set the properties of its item to the contents of the **UITextField**s. When implementing these methods for views appearing and disappearing, it is important to call the superclass's implementation – it has some work to do as well. In DetailViewController.m, implement **viewWillDisappear:**.

```
- (void)viewWillDisappear:(BOOL)animated
{
    [super viewWillDisappear:animated];

    // Clear first responder
    [[self view] endEditing:YES];

    // "Save" changes to item
    [item setItemName:[nameField text]];
    [item setSerialNumber:[serialNumberField text]];
    [item setValueInDollars:[[valueField text] intValue]];
}
```

Notice the use of **endEditing:**. When the message **endEditing:** is sent to a view, if it or any of its subviews is currently the first responder, it will resign its first responder status, and the keyboard will be dismissed. (The argument passed determines whether the first responder should be forced into retirement. Some first responders might refuse to resign, and passing YES ignores that refusal.)

Now the values of the **BNRItem** will be updated when the user taps the Back button on the **UINavigationBar**. When **ItemsViewController** appears back on the screen, it is sent the message **viewWillAppear:**. Take this opportunity to reload the **UITableView** so the user can immediately see the changes. In ItemsViewController.m, override **viewWillAppear:**.

```
- (void)viewWillAppear:(BOOL)animated
{
    [super viewWillAppear:animated];
    [[self tableView] reloadData];
}
```

Build and run your application now. Now you can move back and forth between the **UIViewController**s you created and change the data with ease.

UINavigationBar

The **UINavigationBar** isn't very interesting right now. A **UINavigationBar** should display a descriptive title for the **UIViewController** that is currently on top of the **UINavigationController**'s stack.

Every **UIViewController** has a navigationItem property of type **UINavigationItem**. However, unlike **UINavigationBar**, **UINavigationItem** is not a subclass of **UIView**, so it cannot appear on the screen. Instead, the navigation item supplies the navigation bar with the content it needs to draw. When a **UIViewController** comes to the top of a **UINavigationController**'s stack, the **UINavigationBar** uses the **UIViewController**'s navigationItem to configure itself, as shown in Figure 11.13.

Figure 11.13   UINavigationItem

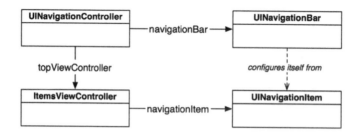

By default, a **UINavigationItem** is empty. At the most basic level, a **UINavigationItem** has a simple title string. When a **UIViewController** is moved to the top of the navigation stack and its navigationItem has a valid string for its title property, the navigation bar will display that string (Figure 11.14).

Figure 11.14   UINavigationItem with title

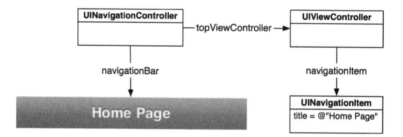

In ItemsViewController.m, modify **init** to set the navigationItem's title to read Homepwner.

```
- (id)init
{
    self = [super initWithStyle:UITableViewStyleGrouped];
    if (self) {
        UINavigationItem *n = [self navigationItem];

        [n setTitle:@"Homepwner"];
    }
    return self;
}
```

Build and run the application. Notice the string Homepwner on the navigation bar. Create and tap on a row and notice that the navigation bar no longer has a title. We need to give the **DetailViewController** a title, too. It would be nice to have the **DetailViewController**'s navigation item title be the name of the **BNRItem** it is displaying. Obviously, you cannot do this in **init** because you don't yet know what its item will be.

Instead, the **DetailViewController** will set its title when it sets its item property. In DetailViewController.m, implement **setItem:**, replacing the synthesized setter method for item.

```
- (void)setItem:(BNRItem *)i
{
    item = i;
    [[self navigationItem] setTitle:[item itemName]];
}
```

Build and run the application. Create and tap a row, and you'll see that the title of the navigation bar is the name of the **BNRItem** you selected.

A navigation item can hold more than just a title string, as shown in Figure 11.15. There are three customizable areas for each **UINavigationItem**: a leftBarButtonItem, a rightBarButtonItem, and a titleView. The left and right bar button items are pointers to instances of **UIBarButtonItem**, which contains the information for a button that can only be displayed on a **UINavigationBar** or a **UIToolbar**.

Figure 11.15   UINavigationItem with everything

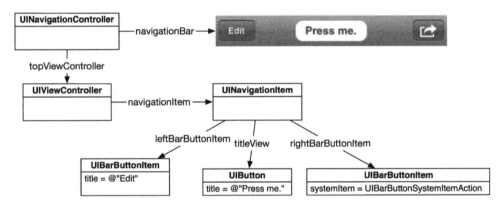

Like **UINavigationItem**, **UIBarButtonItem** is not a subclass of **UIView** but supplies the content that a **UINavigationBar** needs to draw. Consider the **UINavigationItem** and its **UIBarButtonItem**s to be containers for strings, images, and other content. A **UINavigationBar** knows how to look in those containers and draw the content it finds.

The third customizable area of a **UINavigationItem** is its titleView. You can either use a basic string as the title or have a subclass of **UIView** sit in the center of the navigation item. You cannot have both. If it suits the context of a specific view controller to have a custom view (like a button, a slider, an image, or even a map), you would set the titleView of the navigation item to that custom view. Figure 11.15 shows an example of a **UINavigationItem** with a custom view as its titleView. Typically, however, a title string is sufficient, and that's what we'll do in this chapter.

Let's add a **UIBarButtonItem** to the **UINavigationBar**. We want this button to sit on the right side of the navigation bar when the **ItemsViewController** is on top of the stack. When tapped, it should add a new **BNRItem** to the list.

A bar button item has a target-action pair that works like **UIControl**'s target-action mechanism: when tapped, it sends the action message to the target. When you set a target-action pair in a XIB file, you Control-drag from a button to its target and then select a method from the list of IBActions. To programmatically set up a target-action pair, you pass the target and the action to the button.

In `ItemsViewController.m`, create a **UIBarButtonItem** instance and give it its target and action.

```
- (id)init
{
    self = [super initWithStyle:UITableViewStyleGrouped];
    if (self) {
        UINavigationItem *n = [self navigationItem];

        [n setTitle:@"Homepwner"];

        // Create a new bar button item that will send
        // addNewItem: to ItemsViewController
        UIBarButtonItem *bbi = [[UIBarButtonItem alloc]
                        initWithBarButtonSystemItem:UIBarButtonSystemItemAdd
                                             target:self
                                             action:@selector(addNewItem:)];

        // Set this bar button item as the right item in the navigationItem
        [[self navigationItem] setRightBarButtonItem:bbi];
    }
    return self;
}
```

The action is passed as a value of type SEL. Recall that the SEL data type is a pointer to a selector and that a selector is the entire message name including any colons. Note that @selector() doesn't care about the return type, argument types, or names of arguments. Also, remember that @selector() doesn't check to see if the method actually exists. If you give a SEL to a button, that button will send the corresponding message regardless of whether the method is implemented by the target.

Build and run the application. Tap the + button, and a new row will appear in the table. (Note that this is not the only way to set up a bar button item; check the documentation for other initialization messages you can send an instance of **UIBarButtonItem**.)

Now let's add another **UIBarButtonItem** to replace the Edit button in the table view header. In `ItemsViewController.m`, edit the **init** method.

```
- (id)init
{
    self = [super initWithStyle:UITableViewStyleGrouped];
    if (self) {
        UINavigationItem *n = [self navigationItem];

        [n setTitle:@"Homepwner"];

        // Create a new bar button item that will send
        // addNewItem: to ItemsViewController
        UIBarButtonItem *bbi = [[UIBarButtonItem alloc]
                        initWithBarButtonSystemItem:UIBarButtonSystemItemAdd
                                             target:self
                                             action:@selector(addNewItem:)];

        // Set this bar button item as the right item in the navigationItem
        [[self navigationItem] setRightBarButtonItem:bbi];

        [[self navigationItem] setLeftBarButtonItem:[self editButtonItem]];
    }
    return self;
}
```

Surprisingly, that's all the code you need to get an edit button on the navigation bar. Build and run, tap the Edit button, and watch the **UITableView** enter editing mode! Where does **editButtonItem** come from? **UIViewController** has an editButtonItem property, and when sent **editButtonItem**, the view controller creates a **UIBarButtonItem** with the title Edit. Even better, this button comes with a target-action pair: it sends the message **setEditing:animated:** to its **UIViewController** when tapped.

Now that Homepwner has a fully functional navigation bar, you can get rid of the header view and the associated code. In ItemsViewController.m, delete the following methods.

```
- (UIView *)tableView:(UITableView *)aTableView
    viewForHeaderInSection:(NSInteger)section
{
    return [self headerView];
}

- (CGFloat)tableView:(UITableView *)tableView
    heightForHeaderInSection:(NSInteger)section
{
    return [[self headerView] frame].size.height;
}

- (UIView *)headerView
{
    if (!headerView) {
        [[NSBundle mainBundle] loadNibNamed:@"HeaderView" owner:self options:nil];
    }
    return headerView;
}

- (void)toggleEditingMode:(id)sender
{
    if ([self isEditing]) {
        [sender setTitle:@"Edit" forState:UIControlStateNormal];
        [self setEditing:NO animated:YES];
    } else {
        [sender setTitle:@"Done" forState:UIControlStateNormal];
        [self setEditing:YES animated:YES];
    }
}
```

Also remove the following code from ItemsViewController.h.

```
@interface ItemsViewController : UITableViewController
{
    IBOutlet UIView *headerView;
}

- (UIView *)headerView;
- (IBAction)addNewItem:(id)sender;
- (IBAction)toggleEditingMode:(id)sender;

@end
```

You can also remove the file HeaderView.xib from the project navigator.

Build and run again. The old Edit and New buttons are gone, leaving you with a lovely **UINavigationBar** (Figure 11.16).

Figure 11.16   Homepwner with navigation bar

Bronze Challenge: Displaying a Number Pad

The keyboard for the **UITextField** that displays a **BNRItem**'s valueInDollars is a QWERTY keyboard. It would be better if it was a number pad. Change the Keyboard Type of that **UITextField** to the Number Pad. (Hint: you can do this in the XIB file using the attributes inspector.)

Silver Challenge: Dismissing a Number Pad

After completing the bronze challenge, you may notice that there is no return key on the number pad. Devise a way for the user to dismiss the number pad from the screen.

Gold Challenge: Pushing More View Controllers

Right now, **BNRItem**s cannot have their dateCreated property changed. Change **BNRItem** so that it can, and then add a button underneath the dateLabel in **DetailViewController** with the title Change Date. When this button is tapped, push another view controller instance onto the navigation stack. This view controller should have a **UIDatePicker** instance that modifies the dateCreated property of the selected **BNRItem**. Also, have it display text that warns the user against insurance fraud.

12
Camera

In this chapter, you're going to add photos to the Homepwner application. You will present a **UIImagePickerController** so that the user can take and save a picture of each item. The image will then be associated with a **BNRItem** instance, stored in an image store, and viewable in the item's detail view. Then, when the insurance company demands proof, the user will have a visual record of owning that 70" HDTV.

Figure 12.1   Homepwner with camera addition

Displaying Images and UIImageView

Because we want the image to appear in the item's detail view, our first step is to have the **DetailViewController** get and display an image. An easy way to display an image is to put an instance of **UIImageView** on the screen. Open Homepwner.xcodeproj and DetailViewController.xib. Then drag an instance of **UIImageView** onto the view, as shown in Figure 12.2.

Figure 12.2   UIImageView on DetailViewController's view

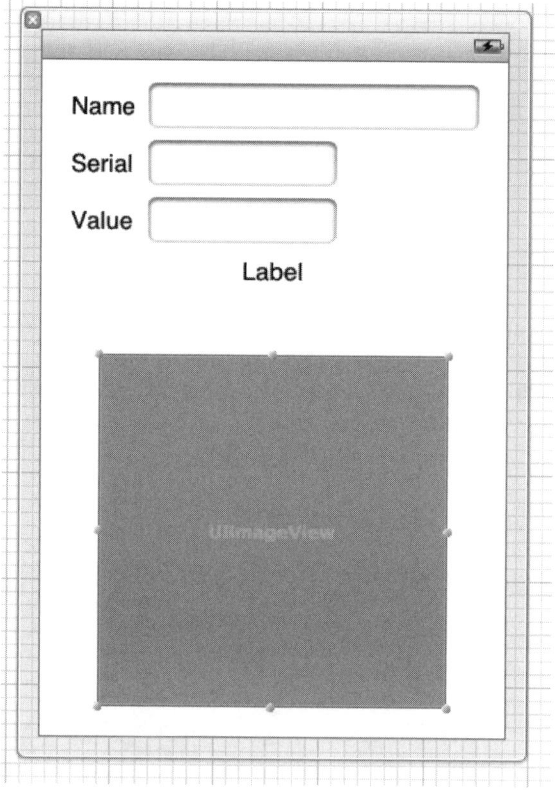

A **UIImageView** displays an image according to its contentMode property. This property determines where to position and how to resize the content within its frame. **UIImageView**'s default value for contentMode is UIViewContentModeScaleToFill, which will adjust the image to exactly match the bounds of the image view. If you keep the default, the image taken by the camera will be contorted to fit into the square **UIImageView**. You have to change the contentMode of the image view so that it resizes the image with the same aspect ratio.

Select the **UIImageView** and open the attributes inspector. Find the Mode attribute and change it to Aspect Fit, as shown in Figure 12.3. This will resize the image to fit within the bounds of the **UIImageView**.

Figure 12.3   Image view attributes

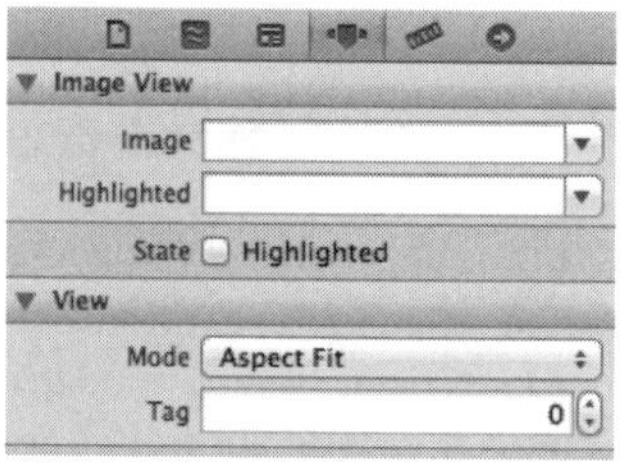

Now, Option-click DetailViewController.h in the project navigator to open it in the assistant editor. Control-drag from the **UIImageView** to the instance variable area in DetailViewController.h. Name the outlet imageView and choose Weak as the storage type. Click Connect.

DetailViewController's instance variable area should now look like this:

```
@interface DetailViewController : UIViewController
{
    __weak IBOutlet UITextField *nameField;
    __weak IBOutlet UITextField *serialNumberField;
    __weak IBOutlet UITextField *valueField;
    __weak IBOutlet UILabel *dateLabel;
    __weak IBOutlet UIImageView *imageView;
}
```

Taking pictures and UIImagePickerController

Now you need a button to initiate the photo-taking process. It would be nice to put this button on the navigation bar, but we will need the navigation bar for another button later. Instead, we will create an instance of **UIToolbar** and place it at the bottom of **DetailViewController**'s view. In DetailViewController.xib, drag a **UIToolbar** onto the bottom of the view.

A **UIToolbar** works a lot like a **UINavigationBar** – you can add **UIBarButtonItem**s to it. However, where a navigation bar has two slots for bar button items, a toolbar has an array of bar button items. You can place as many **UIBarButtonItem**s in a toolbar as can fit on the screen.

By default, a new instance of **UIToolbar** created in a XIB file comes with one **UIBarButtonItem**. Select this bar button item and open the attribute inspector. Change the Identifier to Camera, and the item will show a camera icon (Figure 12.4).

Figure 12.4   UIToolbar with bar button item

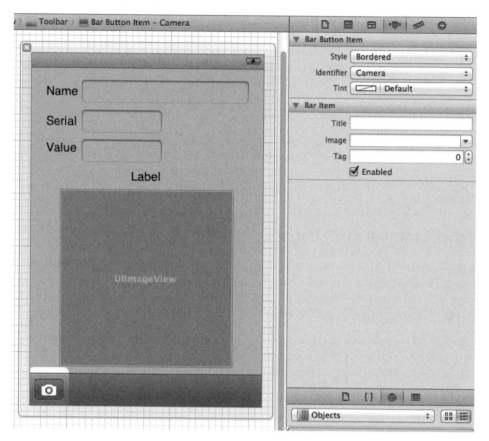

The camera button will need to send a message to the instance of **DetailViewController** when it is tapped. In previous exercises, you connected action methods in two steps: declaring them in the header file and then hooking them up in the XIB file. Just like you did with outlets, you can do both steps at once by opening a source file in the assistant editor and Control-dragging from a XIB file to the file. Option-click DetailViewController.h in the project navigator to open it in the assistant editor .

In DetailViewController.xib, select the camera button and Control-drag from the button to the method declaration area in DetailViewController.h (Figure 12.5).

Figure 12.5   Creating and connecting an action method from a XIB

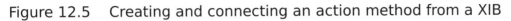

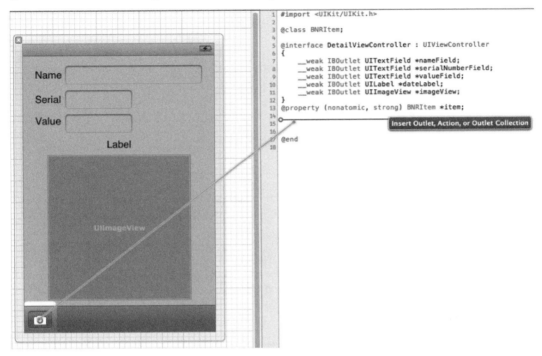

Let go of the mouse, and a window will appear that allows you to specify the type of connection you are creating. From the Connection pop-up menu, choose Action. Then, name this method **takePicture:** and click Connect (Figure 12.6).

Figure 12.6   Creating the action

Now the action method is declared in the header file, and the **UIBarButtonItem** instance in the XIB is hooked up to send this message to the **DetailViewController** when tapped. Connecting an action method in this way also automatically adds a stub implementation in DetailViewController.m:

```
- (IBAction)takePicture:(id)sender
{
}
```

The interface for **DetailViewController** now looks like this:

```
@interface DetailViewController : UIViewController
{
    __weak IBOutlet UITextField *nameField;
    __weak IBOutlet UITextField *serialNumberField;
    __weak IBOutlet UITextField *valueField;
    __weak IBOutlet UILabel *dateLabel;
    __weak IBOutlet UIImageView *imageView;
}
@property (nonatomic, strong) BNRItem *item;

- (IBAction)takePicture:(id)sender;

@end
```

If you made any mistakes while making this connection and later realize it (or realize it now), make sure you open DetailViewController.xib and disconnect any bad connections. (Look for yellow warning signs in the connections inspector.)

Also, notice that Xcode is smart enough to tell you when an action method is connected in the XIB file. See that little circle within a circle in the gutter area next to **takePicture:**'s method name (Figure 12.7)? When this circle is filled in, this action method is connected in a XIB file; an empty circle means it still needs connecting.

Figure 12.7   Source file connection status

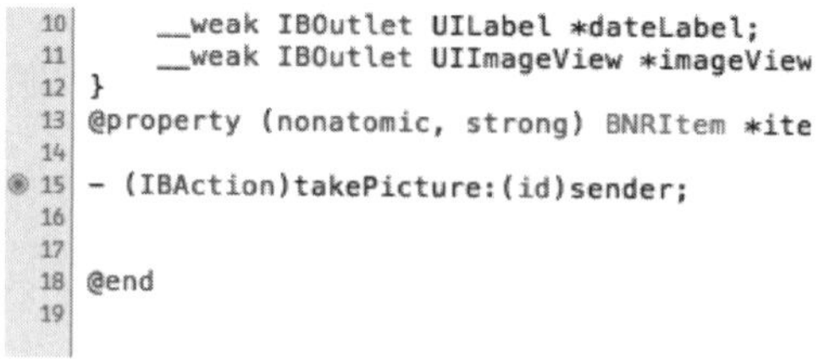

```
10      __weak IBOutlet UILabel *dateLabel;
11      __weak IBOutlet UIImageView *imageView
12 }
13 @property (nonatomic, strong) BNRItem *ite
14
15 - (IBAction)takePicture:(id)sender;
16
17
18 @end
19
```

In the **takePicture:** method, you will instantiate a **UIImagePickerController** and present it on the screen. When creating an instance of **UIImagePickerController**, you must set its sourceType property and assign it a delegate.

The sourceType is a constant that tells the image picker where to get images. It has three possible values:

- UIImagePickerControllerSourceTypeCamera – The user will take a new picture.

- UIImagePickerControllerSourceTypePhotoLibrary – The user will be prompted to select an album and then a photo from that album.

- UIImagePickerControllerSourceTypeSavedPhotosAlbum – The user picks from the most recently taken photos.

Figure 12.8 shows the results of using each constant.

Figure 12.8   UIImagePickerControllerTypes

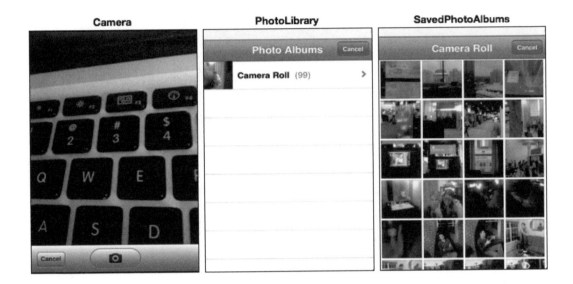

The first source type, UIImagePickerControllerSourceTypeCamera, won't work on a device that doesn't have a camera. So before using this type, you have to check for a camera by sending the message **isSourceTypeAvailable:** to the **UIImagePickerController** class. Sending this message to **UIImagePickerController** with one of the source type constants returns a Boolean value for whether the device supports that source type.

In addition to a source type, the **UIImagePickerController** instance needs a delegate to handle requests from its view. When the user taps the Use Photo button on the **UIImagePickerController**'s interface, the delegate is sent the message **imagePickerController:didFinishPickingMediaWithInfo:**. (The delegate receives another message – **imagePickerControllerDidCancel:** – if the process was cancelled.)

In DetailViewController.m, add the following code to **takePicture:**. (Remember – there's already a stub for this method, so locate the stub in DetailViewController.m and add the following code there.)

```
- (IBAction)takePicture:(id)sender
{
    UIImagePickerController *imagePicker =
            [[UIImagePickerController alloc] init];

    // If our device has a camera, we want to take a picture, otherwise, we
    // just pick from photo library
    if ([UIImagePickerController
            isSourceTypeAvailable:UIImagePickerControllerSourceTypeCamera]) {
        [imagePicker setSourceType:UIImagePickerControllerSourceTypeCamera];
    } else {
        [imagePicker setSourceType:UIImagePickerControllerSourceTypePhotoLibrary];
    }
```

```
    // This line of code will generate a warning right now, ignore it
    [imagePicker setDelegate:self];

}
```

Once the **UIImagePickerController** has a source type and a delegate, it's time to put its view on the screen. Unlike other **UIViewController** subclasses you've used, an instance of **UIImagePickerController** is presented *modally*. When a view controller is *modal*, it takes over the entire screen until it has finished its work.

To present a view modally, **presentViewController:animated:completion:** is sent to the **UIViewController** whose view is on the screen. The view controller to be presented is passed to it, and its view slides up from the bottom of the screen.

In DetailViewController.m, add code to the end of **takePicture:** to present the **UIImagePickerController**.

```
    [imagePicker setDelegate:self];

    // Place image picker on the screen
    [self presentViewController:imagePicker animated:YES completion:nil];

}
```

(Don't worry about the third argument, **completion:**. We'll talk about it more in Chapter 13.)

You can build and run the application now. Select a **BNRItem** to see its details and then tap the camera button on the **UIToolbar**. **UIImagePickerController**'s interface will appear on the screen (Figure 12.9), and you can take a picture (or choose an existing image if you don't have a camera). Tapping the Use Photo button dismisses the **UIImagePickerController**.

(If you are working on the simulator, there won't be any images available. However, you can open Safari in the simulator, navigate to a page with an image, and click and hold on that image. When the action sheet appears, choose Save Image. This image will be saved in the simulator's photo library. But, the simulator can be flaky, so you might have to try a few different images before one actually saves.)

Figure 12.9   UIImagePickerController preview interface

But, oops – you dismissed the controller without keeping a reference to the image anywhere in the code. To hold on to the selected image, you need to implement the delegate method **imagePickerController:didFinishPickingMediaWithInfo:** in **DetailViewController**.

But before you implement this method, let's take care of the two warnings that appeared during the last build telling you that **DetailViewController** does not conform to the UIImagePickerControllerDelegate or the UINavigationControllerDelegate protocol. In DetailViewController.h, add the protocols to the class declaration. (Why UINavigationControllerDelegate? **UIImagePickerController** is a subclass of **UINavigationController**.)

```
@interface DetailViewController : UIViewController
    <UINavigationControllerDelegate, UIImagePickerControllerDelegate>
{
```

That's better. Notice that the two warnings have gone away.

The **imagePickerController:didFinishPickingMediaWithInfo:** message will be sent to the image picker's delegate when a photo is selected. In DetailViewController.m, implement this method to put the image into the **UIImageView** that you created earlier.

```
- (void)imagePickerController:(UIImagePickerController *)picker
didFinishPickingMediaWithInfo:(NSDictionary *)info
{
    // Get picked image from info dictionary
    UIImage *image = [info objectForKey:UIImagePickerControllerOriginalImage];

    // Put that image onto the screen in our image view
    [imageView setImage:image];

    // Take image picker off the screen -
    // you must call this dismiss method
    [self dismissViewControllerAnimated:YES completion:nil];
}
```

Build and run the application again. Take a photo, the image picker is dismissed, and you are returned to the **DetailViewController**'s view. Do you see your image? Oddly enough, you might or you might not. Let's figure out what's going on and fix the problem.

When a photo is taken, that image is loaded into memory. However, the image file is so large that it causes a low-memory warning. Recall that a low-memory warning gives the system the option of requiring view controllers to release their views if they are not currently visible. When a modal view controller is on the screen, its view is visible, and the view of the view controller that presented it is not. In our case, the low-memory warning destroys **DetailViewController**'s view, and the imageView is no longer available when we try to set it.

To get around this problem, we must create a separate store for images. Instead of putting the image directly into the imageView, we will put it into this store. Then when the **DetailViewController**'s view next appears on screen, we'll have the **DetailViewController** grab the image from the image store and put it into its own imageView. In general, this is a best practice: a view controller should re-populate its view's subviews with data whenever it is sent the message **viewWillAppear:** to eliminate the possibility that a low-memory warning could wipe out its content.

Creating BNRImageStore

The image store will hold all the pictures the user will take. In Chapter 14, you will have the **BNRItem** objects write out their instance variables to a file, which will then be read in when the application starts. However, as we've seen, images tend to be very large, so it's a good idea to keep them separate from other data. The image store will fetch and cache the images as they are needed. It will also be able to flush the cache if the device runs low on memory. Create a new **NSObject** subclass called **BNRImageStore**. Open BNRImageStore.h and create its interface:

```
#import <UIKit/UIKit.h>

@interface BNRImageStore : NSObject
{
    NSMutableDictionary *dictionary;
}
+ (BNRImageStore *)sharedStore;

- (void)setImage:(UIImage *)i forKey:(NSString *)s;
- (UIImage *)imageForKey:(NSString *)s;
- (void)deleteImageForKey:(NSString *)s;

@end
```

Like the **BNRItemStore**, the **BNRImageStore** needs to be a singleton. In BNRImageStore.m, write the following code to ensure **BNRImageStore**'s singleton status.

```
@implementation BNRImageStore

+ (id)allocWithZone:(NSZone *)zone
{
    return [self sharedStore];
}

+ (BNRImageStore *)sharedStore
{
    static BNRImageStore *sharedStore = nil;
    if (!sharedStore) {
        // Create the singleton
        sharedStore = [[super allocWithZone:NULL] init];
    }
    return sharedStore;
}

- (id)init
{
    self = [super init];
    if (self) {
        dictionary = [[NSMutableDictionary alloc] init];
    }

    return self;
}
```

Then, implement the other three methods declared in the header file.

```
- (void)setImage:(UIImage *)i forKey:(NSString *)s
{
    [dictionary setObject:i forKey:s];
}

- (UIImage *)imageForKey:(NSString *)s
{
    return [dictionary objectForKey:s];
}

- (void)deleteImageForKey:(NSString *)s
{
    if (!s)
        return;
    [dictionary removeObjectForKey:s];
}
```

NSDictionary

Notice that the dictionary is an instance of **NSMutableDictionary**. A dictionary is a lot like an array: it is a collection object and it has an immutable (**NSDictionary**) and mutable version (**NSMutableDictionary**). However, dictionaries and arrays differ in how they store their objects. An array is an ordered list of pointers to objects that is accessed by an index. When you have an array, you can ask it for the object at the *n*th index:

```
// Put some object at the beginning of an array
[someArray insertObject:someObject atIndex:0];

// Get that same object out
someObject = [someArray objectAtIndex:0];
```

A dictionary's objects are not ordered within the collection. So instead of accessing entries with an index, you use a *key*. The key is usually an instance of **NSString**.

```
// Add some object to a dictionary for the key "MyKey"
[someDictionary setObject:someObject forKey:@"MyKey"];

// Get that same object out
someObject = [someDictionary objectForKey:@"MyKey"];
```

We call each entry in a dictionary a *key-value pair*. The *value* is the object being stored in the collection, and the *key* is a unique value (usually a string) that you use to retrieve the value later. (In other development environments, a dictionary is called a *hash map* or *hash table*, but we still use the term key-value pair to talk about the information they store.)

Figure 12.10   NSDictionary diagram

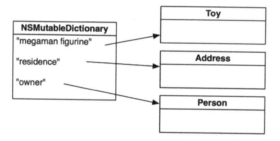

The purpose of a dictionary is difficult to understand if you are new to programming, but the general idea is that a dictionary maps one value to another (Figure 12.10). Consider a robot that responded to the facial expressions of a human. For example, if a human smiled, the robot would wink. Thus, the human-to-robot response would be stored in a dictionary. The "wink" response would be the value stored for the "smile" key. When a human made another facial expression at the robot, it would look up that expression in its dictionary and find the appropriate response.

Consider solving the same human-to-robot response problem with an array as the collection object. One approach would be to store every response in an ordered array. With this approach, you would have to remember the index of every response by assigning a numeric value to each facial expression. If you added a new expression-response pair, you'd have to recompute the indices of each response. At some point early in your programming career, you've probably done something like that:

```
int smileIndex = 0;
int scowlIndex = 1;
RobotResponses responses[2] = { "wink", "scream"};
```

```
if ([human isSmiling])
    response = responses[smileIndex];
else if ([human isScowling])
    response = responses[scowlIndex];
```

Another approach would be to store an object that held both the facial expression and the response in an array. When the human made a facial expression, you would search the list for the appropriate response.

```
for (ExpressionResponsePair *p in allResponses) {
    if ([p expression] == [human facialExpression])
        response = [p response];
}
```

Both of these approaches are inefficient and clumsy. A dictionary makes this lookup process a lot faster and easier to understand:

```
NSMutableDictionary *dictionary = [NSMutableDictionary dictionary];
[dictionary setValue:@"wink" forKey:@"smile"];

response = [dictionary objectForKey:[human facialExpression]];
```

When using a dictionary, there can only be one object for each key. If you add an object to a dictionary with a key that matches the key of an object already present in the dictionary, the earlier object is removed. If you need to store multiple objects under one key, you can put them in an array and add the array to the dictionary as the value.

Finally, note that a dictionary's memory management is like that of an array. Whenever you add an object to a dictionary, the dictionary owns it, and whenever you remove an object from a dictionary, the dictionary releases its ownership.

Creating and using keys

When an image is added to the store, it will be put into a dictionary under a unique key, and the associated **BNRItem** object will be given that key. When the **DetailViewController** wants an image from the store, it will ask its item for the key and search the dictionary for the image. Add a property to BNRItem.h to store the key.

```
@property (nonatomic, readonly, strong) NSDate *dateCreated;
```

@property (nonatomic, copy) NSString *imageKey;

Synthesize this new property in the implementation file.

```
@implementation BNRItem
@synthesize imageKey;
```

The image keys need to be unique in order for your dictionary to work. While there are many ways to hack together a unique string, we're going to use the Cocoa Touch mechanism for creating universally unique identifiers (UUIDs), also known as globally unique identifiers (GUIDs). Objects of type **CFUUIDRef** represent a UUID and are generated using the time, a counter, and a hardware identifier, which is usually the MAC address of the ethernet card.

Import BNRImageStore.h at the top of DetailViewController.m.

```
#import "DetailViewController.h"
#import "BNRItem.h"
#import "BNRImageStore.h"
```

In DetailViewController.m, update **imagePickerController:didFinishPickingMediaWithInfo:** to generate a UUID when a new picture is taken.

```
- (void)imagePickerController:(UIImagePickerController *)picker
        didFinishPickingMediaWithInfo:(NSDictionary *)info
{
    UIImage *image = [info objectForKey:UIImagePickerControllerOriginalImage];

    // Create a CFUUID object - it knows how to create unique identifier strings
    CFUUIDRef newUniqueID = CFUUIDCreate(kCFAllocatorDefault);
```

The prefix CF means **CFUUIDRef** comes from the Core Foundation framework (and remember that the Ref suffix means that it is a pointer). Core Foundation is a collection of C "classes" and functions. Core Foundation objects are created by calling a function that begins with the type of object being created and contains the word **Create** (**CFUUIDCreate**). When creating a Core Foundation object, the first argument specifies how memory is allocated. In practice, you pass kCFAllocatorDefault and let the system make that choice.

Once created, a **CFUUIDRef** is just an array of bytes and, if represented as a string, will look something like this:

```
28153B74-4D6A-12F6-9D61-155EA4C32167
```

This UUID will be used in two ways: it will be the key in the **BNRImageStore**'s dictionary and in a later chapter, it will be the name of the image file on the filesystem. Because keys in a dictionary and paths on the filesystem are typically strings, we want to represent the UUID as a string instead of an array of bytes.

You can create a string object from a **CFUUIDRef** by calling the C function **CFUUIDCreateString**. In DetailViewController.m, add the following line of code in **imagePickerController:didFinishPickingMediaWithInfo:**.

```
- (void)imagePickerController:(UIImagePickerController *)picker
        didFinishPickingMediaWithInfo:(NSDictionary *)info
{
    UIImage *image = [info objectForKey:UIImagePickerControllerOriginalImage];

    CFUUIDRef newUniqueID = CFUUIDCreate (kCFAllocatorDefault);

    // Create a string from unique identifier
    CFStringRef newUniqueIDString =
            CFUUIDCreateString (kCFAllocatorDefault, newUniqueID);
```

Notice that newUniqueIDString's type is **CFStringRef**. The imageKey property of **BNRItem** is an **NSString**. Clearly, you need some way to move between **CFStringRef** and **NSString** to set the imageKey property.

Fortunately, many classes in Core Foundation are *toll-free bridged* with their Objective-C counterpart. For example, **CFStringRef** is toll-free bridged with **NSString**; **CFArrayRef** with **NSArray**. Instances of classes that are toll-free bridged look exactly the same as their counterpart in memory. Therefore, you can use a simple C-style typecast to treat a toll-free bridged Core Foundation object as an Objective-C object.

Typecast newUniqueIDString and set it as the imageKey of the selected **BNRItem** in **imagePickerController:didFinishPickingMediaWithInfo:**. Also, place this image in the **BNRImageStore**.

```
- (void)imagePickerController:(UIImagePickerController *)picker
        didFinishPickingMediaWithInfo:(NSDictionary *)info
{
    UIImage *image = [info objectForKey:UIImagePickerControllerOriginalImage];

    CFUUIDRef newUniqueID = CFUUIDCreate (kCFAllocatorDefault);

    CFStringRef newUniqueIDString =
            CFUUIDCreateString (kCFAllocatorDefault, newUniqueID);

    // Use that unique ID to set our item's imageKey
    NSString *key = (__bridge NSString *)newUniqueIDString;
    [item setImageKey:key];

    // Store image in the BNRImageStore with this key
    [[BNRImageStore sharedStore] setImage:image
                                    forKey:[item imageKey]];
```

Notice the use of __bridge in this typecast. To understand what this keyword does, you must understand how memory is managed for Core Foundation objects.

Core Foundation and toll-free bridging

When a variable that points to an Objective-C object is destroyed, ARC knows that object has lost an owner. ARC doesn't do this with Core Foundation objects. Thus, when a Core Foundation object loses a pointer, you must call a function that tells the object to lose an owner before you lose the pointer. This function is **CFRelease**.

If you do not call **CFRelease** before losing a pointer, the pointed-to object still thinks it has an owner. Losing a pointer to an object before telling it to lose an owner results in a memory leak: you can no longer access that object, and it still has an owner. Add code to **imagePickerController:didFinishPickingMediaWithInfo:** to tell the objects pointed to by newUniqueIDString and newUniqueID to lose an owner since these are both local variables that will be destroyed when this method ends.

```
    [[BNRImageStore sharedStore] setImage:image
                                    forKey:[item imageKey]];

    CFRelease(newUniqueIDString);
    CFRelease(newUniqueID);

    [imageView setImage:image];

    [self dismissViewControllerAnimated:YES completion:nil];
}
```

Here are the memory management rules when it comes to Core Foundation objects.

• A variable only owns the object it points to if the function that created the object has the word **Create** or **Copy** in it.

• If a pointer owns a Core Foundation object, you must call **CFRelease** before you lose that pointer. Remember that a pointer can be lost if it is set to point at something else (including nil) or if the pointer itself is being destroyed.

• Once you call **CFRelease** on a pointer, you cannot access that pointer again.

As you can see, the rules of memory management are a bit more complicated when dealing with Core Foundation because you don't have the luxury of ARC. However, you typically won't use Core Foundation objects as much as Objective-C objects. As long as you stick to these rules, you will be okay.

Now, back to the __bridge keyword. ARC doesn't know how to manage memory with Core Foundation objects very well, so it gets confused if you typecast a Core Foundation pointer into its Objective-C counterpart. Placing __bridge in front of the cast tells ARC, "Hey, don't even worry about it." Thus, when ARC sees this line of code, it doesn't give ownership to the key variable as it normally would:

```
NSString *key = (__bridge NSString *)newUniqueIDString;
```

Once key is an Objective-C pointer, ARC can do its work as normal. When this object is passed to **setImageKey:**, **BNRItem**'s imageKey instance variable takes ownership of that object.

Wrapping up BNRImageStore

Now that the **BNRImageStore** can store images and **BNRItem**s have a key to get that image (Figure 12.11), we need to teach **DetailViewController** how to grab the image for the selected **BNRItem** and place it in its imageView.

Figure 12.11   Cache

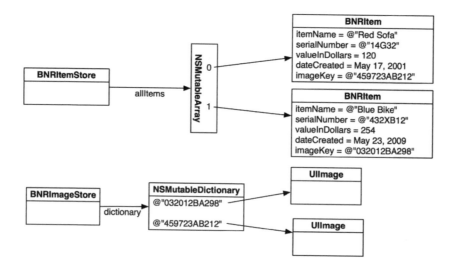

The **DetailViewController**'s view will appear at two times: when the user taps a row in **ItemsViewController** and when the **UIImagePickerController** is dismissed. In both of these situations, the imageView should be populated with the image of the **BNRItem** being displayed. In DetailViewController.m, add code to **viewWillAppear:** to do this.

```
- (void)viewWillAppear:(BOOL)animated
{
    [super viewWillAppear:animated];

    [nameField setText:[item itemName]];
    [serialNumberField setText:[item serialNumber]];
    [valueField setText:[NSString stringWithFormat:@"%d",
                                    [item valueInDollars]]];

    NSDateFormatter *dateFormatter = [[[NSDateFormatter alloc] init]
                                            autorelease];
    [dateFormatter setDateStyle:NSDateFormatterMediumStyle];
    [dateFormatter setTimeStyle:NSDateFormatterNoStyle];

    [dateLabel setText:
            [dateFormatter stringFromDate:[item dateCreated]]];


    NSString *imageKey = [item imageKey];

    if (imageKey) {
        // Get image for image key from image store
        UIImage *imageToDisplay =
                [[BNRImageStore sharedStore] imageForKey:imageKey];

        // Use that image to put on the screen in imageView
        [imageView setImage:imageToDisplay];
    } else {
        // Clear the imageView
        [imageView setImage:nil];
    }
}
```

Notice that if no image exists in the image store for that key (or there is no key for that item), the pointer to the image will be nil. When the image is nil, the **UIImageView** just won't display an image.

Build and run the application. Create a **BNRItem** and select it from the **UITableView**. Then, tap the camera button and take a picture. The image will appear as it should.

There is another detail to take care of: if you select a new image for a **BNRItem**, the old one will still be in the **BNRImageStore**. At the top of **imagePickerController:didFinishPickingMediaWithInfo:** in DetailViewController.m, add some code to tell the **BNRImageStore** to remove the old image.

```
- (void)imagePickerController:(UIImagePickerController *)picker
        didFinishPickingMediaWithInfo:(NSDictionary *)info
{
    NSString *oldKey = [item imageKey];

    // Did the item already have an image?
    if (oldKey) {
```

```
    // Delete the old image
    [[BNRImageStore sharedStore] deleteImageForKey:oldKey];
}

UIImage *image = [info objectForKey:UIImagePickerControllerOriginalImage];
```

Build and run the application again. The behavior should remain the same, but the memory benefits are significant.

Dismissing the keyboard

When the keyboard appears on the screen in the item detail view, it obscures **DetailViewController**'s imageView. This is annoying when you're trying to see an image, so you're going to implement the delegate method **textFieldShouldReturn:** to have the text field resign its first responder status to dismiss the keyboard when the return key is tapped. (This is why you hooked up the delegate outlets earlier.) But first, in DetailViewController.h, have **DetailViewController** conform to the UITextFieldDelegate protocol.

```
@interface DetailViewController : UIViewController
    <UINavigationControllerDelegate, UIImagePickerControllerDelegate,
        UITextFieldDelegate>
```

In DetailViewController.m, implement **textFieldShouldReturn:**.

```
- (BOOL)textFieldShouldReturn:(UITextField *)textField
{
    [textField resignFirstResponder];
    return YES;
}
```

It would be stylish to also dismiss the keyboard if the user taps anywhere else on **DetailViewController**'s view. We can dismiss the keyboard by sending the view the message **endEditing:**, which will cause the text field (as a subview of the view) to resign as first responder. Now let's figure out how to get the view to send a message when tapped.

We have seen how classes like **UIButton** can send an action message to a target when tapped. Buttons inherit this target-action behavior from their superclass, **UIControl**. You're going to change the view of **DetailViewController** from an instance of **UIView** to an instance of **UIControl** so that it can handle touch events.

In DetailViewController.xib, select the main View object. Open the identity inspector and change the view's class to **UIControl** (Figure 12.12).

Figure 12.12   Changing the class of DetailViewController's view

Then, open DetailViewController.h in the assistant editor. Control-drag from the view (now a **UIControl**) to the method declaration area of **DetailViewController**. When the pop-up window appears, select Action from the Connection pop-up menu. Notice that the interface of this pop-up window is slightly different than one you saw when creating and connecting the **UIBarButtonItem**. A **UIBarButtonItem** is a simplified version of **UIControl** – it only sends its target an action message when it is tapped. A **UIControl**, on the other hand, can send action messages in response to a variety of events.

Therefore, you must choose the appropriate event type to trigger the action message being sent. In this case, you want the action message to be sent when the user taps on the view. Configure this pop-up window to appear as it does in Figure 12.13 and click Connect.

Figure 12.13   Configuring a UIControl action

This will create a stub method in **DetailViewController.m**. Enter the following code into that method.

```
- (IBAction)backgroundTapped:(id)sender
{
    [[self view] endEditing:YES];
}
```

Build and run your application and test both ways of dismissing the keyboard.

Bronze Challenge: Editing an Image

UIImagePickerController has a built-in interface for editing an image once it has been selected. Allow the user to edit the image and use the edited image instead of the original image in **DetailViewController**.

Silver Challenge: Removing an Image

Add a button that clears the image for an item.

Gold Challenge: Camera Overlay

A **UIImagePickerController** has a cameraOverlayView property. Make it so that presenting the **UIImagePickerController** shows a crosshair in the middle of the image capture area.

For the More Curious: Recording Video

Once you understand how to use **UIImagePickerController** to take pictures, making the transition to recording video is trivial. Recall that an image picker controller has a sourceType property that determines whether an image comes from the camera, photo library, or saved photos album. Image picker controllers also have a mediaTypes property, which is an array of strings that contains identifiers for what types of media can be selected from the three source types.

There are two types of media a **UIImagePickerController** can select: still images and video. By default, the mediaTypes array only contains the constant string kUTTypeImage. Thus, if you do not change the mediaTypes property of an image picker controller, the camera will only allow the user to take still photos, and the photo library and saved photos album will only display images.

Adding the ability to record video or choose a video from the disk is as simple as adding the constant string kUTTypeMovie to the mediaTypes array. However, not all devices support video through the **UIImagePickerController**. Just like the class method **isSourceTypeAvailable:** allows you to determine if the device has a camera, the **availableMediaTypesForSourceType:** method checks to see if that camera can capture video. To set up an image picker controller that can record video or take still images, you would write the following code:

```
UIImagePickerController *ipc = [[UIImagePickerController alloc] init];
NSArray *availableTypes = [UIImagePickerController
    availableMediaTypesForSourceType:UIImagePickerControllerSourceTypeCamera];
[ipc setMediaTypes:availableTypes];
[ipc setSourceType:UIImagePickerControllerSourceTypeCamera];
[ipc setDelegate:self];
```

Now when this image picker controller interface is presented to the user, there will be a switch that allows them to choose between the still image camera or the video recorder. If the user chooses to record a video, you need to handle that in the **UIImagePickerController** delegate method **imagePickerController:didFinishPickingMediaWithInfo:**.

When dealing with still images, the info dictionary that is passed as an argument contains the full image as a **UIImage** object. However, there is no "UIVideo" class. (Loading an entire video into memory at once would be tough to do with iOS device memory constraints.) Therefore, recorded video is written to disk in a temporary directory. When the user finalizes the video recording, **imagePickerController:didFinishPickingMediaWithInfo:** is sent to the image picker controller's delegate, and the path of the video on the disk is in the info dictionary. You can get the path like so:

```
- (void)imagePickerController:(UIImagePickerController *)picker
didFinishPickingMediaWithInfo:(NSDictionary *)info
{
    NSURL *mediaURL = [info objectForKey:UIImagePickerControllerMediaURL];
}
```

We will talk about the filesystem in Chapter 14, but what you should know now is that the temporary directory is not a safe place to store the video. It needs to be moved to another location.

```
- (void)imagePickerController:(UIImagePickerController *)picker
didFinishPickingMediaWithInfo:(NSDictionary *)info
{
    NSURL *mediaURL = [info objectForKey:UIImagePickerControllerMediaURL];
    if (mediaURL) {

        // Make sure this device supports videos in its photo album
        if (UIVideoAtPathIsCompatibleWithSavedPhotosAlbum([mediaURL path])) {

            // Save the video to the photos album
            UISaveVideoAtPathToSavedPhotosAlbum([mediaURL path], nil, nil, nil);
```

```
                // Remove the video from the temporary directory it was saved at
                [[NSFileManager defaultManager] removeItemAtPath:[mediaURL path]
                                                            error:nil];
        }
    }
}
```

That is really all there is to it. There is just one situation that requires some additional information: suppose you want to restrict the user to choosing *only* videos. Restricting the user to images is simple (leave mediaTypes as the default). Allowing the user to choose between images and videos is just as simple (pass the return value from **availableMediaTypesForSourceType:**). However, to allow video only, you have to jump through a few hoops. First, you must make sure the device supports video, and then you must set the mediaTypes property to an array containing the identifier for video only.

```
    NSArray *availableTypes = [UIImagePickerController
        availableMediaTypesForSourceType:UIImagePickerControllerSourceTypeCamera];

    if ([availableTypes containsObject:(NSString *)kUTTypeMovie])
        [ipc setMediaTypes:[NSArray arrayWithObject:(NSString *)kUTTypeMovie]];
```

Wondering why kUTTypeMovie is cast to an **NSString**? This constant is declared as:

```
    const CFStringRef kUTTypeMovie;
```

If you build this code, it will fail, and the compiler will complain that it has never heard of kUTTypeMovie. Oddly enough, both kUTTypeMovie and kUTTypeImage are declared and defined in another framework – MobileCoreServices. You have to explicitly add this framework and import its header file into your project to use these two constants.

13

UIPopoverController and Modal View Controllers

So far, you have seen four ways to show a view controller's view: setting it as the root view controller of the window, pushing it onto a **UINavigationController**'s stack, adding it to a **UITabBarController**, and presenting it modally.

In this chapter, we will look at **UIPopoverController** and more options for presenting modal view controllers. Some of these options are only available on the iPad, so we'll start by making Homepwner a *universal application* – an application that runs natively on the iPad as well as the iPhone and iPod touch.

Figure 13.1 Homepwner on the iPad

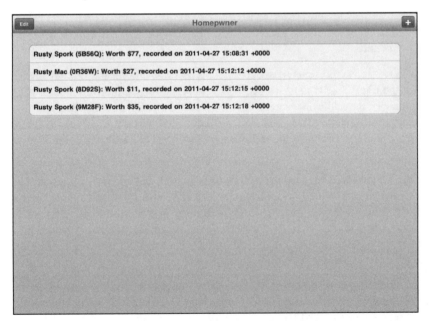

Universalizing Homepwner

Open Homepwner.xcodeproj and select the Homepwner project from the project navigator. Then select the Homepwner target in the editor area. In the Summary pane, change the Devices pop-up to Universal (Figure 13.2).

Figure 13.2   Universalizing Homepwner

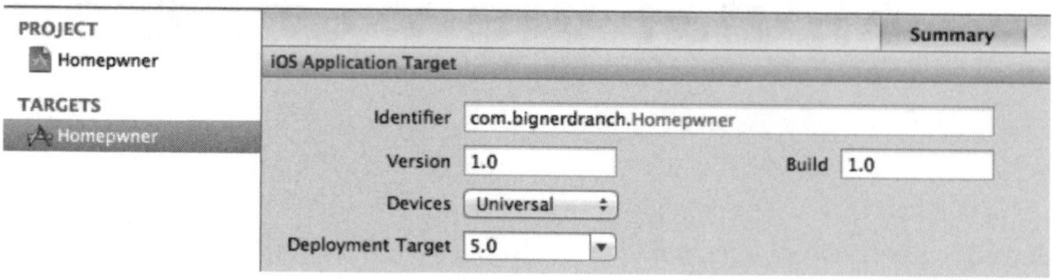

That was it. Homepwner now runs natively on the iPad. Click on the Scheme pop-up button next to the Run button. You'll see that there is now an iPad Simulator option. Select this option and build and run the application.

The **ItemsViewController** view looks great on the iPad, but if you select a row, you'll see that the **DetailViewController**'s interface could use some work. (Also, tapping the button to take a picture throws an exception. We'll fix this shortly.)

One way to improve the looks of the **DetailViewController**'s interface on the iPad is to change the autoresizing masks of the subviews in DetailViewController.xib so that when its view is resized to fit the iPad, all of the subviews are organized nicely. This is what you did when you universalized your HeavyRotation application.

Another way is to create two completely independent XIB files: one for the iPhone device family and the other for the iPad. This is most useful when you want to have a different interface on the iPad that takes advantage of the additional screen space. To do this, you name the iPad-specific XIB file the same as the iPhone version with an added ~ipad suffix, like DetailViewController~ipad.xib. Remember to recreate the entire view hierarchy and re-establish connections in the iPad version of the XIB file.

When you create separate XIB files for the two device families and use the ~ipad suffix, you do not need to write any extra code to load the appropriate XIB file. Every **UIViewController** has a nibName that you pass in the initializer message. (If you pass nil, the nibName is effectively the name of the class.) When a view controller goes to load its view, it loads the XIB file that matches its nibName. However, if the application is running on an iPad, it first checks for a matching XIB file suffixed with ~ipad. If there is one, it loads that XIB file instead.

At this point, we're not focusing on the appearance of the **DetailViewController**'s view, so we have a third option: leave it as it is. But let's do something about the blindingly white background. In **DetailViewController**'s **viewDidLoad** method, the background color of the view is set to be the **groupTableViewBackgroundColor** color. This color is not available on the iPad, which is why you get the all-white background instead. So when the application is running on an iPad, let's set the color to closely match the background color of **ItemsViewController**'s view.

Determining device family

First, we need to check what type of device the application is running on. The object to ask is the **UIDevice** singleton. You get this object by sending the class method **currentDevice** to the **UIDevice** class. Then you can check the value of its userInterfaceIdiom property. At this time, there are only two possible values: UIUserInterfaceIdiomPad (for an iPad) and UIUserInterfaceIdiomPhone (for an iPhone or an iPod touch).

In DetailViewController.m, modify **viewDidLoad**.

```
- (void)viewDidLoad
{
    [super viewDidLoad];
    [[self view] setBackgroundColor:[UIColor groupTableViewBackgroundColor]];

    UIColor *clr = nil;
    if ([[UIDevice currentDevice] userInterfaceIdiom] == UIUserInterfaceIdiomPad) {
        clr = [UIColor colorWithRed:0.875 green:0.88 blue:0.91 alpha:1];
    } else {
        clr = [UIColor groupTableViewBackgroundColor];
    }
    [[self view] setBackgroundColor:clr];
}
```

Build and run the application on the iPad simulator or on an iPad. Navigate to the **DetailViewController** and sigh in relief at the much nicer background color.

iPad users expect applications to work in all orientations, so add the following method to both ItemsViewController.m and DetailViewController.m:

```
- (BOOL)shouldAutorotateToInterfaceOrientation:(UIInterfaceOrientation)io
{
    if ([[UIDevice currentDevice] userInterfaceIdiom] == UIUserInterfaceIdiomPad) {
        return YES;
    } else {
        return (io == UIInterfaceOrientationPortrait);
    }
}
```

Build and run the application on both the iPhone and iPad (or their respective simulators). Notice that rotating on the iPhone does nothing and rotating on the iPad rotates the view of the view controller that is on the screen.

Now that Homepwner can run on the iPad, let's take advantage of some iPad-only ways to present view controllers, starting with **UIPopoverController**.

UIPopoverController

It is common for an application to present a view controller so that the user can make a choice about what the application should do next. For example, the **UIImagePickerController** shows the user a table of images to choose from.

On the iPhone and iPod touch, view controllers like this are presented modally and take up the entire screen. However, the iPad, having more screen real estate, offers another option: **UIPopoverController**.

A popover controller displays another view controller's view in a bordered window that floats above the rest of the application's interface. When you create a **UIPopoverController**, you set this other view controller as the popover controller's contentViewController.

In this chapter, you will present the **UIImagePickerController** in a **UIPopoverController** when the user taps the camera bar button item in the **DetailViewController**'s view.

Figure 13.3   UIPopoverController

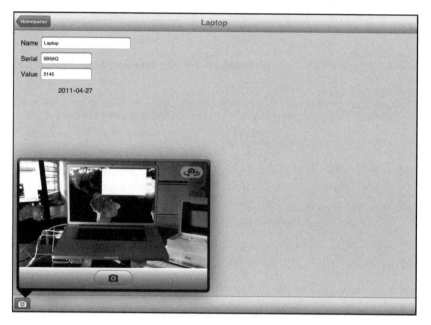

In DetailViewController.h, add an instance variable to hold the popover controller. Also, declare that **DetailViewController** conforms to the UIPopoverControllerDelegate protocol.

```
@interface DetailViewController : UIViewController
    <UINavigationControllerDelegate, UIImagePickerControllerDelegate,
     UITextFieldDelegate, UIPopoverControllerDelegate>
{
    __weak IBOutlet UITextField *nameField;
    __weak IBOutlet UITextField *serialNumberField;
    __weak IBOutlet UITextField *valueField;
    __weak IBOutlet UILabel *dateLabel;
    __weak IBOutlet UIImageView *imageView;

    UIPopoverController *imagePickerPopover;
}
```

In DetailViewController.m, add the following code to the end of **takePicture:**.

```
[imagePicker setDelegate:self];

[self presentViewController:imagePicker animated:YES completion:nil];

// Place image picker on the screen
```

```
        // Check for iPad device before instantiating the popover controller
        if ([[UIDevice currentDevice] userInterfaceIdiom] == UIUserInterfaceIdiomPad) {
            // Create a new popover controller that will display the imagePicker
            imagePickerPopover = [[UIPopoverController alloc]
                    initWithContentViewController:imagePicker];

            [imagePickerPopover setDelegate:self];

            // Display the popover controller; sender
            // is the camera bar button item
            [imagePickerPopover presentPopoverFromBarButtonItem:sender
                            permittedArrowDirections:UIPopoverArrowDirectionAny
                            animated:YES];
        } else {
            [self presentViewController:imagePicker animated:YES completion:nil];
        }
    }
```

Notice that we check for the device before creating the **UIPopoverController**. It is critical to do this. You can only instantiate **UIPopoverController**s on the iPad family of devices, and trying to create one on an iPhone will throw an exception.

Build and run the application on the iPad simulator or on an iPad. Navigate to the **DetailViewController** and tap the camera icon. The popover will appear and show the **UIImagePickerController**'s view. Select an image from the picker, and it will appear in **DetailViewController**'s view.

You can dismiss the popover controller by tapping anywhere else on the screen. When a popover is dismissed in this way, it sends the message **popoverControllerDidDismissPopover:** to its delegate. Implement this method in DetailViewController.m.

```
- (void)popoverControllerDidDismissPopover:(UIPopoverController *)popoverController
{
    NSLog(@"User dismissed popover");
    imagePickerPopover = nil;
}
```

Notice that you set imagePickerPopover to nil here to destroy the popover. You will create a new one each time the camera button is tapped.

The popover should also be dismissed when you select an image from the image picker. In DetailViewController.m, at the end of **imagePickerController:didFinishPickingMediaWithInfo:**, dismiss the popover when an image is selected.

```
    [imageView setImage:image];

    [self dismissViewControllerAnimated:YES completion:nil];

    if ([[UIDevice currentDevice] userInterfaceIdiom] == UIUserInterfaceIdiomPhone) {
        // If on the phone, the image picker is presented modally. Dismiss it.
        [self dismissViewControllerAnimated:YES completion:nil];
    } else {
        // If on the pad, the image picker is in the popover. Dismiss the popover.
        [imagePickerPopover dismissPopoverAnimated:YES];
        imagePickerPopover = nil;
    }
}
```

When you explicitly send the message **dismissPopoverAnimated:** to dismiss the popover controller, it does not send **popoverControllerDidDismissPopover:** to its delegate, so you must set imagePickerPopover to nil in **dismissPopoverAnimated:**.

There is a small bug to fix. If the **UIPopoverController** is visible and the user taps on the camera button again, the application will crash. This crash occurs because the **UIPopoverController** that is on the screen is destroyed when imagePickerPopover is set to point at the new **UIPopoverController** in **takePicture:**. You can ensure that the destroyed **UIPopoverController** is not visible and cannot be tapped by adding the following code to the top of **takePicture:** in DetailViewController.m.

```
- (IBAction)takePicture:(id)sender
{
    if ([imagePickerPopover isPopoverVisible]) {
        // If the popover is already up, get rid of it
        [imagePickerPopover dismissPopoverAnimated:YES];
        imagePickerPopover = nil;
        return;
    }

    UIImagePickerController *imagePicker =
            [[UIImagePickerController alloc] init];
```

Build and run the application. Tap the camera button to show the popover and then tap it again – the popover will disappear.

More Modal View Controllers

In this part of the chapter, you will update Homepwner to present the **DetailViewController** modally when the user creates a new **BNRItem**. When the user selects an existing **BNRItem**, the **DetailViewController** will be pushed onto the **UINavigationController**'s stack as before.

Figure 13.4   New item

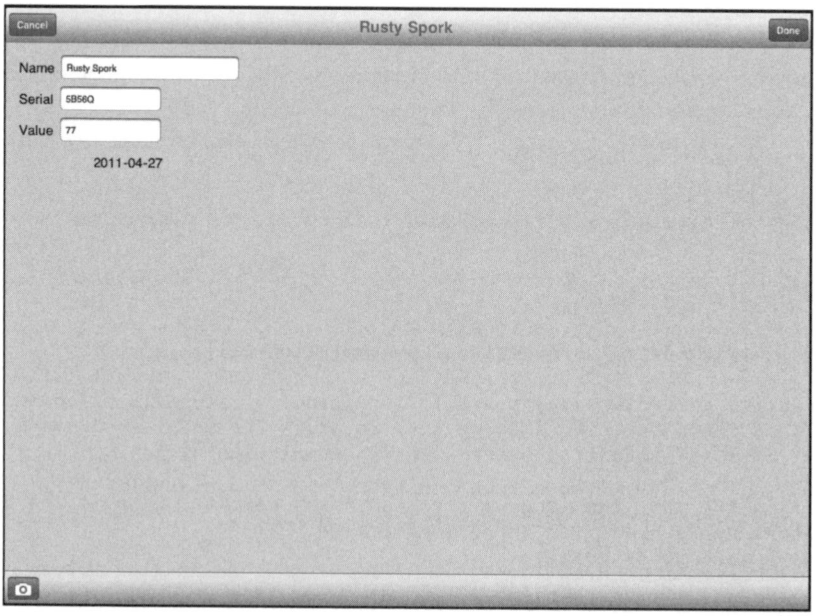

To implement this dual usage of **DetailViewController**, you will give it a new designated initializer, **initForNewItem:**. This initializer will check whether the instance is being used to create a new **BNRItem** or to show an existing one. Then it will configure the interface accordingly.

In DetailViewController.h, declare this initializer.

```
}
- (id)initForNewItem:(BOOL)isNew;

@property (nonatomic, strong) BNRItem *item;
```

If the **DetailViewController** is being used to create a new **BNRItem**, we want it to show a Done button and a Cancel button on its navigation item. Implement this method in DetailViewController.m.

```
- (id)initForNewItem:(BOOL)isNew
{
    self = [super initWithNibName:@"DetailViewController" bundle:nil];

    if (self) {
        if (isNew) {
            UIBarButtonItem *doneItem = [[UIBarButtonItem alloc]
                    initWithBarButtonSystemItem:UIBarButtonSystemItemDone
                                         target:self
                                         action:@selector(save:)];
            [[self navigationItem] setRightBarButtonItem:doneItem];

            UIBarButtonItem *cancelItem = [[UIBarButtonItem alloc]
                    initWithBarButtonSystemItem:UIBarButtonSystemItemCancel
                                         target:self
                                         action:@selector(cancel:)];
            [[self navigationItem] setLeftBarButtonItem:cancelItem];
        }
    }

    return self;
}
```

In the past, when you've changed the designated initializer of a class from its superclass's designated initializer, you've overridden the superclass's initializer to call the new one. In this case, you're just going to make it illegal to use the superclass's designated initializer by throwing an exception when anyone calls it.

In DetailViewController.m, override **UIViewController**'s designated initializer.

```
- (id)initWithNibName:(NSString *)nibName bundle:(NSBundle *)bundle
{
    @throw [NSException exceptionWithName:@"Wrong initializer"
                                  reason:@"Use initForNewItem:"
                                userInfo:nil];
    return nil;
}
```

This code creates an instance of **NSException** with a name and a reason and then throws the exception. This halts the application and shows the exception in the console.

To confirm that this exception will be thrown, let's return to where this **initWithNibName:bundle:** method is currently called – the **tableView:didSelectRowAtIndexPath:** method of

ItemsViewController. In this method, **ItemsViewController** creates an instance of **DetailViewController** and sends it the message **init**, which eventually calls **initWithNibName:bundle:**. Therefore, selecting a row in the table view will result in the "Wrong initializer" exception being thrown.

Build and run the application and tap a row. You application will halt, and you will see an exception in the console. Notice that the name and the reason are part of the console message.

You don't want to see this exception again, so in ItemsViewController.m, update **tableView:didSelectRowAtIndexPath:** to use the new initializer.

```
- (void)tableView:(UITableView *)tableView
    didSelectRowAtIndexPath:(NSIndexPath *)indexPath
{
    DetailViewController *detailViewController =
            [[DetailViewController alloc] init];

    DetailViewController *detailViewController =
        [[DetailViewController alloc] initForNewItem:NO];

    NSArray *items = [[BNRItemStore sharedStore] allItems];
```

Build and run the application again. Nothing new and exciting will happen, but your application will no longer crash when you select a row in the table.

Now that we've got our new initializer in place, let's change what happens when the user adds a new item.

In ItemsViewController.m, edit the **addNewItem:** method to create an instance of **DetailViewController** in a **UINavigationController** and present the navigation controller modally.

```
- (IBAction)addNewItem:(id)sender
{
    BNRItem *newItem = [[BNRItemStore sharedStore] createItem];
    int lastRow = [[[BNRItemStore sharedStore] allItems] indexOfObject:newItem];

    NSIndexPath *ip = [NSIndexPath indexPathForRow:lastRow inSection:0];

    [[self tableView] insertRowsAtIndexPaths:[NSArray arrayWithObject:ip]
                        withRowAnimation:UITableViewRowAnimationTop];

    DetailViewController *detailViewController =
            [[DetailViewController alloc] initForNewItem:YES];

    [detailViewController setItem:newItem];

    UINavigationController *navController = [[UINavigationController alloc]
                                initWithRootViewController:detailViewController];

    [self presentViewController:navController animated:YES completion:nil];
}
```

Build and run the application and tap the New button to create a new item. An instance of **DetailViewController** will slide up from the bottom of the screen with a Done button and a Cancel button on its navigation item. (Tapping these buttons, of course, will throw an exception since you haven't implemented the action methods yet.)

Dismissing modal view controllers

To dismiss a modally-presented view controller, you must send the message
dismissViewControllerAnimated:completion: to the view controller that presented it. You've done this before with **UIImagePickerController** – the **DetailViewController** presented it, and when the image picker told the **DetailViewController** it was done, the **DetailViewController** dismissed it.

Now, we have a slightly different situation. When a new item is created, the **ItemsViewController** presents the **DetailViewController** modally. The **DetailViewController** has two buttons on its navigationItem that will dismiss it when tapped: Cancel and Done. There is a problem here: the action messages for these buttons are sent to the **DetailViewController**, but it is the responsibility of the **ItemsViewController** to do the dismissing. The **DetailViewController** needs a way to tell the view controller that presented it, "Hey, I'm done, you can dismiss me now."

Fortunately, every **UIViewController** has a presentingViewController property that points to the view controller that presented it. The **DetailViewController** will grab a pointer to its presentingViewController and send it the message **dismissViewControllerAnimated:completion:**. Implement the action method for the Save button in DetailViewController.m.

```
- (void)save:(id)sender
{
    [[self presentingViewController] dismissViewControllerAnimated:YES
                                                       completion:nil];
}
```

The Cancel button has a little bit more going on. When the user taps the button on the **ItemsViewController** to add a new item to the list, a new instance of **BNRItem** is created, added to the store, and then the **DetailViewController** slides up to edit this new item. If the user cancels the item's creation, then that **BNRItem** needs to be removed from the store. At the top of DetailViewController.m, import the header for **BNRItemStore**.

```
#import "DetailViewController.h"
#import "BNRItem.h"
#import "BNRImageStore.h"
#import "BNRItemStore.h"

@implementation DetailViewController
```

Now implement the action method for the Cancel button in DetailViewController.m.

```
- (void)cancel:(id)sender
{
    // If the user cancelled, then remove the BNRItem from the store
    [[BNRItemStore sharedStore] removeItem:item];

    [[self presentingViewController] dismissViewControllerAnimated:YES
                                                       completion:nil];
}
```

Build and run the application. Create a new item and tap the Cancel button. The instance of **DetailViewController** will slide off the screen, and nothing will be added to the table view. Then, create a new item and tap the Done button. The **DetailViewController** will slide off the screen, and your new **BNRItem** will appear in the table view.

269

Note that the **cancel:** and **save:** methods are not declared anywhere. This is okay. Remember that declaring a method lets the compiler know that the method exists. For most methods, the compiler will give you an error when you try to send a message whose method has not been declared. However, when setting the action of a **UIBarButtonItem** or **UIControl**, the compiler does not validate the action message because it isn't being called at that point. Instead, the message is validated at runtime when it is actually sent. If the method is defined, all goes well; if not, you get an unrecognized selector exception.

There is one final note to make. We've said that the **ItemsViewController** presents the **DetailViewController** modally. This is true in spirit, but the actual relationships are more complicated than that. The **DetailViewController**'s presentingViewController is really the **UINavigationController** that has the **ItemsViewController** on its stack. You can tell this the case because when the **DetailViewController** is presented modally, it covers up the navigation bar. If the **ItemsViewController** was handling the modal presentation, then the **DetailViewController**'s view would fit within the view of the **ItemsViewController**, and the navigation bar would not be obscured.

For the purposes of presenting and dismissing modal view controllers, this doesn't matter; the modal view controller doesn't care who its presentingViewController is as long as it can send it a message and get dismissed. But, we shouldn't lie to you (sorry about that), so we'll go into the fascinating details of view controller relationships at the end of this chapter.

Modal view controller styles

On the iPhone or iPod touch, a modal view controller takes over the entire screen. This is the default behavior and the only possibility on these devices. On the iPad, you have two additional options: a form sheet style and a page sheet style. You can change the presentation of the modal view controller by setting its modalPresentationStyle property to a pre-defined constant – UIModalPresentationFormSheet or UIModalPresentationPageSheet.

The form sheet style shows the modal view controller's view in a rectangle in the center of the iPad's screen and dims out the presenting view controller's view (Figure 13.5).

Figure 13.5   An example of the form sheet style

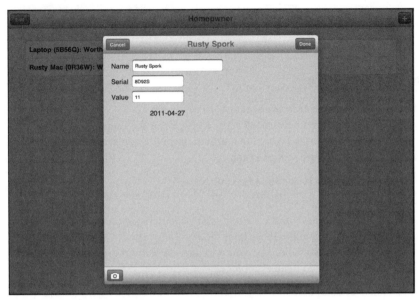

The page sheet style is the same as the default full-screen style in portrait mode. In landscape mode, it keeps its width the same as in portrait mode and dims the left and right edges of the presenting view controller's view that stick out behind it.

In `ItemsViewController.m`, modify the **addNewItem:** method to change the presentation style of the **UINavigationController** that is being presented.

```
UINavigationController *navController = [[UINavigationController alloc]
                         initWithRootViewController:detailViewController];

[navController setModalPresentationStyle:UIModalPresentationFormSheet];

[self presentViewController:navController animated:YES completion:nil];
```

Notice that we change the presentation style of the **UINavigationController**, not the **DetailViewController**, since it is the one that is being presented modally.

Build and run the application on the iPad simulator or on an iPad. Tap the button to add a new item and watch the modal view controller slide onto the screen. Add some item details and then tap the Done button. The table view reappears, but your new **BNRItem** isn't there. What happened?

Before you changed its presentation style, the modal view controller took up the entire screen, which caused the view of the **ItemsViewController** to disappear. When the modal view controller was dismissed, the **ItemsViewController** was sent the messages **viewWillAppear:** and **viewDidAppear:** and took this opportunity to reload its table to catch any updates to the **BNRItemStore**.

With the new presentation style, the **ItemsViewController**'s view doesn't disappear when it presents the view controller. So it isn't sent the re-appearing messages when the modal view controller is dismissed, and it doesn't get the chance to reload its table view.

We have to find another opportunity to reload the data. The code for the **ItemsViewController** to reload its table view is simple. It looks like this:

```
[[self tableview] reloadData];
```

What we need to do is to package up this code and have it executed right when the modal view controller is dismissed. Fortunately, there is a built-in mechanism in **dismissViewControllerAnimated:completion:** that we can use to accomplish this.

Completion blocks

In both **dismissViewControllerAnimated:completion:** and **presentViewController:animated:completion:**, we've been passing `nil` as the last argument. Take a look at the type of that argument in the declaration for **dismissViewControllerAnimated:completion:**.

```
- (void)dismissViewControllerAnimated:(BOOL)flag
                           completion:(void (^)(void))completion;
```

Looks strange, huh? This method expects a *block* as an argument, and passing a block here is the solution to our problem. So we need to talk about blocks. However, the concepts and syntax of blocks can take a while to get used to, so we're just going to introduce them briefly. We will return to blocks in Chapter 27, which is entirely dedicated to blocks.

A block is both a chunk of code and an object at the same time. Blocks are a lot like C functions, but they are defined inside another method. Once defined, you can have a variable point at that block – just like a variable points at an object. Because you have this variable, you can pass a pointer to a block as an argument to a method or keep it as an instance variable – just like you can pass a pointer to an object as an argument to a method or keep a pointer to an object as an instance variable.

Here's the important part to understand right now: We can put the code to reload the table view into a block and pass it to **dismissViewControllerAnimated:completion:**. Then, that code will be executed right after the modal view controller is dismissed.

In DetailViewController.h, add a new property for a pointer to a block.

@property (nonatomic, copy) void (^dismissBlock)(void);

This says **DetailViewController** has a property named `dismissBlock` that points to a block. Like a C function, a block has a return value and a list of arguments. These function-like characteristics are included in the declaration of a block. This particular block returns `void` and takes no arguments.

Synthesize this property in DetailViewController.m.

```
@implementation DetailViewController
@synthesize dismissBlock;
```

We can't create the block itself in **DetailViewController**, though. We have to create it in **ItemsViewController** because the **ItemsViewController** is the only object that knows about its `tableView`.

In ItemsViewController.m, create a block that reloads the **ItemsViewController**'s table and pass the block to the **DetailViewController**. Do this in the **addNewItem:** method in ItemsViewController.m.

```
- (IBAction)addNewItem:(id)sender
{
    // Create a new BNRItem and add it to the store
    BNRItem *newItem = [[BNRItemStore sharedStore] createItem];
```

```
DetailViewController *detailViewController =
        [[DetailViewController alloc] initForNewItem:YES];

[detailViewController setItem:newItem];

[detailViewController setDismissBlock:^{
    [[self tableView] reloadData];
}];

UINavigationController *navController = [[UINavigationController alloc]
                            initWithRootViewController:detailViewController];
```

Now when the user taps a button to add a new item, a block that reloads the **ItemsViewController**'s table is created and set as the dismissBlock of the **DetailViewController**. The **DetailViewController** will hold on to this block until the **DetailViewController** needs to be dismissed.

At that point, the **DetailViewController** will pass this block to **dismissViewControllerAnimated:completion:**. In DetailViewController.m, modify the implementations of **save:** and **cancel:** to send the message **dismissViewControllerAnimated:completion:** with dismissBlock as an argument.

```
- (IBAction)save:(id)sender
{
    [[self presentingViewController] dismissViewControllerAnimated:YES
                                                      completion:nil];
    [[self presentingViewController] dismissViewControllerAnimated:YES
                                            completion:dismissBlock];
}

- (IBAction)cancel:(id)sender
{
    [[BNRItemStore sharedStore] removeItem:item];

    [[self presentingViewController] dismissViewControllerAnimated:YES
                                                      completion:nil];
    [[self presentingViewController] dismissViewControllerAnimated:YES
                                            completion:dismissBlock];
}
```

Build and run the application. Tap the button to create a new item and then tap Done. The new **BNRItem** will appear in the table.

Once again, don't worry if the syntax or the general idea of blocks doesn't make sense at this point. Hold on until Chapter 27, and we will hit all the gory details there.

Modal view controller transitions

In addition to changing the presentation style of a modal view controller, you can change the animation that places it on screen. Like presentation styles, there is a view controller property (modalTransitionStyle) that you can set with a pre-defined constant. By default, the animation will slide the modal view controller up from the bottom of the screen. You can also have the view controller fade in, flip in, or appear underneath a page curl (like in the Maps application).

In `ItemsViewController.m`, update the **addNewItem:** method to use a different transition.

```
[navController setModalPresentationStyle:UIModalPresentationFormSheet];
[navController setModalTransitionStyle:UIModalTransitionStyleFlipHorizontal];

[self presentViewController:navController animated:YES completion:nil];
```

Build and run the application and notice the change in animation. Try out some of the other options, but make sure to read the fine print in the documentation. For instance, you can't use the page curl transition unless the presentation style is full screen. Also, note that these transitions will still work if you switch back to deploying on an iPhone. The presentation style, however, will always be full screen.

Bronze Challenge: Universalizing Whereami

Go back to Chapter 5 and universalize Whereami. Make sure its interface appears just right on both the iPad and iPhone.

Silver Challenge: Peeling Away the Layers

Have the **DetailViewController** be presented with the UIModalTransitionStylePartialCurl style when creating a new item.

Gold Challenge: Popover Appearance

You can change the appearance of a **UIPopoverController**. Do this for the popover that presents the **UIImagePickerController**. (Hint: check out the popoverBackgroundViewClass property in **UIPopoverController**.)

For the More Curious: View Controller Relationships

The relationships between view controllers are important for understanding where and how a view controller's view appears on the screen. Overall, there are two different types of relationships between view controllers: *parent-child* relationships and *presenting-presenter* relationships. Let's look at each one individually.

Parent-child relationships

Parent-child relationships are formed when using *view controller containers*. Examples of view controller containers are **UINavigationController**, **UITabBarController**, and **UISplitViewController** (which you will see in Chapter 26). You can identify a view controller container because it has a viewControllers property that is an array of the view controllers it contains.

A view controller container is always a subclass of **UIViewController** and thus has a view. The behavior of a view controller container is that it adds the views of its viewControllers as subviews of its own view. A container has its own built-in interface, too. For example, a **UINavigationController**'s view shows a navigation bar and the view of its topViewController.

View controllers in a parent-child relationship form a *family*. So, a **UINavigationController** and its viewControllers are in the same family. A family can have multiple levels. For example, imagine a situation where a **UITabBarController** contains a **UINavigationController** that contains a **UIViewController**. These three view controllers are in the same family (Figure 13.6). The container classes have access to their children through the viewControllers array, and the children have access to their ancestors through four properties of **UIViewController**.

Figure 13.6   A view controller family

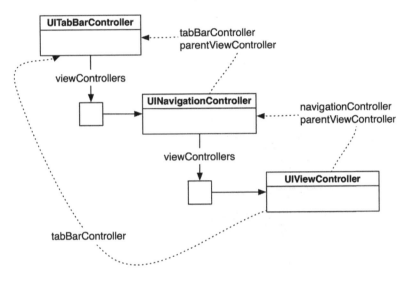

The first three ancestor-accessing properties of **UIViewController** are navigationController, tabBarController, and splitViewController. When a view controller is sent one of these messages, it starts traversing the family tree until it finds the appropriate type of view controller container. If there is no ancestor of the appropriate type, these methods return nil.

Additionally, every **UIViewController** has a parentViewController property. This property holds the closest view controller ancestor in the family. Thus, it could return a **UINavigationController**, **UITabBarController**, or a **UISplitViewController** depending on the makeup of the family tree.

Presenting-presenter relationships

The other kind of relationship is a presenting-presenter relationship, which occurs when a view controller is presented modally. When a view controller is presented modally, its view is added *on top of* the view controller's view that presented it. This is different than a view controller container, which intentionally keeps a spot open on its interface to swap in the views of the view controllers it contains. Any **UIViewController** can present another view controller modally.

Figure 13.7   Presenting-presenter relationship

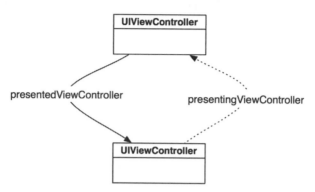

There are two built-in properties for managing the relationship between presenter and presentee. A modally-presented view controller's `presentingViewController` will point back to the view controller that presented it, while the presenter will keep a pointer to the presentee in its `presentedViewController` property (Figure 13.7).

Inter-family relationships

A presented view controller and its presenter are *not* in the same view controller family. Instead, the presented view controller has its own family. Sometimes, this family is just one **UIViewController**; other times, this family is made up of multiple view controllers.

Understanding the difference in families will help you understand the values of properties like `presentedViewController` and `navigationController`. Consider the view controllers in Figure 13.8. There are two families, each with multiple view controllers. This diagram shows the values of the view controller relationship properties.

Figure 13.8   A view controller hierarchy

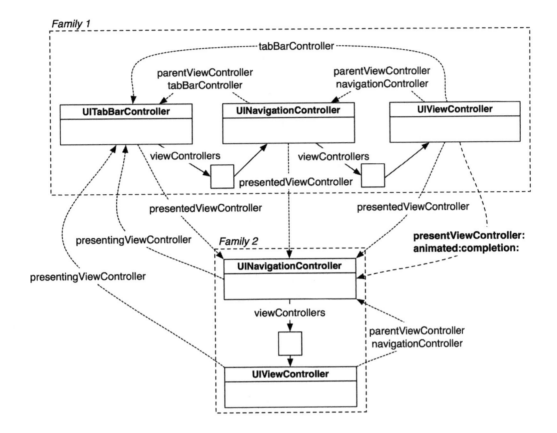

First, notice that the properties for parent-child relationships can never cross over family boundaries. Thus, sending **tabBarController** to a view controller in Family 2 will not return the **UITabBarController** in Family 1. Likewise, sending **navigationController** to the view controller in Family 2 returns its **UINavigationController** parent in Family 2 and not the **UINavigationController** in Family 1.

Perhaps the oddest view controller relationships are the ones between families. When a view controller is presented modally, the actual presenter is the oldest member of the presenting family. For example, in Figure 13.8, the **UITabBarController** is the presentingViewController for the view controllers in Family 2. It doesn't matter which view controller in Family 1 was sent **presentViewController:animated:completion:**, the **UITabBarController** is always the presenter.

This behavior explains why the **DetailViewController** obscures the **UINavigationBar** when presented modally but not when presented normally in the **UINavigationController**'s stack. Even though the **ItemsViewController** is told to do the modal presenting, its oldest ancestor, the **UINavigationController**, actually carries out the task. The **DetailViewController** is put on top of the **UINavigationController**'s view and thus obscures the **UINavigationBar**.

Notice also that the presentingViewController and presentedViewController are valid for every view controller in each family and always point to the oldest ancestor in the other family.

You can actually override this oldest-ancestor behavior (but only on the iPad). By doing so, you can specify where the views of the presented view controller family appear on the screen. For example, you could present the **DetailViewController** and its navigationController so that it only obscures the **UITableView** but not the **UINavigationBar**.

Every **UIViewController** has a definesPresentationContext property for this purpose. By default, this property is NO, which means the view controller will always pass presentation off to its next ancestor, until there are no more ancestors left. Setting this property to YES interrupts the search for the oldest ancestor, allowing a view controller to present the modal view controller in its own view (Figure 13.9). Additionally, you must set the modalPresentationStyle for the presented view controller to UIModalPresentationCurrentContext.

Figure 13.9   Presentation context

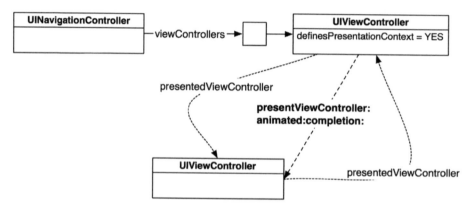

You can test this out by changing the code in ItemsViewController.m's **addNewItem:** method.

```
UINavigationController *navController = [[UINavigationController alloc]
                              initWithRootViewController:detailViewController];

[navController setModalPresentationStyle:UIModalPresentationFormSheet];
[navController setModalPresentationStyle:UIModalPresentationCurrentContext];
[self setDefinesPresentationContext:YES];

[navController setModalTransitionStyle:UIModalTransitionStyleFlipHorizontal];

    [self presentViewController:navController animated:YES completion:nil];
}
```

After building and running on the iPad, tap the + icon. Notice that the **DetailViewController** does not obscure the **UINavigationBar**. Make sure you undo this code before moving on to the next chapter.

14

Saving, Loading, and Application States

There are many ways to save and load data in an iOS application. This chapter will take you through some of the most common mechanisms as well as the concepts you need to understand to write to or read from the filesystem on iOS.

Archiving

Any iOS application is really doing one thing: providing an interface for a user to manipulate data. Every object in an application has a role in this process. Model objects, as you know, are responsible for holding on to the data that the user manipulates. View objects simply reflect that data, and controllers are responsible for what is going on while the application is running. Therefore, when talking about saving and loading data, we are almost always talking about saving and loading model objects.

In Homepwner, the model objects that a user manipulates are instances of **BNRItem**. Homepwner would actually be a useful application if instances of **BNRItem** persisted between runs of the application, and in this chapter, we will use *archiving* to save and load **BNRItem**s.

Archiving is one of the most common ways of persisting model objects on iOS. Archiving an object involves recording all of its instance variables and saving them to the filesystem. Unarchiving an object loads the data from the filesystem and creates objects from that record.

Classes whose instances need to be archived and unarchived must conform to the NSCoding protocol and implement its two required methods, **encodeWithCoder:** and **initWithCoder:**.

```
@protocol NSCoding

- (void)encodeWithCoder:(NSCoder *)aCoder;
- (id)initWithCoder:(NSCoder *)aDecoder;

@end
```

Make **BNRItem** conform to NSCoding. Open Homepwner.xcodeproj and add this protocol declaration in BNRItem.h.

```
@interface BNRItem : NSObject <NSCoding>
```

Now we need to implement the required methods. Let's start with **encodeWithCoder:**. When a **BNRItem** is sent the message **encodeWithCoder:**, it will encode all of its instance variables into the **NSCoder** object that is passed as an argument. You can think of this **NSCoder** object as a container for data that is responsible for organizing that data and writing it to the filesystem. It organizes the data in key-value pairs.

In BNRItem.m, implement **encodeWithCoder:** to add the instance variables to the container.

```
- (void)encodeWithCoder:(NSCoder *)aCoder
{
    [aCoder encodeObject:itemName forKey:@"itemName"];
    [aCoder encodeObject:serialNumber forKey:@"serialNumber"];
    [aCoder encodeObject:dateCreated forKey:@"dateCreated"];
    [aCoder encodeObject:imageKey forKey:@"imageKey"];

    [aCoder encodeInt:valueInDollars forKey:@"valueInDollars"];
}
```

Notice that pointers to objects are encoded with **encodeObject:forKey:**, but valueInDollars is encoded with **encodeInt:forKey:**. Check the documentation for **NSCoder** to see all of the types you can encode. Regardless of the type of the encoded value, there is always a key, which is a string that identifies which instance variable is being encoded. By convention, this key is the name of the instance variable being encoded.

When an object is encoded, that object is sent **encodeWithCoder:**. When an object is sent **encodeWithCoder:**, it encodes its instance variables in the same way – by sending them **encodeWithCoder:** (Figure 14.1). Thus, encoding an object is a recursive process where objects encode other objects.

Figure 14.1   Encoding an object

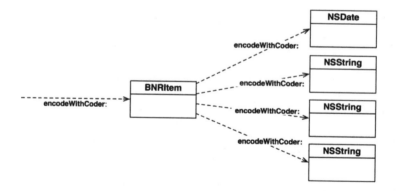

To be encoded, these objects must also conform to NSCoding. Check out the documentation for **NSString** and **NSDate**: they are NSCoding compliant.

The purpose of the key used when encoding is to retrieve the encoded value when this **BNRItem** is loaded from the filesystem later. Objects being loaded from an archive are sent the message **initWithCoder:**. This method should grab all of the objects that were encoded in **encodeWithCoder:** and assign them to the appropriate instance variable. Implement this method in BNRItem.m.

```
- (id)initWithCoder:(NSCoder *)aDecoder
{
```

```
    self = [super init];
    if (self) {
        [self setItemName:[aDecoder decodeObjectForKey:@"itemName"]];
        [self setSerialNumber:[aDecoder decodeObjectForKey:@"serialNumber"]];
        [self setImageKey:[aDecoder decodeObjectForKey:@"imageKey"]];

        [self setValueInDollars:[aDecoder decodeIntForKey:@"valueInDollars"]];

        dateCreated = [aDecoder decodeObjectForKey:@"dateCreated"];
    }
    return self;
}
```

Notice that this method has an **NSCoder** argument, too. In **initWithCoder:**, the **NSCoder** is full of data to be consumed by the **BNRItem** being initialized. Also notice that you sent **decodeObjectForKey:** to the container to get objects back and **decodeIntForKey:** to get the valueInDollars.

In Chapter 2, we talked about the initializer chain and designated initializers. The **initWithCoder:** method isn't part of this design pattern; you will keep **BNRItem**'s designated initializer the same, and **initWithCoder:** will not call it.

(By the way, archiving is how XIB files are created. **UIView** conforms to NSCoding. Instances of **UIView** are created when you drag them onto the canvas area. When the XIB file is saved, these views are archived into the XIB file. When your application launches, it unarchives the views from the XIB file. There are some minor differences between a XIB file and a standard archive, but overall, it's the same process.)

BNRItems are now NSCoding compliant and can be saved to and loaded from the filesystem using archiving. You can build the application to make sure there are no syntax errors, but, we still need a way to kick off the saving and loading. We also need a place on the filesystem to store the saved **BNRItem**s.

Application Sandbox

Every iOS application has its own *application sandbox*. An application sandbox is a directory on the filesystem that is barricaded from the rest of the filesystem. Your application must stay in its sandbox, and no other application can access your sandbox.

Figure 14.2   Application sandbox

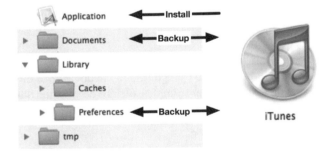

The application sandbox contains a number of directories:

application bundle	This directory contains all the resources and the executable. It is read-only.
Library/Preferences/	This directory is where any preferences are stored and where the Settings application looks for application preferences. Library/Preferences is handled automatically by the class **NSUserDefaults** (which you will learn about in Chapter 18) and is backed up when the device is synchronized with iTunes or iCloud. (We'll see how to synchronize with iCloud in Chapter 30.)
tmp/	This directory is where you write data that you will use temporarily during an application's runtime. You should remove files from this directory when done with them, and the operating system may purge them while your application is not running. It does not get backed up when the device is synchronized with iTunes or iCloud. To get the path to the tmp directory in the application sandbox, you can use the convenience function **NSTemporaryDirectory**.
Documents/	This directory is where you write data that the application generates during runtime and that you want to persist between runs of the application. It is backed up when the device is synchronized with iTunes or iCloud. If something goes wrong with the device, files in this directory can be restored from iTunes or iCloud. For example, in a game application, the saved game files would be stored here.
Library/Caches/	This directory is where you write data that the application generates during runtime and that you want to persist between runs of the application. However, unlike the Documents directory, it does not get backed up when the device is synchronized with iTunes or iCloud. A major reason for not backing up cached data is that the data can be very large and extend the time it takes to synchronize your device. Data stored somewhere else – like a web server – can be placed in this directory. If the user needs to restore the device, this data can be downloaded from the web server again.

Constructing a file path

The **BNRItem**s from Homepwner will be saved to a single file in the Documents directory. The **BNRItemStore** will handle writing to and reading from that file. To do this, the **BNRItemStore** needs to construct a path to this file.

Open BNRItemStore.h and declare a new method.

```
- (NSString *)itemArchivePath;
```

Implement this method in BNRItemStore.m.

```
- (NSString *)itemArchivePath
{
    NSArray *documentDirectories =
        NSSearchPathForDirectoriesInDomains(NSDocumentDirectory,
                                            NSUserDomainMask, YES);

    // Get one and only document directory from that list
    NSString *documentDirectory = [documentDirectories objectAtIndex:0];

    return [documentDirectory stringByAppendingPathComponent:@"items.archive"];
}
```

You can build to check for syntax errors.

The function **NSSearchPathForDirectoriesInDomains** searches the filesystem for a path that meets the criteria given by the arguments. On iOS, the last two arguments are always the same. (This function is borrowed from Mac OS X, where there are significantly more options.) The first argument is a constant that specifies the directory in the sandbox you want the path to. For example, searching for NSCachesDirectory will return the Caches directory in the application's sandbox.

You can search the documentation for one of the constants you already know – like NSDocumentDirectory – to locate the other options. Remember that these constants are shared by iOS and Mac OS X, so not all of them will work on iOS.

The return value of **NSSearchPathForDirectoriesInDomains** is an array of strings. It is an array of strings because, on Mac OS X, there may be multiple paths that meet the search criteria. On iOS, however, there will only be one (if the directory you searched for is an appropriate sandbox directory). Therefore, the name of the archive file is appended to the first and only path in the array. This will be where **BNRItem**s live.

NSKeyedArchiver and NSKeyedUnarchiver

You now have a place to save data on the filesystem and a model object that can be saved to the filesystem. The final two questions we must answer are: how do we kick off the saving and loading processes and when do we do it? To save **BNRItem**s, you will use the class **NSKeyedArchiver** when the application "exits."

In BNRItemStore.h, declare a new method.

```
- (BOOL)saveChanges;
```

Implement this method in BNRItemStore.m to send the message **archiveRootObject:toFile:** to the **NSKeyedArchiver** class.

```
- (BOOL)saveChanges
{
    // returns success or failure
    NSString *path = [self itemArchivePath];

    return [NSKeyedArchiver archiveRootObject:allItems
                                       toFile:path];
}
```

The **archiveRootObject:toFile:** method takes care of saving every single **BNRItem** in allItems to the **itemArchivePath**. Yes, it is that simple. Here's how it works.

The method begins by creating an instance of **NSKeyedArchiver**. Then, it sends the message **encodeWithCoder:** to the root object (in our case, allItems). **NSKeyedArchiver** is a subclass of **NSCoder**, so we can pass this new instance of **NSKeyedArchiver** as the argument to **encodeWithCoder:**.

The allItems array then sends **encodeWithCoder:** to all of the objects it contains, passing the same **NSKeyedArchiver**. The contents of this array – a bunch of **BNRItem**s – then encode their instance variables into the very same **NSKeyedArchiver** (Figure 14.3). Once all of these objects have been encoded, the **NSKeyedArchiver** writes the data it collected to the path.

Figure 14.3   Archiving an array

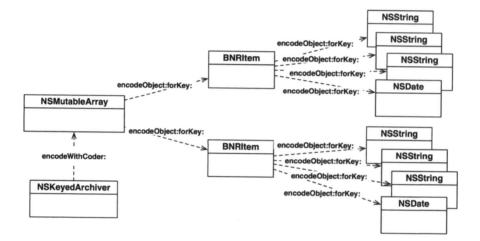

When the user presses the home button on the device, the message **applicationDidEnterBackground:** is sent to the **HomepwnerAppDelegate**. That's when we want to send **saveChanges** to the **BNRItemStore**.

In HomepwnerAppDelegate.m, implement **applicationDidEnterBackground:** to kick off saving the **BNRItem**s. Make sure to import the header file for **BNRItemStore** at the top of this file.

```
#import "BNRItemStore.h"

@implementation HomepwnerAppDelegate

- (void)applicationDidEnterBackground:(UIApplication *)application
{
    BOOL success = [[BNRItemStore sharedStore] saveChanges];
    if (success) {
        NSLog(@"Saved all of the BNRItems");
    } else {
        NSLog(@"Could not save any of the BNRItems");
    }
}
```

(This method may have already been implemented by the template. If so, make sure to add code to the existing method instead of writing a brand new one.)

Build and run the application on the simulator. Create a few **BNRItem**s. Then, click the home button to leave the application. Check the console, and you should see that all of the **BNRItem**s were saved. (If they were not, double-check the NSCoding implementations in BNRItem.m.)

While you cannot load these **BNRItem**s back into the application yet, you can still verify that *something* was saved. In Finder, hit Command-Shift-G. Then, type in ~/Library/Application Support/iPhone Simulator and hit return. This is where all of the applications and their sandboxes are stored for the simulator.

Open the directory 5.0 (or, if you are working with another version of iOS, select that directory). Open Applications to see the list of every application that has run on your simulator using iOS 5.0. Unfortunately, these applications have really unhelpful names. You have to dig into each directory to find the one that contains Homepwner.

Figure 14.4   Homepwner's sandbox

In Homepwner's directory, navigate into the Documents directory (Figure 14.4). You will see the items.archive file. Here's a tip: make an alias to the iPhone Simulator directory somewhere convenient to make it easy to check the sandboxes of your applications.

Now let's turn to loading these files. To load **BNRItem**s when the application launches, you will use the class **NSKeyedUnarchiver** when the **BNRItemStore** is created. In BNRItemStore.m, add the following code to **init**.

```
- (id)init
{
    self = [super init];
    if (self) {
        allItems = [[NSMutableArray alloc] init];

        NSString *path = [self itemArchivePath];
        allItems = [NSKeyedUnarchiver unarchiveObjectWithFile:path];

        // If the array hadn't been saved previously, create a new empty one
        if (!allItems)
            allItems = [[NSMutableArray alloc] init];
    }
    return self;
}
```

The **unarchiveObjectWithFile:** method will create an instance of **NSKeyedUnarchiver** and load the archive located at the **itemArchivePath** into that instance. The **NSKeyedUnarchiver** will then inspect the type of the root object in the archive and create an instance of that type. In this case, the type will be an **NSMutableArray** because you created this archive with a root object of this type. (If the root object was a **BNRItem** instead, **unarchiveObjectWithFile:** would return an instance of **BNRItem**.)

The newly allocated **NSMutableArray** is then sent **initWithCoder:** and, as you may have guessed, the **NSKeyedUnarchiver** is passed as the argument. The array starts decoding its contents (instances of **BNRItem**) from the **NSKeyedUnarchiver** and sends each of these objects the message **initWithCoder:** passing the same **NSKeyedUnarchiver**.

The clever part about **NSKeyedUnarchiver** is that it knows which object is currently decoding its instance variables. Thus, you don't need to uniquely identify each object in an archive. You only need to identify the relationship between an object and its instance variables, and this relationship is already identified by the key used to encode and decode the object in the NSCoding protocol methods.

You can now build and run the application. Any **BNRItem**s a user enters will be available until the user explicitly deletes them. One thing to note about testing your saving and loading code: If you kill Homepwner from Xcode, the **BNRItem**s will not be saved. You must hit the home button first and then kill it from Xcode by clicking the Stop button.

Now that you can save and load **BNRItem**s, there is no reason to auto-populate each one with random data. In BNRItemStore.m, modify the implementation of **createItem** so that it creates an empty **BNRItem** instead of one with random data.

```
- (BNRItem *)createItem
{
    BNRItem *p = [BNRItem randomItem];
    BNRItem *p = [[BNRItem alloc] init];

    [allItems addObject:p];

    return p;
}
```

Application States and Transitions

In Homepwner, **BNRItem**s are archived when the application enters the *background state*. It is useful to understand all of the states an application can be in, what causes them to transition between states, and how your code can be notified of these transitions. This information is summarized in Figure 14.5.

Figure 14.5   States of typical application

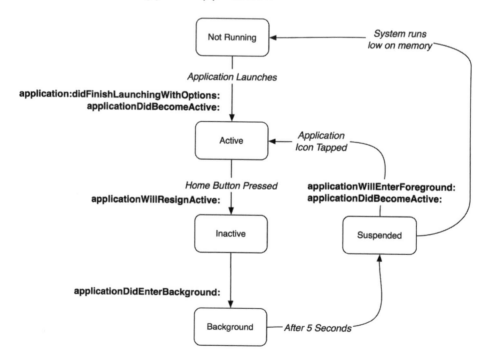

When an application is not running, it is in the *not running* state, and it does not execute any code or have any memory reserved in RAM.

After the user launches an application, it enters the *active state*. When in the active state, an application's interface is on the screen, it is accepting events, and its code is handling those events.

While in the active state, an application can be temporarily interrupted by a system event like an SMS message, push notification, phone call, or alarm. An overlay will appear on top of your application to handle this event. This state is known as the *inactive state*. In the inactive state, an application is mostly visible (an alert view will appear and obscure part of the interface) and is executing code, but it is not receiving events. Applications typically spend very little time in the inactive state. You can force an active application into the inactive state by pressing the lock button at the top of the device. The application will stay inactive until the device is unlocked.

When the user presses the home button or switches to another application in some other way, the application enters the *background state*. (Actually, it spends a brief moment in the inactive state before transitioning to the background.) In the background, an application's interface is not visible or receiving events, but it can still execute code. By default, an application that enters the background state has five seconds before it enters the *suspended state*.

An application in the suspended state cannot execute code, you cannot see its interface, and any resources it doesn't need while suspended are destroyed. A suspended application is essentially freeze-dried and can be quickly thawed when the user relaunches it. The resources that are destroyed are ones that can be reloaded, like cached images, system-managed caches, and other graphics data. (You don't have to worry about destroying and reloading these resources; your application handles it automatically.) Table 14.1 summarizes the characteristics of the different application states.

Table 14.1   Application states

State	Visible	Receives Events	Executes Code
Not Running	No	No	No
Active	Yes	Yes	Yes
Inactive	Mostly	No	Yes
Background	No	No	Yes
Suspended	No	No	No

You can see what applications are in the background or suspended by double-clicking the home button on your device. (Recently run applications that have been terminated may also appear in this list.)

Figure 14.6   Background and suspended applications in the dock

An application in the suspended state will remain in that state as long as there is adequate system memory. When the operating system decides memory is getting low, it terminates suspended applications as needed. And it will do so without warning. A suspended application gets no notification that it is about to be terminated; it is simply removed from memory. (An application may remain in the dock after it has been terminated, but it will have to be relaunched when tapped.)

When an application changes its state, the application delegate is sent a message. Here are some of the messages from the UIApplicationDelegate protocol that announce application state transitions.

- application:didFinishLaunchingWithOptions:
- applicationDidBecomeActive:
- applicationWillResignActive:
- applicationDidEnterBackground:
- applicationWillEnterForeground:

You can implement code in these methods to take the appropriate actions for your application. Transitioning to the background state is where you should always save any outstanding changes and the state of the application because it is the last time your application can execute code before it enters the suspended state. Once in the suspended state, an application can be terminated at the whim of the operating system.

Writing to the Filesystem with NSData

Our archiving in Homepwner saves and loads the imageKey for each **BNRItem**, but what about the images themselves? Let's extend the image store to save images as they are added and fetch them as they are needed.

The images for **BNRItem** instances are created by user interaction and are only stored within the application. Therefore, the Documents directory is the best place to store them. You can use the image key generated when the user takes a picture to name the image in the filesystem.

Open BNRImageStore.h and add a new method declaration.

```
- (NSString *)imagePathForKey:(NSString *)key;
```

Implement **imagePathForKey:** in BNRImageStore.m to create a path in the documents directory using a given key.

```
- (NSString *)imagePathForKey:(NSString *)key
{
    NSArray *documentDirectories =
            NSSearchPathForDirectoriesInDomains(NSDocumentDirectory,
                                                NSUserDomainMask,
                                                YES);

    NSString *documentDirectory = [documentDirectories objectAtIndex:0];

    return [documentDirectory stringByAppendingPathComponent:key];
}
```

To save and load an image, you are going to copy the JPEG representation of the image into a buffer in memory. Instead of just malloc'ing a buffer, Objective-C programmers have a handy class to create, maintain, and destroy these sorts of buffers – **NSData**. An **NSData** instance holds some number of bytes of binary data, and you will use **NSData** store image data.

In BNRImageStore.m, modify **setImage:forKey:** to get a path and save the image.

```
- (void)setImage:(UIImage *)i forKey:(NSString *)s
{
    [dictionary setObject:i forKey:s];

    // Create full path for image
    NSString *imagePath = [self imagePathForKey:s];

    // Turn image into JPEG data,
    NSData *d = UIImageJPEGRepresentation(i, 0.5);

    // Write it to full path
    [d writeToFile:imagePath atomically:YES];
}
```

Let's examine this code more closely. The function **UIImageJPEGRepresentation** takes two parameters: a **UIImage** and a compression quality. The compression quality is a float from 0 to 1, where 1 is the highest quality. The function returns an instance of **NSData**.

This **NSData** instance can be written to the filesystem by sending it the message **writeToFile:atomically:**. The bytes held in this **NSData** are then written to the path specified by the first parameter. The second parameter, **atomically**, is a Boolean value. If it is YES, the file is written to a temporary place on the filesystem, and, once the writing operation is complete, that file is renamed to the path of the first parameter, replacing any previously existing file. Writing atomically prevents data corruption should your application crash during the write procedure.

It is worth noting that this way of writing data to the filesystem is *not* archiving. While **NSData** instances can be archived, using the method **writeToFile:atomically:** is a binary write to the filesystem.

In BNRImageStore.m, make sure that when an image is deleted from the store, it is also deleted from the filesystem:

```
- (void)deleteImageForKey:(NSString *)s
{
    if (!s)
        return;
    [dictionary removeObjectForKey:s];

    NSString *path = [self imagePathForKey:s];
    [[NSFileManager defaultManager] removeItemAtPath:path
                                               error:NULL];
}
```

Now that the image is stored in the filesystem, the **BNRImageStore** will need to load that image when it is requested. The class method **imageWithContentsOfFile:** of **UIImage** will read in an image from a file, given a path.

In BNRImageStore.m, replace the method **imageForKey:** so that the **BNRImageStore** will load the image from the filesystem if it doesn't already have it.

```
- (UIImage *)imageForKey:(NSString *)s
{
    return [dictionary objectForKey:s];

    // If possible, get it from the dictionary
    UIImage *result = [dictionary objectForKey:s];

    if (!result) {
        // Create UIImage object from file
        result = [UIImage imageWithContentsOfFile:[self imagePathForKey:s]];

        // If we found an image on the file system, place it into the cache
        if (result)
            [dictionary setObject:result forKey:s];
        else
            NSLog(@"Error: unable to find %@", [self imagePathForKey:s]);
    }
    return result;
}
```

When a **BNRItem** is removed from the store, its image should also be removed from the filesystem. At the top of BNRItemStore.m, import the header for the **BNRImageStore** and add the following code to **removeItem:**.

```
#import "BNRImageStore.h"

@implementation BNRItemStore

- (void)removeItem:(BNRItem *)p
{
    NSString *key = [p imageKey];
    [[BNRImageStore sharedStore] deleteImageForKey:key];

    [allItems removeObjectIdenticalTo:p];
}
```

Build and run the application again. Take a photo for a item, exit the application, and then kill it from the dock. Launch the application again. Selecting that same item will show all its saved details – including the photo you just took.

Also, notice that the images were saved immediately after being taken, while the **BNRItem**s were saved only when the application entered background. We saved the images right away because they are just too big to keep in memory for long.

More on Low-Memory Warnings

You have seen how view controllers handle low-memory warnings – they are sent the message **didReceiveMemoryWarning** and destroy their views if they are not on the screen. This is an appropriate solution to handling a low-memory warning: an object gets rid of anything it isn't currently using and can recreate later. Objects other than view controllers may have data that they aren't using and can recreate later. The **BNRImageStore** is such an object – when its images aren't on the screen, it is okay to destroy them because they can be loaded from the filesystem when they're needed again.

Whenever a low-memory warning occurs, UIApplicationDidReceiveMemoryWarningNotification is posted to the notification center. Objects that want to implement their own low-memory warning handlers can register for this notification. In BNRImageStore.m, edit the **init** method to register the image store as an observer of this notification.

```
- (id)init
{
    self = [super init];
    if (self) {
        dictionary = [[NSMutableDictionary alloc] init];

        NSNotificationCenter *nc = [NSNotificationCenter defaultCenter];
        [nc addObserver:self
               selector:@selector(clearCache:)
                   name:UIApplicationDidReceiveMemoryWarningNotification
                 object:nil];

    }

    return self;
}
```

Now, a low-memory warning will send the message **clearCache:** to the **BNRImageStore** instance. In BNRImageStore.m, implement **clearCache:** to remove all the **UIImage** objects from the **BNRImageStore**'s dictionary.

```
- (void)clearCache:(NSNotification *)note
{
    NSLog(@"flushing %d images out of the cache", [dictionary count]);
    [dictionary removeAllObjects];
}
```

Removing an object from a dictionary relinquishes ownership of the object, so flushing the cache causes all of the images to lose an owner. Images that aren't being used by other objects are destroyed, and when they are needed again, they will be reloaded from the filesystem. If an image is currently displayed in the **DetailViewController**'s imageView, then it will not be destroyed since it is owned by the imageView. When the **DetailViewController**'s imageView loses ownership of that image (either because the `DetailViewController` was popped off the stack or a new image was taken), then it is destroyed. It will be reloaded later if needed.

Model-View-Controller-Store Design Pattern

In this exercise, we expanded on the `BNRItemStore` to allow it to save and load `BNRItem` instances from the filesystem. The controller object asks the `BNRItemStore` for the model objects it needs, but it doesn't have to worry about where those objects actually came from. As far as the controller is concerned, if it wants an object, it will get one; the `BNRItemStore` is responsible for making sure that happens.

The standard Model-View-Controller design pattern calls for the controller to bear the burden of saving and loading model objects. However, in practice, this can become overwhelming – the controller is simply too busy handling the interactions between model and view objects to deal with the details of how objects are fetched and saved. Therefore, it is useful to move the logic that deals with where model objects come from and where they are saved to into another type of object: a *store*.

A store exposes a number of methods that allow a controller object to fetch and save model objects. The details of where these model objects come from or how they get there is left to the store. In this chapter, the store worked with a simple file. However, the store could also access a database, talk to a web service, or use some other method to produce the model objects for the controller.

One benefit of this approach, besides simplified controller classes, is that you can swap out *how* the store works without modifying the controller or the rest of your application. This can be a simple change, like the directory structure of the data, or a much larger change, like the format of the data. Thus, if an application has more than one controller object that needs to save and load data, you only have to change the store object.

You can also apply the idea of a store to objects like `CLLocationManager`. The location manager is a store that returns model objects of type `CLLocation`. The basic idea still stands: a model object is returned to the controller, and the controller doesn't care where it came from.

Thus, we introduce a new design pattern called *Model-View-Controller-Store*, or simply MVCS. It's the hip, new design pattern that programmers are talking about everywhere. This design pattern will be expanded on in Chapter 28.

Bronze Challenge: PNG

Instead of saving each image as a JPEG, save it as a PNG instead.

Silver Challenge: Archiving Whereami

Another application you wrote could benefit from archiving: Whereami. In Whereami, archive the `MapPoint` objects so that they can be reused. (Hint: You cannot archive structures. However, you can break up structures into their primitive types....)

For The More Curious: Application State Transitions

Let's write some quick code to get a better understanding of the different application state transitions.

You already know about `self`, an implicit variable that points to the instance that is executing the current method. There is another implicit variable called `_cmd`, which is the selector for the current method. You can get the **NSString** representation of a selector with the function **NSStringFromSelector**.

In `HomepwnerAppDelegate.m`, implement the application state transition delegate methods so that they print out the name of the method. You'll need to add four more methods. (Check to make sure the template hasn't already created these methods before writing brand new ones.)

```
- (void)applicationWillResignActive:(UIApplication *)application
{
    NSLog(@"%@", NSStringFromSelector(_cmd));
}

- (void)applicationWillEnterForeground:(UIApplication *)application
{
    NSLog(@"%@", NSStringFromSelector(_cmd));
}

- (void)applicationDidBecomeActive:(UIApplication *)application
{
    NSLog(@"%@", NSStringFromSelector(_cmd));
}
- (void)applicationWillTerminate:(UIApplication *)application
{
    NSLog(@"%@", NSStringFromSelector(_cmd));
}
```

Now, add the following **NSLog** statements to the top of **application:didFinishLaunchingWithOptions:** and **applicationDidEnterBackground:**.

```
- (BOOL)application:(UIApplication *)application
  didFinishLaunchingWithOptions:(NSDictionary *)launchOptions
{
    NSLog(@"%@", NSStringFromSelector(_cmd));
    ...
}

- (void)applicationDidEnterBackground:(UIApplication *)application
{
    NSLog(@"%@", NSStringFromSelector(_cmd));
    [[BNRItemStore sharedStore] saveChanges];
}
```

Build and run the application. You will see that the application gets sent **application:didFinishLaunchingWithOptions:** and then **applicationDidBecomeActive:**. Play around some to see what actions cause what transitions.

Click the Home button, and the console will report that the application briefly inactivated and then went to the background state. Relaunch the application by tapping its icon on the Home screen or in the dock. The console will report that the application entered the foreground and then became active.

Click the Home button to exit the application again. Then, Double-click the Home button to launch the dock and then touch and hold the Homepwner icon until it begins to jiggle. Tap the red terminate button in the icon's upper left corner. Note that no message is sent to your application delegate at this point – it is simply terminated.

For the More Curious: Reading and Writing to the Filesystem

In addition to archiving and **NSData**'s binary read and write methods, there are a few more methods for transferring data to and from the filesystem. One of them, Core Data, is coming up in Chapter 16. A couple of others are worth mentioning here.

You have access to the standard file I/O functions from the C library. These functions look like this:

```
FILE *inFile = fopen("textfile", "rt");
char *buffer = malloc(someSize);
fread(buffer, byteCount, 1, inFile);

FILE *outFile = fopen("binaryfile", "w");
fwrite(buffer, byteCount, 1, outFile);
```

However, you won't see these functions used much because there are more convenient ways of reading and writing binary and text data. Using **NSData** works well for binary data. For text data, **NSString** has two instance methods **writeToFile:atomically:encoding:error:** and **initWithContentsOfFile:**. They are used as follows:

```
// A local variable to store an error object if one comes back
NSError *err;

NSString *someString = @"Text Data";
BOOL success = [someString writeToFile:@"/some/path/file"
                           atomically:YES
                             encoding:NSUTF8StringEncoding
                                error:&err];
if (!success) {
    NSLog(@"Error writing file: %@", [err localizedDescription]);
}

NSString *x = [[NSString alloc] initWithContentsOfFile:@"/some/path/file"
                                          encoding:NSUTF8StringEncoding
                                             error:&err];
if (!x) {
    NSLog(@"Error reading file: %@", [err localizedDescription]);
}
```

What's that **NSError** object? Some methods might fail for a variety of reasons. For example, writing to the filesystem might fail because the path is invalid or the user doesn't have permission to write to the specified path. An **NSError** object contains the reason for a failure. You can send the message **localizedDescription** to an instance of **NSError** for a human-readable description of the error. This is something you can show to the user or print to a debug console.

Error objects also have code and domain properties. The code is an integer representing the error. The domain represents the error domain. For example, not having permission to write to a directory results in error code 513 in error domain NSCocoaErrorDomain. Each domain has its own set of error codes, and codes within different domains can have the same integer value, so an error is uniquely specified by its code and error domain. You can check out the error codes for the NSCocoaErrorDomain in the file Foundation/FoundationErrors.h.

The syntax for getting back an **NSError** instance is a little strange. An error object is only created if an error occurred; otherwise, there is no need for the object. When a method can return an error through one of its arguments, you create a local variable that is a pointer to an **NSError** object. Notice that you don't instantiate the error object – that is the job of the method you are calling. Instead, you pass the *address* of your pointer variable (&err) to the method that might generate an error. If an error occurs in the implementation of that method, an **NSError** instance is created, and your pointer is set to point at that new object. If you don't care about the error object, you can always pass nil.

Sometimes you want to show the error to the user. This is typically done with an **UIAlertView**:

```
NSString *x = [[NSString alloc] initWithContentsOfFile:@"/some/path/file"
                                  encoding:NSUTF8StringEncoding
                                     error:&err];
if (!x) {
    UIAlertView *a = [[UIAlertView alloc] initWithTitle:@"Read Failed"
                                   message:[err localizedDescription]
                                  delegate:nil
                         cancelButtonTitle:@"OK"
                         otherButtonTitles:nil];
    [a show];
}
```

Figure 14.7   UIAlertView

Like **NSString**, the classes **NSDictionary** and **NSArray** have **writeToFile:** and **initWithContentsOfFile:** methods. To write collection objects to the filesystem with these methods, the collection objects must contain only *property list serializable* objects. The only objects that are *property list serializable* are **NSString**, **NSNumber**, **NSDate**, **NSData**, **NSArray**, and **NSDictionary**. When an **NSArray** or **NSDictionary** is written to the filesystem with these methods, an *XML property list* is created. An XML property list is a collection of tagged values:

```
<?xml version="1.0" encoding="UTF-8"?>
<!DOCTYPE plist PUBLIC "-//Apple//DTD PLIST 1.0//EN"
      "http://www.apple.com/DTDs/PropertyList-1.0.dtd">
<plist version="1.0">
<array>
    <dict>
        <key>firstName</key>
        <string>Joe</string>
        <key>lastName</key>
        <string>Conway</string>
    </dict>
    <dict>
        <key>firstName</key>
        <string>Aaron</string>
        <key>lastName</key>
```

```
      <string>Hillegass</string>
   </dict>
</array>
</plist>
```

XML property lists are a convenient way to store data because they can be read on nearly any system. Many web service applications use property lists as input and output. The code for writing and reading a property list looks like this:

```
NSMutableDictionary *d = [NSMutableDictionary dictionary];
[d setObject:@"A string" forKey:@"String"];
[d writeToFile:@"/some/path/file" atomically:YES];

NSMutableDictionary *anotherD = [[NSMutableDictionary alloc]
                     initWithContentsOfFile:@"/some/path/file"];
```

For the More Curious: The Application Bundle

When you build an iOS application project in Xcode, you create an *application bundle*. The application bundle contains the application executable and any resources you have bundled with your application. Resources are things like XIB files, images, audio files – any files that will be used at runtime. When you add a resource file to a project, Xcode is smart enough to realize that it should be bundled with your application and categorizes it accordingly.

How can you tell which files are being bundled with your application? Select the Homepwner project from the project navigator. Check out the Build Phases pane in the Homepwner target. Everything under Copy Bundle Resources will be added to the application bundle when it is built.

Each item in the Homepwner target group is one of the phases that occurs when you build a project. The Copy Bundle Resources phase is where all of the resources in your project get copied into the application bundle.

You can check out what an application bundle looks like on the filesystem after you install an application on the simulator. Navigate to ~/Library/Application Support/iPhone Simulator/ (version number)/Applications. The directories within this directory are the application sandboxes for applications installed on your computer's iOS simulator. Opening one of these directories will show you what you expect in an application sandbox: an application bundle and the Documents, tmp, and Library directories. Right or Command-click the application bundle and choose Show Package Contents from the contextual menu.

Figure 14.8   Viewing an application bundle

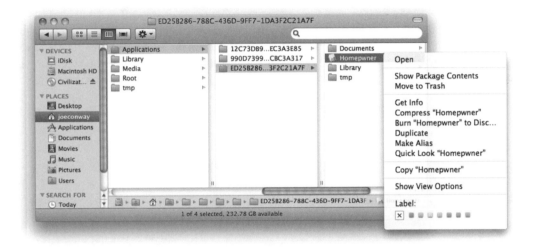

A Finder window will appear showing you the contents of the application bundle. When a user downloads your application from the App Store, these files are copied to their device.

Figure 14.9   The application bundle

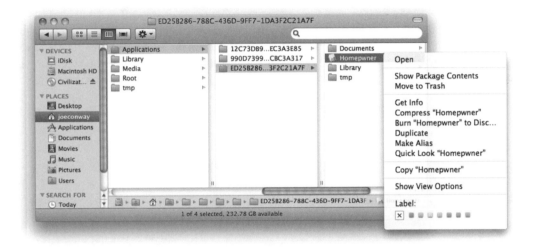

You can load files from the application's bundle at runtime. To get the full path for files in the application bundle, you need to get a pointer to the application bundle and then ask it for the path of a resource.

```
// Get a pointer to the application bundle
NSBundle *applicationBundle = [NSBundle mainBundle];

// Ask for the path to a resource named myImage.png in the bundle
NSString *path = [applicationBundle pathForResource:@"myImage"
                                             ofType:@"png"];
```

If you ask for the path to a file that is not in the application's bundle, this method will return nil. If the file does exist, then the full path is returned, and you can use this path to load the file with the appropriate class.

Also, files within the application bundle are read-only. You cannot modify them nor can you dynamically add files to the application bundle at runtime. Files in the application bundle are typically things like button images, interface sound effects, or the initial state of a database you ship with your application. You will use this method in later chapters to load these types of resources at runtime.

15

Subclassing UITableViewCell

A **UITableView** displays a list of **UITableViewCell**s. For many applications, the basic cell with its textLabel, detailTextLabel, and imageView is sufficient. However, when you need a cell with more detail or a different layout, you subclass **UITableViewCell**.

In this chapter, you will create a custom subclass of **UITableViewCell** named **HomepwnerItemCell** that will display **BNRItem** instances more eloquently. Each of these cells will show a **BNRItem**'s name, its value in dollars, its serial number, and a thumbnail of its image (Figure 15.1).

Figure 15.1   Homepwner with subclassed UITableViewCells

Creating HomepwnerItemCell

UITableViewCell is a **UIView** subclass. When subclassing **UIView** (or any of its subclasses), you typically override its **drawRect:** method to customize the view's appearance. However, when subclassing **UITableViewCell**, you don't change the cell's appearance directly.

Each cell has a subview named contentView, which is a container for the view objects that make up the layout of a cell subclass (Figure 15.2). You subclass **UITableViewCell** by changing the view objects in a cell's contentView. For instance, you could create instances of the classes **UITextField**, **UILabel**, and **UIButton** and add them to the contentView. (If you wanted something even more daring, you could create a **UIView** subclass, override its **drawRect:**, and add an instance of it to the contentView.)

Figure 15.2   HomepwnerItemCell hierarchy

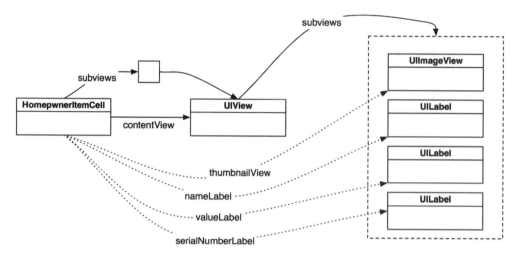

Adding subviews to the contentView instead of directly to the **UITableViewCell** subclass is important because the cell will resize the contentView at certain times. For example, when a table view enters editing mode, the contentView resizes itself to make room for the editing controls (Figure 15.3). If you were to add subviews directly to the **UITableViewCell**, these editing controls would obscure the subviews. The cell can't adjust its size when entering edit mode, but the contentView can and does.

Figure 15.3   Table view cell layout in standard and editing mode

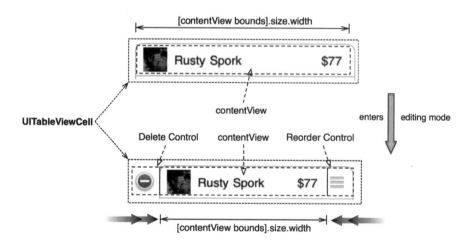

Open Homepwner.xcodeproj. Create a new **NSObject** subclass and name it **HomepwnerItemCell**. In HomepwnerItemCell.h, change the superclass to **UITableViewCell**.

```
@interface HomepwnerItemCell : NSObject
@interface HomepwnerItemCell : UITableViewCell
```

Configuring a UITableViewCell subclass's interface

Deciding how to lay out a cell's interface is just like deciding how to lay out any other interface: if there is more than one view, you do it in a XIB file. Create a new Empty XIB file and name this file `HomepwnerItemCell.xib`. (The Device Family is irrelevant for this file.)

Open `HomepwnerItemCell.xib` and drag a **UITableViewCell** instance from the library to the canvas. (Make sure you choose **UITableViewCell**, not **UITableView** or **UITableViewController**.)

This cell needs to display three text elements and an image, so drag three **UILabel**s and one **UIImageView** onto the cell. Configure them as shown in Figure 15.4. Make the text of the bottom label a little smaller and a dark shade of gray.

Figure 15.4   HomepwnerItemCell's layout

While this cell has a specified width and height in the XIB file, we don't know what the actual width and height will be in the application. Since our application will run on the iPhone and on the iPad (in both portrait and landscape orientations), the cell will need to adjust horizontally to fit the window it is on. Thus, you must set the autoresizing mask for each subview. In the size inspector, change the subviews' autoresizing masks to what is shown in Figure 15.5.

Figure 15.5   Autoresizing masks for HomepwnerItemCell

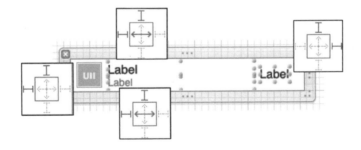

When the cell resizes horizontally (which it will depending on the orientation and the device), the label on the righthand side will stay fixed to the righthand side. The rest of the subviews will stay fixed to the lefthand side, and the two labels in the center will grow wider.

Figure 15.6   Changing the cell class

Finally, click on the cell in the outline view and select the identity inspector. Change the Class to `HomepwnerItemCell` (Figure 15.6).

Exposing the properties of HomepwnerItemCell

This cell looks nice, and it is almost ready to use in Homepwner, but there is one problem. When an instance of `HomepwnerItemCell` is created in `tableView:cellForRowAtIndexPath:`, you will need to set the text of each of these labels and the image of the `UIImageView`. (A cell that you can't configure would be pretty useless.) Thus, `HomepwnerItemCell` needs properties to access each of the subviews that makes up its interface.

The next step, then, is to create and connect outlets on `HomepwnerItemCell` for each of its subviews. You will use the same technique you have been using the last few chapters of Control-dragging into the source file to create the outlets. However, there will be a small difference for `HomepwnerItemCell`'s outlets: they will be properties instead of simply instance variables.

In `DetailViewController`, none of the outlets to the `UITextField`s were exposed as properties because no other object was supposed to have access to them. In this case, the table view's data source must configure each subview. By exposing the subviews as properties, the data source (`ItemsViewController`) will have the access it needs to do this.

Option-click on HomepwnerItemCell.h while HomepwnerItemCell.xib is open. Control-drag from each subview to the method declaration area in HomepwnerItemCell.h. (If there is an instance variable area defined in your file, you want to drag to the area after the closing bracket.) Name each outlet and configure the other attributes of the connection, as shown in Figure 15.7. (Pay attention to the Connection, Storage, and Object fields.)

Figure 15.7   HomepwnerItemCell connections

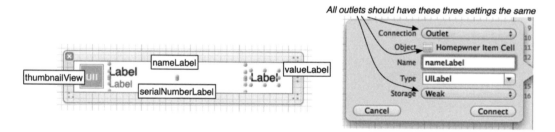

Double-check that HomepwnerItemCell.h looks like this:

```
@interface HomepwnerItemCell : UITableViewCell

@property (weak, nonatomic) IBOutlet UIImageView *thumbnailView;
@property (weak, nonatomic) IBOutlet UILabel *nameLabel;
@property (weak, nonatomic) IBOutlet UILabel *serialNumberLabel;
@property (weak, nonatomic) IBOutlet UILabel *valueLabel;

@end
```

You can also see in HomepwnerItemCell.m that making a property outlet connection automatically adds a @synthesize statement for the property.

Finally, note that you did not specify the File's Owner class or make any connections with it. In the case of **UITableViewCell** XIBs, the File's Owner is not used.

Using HomepwnerItemCell

In **ItemsViewController**'s **tableView:cellForRowAtIndexPath:** method, you will create an instance of **HomepwnerItemCell** for every row in the table. At the top of ItemsViewController.h, import the header file for **HomepwnerItemCell** so that **ItemsViewController** knows about it.

```
#import "HomepwnerItemCell.h"
```

In earlier implementations of **tableView:cellForRowAtIndexPath:**, you would ask the table view if it had any reusable cells first and create a brand new one if it did not. When using a XIB file to load a **UITableViewCell** subclass, the process is a little different: you register this XIB file with the **UITableView** for a given reuse identifier when the table first loads.

In ItemsViewController.m, override **viewDidLoad** to register HomepwnerItemCell.xib for the HomepwnerItemCell reuse identifier.

```
- (void)viewDidLoad
{
    [super viewDidLoad];

    // Load the NIB file
    UINib *nib = [UINib nibWithNibName:@"HomepwnerItemCell" bundle:nil];

    // Register this NIB which contains the cell
    [[self tableView] registerNib:nib
            forCellReuseIdentifier:@"HomepwnerItemCell"];
}
```

Notice that we waited until **viewDidLoad** to register the XIB. If we registered it in the designated initializer, the table view would only see this registration once. A low-memory warning, in this situation, would effectively unregister this XIB file because a new instance of **UITableView** would be created without re-registering it.

To get an instance of **HomepwnerItemCell**, all you do is ask the table view to dequeue a cell for the HomepwnerItemCell reuse identifier. If the table has a reusable instance of **HomepwnerItemCell**, it will return that. If it doesn't, it will load HomepwnerItemCell.xib and give you an instance of the archived cell. In ItemsViewController.m, locate **tableView:cellForRowAtIndexPath:** and modify it like so:

```
- (UITableViewCell *)tableView:(UITableView *)tableView
         cellForRowAtIndexPath:(NSIndexPath *)indexPath
{
    UITableViewCell *cell =
            [tableView dequeueReusableCellWithIdentifier:@"UITableViewCell"];

    if (!cell) {
        cell = [[UITableViewCell alloc]
                  initWithStyle:UITableViewCellStyleDefault
                reuseIdentifier:@"UITableViewCell"];
    }

    BNRItem *p = [[[BNRItemStore sharedStore] allItems]
                                 objectAtIndex:[indexPath row]];
    [[cell textLabel] setText:[p description]];
```

```
        // Get the new or recycled cell
        HomepwnerItemCell *cell = [tableView
                dequeueReusableCellWithIdentifier:@"HomepwnerItemCell"];

        // Configure the cell with the BNRItem
        [[cell nameLabel] setText:[p itemName]];
        [[cell serialNumberLabel] setText:[p serialNumber]];
        [[cell valueLabel] setText:
                [NSString stringWithFormat:@"$%d", [p valueInDollars]]];

        return cell;
}
```

Build and run the application. Your cells should look like the cells in Figure 15.8.

Figure 15.8   HomepwnerItemCell in action

Let's go back to the **UINib** class you used when loading HomepwnerItemCell.xib. An instance of **UINib** knows how to read a XIB file. (Remember, XIB and NIB are used interchangeably; technically, an application loads NIBs, but we work with XIBs, so it's easier to call them that.)

An instance of **UINib** is created with the contents of a XIB file. It loads the data in that file and holds on to it as long as it lives. When it is sent the message **instantiateWithOwner:options:**, the **UINib** parses that data: all of the archived objects come alive, and all of the connections are established. (The object passed as the first argument is the File's Owner.)

In Chapter 10, you loaded a XIB file by sending the message **loadNibNamed:owner:options:** to the main **NSBundle** without ever using **UINib**. Well, **loadNibNamed:owner:options:** uses **UINib** under the hood. It creates an instance of **UINib** and sends it the message **instantiateWithOwner:options:**, relaying the options and owner arguments.

Both of these methods return an **NSArray**. This array contains all of the top-level objects in the XIB file (the ones that aren't under a disclosure tab in the outline view of the XIB). When you register a XIB file with a table view, it scans this array for an instance of **UITableViewCell** or a subclass of it and returns it to your data source.

Since the table view just scans the XIB file for a **UITableViewCell**, it is important that you only put one instance of **UITableViewCell** in a XIB file used for this purpose. Otherwise, the table view will get confused and throw an exception.

Image Manipulation

To display an image within a cell, you could just resize the large image of the item from the image store. However, doing so would incur a performance penalty because a large number of bytes would need to be read, filtered, and resized to fit within the cell. A better idea is to create and use a thumbnail of the image instead.

To create a thumbnail of a **BNRItem** image, you are going to draw a scaled-down version of the full image to an offscreen context and keep a pointer to that new image inside a **BNRItem** instance. You also need a place to store this thumbnail image so that it can be reloaded when the application launches again.

In Chapter 12, we put the full-sized images in the **BNRImageStore** so that they can be flushed if necessary. However, the thumbnail images will be small enough that we can archive them with the other **BNRItem** instance variables.

Big problem, though: the thumbnail will be an instance of **UIImage**. **UIImage** doesn't conform to the NSCoding protocol, so you can't encode the thumbnail directly in an **NSCoder**. What you can do is encode the thumbnail as data (PNG format) and wrap it in an **NSData** object, which does conform to NSCoding.

Open BNRItem.h. Declare two new properties: a **UIImage** and an **NSData**. You will also want a method to turn a full-sized image into a thumbnail.

```
@property (nonatomic, copy) NSString *imageKey;

@property (nonatomic, strong) UIImage *thumbnail;
@property (nonatomic, strong) NSData *thumbnailData;

- (void)setThumbnailDataFromImage:(UIImage *)image;
@end
```

Synthesize these properties in BNRItem.m. You will eventually override the default setter and getter methods for these properties, but synthesizing automatically generates the two instances variables you need.

```
@implementation BNRItem

@synthesize thumbnail, thumbnailData;
```

When an image is chosen for this **BNRItem**, you will give that image to the **BNRItem**. It will chop it down to a much smaller size and then keep that smaller-sized image as its thumbnail. It will also create an **NSData** object that is the PNG representation of that image and set it as its thumbnailData. The thumbnailData will be archived with the **BNRItem**, and every time it is loaded from an archive, it will recreate its thumbnail from this data.

In BNRItem.m, create a getter method for thumbnail that will create it from the data if necessary:

```
- (UIImage *)thumbnail
{
    // If there is no thumbnailData, then I have no thumbnail to return
    if (!thumbnailData) {
        return nil;
    }
}
```

```
    // If I have not yet created my thumbnail image from my data, do so now
    if (!thumbnail) {

        // Create the image from the data
        thumbnail = [UIImage imageWithData:thumbnailData];
    }
    return thumbnail;
}
```

Now let's turn to the **setThumbnailDataFromImage:** method. This method will take a full-sized image, create a smaller representation of it in an offscreen context object, and set the thumbnail pointer to the image produced by the offscreen context.

iOS provides a convenient suite of functions to create offscreen contexts and produce images from them. To create an offscreen image context, you use the function **UIGraphicsBeginImageContextWithOptions**. This function accepts a CGSize structure that specifies the width and height of the image context, a scaling factor, and whether the image should be opaque. When this function is called, a new **CGContextRef** is created and becomes the current context.

To draw to a **CGContextRef**, you use Core Graphics, just as though you were implementing a **drawRect:** method for a **UIView** subclass. To get a **UIImage** from the context after it has been drawn, you call the function **UIGraphicsGetImageFromCurrentImageContext**.

Once you have produced an image from an image context, you must clean up the context with the function **UIGraphicsEndImageContext**.

In BNRItem.m, implement the following methods to create a thumbnail using an offscreen context.

```
- (void)setThumbnailDataFromImage:(UIImage *)image
{
    CGSize origImageSize = [image size];

    // The rectangle of the thumbnail
    CGRect newRect = CGRectMake(0, 0, 40, 40);

    // Figure out a scaling ratio to make sure we maintain the same aspect ratio
    float ratio = MAX(newRect.size.width / origImageSize.width,
                      newRect.size.height / origImageSize.height);

    // Create a transparent bitmap context with a scaling factor
    // equal to that of the screen
    UIGraphicsBeginImageContextWithOptions(newRect.size, NO, 0.0);

    // Create a path that is a rounded rectangle
    UIBezierPath *path = [UIBezierPath bezierPathWithRoundedRect:newRect
                                                   cornerRadius:5.0];
    // Make all subsequent drawing clip to this rounded rectangle
    [path addClip];

    // Center the image in the thumbnail rectangle
    CGRect projectRect;
    projectRect.size.width = ratio * origImageSize.width;
    projectRect.size.height = ratio * origImageSize.height;
    projectRect.origin.x = (newRect.size.width - projectRect.size.width) / 2.0;
    projectRect.origin.y = (newRect.size.height - projectRect.size.height) / 2.0;

    // Draw the image on it
```

```
    [image drawInRect:projectRect];

    // Get the image from the image context, keep it as our thumbnail
    UIImage *smallImage = UIGraphicsGetImageFromCurrentImageContext();
    [self setThumbnail:smallImage];

    // Get the PNG representation of the image and set it as our archivable data
    NSData *data = UIImagePNGRepresentation(smallImage);
    [self setThumbnailData:data];

    // Cleanup image context resources, we're done
    UIGraphicsEndImageContext();
}
```

In `DetailViewController.m`, add the following line of code to
imagePickerController:didFinishPickingMediaWithInfo: to create a thumbnail when the camera
takes the original image.

```
- (void)imagePickerController:(UIImagePickerController *)picker
didFinishPickingMediaWithInfo:(NSDictionary *)info
{
    NSString *oldKey = [item imageKey];

    if (oldKey) {
        [[BNRImageStore sharedStore] deleteImageForKey:oldKey];
    }

    UIImage *image = [info objectForKey:UIImagePickerControllerOriginalImage];

    [item setThumbnailDataFromImage:image];
```

Now that **BNRItem**s have a thumbnail, you can use this thumbnail in **ItemsViewController**'s table
view. In `ItemsViewController.m`, update **tableView:cellForRowAtIndexPath:**.

```
    [[cell valueLabel] setText:
                [NSString stringWithFormat:@"$%d", [p valueInDollars]]];

    [[cell thumbnailView] setImage:[p thumbnail]];

    return cell;
}
```

Now build and run the application. Take a picture for a **BNRItem** instance and return to the table view.
That row will display a thumbnail image along with the name and value of the **BNRItem**. (Note that you
will have to retake pictures for existing **BNRItem**s.)

Don't forget to add the thumbnail data to your archive! Open BNRItem.m:

```
- (id)initWithCoder:(NSCoder *)aDecoder
{
    self = [super init];

    if (self) {
        [self setItemName:[aDecoder decodeObjectForKey:@"itemName"]];
        [self setSerialNumber:[aDecoder decodeObjectForKey:@"serialNumber"]];
        [self setImageKey:[aDecoder decodeObjectForKey:@"imageKey"]];

        [self setValueInDollars:[aDecoder decodeIntForKey:@"valueInDollars"]];
```

```
        dateCreated = [aDecoder decodeObjectForKey:@"dateCreated"];

        thumbnailData = [aDecoder decodeObjectForKey:@"thumbnailData"];
    }

    return self;
}

- (void)encodeWithCoder:(NSCoder *)aCoder
{
    [aCoder encodeObject:itemName forKey:@"itemName"];
    [aCoder encodeObject:serialNumber forKey:@"serialNumber"];
    [aCoder encodeObject:dateCreated forKey:@"dateCreated"];
    [aCoder encodeObject:imageKey forKey:@"imageKey"];

    [aCoder encodeInt:valueInDollars forKey:@"valueInDollars"];

    [aCoder encodeObject:thumbnailData forKey:@"thumbnailData"];
}
```

Build and run the application. Take some photos of items and then exit and relaunch the application. The thumbnails will now appear for saved item objects.

Relaying Actions from UITableViewCells

Sometimes, it is useful to add a **UIControl** or one of its subclasses, like a **UIButton**, to a **UITableViewCell**. For instance, we want users to be able to tap the thumbnail image in a cell and see a full-size image for that item. In this section, we'll do that by adding a clear button on top of the thumbnail. Tapping this button will show the full-size image in a **UIPopoverController** when the application is running on an iPad.

Open HomepwnerItemCell.xib and drag a **UIButton** on top of the **UIImageView** that is already there. Resize this button to match the exact width and height of the **UIImageView**.

Then, Option-click on HomepwnerItemCell.h to open it in the assistant editor. Control-drag from the button to the method area of this file and configure this connection as shown in Figure 15.9.

Figure 15.9   Button connection

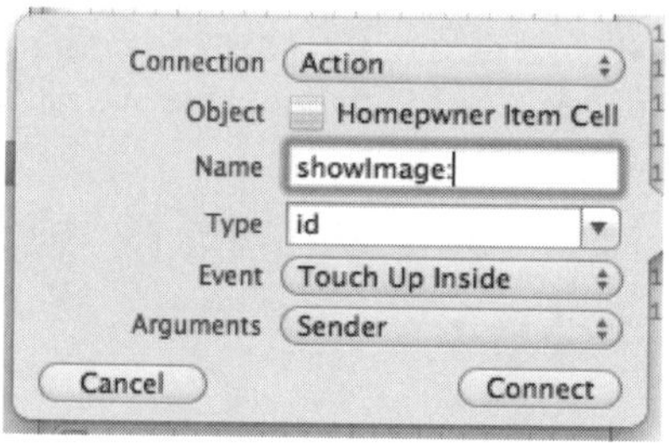

This connection will add the following code to HomepwnerItemCell.h.

```
- (IBAction)showImage:(id)sender;
```

Obviously, we don't want this button to obscure the image underneath it. In the attributes inspector, change the button's type to Custom (Figure 15.10).

Figure 15.10   Setting a UIButton's type

A custom button doesn't do any drawing by default (unlike, for example, a rounded rectangle button that draws a white pill with a blue outline). This means it starts out as a transparent button with nothing on it. If we wanted to, we could use an image or subclass **UIButton** and override **drawRect:** to give this button a totally custom look. But in our case, we just want a transparent button, so we're done.

At this point, though, we run into a problem: the action message of the button will be sent to the **HomepwnerItemCell**. But **HomepwnerItemCell** is not a controller and doesn't have access to any of the image data necessary to get the full-size image. In fact, it doesn't even have access to the **BNRItem** whose thumbnail it is displaying.

We could consider letting **HomepwnerItemCell** keep a pointer to the **BNRItem** it displays. But, table view cells are view objects, and they shouldn't manage model objects or be able to present additional interfaces (like the **UIPopoverController**).

So our plan, instead, is to give **HomepwnerItemCell** a pointer to **ItemsViewController**. (**ItemsViewController** is the controller object that manages the **UITableView** that **HomepwnerItemCell**s belong to, so it is also the controller of every **HomepwnerItemCell**.) Then, when the **HomepwnerItemCell** receives the action message from the button, it will send a new message to the **ItemsViewController** so that the controller can fetch the image and present it in the **UIPopoverController**.

Adding pointers to cell subclass

Now we need to give **HomepwnerItemCell** that pointer to the controller as well as a pointer to the table view that the cell belongs to. In HomepwnerItemCell.h, add the following two properties.

```
@property (weak, nonatomic) id controller;
@property (weak, nonatomic) UITableView *tableView;
```

These properties are weak because the **HomepwnerItemCell** is owned by its tableView already. Its tableView is owned by its controller. Thus, making either of these properties strong references would create a retain cycle because a child (the cell) would have a strong reference to its parent (the **UITableView**) or its grandparent (the controller).

In HomepwnerItemCell.m, synthesize these properties.

```
@synthesize controller;
@synthesize tableView;
```

Now we need to set these properties when the cell is created. In ItemsViewController.m, locate the **tableView:cellForRowAtIndexPath:** method and add the following code.

```
HomepwnerItemCell *cell = [tableView
                dequeueReusableCellWithIdentifier:@"HomepwnerItemCell"];

[cell setController:self];
[cell setTableView:tableView];
```

```
[[cell nameLabel] setText:[p itemName]];
```

Why do we need to give the cell a pointer to the table view when the controller already has a pointer to that table view? Wouldn't it be simpler just to have the cell pass itself and let the controller determine the table view? Yes, it would. But we're doing it this way so that, later in the chapter, the cell can pass its own index path to enable some cool Objective-C techniques. And serious bonus points for having these questions.

Relaying the message to the controller

Every cell will now know its controller and the table view it is displayed on. When the message `showImage:` is sent to a `HomepwnerItemCell`, we want the `HomepwnerItemCell` to turn around and tell the `ItemsViewController` to show the image for the item at the cell's index path.

In `HomepwnerItemCell.m`, implement `showImage:` to get its index path from the table view and then send its controller the `showImage:atIndexPath:` message. (We'll get to the implementation of `showImage:atIndexPath:` in a moment.)

```
- (IBAction)showImage:(id)sender
{
    NSIndexPath *indexPath = [[self tableView] indexPathForCell:self];

    [[self controller] showImage:sender
                     atIndexPath:indexPath];
}
```

Now, whenever the button overlaid on the thumbnail is tapped, `ItemsViewController` will be sent `showImage:atIndexPath:`. The first argument is a pointer to the button that sent the original `showImage:` message, and the second argument is the `NSIndexPath` of the cell that this button is on. At least that is what should happen. Unfortunately, `HomepwnerItemCell` doesn't know the details of `ItemsViewController`. Thus, it doesn't know that `ItemsViewController` implements `showImage:atIndexPath:`, and this code will generate an error.

One approach would be to import `ItemsViewController.h` into `HomepwnerItemCell.m`. However, this creates a dependency between `HomepwnerItemCell` and `ItemsViewController` and `HomepwnerItemCell` could not be used with any other view controller. Let's take a different approach that will keep the two classes separate and give us some flexibility down the road.

Objective-C selector magic

We can use the flexible power of Objective-C's runtime messaging to generalize the implementation of `showImage:`. Instead of explicitly sending `showImage:atIndexPath:` to the controller when `showImage:` is called, we are going to send the message `performSelector:withObject:withObject:`. This method takes a `SEL` that is the selector of the message to be sent, and the next two arguments are the arguments to be passed in that message (in order). The controller then searches for the method whose name matches the passed-in selector and executes it.

This is an interesting way of doing things, but we'll see why it is useful in a moment. First, remember that a selector is just the name of a message. You can turn a selector into a string, and you can turn a string back into a selector. In between these two steps, you can modify the string that becomes the selector. This is what you will do for `HomepwnerItemCell` – when it is sent the message `showImage:`, it will get that selector, append `atIndexPath:` to it, and send the new selector to its controller in

performSelector:withObject:withObject:. The two arguments will be the sender of **showImage:** and the cell's index path.

In HomepwnerItemCell.m, modify the implementation of **showImage:** to construct the selector and send this information to the controller.

```
- (IBAction)showImage:(id)sender
{
    // Get this name of this method, "showImage:"
    NSString *selector = NSStringFromSelector(_cmd);
    // selector is now "showImage:atIndexPath:"
    selector = [selector stringByAppendingString:@"atIndexPath:"];

    // Prepare a selector from this string
    SEL newSelector = NSSelectorFromString(selector);

    NSIndexPath *indexPath = [[self tableView] indexPathForCell:self];
    [[self controller] showImage:sender
                     atIndexPath:indexPath];

    // Ignore warning for this line - may or may not appear, doesn't matter
    [[self controller] performSelector:newSelector
                            withObject:sender
                            withObject:indexPath];
}
```

(As you might expect, there's also **performSelector:** for messages with no arguments, **performSelector:withObject:** for messages with one argument, and so on for all the possible message sends.)

At this point, we hope your Objective-C programmer warning sirens are going off. Are you thinking, "If we can just invent messages to send, then isn't it too easy to send a message that an object won't respond to?" With great power comes great responsibility. Only you can prevent unrecognized selector exceptions by checking with the receiver first.

In HomepwnerItemCell.m, check to see if the controller implements **showImage:atIndexPath:** first.

```
- (IBAction)showImage:(id)sender
{
    NSString *selector = NSStringFromSelector(_cmd);
    selector = [selector stringByAppendingString:@"atIndexPath:"];

    SEL newSelector = NSSelectorFromString(selector);

    NSIndexPath *indexPath = [[self tableView] indexPathForCell:self];
    if (indexPath) {
        if ([[self controller] respondsToSelector:newSelector]) {

            // Ignore warning for this line - may or may not appear, doesn't matter
            [[self controller] performSelector:newSelector
                                    withObject:sender
                                    withObject:indexPath];
        }
    }
}
```

Let's verify this all works according to plan. In ItemsViewController.m, implement showImage:atIndexPath: to print out the index path.

```
- (void)showImage:(id)sender atIndexPath:(NSIndexPath *)ip
{
    NSLog(@"Going to show the image for %@", ip);
}
```

Build and run the application. Tap a thumbnail (or, more accurately, the clear button on top of the thumbnail) and check the message in the console.

All of this code may seem like overkill, and for one message, it really is. However, this approach has bought us two things: the decoupling the cell from the controller and a general purpose format for cells to relay messages to their controller. In the Silver Challenge for this exercise, you will see how easy it is to use this technique in a general way to give all of your cells the ability to relay messages.

Presenting the image in a popover controller

Now, ItemsViewController needs to change showImage:atIndexPath: to grab the BNRItem associated with the cell whose button was tapped and display its image in a UIPopoverController.

To display an image in a popover, you need a UIViewController whose view shows an image as the popover's content view controller. Create a new UIViewController subclass from the UIViewController template. Name this new class ImageViewController, select UIViewController as its superclass, and check only the With XIB for user interface box.

Open ImageViewController.xib. First, drag a UIScrollView onto the View. Then, drag a UIImageView onto the UIScrollView.

Figure 15.11   ImageViewController XIB

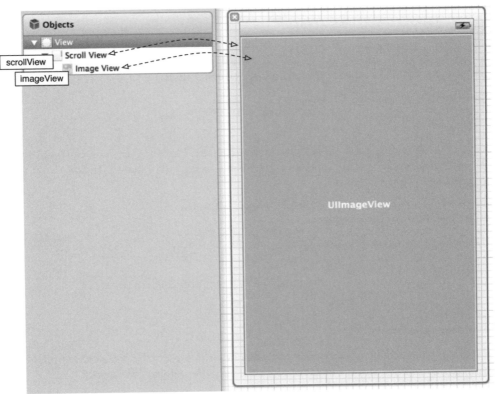

One of the issues of configuring a XIB file that has views stacked on top of each other is that it is difficult to select the views that are totally obscured. When this happens, you can make connections by dragging from the objects in the outline view instead of their visual representations on the canvas.

In ImageViewController.h, add curly brackets to **ImageViewController**'s interface and then make the connections shown in Figure 15.11. These connections should be instance variable outlets with weak storage.

Now add a property in ImageViewController.h to hold the image.

```
@interface ImageViewController : UIViewController
{
    __weak IBOutlet UIImageView *imageView;
    __weak IBOutlet UIScrollView *scrollView;
}
@property (nonatomic, strong) UIImage *image;
@end
```

When an instance of **ImageViewController** is created, it will be given an image. Anytime it is displayed, it will resize its imageView to fit the image and tell its scrollView to update its content size to match. In ImageViewController.m, synthesize the image property and implement **viewWillAppear:** to configure the views.

```
@implementation ImageViewController
@synthesize image;
```

```
- (void)viewWillAppear:(BOOL)animated
{
    [super viewWillAppear:animated];

    CGSize sz = [[self image] size];
    [scrollView setContentSize:sz];
    [imageView setFrame:CGRectMake(0, 0, sz.width, sz.height)];

    [imageView setImage:[self image]];
}
@end
```

Now you can finish implementing **showImage:atIndexPath:**. First, in ItemsViewController.h, declare that **ItemsViewController** conforms to UIPopoverControllerDelegate and give it an instance variable to hold the popover.

```
@interface ItemsViewController : UITableViewController
    <UIPopoverControllerDelegate>
{
    UIPopoverController *imagePopover;
}
```

Next, import the appropriate header files at the top of ItemsViewController.m.

```
#import "BNRImageStore.h"
#import "ImageViewController.h"
```

Flesh out the implementation of **showImage:atIndexPath:** to present the popover controller that displays the full-size image for the **BNRItem** represented by the cell that was tapped.

```
- (void)showImage:(id)sender atIndexPath:(NSIndexPath *)ip
{
    NSLog(@"Going to show the image for %@", ip);

    if ([[UIDevice currentDevice] userInterfaceIdiom] == UIUserInterfaceIdiomPad) {
        // Get the item for the index path
        BNRItem *i = [[[BNRItemStore sharedStore] allItems] objectAtIndex:[ip row]];

        NSString *imageKey = [i imageKey];

        // If there is no image, we don't need to display anything
        UIImage *img = [[BNRImageStore sharedStore] imageForKey:imageKey];
        if (!img)
            return;

        // Make a rectangle that the frame of the button relative to
        // our table view
        CGRect rect = [[self view] convertRect:[sender bounds] fromView:sender];

        // Create a new ImageViewController and set its image
        ImageViewController *ivc = [[ImageViewController alloc] init];
        [ivc setImage:img];

        // Present a 600x600 popover from the rect
        imagePopover = [[UIPopoverController alloc]
                        initWithContentViewController:ivc];
        [imagePopover setDelegate:self];
        [imagePopover setPopoverContentSize:CGSizeMake(600, 600)];
```

```
    [imagePopover presentPopoverFromRect:rect
                          inView:[self view]
        permittedArrowDirections:UIPopoverArrowDirectionAny
                        animated:YES];
    }
}
```

Finally, in `ItemsViewController.m`, get rid of the popover if the user taps anywhere outside of it .

```
- (void)popoverControllerDidDismissPopover:(UIPopoverController *)popoverController
{
    [imagePopover dismissPopoverAnimated:YES];
    imagePopover = nil;
}
```

Build and run the application. Tap on the thumbnails in each row to see the full-size image in the popover. Tap anywhere else to dismiss the popover.

Bronze Challenge: Color Coding

If a **BNRItem** is worth more than $50, make its value label text appear in green. If it is worth less than $50, make it appear in red.

Silver Challenge: Cell Base Class

The need for a cell to forward an action message to its controller is pretty common. If your cell subclasses inherit this ability, then you don't have to re-implement this functionality in each subclass. Make a **UITableViewCell** subclass as a cell base class that just implements the ability to forward action messages to a controller. Make **HomepwnerItemCell** a subclass of this base class. To test your base class further, create another subclass of it that has a **UIStepper** on it that will adjust the value of a **BNRItem**.

Figure 15.12 Cell class hierarchy

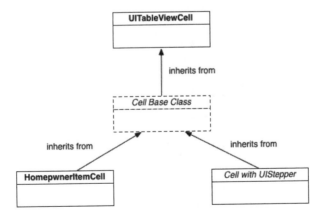

Gold Challenge: Zooming

The **ImageViewController** should center its image and allow zooming. Implement this behavior in `ImageViewController.m`.

16

Core Data

When deciding between approaches to saving and loading for iOS applications, the first question is typically "Local or remote?" If you want to save data to a remote server, this is typically done with a web service. Web services are covered in Chapter 25, so let's assume that you want to store data locally. The next question is typically "Archiving or Core Data?"

At the moment, Homepwner uses keyed archiving to save item data to the filesystem. The biggest drawback to archiving is its all-or-nothing nature: to access anything in the archive, you must unarchive the entire file; to save any changes, you must rewrite the entire file. Core Data, on the other hand, can fetch a small subset of the stored objects. And if you change any of those objects, you can update just that part of the file. This incremental fetching, updating, deleting, and inserting can radically improve the performance of your application when you have a lot of model objects being shuttled between the filesystem and RAM.

Object-Relational Mapping

Core Data is a framework that provides *object-relational mapping*. In other words, Core Data can turn Objective-C objects into data that is stored in a SQLite database file and vice-versa. SQLite is a relational database that is stored in a single file. (Technically, SQLite is the library that manages the database file, but we use the word to mean both the file and the library.) It is important to note that SQLite is not a full-fledged relational database server like Oracle, MySQL, or SQLServer, which are their own applications that clients can connect to over a network.

Core Data gives us the ability to fetch and store data in a relational database without having to know SQL. However, you do have to understand a bit about how relational databases work. This chapter will give you that understanding as you replace keyed archiving with Core Data in Homepwner's `BNRItemStore`.

Moving Homepwner to Core Data

Your Homepwner application currently uses archiving to save and reload its data. For a moderately sized object model (say, fewer than 1000 objects), this is fine. As your object model gets larger, however, you will want to be able to do incremental fetches and updates, and Core Data can do this.

The very first step is to add the Core Data framework to your project. Select the Homepwner target and under Build Phases, open the Link Binary With Libraries build phase. Click the + button to add the Core Data framework.

Figure 16.1   Add Core Data framework

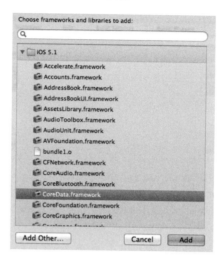

The model file

In a relational database, we have something called a *table*. A table represents some type; you can have a table of people, a table of a credit card purchases, or a table of real-estate listings. Each table has a number of columns to hold pieces of information about that thing. A table that represents people might have a column for the person's name, social security number, height, and age. Every row in the table represents a single person.

Figure 16.2   Role of Core Data

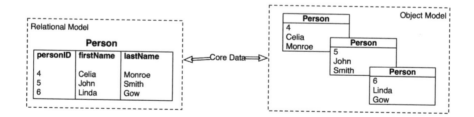

This organization translates well to Objective-C. Every table is like an Objective-C class. Every column is one of the class's instance variables. Every row is an instance of that class. Thus, Core Data's job is to move data to and from these two organizations (Figure 16.2).

Core Data uses different terminology to describe these ideas: a table/class is called a *entity*, and the columns/instance variables are called *attributes*. A Core Data model file is the description of every entity along with its attributes in your application. In Homepwner, you're going to describe a **BNRItem** entity in a model file and give it attributes like itemName, serialNumber, and valueInDollars.

Open Homepwner.xcodeproj. From the File menu, create a new file. Select Core Data in the iOS section and create a new Data Model. Name it Homepwner.

Figure 16.3   Create the model File

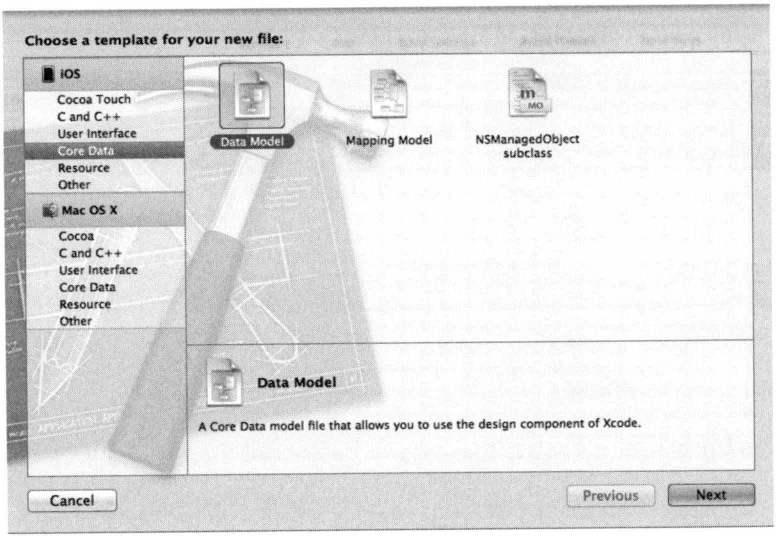

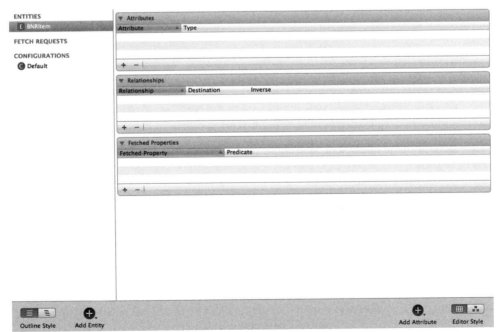

This will create a `Homepwner.xcdatamodeld` file and add it to your project. Select this file from the project navigator, and the editor area will reveal the user interface for manipulating a Core Data model file.

Find the Add Entity button at the bottom left of the window and click it. A new Entity will appear in the list of entities in the lefthand table. Double-click this entity and change its name to **BNRItem** (Figure 16.4).

Figure 16.4   Create the BNRItem entity

Now your **BNRItem** entity needs attributes. Remember that these will be the instance variables of the **BNRItem** class. The necessary attributes are listed below. For each attribute, click the + button in the Attributes section and edit the Attribute and Type values:

- itemName is a String

- serialNumber is a String

- valueInDollars is an Integer 32

- dateCreated is a Date

- imageKey is a String

- thumbnailData is a Binary Data

- thumbnail is an Undefined (It's a **UIImage**, but that isn't one of the possibilities.)

Select thumbnail from the Attributes list and then click the ▣ icon in the inspector selector to show the *data model inspector*. Check the box for Transient (Figure 16.5; you can also verify your attributes with this figure). Making this attribute transient lets Core Data know that thumbnail will be created at runtime instead of saved and loaded from the file. instead.

Figure 16.5 BNRItem attributes and the data model inspector

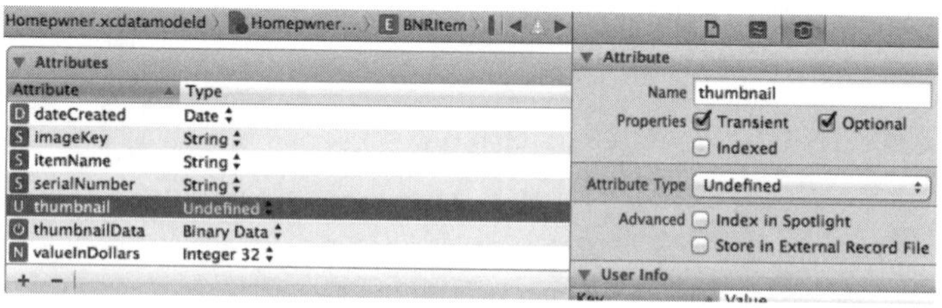

There is one more attribute to add. In Homepwner, users can order items by changing their positions in the table view. Archiving items in an array naturally respects this order. However, relational tables don't order their rows. Instead, when you fetch a set of rows, you specify their order using one of the attributes ("Fetch me all the **Employee** objects ordered by lastName.").

To maintain the order of items, you need to create an attribute to record each item's position in the table view. Then when you fetch items, you can ask for them to be ordered by this attribute. (You'll also need to update that attribute when the items are reordered.) Create this final attribute: name it orderingValue and make it a Double.

At this point, your model file is sufficient to save and load items. However, one of the benefits to using Core Data is that entities can be related to one another, so we're going to add a new entity called **BNRAssetType** that describes a category of items. For example, a painting might be of the Art asset type. **BNRAssetType** will be an entity in the model file, and each row of that table will be mapped to an Objective-C object at runtime.

Add another entity called **BNRAssetType** to your model file. Give it an attribute called label of type String. This will be the name of the category the **BNRAssetType** represents.

Figure 16.6   Create the BNRAssetType entity

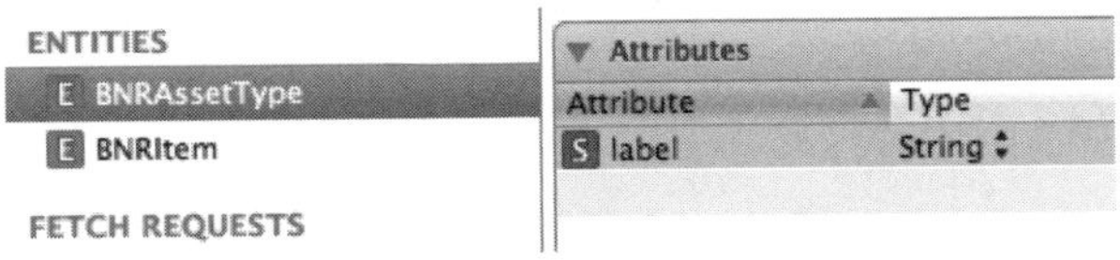

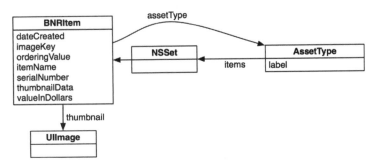

Now, you need to establish relationships between **BNRAssetType** and **BNRItem**. Relationships between entities are mapped as pointers. There are two kinds of relationships: *to-many* and *to-one*. When an entity has a to-one relationship, each instance of that entity will have a pointer to an instance in the entity it has a relationship to. For example, the **BNRItem** entity will have a to-one relationship to the **BNRAssetType** entity. Thus, a **BNRItem** instance will have a pointer to a **BNRAssetType** instance.

When an entity has a to-many relationship, each instance of that entity has a pointer to an **NSSet**. This set contains the instances of the entity that it has a relationship with. For example, the **BNRAssetType** entity will have a to-many relationship to **BNRItem** because many **BNRItem**s can have the same **BNRAssetType**. Thus, a **BNRAssetType** object will have a set of all the **BNRItem**s that are its type of asset.

With these relationships, we can ask a **BNRAssetType** object for the set of **BNRItem**s that fall into its category, and we can ask a **BNRItem** which **BNRAssetType** it falls under. Figure 16.7 diagrams the relationships between **BNRAssetType** and **BNRItem**.

Figure 16.7   Entities in Homepwner

Let's add these relationships to our model file. Select the BNRAssetType entity and then click the + button in the Relationships section. Name this relationship items in the Relationship column. Then, select BNRItem from the Destination column. In the data model inspector, check the box for To-Many Relationship (Figure 16.8).

Figure 16.8   Create the items relationship

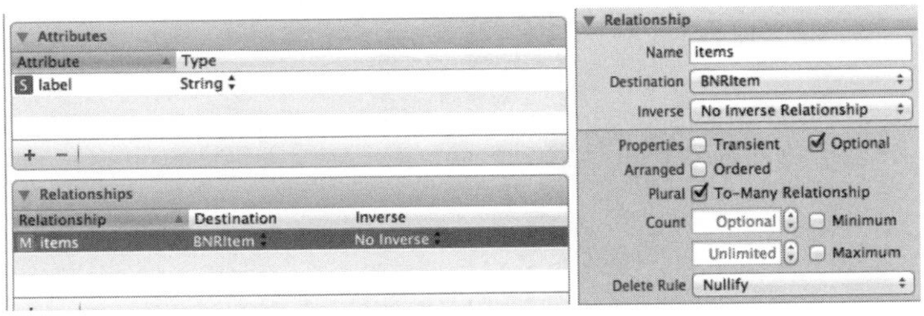

Now go back to the **BNRItem** entity. Add a relationship named `assetType` and pick BNRAssetType as its destination. In the Inverse column, select items (Figure 16.9).

Figure 16.9   Create the assetType relationship

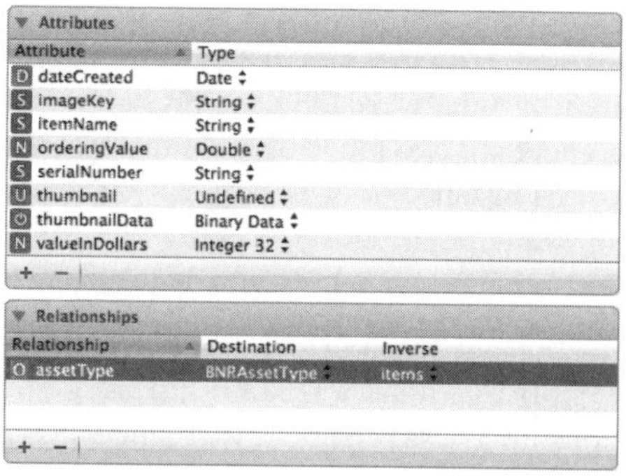

One final note on terminology: in the language of entity-relationship modeling, the attributes and relationships of an entity are collectively known as its *properties*.

NSManagedObject and subclasses

When an object is fetched with Core Data, its class, by default, is **NSManagedObject**. **NSManagedObject** is a subclass of **NSObject** that knows how to cooperate with the rest of Core Data. An **NSManagedObject** works a bit like a dictionary: it holds a key-value pair for every property (attribute or relationship) in the entity.

An **NSManagedObject** is little more than a data container. If you need your model objects to *do* something in addition to holding data, you must subclass **NSManagedObject**. Then, in your model file, you specify that this entity is represented by instances of your subclass, not the standard **NSManagedObject**.

Select the BNRItem entity. Show the data model inspector and change the Class field to **BNRItem**, as shown in Figure 16.10. Now, when a **BNRItem** entity is fetched with Core Data, the type of this object will be **BNRItem**. (**BNRAssetType** instances will still be of type **NSManagedObject**.)

Figure 16.10   Changing the class of an entity

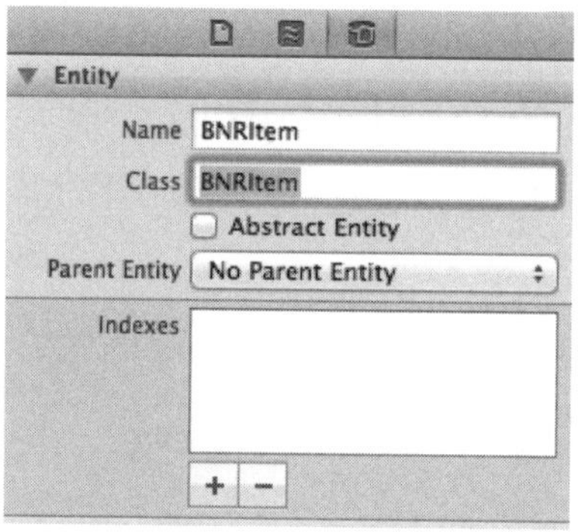

There is one problem: the **BNRItem** class already exists, and it does not inherit from **NSManagedObject**. Changing the superclass of the existing **BNRItem** to **NSManagedObject** will require considerable modifications. Thus, the easiest solution is to remove your current **BNRItem** class files, have Core Data generate a new **BNRItem** class, and then add your behavior methods back to the new class files.

In Finder, drag both BNRItem.h and BNRItem.m to your desktop for safekeeping. Then, in Xcode, delete these two files from the project navigator. (They will appear in red after you have moved the files).

Now, open Homepwner.xcdatamodeld again and select the **BNRItem** entity. Then, select New File... from the New menu.

From the iOS section, select Core Data, choose the NSManagedObject subclass option, and hit Next. When prompted to save, check the box for Use scalar properties for primitive data types.

Xcode will generate two new BNRItem.h and BNRItem.m files. Open BNRItem.h and see what Core Data has wrought. Change the type of the thumbnail property to **UIImage** and add the method declaration from the previous **BNRItem**.

```
#import <Foundation/Foundation.h>
#import <CoreData/CoreData.h>

@interface BNRItem : NSManagedObject

@property (nonatomic, strong) NSString * itemName;
@property (nonatomic, strong) NSString * serialNumber;
@property (nonatomic) int32_t valueInDollars;
@property (nonatomic) NSTimeInterval dateCreated;
@property (nonatomic, strong) NSString * imageKey;
@property (nonatomic, strong) NSData * thumbnailData;
@property UNKNOWN_TYPE UNKNOWN_TYPE thumbnail;
@property (nonatomic, strong) UIImage *thumbnail;
@property (nonatomic) double orderingValue;
@property (nonatomic, strong) NSManagedObject *assetType;

- (void)setThumbnailDataFromImage:(UIImage *)image;

@end
```

Notice that the types of a few properties have changed, like valueInDollars and dateCreated. The type int32_t is just like an int, so we don't have to worry about that. However, dateCreated is now an NSTimeInterval instead of an **NSDate**.

NSDate, as we know it, represents a date. You might expect for it to store the current year, month, day, hour, etc., but this would cause issues for other types of calendars. (We use the Gregorian calender; other nations may not.) Instead, an **NSDate** stores the number of seconds since a fixed point in time: January 1st, 2001 in Gregorian. Thus, it is perfectly reasonable to represent an **NSDate** as an NSTimeInterval, which is just a type definition for double.

However, this change in type causes an issue with the code in Homepwner where we treat this variable as an **NSDate** object. In DetailViewController.m, locate **viewWillAppear:** and substitute the following line of code:

~~[dateLabel setText:[dateFormatter stringFromDate:[item dateCreated]]];~~

```
// Convert time interval to NSDate
NSDate *date = [NSDate dateWithTimeIntervalSinceReferenceDate:[item dateCreated]];
[dateLabel setText:[dateFormatter stringFromDate:date]];
```

Next, in BNRItem.m, copy the **setThumbnailFromImage:** method from your old BNRItem.m to the new one:

```
- (void)setThumbnailDataFromImage:(UIImage *)image
{
    CGSize origImageSize = [image size];

    CGRect newRect = CGRectMake(0, 0, 40, 40);

    float ratio = MAX(newRect.size.width / origImageSize.width,
                      newRect.size.height / origImageSize.height);

    UIGraphicsBeginImageContextWithOptions(newRect.size, NO, 0.0);

    UIBezierPath *path = [UIBezierPath bezierPathWithRoundedRect:newRect
                                                    cornerRadius:5.0];
    [path addClip];

    CGRect projectRect;
    projectRect.size.width = ratio * origImageSize.width;
    projectRect.size.height = ratio * origImageSize.height;
    projectRect.origin.x = (newRect.size.width - projectRect.size.width) / 2.0;
    projectRect.origin.y = (newRect.size.height - projectRect.size.height) / 2.0;

    [image drawInRect:projectRect];

    UIImage *smallImage = UIGraphicsGetImageFromCurrentImageContext();
    [self setThumbnail:smallImage];

    NSData *data = UIImagePNGRepresentation(smallImage);
    [self setThumbnailData:data];

    UIGraphicsEndImageContext();
}
```

The thumbnail attribute is not going to be saved – it is a transient attribute. You'll need to update thumbnail from the thumbnailData when the object first emerges from the filesystem. When Homepwner used keyed archiving, we did this in **initWithCoder:**. Now that we're using Core Data, objects are initialized by another Core Data object, which you will meet in a moment. Thus, you do not implement **init** methods for **NSManagedObject** subclasses. Instead, to configure an object after it has been created, you override the method **awakeFromFetch**. Implement **awakeFromFetch** in BNRItem.m to set the thumbnail from the thumbnailData (which is saved).

```
- (void)awakeFromFetch
{
    [super awakeFromFetch];

    UIImage *tn = [UIImage imageWithData:[self thumbnailData]];
    [self setPrimitiveValue:tn forKey:@"thumbnail"];
}
```

This adds the extra behavior of **BNRItem**'s old implementation of **initWithCoder:**.

Of course, when you first launch an application, there are no saved **BNRItem**s or **BNRAssetType**s. When the user creates a new **BNRItem** instance, it will be added to the database. When objects are added to the database, they are sent the message **awakeFromInsert**. Here is where you will set the dateCreated instance variable of a **BNRItem**. Implement **awakeFromInsert** in BNRItem.m.

```
- (void)awakeFromInsert
{
    [super awakeFromInsert];
    NSTimeInterval t = [[NSDate date] timeIntervalSinceReferenceDate];
    [self setDateCreated:t];
}
```

This adds the extra behavior of **BNRItem**'s old designated initializer. Build the application to check for syntax errors, but do not run it.

Updating BNRItemStore

The portal through which you talk to the database is the **NSManagedObjectContext**. The **NSManagedObjectContext** uses an **NSPersistentStoreCoordinator**. You ask the persistent store coordinator to open a SQLite database at a particular filename. The persistent store coordinator uses the model file in the form of an instance of **NSManagedObjectModel**. In Homepwner, these objects will work with the **BNRItemStore**. These relationships are shown in Figure 16.11.

Figure 16.11   BNRItemStore and NSManagedObjectContext

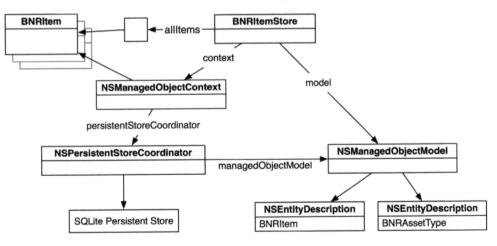

In BNRItemStore.h, import Core Data and add three instance variables.

```
#import <CoreData/CoreData.h>

@class BNRItem;

@interface BNRItemStore : NSObject
{
    NSMutableArray *allItems;
    NSMutableArray *allAssetTypes;
    NSManagedObjectContext *context;
    NSManagedObjectModel *model;
}
```

In BNRItemStore.m, change the implementation of **itemArchivePath** to return a different path that Core Data will use to save data.

```
- (NSString *)itemArchivePath
{
    NSArray *documentDirectories =
        NSSearchPathForDirectoriesInDomains(NSDocumentDirectory,
                                            NSUserDomainMask,
                                            YES);

    // Get one and only document directory from that list
    NSString *documentDirectory = [documentDirectories objectAtIndex:0];

    return [documentDirectory stringByAppendingPathComponent:@"items.archive"];

    return [documentDirectory stringByAppendingPathComponent:@"store.data"];
}
```

When the **BNRItemStore** is initialized, it needs to set up the **NSManagedObjectContext** and a **NSPersistentStoreCoordinator**. The persistent store coordinator needs to know two things: "What are all of my entities and their attribute and relationships?" and "Where am I saving and loading data from?" To answer these questions, we need to create an instance of **NSManagedObjectModel** to hold the entity information of Homepwner.xcdatamodeld and initialize the persistent store coordinator with this object. Then, we will create the instance of **NSManagedObjectContext** and specify that it use this persistent store coordinator to save and load objects.

In BNRItemStore.m, update **init**.

```
- (id)init
{
    self = [super init];

    if (self) {
        NSString *path = [self itemArchivePath];
        allItems = [NSKeyedUnarchiver unarchiveObjectWithFile:path];

        if (!allItems)
            allItems = [[NSMutableArray alloc] init];

        // Read in Homepwner.xcdatamodeld
        model = [NSManagedObjectModel mergedModelFromBundles:nil];

        NSPersistentStoreCoordinator *psc =
            [[NSPersistentStoreCoordinator alloc] initWithManagedObjectModel:model];
```

```
    // Where does the SQLite file go?
    NSString *path = [self itemArchivePath];
    NSURL *storeURL = [NSURL fileURLWithPath:path];

    NSError *error = nil;

    if (![psc addPersistentStoreWithType:NSSQLiteStoreType
                           configuration:nil
                                     URL:storeURL
                                 options:nil
                                   error:&error]) {
        [NSException raise:@"Open failed"
                    format:@"Reason: %@", [error localizedDescription]];
    }

    // Create the managed object context
    context = [[NSManagedObjectContext alloc] init];
    [context setPersistentStoreCoordinator:psc];

    // The managed object context can manage undo, but we don't need it
    [context setUndoManager:nil];
}

    return self;
}
```

Before, **BNRItemStore** would write out the entire **NSMutableArray** of **BNRItem**s when you asked it to save using keyed archiving. Now, you will have it send the message **save:** to the **NSManagedObjectContext**. The context will update all of the records in store.data with any changes since the last time it was saved. In BNRItemStore.m, change **saveChanges**.

```
- (BOOL)saveChanges
{
    NSString *path = [self itemArchivePath];
    return [NSKeyedArchiver archiveRootObject:allItems
                                       toFile:[self itemArchivePath]];

    NSError *err = nil;
    BOOL successful = [context save:&err];
    if (!successful) {
        NSLog(@"Error saving: %@", [err localizedDescription]);
    }
    return successful;
}
```

Note that this method is already called when the application is moved to the background.

NSFetchRequest and NSPredicate

In this application, we will fetch all of the **BNRItem**s in store.data the first time we need them. To get objects back from the **NSManagedObjectContext**, you must prepare and execute an **NSFetchRequest**. After a fetch request is executed, you will get an array of all the objects that match the parameters of that request.

A fetch request needs an entity description that defines which entity you want to get objects from. To fetch **BNRItem** instances, you specify the **BNRItem** entity. You can also set the request's *sort descriptors* to specify the order of the objects in the array. A sort descriptor has a key that maps to an attribute of the entity and a BOOL that indicates if the order should be ascending or descending. We want to sort the returned **BNRItem**s by orderingValue in ascending order. In BNRItemStore.h, declare a new method.

```
- (void)loadAllItems;
```

In BNRItemStore.m, define **loadAllItems** to prepare and execute the fetch request and save the results into the allItems array.

```
- (void)loadAllItems
{
    if (!allItems) {
        NSFetchRequest *request = [[NSFetchRequest alloc] init];

        NSEntityDescription *e = [[model entitiesByName] objectForKey:@"BNRItem"];
        [request setEntity:e];

        NSSortDescriptor *sd = [NSSortDescriptor
                                  sortDescriptorWithKey:@"orderingValue"
                                              ascending:YES];
        [request setSortDescriptors:[NSArray arrayWithObject:sd]];

        NSError *error;
        NSArray *result = [context executeFetchRequest:request error:&error];
        if (!result) {
                [NSException raise:@"Fetch failed"
                            format:@"Reason: %@", [error localizedDescription]];
        }

        allItems = [[NSMutableArray alloc] initWithArray:result];
    }
}
```

In BNRItemStore.m, send this message to the **BNRItemStore** at the end of **init**.

```
        [context setUndoManager:nil];

        [self loadAllItems];
    }
    return self;
}
```

You can build to check for syntax errors. You will see a warning that **allAssetTypes** hasn't been implemented yet – that's okay for now.

In this application, you immediately fetched all the instances of the **BNRItem** entity. This is a simple request. In an application with a much larger data set, you would carefully fetch just the instances you needed. To selectively fetch instances, you add a *predicate* (an **NSPredicate**) to your fetch request, and only the objects that satisfy the predicate are returned.

A predicate contains a condition that can be true or false. For example, if you only wanted the items worth more than $50, you would create a predicate and add it to the fetch request like this:

```
NSPredicate *p = [NSPredicate predicateWithFormat:@"valueInDollars > 50"];
[request setPredicate:p];
```

The format string for a predicate can be very long and complex. Apple's *Predicate Programming Guide* is a complete discussion of what is possible.

Predicates can also be used to filter the contents of an array. So, even if you had already fetched the allItems array, you could still use a predicate:

```
NSArray *expensiveStuff = [allItems filteredArrayUsingPredicate:p];
```

Adding and deleting items

This handles saving and loading, but what about adding and deleting? When the user wants to create a new **BNRItem**, you will not allocate and initialize this new **BNRItem**. Instead, you will ask the **NSManagedObjectContext** to insert a new object from the **BNRItem** entity. It will then return an instance of **BNRItem**. In BNRItemStore.m, edit the **createItem** method.

```
- (BNRItem *)createItem
{
    BNRItem *p = [[BNRItem alloc] init];
    double order;
    if ([allItems count] == 0) {
        order = 1.0;
    } else {
        order = [[allItems lastObject] orderingValue] + 1.0;
    }
    NSLog(@"Adding after %d items, order = %.2f", [allItems count], order);

    BNRItem *p = [NSEntityDescription insertNewObjectForEntityForName:@"BNRItem"
                                              inManagedObjectContext:context];

    [p setOrderingValue:order];

    [allItems addObject:p];

    return p;
}
```

When a user deletes a **BNRItem**, you must inform the context so that it is removed from the database. In BNRItemStore.m, add the following code to **removeItem:**.

```
- (void)removeItem:(BNRItem *)p
{
    NSString *key = [p imageKey];
    [[BNRImageStore sharedStore] deleteImageForKey:key];
    [context deleteObject:p];
    [allItems removeObjectIdenticalTo:p];
}
```

Reordering items

The last bit of functionality you need to replace for **BNRItem** is the ability to re-order **BNRItem**s in the **BNRItemStore**. Because Core Data will not handle ordering automatically, we must update a **BNRItem**'s orderingValue every time it is moved in the table view.

This would get rather complicated if the orderingValue was an integer: every time a **BNRItem** was placed in a new index, we would have to change the orderingValue's of other **BNRItem**s. This is why we created orderingValue as a double. We can take the orderingValues of the **BNRItem** that will be before and after the moving item, add them together, and divide by two. The new orderingValue will fall directly in between the values of the **BNRItem**s that surround it. In BNRItemStore.m, modify **moveItemAtIndex:toIndex:** to handle reordering items.

```
- (void)moveItemAtIndex:(int)from
              toIndex:(int)to
{
    if (from == to) {
        return;
    }
    BNRItem *p = [allItems objectAtIndex:from];

    [allItems removeObjectAtIndex:from];

    [allItems insertObject:p atIndex:to];

    // Computing a new orderValue for the object that was moved
    double lowerBound = 0.0;

    // Is there an object before it in the array?
    if (to > 0) {
        lowerBound = [[allItems objectAtIndex:to - 1] orderingValue];
    } else {
        lowerBound = [[allItems objectAtIndex:1] orderingValue] - 2.0;
    }

    double upperBound = 0.0;

    // Is there an object after it in the array?
    if (to < [allItems count] - 1) {
        upperBound = [[allItems objectAtIndex:to + 1] orderingValue];
    } else {
        upperBound = [[allItems objectAtIndex:to - 1] orderingValue] + 2.0;
    }

    double newOrderValue = (lowerBound + upperBound) / 2.0;

    NSLog(@"moving to order %f", newOrderValue);
    [p setOrderingValue:newOrderValue];
}
```

Finally, you can build and run your application. Of course, the behavior is the same as it always was, but it is now using Core Data.

Adding BNRAssetTypes to Homepwner

In the model file, you described a new entity, **BNRAssetType**, that every item will have a to-one relationship to. You need a way for the user to set the **BNRAssetType** of **BNRItem**s and create new **BNRAssetType**s. Also, the **BNRItemStore** will need a way to fetch the **BNRAssetType**s. (Creating new **BNRAssetType**s is left as a challenge at the end of this chapter.)

In BNRItemStore.h, declare a new method.

```
- (NSArray *)allAssetTypes;
```

In BNRItemStore.m, define this method. If this is the first time the application is being run – and therefore there are no **BNRAssetType**s in the store – create three default types.

```
- (NSArray *)allAssetTypes
{
```

```
    if (!allAssetTypes) {
        NSFetchRequest *request = [[NSFetchRequest alloc] init];

        NSEntityDescription *e = [[model entitiesByName]
                                    objectForKey:@"BNRAssetType"];

        [request setEntity:e];

        NSError *error;
        NSArray *result = [context executeFetchRequest:request error:&error];
        if (!result) {
            [NSException raise:@"Fetch failed"
                        format:@"Reason: %@", [error localizedDescription]];
        }
        allAssetTypes = [result mutableCopy];
    }

    // Is this the first time the program is being run?
    if ([allAssetTypes count] == 0) {
        NSManagedObject *type;

        type = [NSEntityDescription insertNewObjectForEntityForName:@"BNRAssetType"
                                        inManagedObjectContext:context];
        [type setValue:@"Furniture" forKey:@"label"];
        [allAssetTypes addObject:type];

        type = [NSEntityDescription insertNewObjectForEntityForName:@"BNRAssetType"
                                        inManagedObjectContext:context];
        [type setValue:@"Jewelry" forKey:@"label"];
        [allAssetTypes addObject:type];

        type = [NSEntityDescription insertNewObjectForEntityForName:@"BNRAssetType"
                                        inManagedObjectContext:context];
        [type setValue:@"Electronics" forKey:@"label"];
        [allAssetTypes addObject:type];

    }
    return allAssetTypes;
}
```

Now you need change the user interface so that the user can see and change the **BNRAssetType** of the **BNRItem** in the **DetailViewController**.

Figure 16.12   Interface for BNRAssetType

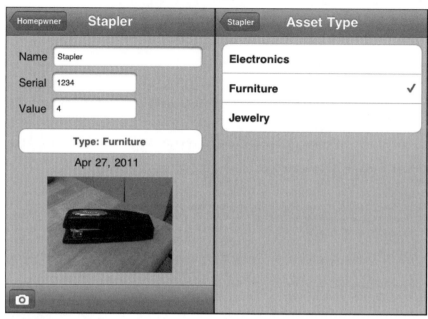

Create a new Objective-C class template file and choose NSObject as the superclass. Name this class **AssetTypePicker**.

In AssetTypePicker.h, forward declare **BNRItem**, change the superclass to **UITableViewController**, and give it a **BNRItem** property.

```
#import <UIKit/UIKit.h>

@class BNRItem;

@interface AssetTypePicker : NSObject
@interface AssetTypePicker : UITableViewController

@property (nonatomic, strong) BNRItem *item;

@end
```

This table view controller will show a list of the available **BNRAssetType**s. Tapping a button on the **DetailViewController**'s view will display it. Implement the data source methods and import the appropriate header files in AssetTypePicker.m. (You've seen all this stuff before.)

```
#import "AssetTypePicker.h"
#import "BNRItemStore.h"
#import "BNRItem.h"


@implementation AssetTypePicker

@synthesize item;

- (id)init
{
    return [super initWithStyle:UITableViewStyleGrouped];
```

```
}
- (id)initWithStyle:(UITableViewStyle)style
{
    return [self init];
}

- (NSInteger)tableView:(UITableView *)tableView
 numberOfRowsInSection:(NSInteger)section
{
    return [[[BNRItemStore sharedStore] allAssetTypes] count];
}

- (UITableViewCell *)tableView:(UITableView *)tableView
         cellForRowAtIndexPath:(NSIndexPath *)ip
{
    UITableViewCell *cell =
        [tableView dequeueReusableCellWithIdentifier:@"UITableViewCell"];

    if (cell == nil) {
        cell = [[UITableViewCell alloc] initWithStyle:UITableViewCellStyleDefault
                                      reuseIdentifier:@"UITableViewCell"];
    }

    NSArray *allAssets = [[BNRItemStore sharedStore] allAssetTypes];
    NSManagedObject *assetType = [allAssets objectAtIndex:[ip row]];

    // Use key-value coding to get the asset type's label
    NSString *assetLabel = [assetType valueForKey:@"label"];
    [[cell textLabel] setText:assetLabel];

    // Checkmark the one that is currently selected
    if (assetType == [item assetType]) {
        [cell setAccessoryType:UITableViewCellAccessoryCheckmark];
    } else {
        [cell setAccessoryType:UITableViewCellAccessoryNone];
    }

    return cell;
}

- (void)tableView:(UITableView *)tableView
didSelectRowAtIndexPath:(NSIndexPath *)ip
{
    UITableViewCell *cell = [tableView cellForRowAtIndexPath:ip];

    [cell setAccessoryType:UITableViewCellAccessoryCheckmark];

    NSArray *allAssets = [[BNRItemStore sharedStore] allAssetTypes];
    NSManagedObject *assetType = [allAssets objectAtIndex:[ip row]];
    [item setAssetType:assetType];

    [[self navigationController] popViewControllerAnimated:YES];
}

@end
```

In `DetailViewController.xib`, add a new **UIButton** to the view. Create and connect the outlet and action as shown in Figure 16.13. The outlet `assetTypeButton` should be a weak instance variable. (Remember, you create and connect outlets by Control-dragging to `DetailViewController.h`.)

Figure 16.13   Add a UIButton

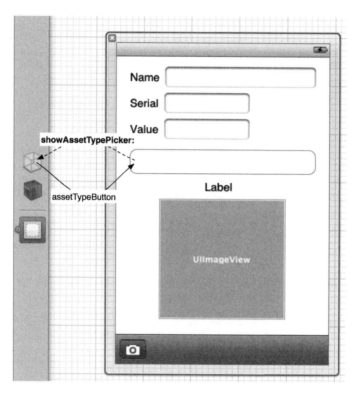

The following method and instance variable should now be declared in `DetailViewController.h`.

```
__weak IBOutlet UIButton *assetTypeButton;
```

```
- (IBAction)showAssetTypePicker:(id)sender;
```

At the top of `DetailViewController.m`, import the header for this new table view controller.

```
#import "DetailViewController.h"
```

#import "AssetTypePicker.h"

Implement **showAssetTypePicker:** in `DetailViewController.m`.

```
- (IBAction)showAssetTypePicker:(id)sender
{
    [[self view] endEditing:YES];

    AssetTypePicker *assetTypePicker = [[AssetTypePicker alloc] init];
    [assetTypePicker setItem:item];

    [[self navigationController] pushViewController:assetTypePicker
                                          animated:YES];
}
```

And finally, update the title of the button to show the asset type of a **BNRItem**. In `DetailViewController.m`, add the following code to **viewWillAppear:**.

```
    if (imageKey) {
        // Get image for image key from image cache
        UIImage *imageToDisplay = [[BNRImageStore sharedStore]
                                                imageForKey:imageKey];

        // Use that imge to put on the screen in imageView
        [imageView setImage:imageToDisplay];
    } else {
        // clear the imageView
        [imageView setImage:nil];
    }
    NSString *typeLabel = [[item assetType] valueForKey:@"label"];
    if (!typeLabel)
        typeLabel = @"None";

    [assetTypeButton setTitle:[NSString stringWithFormat:@"Type: %@", typeLabel]
                    forState:UIControlStateNormal];
}
```

Build and run the application. Select a **BNRItem** and set its asset type.

More About SQL

In this chapter, you used SQLite via Core Data. If you're curious about what SQL commands Core Data is executing, you can use a command-line argument to log all communications with the SQLite database to the console. From the Product menu, choose Edit Scheme.... Select the Run Homepwner.app item and the Arguments tab. Add two arguments: -com.apple.CoreData.SQLDebug and 1.

Figure 16.14   Turning on Core Data logging

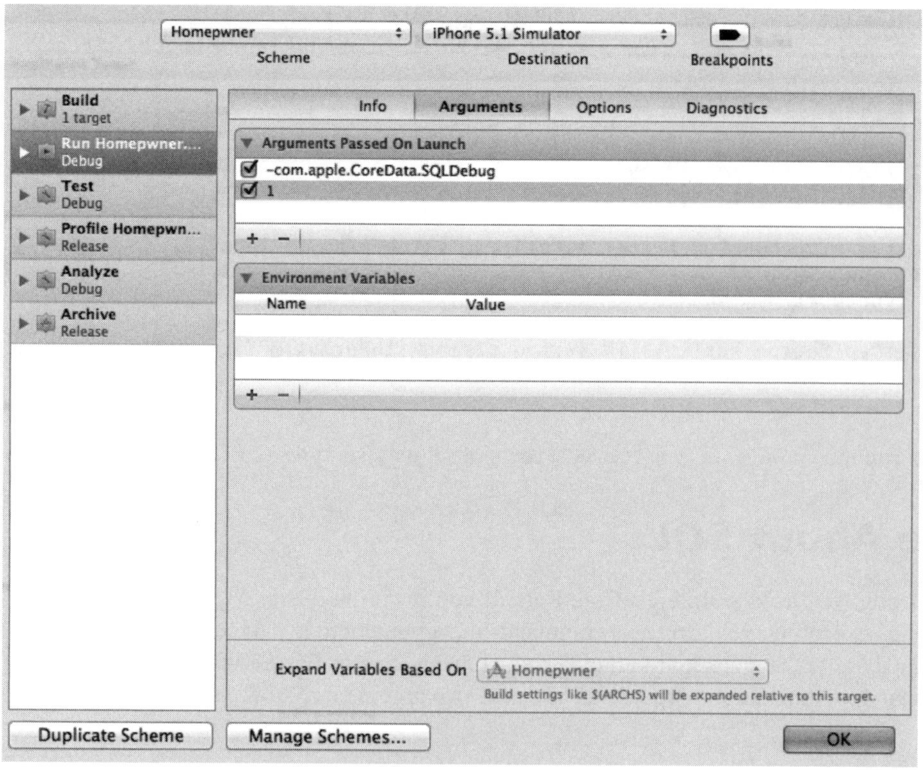

Build and run the application again. Make sure the debug area and console are visible so you can see the SQL logging. Add a few locations and inventory items; then navigate around the application looking at various items.

Faults

Relationships are fetched in a lazy manner. When you fetch a managed object with relationships, the objects at the other end of those relationship are *not* fetched. Instead, Core Data uses *faults*. There are to-many faults (which stand in for sets) and to-one faults (which stand in for managed objects). So, for example, when the instances of **BNRItem** are fetched into your application, the instances of **BNRAssetType** are not. Instead, fault objects are created that stand in for the **BNRAssetType** objects until they are really needed.

Figure 16.15   Object faults

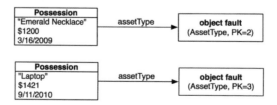

An object fault knows what entity it is from and what its primary key is. So, for example, when you ask a fault that represents an asset type what its label is, you'll see SQL executed that looks something like this:

```
SELECT t0.Z_PK, t0.Z_OPT, t0.ZLABEL FROM ZBNRASSETTYPE t0 WHERE t0.Z_PK = 2
```

(Why is everything prefixed with Z_? I don't know. What is OPT? I don't know, but I would guess it is short for "optimistic locking." These details are not important.) The fault is replaced, in the exact same location in memory, with a managed object containing the real data.

Figure 16.16 After one fault is replaced

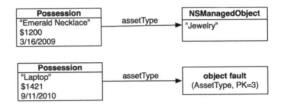

This lazy fetching makes Core Data not only easy to use, but also quite efficient.

What about to-many faults? Imagine that your application worked the other way: the user is presented with a list of **BNRAssetType** objects to select from. Then, the items for that asset type are fetched and displayed. How would this work? When the assets are first fetched, each one has a set fault that is standing in for the **NSSet** of item objects:

Figure 16.17 Set faults

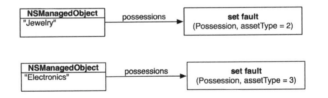

When the set fault is sent a message that requires the **BNRItem** objects, it fetches them and replaces itself with an **NSSet**:

Figure 16.18 Set fault replaced

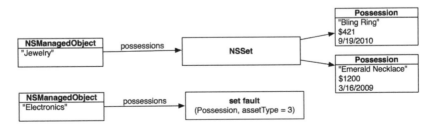

Core Data is a very powerful and flexible persistence framework, and this chapter has been just a quick introduction to its capabilities. For more details, we strongly suggest that you read Apple's *Core Data Programming Guide*. Here are some of the things we have not delved into:

- **NSFetchRequest** is a powerful mechanism for specifying data you want from the persistent store. We used it a little, but you will want to go deeper. You should also explore the following related classes: **NSPredicate**, **NSSortOrdering**, **NSExpressionDescription**, and **NSExpression**. Also, fetch request templates can be created as part of the model file.

- A *fetched property* is a little like a to-many relationship and a little like an **NSFetchRequest**. You typically specify them in the model file.

- As your app evolves from version to version, you'll need to change the data model over time. This can be tricky – in fact, Apple has an entire book about it: *Data Model Versioning and Data Migration Programming Guide*.

- There is good support for validating data as it goes into your instances of **NSManagedObject** and again as it moves from your managed object into the persistent store.

- You can have a single **NSManagedObjectContext** working with more than one persistent store. You partition your model into *configurations* and then assign each configuration to a particular persistent store. You are not allowed to have relationships between entities in different stores, but you can use fetched properties to achieve a similar result.

Trade-offs of Persistence Mechanisms

At this point, you can start thinking about the tradeoffs between the common ways that iOS applications can store their data Which is best for your application? Use Table 16.1 to help you decide.

Table 16.1   Data storage pros and cons

Technique	Pros	Cons
Archiving	Allows ordered relationships (arrays, not sets). Easy to deal with versioning.	Reads all the objects in (no faulting). No incremental updates.
Web Service	Makes it easy to share data with other devices and applications.	Requires a server and a connection to the Internet.
Core Data	Lazy fetches by default. Incremental updates.	Versioning is awkward (but can certainly be done using an **NSModelMapping**). No real ordering within an entity, although to-many relationships can be ordered.

Bronze Challenge: Assets on the iPad

On the iPad, present the **AssetTypePicker** in a **UIPopoverController**.

Silver Challenge: New Asset Types

Make it possible for the user to add new asset types by adding a button to the **AssetTypePicker**'s
`navigationItem`.

Gold Challenge: Showing Assets of a Type

In the **AssetTypePicker** view controller, create a second section in the table view. This section should
show all of the assets that belong to the selected asset type.

17
Localization

The appeal of iOS is global – iOS users live in many different countries and speak many different languages. You can ensure that your application is ready for this global audience through the processes of internationalization and localization. *Internationalization* is making sure your native cultural information is not hard-coded into your application. (By cultural information, we mean language, currency, date formats, number formats, and more.)

Localization, on the other hand, is providing the appropriate data in your application based on the user's Language and Region Format settings. You can find these settings in the Settings application. Select the General row and then the International row.

Figure 17.1 International settings

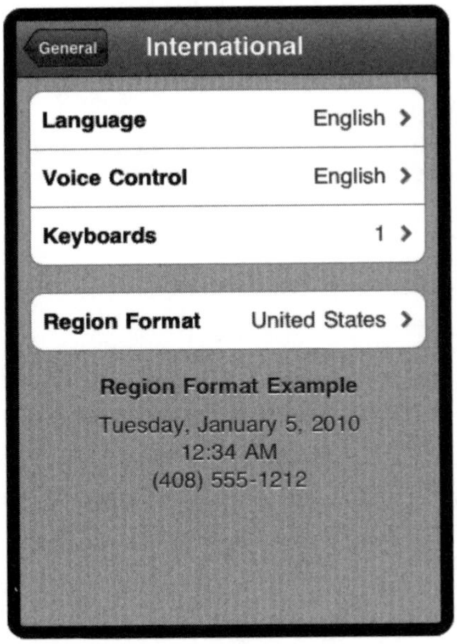

Apple makes these processes relatively simple. An application that takes advantage of the localization APIs does not even need to be recompiled to be distributed in other languages or regions. In this chapter, you're going to localize the item detail view of Homepwner. (By the way, internationalization and localization are big words. You will sometimes see people abbreviate them to i18n and L10n, respectively.)

Internationalization Using NSLocale

In this first section, you will use the class **NSLocale** to internationalize the currency symbol for the value of an item.

NSLocale knows how different regions display symbols, dates, and decimals and whether they use the metric system. An instance of **NSLocale** represents one region's settings for these variables. In the Settings application, the user can choose a region like United States or United Kingdom. (Why does Apple use "region" instead of "country?" Some countries have more than one region with different settings. Scroll through the options in Region Format to see for yourself.)

When you send the message **currentLocale** to **NSLocale**, the instance of **NSLocale** that represents the user's region setting is returned. Once you have a pointer to that instance of **NSLocale**, you can ask it questions like, "What's the currency symbol for this region?" or "Does this region use the metric system?"

To ask one of these questions, you send the **NSLocale** instance the message **objectForKey:** with one of the **NSLocale** constants as an argument. (You can find all of these constants in the **NSLocale** documentation page.)

Let's internationalize the currency symbol displayed in each **HomepwnerItemCell**. Open Homepwner.xcodeproj and, in ItemsViewController.m, locate the method **tableView:cellForRowAtIndexPath:**. When the text of the cell's valueLabel is set in this method, the string "$%d" is used, which makes the currency symbol always a dollar sign. Replacing that code with the following will get and display the appropriate currency symbol for the user's region.

```
    [[cell serialNumberLabel] setText:[p serialNumber]];
    [[cell valueLabel] setText:[NSString stringWithFormat:@"$%d",
                        [p valueInDollars]]];

    NSString *currencySymbol = [[NSLocale currentLocale]
                        objectForKey:NSLocaleCurrencySymbol];
    [[cell valueLabel] setText:[NSString stringWithFormat:@"%@%d",
                        currencySymbol,
                        [p valueInDollars]]];

    [[cell thumbnailView] setImage:[p thumbnail]];

    return cell;
}
```

Build and run the application. If the currency symbol is the dollar sign in your region, you'll need to change your region format in order to test this code. Exit the Homepwner application and kill it in the dock. Then, in the Settings application, change Region Format to United Kingdom (General → International → Region Format).

Run your application again. This time, you will see values displayed in pounds (£). (Note that this is not a currency conversion from dollars to pounds; you're just replacing the symbol.)

While your region format is set to the UK, check out the date format of the date an item was created: it is *Day Month Year*. Now exit and kill Homepwner and change your region to US. Relaunch Homepwner and navigate to an item's details. The date format is now *Month Day, Year*. The text for the date label has already been internationalized. When did this happen?

In Chapter 11, you used an instance of **NSDateFormatter** to set the text of the date label of **DetailViewController**. **NSDateFormatter** has a **locale** property, which is set to the device's current locale. Whenever you use an **NSDateFormatter** to create a date, it checks its **locale** property and sets the format accordingly. So the text of the date label has been internationalized from the start.

Localizing Resources

When internationalizing, you ask the instance of **NSLocale** questions. But the **NSLocale** only has a few region-specific variables. This is where localization comes into play: Localization is the process by which application-specific substitutions are created for different region and language settings. Localization usually means one of two things:

- generating multiple copies of resources like images, sounds, and interfaces for different regions and languages

- creating and accessing *strings tables* to translate text into different languages

Any resource, whether it's an image or a XIB file, can be localized. Localizing a resource puts another copy of the resource in the application bundle. These resources are organized into language-specific directories, known as lproj directories. Each one of these directories is the name of the localization suffixed with lproj. For example, the American English localization is en_US: where en is the English language code and US is the United States of America region code. (The region can be omitted if you don't need to make regional distinctions in your resource files.) These language and region codes are standard on all platforms, not just iOS.

When a bundle is asked for the path of a resource file, it first looks at the root level of the bundle for a file of that name. If it does not find one, it looks at the locale and language settings of the device, finds the appropriate lproj directory, and looks for the file there. Thus, just by localizing resource files, your application will automatically load the correct file.

In this section, you're going to localize one of Homepwner's interfaces: the DetailViewController.xib file. You will create English and Spanish localizations, which will create two lproj directories that will each contain a version of DetailViewController.xib. Select DetailViewController.xib in the project navigator. Then, show the utilities area.

Click the 🗋 icon in the inspector selector to open the file inspector. Find the section in this inspector named Localization and click the + button at the bottom. This signifies to Xcode that this file can be localized, automatically creates en.lproj, and moves the DetailViewController.xib file to it.

Click the + button again and select Spanish. This creates an es.lproj folder and adds a copy of DetailViewController.xib to it. The file inspector should look like Figure 17.2.

Figure 17.2   Localizing DetailViewController.xib

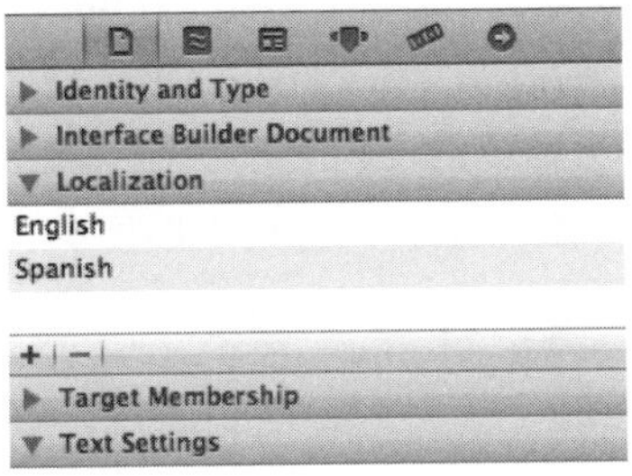

Back in Xcode, look in the project navigator. Click the disclosure button next to DetailViewController.xib (Figure 17.3) and then Control-click on each of these XIB files and select Show in Finder to show that file in its lproj directory. Keep these windows open; you'll need them shortly.

Figure 17.3   Localized XIB in the project navigator

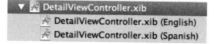

In the project navigator, click the Spanish version of DetailViewController.xib. When this file opens, the text is not in Spanish. You have to translate localized files yourself; Xcode isn't *that* smart.

One option is to manually edit each string in this XIB file in Xcode. However, this approach does not scale well if you're planning multiple localizations. What happens when you add a new label or button to your localized XIB? You have to add this view to the XIB for every language. This is not fun.

Instead, you can use a command-line tool named ibtool to suck the strings from your native language XIB file into a file. Then, you can translate these strings and create a new XIB file for each language. To get started, open Terminal.app in the Applications/Utilities directory.

Once Terminal launches, you'll need to navigate to the location of en.lproj. If you are familiar with Unix, have at it. If not, you're about to learn a cool trick. In Terminal, type the following:

```
cd
```

followed by a space. Drag the en.lproj folder's icon from the Finder onto the Terminal window. Terminal will fill out the path for you. Hit return. The current working directory of Terminal is now this directory. For example, my terminal command looks like this:

```
cd /iphone/Homepwner/Homepwner/en.lproj
```

Next, you will use ibtool to suck the strings from this XIB file. Enter the following terminal command and enter it all on the same line. (We only broke it up so that it would fit on the page.)

```
ibtool --export-strings-file ~/Desktop/DetailViewController.strings
            DetailViewController.xib
```

This will create a DetailViewController.strings file on your desktop that contains all of the strings in your XIB file. Edit this file according to the following text. The numbers and order may be different in your file, but you can use the text field in the comment to match up the translations.

```
/* Class = "IBUILabel"; text = "Name"; ObjectID = "4"; */
"4.text" = "Nombre";

/* Class = "IBUILabel"; text = "Serial"; ObjectID = "5"; */
"5.text" = "Numéro de serie";

/* Class = "IBUILabel"; text = "Value"; ObjectID = "6"; */
"6.text" = "Valor";
```

```
/* Class = "IBUILabel"; text = "Label"; ObjectID = "7"; */
"7.text" = "Label";
```

Notice that we do not change the Label text because it will be created at runtime. Save this file.

Now you will use ibtool to create a new Spanish XIB file. This file will be based on the English version of DetailViewController.xib but will replace all of the strings with the values from DetailViewController.strings. To pull this off, you need to know the path of your English XIB file and the path of your Spanish directory in this project's directory. Remember, you opened these windows in Finder earlier.

In Terminal.app, enter the following command, followed by a space after write. (But don't hit return yet!)

```
ibtool --import-strings-file ~/Desktop/DetailViewController.strings --write
```

Next, find DetailViewController.xib in es.lproj and drag it onto the terminal window. Then, find DetailViewController.xib in the en.lproj folder and drag it onto the terminal window. Your command should look similar to this:

```
ibtool --import-strings-file ~/Desktop/DetailViewController.strings --write
    /iphone/Homepwner/Homepwner/es.lproj/DetailViewController.xib
    /iphone/Homepwner/Homepwner/en.lproj/DetailViewController.xib
```

This command says, "Create DetailViewController.xib in es.lproj from the DetailViewController.xib in en.lproj, and then replace all of the strings with the values from DetailViewController.strings."

Hit return. (You might see some sort of warning where ibtool complains about GSCapabilities; you can ignore it.)

Open DetailViewController.xib (Spanish) in Xcode. This XIB file is now localized to Spanish. To finish things off, resize the label and text field for the serial number, as shown in Figure 17.4.

Figure 17.4   Spanish DetailViewController.xib

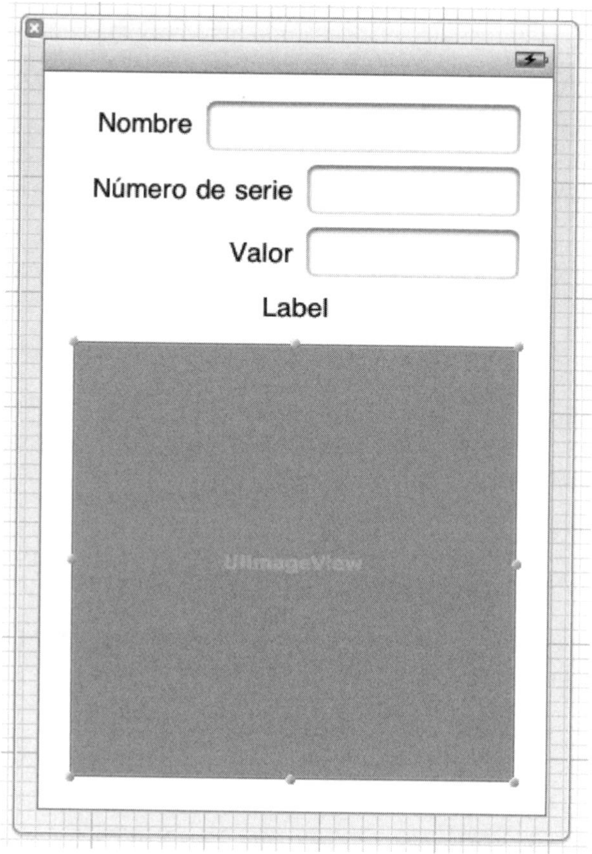

Now that you have finished localizing this XIB file, let's test it out. First, there is a little Xcode glitch to be aware of: sometimes Xcode just ignores a resource file's changes when you build an application. To ensure your application is being built from scratch, first delete the application from your device or simulator. Then, choose Clean from the Product menu. This will force the application to be entirely re-compiled, re-bundled, and re-installed.

Homepwner's detail view will not appear in Spanish until you change the language settings on the device. In Settings, change the language settings to Español (General → International → Language) and then relaunch your application. Select an item row, and you will see the interface in Spanish.

NSLocalizedString and Strings Tables

In many places in your applications, you create NSString instances dynamically or display string literals to the user. To display translated versions of these strings, you must create a *strings table*. A strings table is a file containing a list of key-value pairs for all of the strings that your application uses and their associated translations. It's a resource file that you add to your application, but you don't need to do a lot of work to get data from it.

Whenever you have a string in your code, it appears like this:

```
@"Hello!"
```

To internationalize a string in your code, you replace literal strings with the function
NSLocalizedString.

```
NSString *translatedString =
    NSLocalizedString(@"Hello!", @"The greeting for the user");
```

This function takes two arguments: a key and a comment that describes the string's use. The key is
the lookup value in a strings table. At runtime, the **NSLocalizedString** function will look through the
strings tables bundled with your application for a table that matches the user's language settings. Then,
in that table, the function gets the translated string that matches the key.

Now you're going to internationalize the string "Homepwner" that is displayed in the navigation bar. In
`ItemsViewController.m`, locate the **init** method and change the line of code that sets the title of the
navigationItem.

```
- (id)init
{
    // Call the superclass's designated initializer
    self = [super initWithStyle:UITableViewStyleGrouped];
    if (self) {
        UINavigationItem *n = [self navigationItem];

        [n setTitle:@"Homepwner"];

        [n setTitle:NSLocalizedString(@"Homepwner", @"Name of application")];
```

Once you have a file that has been internationalized with the **NSLocalizedString** function, you can
generate strings tables with a command-line application.

Open Terminal.app and navigate to the location of `ItemsViewController.m`. My command looks like
this:

```
cd /iphone/Homepwner/Homepwner/
```

At this point, you can use the terminal command `ls` to print out the directory contents and confirm that
`ItemsViewController.m` is in that list.

To generate the strings table, enter the following into Terminal and hit return:

```
genstrings ItemsViewController.m
```

This creates a file named `Localizable.strings` in the same directory as `ItemsViewController.m`.
Drag this file into the project navigator. When the application is compiled, this resource will be copied
into the main bundle.

Oddly enough, Xcode sometimes has a problem with strings tables. Open the `Localizable.strings`
file in the editor area. If you see a bunch of upside-down question marks, you need to reinterpret this
file as Unicode (UTF-16). Show the utilities area and select the file inspector. Locate the area named
Text Settings and change the pop-up menu next to Text Encoding to Unicode (UTF-16) (Figure 17.5). It
will ask if you want to reinterpret or convert. Choose Reinterpret.

Figure 17.5   Changing encoding of a file

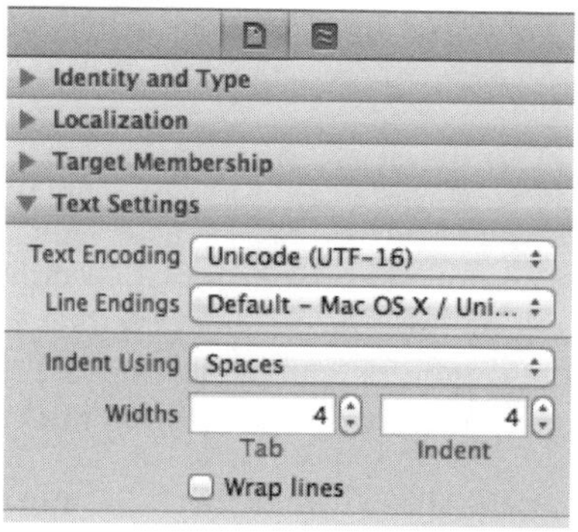

The file should look like this:

```
/* Name of application */
"Homepwner" = "Homepwner";
```

Notice that the comment above your string is the second argument you supplied to the
NSLocalizedString function. Even though the function doesn't require the comment argument,
including it will make your localizing life easier.

Now that you've created Localizable.strings, localize it in Xcode the same way you did the XIB
file. Select the file in the project navigator and click the plus button in the utilities area. Add the
Spanish localization and then open the Spanish version of Localizable.strings. The string on
the lefthand side is the *key* that is passed to the **NSLocalizedString** function, and the string on the
righthand side is what is returned. Change the text on the righthand side to the Spanish translation
shown below.

```
/* Name of application */
"Homepwner" = "Dueño de casa"
```

Build and run the application again. The title of the navigation bar will appear in Spanish. If it doesn't,
you might need to delete the application, clean your project, and rebuild. (Or check your user language
setting.)

Bronze Challenge: Another Localization

Practice makes perfect. Localize Homepwner for another language.

For the More Curious: NSBundle's Role in Internationalization

The real work of adding a localization is done for you by the class **NSBundle**. For example, when a
UIViewController is initialized, it is given two arguments: the name of a XIB file and an **NSBundle**
object. The bundle argument is typically nil, which is interpreted as the application's *main bundle*.
(The main bundle is another name for the application bundle – all of the resources and the executable
for the application. When an application is built, all of the lproj directories are copied into this
bundle.)

When the view controller loads its view, it asks the bundle for the XIB file. The bundle, being very smart, checks the current language settings of the device and looks in the appropriate lproj directory. The path for the XIB file in the lproj directory is returned to the view controller and loaded.

NSBundle knows how to search through localization directories for every type of resource using the instance method **pathForResource:ofType:**. When you want a path to a resource bundled with your application, you send this message to the main bundle. Here's an example using the resource file myImage.png:

```
NSString *path = [[NSBundle mainBundle] pathForResource:@"myImage"
                                                 ofType:@"png"];
```

The bundle first checks to see if there is a myImage.png file in the top level of the application bundle. If so, it returns the full path to that file. If not, the bundle gets the device's language settings and looks in the appropriate lproj directory to construct the path. If no file is found, it returns nil.

This is why you must delete and clean an application when you localize a file. The previous un-localized file will still be in the root level of the application bundle because Xcode will not delete a file from the bundle when you re-install. Even though there are lproj folders in the application bundle, the bundle finds the top-level file first and returns its path.

18

NSUserDefaults

Many applications include preferences that users can set. Whether users are picking the size of the text or storing usernames, there is a standard way of enabling iOS application preferences. In this chapter, you're going to use the **NSUserDefaults** class to add a preference to your Whereami application. This preference will specify the map type of the **MKMapView**.

Updating Whereami

Every **MKMapView** has a mapType property that specifies whether it shows roads, satellite imagery, or both. You will allow the user to change this property by adding a **UISegmentedControl** that toggles the map type. The user's choice will be saved as a preference, and the next time the application is launched, the preferred type of map will be displayed.

Open the Whereami project. Then open WhereamiViewController.xib and add a **UISegmentedControl** to the interface. Change its style and number of segments to what is shown in Figure 18.1.

Figure 18.1   UISegmentedControl attributes

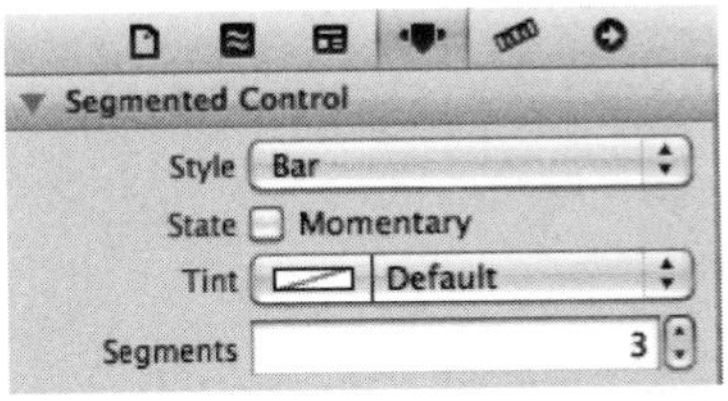

Make an outlet and an action connection between this object and the **WhereamiViewController** (Figure 18.2). The outlet will be a weak instance variable.

Figure 18.2   Adding to Whereami's interface

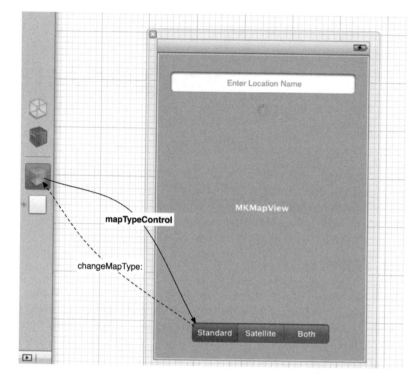

After making connections, WhereamiViewController.h should look like this:

```
    __weak IBOutlet UISegmentedControl *mapTypeControl;
}
- (IBAction)changeMapType:(id)sender;
```

In WhereamiViewController.m, implement **changeMapType:**.

```
- (IBAction)changeMapType:(id)sender
{
    switch ([sender selectedSegmentIndex])
    {
        case 0:
        {
            [worldView setMapType:MKMapTypeStandard];
        } break;
        case 1:
        {
            [worldView setMapType:MKMapTypeSatellite];
        } break;
        case 2:
        {
            [worldView setMapType:MKMapTypeHybrid];
        } break;
    }
}
```

Build and run the application and change the map type. However, if you quit the application (and kill it from Xcode), it won't remember the preference on the next launch.

Using NSUserDefaults

What we need to do now is store a value to specify the map type that the user last selected so that the chosen type will automatically be displayed when the user launches the application again. This value will be stored in an instance of **NSUserDefaults**.

Every application has an instance of **NSUserDefaults** that it can access by sending the class message **standardUserDefaults** to the **NSUserDefaults** class. This instance of **NSUserDefaults** is like an **NSMutableDictionary**; you can access objects in it using a key. It is also automatically read from disk when the application first accesses it and written to disk when it is modified.

The keys of an **NSUserDefaults** are always of type **NSString**. A key identifies a preference. An object represents the value of a preference. These objects must be property list serializable or primitives. For example, if you created a key "Text Size" and assigned the integer 16, it would mean the user's preferred text size is 16 points.

But that "Text Size" key is a completely hypothetical example. There isn't a built-in key that magically resizes all of your text. In fact, there are no built-in keys at all. Instead, you create your own keys specific to your application and give them values that mean something to your application.

The key you will create for Whereami is a string, and it will be used for both reading and setting the value. You will define it as a static variable so that you can pass a variable as the key instead of a hard-coded string. (If you mistype a variable name, the compiler will give you an error. But it can't help if you've mistyped a string.)

At the top of WhereamiViewController.m, declare a new static variable to hold the preference name for the map type.

```
NSString * const WhereamiMapTypePrefKey = @"WhereamiMapTypePrefKey";

@implementation WhereamiViewController
```

Notice that the key is the name of the application, the name of the preference, and the words PrefKey. This is the typical pattern for naming preference keys.

To add or change the value of a preference in an **NSUserDefaults**, you use **setObject:forKey:** just like you would with an **NSMutableDictionary**. In addition, **NSUserDefaults** has some convenience methods for putting primitives into preferences, like **setInteger:forKey:**.

In WhereamiViewController.m, add the following line of code to **changeMapType:**.

```
- (IBAction)changeMapType:(id)sender
{
    [[NSUserDefaults standardUserDefaults]
                setInteger:[sender selectedSegmentIndex]
                    forKey:WhereamiMapTypePrefKey];

    switch([sender selectedSegmentIndex])
    {
        case 0:
        {
            [worldView setMapType:MKMapTypeStandard];
        }break;
        case 1:
        {
            [worldView setMapType:MKMapTypeSatellite];
```

```
        }break;
        case 2:
        {
            [worldView setMapType:MKMapTypeHybrid];
        }break;
    }
}
```

Now, whenever the user changes the map type, that value will be written to the **NSUserDefaults**, which will then be saved to disk. When the **NSUserDefaults** saves its data to disk, it saves it to the Library/ Preferences directory. The name of that file will be the bundle identifier for your application.

When your application firsts asks for the **standardUserDefaults**, it will load this file from disk, and all of the saved preferences will be available to your application. In WhereamiViewController.m, update the method **viewDidLoad** to read in this value and set the map type accordingly.

```
- (void)viewDidLoad
{
    [worldView setShowsUserLocation:YES];

    NSInteger mapTypeValue = [[NSUserDefaults standardUserDefaults]
                                   integerForKey:WhereamiMapTypePrefKey];

    // Update the UI
    [mapTypeControl setSelectedSegmentIndex:mapTypeValue];

    // Update the map
    [self changeMapType:mapTypeControl];
}
```

Build and run Whereami and change the map type. Exit the application by pressing the Home button and kill it from Xcode. Then, relaunch it, and the map will display the type of map you previously selected.

When your application first launches, the value for the key WhereamiMapTypePrefKey does not exist, and it defaults to 0. For this application, that works fine, but some preferences may need a temporary, non-zero default value (i.e., a "factory setting") for the application to run correctly. These temporary defaults are placed in the *registration domain* of **NSUserDefaults**. Any preferences set by the user are stored in a different domain, the *application domain*.

By default, the application domain is empty: there are no keys and no values. The first time a user changes a setting, a value is added to the application domain for the specified key. When you ask the **NSUserDefaults** for the value of a preference, it first looks in the application domain. If there is a value for that key, then the user has set a preference, and the **NSUserDefaults** returns that value. If not, the **NSUserDefaults** looks in the registration domain and finds the temporary default.

The application domain is always saved to disk; that's why it remembers user preferences on the next launch. The registration domain is not, and its values must be set every time the application launches. To set the values of the registration domain, you create an **NSDictionary** with a key-value pair for each preference you plan on using in your application. Then, you send the dictionary as an argument to the method **registerDefaults:** of NSUserDefaults.

Typically, you send the **registerDefaults:** message before any object is able to access the instance of **NSUserDefaults**. This means before the instance of the application delegate is created. What comes before the creation of the **WhereamiViewController**? The creation of the **WhereamiViewController** *class*. Like any object, a class also must be initialized before it can receive messages. So, after a class is created but before it receives its first message, it is sent the message **initialize**.

In WhereamiViewController.m, override the class method **initialize** to register defaults, including setting the map type preference to 1.

```
+ (void)initialize
{
    NSDictionary *defaults = [NSDictionary
                              dictionaryWithObject:[NSNumber numberWithInt:1]
                                            forKey:WhereamiMapTypePrefKey];
    [[NSUserDefaults standardUserDefaults] registerDefaults:defaults];
}
```

Delete the application from your device to remove the previously saved preferences. Then, build and run again. The first time the application launches, the default satellite map will be displayed. If you change the map type, the preference is added to the application domain, and your application will use that value from then on. The default value in the registration domain will be ignored.

NSUserDefaults is a simple class but a useful one. In addition to storing preferences, many developers use **NSUserDefaults** to store little pieces of information that are important but don't really need to be kept in distinct files. For example, if you want to display an alert to a user every 3rd time the application is launched, you could store the number of times the application has been launched in the **NSUserDefaults**.

Silver Challenge: Initial Location

Every time the application finds a new location, note the latitude and longitude in **NSUserDefaults**. When the application launches, zoom in on this coordinate. Make sure you register a default!

Gold Challenge: Concise Coordinates

The silver challenge revealed that you would have to separate the latitude and longitude into separate key-value pairs in **NSUserDefaults**. Make it so both the latitude and longitude are stored as one value under one key. (Hint: You will need to use **NSKeyedArchiver** and **NSKeyedUnarchiver**, and not **NSUserDefaults**' **setObject:forKey:**.)

For the More Curious: The Settings Application

Every iOS device has a Settings application. Applications that register some or all of their preferences with Settings get an entry in this application where those preferences can be changed. However, most applications do not use Settings to store their preferences: why leave the application, find Settings, change a value, and then re-open the application when you could have your own built-in interface?

But, in case it's something you want to do, here's how. To register for an entry in Settings, you add a Settings.bundle to your application. This bundle contains a property list that has an entry for each preference you want to expose in the Settings application. (There is a template for this bundle when you create a new file.)

Each entry contains a key that is a string that matches the name of the preference keys you use with **NSUserDefaults**. Additionally, you set a *preference specifier* key with one of the pre-defined constants. These constants indicate the type of control that will appear for this preference in the

Settings application. They are things like text fields, switches, and sliders. You also add a key for a default value. Some preference specifiers require you to add additional keys. For example, a slider preference will need a minimum and a maximum value.

If you choose to use a settings bundle, you must take care to respect the changes made in the Settings application when transitioning between application states. If your application is terminated and then the user changes a value in Settings, those changes will be written to disk, and the next time your application launches, it will get the correct values. However, most iOS applications are not terminated when the user presses the Home button. Thus, when your application returns from being suspended, you should check to see if any of the preferences were changed while it was suspended.

An application returning from the suspended state that has had preferences changed will be notified via the **NSNotificationCenter**. You can register for the NSUserDefaultsDidChangeNotification notification to be informed of these changes. (You typically register for this notification when the application first launches.)

19

Touch Events and UIResponder

In Chapter 6, you created a **UIScrollView** that handled touch events to scroll a view and even handled a multi-touch event to zoom. The **UIScrollView** class makes scrolling and zooming easy to implement. But what if you want to do something else, something special or unique, with touch events?

In this chapter, you are going to create a view that lets the user draw lines by dragging across the view (Figure 19.1). Using multi-touch, the user will be able to draw more than one line at a time. Double-tapping will clear the screen and allow the user to begin again.

Figure 19.1 A drawing program

Touch Events

As a subclass of **UIResponder**, your view can override four methods to handle the four distinct touch events:

- a finger or fingers touches the screen

  ```
  - (void)touchesBegan:(NSSet *)touches
          withEvent:(UIEvent *)event;
  ```

- a finger or fingers move across the screen (This message is sent repeatedly as a finger moves.)

  ```
  - (void)touchesMoved:(NSSet *)touches
          withEvent:(UIEvent *)event;
  ```

- a finger or fingers are removed from the screen

  ```
  - (void)touchesEnded:(NSSet *)touches
          withEvent:(UIEvent *)event;
  ```

- a system event, like an incoming phone call, interrupts a touch before it ends

  ```
  - (void)touchesCancelled:(NSSet *)touches
          withEvent:(UIEvent *)event;
  ```

When a finger touches the screen, an instance of **UITouch** is created. The **UIView** that this finger touched is sent the message **touchesBegan:withEvent:** and the **UITouch** is in the **NSSet** of touches.

As that finger moves around the screen, the touch object is updated to contain the current location of the finger on the screen. Then, the same **UIView** that the touch began on is sent the message **touchesMoved:withEvent:**. The **NSSet** that is passed as an argument to this method contains the same **UITouch** that originally was created when the finger it represents touched the screen.

When a finger is removed from the screen, the touch object is updated one last time to contain the current location of the finger, and the view that the touch began on is sent the message **touchesEnded:withEvent:**. After that method finishes executing, the **UITouch** object is destroyed.

From this information, we can draw a few conclusions about how touch objects work:

- One **UITouch** corresponds to one finger on the screen. This touch object lives as long as the finger is on the screen and always contains the current position of the finger on the screen.

- The view that the finger started on will receive every touch event message for that finger no matter what. If the finger moves outside of the **UIView**'s frame that it began on, that view still receives the **touchesMoved:withEvent:** and **touchesEnded:withEvent:** messages. Thus, if a touch begins on a view, then that view owns the touch for the life of the touch.

- You don't have to – nor should you ever – keep a reference to a **UITouch** object. The application will give you access to a touch object when it changes state.

Every time a touch does something, like begins, moves, or ends, a *touch event* is added to a queue of events that the **UIApplication** object manages. In practice, the queue rarely fills up, and events are delivered immediately. The delivery of these touch events involves sending one of the **UIResponder** messages to the view that owns the touch. (If your touches are sluggish, then one of your methods is hogging the CPU, and events are waiting in line to be delivered. Chapter 21 will show you how to catch these problems.)

What about multiple touches? If multiple fingers do the same thing at the exact same time to the same view, all of these touch events are delivered at once. Each touch object – one for each finger – is included in the **NSSet** passed as an argument in the **UIResponder** messages. However, the window of opportunity for the "exact same time" is fairly short. So, instead of one responder message with all of the touches, there are usually multiple responder messages with one or more of the touches.

Creating the TouchTracker Application

Now let's get started with your application. In Xcode, create a new Empty Application iPhone project and name it TouchTracker. Don't specify a Class Prefix and only check the box for Automatic Reference Counting.

First, you will need a model object that describes a line. Create a new **NSObject** and name it **Line**. In Line.h, declare two CGPoint properties:

```
#import <Foundation/Foundation.h>

@interface Line : NSObject

@property (nonatomic) CGPoint begin;
@property (nonatomic) CGPoint end;
@end
```

In Line.m, synthesize the properties:

```
#import "Line.h"

@implementation Line

@synthesize begin, end;

@end
```

Next, create a new **NSObject** called **TouchDrawView**. In TouchDrawView.h, change the superclass to **UIView**. Also, declare two collection objects: an array to hold complete lines and a dictionary to hold lines that are still being drawn. You'll see why we're using different collection objects shortly.

```
#import <Foundation/Foundation.h>

@interface TouchDrawView : NSObject
@interface TouchDrawView : UIView
{
    NSMutableDictionary *linesInProcess;
    NSMutableArray *completeLines;
}
- (void)clearAll;
@end
```

Now you need a view controller to manage an instance of **TouchDrawView** in TouchTracker. Create a new **NSObject** subclass named **TouchViewController**. In TouchViewController.h, change the superclass to **UIViewController**.

```
@interface TouchViewController : NSObject
@interface TouchViewController : UIViewController
```

In TouchViewController.m, override **loadView** to set up an instance of **TouchDrawView** as **TouchViewController**'s view. Make sure to import the header file for **TouchDrawView** at the top of this file.

```
#import "TouchViewController.h"
#import "TouchDrawView.h"

@implementation TouchViewController

- (void)loadView
{
    [self setView:[[TouchDrawView alloc] initWithFrame:CGRectZero]];
}

@end
```

In AppDelegate.m, create an instance of **TouchViewController** and set it as the rootViewController of the window. Don't forget to import the header file for **TouchViewController** in this file.

```
#import "AppDelegate.h"
#import "TouchViewController.h"

@implementation AppDelegate

@synthesize window = _window;

- (BOOL)application:(UIApplication *)application
    didFinishLaunchingWithOptions:(NSDictionary *)launchOptions
{
    self.window = [[UIWindow alloc] initWithFrame:[[UIScreen mainScreen] bounds]];
    // Override point for customization after application launch.

    TouchViewController *tvc = [[TouchViewController alloc] init];
    [[self window] setRootViewController:tvc];

    self.window.backgroundColor = [UIColor whiteColor];
    [self.window makeKeyAndVisible];
    return YES;
}
```

Drawing with TouchDrawView

TouchDrawView will keep track of all of the lines that have been drawn and any that are currently being drawn. In TouchDrawView.m, create the two collections and import the header for the **Line** class.

```
#import "TouchDrawView.h"
#import "Line.h"

@implementation TouchDrawView

- (id)initWithFrame:(CGRect)r
{
    self = [super initWithFrame:r];
```

```
    if (self) {
        linesInProcess = [[NSMutableDictionary alloc] init];

        // Don't let the autocomplete fool you on the next line,
        // make sure you are instantiating an NSMutableArray
        // and not an NSMutableDictionary!
        completeLines = [[NSMutableArray alloc] init];

        [self setBackgroundColor:[UIColor whiteColor]];

        [self setMultipleTouchEnabled:YES];
    }

    return self;
}
```

Notice that you explicitly enabled multi-touch events by sending the message
setMultipleTouchEnabled:. Without this, only one touch at a time can be active on a view. If another
finger touches the view, it will be ignored, and the view will not be sent **touchesBegan:withEvent:** or
any of the other **UIResponder** messages.

Now override the **drawRect:** method to create lines using functions from Core Graphics:

```
- (void)drawRect:(CGRect)rect
{
    CGContextRef context = UIGraphicsGetCurrentContext();
    CGContextSetLineWidth(context, 10.0);
    CGContextSetLineCap(context, kCGLineCapRound);

    // Draw complete lines in black
    [[UIColor blackColor] set];
    for (Line *line in completeLines) {
        CGContextMoveToPoint(context, [line begin].x, [line begin].y);
        CGContextAddLineToPoint(context, [line end].x, [line end].y);
        CGContextStrokePath(context);
    }

    // Draw lines in process in red (Don't copy and paste the previous loop;
    // this one is way different)
    [[UIColor redColor] set];
    for (NSValue *v in linesInProcess) {
        Line *line = [linesInProcess objectForKey:v];
        CGContextMoveToPoint(context, [line begin].x, [line begin].y);
        CGContextAddLineToPoint(context, [line end].x, [line end].y);
        CGContextStrokePath(context);
    }
}
```

Finally, write a method that will clear the collections and redraw the view in TouchDrawView.m.

```
- (void)clearAll
{
    // Clear the collections
    [linesInProcess removeAllObjects];
    [completeLines removeAllObjects];

    // Redraw
    [self setNeedsDisplay];
}
```

Turning Touches Into Lines

A line (remember 9th grade geometry class?) is defined by two points. Our **Line** stores these points as properties named begin and end. When a touch begins, you'll create a line and set both begin and end to the point where the touch began. When the touch moves, you will update end. When the touch ends, you will have your complete line.

There are two collection objects that hold **Line** instances. Lines that have been completed are stored in the completeLines array. Lines that are still being drawn, however, are stored in an **NSMutableDictionary**. Why do we need a dictionary? We've enabled multi-touch, so a user can draw more than one line at a time. This means we have to keep track of which touch events go with which line. For instance, imagine the user touches the screen with two fingers creating two instances of **Line**. Then one of those fingers moves. The **TouchDrawView** is sent a message for the event, but how can it know which line to update?

This is why we're using a dictionary instead of an array for the lines in process. When a touch begins, we will grab the address of the **UITouch** object that is passed in and wrap it in an **NSValue** instance. A new **Line** will be created and added to the dictionary, and the **NSValue** will be its key. As we receive more touch events, we can use the address of the **UITouch** that is passed in to access and update the right line (Figure 19.2).

Figure 19.2   Object diagram for TouchTracker

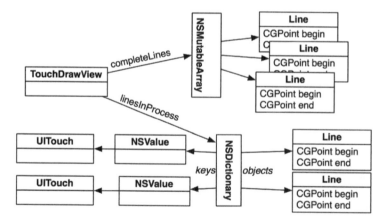

Now let's return to the methods for handling touch events. First, in TouchDrawView.m, override **touchesBegan:withEvent:** to create a new **Line** instance and store it in an **NSMutableDictionary**.

```
- (void)touchesBegan:(NSSet *)touches
          withEvent:(UIEvent *)event
{
    for (UITouch *t in touches) {

        // Is this a double tap?
        if ([t tapCount] > 1) {
            [self clearAll];
            return;
        }
    }
```

```
        // Use the touch object (packed in an NSValue) as the key
        NSValue *key = [NSValue valueWithNonretainedObject:t];

        // Create a line for the value
        CGPoint loc = [t locationInView:self];
        Line *newLine = [[Line alloc] init];
        [newLine setBegin:loc];
        [newLine setEnd:loc];

        // Put pair in dictionary
        [linesInProcess setObject:newLine forKey:key];
    }
}
```

Next, in TouchDrawView.m, override **touchesMoved:withEvent:** to update the end point of the line associated with the moving touch.

```
- (void)touchesMoved:(NSSet *)touches
          withEvent:(UIEvent *)event
{
    // Update linesInProcess with moved touches
    for (UITouch *t in touches) {
        NSValue *key = [NSValue valueWithNonretainedObject:t];

        // Find the line for this touch
        Line *line = [linesInProcess objectForKey:key];

        // Update the line
        CGPoint loc = [t locationInView:self];
        [line setEnd:loc];
    }
    // Redraw
    [self setNeedsDisplay];
}
```

When a touch ends, you need to finalize the line. However, a touch can end for two reasons: the user lifts the finger off the screen (**touchesEnded:withEvent:**) or the operating system interrupts your application (**touchesCancelled:withEvent:**). A phone call, for example, will interrupt your application.

In many applications, you'll want to handle these two events differently. However, for TouchTracker, you will write one method to handle both cases. Declare a new method in TouchDrawView.h.

```
- (void)endTouches:(NSSet *)touches;
```

In TouchDrawView.m, implement **endTouches:**.

```
- (void)endTouches:(NSSet *)touches
{
    // Remove ending touches from dictionary
    for (UITouch *t in touches) {
        NSValue *key = [NSValue valueWithNonretainedObject:t];
        Line *line = [linesInProcess objectForKey:key];

        // If this is a double tap, 'line' will be nil,
        // so make sure not to add it to the array
        if (line) {
            [completeLines addObject:line];
            [linesInProcess removeObjectForKey:key];
```

```
        }
    }
    // Redraw
    [self setNeedsDisplay];
}
```

Finally, override the two methods from **UIResponder** to call **endTouches:** in TouchDrawView.m.

```
- (void)touchesEnded:(NSSet *)touches
            withEvent:(UIEvent *)event
{
    [self endTouches:touches];
}

- (void)touchesCancelled:(NSSet *)touches
               withEvent:(UIEvent *)event
{
    [self endTouches:touches];
}
```

Build and run the application. Then make beautiful line art with one or more fingers.

The Responder Chain

In Chapter 5, we talked briefly about **UIResponder** and the first responder. A **UIResponder** can receive touch events. **UIView** is one example of a **UIResponder** subclass, but there are many others, including **UIViewController**, **UIApplication**, and **UIWindow**. You are probably thinking, "But you can't touch a **UIViewController**. It's not an on-screen object." You are right – you can't send a touch event *directly* to a **UIViewController**, but view controllers can receive events through the *responder chain*. (By the way, you get two bonus points for keeping the view controller and its view separate in your brain.)

Every **UIResponder** has a pointer called nextResponder, and together these objects make up the responder chain (Figure 19.3). A touch event starts at the view that was touched. The nextResponder of a view is typically its **UIViewController** (if it has one) or its superview (if it doesn't). The nextResponder of a view controller is typically its view's superview. The top-most superview is the window. The window's nextResponder is the singleton instance of **UIApplication**. If the application doesn't handle the event, then it is discarded. (Note that the window and application don't do anything with an event unless you subclass them.)

Figure 19.3   Responder chain

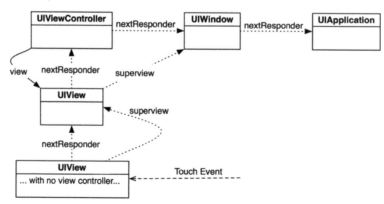

How does a **UIResponder** *not* handle an event? It forwards the same message to its nextResponder. That is what the default implementation of methods like **touchesBegan:withEvent:** do. So if a method is not overridden, its next responder will attempt to handle the touch event.

You can explicitly send a message to a next responder, too. Let's say there is a view that tracks touches, but if a double tap occurs, its next responder should handle it. The code would look like this:

```
- (void)touchesBegan:(NSSet *)touches withEvent:(UIEvent *)event
{
    UITouch *touch = [touches anyObject];
    if ([touch tapCount] == 2) {
        [[self nextResponder] touchesBegan:touches withEvent:event];
        return;
    }

    ... Go on to handle touches that aren't double taps
}
```

Bronze Challenge: Saving and Loading

Save the lines when the application terminates. Reload them when the application resumes.

Silver Challenge: Colors

Make it so the angle at which a line is drawn dictates its color once it has been added to completeLines.

Gold Challenge: Circles

Use two fingers to draw circles. Try having each finger represent one corner of the bounding box around the circle. You can simulate two fingers on the simulator by holding down the option button. (Hint: This is much easier if you track touches that are working on a circle in a separate dictionary.)

For the More Curious: UIControl

The class **UIControl** is the superclass for several classes in Cocoa Touch, including **UIButton** and **UISlider**. We've seen how to set the targets and actions for these controls. Now we can take a closer look at how **UIControl** overrides the same **UIResponder** methods you implemented in this chapter.

In **UIControl**, each possible *control event* is associated with a constant. Buttons, for example, typically send action messages on the UIControlEventTouchUpInside control event. A target registered for this control event will only receive its action message if the user touches the control and then lifts the finger off the screen inside the frame of the control. Essentially, it is a tap.

For a button, however, you can have actions on other event types. For example, you might trigger a method if the user removes the finger *inside or outside* the frame. Assigning the target and action programmatically would look like this:

```
[rButton addTarget:tempController
            action:@selector(resetTemperature:)
  forControlEvents:UIControlEventTouchUpInside | UIControlEventTouchUpOutside];
```

Now consider how **UIControl** handles UIControlEventTouchUpInside.

```
// Not the exact code. There is a bit more going on!
- (void)touchesEnded:(NSSet *)touches withEvent:(UIEvent *)event
{
    // Reference to the touch that is ending
    UITouch *touch = [touches anyObject];

    // Location of that point in this control's coordinate system
    CGPoint touchLocation = [touch locationInView:self];

    // Is that point still in my viewing bounds?
    if (CGRectContainsPoint([self bounds], touchLocation))
    {
        // Send out action messages to all targets registered for this event!
        [self sendActionsForControlEvents:UIControlEventTouchUpInside];
    } else {
        // The touch ended outside the bounds, different control event
        [self sendActionsForControlEvents:UIControlEventTouchUpOutside];
    }
}
```

So how do these actions get sent to the right target? At the end of the **UIResponder** method implementations, the control sends the message **sendActionsForControlEvents:** to itself. This method looks at all of the target-action pairs the control has, and if any of them are registered for the control event passed as the argument, those targets are sent an action message.

However, a control never sends a message directly to its targets. Instead, it routes these messages through the **UIApplication** object. Why not have controls send the action messages directly to the targets? Controls can also have nil-targeted actions. If a **UIControl**'s target is nil, the **UIApplication** finds the *first responder* of its **UIWindow** and sends the action message to it.

20

UIGestureRecognizer and UIMenuController

In Chapter 19, you handled raw touches and determined their course by implementing methods from **UIResponder**. Sometimes, you want to detect a specific pattern of touches that make a gesture, like a pinch or a swipe. Instead of writing code to detect common gestures yourself, you can use instances of **UIGestureRecognizer**.

A **UIGestureRecognizer** intercepts touches that are on their way to being handled by a view. When it recognizes a particular gesture, it sends a message to the object of your choice. There are several types of gesture recognizers built into the SDK. In this chapter, we will use three of them to allow TouchTracker users to select, move, and delete lines. We'll also see how to use another interesting iOS class, **UIMenuController**.

Figure 20.1 TouchTracker by the end of the chapter

UIGestureRecognizer Subclasses

You don't instantiate **UIGestureRecognizer** itself. Instead, there are a number of subclasses of **UIGestureRecognizer**, and each one is responsible for recognizing a particular gesture.

To use an instance of a **UIGestureRecognizer** subclass, you give it a target-action pair and attach it to a view. Whenever the gesture recognizer recognizes its gesture on the view, it will send the action message to its target. All **UIGestureRecognizer** action messages have the same form:

```
- (void)action:(UIGestureRecognizer *)gestureRecognizer;
```

When recognizing a gesture, the gesture recognizer intercepts the touches destined for the view (Figure 20.2). Thus, a view with gesture recognizers may not receive the typical **UIResponder** messages like **touchesBegan:withEvent:**.

Figure 20.2   UIGestureRecognizers intercept UITouches

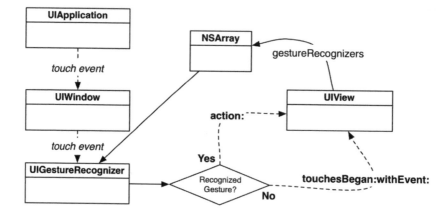

Detecting Taps with UITapGestureRecognizer

The first **UIGestureRecognizer** subclass you will use is **UITapGestureRecognizer**. When the user taps a line in TouchTracker, you will present a menu that allows them to delete it. Open TouchTracker.xcodeproj from Chapter 19.

In the first part of this section, we are going to recognize a tap, determine which line is close to where the tap occurred, store a reference to that line, and change that line's color to green so that the user knows it has been selected.

In TouchDrawView.m, edit the **initWithFrame:** method to create an instance of **UITapGestureRecognizer** and attach it to the **TouchDrawView** being initialized.

```
- (id)initWithFrame:(CGRect)r
{
    self = [super initWithFrame:r];

    if (self) {
        linesInProcess = [[NSMutableDictionary alloc] init];
        completeLines = [[NSMutableArray alloc] init];
```

```
        [self setBackgroundColor:[UIColor whiteColor]];

        [self setMultipleTouchEnabled:YES];

        UITapGestureRecognizer *tapRecognizer =
        [[UITapGestureRecognizer alloc] initWithTarget:self
                                        action:@selector(tap:)];

        [self addGestureRecognizer:tapRecognizer];
    }
    return self;
}
```

Now whenever a tap occurs on this **TouchDrawView**, the **UITapGestureRecognizer** will send it the message **tap:**. In TouchDrawView.m, implement the **tap:** method. For now, just have it log something to the console.

```
- (void)tap:(UIGestureRecognizer *)gr
{
    NSLog(@"Recognized tap");
}
```

Build and run the application and then tap on the screen. You should notice two things: the console reports that a tap was recognized, and a dot is drawn on the view. That dot is a very short line and a bug. In this application, we don't want anything drawn in response to a tap. Add the following code to **tap:** to remove any lines in process and redisplay the view.

```
- (void)tap:(UIGestureRecognizer *)gr
{
    NSLog(@"Recognized tap");

    // If we just tapped, remove all lines in process
    // so that a tap doesn't result in a new line
    [linesInProcess removeAllObjects];

    [self setNeedsDisplay];
}
```

Build and run again. Now a tap should have no effect except for logging a statement to the console.

Now, in order to "select a line," we need to find a line close to where the tap occurred and then store a reference to that line for later. In TouchDrawView.h, declare a new method and a new property. Also, at the top of this file, forward declare the **Line** class.

```
@class Line;

@interface TouchDrawView : UIView
{
    NSMutableDictionary *linesInProcess;
    NSMutableArray *completeLines;
}
@property (nonatomic, weak) Line *selectedLine;

- (Line *)lineAtPoint:(CGPoint)p;

- (void)clearAll;
- (void)endTouches:(NSSet *)touches;

@end
```

Synthesize `selectedLine` in TouchDrawView.m.

```
@implementation TouchDrawView
@synthesize selectedLine;
```

Implement **lineAtPoint:** in TouchDrawView.m to get a **Line** close to the given point.

```
- (Line *)lineAtPoint:(CGPoint)p
{
    // Find a line close to p
    for (Line *l in completeLines) {
        CGPoint start = [l begin];
        CGPoint end = [l end];

        // Check a few points on the line
        for (float t = 0.0; t <= 1.0; t += 0.05) {
            float x = start.x + t * (end.x - start.x);
            float y = start.y + t * (end.y - start.y);

            // If the tapped point is within 20 points, let's return this line
            if (hypot(x - p.x, y - p.y) < 20.0) {
                return l;
            }
        }
    }

    // If nothing is close enough to the tapped point, then we didn't select a line
    return nil;
}
```

(There are better ways to implement **lineAtPoint:**, but this simplistic implementation is okay for our purposes.)

The point we are interested in, of course, is where the tap occurred. We can easily get this information. Every **UIGestureRecognizer** has a **locationInView:** method. Sending this message to the gesture recognizer will give you the coordinate where the gesture occurred in the coordinate system of the view that is passed as the argument.

In TouchDrawView.m, send the **locationInView:** message to the gesture recognizer, pass the result to **lineAtPoint:**, and make the returned line the `selectedLine`.

```
- (void)tap:(UIGestureRecognizer *)gr
{
    NSLog(@"Recognized tap");

    CGPoint point = [gr locationInView:self];
    [self setSelectedLine:[self lineAtPoint:point]];

    // If we just tapped, remove all lines in process so a new one
    // isn't drawn on every tap
    [linesInProcess removeAllObjects];

    [self setNeedsDisplay];
}
```

Finally, in TouchDrawView.m, update **drawRect:** to draw the `selectedLine` in green. Make sure this code comes after you draw the complete and in progress lines.

```
    [[UIColor redColor] set];
```

```
    for (NSValue *v in linesInProcess) {
        Line *line = [linesInProcess objectForKey:v];
        CGContextMoveToPoint(context, [line begin].x, [line begin].y);
        CGContextAddLineToPoint(context, [line end].x, [line end].y);
        CGContextStrokePath(context);
    }

    // If there is a selected line, draw it
    if ([self selectedLine]) {
        [[UIColor greenColor] set];
        CGContextMoveToPoint(context, [[self selectedLine] begin].x,
                                      [[self selectedLine] begin].y);
        CGContextAddLineToPoint(context, [[self selectedLine] end].x,
                                         [[self selectedLine] end].y);
        CGContextStrokePath(context);
    }

}
```

Build and run the application. Draw a few lines and then tap on one. The tapped line should appear in green.

UIMenuController

When the user selects a line, we want a menu to appear right where the user tapped that offers the option to delete that line. There is a built-in class for providing this sort of menu called **UIMenuController**. A menu controller has a list of menu items and is presented in an existing view. Each item has a title (what shows up in the menu) and an action (the message it sends the view it is being presented in).

Figure 20.3   A UIMenuController

There is only one **UIMenuController** per application. When you wish to present this instance, you fill it with menu items, give it a rectangle to present from, and set it to be visible. Do this in TouchDrawView.m's **tap:** method if the user has tapped on a line. If the user tapped somewhere that is not near a line, the currently selected line will be deselected, and the menu controller will hide.

```
- (void)tap:(UIGestureRecognizer *)gr
{
    NSLog(@"Recognized tap");
    CGPoint point = [gr locationInView:self];
    [self setSelectedLine:[self lineAtPoint:point]];

    [linesInProcess removeAllObjects];

    if ([self selectedLine]) {
        // We'll talk about this shortly
        [self becomeFirstResponder];

        // Grab the menu controller
        UIMenuController *menu = [UIMenuController sharedMenuController];
```

```
        // Create a new "Delete" UIMenuItem
        UIMenuItem *deleteItem = [[UIMenuItem alloc] initWithTitle:@"Delete"
                                                action:@selector(deleteLine:)];
        [menu setMenuItems:[NSArray arrayWithObject:deleteItem]];

        // Tell the menu where it should come from and show it
        [menu setTargetRect:CGRectMake(point.x, point.y, 2, 2) inView:self];
        [menu setMenuVisible:YES animated:YES];
    } else {
        // Hide the menu if no line is selected
        [[UIMenuController sharedMenuController] setMenuVisible:NO animated:YES];
    }
    [self setNeedsDisplay];
}
```

For a menu controller to appear, the view that is presenting the menu controller must be the first responder of the window. So we sent the message **becomeFirstResponder** to the **TouchDrawView** before getting the menu controller. However, you might remember from Chapter 6 that you must override **canBecomeFirstResponder** in a view if it needs to become the first responder.

In TouchDrawView.m, override this method to return YES.

```
- (BOOL)canBecomeFirstResponder
{
    return YES;
}
```

You can build and run the application now, but when you select a line, the menu won't appear. This is because menu controllers are smart: When a menu controller is to be displayed, it goes through each menu item and asks its view if it implements the action message for that item. If the view does not implement that method, then the menu controller won't show the associated menu item. To get the Delete menu item to appear, implement **deleteLine:** in TouchDrawView.m.

```
- (void)deleteLine:(id)sender
{
    // Remove the selected line from the list of completeLines
    [completeLines removeObject:[self selectedLine]];

    // Redraw everything
    [self setNeedsDisplay];
}
```

Build and run the application. Draw a line, tap on it, and then select Delete from the menu item. Bonus feature: the selectedLine property was declared as weak, so when it is removed from the completeLines array, selectedLine is automatically set to nil.

UILongPressGestureRecognizer

Let's test out two other subclasses of **UIGestureRecognizer**: **UILongPressGestureRecognizer** and **UIPanGestureRecognizer**. When the user holds down on a line (a long press), that line should be selected. While a line is selected in this way, the user should be able to drag the line (a pan) to a new position.

In this section, we'll focus on the long press recognizer. In TouchDrawView.m, instantiate a **UILongPressGestureRecognizer** in **initWithFrame:** and add it to the **TouchDrawView**.

```
[self addGestureRecognizer:tapRecognizer];

UILongPressGestureRecognizer *pressRecognizer =
    [[UILongPressGestureRecognizer alloc] initWithTarget:self
                                          action:@selector(longPress:)];
[self addGestureRecognizer:pressRecognizer];
```

Now when the user holds down on the **TouchDrawView**, the message **longPress:** will be sent to it. By default, a touch must be held 0.5 seconds to become a long press, but you can change the minimumPressDuration of the gesture recognizer if you like.

A tap is a simple gesture. By the time it is recognized, the gesture is over, and a tap has occurred. A long press, on the other hand, is a gesture that occurs over time and is defined by three separate events.

For example, when the user touches a view, the long press recognizer notices a *possible* long press but must wait and see whether this touch is held long enough to become a long press gesture.

Once the user holds the touch long enough, the long press is recognized and the gesture has *begun*. When the user removes the finger, the gesture has *ended*.

Each of these events causes a change in the gesture recognizer's state property. For instance, the state of the long press recognizer described above would be UIGestureRecognizerStatePossible, then UIGestureRecognizerStateBegan, and finally UIGestureRecognizerStateEnded.

When a gesture recognizer transitions to any state other than the possible state, it sends its action message to its target. This means the long press recognizer's target receives the same message when a long press begins and when it ends. The gesture recognizer's state allows the target to determine why it has been sent the action message and take the appropriate action.

Here's the plan for implementing our action method **longPress:**. When the view receives **longPress:** and the long press has just begun, we will select the closest line to where the gesture occurred. This allows the user to select a line while keeping the finger on the screen (which is important in the next section when we implement panning). When the view receives **longPress:** and the long press has ended, we will deselect the line.

In TouchDrawView.m, implement **longPress:**.

```
- (void)longPress:(UIGestureRecognizer *)gr
{
    if ([gr state] == UIGestureRecognizerStateBegan) {
        CGPoint point = [gr locationInView:self];
        [self setSelectedLine:[self lineAtPoint:point]];

        if ([self selectedLine]) {
            [linesInProcess removeAllObjects];
        }
```

```
    } else if ([gr state] == UIGestureRecognizerStateEnded) {
        [self setSelectedLine:nil];
    }
    [self setNeedsDisplay];
}
```

Build and run the application. Draw a line and then hold down on it; the line will turn green and be selected and will stay that way until you let go.

UIPanGestureRecognizer and Simultaneous Recognizers

Once a line is selected during a long press, we want the user to be able to move that line around the screen by dragging it with a finger. So we need a gesture recognizer for a finger moving around the screen. This gesture is called *panning*, and its gesture recognizer subclass is **UIPanGestureRecognizer**.

Normally, a gesture recognizer does not share the touches it intercepts. Once it has recognized its gesture, it "eats" that touch, and no other recognizer gets a chance to handle it. In our case, this is bad: the entire pan gesture we want to recognize happens within a long press gesture. We need the long press recognizer and the pan recognizer to be able to recognize their gestures simultaneously. Let's see how to do that.

First, in TouchDrawView.h, declare that **TouchDrawView** conforms to the UIGestureRecognizerDelegate protocol and declare a **UIPanGestureRecognizer** as an instance variable.

```
@interface TouchDrawView : UIView
    <UIGestureRecognizerDelegate>
{
    NSMutableDictionary *linesInProcess;
    NSMutableArray *completeLines;

    UIPanGestureRecognizer *moveRecognizer;
}
```

In TouchDrawView.m, add code to **initWithFrame:** to instantiate a **UIPanGestureRecognizer**, set two of its properties, and attach it to the **TouchDrawView**.

```
[self addGestureRecognizer:pressRecognizer];

moveRecognizer = [[UIPanGestureRecognizer alloc]
                    initWithTarget:self action:@selector(moveLine:)];
[moveRecognizer setDelegate:self];
[moveRecognizer setCancelsTouchesInView:NO];
[self addGestureRecognizer:moveRecognizer];
```

There are a number of methods in the UIGestureRecognizerDelegate protocol, but we are only interested in one – **gestureRecognizer:shouldRecognizeSimultaneouslyWithGestureRecognizer:**. A gesture recognizer will send this message to its delegate when it recognizes its gesture but realizes that another gesture recognizer has recognized its gesture, too. If this method returns YES, the recognizer will share its touches with other gesture recognizers.

Invoice for/Bon de livraison pour

Your order of/Votre commande du:November 29, 2012   Invoice number/N° bon de livraison DnN1v3kSR November 29, 2012
Order ID/N° commande: 701-2951240-1902661

SDnN1v3kSR

Quantity/Quantité	Item/Article	Description/Description	Our Price/Notre prix	Total/Total
1	iOS Programming: The Big Nerd Ranch Guide (3rd Edition) (** P-1-A147H512 **) **0321821521**	Paperback		

Happy learning! Stephen

This completes your gift order.
Cette livraison complète votre commande de cadeau.

Amazon.com.ca,Inc. 410 Terry Avenue North Seattle, WA 98109-5210

JM8

0/DnN1v3kSR/-1 of 1-//UPS-STD/second-ca/4092325/1129-16:30/1129-13:23

In TouchDrawView.m, return YES when the moveRecognizer sends the message to its delegate.

```
- (BOOL)gestureRecognizer:(UIGestureRecognizer *)gestureRecognizer
    shouldRecognizeSimultaneouslyWithGestureRecognizer:(UIGestureRecognizer *)other
{
    if (gestureRecognizer == moveRecognizer)
        return YES;
    return NO;
}
```

Now when the user begins a long press, the **UIPanGestureRecognizer** will be allowed to keep track of this finger, too. When the finger begins to move, the pan recognizer will transition to the began state. If these two recognizers could not work simultaneously, the long press recognizer would start, and the pan recognizer would never transition to the began state or send its action message to its target.

In addition to the states we've seen previously, a pan gesture recognizer supports the *changed* state. When a finger starts to move, the pan recognizer enters the began state and sends a message to its target. While the finger moves around the screen, the recognizer transitions to the changed state and sends its action message to its target repeatedly. Finally, when the finger leaves the screen, the recognizer's state is set to ended, and the final message is delivered to the target.

Now we need to implement the **moveLine:** method that the pan recognizer sends its target. In this implementation, you will send the message **translationInView:** to the pan recognizer. This **UIPanGestureRecognizer** method returns how far the pan has moved as a CGPoint in the coordinate system of the view passed as the argument. Therefore, when the pan gesture begins, this property is set to the zero point (where both x and y equal zero). As the pan moves, this value is updated – if the pan goes very far to the right, it has a high x value; if the pan returns to where it began, its translation goes back to the zero point.

In TouchDrawView.m, implement **moveLine:**. Notice that because we will send the gesture recognizer a method from the **UIPanGestureRecognizer** class, the parameter of this method must be a pointer to an instance of **UIPanGestureRecognizer** rather than **UIGestureRecognizer**.

```
- (void)moveLine:(UIPanGestureRecognizer *)gr
{
    // If we haven't selected a line, we don't do anything here
    if (![self selectedLine])
        return;

    // When the pan recognizer changes its position...
    if ([gr state] == UIGestureRecognizerStateChanged) {
        // How far has the pan moved?
        CGPoint translation = [gr translationInView:self];

        // Add the translation to the current begin and end points of the line
        CGPoint begin = [[self selectedLine] begin];
        CGPoint end = [[self selectedLine] end];
        begin.x += translation.x;
        begin.y += translation.y;
        end.x += translation.x;
        end.y += translation.y;

        // Set the new beginning and end points of the line
        [[self selectedLine] setBegin:begin];
        [[self selectedLine] setEnd:end];
```

```
        // Redraw the screen
        [self setNeedsDisplay];
    }
}
```

Build and run the application. Touch and hold on a line and begin dragging – and you'll immediately notice that the line and your finger are way out of sync. This makes sense because you are adding the current translation over and over again to the line's original end points. We really need the gesture recognizer to report the translation since the last time this method was called instead. Fortunately, we can do this. You can set the translation of a pan gesture recognizer back to the zero point every time it reports a change. Then, the next time it reports a change, it will have the translation since the last event.

Near the bottom of **moveLine:** in TouchDrawView.m, add the following line of code.

```
        [self setNeedsDisplay];

        [gr setTranslation:CGPointZero inView:self];
    }
}
```

Build and run the application and move a line around. Works great!

Before moving on, let's take a look at a property you set in the pan gesture recognizer – cancelsTouchesInView. Every **UIGestureRecognizer** has this property and, by default, this property is YES. This means that the gesture recognizer will eat any touch it recognizes so that the view will not have a chance to handle it via the traditional **UIResponder** methods, like **touchesBegan:withEvent:**.

Usually, this is what you want, but not always. In our case, the gesture that the pan recognizer recognizes is the same kind of touch that the view handles to draw lines using the **UIResponder** methods. If the gesture recognizer eats these touches, then users will not be able to draw lines.

When you set cancelsTouchesInView to NO, touches that the gesture recognizer recognizes also get delivered to the view via the **UIResponder** methods. This allows both the recognizer and the view's **UIResponder** methods to handle the same touches. If you're curious, comment out the line that sets cancelsTouchesInView to NO and build and run again to see the effects.

For the More Curious: UIMenuController and UIResponderStandardEditActions

The **UIMenuController** is typically responsible for showing the user an "edit" menu when it is displayed; think of a text field or text view when you press and hold. Therefore, an unmodified menu controller (one that you don't set the menu items for) already has default menu items that it presents, like Cut, Copy, and other familiar friends. Each item has an action message wired up. For example, **cut:** is sent to the view presenting the menu controller when the Cut menu item is tapped.

All **UIResponder**s implement these methods, but, by default, these methods don't do anything. Subclasses like **UITextField** override these methods to do something appropriate for their context, like cut the currently selected text. The methods are all declared in the UIResponderStandardEditActions protocol.

If you override a method from UIResponderStandardEditActions in a view, its menu item will automatically appear in any menu you show for that view. This works because the menu controller sends the message **canPerformAction:withSender:** to its view, which returns YES or NO depending on whether the view implements this method.

If you want to implement one of these methods but *don't* want it to appear in the menu, you can override **canPerformAction:withSender:** to return NO.

```
- (BOOL)canPerformAction:(SEL)action withSender:(id)sender
{
    if (action == @selector(copy:))
        return NO;

    // The superclass' implementation will return YES if the method is in the .m file
    return [super canPerformAction:action withSender:sender];
}
```

For the More Curious: More on UIGestureRecognizer

We've only scratched the surface of **UIGestureRecognizer**; there are more subclasses, more properties, and more delegate methods, and you can even create recognizers of your own. This section will give you an idea of what **UIGestureRecognizer** is capable of, and then you can study the documentation for **UIGestureRecognizer** to learn even more.

When a gesture recognizer is on a view, it is really handling all of the **UIResponder** methods, like **touchesBegan:withEvent:**, for you. Gesture recognizers are pretty greedy, so they typically don't let a view receive touch events or they at least delay the delivery of those events. You can set properties on the recognizer, like **delaysTouchesBegan**, **delaysTouchesEnded**, and **cancelsTouchesInView**, to change this behavior. If you need finer control than this all-or-nothing approach, you can implement delegate methods for the recognizer.

At times, you may have two gesture recognizers looking for very similar gestures. You can chain recognizers together so that one is required to fail for the next one to start using the method **requireGestureRecognizerToFail:**.

One thing you must understand to master gesture recognizers is how they interpret their state. Overall, there are seven states a recognizer can enter:

- UIGestureRecognizerStatePossible
- UIGestureRecognizerStateBegan
- UIGestureRecognizerStateChanged
- UIGestureRecognizerStateEnded

- UIGestureRecognizerStateFailed
- UIGestureRecognizerStateCancelled
- UIGestureRecognizerStateRecognized

Most of the time, a recognizer will stay in the possible state. When a recognizer recognizes its gesture, it goes into the began state. If the gesture is something that can continue, like a pan, it will go into and stay in the changed state until it ends. When any of its properties change, it sends another message to its target. When the gesture ends (typically when the user lifts the finger), it enters the ended state.

Not all recognizers begin, change, and end. For gesture recognizers that pick up on a discrete gesture like a tap, you will only ever see the recognized state (which has the same value as the ended state).

Finally, a recognizer can be cancelled (by an incoming phone call, for example) or fail (because no amount of finger contortion can make the particular gesture from where the fingers currently are). When these states are transitioned to, the action message of the recognizer is sent, and the state property can be checked to see why.

The three built-in recognizers we did not implement in this chapter are **UIPinchGestureRecognizer**, **UISwipeGestureRecognizer**, and **UIRotationGestureRecognizer**. Each of these have properties that allow you to fine-tune their behavior. The documentation will show you the way.

Finally, if there is a gesture you want to recognize that isn't implemented by the built-in subclasses of **UIGestureRecognizer**, you can subclass **UIGestureRecognizer** yourself. This is an intense undertaking and outside the scope of this book. You can read the Subclassing Notes in the **UIGestureRecognizer** documentation to learn what's required.

Bronze Challenge: Clearing Lines

Right now, the **TouchDrawView** clears its lines whenever the user double taps. Keep this same functionality but have a gesture recognizer perform the recognition of the double tap instead of **touchesBegan:withEvent:**. Make sure you remove the following code from **touchesBegan:withEvent:**.

```
if ([t tapCount] > 1) {
    [self clearAll];
    return;
}
```

Silver Challenge: Mysterious Lines

There is a bug in the application. If you tap on a line and then start drawing a new one while the menu is visible, you'll drag the selected line and draw a new line at the same time. Fix this bug.

Gold Challenge: Speed and Size

Piggy-back off of the pan gesture recognizer to record the velocity of the pan when you are drawing a line. Adjust the thickness of the line being drawn based on this speed. Make no assumptions about how small or large the velocity value of the pan recognizer can be. (In other words, log a variety of velocities to the console first.)

Mega-Gold Challenge: Colors

Have a three-finger swipe upwards bring up a panel that shows some colors. Selecting one of those colors should make any lines you draw afterwards appear in that color. No extra lines should be drawn by putting up that panel – or at least any lines drawn should be immediately deleted when the application realizes that it is dealing with a three-finger swipe.

21

Instruments

In Chapter 4, you learned about using the debugger to find and fix problems in your code. Now we're going to look at other tools available to iOS programmers and how you can integrate them into your application development.

Static Analyzer

When you build an application, you can ask Xcode to analyze your code. The static analyzer then makes educated guesses about what would happen if that code were to be executed and informs you of potential problems. It does this without executing the code.

When the static analyzer checks the code, it examines each function and method individually by iterating over every possible *code path*. A method can have a number of control statements (`if`, `for`, `switch`, etc.). The conditions of these statements will dictate which code is actually executed. A code path is one of the possible paths the code will take given these control statements. For example, a method that has a single `if` statement has two code paths: one if the condition fails and one if the condition succeeds.

Open `TouchTracker.xcodeproj`.

Right now, `TouchTracker` doesn't have any code that offends the static analyzer. So, we will introduce some code that does. In `TouchDrawView.m`, implement the following method.

```
- (int)numberOfLines
{
    int count;

    // Check that they are non-nil before we add their counts...
    if (linesInProcess && completeLines)
        count = [linesInProcess count] + [completeLines count];

    return count;
}
```

To start the static analyzer, click and hold the Run button in the top-left corner of the workspace. In the pop-up window that appears, choose Analyze (Figure 21.1). Alternatively, you can use the keyboard shortcut: Command-Shift-B.

Figure 21.1   Using the static analyzer

Analysis results appear in the issue navigator. You will see one Logic error in your code at the return point of **numberOfLines**. The analyzer believes there is a code path that will result in an undefined or garbage value being returned to the caller. In English, that means it is possible that the variable count will not be given a value before it is returned from **numberOfLines**.

Figure 21.2   Analyzer results

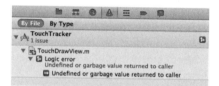

The analyzer can show us how it came to this conclusion. Click the disclosure button next to the analyzer result to reveal the detailed information underneath it. Click the item underneath the disclosure button. In the editor area, curvy blue lines will appear inside the **numberOfLines** method (Figure 21.3). (If you don't see line numbers in the gutter, you can turn them on by selecting Preferences from the Xcode menu. Choose the Text Editing tab and click the checkbox Show Line Numbers.)

Figure 21.3   Expanded analysis

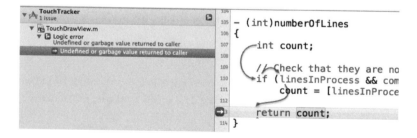

The code path shown by the analyzer lines is as follows:

1. The variable count is created and not initialized.

2. The if statement fails, so count does not get a value.

3. The variable count is returned without being assigned a value.

You can fix this issue by initializing count to zero.

```
- (int)numberOfLines
{
    int count;
    int count = 0;

    // Check that they are non-nil before we add their counts...
    if (linesInProcess && completeLines)
        count = [linesInProcess count] + [completeLines count];

    return count;
}
```

Analyze this code again, and no issues will be reported now that count is always initialized with a value.

When you analyze your code (which you will do on a regular basis because you are a smart programmer), you'll see issues other than the one described here. Many times, we see novice programmers shy away from analyzer issues because of the technical language. Don't do this. Take the time to expand the analysis and understand what the analyzer is trying to tell you. It will be worth it for the development of your application and for your development as a programmer.

Instruments

The static analyzer is useful for catching issues that can be recognized at compile time. However, some problems can't be recognized until runtime. This is where Instruments excels. The Instruments tool monitors your application while it is running and can find real issues as they are happening. Instruments is made up of several plug-ins that enable you to inspect things like what objects are allocated, where the CPU is spending its time, file I/O, network I/O, and others. Each plug-in is known as an Instrument. Together, they help you track down inefficiencies in your application and optimize your code.

When you use Instruments to monitor your application, you are *profiling* the application. While you can profile the application running on the simulator, you will get more accurate data on a device.

Allocations Instrument

The Allocations instrument tells us about every object that has been created and how much memory it takes up.

To profile an application, click and hold the Run button in the top left corner of the workspace. In the pop-up menu that appears, select Profile (Figure 21.4).

Figure 21.4   Profiling an application

Instruments will launch and ask which instrument to use. Choose Allocations and click Profile.

Figure 21.5   Choosing an instrument

TouchTracker will launch, and a window will open in Instruments (Figure 21.6). The interface may be overwhelming at first, but, like Xcode's workspace window, it will become familiar with time and use. First, make sure you can see everything by turning on all of the areas in the window. In the View control at the top of the window, click all three buttons to reveal the three main areas. The window should look like Figure 21.6.

Figure 21.6 Allocations instrument

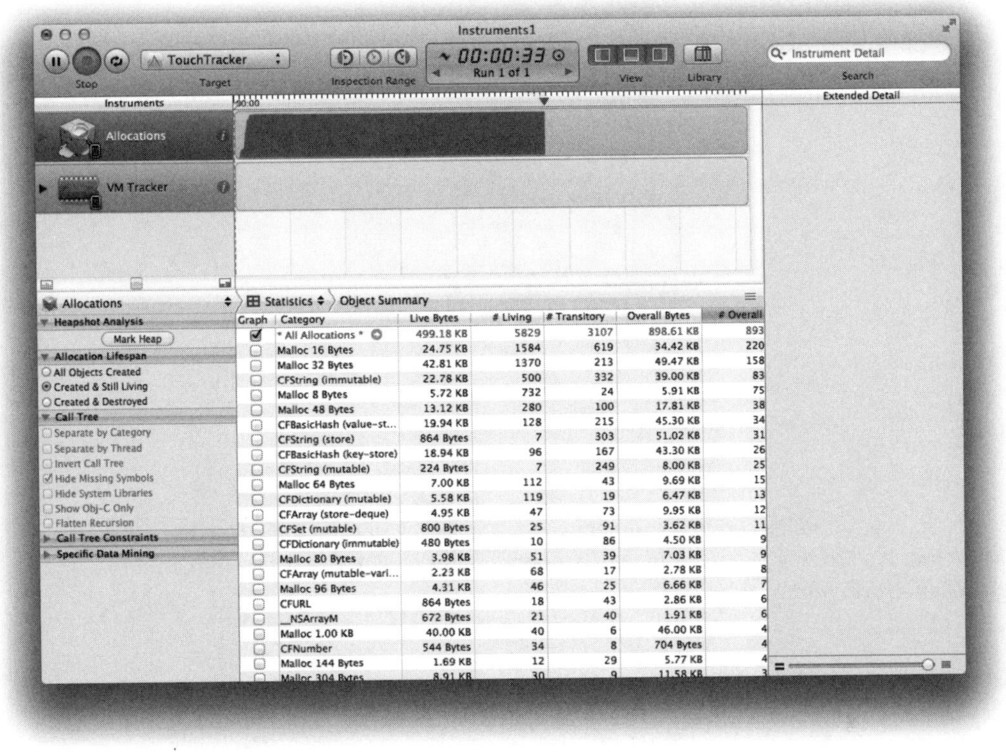

This table shows every memory allocation in the application. There are a lot of objects here, but let's look at the objects that your code is responsible for creating. First, draw some lines in TouchTracker. Then, type Line in the Instrument Detail search box in the top right corner of the window.

This will filter the list of objects in the Object Summary table so that it only shows instances of **Line** (Figure 21.7).

Figure 21.7 Allocated Lines

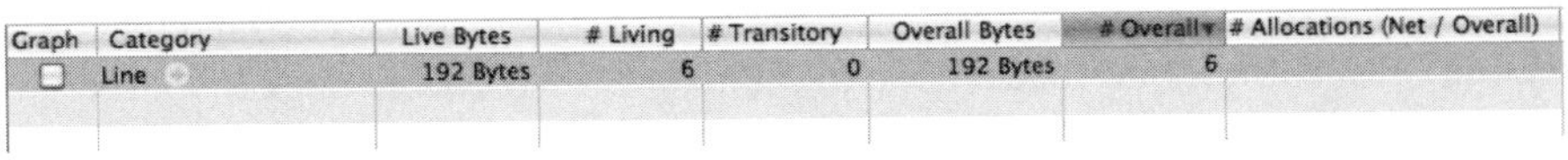

Graph	Category	Live Bytes	# Living	# Transitory	Overall Bytes	# Overall▼	# Allocations (Net / Overall)
☐	Line	192 Bytes	6	0	192 Bytes	6	

The # Living column shows you how many line objects are currently allocated. Live Bytes shows how much memory these living instances take up. The # Overall column shows you how many lines have been created during the course of the application – even if they have since been deallocated.

As you would expect, the number of lines living and the number of lines overall are equal at the moment. Now double-tap the screen in TouchTracker and erase your lines. In Instruments, notice that the **Line** instances disappear from the table. The Allocations instrument is currently set to show only objects that are created and still living. To change this, select All Objects Created from the Allocation Lifespan section of the lefthand panel (Figure 21.8).

Figure 21.8   Allocations options

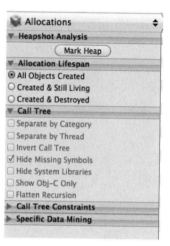

Let's see what else the Allocations instrument can tell us about our lines. In the table, select the row that says Line. An arrow will appear in the Category column; click that arrow to see more details about these allocations (Figure 21.9).

Figure 21.9   Line summary

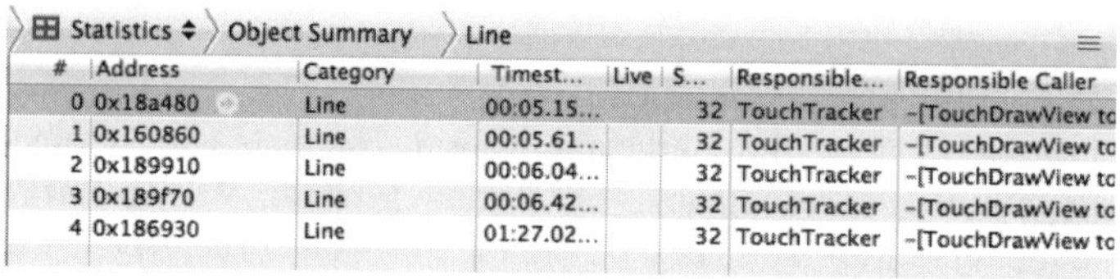

#	Address	Category	Timest...	Live	S...	Responsible...	Responsible Caller
0	0x18a480	Line	00:05.15...		32	TouchTracker	–[TouchDrawView to
1	0x160860	Line	00:05.61...		32	TouchTracker	–[TouchDrawView to
2	0x189910	Line	00:06.04...		32	TouchTracker	–[TouchDrawView to
3	0x189f70	Line	00:06.42...		32	TouchTracker	–[TouchDrawView to
4	0x186930	Line	01:27.02...		32	TouchTracker	–[TouchDrawView to

Each row in this table shows a single instance of **Line** that has been created. Select one of the rows and check out the stack trace that appears in the Extended Detail area on the right side of the Instruments window (Figure 21.10). This stack trace shows you where that instance of **Line** was created. Grayed-out items in the trace are system library calls. Items in black text are your code. Find the top-most item that is your code (-[TouchDrawView touchesBegan:withEvent:]) and double-click it.

Figure 21.10   Stack trace

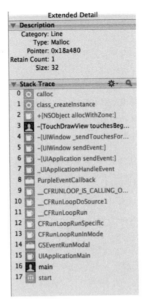

The source code for this implementation will replace the table of **Line** instances (Figure 21.11). The percentages you see are the amount of memory these method calls allocate compared to the other calls in this method. For example, the **Line** instance makes up about 47 percent of the memory allocated by **touchesBegan:withEvent:**.

Figure 21.11   Source code in Instruments

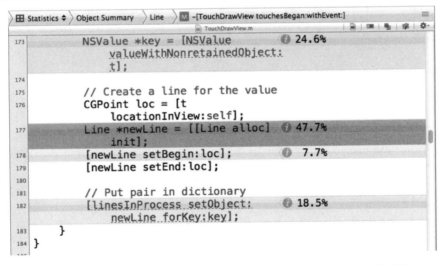

Notice that above the summary area is a breadcrumb navigation bar (Figure 21.12). You can click on an item in this bar to return to a previous set of information.

Figure 21.12   Navigation for summary area

Click on the Line item in the breadcrumb bar to get back to the list of all **Line** instances. Click on a single instance and then click the arrow icon on that row. This will show you the history of this object. There are two events: when the **Line** was created and when it was destroyed. You can select an event row to see the stack trace that resulted in the event in the extended detail area.

Settings in Allocations

Let's look at some of the options in the Allocations instrument. First, click the Stop button in the top left corner of the Instruments window. (The options we are going to configure must be set before Instruments begins monitoring the application.)

Click the info button next to the Allocations tool underneath the Stop button. This will show a panel with the settings for the Allocations instrument: check the box for Record reference counts (Figure 21.13).

Figure 21.13   Enable recording of reference counts

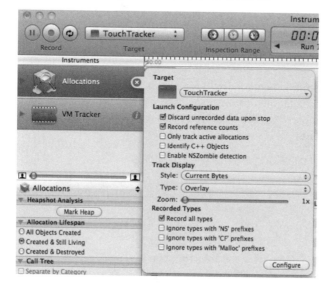

The Record reference counts option instructs Instruments to note every time an object gains or loses an owner. Click the red Record button again to start profiling with this option turned on. (Instruments can't build an application itself, so it uses the most recent build from Xcode.)

Draw some lines in TouchTracker and then double-tap to delete them. Now select the **Line** row and click the arrow next to it. Then select one of the **Line** instances that appear and click its arrow. This new table shows you the reference count history of an individual **Line** object (Figure 21.14).

Figure 21.14   Object's lifespan

#	Category	Event Type	RefCt	Timestamp	Address	Size	Responsible Li...	Responsible Caller
0	Line	Malloc	1	00:59.938.257	0x8007da0	32	TouchTracker	-[TouchDrawView touch...
1	Line	Retain	2	00:59.938.297	0x8007da0	0	TouchTracker	-[TouchDrawView touch...
2	Line	Release	1	00:59.938.304	0x8007da0	0	TouchTracker	-[TouchDrawView touch...
3	Line	Retain	2	01:00.127.439	0x8007da0	0	TouchTracker	-[TouchDrawView endTo...
4	Line	Release	1	01:00.127.443	0x8007da0	0	TouchTracker	-[TouchDrawView endTo...
5	Line	Release	0	01:08.933.142	0x8007da0	0	TouchTracker	-[TouchDrawView clearAll]
6	Line	Free	0	01:08.933.142	0x8007da0	-32	TouchTracker	-[TouchDrawView clearAll]

You've seen this information before, but after turning on Record reference counts, there is much more of it. Each time the selected **Line** instance gained an owner, a Retain event was added to this table. Each time the line lost an owner, a Release event was added to the table. The RefCt column tells you the number of owners a **Line** has after that event. You can click on a row to see the stack trace that caused that event.

Heapshot analysis

The last item we'll examine in the Allocations instrument is Heapshot Analysis. First, clear the search box so that you aren't filtering results anymore. Then, find the Heapshot Analysis category on the left side of the Instruments window and click Mark Heap. A category named Baseline will appear in the table. You can click the disclosure button next to this category to see all of the allocations that took place before you marked the heapshot. Now draw more lines in TouchTracker and click Mark Heap again. Another category will appear named Heapshot 1. Click the disclosure button next to Heapshot 1 (Figure 21.15).

Figure 21.15 Heapshot

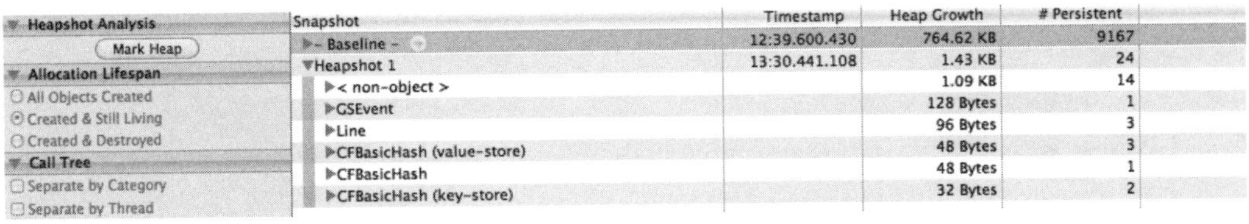

	Snapshot	Timestamp	Heap Growth	# Persistent
▼ Heapshot Analysis	▶ - Baseline - ⊙	12:39.600.430	764.62 KB	9167
(Mark Heap)	▼ Heapshot 1	13:30.441.108	1.43 KB	24
▼ Allocation Lifespan	▶ < non-object >		1.09 KB	14
○ All Objects Created	▶ GSEvent		128 Bytes	1
⊙ Created & Still Living	▶ Line		96 Bytes	3
○ Created & Destroyed	▶ CFBasicHash (value-store)		48 Bytes	3
▼ Call Tree	▶ CFBasicHash		48 Bytes	1
☐ Separate by Category	▶ CFBasicHash (key-store)		32 Bytes	2
☐ Separate by Thread				

Every allocation that took place after the first heapshot is in this category. You can see the **Line** instances that you just created as well as a few objects that were used to handle other code during this time. You can take as many heapshots as you like; they are very useful for seeing what objects get allocated for a specific event. Double-tap the screen in TouchTracker to clear the lines and notice that the objects in this heapshot disappear.

To return to the full object list where we started, select the pop-up button in the breadcrumb bar that currently says Heapshots and change it to Statistics.

Time Profiler Instrument

The Time Profiler instrument finds wasted CPU cycles in an application. To see how this works, add the following CPU cycle-wasting code to the end of your **drawRect:** method:

```
float f = 0.0;
for (int i = 0; i < 1000; i++) {
    f = f + sin(sin(time(NULL) + i));
}
NSLog(@"f = %f", f);
```

Build and profile the application. When Instruments asks which instrument to use, choose Time Profiler (Figure 21.16). When Instruments launches the application and its window appears, make sure that all three areas are visible by clicking the buttons in the View control to blue.

Figure 21.16   Time Profiler instrument

Touch and hold your finger on the TouchTracker screen. Move your finger around but keep it on the screen. This sends **touchesMoved:withEvent:** over and over to the **TouchDrawView**. Each **touchesMoved:withEvent:** message causes **drawRect:** to be sent, which in turn causes the silly sin code to run repeatedly.

As you move your finger, watch the table in Instruments shuffle around its items. Then click the pause button (to the left of the Stop button) and examine the table's contents. Each row is one function or method call. In the left column, the amount of time spent in that function (expressed in milliseconds and as a percentage of the total run time) is displayed (Figure 21.17). This gives you an idea of where your application is spending its execution time.

Figure 21.17   Time Profiler results

Running (Self)		Symbol Name
761.0ms	25.7%	▶aa_write_word CoreGraphics
610.0ms	20.6%	▶CGSFillDRAM8by1 CoreGraphics
423.0ms	14.3%	▶CGSColorMaskCopyARGB8888 CoreGraphics
382.0ms	12.9%	▶aa_render CoreGraphics
107.0ms	3.6%	▶mach_absolute_time libSystem.B.dylib
70.0ms	2.3%	▶aa_cubeto CoreGraphics
51.0ms	1.7%	▶mach_msg_trap libSystem.B.dylib
28.0ms	0.9%	cos libSystem.B.dylib
21.0ms	0.7%	▶__udivsi3 libgcc_s.1.dylib
20.0ms	0.6%	▶munmap libSystem.B.dylib
20.0ms	0.6%	▶objc_msgSend libobjc.A.dylib
19.0ms	0.6%	▶sin libSystem.B.dylib
14.0ms	0.4%	▶__mmap libSystem.B.dylib
12.0ms	0.4%	▶aa_distribute_edges CoreGraphics

There is no rule that says, "If X percentage of time is spent in this function, your application has a problem." Instead, use Time Profiler if you notice your application acting sluggish while testing it as a user. For example, you should notice that drawing in TouchTracker is less responsive since we added the wasteful `sin` code.

We know that when drawing a line, two things are happening: **touchesMoved:withEvent:** and **drawRect:** are being sent to the **TouchDrawView** view. In Time Profiler, we can check to see how much time is spent in these two methods relative to the rest of the application. If an inordinate amount of time is being spent in one of these methods, we know that's where the problem is.

(Keep in mind that some things just take time. Redrawing the entire screen every time the user's finger moves, as is done in TouchTracker, is an expensive operation. If it was hindering the user experience, you could find a way to reduce the number of times the screen is redrawn. For example, you could redraw only every tenth of a second regardless of how many touch events were sent.)

Time Profiler shows you nearly every function and method call in the application. If you want to focus on certain parts of the application's code, you can prune down its results. For example, sometimes the **mach_msg_trap** function will be very high on the sample list. This function is where the main thread sits when it is waiting for input. It is not a bad thing to spend time in this function, so you might want to ignore this time when looking at your Time Profiler results.

Use the search box in the top right corner of the Instruments window to find **mach_msg_trap**. Then, select it from the table. On the left side of the screen, click the Symbol button under Specific Data Mining. The **mach_msg_trap** function appears in the table under Specific Data Mining, and the pop-up button next to it displays Charge. Click on Charge and change it to Prune. Then, clear the text from the search box. Now, the list is adjusted so that any time spent in **mach_msg_trap** is ignored. You can click on Restore while **mach_msg_trap** is selected in the Specific Data Mining table to add it back to the total time.

Figure 21.18 Pruning a symbol

Other options for reducing the list of symbols in Time Profiler include showing only Objective-C calls, hiding system libraries, and charging calls to callers. The first two are obvious, but let's look at charging calls to callers. Select the row that holds **mach_absolute_time**. (If you are running on the simulator, select **_nanotime** instead.) Then, click the Symbol button. This function disappears from the main table and reappears in the Specific Data Mining table. Notice that it is listed as a Charge. This means that the time spent in this function will be attributed to the function or method that called it.

Back in the main table, notice that **mach_absolute_time** has been replaced with the function that calls it, **gettimeofday**. If you take the same steps to charge **gettimeofday**, it will be replaced with its caller, **time**. If you charge **time**, it will be replaced with its caller, **drawRect:**. The **drawRect:** method will move to near the top of the list; it now is now charged with **time**, **gettimeofday**, and **mach_absolute_time**.

Some common function calls always use a lot of CPU time. Most of the time, these are harmless and unavoidable. For example, the **objc_msgSend** function is the central dispatch function for any Objective-C message. It occasionally creeps to the top of the list when you are sending lots of messages to objects. Usually, it's nothing to worry about. However, if you are spending more time dispatching messages than actually doing work in the triggered methods *and* your application isn't performing well, you have a problem that needs solving.

As a real world example, an overzealous Objective-C developer might be tempted to create classes for things like vectors, points, and rectangles. These classes would likely have methods to add, subtract, or multiply instances as well as accessor methods to get and set instance variables. When these classes are used for drawing, the code has to send a lot of messages to do something simple, like creating two vectors and adding them together. The messages add excessive overhead considering the simplicity of the operation. Therefore, the better alternative is to create data types like these as structures and access their memory directly. (This is why CGRect and CGPoint are structures and not Objective-C classes.)

Don't forget to remove the CPU cycle-wasting code in **drawRect:**!

Leaks Instrument

Another useful instrument is Leaks. Although this instrument is less useful now that ARC handles memory management, we know that there is still a possibility of leaking memory with a retain cycle. Leaks can help us find retain cycles.

First, we need to introduce a retain cycle into our application. Let's pretend that every **Line** needs to know what array of lines it belongs to. Add a new property to Line.h.

@property (nonatomic, strong) NSMutableArray *containingArray;

Synthesize this property in Line.m.

```
@implementation Line
@synthesize begin, end;
@synthesize containingArray;
@end
```

In TouchDrawView.m, set every completed line's containingArray property in **endTouches:**.

```
- (void)endTouches:(NSSet *)touches
{
    for (UITouch *t in touches) {
        NSValue *key = [NSValue valueWithNonretainedObject:t];
        Line *line = [linesInProcess objectForKey:key];

        if (line) {
            [completeLines addObject:line];
            [linesInProcess removeObjectForKey:key];
            [line setContainingArray:completeLines];
        }
    }
    [self setNeedsDisplay];
}
```

Finally, in **clearAll** of TouchDrawView.m, comment out the code that removes all of the objects from the completeLines and create a new instance of **NSMutableArray** instead.

```
- (void)clearAll
{
    [linesInProcess removeAllObjects];
//    [completeLines removeAllObjects];

    completeLines = [[NSMutableArray alloc] init];

    [self setNeedsDisplay];
}
```

Build and profile the application. Choose Leaks as the instrument to use.

Draw a few lines and then double tap the screen to clear it. Select the Leaks instrument from the top left table and wait a few seconds. Three items will appear in the summary table: an **NSMutableArray**, a few **Line** instances, and a Malloc 16 Bytes block. This memory has been leaked.

Select the Leaks pop-up button in the breadcrumb bar and change it to Cycles & Roots (Figure 21.19). This view gives you a lovely graphical representation of the retain cycle: an **NSMutableArray** (our completeLines array) has a reference to a list of **Line**s, and each **Line** has a reference back to its containingArray.

Figure 21.19   Cycles and Roots

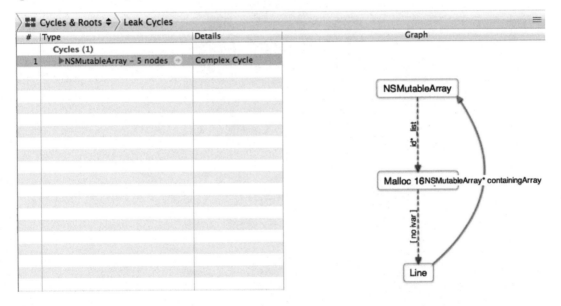

You can of course fix this problem by making the containingArray property a weak reference. Or just remove the property and undo your changes to **endTouches:** and **clearAll**.

This should give you a good start with the Instruments application. The more you play with it, the more adept at using it you will become. One final word of warning before you invest a significant amount of your development time using Instruments: If there is no performance problem, don't fret over every little row in Instruments. It is a tool for diagnosing existing problems, not for finding new ones. Write clean code that works first; then, if there is a problem, you can find and fix it with the help of Instruments.

Xcode Schemes

In Xcode, a workspace is a collection of projects, and a project is a collection targets and files. A target has a number of build settings and phases that reference files from its project. When built, a target creates a product, which is usually an application.

A *scheme* contains one or more targets *and* specifies what to do with the product or products (Figure 21.20).

Figure 21.20   Xcode containers

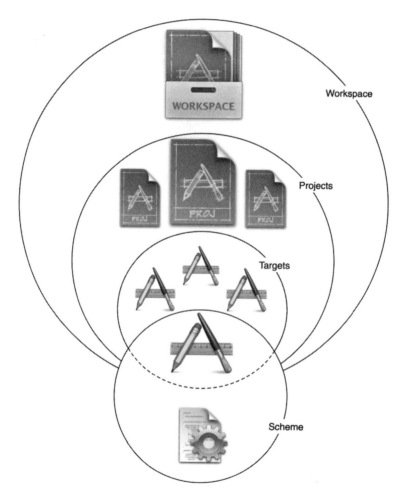

When you create a new project, a scheme with the same name as the project is created for you. For instance, the TouchTracker project has a TouchTracker scheme, and this scheme contains the TouchTracker target, which is responsible for building the TouchTracker iOS application.

To view the details of a scheme, click the Scheme pop-up menu at the top left of the Xcode window and select Edit Scheme.... The *scheme editor* will drop down into the workspace (Figure 21.21).

Figure 21.21   Editing a scheme

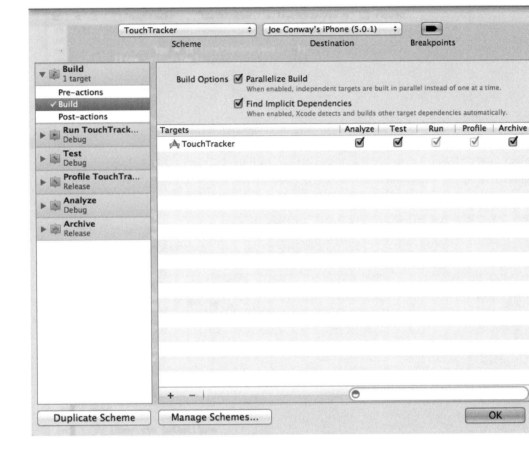

On the left side of the scheme editor is the list of actions that every scheme can do. (Notice that these scheme actions are also the choices you see when you click and hold the Run button in the Xcode workspace with the exception of Archive.) Selecting a scheme action here shows its options in the details pane. Take a moment to look over the actions and the available options. Notice that some actions have multiple tabs that categorize their options.

Creating a new scheme

As projects become larger and more complicated, they require more specific testing and debugging. To avoid having to constantly edit one scheme, we typically create new schemes for common situations. For example, if we have an application that consumes a lot of memory, we might want to routinely run the Allocations instrument on it. Instead of having Instruments ask which instrument to use when we profile the application, we can set up a new scheme that always runs Allocations.

Let's set up this scheme for the TouchTracker target. From the Scheme pop-up menu, select New Scheme.... When the sheet drops down, enter Allocations into the name and make sure TouchTracker is selected as the target (Figure 21.22). Click OK.

Figure 21.22 Creating a new scheme

Reopen the scheme editor sheet either by selecting Edit Scheme... from the Scheme pop-up menu or using the keyboard shortcut Command-Shift-<. Then click the Scheme pop-up menu in the scheme editor and select Allocations. Select the Profile action from the left table. On the detail pane, change the Instrument pop-up to Allocations and click OK (Figure 21.23).

Figure 21.23 An allocations-only scheme

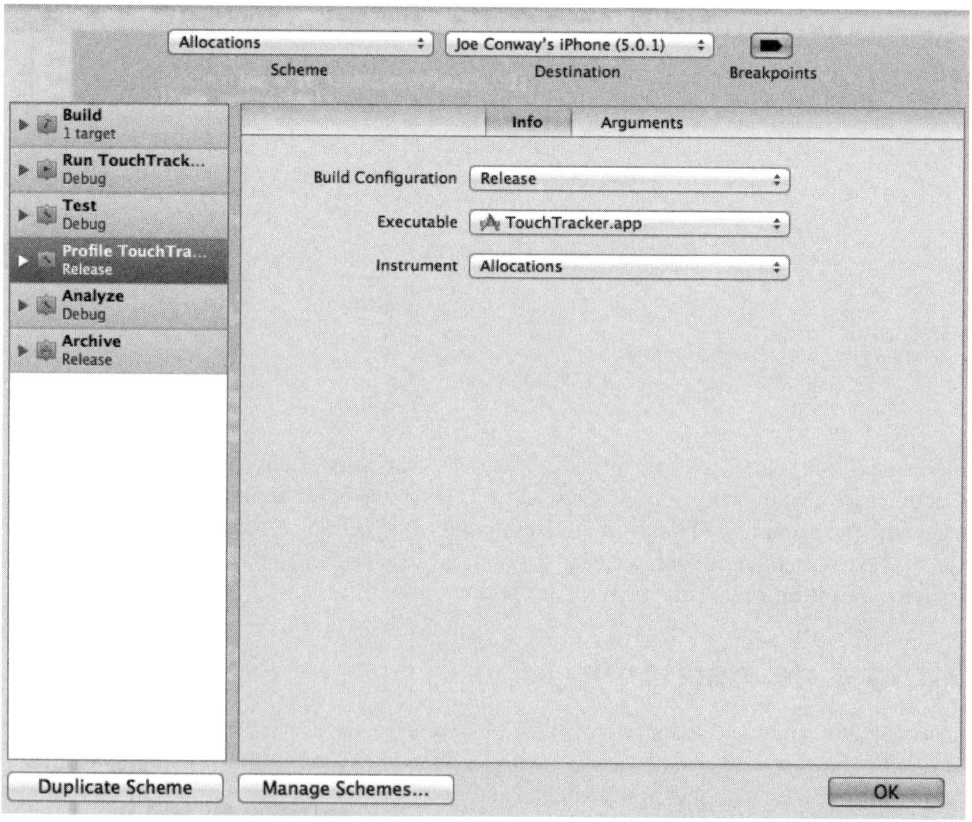

To use your new scheme, click the Scheme pop-up menu back on the workspace window. Here you can choose which scheme to use and a destination device for that scheme. Choose one of the destination options under the Allocations heading (Figure 21.24). Then, profile your application. Instruments will launch your application and automatically start the Allocations instrument.

Figure 21.24 Choosing a scheme

Profile
Stop
Allocations
Joe Conway's iPhone
TouchTracker
✓ Allocations
Edit Scheme...
New Scheme...
Manage Schemes...
✓ Joe Conway's iPhone
iPad 5.0 Simulator
iPhone 5.0 Simulator
Update Simulators...

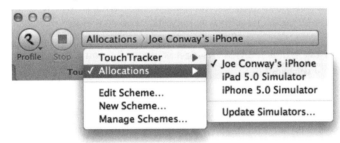

Switch back to the default TouchTracker scheme and profile again. This time, Instruments will again ask you to choose an instrument.

Here's a handy scheme tip: hold down the Option key when selecting a scheme action from the Run button. This automatically opens the scheme editor and allows you to quickly review and change the settings of the selected scheme before performing the action. In fact, holding down the Option key will open the scheme editor whether you select the action from the Run pop-up button, from the Product menu, or use a keyboard shortcut.

Build Settings

Every target includes *build settings* that describe how it should be built. Every project also has build settings that serve as defaults for all the targets within the project. Let's take a look at the project build settings for TouchTracker. Select the project from the project navigator and then select the TouchTracker project in the editor area.

Click the Build Settings tab at the top of the editor area. These are the project-level build settings – the default values that targets inherit. In the top-right corner of the editor area is a search box that you can use to search for a specific setting. Start typing `iOS Deployment Target` in the box, and the list will adjust to show this setting. (The deployment target specifies the lowest version of the OS that can run the application.)

Next to the search box are two sets of options: Basic or All and Combined and Levels. The first pair determines which settings are shown. To see the difference between the second pair, let's look at the target's build settings.

In the left table of the editor area, select the TouchTracker target. Then select the Build Settings tab. These are the build settings for this specific target. Find the iOS Deployment Target setting again and click on Levels.

Figure 21.25 Build Settings - Levels

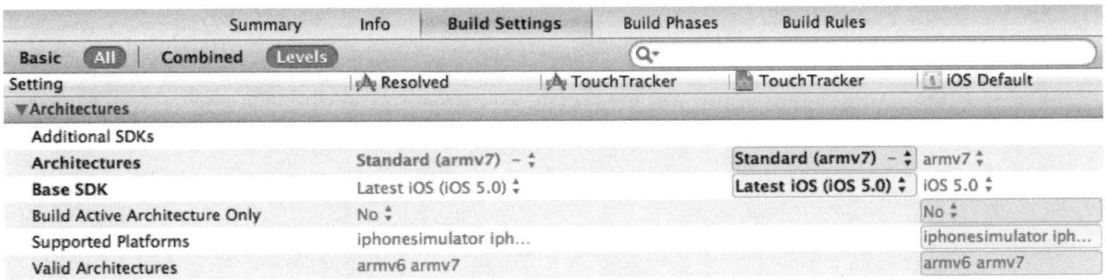

Summary
Info
Build Settings
Build Phases
Build Rules
Basic
All
Combined
Levels
Setting
Resolved
TouchTracker
TouchTracker
iOS Default
▼Architectures
Additional SDKs
Architectures
Standard (armv7)
Standard (armv7)
armv7
Base SDK
Latest iOS (iOS 5.0)
Latest iOS (iOS 5.0)
iOS 5.0
Build Active Architecture Only
No
No
Supported Platforms
iphonesimulator iph...
iphonesimulator iph...
Valid Architectures
armv6 armv7
armv6 armv7

When viewing the build settings with this option, you can see each setting's value at the three different levels: OS, project, and target. (Figure 21.25). The far right column shows the iOS Default settings; these serve as the project's defaults, which it can override. The next column to the left shows the project's settings, and the one after that shows the currently selected target's settings. The Resolved column shows which setting will actually be used; it is always be equal to the left-most specified value. You can click in each column to set the value for that level. When you're done looking around, change the setting back to Combined.

Each target and project has multiple *build configurations*. A build configuration is a set of build settings. When you create a project, there are two build configurations: debug and release. The build settings for the debug configuration make it easier to debug your application, while the release settings turn on optimizations to speed up execution.

Let's take a look at the build settings and configurations for TouchTracker. Select the project from the project navigator and the TouchTracker project in the editor area. Then, select Info from the tabs on top of the editor area (Figure 21.26).

Figure 21.26   Build configurations list

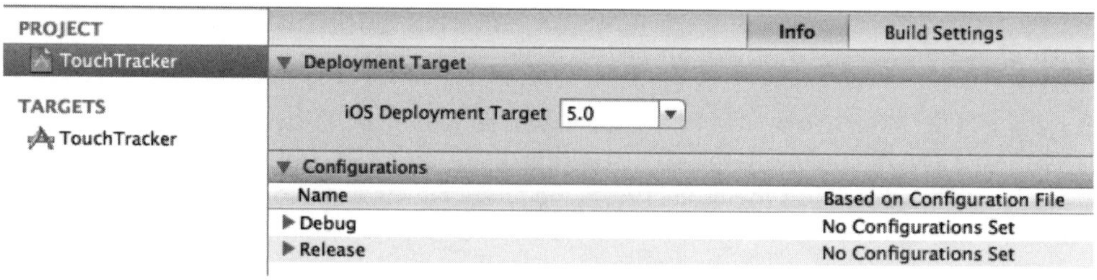

The Configurations section shows you the available build configurations in the project and targets. You can add and remove build configurations with the buttons at the bottom of this section.

When performing a scheme action, the scheme will use one of these configurations when building its targets. You can specify the build configuration that the scheme uses in the scheme editor in the option for Build Configuration in the Info pane.

Enough talk – time to do something useful. Let's change the value of the target build setting Preprocessor Macros. Preprocessor macros allow you to compile code conditionally. They are either defined or not defined at the start of a build. If you wrap a block of code in a preprocessor directive, it will only be compiled if that macro has been defined. The Preprocessor Macros setting lists preprocessor macros that are defined when a certain build configuration is used by a scheme to build a target.

Select the TouchTracker target, and in its Build Settings pane, search for the Preprocessor Macros build setting. Double-click on the value column for the Debug configuration under Preprocessor Macros. In the table that appears, add a new item: VIEW_DEBUG, as shown in Figure 21.27.

Figure 21.27   Changing a build setting

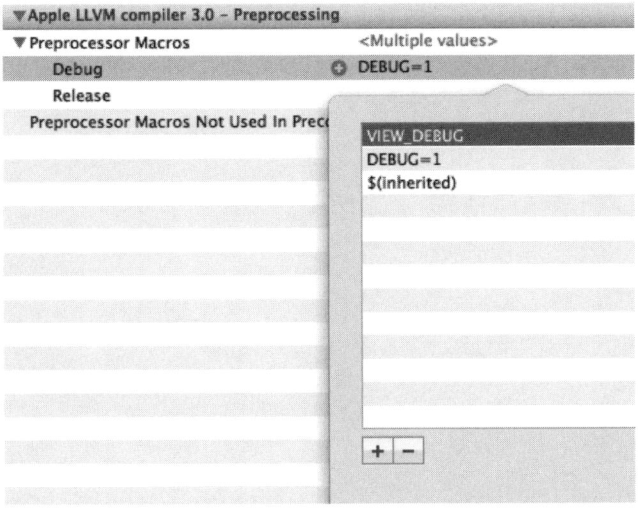

Adding this value to this setting says, "When you are building the TouchTracker target with the debug configuration, a preprocessor macro VIEW_DEBUG is defined."

Let's add some debugging code to TouchTracker that will only be compiled when the target is built with the debug configuration. **UIView** has a private method **recursiveDescription** that prints out the entire view hierarchy of an application. However, you cannot call this method in an application that you deploy to the App Store, so you will only allow it to be called if VIEW_DEBUG is defined.

In AppDelegate.m, add the following code to **application:didFinishLaunchingWithOptions:**.

```
    [self.window makeKeyAndVisible];
#ifdef VIEW_DEBUG
    NSLog(@"%@", [[self window] performSelector:@selector(recursiveDescription)]);
#endif
    return YES;
}
```

This code will send the message **recursiveDescription** to the window. (Notice the use of **performSelector:**. **recursiveDescription** is a private method, so we have to dispatch it in this way.) **recursiveDescription** will print a view's description, then all of its subviews, and its subviews' subviews and so on. You can leave this code in for all builds. Because the preprocessor macro will not be defined for a release build, the code will not be compiled when you build for the App Store.

Now let's test out this code. Hold down the Option key and run the application. When the scheme editor drops down, make sure that the debug configuration is selected. Check out the console and you will see the view hierarchy of your application, starting at the window. (Don't worry about the warning that this line of code generates.)

22

Core Animation Layer

Animation is a hallmark of the iOS interface. When used properly, it gives the user visual cues about the application's workflow. The classes and functions needed to animate an application's interface are in the Core Animation API. To use any part of Core Animation, you need to add the QuartzCore framework to your project.

Open your HypnoTime project and select the project from the project navigator. Then, select the HypnoTime target and the Build Phases pane. Add `QuartzCore.framework` to Link Binary With Libraries, as shown in Figure 22.1.

Figure 22.1   QuartzCore.framework

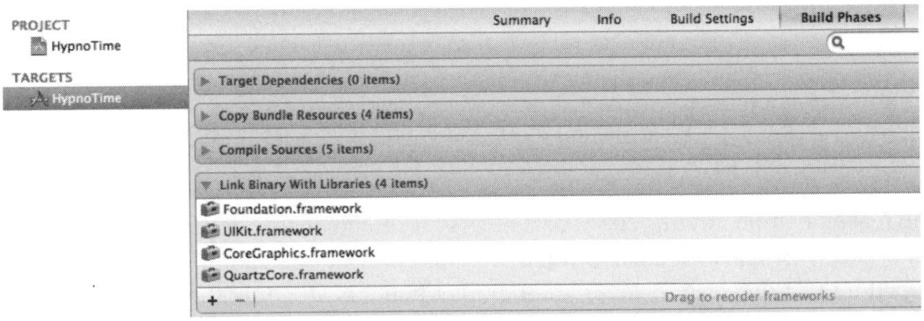

There are two classes that make Core Animation work: **CALayer** and **CAAnimation**.

At its core, an instance of **CALayer** is a buffer containing a bitmap. When you draw a layer (or a stack of layers), the rendering is hardware-accelerated. This makes drawing a layer to the screen incredibly fast. Like views, layers are arranged hierarchically – each layer can have sublayers.

A **CAAnimation** object causes a change over time. Typically, it changes one property (like `opacity`) of a layer.

In this chapter, we will focus on **CALayer**, and in the next chapter, we'll focus on **CAAnimation**.

Layers and Views

In Chapter 6, you learned that every view has an image and that it is a view's image that gets drawn to the screen. This image is an instance of **CALayer**.

When you instantiate a view, it creates a layer, and when the screen is redrawn, the layers of each view in the window's hierarchy are drawn (including the window's layer). We call layers created by views *implicit layers*. Because every view has a layer, there is a matching layer hierarchy that mimics the view hierarchy (Figure 22.2).

After the views draw on their layers, the layers are copied to the screen. When we talk about copying a bunch of layers to the screen in a particular order and respecting each pixel's opacity, we use the word *composite*. Thus, the full description is "Each view renders to its layer, and then all the layers are composited to the screen."

Figure 22.2   View and corresponding layer hierarchy

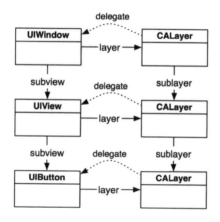

Notice in Figure 22.2 that each view has a layer and each view is its layer's delegate. We'll come back to the delegate relationship later in the chapter.

So what's the reason behind having views *and* layers? Remember that **UIView** is a subclass of **UIResponder**. A view is really an abstraction of a visible object that can be interacted with on the screen, wrapped into a tidy class. A layer, on the other hand, is all about the drawing.

Creating a CALayer

Not all layers are implicit layers. You can create a layer by sending **alloc** to the class **CALayer**. Layers created this way are called *explicit layers*. In this section, you're going to create a layer and then make it a sublayer of the implicit layer of your **HypnosisView** (Figure 22.3).

Figure 22.3   Object diagram

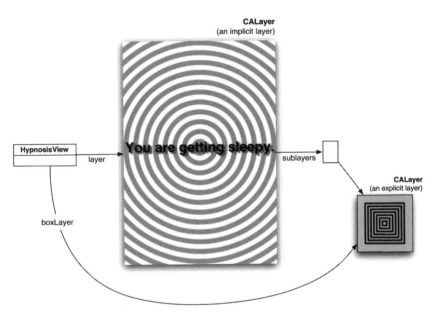

In HypnosisView.h, import the QuartzCore framework and add an instance variable to hold on to the layer object you are about to create:

```
#import <Foundation/Foundation.h>
#import <QuartzCore/QuartzCore.h>

@interface HypnosisView : UIView
{
    CALayer *boxLayer;
}
@property (nonatomic, strong) UIColor *circleColor;
@end
```

The designated initializer for a **CALayer** is simply **init**. After you instantiate a layer, you set its size, position (relative to its superlayer), and contents. In HypnosisView.m, change the **initWithFrame:** method to create a new layer and add it as a sublayer to **HypnosisView**'s layer.

```
- (id)initWithFrame:(CGRect)r
{
    self = [super initWithFrame:r];

    if (self) {
        [self setBackgroundColor:[UIColor clearColor]];
        [self setCircleColor:[UIColor lightGrayColor]];

        // Create the new layer object
        boxLayer = [[CALayer alloc] init];

        // Give it a size
        [boxLayer setBounds:CGRectMake(0.0, 0.0, 85.0, 85.0)];
```

```
    // Give it a location
    [boxLayer setPosition:CGPointMake(160.0, 100.0)];

    // Make half-transparent red the background color for the layer
    UIColor *reddish = [UIColor colorWithRed:1.0 green:0.0 blue:0.0 alpha:0.5];

    // Get a CGColor object with the same color values
    CGColorRef cgReddish = [reddish CGColor];
    [boxLayer setBackgroundColor:cgReddish];

    // Make it a sublayer of the view's layer
    [[self layer] addSublayer:boxLayer];
}

    return self;
}
```

Build and run the application. You will see a semi-transparent red block appear on the view, as shown in Figure 22.4.

Figure 22.4   Red layer

Notice that layers interpret their size and position differently than views do. With a **UIView**, we typically define the frame of the view to establish its size and position. The origin of the frame rectangle is the upper-left corner of the view, and the size stretches right and down from the origin.

For a **CALayer**, instead of defining a frame, you set the bounds and position properties of the layer. The default setting for position is the *center* of the layer in its superlayer. (The anchorPoint property determines where the position lies inside the layer's bounds, and its default value is (0.5, 0.5), otherwise known as the center.) Therefore, if you change the size of the layer but leave the position constant, the layer will remain centered on the same point.

Even though a layer doesn't have a frame property, you can still get and set its "frame" by sending it the messages frame and setFrame:. When a layer is sent the message frame, it computes a rectangle from its position and bounds properties. Similarly, when sending a layer the message setFrame:, it does some math and then sets the bounds and position properties accordingly.

However, it is better to think of layers in terms of their position and bounds properties. The mental math needed to animate a layer is much simpler if you stick to setting the bounds and position properties directly.

Layer Content

A layer contains a bitmap called its contents, which can be set programmatically or with an image. To set the contents programmatically, you either subclass **CALayer** or assign a delegate to an instance of **CALayer**. The delegate then implements drawing routines. (This is how implicit layers work; the view is its layer's delegate.)

We will discuss drawing to a layer programmatically at the end of this chapter. For now, you're going to set the contents of the layer using an image file.

In HypnosisView.m, add the following code to the **initWithFrame:** method:

```
[boxLayer setBackgroundColor:cgReddish];

// Create a UIImage
UIImage *layerImage = [UIImage imageNamed:@"Hypno.png"];

// Get the underlying CGImage
CGImageRef image = [layerImage CGImage];

// Put the CGImage on the layer
[boxLayer setContents:(__bridge id)image];

// Inset the image a bit on each side
[boxLayer setContentsRect:CGRectMake(-0.1, -0.1, 1.2, 1.2)];

// Let the image resize (without changing the aspect ratio)
// to fill the contentRect
[boxLayer setContentsGravity:kCAGravityResizeAspect];

[[self layer] addSublayer:boxLayer];
```

In this code, we create an image and then get the underlying **CGImage** to use with Core Graphics drawing. Then we set the image as the layer's contents and make adjustments for how the contents appear within the layer.

Notice the use of **CGImageRef** and **CGColorRef** in this method. Why doesn't Core Animation use **UIImage** and **UIColor**?

The QuartzCore framework (which supplies the classes **CALayer** and **CAAnimation**) and Core Graphics framework (which supplies CGImageRef) exist on both iOS and on the Mac. UIKit (where we get **UIImage** and anything else prefixed with **UI**) only exists on iOS. To maintain its portability, QuartzCore must use CGImageRef instead of **UIImage**. Fortunately, UIKit objects have methods to easily access their Core Graphics counterparts, like **UIImage**'s **CGImage** method you used in the previous code.

Build and run the application. Now your layer has an image for its contents, as shown in Figure 22.5.

Figure 22.5   Layer with image

Because layers exist in a hierarchy, they can have sublayers, and each layer has a pointer back to its parent layer called superlayer. When a layer is composited to the screen, it is copied to the screen, and then each sublayer is composited atop it. Therefore, a layer always draws on top of its superlayer.

In a view hierarchy, sibling views (views with the same parent) typically do not have overlapping bounds. For instance, imagine a view with two subviews that are buttons. What would be the point of them overlapping and obscuring each other? It would confuse and frustrate the user trying to tap one or the other.

The layer hierarchy, however, is a different story. Siblings are far more likely to overlap because layers are about visual effects and drawing, not user interaction. Which sibling is composited over the other? Each layer has a property called zPosition. If two layers are siblings and they overlap, then the layer with the higher zPosition is composited on top of the layer with the lower zPosition. (A sublayer *always* draws on top of its superlayer, regardless of zPosition.)

A layer's zPosition defaults to 0 and can be set to a negative value.

```
[underLayer setZPosition:-5];
[overLayer setZPosition:5];
[parentLayer addSublayer:underLayer];
[parentLayer addSublayer:overLayer];

// overLayer is composited on top of underLayer!
```

When the Z-axis is discussed, some developers imagine that perspective is applied, and they expect a layer to appear larger as its zPosition increases. However, Core Animation layers are presented orthographically; they do not appear as different sizes based on their zPositions.

Figure 22.6   Perspective vs. orthographic

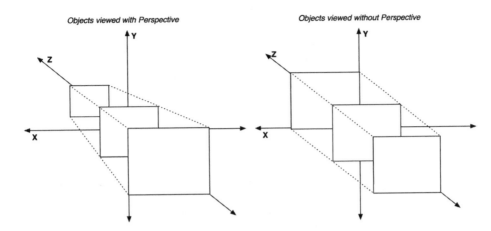

Implicitly Animatable Properties

Several of the properties of **CALayer** are *implicitly animatable*. This means that changes to these properties are automatically animated when their setters are called. The property position is an implicitly animatable property. Sending the message **setPosition:** to a **CALayer** doesn't just move the layer to a new position; it animates the change from the old position to the new one.

In this section, you will have the application respond to user taps: the boxLayer will move to wherever the user starts a touch. This change in position will be animated because position is an implicitly animatable property.

In HypnosisView.m, implement **touchesBegan:withEvent:** to change the layer's position.

```
- (void)touchesBegan:(NSSet *)touches
          withEvent:(UIEvent *)event
{
    UITouch *t = [touches anyObject];
    CGPoint p = [t locationInView:self];
    [boxLayer setPosition:p];
}
```

Build and run the application. The layer will move smoothly from its current position to where you tap. All you had to do to get this animation was send **setPosition:**. Pretty cool, huh?

If the user drags rather than taps, let's have the layer follow the user's finger. In HypnosisView.m, implement **touchesMoved:withEvent:** to send **setPosition:** to the layer.

```
- (void)touchesMoved:(NSSet *)touches
          withEvent:(UIEvent *)event
{
    UITouch *t = [touches anyObject];
    CGPoint p = [t locationInView:self];
    [boxLayer setPosition:p];
}
```

Build and run the application. This is not so cool. Notice how the animation makes the layer lag behind your dragging finger, making the application seem sluggish.

Why the poor response? An implicitly animatable property changes to its destination value over a constant time interval. However, changing a property while it is being animated starts another implicit animation. Therefore, if a layer is in the middle of traveling from point A to point B, and you tell it to go to point C, it will never reach B; and that little change of direction coupled with the timer restarting makes the animation seem choppy. (Figure 22.7)

Figure 22.7   Animation missing waypoints

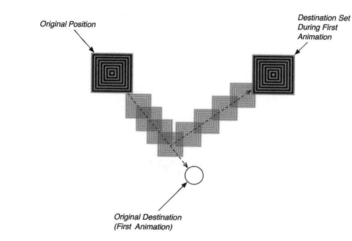

To disable an implicit animation, you can use an *animation transaction*. Animation transactions allow you to batch animations and set their parameters, like the duration and animation curve. To begin a transaction, you send the message **begin** to the class **CATransaction**. To end a transaction, you send **commit** to CATransaction. Within the **begin** and **commit** block, you can set properties of a layer and also set values for the transaction as a whole.

Animation transactions can be used for lots of things, but here we'll use it to disable the animation of the layer's change in position. In HypnosisView.m, edit **touchesMoved:withEvent:**.

```
- (void)touchesMoved:(NSSet *)touches
            withEvent:(UIEvent *)event
{
    UITouch *t = [touches anyObject];
    CGPoint p = [t locationInView:self];
    [CATransaction begin];
    [CATransaction setDisableActions:YES];
    [boxLayer setPosition:p];
    [CATransaction commit];
}
```

Build and run the application. Now the dragging should feel much more responsive.

Bronze Challenge: Another Layer

Add another layer as a sublayer of the boxLayer – with any image you choose. Make it so the sublayer sits in the center of the boxLayer at all times and is half the size of the boxLayer.

Silver Challenge: Corner Radius

Have the **CALayer** draw with rounded corners.

Gold Challenge: Shadowing

Have the **CALayer** draw with a shadow. Make sure that, even though the image is translucent, the shadow only appears at the edges of the layer.

For the More Curious: Programmatically Generating Content

In this chapter, you set a layer's contents with an image file. Now let's look at how to set a layer's contents programmatically. There are two ways to draw to a layer using Core Graphics: subclassing and delegation. In practice, subclassing is the last thing you want to do. The only reason to subclass **CALayer** to provide custom content is if you need to draw differently depending on some state of the layer. If this is the approach you wish to take, you must override the method **drawInContext:**.

```
@implementation LayerSubclass

- (void)drawInContext:(CGContextRef)ctx
{
    UIImage *layerImage = nil;
    if (hypnotizing)
        layerImage = [UIImage imageNamed:@"Hypno.png"];
    else
        layerImage = [UIImage imageNamed:@"Plain.png"];

    CGRect boundingBox = CGContextGetClipBoundingBox(ctx);
    CGContextDrawImage(ctx, boundingBox, [layerImage CGImage]);
}
@end
```

Delegation is the more common way to programmatically draw to a layer. This is how implicit layers work, but you can also give an explicit layer a delegate. However, it is not a good idea to assign a **UIView** as the delegate of an explicit layer. Use a controller object instead. (A **UIView** is already the delegate of another layer, and bad things happen when a view is the delegate of two layers.)

A layer sends the message **drawLayer:inContext:** to its delegate object when it is being displayed. The delegate can then perform Core Graphics calls on this context.

```
@implementation Controller

- (void)drawLayer:(CALayer *)layer inContext:(CGContextRef)ctx
{
    if (layer == hypnoLayer)
    {
        UIImage *layerImage = [UIImage imageNamed:@"Hypno.png"];
        CGRect boundingBox = CGContextGetClipBoundingBox(ctx);
        CGContextDrawImage(ctx, boundingBox, [layerImage CGImage]);
    }
}
@end
```

For both subclassing and delegation, you must send an explicit **setNeedsDisplay** to the layer in order for these methods to be invoked. Otherwise, the layer thinks it doesn't have any content and won't draw.

For the More Curious: Layers, Bitmaps, and Contexts

A layer is simply a bitmap – a chunk of memory that holds the red, green, blue, and alpha values of each pixel. When you send the message **setNeedsDisplay** to a **UIView** instance, that method is forwarded to the view's layer. After the run loop is done processing an event, every layer marked for re-display prepares a **CGContextRef**. Drawing routines called on this context generate pixels that end up in the layer's bitmap.

How do drawing routines get called on the layer's context? After a layer prepares its context, it sends the message **drawLayer:inContext:** to its delegate. The delegate of an implicit layer is its view, so in the implementation for **drawLayer:inContext:**, the view sends **drawRect:** to itself. Therefore, when you see this line at the top of your **drawRect:** implementations...

```
- (void)drawRect:(CGRect)r
{
    CGContextRef ctx = UIGraphicsGetCurrentContext();
}
```

you are getting a pointer to the layer's context. All of the drawing in **drawRect:** is filling the layer's bitmap, which is then copied to the screen.

Need to see this for yourself? Set an Xcode breakpoint in **HypnosisView**'s **drawRect:** and check out the stack trace in the debug navigator, as shown in Figure 22.8.

Figure 22.8   Stack trace in drawRect:

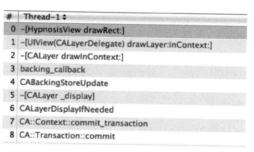

A few paragraphs up, we said that the pixels generated by drawing routines "end up in the layer's bitmap." What does that mean? When you want to create a bitmap context in Cocoa Touch (as you did when you created the thumbnails for the possessions), you typically do something like this:

```
// Create context
UIGraphicsBeginImageContextWithOptions(size, NO, [[UIScreen mainScreen] scale]);
    ... Do drawing here ...

// Get image result
UIImage *result = UIGraphicsGetImageFromCurrentImageContext();
```

```
// Clean up image context
UIGraphicsEndImageContext();
```

A bitmap context is created and drawn to, and the resulting pixels are stored in a **UIImage** instance.

The UIGraphics suite of functions provides a convenient way of creating a bitmap **CGContextRef** and writing that data to a **UIImage** object:

```
// Create a color space to use for the context
CGColorSpaceRef colorSpace = CGColorSpaceCreateDeviceRGB();

// Create a context of appropriate width and height
// with 4 bytes per pixel - RGBA
CGContextRef ctx =
    CGBitmapContextCreate(NULL, width, height, 8, width * 4,
            colorSpace, kCGImageAlphaPremultipliedLast);

// Make this context the current one
UIGraphicsPushContext(ctx);

... Do drawing here ...

// Get image result
CGImageRef image = CGBitmapContextCreateImage(ctx);
UIImage *result = [[[UIImage alloc] initWithCGImage:image] autorelease];

// Clean up image context - make previous context current if one exists
UIGraphicsPopContext();
CGImageRelease(image);
CGContextRelease(ctx);
CGColorSpaceRelease(colorSpace);
```

A layer creates the same kind of context when it needs to redraw its contents. However, a layer does it a little differently. See the NULL as the first parameter to **CGBitmapContextCreate**? That is where you pass a data buffer to hold the pixels generated by drawing routines in this context. By passing NULL, we say, "Core Graphics, figure out how much memory is needed for this buffer, create it, and then dispose of it when the context is destroyed." A **CALayer** already has a buffer (its contents), so it would call the function as follows:

```
CGContextRef ctx =
    CGBitmapContextCreate(myBitmapPixels, width, height, 8, width * 4,
            colorSpace, kCGImageAlphaPremultipliedLast);
```

Then, when this context is drawn to, all of the resulting pixels are immediately written to the bitmap that is the layer.

23

Controlling Animation with CAAnimation

An animation object drives change over time. An animation object is an instruction set ("move from point A to point B over 2 seconds") that can be added to a **CALayer** instance. When an animation object is added to a layer, that layer begins following the instructions of the animation. Many properties of **CALayer** can be animated by animation objects: opacity, position, transform, bounds, and contents are just a few.

Animation Objects

While you have not yet used animations objects explicitly, all animation in iOS is driven by them, including the animations you saw in the last chapter. The abstract superclass for all animation objects is **CAAnimation**. **CAAnimation** is responsible for handling timing; for instance, it has a duration property that specifies the length of the animation. As an abstract superclass, you do not use **CAAnimation** objects directly. Instead, you use one of its concrete subclasses shown in Figure 23.1.

Figure 23.1   Inheritance

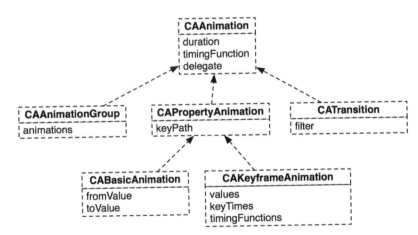

CAPropertyAnimation is a subclass of **CAAnimation** that extends the ability of its superclass by adding the ability to change the properties of a layer. Each property animation has a *key path* of type **NSString**. This string is the name of an animatable property of a **CALayer**. Many of **CALayer**'s properties are animatable. Check the documentation for a list. Search for "animatable properties" and look under the Core Animation Programming Guide (Figure 23.2).

Figure 23.2   Animatable properties in the documentation

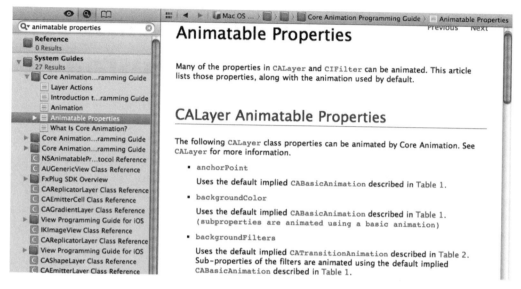

Typically, the key path matches the name of the property. For example, a property animation that will animate a layer's opacity property will have a key path of opacity.

Sometimes a property whose type is a structure (like position, whose type is CGPoint) can have each of its members accessed by a key path. (The available options for this are in the documentation under Core Animation Extensions To Key-Value Coding.)

However, like **CAAnimation**, **CAPropertyAnimation** is an abstract superclass. To create an animation object that modifies a property of a layer, you use one of the two concrete subclasses of **CAPropertyAnimation**: **CABasicAnimation** and **CAKeyframeAnimation**. Most of the time you will spend with Core Animation will involve these two classes.

CABasicAnimation is the simpler of the two classes. It has two properties: fromValue and toValue, and it inherits **CAAnimation**'s duration property. When a basic animation is added to a layer, the property to be animated is set to the value in fromValue. Over the time specified by duration, the value of the property is interpolated linearly from fromValue to toValue, as shown in Figure 23.3.

Figure 23.3   Interpolating a CABasicAnimation that animates the position of a layer

Here's an example of an animation object that acts on a layer's opacity property.

```
// Create an animation that will change the opacity of a layer
CABasicAnimation *fader = [CABasicAnimation animationWithKeyPath:@"opacity"];

// It will last 2 seconds
[fader setDuration:2.0];

// The layer's opacity will start at 1.0 (completely opaque)
[fader setFromValue:[NSNumber numberWithFloat:1.0]];

// And will end at 0.0 (completely transparent)
[fader setToValue:[NSNumber numberWithFloat:0.0]];

// Add it to the layer
[rexLayer addAnimation:fader forKey:@"BigFade"];
```

The key, "BigFade" in this case, is ignored by the system. However, you could use it to access the animation later if, for example, you needed to cancel it mid-fade.

In this code, the fromValue and toValue take **NSNumber**s as arguments. The type of these properties however, is id because animation objects need to be able to support different data types. For example, an animation that changes the position of a layer would need values that are of type CGPoint.

You can't just pass any object for any property; **CABasicAnimation** expects the appropriate object based on the key path. For scalar values, like opacity, you can wrap a number in an **NSNumber** instance. For properties represented by structures, like position, you wrap the structures in instances of **NSValue**.

```
CABasicAnimation *mover = [CABasicAnimation animationWithKeyPath:@"position"];
[mover setDuration:1.0];
[mover setFromValue:[NSValue valueWithCGPoint:CGPointMake(0.0, 100.0)]];
[mover setToValue:[NSValue valueWithCGPoint:CGPointMake(100.0, 100.0)]];
```

Figure 23.4   CAKeyframeAnimation

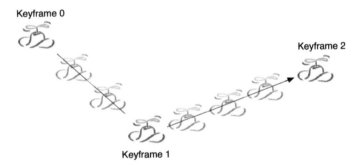

The difference between **CABasicAnimation** and **CAKeyframeAnimation** is that a basic animation only interpolates two values while a keyframe animation can interpolate as many values as you give it (Figure 23.4). These values are put into an **NSArray** in the order in which they are to occur. This array is then set as the values property of a **CAKeyframeAnimation** instance.

```
CAKeyframeAnimation *mover = [CAKeyframeAnimation animationWithKeyPath:@"position"];
NSArray *vals = [NSMutableArray array];
[vals addObject:[NSValue valueWithCGPoint:CGPointMake(0.0, 100.0)]];
[vals addObject:[NSValue valueWithCGPoint:CGPointMake(100.0, 100.0)]];
[mover setValues:vals];
[mover setDuration:1.0];
```

Each value in the `values` property is called a *keyframe*. Keyframes are the values that the animation will interpolate; the animation will take the property it is animating through each of these keyframes over its duration. A basic animation is really a keyframe animation that is limited to two keyframes. (In addition to allowing more than two keyframes, **CAKeyframeAnimation** adds the ability to change the timing of each of the keyframes, but that's more advanced than what we want to talk about right now.)

There are two more **CAAnimation** subclasses, but they are used less often. A **CAAnimationGroup** instance holds an array of animation objects. When an animation group is added to a layer, the animations run concurrently.

```
CABasicAnimation *mover = [CABasicAnimation animationWithKeyPath:@"position"];
[mover setDuration:1.0];
[mover setFromValue:[NSValue valueWithCGPoint:CGPointMake(0.0, 100.0)]];
[mover setToValue:[NSValue valueWithCGPoint:CGPointMake(100.0, 100.0)]];

CABasicAnimation *fader = [CABasicAnimation animationWithKeyPath:@"opacity"];
[fader setDuration:1.0];
[fader setFromValue:[NSNumber numberWithFloat:1.0]];
[fader setToValue:[NSNumber numberWithFloat:0.0]];

CAAnimationGroup *group = [CAAnimationGroup animation];
[group setAnimations:[NSArray arrayWithObjects:fader, mover, nil]];
```

CATransition animates layers as they are transitioning on and off the screen. On Mac OS X, **CATransition** is made very powerful by Core Image Filters. In iOS, it can only do a couple of simple transitions like fading and sliding. (**CATransition** is used by **UINavigationController** when pushing a view controller's view onto the screen.)

Spinning with CABasicAnimation

In this section, you are going to use an animation object to spin the implicit layer of the time field in HypnoTime's **TimeViewController** whenever it is updated (Figure 23.5). (Recall that an implicit layer is a layer created by a view when the view is instantiated. The time field is a **UILabel**, which is a subclass of **UIView**, so it has an implicit layer that we can animate.)

Figure 23.5   Current time mid-spin

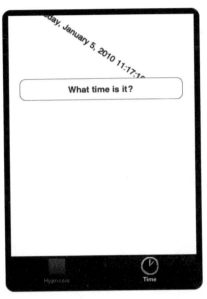

Open `HypnoTime.xcodeproj`.

The Core Animation code you will write in this exercise will be in `TimeViewController.m`. So import the header from the QuartzCore framework at the top of this file.

#import <QuartzCore/QuartzCore.h>

`@implementation TimeViewController`

In order to spin the `timeLabel`, you need an animation object that will apply a 360-degree rotation over time to a layer. So we need to determine four things:

- Which type of animation object suits this purpose?

- What key path handles rotation?

- How long should the animation take to complete?

- What values should the animation interpolate?

To answer the first question, think about the number of keyframes an animation would need to make a complete revolution. It only needs two: a non-rotated value and a fully-rotated value, so **CABasicAnimation** can handle this task.

To determine the key path, we use the property of **CALayer** that deals with rotation. This property is its `transform`, the transformation matrix that is applied to the layer when it draws. The `transform` of a layer can rotate, scale, translate, and skew its frame. (For more details, go to Core Animation Extensions To Key-Value Coding in the documentation.) This exercise only calls for rotating the layer, and, fortunately, you can isolate the rotation of the `transform` in a key path (Figure 23.6). Therefore, the key path of the basic animation will be `transform.rotation`.

Figure 23.6   Core Animation Extensions to Key-Value Coding documentation

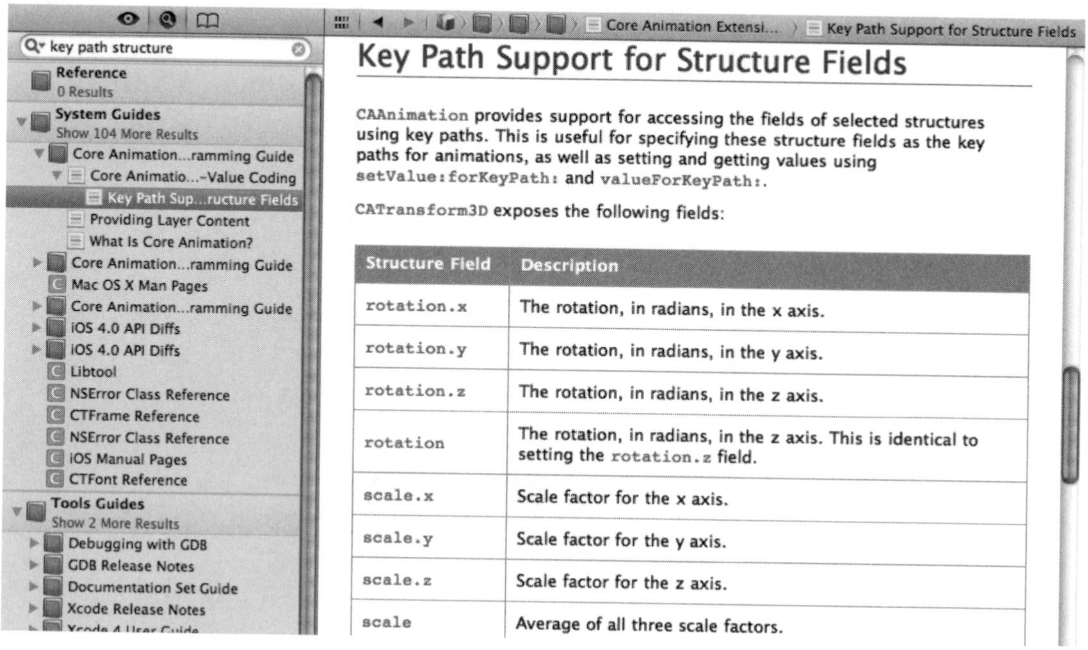

Let's make the duration of this animation one second. That's enough time for the user to see the spin but not so much time that they get bored waiting for it to complete.

Lastly, we need the values of the two keyframes: the fromValue and the toValue. The documentation says that the transform.rotation is in radians, so that's how we'll pass these values. A little geometry research tells us that no rotation is 0 radians and a full rotation is 2 * PI radians. When using a **CABasicAnimation**, if you do not supply a fromValue, the animation assumes that fromValue is the current value of that property. The default value of the transform property is the identity matrix – no rotation. This means you only have to supply the final keyframe to this animation object.

In TimeViewController.h, declare a new method.

```
- (void)spinTimeLabel;
```

In TimeViewController.m, edit the method **showCurrentTime:** to call this method.

```
- (IBAction)showCurrentTime:(id)sender
{
    NSDate *now = [NSDate date];
    NSDateFormatter *formatter = [[NSDateFormatter alloc] init];
    [formatter setTimeStyle:NSDateFormatterMediumStyle];

    [timeLabel setText:[formatter stringFromDate:now]];

    [self spinTimeLabel];
}
```

In TimeViewController.m, create an animation object that will spin a layer around in one second.

```
- (void)spinTimeLabel
{
    // Create a basic animation
    CABasicAnimation *spin =
            [CABasicAnimation animationWithKeyPath:@"transform.rotation"];

    // fromValue is implied
    [spin setToValue:[NSNumber numberWithFloat:M_PI * 2.0]];
    [spin setDuration:1.0];
}
```

Now that you have an animation object, it needs to be applied to a layer for it to have any effect. CALayer instances implement the method addAnimation:forKey: for this purpose. This method takes two arguments: an animation object and a key. Once again: this key is *not* the key path; it is simply a human-readable name for this animation.

In spinTimeLabel, add your animation object to timeLabel's layer to start the animation.

```
    [spin setToValue:[NSNumber numberWithFloat:M_PI * 2.0]];
    [spin setDuration:1.0];

    // Kick off the animation by adding it to the layer
    [[timeLabel layer] addAnimation:spin
                        forKey:@"spinAnimation"];
}
```

Build and run the application. The label field will spin 360 degrees when the user updates it – either by switching to the Time tab or tapping the button.

Note that the animation object exists independently of the layer it is applied to. This animation object could be added to any layer to rotate it 360 degrees. You can create animation objects and keep them around for later use in the application.

Timing functions

You may notice that the rotation of the label field's layer starts and stops suddenly; it would look nicer if it gradually accelerated and decelerated. This sort of behavior is controlled by the animation's timing function, which is an instance of the class CAMediaTimingFunction. By default, the timing function is linear – the values are interpolated linearly. Changing the timing function changes how these animations are interpolated. It doesn't change the duration or the keyframes.

In spinTimeLabel, change the timing function to "ease" in and out of the animation.

```
    [spin setDuration:1.0];

    // Set the timing function
    CAMediaTimingFunction *tf = [CAMediaTimingFunction
                    functionWithName:kCAMediaTimingFunctionEaseInEaseOut];
    [spin setTimingFunction:tf];

    [[timeLabel layer] addAnimation:spin
                        forKey:@"spinAnimation"];
}
```

Build and run the application and see how the animation changes.

There are four timing functions, you have seen linear and kCAMediaTimingFunctionEaseInEaseOut. The other two are kCAMediaTimingFunctionEaseIn (accelerates gradually, stops suddenly) and kCAMediaTimingFunctionEaseOut (accelerates suddenly, stops slowly). You can also create your own timing functions with **CAMediaTimingFunction**. See the doc for details.

Animation completion

Sometimes you want to know when an animation is finished. For instance, you might want to chain animations or update another object when an animation completes. How can you know when an animation is complete? Every animation object can have a delegate, and the animation object sends the message **animationDidStop:finished:** to its delegate when an animation stops.

Edit TimeViewController.m so that it logs a message to the console whenever an animation stops.

```
- (void)animationDidStop:(CAAnimation *)anim finished:(BOOL)flag
{
    NSLog(@"%@ finished: %d", anim, flag);
}
- (void)spinTimeLabel
{
    // Create a basic animation
    CABasicAnimation *spin =
                [CABasicAnimation animationWithKeyPath:@"transform.rotation"];

    [spin setDelegate:self];

    // fromValue is implied
    [spin setToValue:[NSNumber numberWithFloat:M_PI * 2.0]];
    [spin setDuration:1.0];

    // Set the timing function
    CAMediaTimingFunction *tf = [CAMediaTimingFunction
                        functionWithName:kCAMediaTimingFunctionEaseInEaseOut];
    [spin setTimingFunction:tf];

    // Kick off the animation by adding it to the layer
    [[timeLabel layer] addAnimation:spin
                            forKey:@"spinAnimation"];
}
```

Build and run the application. Notice the log statements when the animation is complete. If you press the button several times quickly, the animation in progress will be interrupted by a new one. The interrupted animation will still send the message **animationDidStop:finished:** to its delegate; however, the finished flag will be NO.

Bouncing with a CAKeyframeAnimation

For practice with **CAKeyframeAnimation**, you are going to make the time label grow and shrink to give it a bouncing effect (Figure 23.7).

Figure 23.7 Current time mid-bounce

Declare a new method in `TimeViewController.h`.

- (void)bounceTimeLabel;

In `TimeViewController.m`, replace the code that spins the label in **showCurrentTime:** with a call to **bounceTimeLabel**.

```
- (IBAction)showCurrentTime:(id)sender
{
    NSDate *now = [NSDate date];
    static NSDateFormatter *formatter = nil;
    if (!formatter) {
        formatter = [[NSDateFormatter alloc] init];
        [formatter setDateStyle:NSDateFormatterMediumStyle];
    }
    [timeLabel setText:[formatter stringFromDate:now]];

    [self spinTimeLabel];
    [self bounceTimeLabel];
}
```

Then, implement **bounceTimeLabel** in `TimeViewController.m`.

```
- (void)bounceTimeLabel
{
    // Create a key frame animation
    CAKeyframeAnimation *bounce =
                [CAKeyframeAnimation animationWithKeyPath:@"transform"];

    // Create the values it will pass through
    CATransform3D forward = CATransform3DMakeScale(1.3, 1.3, 1);
    CATransform3D back = CATransform3DMakeScale(0.7, 0.7, 1);
    CATransform3D forward2 = CATransform3DMakeScale(1.2, 1.2, 1);
    CATransform3D back2 = CATransform3DMakeScale(0.9, 0.9, 1);
```

419

```
[bounce setValues:[NSArray arrayWithObjects:
                   [NSValue valueWithCATransform3D:CATransform3DIdentity],
                   [NSValue valueWithCATransform3D:forward],
                   [NSValue valueWithCATransform3D:back],
                   [NSValue valueWithCATransform3D:forward2],
                   [NSValue valueWithCATransform3D:back2],
                   [NSValue valueWithCATransform3D:CATransform3DIdentity],
                   nil]];
// Set the duration
[bounce setDuration:0.6];

// Animate the layer
[[timeLabel layer] addAnimation:bounce
                    forKey:@"bounceAnimation"];
}
```

Build and run the application. The time field should now scale up and down and up and down when it is updated. The constant CATransform3DIdentity is the *identity matrix*. When the transform of a layer is the identity matrix, no scaling, rotation, or translation is applied to the layer: it sits squarely within its bounding box at its position. So, this animation starts at no transformation, scales a few times, and then reverts back to no transformation.

Once you understand layers and the basics of animation, there isn't a whole lot to it – other than finding the appropriate key path and getting the timing of things right. Core Animation is one of those things you can play around with and see results immediately. So play with it!

Bronze Challenge: More Animation

When the time label bounces, it should also change its opacity. Try and match the fading of the opacity with the shrinking and growing of the label.

Silver Challenge: Even More Animation

After the TimeViewController's view appears onto the screen, have the What time is it? button slide in from the side.

Gold Challenge: Chaining Animations

After completing the silver challenge, make it so the What time is it? button starts to fade in and out over and over again. This animation should only begin once the button has slid into place.

For the More Curious: The Presentation Layer and the Model Layer

You can think of an instance of CALayer as having two parts: the content that gets composited onto the screen and a set of parameters that describe how it should be composited (opacity, transform, position, etc.). When a layer is being animated, it actually has two copies of these parameters: the model version and the presentation version. The presentation parameters are the ones that are being smoothly changed by the animation object. The model parameters are the persistent ones – the ones that will be used once the animation is over.

So, when a layer is being animated, its content is composited to the screen using the presentation parameters. When it is animation-less, the model parameters are used.

Apple calls these sets of parameters the *model layer* and the *presentation layer*.

When you ask a layer for its position, you are getting the position of the model layer. To get the presentation version, you ask for the **presentationLayer** first.

```
CGPoint whereIsItWhenAnimationStops = [layer position];
CGPoint whereIsItNow = [[layer presentationLayer] position];
```

Why is this useful? Imagine a game that has animating objects on the screen, and if the user taps one of the objects, it blows up. Only the presentation layer knows where the object currently is on the screen, which you must know in order to judge the accuracy of the user's tap.

In this chapter, our examples have had the animated objects return to their original states after the animation is complete. Often, however, you want to animate an object to a state and then have it stay there once the animation is over. To do this, you must keep the presentation and model layers clear in your mind. Not doing so leads to two common errors:

- *Your animation goes great, but at the end it snaps back to its initial position (or opacity or whatever) when you wanted it to remain where it was.* This happens because you forgot to update the model parameters to match the final state of your animation. Try using an explicit animation in **touchesBegan:withEvent:** method in HypnosisView.m. (Also comment out **touchesMoved:withEvent:**.)

```
- (void)touchesBegan:(NSSet *)touches withEvent:(UIEvent *)event
{
    UITouch *t = [touches anyObject];
    CGPoint p = [t locationInView:self];
    CABasicAnimation *ba = [CABasicAnimation animationWithKeyPath:@"position"];
    [ba setFromValue:[NSValue valueWithCGPoint:[boxLayer position]]];
    [ba setToValue:[NSValue valueWithCGPoint:p]];
    [ba setDuration:3.0];

    // Update the model layer
    [boxLayer setPosition:p];

    // Add animation that will gradually update presentation layer
    [boxLayer addAnimation:ba forKey:@"foo"];
}
- (void)touchesMoved:(NSSet *)touches
            withEvent:(UIEvent *)event
{
//     UITouch *t = [touches anyObject];
//     CGPoint p = [t locationInView:self];
//     [CATransaction begin];
//     [CATransaction setDisableActions:YES];
//     [boxLayer setPosition:p];
//     [CATransaction commit];

}
```

In this animation, If you build and run now and tap the screen, you will see the boxLayer slowly move to wherever you touched the screen.

If you comment out the line that says [boxLayer setPosition:p], you'll see that the layer bounces back to its starting position once the animation ends. For beginners, this is a very common error.

- *No animation happens. Your layer leaps directly to its final state.* When an animation begins, if there is no `fromValue`, the `fromValue` is taken from the model layer. If you update the model to the final state before starting the animation, your `fromValue` and `toValue` end up the same. Usually the fix is to give the animation an explicit `fromValue`.

24

UIStoryboard

In your projects so far, you've laid out the interfaces of your view controllers in separate XIB files and then instantiated the view controllers programmatically. In this chapter, you will use a *storyboard* instead. Storyboards are a feature of iOS that allows you to instantiate and lay out all of your view controllers in one XIB-like file. Additionally, you can wire up view controllers in the storyboard to dictate how they get presented to the user.

The purpose of a storyboard is to minimize some of the simple code a programmer has to write to create and set up view controllers and the interactions between them. To see this simplification – and its drawbacks – let's create an application that uses a storyboard.

Creating a Storyboard

Create a new iOS Empty Application and name it Storytime (Figure 24.1).

Figure 24.1   Creating Storytime

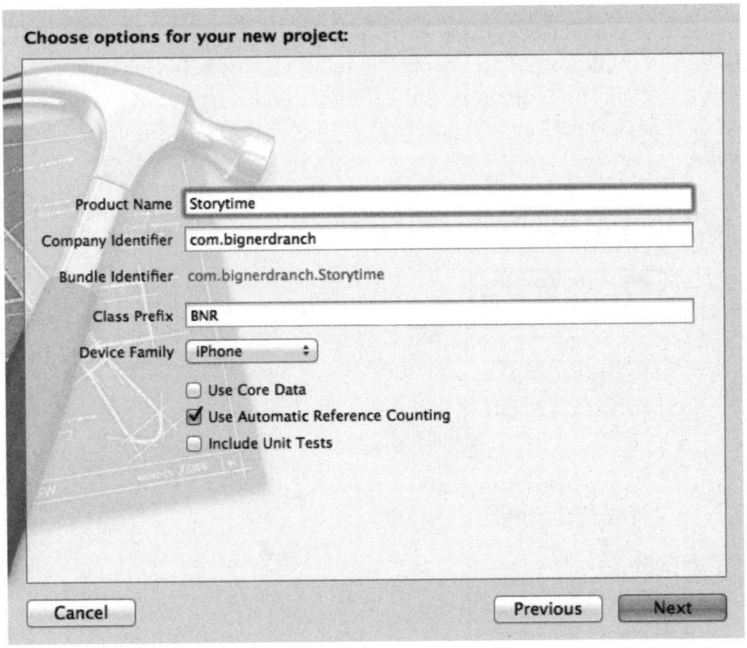

Then, select New File... from the New menu. Select User Interface from the iOS section. Then, select the Storyboard template and hit Next (Figure 24.2).

Figure 24.2   Creating a storyboard

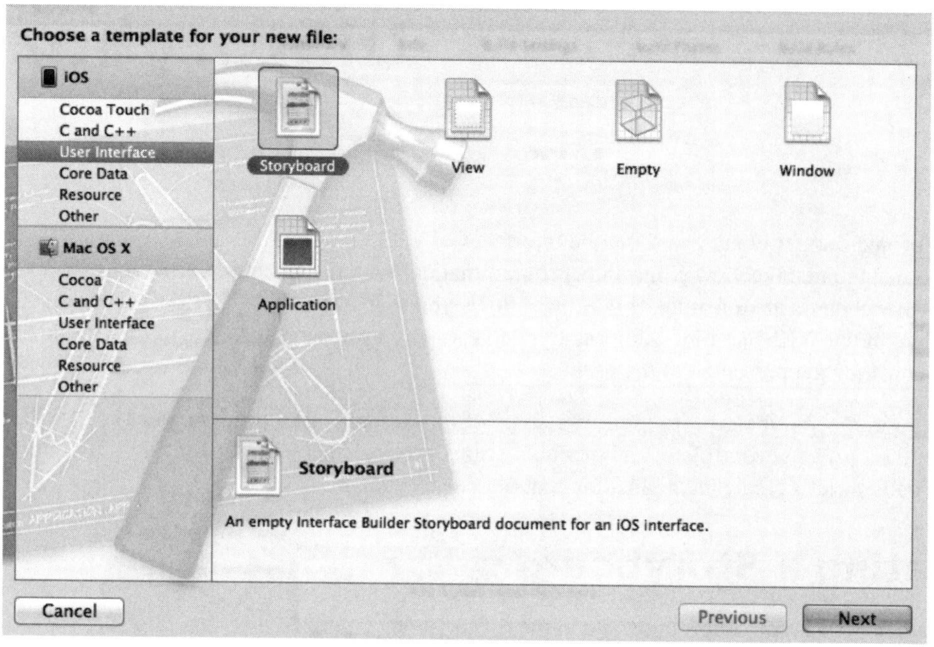

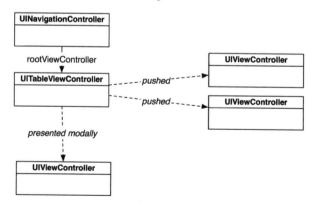

On the next pane, select iPhone from the Device Family pop-up menu and click Next. Then, name this file Storytime.

This will create a new file named Storytime.storyboard and open it in the editor area. A storyboard is a lot like a XIB, except it allows you to lay out the relationships between view controllers in addition to laying out their interfaces. The Storytime application will have a total of five view controllers, including a **UINavigationController** and a **UITableViewController**. Figure 24.3 shows an object diagram of Storytime.

Figure 24.3   Object diagram for Storytime

Using a storyboard, we can set up the relationships shown in Figure 24.3 without writing any code.

To get started, open the utilities area and the Object Library. Drag a Navigation Controller onto the canvas. The canvas will now look like Figure 24.4.

Figure 24.4 Navigation controller in storyboard

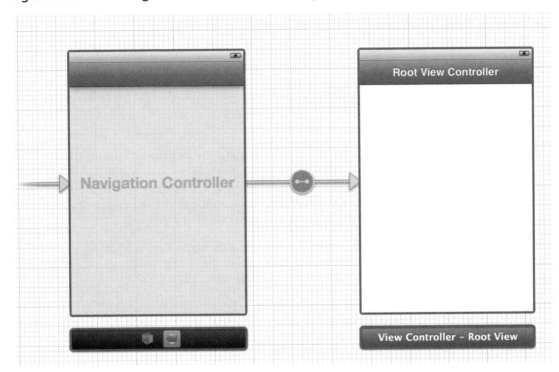

In addition to the **UINavigationController** object you asked for, the storyboard took the liberty of creating three other objects: the view of the navigation controller, a **UIViewController**, and the view of the **UIViewController**. In addition, the **UIViewController** has been made the root view controller of the navigation controller.

The two view controller instances are represented by the black bars on the canvas, and their views are shown above them. You configure the view the same as you would in a normal XIB file. To configure the view controller itself, you select the black bar.

Before we go any further, we need to tell our application about this storyboard file. Select the Storytime project from the project navigator. Then, select the Storytime target and the Summary tab. Locate the Main Storyboard field and enter Storytime (Figure 24.5). This tells Storytime to load the Storytime.storyboard file when the application launches.

Figure 24.5   Setting the main storyboard

When an application has a main storyboard file, it will automatically load that storyboard when the application launches. In addition to loading the storyboard and its view controllers, it will also create a window and set the initial view controller of the storyboard as the root view controller of the window. You can tell which view controller is the initial view controller by looking at the canvas in the storyboard file – the initial view controller has an arrow that fades in as it points to it.

Since a storyboard file supplies the window for an application, the application delegate doesn't need to create a window. In BNRAppDelegate.m, remove the code from application:didFinishLaunchingWithOptions: that creates the window.

```
- (BOOL)application:(UIApplication *)application
    didFinishLaunchingWithOptions:(NSDictionary *)launchOptions
{
    self.window = [[UIWindow alloc] initWithFrame:[[UIScreen mainScreen] bounds]];
    self.window.backgroundColor = [UIColor whiteColor];
    [self.window makeKeyAndVisible];
    return YES;
}
```

Build and run the application, and you'll see a view of a view controller and a navigation bar that says Root View Controller (Figure 24.6). All of this came from the storyboard file – you didn't even have to write any code.

Figure 24.6   Initial Storytime screen

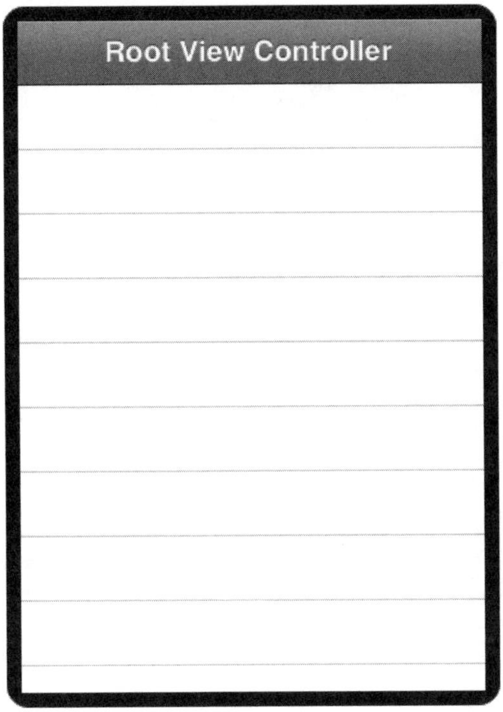

UITableViewControllers in Storyboards

When using a **UITableViewController**, you typically implement the appropriate data source methods to return the content of each cell. This makes sense when you have dynamic content – like a list of **BNRItem**s that may change – but it is a lot of work when you have a table whose content never changes. Storyboards allow you to add static content to a table view without having to implement the data source methods.

To see how easy this is, we're going to add a **UITableViewController** to the storyboard and give it static content. (Depending on a number of factors, the root view controller of the **UINavigationController** may already be a **UITableViewController**. If this is the case in your storyboard, go through the following steps anyway for the practice.)

First, you need to delete the current root view controller of the navigation controller. In Storytime.storyboard, select the black bar that represents the **UIViewController** that is the root view controller. Then press the Delete key. That view controller is now gone, and the navigation controller no longer has a root view controller.

Next, drag a **UITableViewController** from the library onto the canvas. To set this table view controller as the root view controller of the navigation controller, Control-drag from the navigation controller's view to the table view controller. Let go, and from the black panel that appears, select Relationship - rootViewController (Figure 24.7).

Figure 24.7   Setting a relationship

This establishes the **UITableViewController** as the root view controller of the **UINavigationController**. There will now be an arrow from the navigation controller to the table view controller. In the middle of this arrow is an icon that represents the type of relationship between the two view controllers (Figure 24.8).

Figure 24.8   UINavigationController and UITableViewController

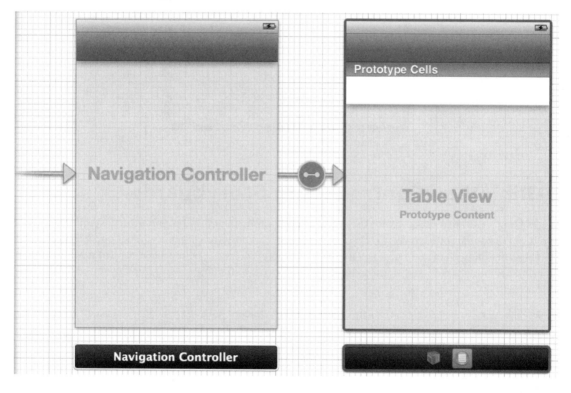

(Notice the zoom in and out controls in the bottom right corner? You can zoom in and out to see more of the canvas. This is especially useful when you have a lot of view controllers. However, you cannot select the view objects when zoomed out.)

Next, select the Table View of the **UITableViewController**. In the attributes inspector, change the Content pop-up menu to Static Cells (Figure 24.9).

Figure 24.9   Static cells

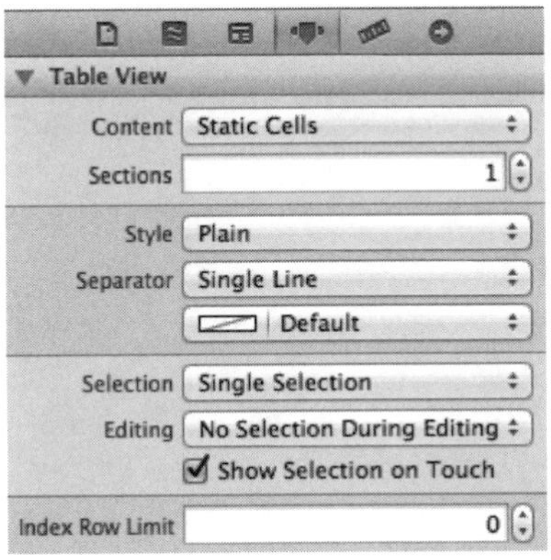

Three **UITableViewCell**s will appear on the table view. You can now select and configure each one individually. Select the top-most cell and, in the attributes inspector, change its Style to Basic (Figure 24.10).

Figure 24.10   Basic UITableViewCell

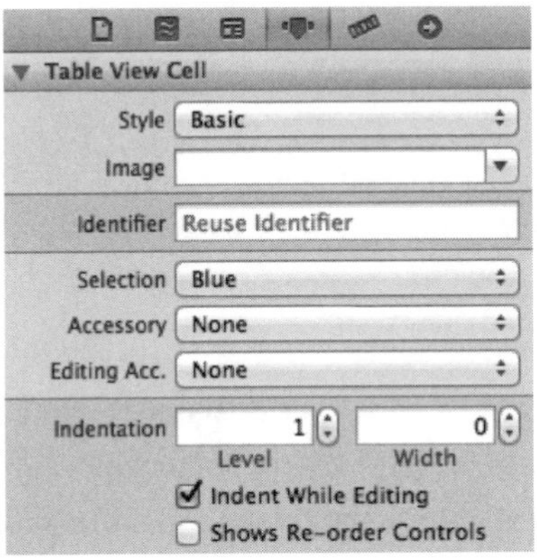

Back on the canvas, the selected cell will now say Title. Double-click on the text and change it to Red.

Repeat the same steps for the second cell but have the title read White. Let's get rid of the third cell; select it and press Delete. Figure 24.11 shows the updated table view.

Figure 24.11 Configured cells

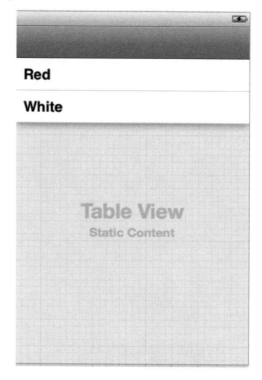

Build and run the application. You will see exactly what you have laid out in the storyboard file – a table view underneath a navigation bar. The table view has two cells that read Red and White. And you didn't have to write any data source methods.

Segues

Most iOS applications have a number of view controllers that users navigate between. Storyboards allow you to set up these interactions as *segues* without having to write code.

A segue moves another view controller onto the screen when triggered and is represented by an instance of **UIStoryboardSegue**. Each segue has a style, an action item, and an identifier. The *style* of a segue determines how the view controller will be presented, such as pushed onto the stack or presented modally. The *action item* is the view object in the storyboard file that triggers the segue, like a button, a bar button item, or another **UIControl**. The *identifier* is used to programmatically access the segue. This is useful when you want to trigger a segue that doesn't come from an action item, like a shake or some other interface element that can't be set up in the storyboard file.

Let's start with two push segues. A push segue pushes a view controller onto the stack of a navigation controller. We'll need to set up two more view controllers in our storyboard, one whose view's background is red, and the other, white. The segues will be between the table view controller and these two new view controllers. The action items will be the table view's cells; tapping a cell will push the appropriate view controller onto the navigation controller's stack.

Drag two **UIViewController**s onto the canvas. Select the View of one of the view controllers and, in the attributes inspector, change its background color to red.

Next, select the cell titled Red. Control-drag to the view controller whose view has the red background. A black panel titled Storyboard Segues will appear. This panel lists the possible styles for this segue. Select Push.

Then, select the White cell and Control-drag to the other view controller. Your canvas should look like Figure 24.12.

Figure 24.12   Setting up two segues

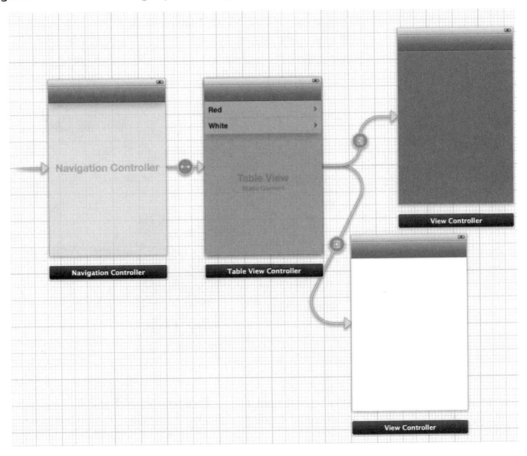

Notice the arrows that come from the table view controller to the other two view controllers. Each of these is a segue. The icon in the circle tells us that these segues are push segues.

Build and run the application. Tap on each row, and you will be taken to the appropriate view controller. You can even move back in the navigation stack to the table view controller like you would expect. The best part about this? We haven't written any code yet.

Note that push segues only work if the origin of the segue is inside a navigation controller. Fortunately for us, the origin of these segues is the table view controller, which meets this requirement.

Now let's look at another style a segue – a Modal segue. Drag a new **UIViewController** onto the canvas. We want this segue's action item to be a bar button item on the table view controller's navigation item.

Drag a Bar Button Item from the library onto the right corner of the navigation bar at the top of the table view controller's view. Then, Control-drag from this bar button item to the view controller you just dropped on the canvas. Select Modal from the black panel. The storyboard canvas now looks like Figure 24.13. (Notice that the icon for the modal segue is different from the icon for the push segues.)

Figure 24.13   A modal segue

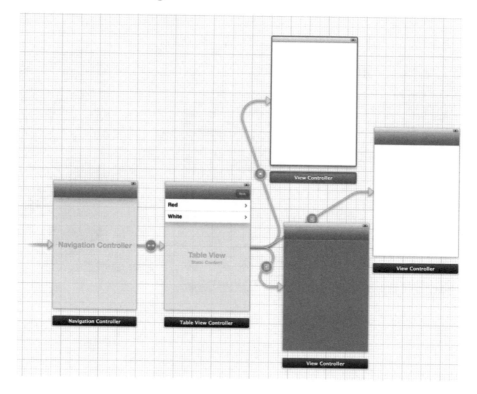

Build and run the application. Tap the bar button item, and a view controller with a white view will slide onto the screen. All is well – except you can't dismiss this view controller. You'll have to write some actual code to do that.

Right now, every view controller in the storyboard is a standard instance of **UIViewController** or one of its standard subclasses. We cannot write code for any of these as they are. To write code for a view controller in a storyboard, you have to create a subclass of **UIViewController** and specify in the storyboard that the view controller is an instance of your subclass.

Let's create a new **UIViewController** subclass to see how this works. Create a new file from the **UIViewController** template. Name it **ModalViewController** and configure it as shown in Figure 24.14.

Figure 24.14 ModalViewController

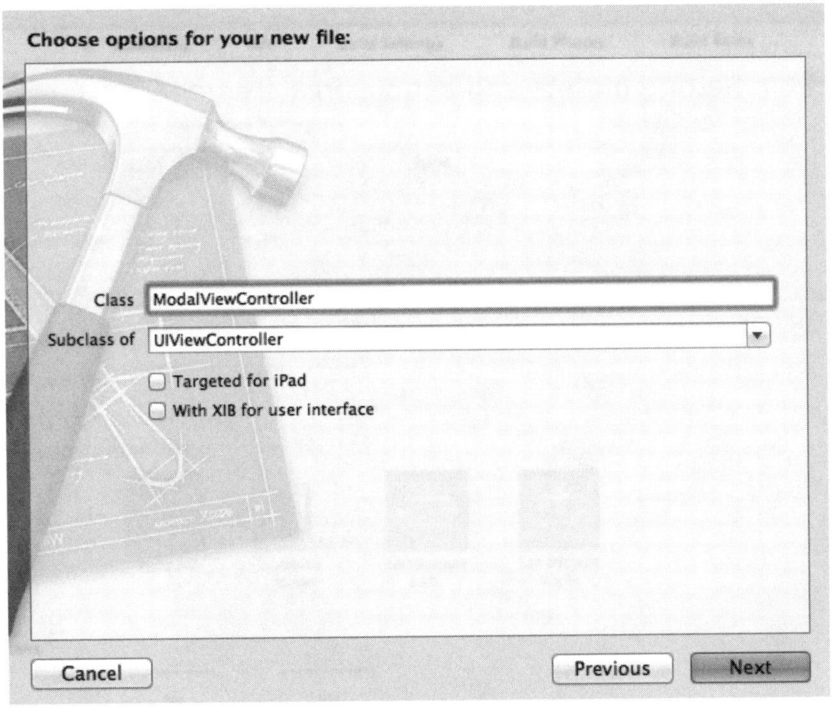

![ModalViewController new file options dialog showing Class field with "ModalViewController" and Subclass of "UIViewController", with Targeted for iPad and With XIB for user interface unchecked]

In `ModalViewController.h`, declare a new `IBAction`.

```
@interface ModalViewController : UIViewController

- (IBAction)dismiss:(id)sender;

@end
```

In `ModalViewController.m`, implement this method to dismiss the instance of **ModalViewController**.

```
- (IBAction)dismiss:(id)sender
{
    [[self presentingViewController] dismissViewControllerAnimated:YES
                                                       completion:nil];
}
```

Open `Storytime.storyboard` again. Select the black bar underneath the modally presented view controller. In the identity inspector, change the Class to **ModalViewController** (Figure 24.15).

Figure 24.15 Changing view controller to ModalViewController

Now, after making sure you are zoomed in, drag a Round Rect Button onto the **ModalViewController**'s view. Label this button Dismiss.

Select the button and notice that the black bar that represents the view controller now shows two icons: the second icon is the view controller object. Control-drag from the button to this view controller icon and let go – when the panel appears, select the **dismiss:** method (Figure 24.16).

Figure 24.16   Setting outlets and actions in a storyboard

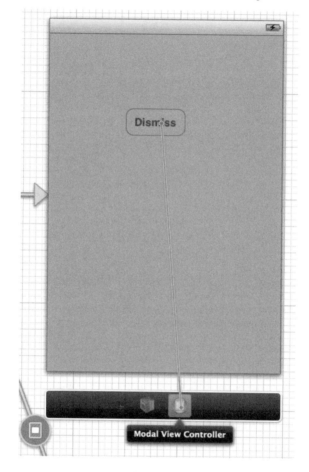

This button is now hooked up to send the message **dismiss:** to its **ModalViewController** whenever tapped. Build and run the application, present the **ModalViewController**, and then tap on the Dismiss button. Voilà!

More on Storyboards

In this exercise, you created a storyboard, set up a few view controllers, laid out their interfaces, and created some segues between them. This is the basic idea behind storyboards, and while there are a few more flavors of segues and types of view controllers you can set up, you get the idea. A storyboard replaces lines of code.

For example, the push segues in this application replace this code:

```
- (void)tableView:(UITableView *)tableView
    didSelectRowAtIndexPath:(NSIndexPath *)ip
{
    UIViewController *vc = [[UIViewController alloc] init];
    [[self navigationController] pushViewController:vc];
}
```

While this seems nice, storyboarding, in our opinion, is not very useful. Let's go through the pros and cons. First, the pros:

• Storyboards can be used to easily show off the flow of an application to a client or a colleague.

• Storyboards remove some simple code from your source files.

• Tables with static content are easy to create.

• Storyboards sure do look pretty.

The cons, unfortunately, outweigh the pros:

• Storyboards are difficult to work with in a team. Typically, a team of iOS programmers breaks up the work by having each member focus on a particular view controller. With a storyboard, everyone has to do their work in the same storyboard file. This can quickly lead to clutter.

• Storyboards screw up version control. If two people are working on the storyboard at the same time – which happens every day in a team environment – your version control system, like Subversion, will find conflicts that you must resolve manually.

• Storyboards disrupt the flow of programming. Let's say you are writing a view controller and adding the code for a button that presents a view controller modally. We can do that pretty easily in code – alloc and init the view controller, and send presentViewController:animated:completion: to self. With storyboards, you have to load up the storyboard file, drag some stuff onto the canvas, set the Class in the identity inspector, connect the segue, and then configure the segue.

• Storyboards sacrifice flexibility and control for ease of use. When you need to get your hands dirty, which is often, a storyboard is more of a wall than a trampoline. The work required to add advanced functionality to the basic functionality of a storyboard is often more than the work required to put together the advanced and basic functionality in code.

• Storyboards always create new view controller instances. Each time you perform a segue, a new instance of the destination view controller is created. Sometimes, though, you'd like to keep a view controller around instead of destroying it each time it disappears off the screen. Storyboarding does not allow you to do this.

Overall, storyboards make easy code easier and difficult code more difficult. We won't be using them in this book, and we do not use them when writing our own applications. It is up to you to decide if a particular application would benefit from storyboarding. Of course, your opinion may change as your project gets more complex. Don't say we didn't warn you!

25

Web Services and UIWebView

In this chapter, you will lay the foundation of an application that reads the RSS feed from the Big Nerd Ranch Forums (Figure 25.1). Forum posts will be listed in a table view, and selecting a post from the table will display it from the site. Figure 25.1 shows the Nerdfeed application at the end of this chapter.

Figure 25.1   Nerdfeed

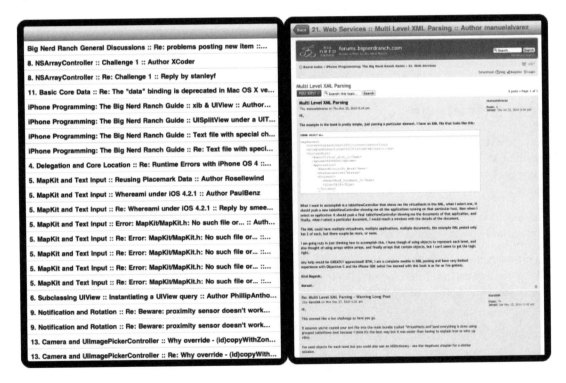

We will divide the work into two parts. The first is connecting to and collecting data from a web service and using that data to create model objects. The second part is using the **UIWebView** class to display web content. Figure 25.2 shows an object diagram for Nerdfeed.

Figure 25.2   Nerdfeed object diagram

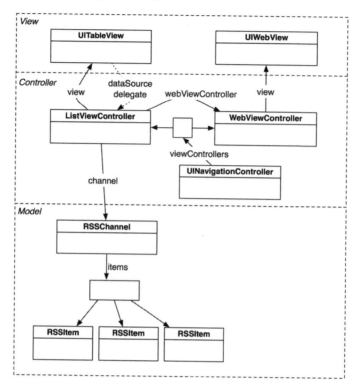

Web Services

Your handy web browser uses the HTTP protocol to communicate with a web server. In the simplest interaction, the browser sends a request to the server specifying a URL. The server responds by sending back the requested page (typically HTML and images), which the browser formats and displays.

In more complex interactions, browser requests include other parameters, like form data. The server processes these parameters and returns a customized, or dynamic, web page.

Web browsers are widely used and have been around for a long time. So the technologies surrounding HTTP are stable and well-developed: HTTP traffic passes neatly through most firewalls, web servers are very secure and have great performance, and web application development tools have become easy to use.

You can write a client application for iOS that leverages the HTTP infrastructure to talk to a web-enabled server. The server side of this application is a *web service*. Your client application and the web service can exchange requests and responses via HTTP.

Because the HTTP protocol doesn't care what data it transports, these exchanges can contain complex data. This data is typically in XML or JSON (JavaScript Object Notation) format. If you control the web server as well as the client, you can use any format you like; if not, you have to build your application to use whatever the server supports.

In this chapter, you will create a client application that will make a request to the smartfeed web service hosted at http://forums.bignerdranch.com. You will pass a number of arguments to this service that determine the format of the data that is returned. This data will be XML that describes the most recent posts at our developer forums.

Starting the Nerdfeed application

Create a new Empty Application for the iPad Device Family. Name this application Nerdfeed, as shown in Figure 25.3. (If you don't have an iPad to deploy to, use the iPad simulator.)

Figure 25.3 Creating an iPad Empty Application

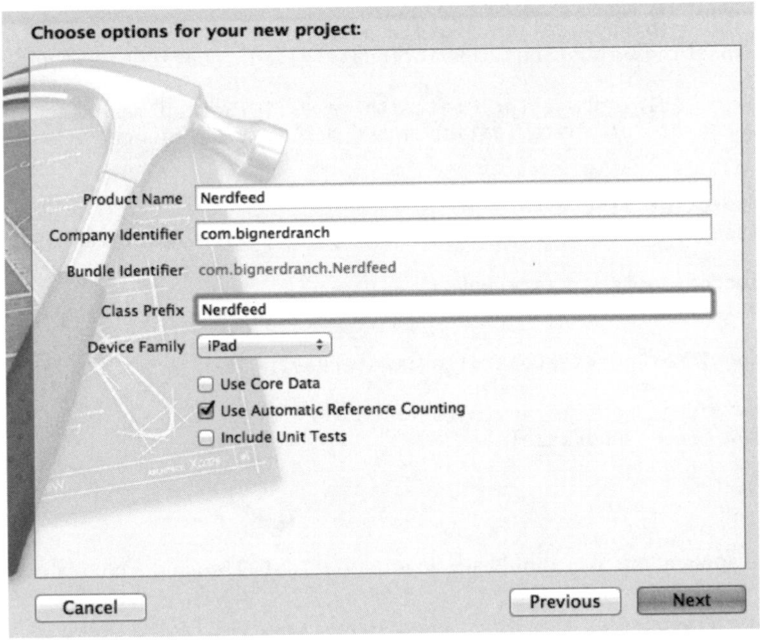

Let's knock out the basic UI before focusing on web services. Create a new **NSObject** subclass and name it **ListViewController**. In ListViewController.h, change the superclass to **UITableViewController**.

```
@interface ListViewController : NSObject
@interface ListViewController : UITableViewController
```

In ListViewController.m, write stubs for the required data source methods so that we can build and run as we go through this exercise.

```
- (NSInteger)tableView:(UITableView *)tableView
  numberOfRowsInSection:(NSInteger)section
{
    return 0;
}
```

```
- (UITableViewCell *)tableView:(UITableView *)tableView
        cellForRowAtIndexPath:(NSIndexPath *)indexPath
{
    return nil;
}
```

In NerdfeedAppDelegate.m, create an instance of **ListViewController** and set it as the root view controller of a navigation controller. Make that navigation controller the root view controller of the window.

```
#import "NerdfeedAppDelegate.h"
#import "ListViewController.h"

@implementation NerdfeedAppDelegate
@synthesize window;

- (BOOL)application:(UIApplication *)application
    didFinishLaunchingWithOptions:(NSDictionary *)launchOptions
{
    self.window = [[UIWindow alloc] initWithFrame:[[UIScreen mainScreen] bounds]];
    // Override point for customization after application launch.

    ListViewController *lvc =
        [[ListViewController alloc] initWithStyle:UITableViewStylePlain];

    UINavigationController *masterNav =
        [[UINavigationController alloc] initWithRootViewController:lvc];

    [[self window] setRootViewController:masterNav];

    self.window.backgroundColor = [UIColor whiteColor];
    [self.window makeKeyAndVisible];

    return YES;
}
```

Build and run the application. You should see an empty **UITableView** and a navigation bar.

NSURL, NSURLRequest, and NSURLConnection

The Nerdfeed application will fetch data from a web server using three handy classes: **NSURL**, **NSURLRequest**, and **NSURLConnection** (Figure 25.4).

Figure 25.4   Relationship of web service classes

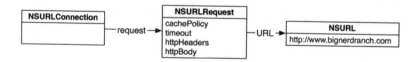

Each of these classes has an important role in communicating with a web server:

- An **NSURL** instance contains the location of a web application in URL format. For many web services, the URL will be composed of the base address, the web application you are communicating with, and any arguments that are being passed.

- An **NSURLRequest** instance holds all the data necessary to communicate with a web server. This includes an **NSURL** object, as well as a caching policy, a limit on how long you will give the web server to respond, and additional data passed through the HTTP protocol. (**NSMutableURLRequest** is the mutable subclass of **NSURLRequest**.)

- An **NSURLConnection** instance is responsible for actually making the connection to a web server, sending the information in its **NSURLRequest**, and gathering the response from the server.

Formatting URLs and requests

The form of a web service request varies depending on who implements the web service; there are no set-in-stone rules when it comes to web services. You will need to find the documentation for the web service to know how to format a request. As long as a client application sends the server what it wants, you have a working exchange.

The Big Nerd Ranch Forum's RSS feed wants a URL that looks like this:

```
http://forums.bignerdranch.com/smartfeed.php?limit=1_DAY&sort_by=standard
&feed_type=RSS2.0&feed_style=COMPACT
```

You can see that the base URL is forums.bignerdranch.com, the web application is smartfeed, and there are five arguments. These arguments are required by the smartfeed web application.

This is a pretty common form for a web service request. Generally, a request URL looks like this:

```
http://baseURL.com/serviceName?argumentX=valueX&argumentY=valueY
```

At times, you will need to make a string "URL-safe." For example, space characters and quotes are not allowed in URLs; They must be replaced with escape-sequences. Here is how that is done.

```
NSString *search = @"Play some \"Abba\"";
NSString *escaped =
    [search stringByAddingPercentEscapesUsingEncoding:NSUTF8StringEncoding];

// escaped is now "Play%20some%20%22Abba%22"
```

When the request to the Big Nerd Ranch forums is processed, the server will return XML data that contains the last 20 posts. The **ListViewController**, who made the request, will populate its table view with the titles of the posts.

In ListViewController.h, add an instance variable for the connection and one for the data that is returned from that connection. Also add a new method declaration.

```
@interface ListViewController : UITableViewController
{
    NSURLConnection *connection;
    NSMutableData *xmlData;
}
- (void)fetchEntries;
@end
```

Working with NSURLConnection

An **NSURLConnection** instance can communicate with a web server either synchronously or asynchronously. Because passing data to and from a remote server can take some time, synchronous connections are generally frowned upon because they stall your application until the connection

completes. This chapter will teach you how to perform an asynchronous connection with
NSURLConnection.

When an instance of **NSURLConnection** is created, it needs to know the location of the web application
and the data to pass to that web server. It also needs a delegate. When told to start communicating with
the web server, **NSURLConnection** will initiate a connection to the location, begin passing it data, and
possibly receive data back. It will update its delegate each step of the way with useful information.

In ListViewController.m, implement the **fetchEntries** method to create an **NSURLRequest** that
connects to http://forums.bignerdranch.com and asks for the last 20 posts in RSS 2.0 format. Then,
create an **NSURLConnection** that transfers this request to the server.

```
- (void)fetchEntries
{
    // Create a new data container for the stuff that comes back from the service
    xmlData = [[NSMutableData alloc] init];

    // Construct a URL that will ask the service for what you want -
    // note we can concatenate literal strings together on multiple
    // lines in this way - this results in a single NSString instance
    NSURL *url = [NSURL URLWithString:
        @"http://forums.bignerdranch.com/smartfeed.php?"
        @"limit=1_DAY&sort_by=standard&feed_type=RSS2.0&feed_style=COMPACT"];


    // For Apple's Hot News feed, replace the line above with
    // NSURL *url = [NSURL URLWithString:@"http://www.apple.com/pr/feeds/pr.rss"];

    // Put that URL into an NSURLRequest
    NSURLRequest *req = [NSURLRequest requestWithURL:url];

    // Create a connection that will exchange this request for data from the URL
    connection = [[NSURLConnection alloc] initWithRequest:req
                                      delegate:self
                               startImmediately:YES];
}
```

Kick off the exchange whenever the **ListViewController** is created. In ListViewController.m,
override **initWithStyle:**.

```
- (id)initWithStyle:(UITableViewStyle)style
{
    self = [super initWithStyle:style];

    if (self) {
        [self fetchEntries];
    }

    return self;
}
```

Build the application to make sure there are no syntax errors.

Collecting XML data

This code, as it stands, will make the connection to the web service and retrieve the last 20 posts.
However, there is one problem: you don't see those posts anywhere. You need to implement delegate
methods for **NSURLConnection** to collect the XML data returned from this request.

Figure 25.5   NSURLConnection flow chart

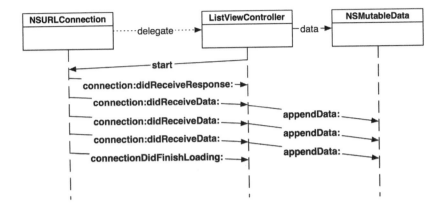

The delegate of an **NSURLConnection** is responsible for overseeing the connection and for collecting the data returned from the request. (This data is typically an XML or JSON document; for this web service, it is XML.) However, the data returned usually comes back in pieces, and it is the delegate's job to collect the pieces and put them together.

In ListViewController.m, implement **connection:didReceiveData:** to put all of the data received by the connection into the instance variable xmlData.

```
// This method will be called several times as the data arrives
- (void)connection:(NSURLConnection *)conn didReceiveData:(NSData *)data
{
    // Add the incoming chunk of data to the container we are keeping
    // The data always comes in the correct order
    [xmlData appendData:data];
}
```

When a connection has finished retrieving all of the data from a web service, it sends the message **connectionDidFinishLoading:** to its delegate. In this method, you are guaranteed to have the complete response from the web service request and can start working with that data. For now, implement **connectionDidFinishLoading:** in ListViewController.m to print out the string representation of that data to the console to make sure good stuff is coming back.

```
- (void)connectionDidFinishLoading:(NSURLConnection *)conn
{
    // We are just checking to make sure we are getting the XML
    NSString *xmlCheck = [[NSString alloc] initWithData:xmlData
                                    encoding:NSUTF8StringEncoding];
    NSLog(@"xmlCheck = %@", xmlCheck);
}
```

There is a possibility that a connection will fail. If an instance of **NSURLConnection** cannot make a connection to a web service, it sends its delegate the message **connection:didFailWithError:**. Note that this message gets sent for a *connection* failure, like having no Internet connectivity or if the server doesn't exist. For other types of errors, such as data sent to a web service in the wrong format, the error information is returned in **connection:didReceiveData:**.

In `ListViewController.m`, implement **connection:didFailWithError:** to inform your application of a connection failure.

```
- (void)connection:(NSURLConnection *)conn
  didFailWithError:(NSError *)error
{
    // Release the connection object, we're done with it
    connection = nil;

    // Release the xmlData object, we're done with it
    xmlData = nil;

    // Grab the description of the error object passed to us
    NSString *errorString = [NSString stringWithFormat:@"Fetch failed: %@",
                            [error localizedDescription]];

    // Create and show an alert view with this error displayed
    UIAlertView *av = [[UIAlertView alloc] initWithTitle:@"Error"
                                                 message:errorString
                                                delegate:nil
                                       cancelButtonTitle:@"OK"
                                       otherButtonTitles:nil];
    [av show];
}
```

Try building and running your application. You should see the XML results in the console shortly after you launch the application. If you put your device in Airplane Mode (or if it is not connected to a network), you should see a friendly error message when you try to fetch again. (For now, you will have to restart the application from Xcode in order to refetch the data after you've received the error.)

The XML that comes back from the server looks something like this:

```
<?xml version="1.0" encoding="utf-8"?>
<rss version="2.0" xmlns:atom="http://www.w3.org/2005/Atom">
  <channel>
    <title>forums.bignerdranch.com</title>
    <description>Books written by Big Nerd Ranch</description>
        ...
    <item>
      <title>Big Nerd Ranch General Discussions :: Big Nerd Ranch!</title>
      <link>http://forums.bignerdranch.com/viewtopic.php?f=4&t=532</link>
      <author>no_email@example.com (bignerd)</author>
      <category>Big Nerd Ranch General Discussions</category>
      <comments>http://forums.bignerdranch.com/posting.php?mode=reply</comments>
      <pubDate>Mon, 27 Dec 2010 11:27:01 GMT</pubDate>
    </item>
    ...
  </channel>
</rss>
```

(If you aren't seeing anything like this in your console, verify that you typed the URL correctly.)

Let's break down the XML the server returned. The top-level element in this document is an `rss` element. It contains a `channel` element. That `channel` element has some metadata that describes it (a title and a description). Then, there is a series of `item` elements. Each `item` has a title, link, author, etc. and represents a single post on the forum.

In a moment, you will create two new classes, **RSSChannel** and **RSSItem**, to represent the `channel` and `item` elements. The **ListViewController** will have an instance variable for the **RSSChannel**. The

RSSChannel will hold an array of RSSItems. Each RSSItem will be displayed as a row in the table view. Both RSSChannel and RSSItem will retain some of their metadata as instance variables, as shown in Figure 25.6.

Figure 25.6   Model object graph

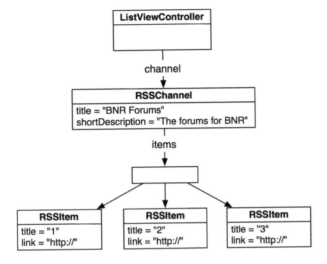

Parsing XML with NSXMLParser

To parse the XML, you will use the class **NSXMLParser**. An **NSXMLParser** instance takes a chunk of XML data and reads it line by line. As it finds interesting information, it sends messages to its delegate, like, "I found a new element tag," or "I found a string inside of an element." The delegate object is responsible for interpreting what these messages mean in the context of the application.

In ListViewController.m, delete the code you wrote in **connectionDidFinishLoading:** to log the XML. Replace it with code to kick off the parsing and set the parser's delegate to point at the instance of **ListViewController**.

```
- (void)connectionDidFinishLoading:(NSURLConnection *)conn
{
    NSString *xmlCheck = [[NSString alloc] initWithData:xmlData
                                          encoding:NSUTF8StringEncoding];
    NSLog(@"xmlCheck = %@", xmlCheck);

    // Create the parser object with the data received from the web service
    NSXMLParser *parser = [[NSXMLParser alloc] initWithData:xmlData];

    // Give it a delegate - ignore the warning here for now
    [parser setDelegate:self];

    // Tell it to start parsing - the document will be parsed and
    // the delegate of NSXMLParser will get all of its delegate messages
    // sent to it before this line finishes execution - it is blocking
    [parser parse];
```

```
    // Get rid of the XML data as we no longer need it
    xmlData = nil;

    // Get rid of the connection, no longer need it
    connection = nil;

    // Reload the table.. for now, the table will be empty.
    [[self tableView] reloadData];
}
```

The delegate of the parser, **ListViewController**, will receive a message when the parser finds a new element, another message when it finds a string within an element, and another when an element is closed.

For example, if a parser saw this XML:

```
<title>Big Nerd Ranch</title>.
```

it would send its delegate three consecutive messages: "I found a new element: 'title'," then, "I found a string: 'Big Nerd Ranch'," and finally, "I found the end of an element: 'title'." These messages are found in the NSXMLParserDelegate protocol:

```
// The "I found a new element" message
  - (void)parser:(NSXMLParser *)parser          // Parser that is sending message
 didStartElement:(NSString *)elementName        // Name of the element found
    namespaceURI:(NSString *)namespaceURI
   qualifiedName:(NSString *)qualifiedName
      attributes:(NSDictionary *)attributeDict;

// The "I found a string" message
  - (void)parser:(NSXMLParser *)parser          // Parser that is sending message
 foundCharacters:(NSString *)string;            // Contents of element (string)

// The "I found the end of an element" message
- (void)parser:(NSXMLParser *)parser            // Parser that is sending message
  didEndElement:(NSString *)elementName         // Name of the element found
   namespaceURI:(NSString *)namespaceURI
  qualifiedName:(NSString *)qName;
```

The namespaceURI, qualifiedName, and attributes arguments are for more complex XML, and we'll return to them at the end of the chapter.

Constructing the tree of model objects

It is up to the **ListViewController** to make sense of that series of messages, and it does this by constructing an object tree that represents the XML feed. In this case, after the XML is parsed, there will be an instance of **RSSChannel** that contains a number of **RSSItem** instances. Here are the steps to constructing the tree:

- When the parser reports it found the start of the channel element, create an instance of **RSSChannel**.

- When the parser finds a title or description element and it is currently inside a channel element, set the appropriate property of the **RSSChannel** instance.

- When the parser finds an item element, create an instance of **RSSItem** and add it to the items array of the **RSSChannel**.

- When the parser finds a title or link element and it is currently inside a item element, set the appropriate property of the **RSSItem** instance.

This list doesn't seem too daunting. However, there is one issue that makes it difficult: the parser doesn't remember anything about what it has parsed. A parser may report, "I found a title element." Its next report is "Now I've found the string inside an element." At this point, if you asked the parser which element that string was inside, it couldn't tell you. It only knows about the string it just found. This leaves the burden of tracking state on the parser's delegate, and maintaining the state for an entire tree of objects in a single object is cumbersome.

Instead, you will spread out the logic for handling messages from the parser among the classes involved. If the last found element is a channel, then that instance of **RSSChannel** will be responsible for handling what the parser spits out next. The same goes for **RSSItem**; it will be responsible for grabbing its own title and link strings.

"But the parser can only have one delegate," you say. And you're right; it can only have one delegate *at a time*. We can change the delegate of an **NSXMLParser** whenever we please, and the parser will keep chugging through the XML and sending messages to its current delegate. The flow of the parser and the related objects is shown in Figure 25.7.

Figure 25.7   Flow diagram of XML being parsed into a tree, creating the tree

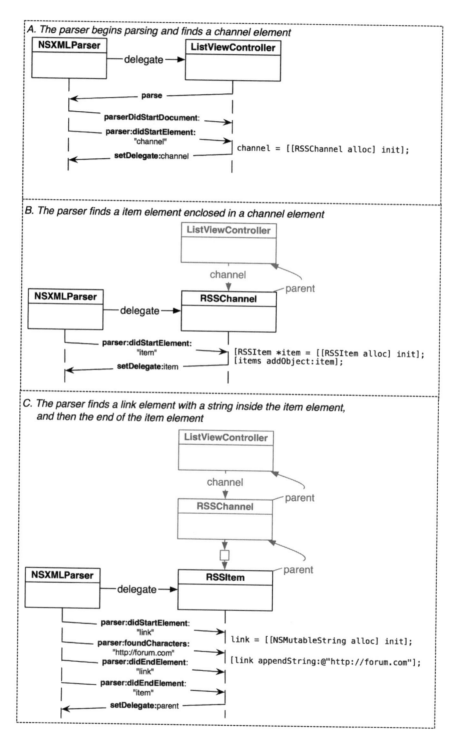

When the parser finds the end of an element, it tells its delegate. If the delegate is the object that represents that element, that object returns control to the previous delegate (Figure 25.8).

Figure 25.8   Flow diagram of XML being parsed into a tree, back up the tree

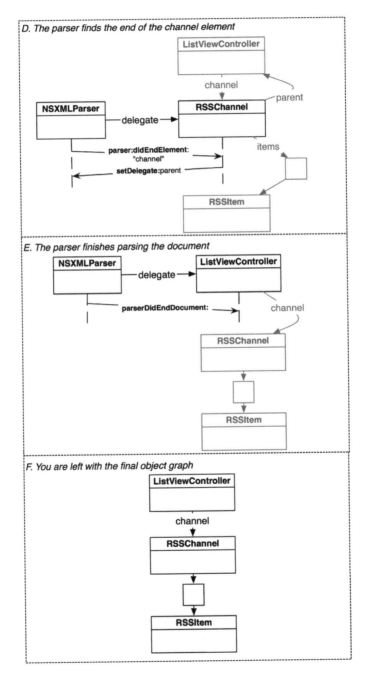

Now that we have a plan, let's get to work. Create a new **NSObject** subclass named **RSSChannel**. A channel object needs to hold some metadata, an array of **RSSItem** instances, and a pointer back to the previous parser delegate. In RSSChannel.h, add these properties:

```
@interface RSSChannel : NSObject

@property (nonatomic, weak) id parentParserDelegate;

@property (nonatomic, strong) NSString *title;
@property (nonatomic, strong) NSString *infoString;
@property (nonatomic, readonly, strong) NSMutableArray *items;

@end
```

In RSSChannel.m, synthesize the properties and override **init**.

```
@implementation RSSChannel
@synthesize items, title, infoString, parentParserDelegate;

- (id)init
{
    self = [super init];

    if (self) {
        // Create the container for the RSSItems this channel has;
        // we'll create the RSSItem class shortly.
        items = [[NSMutableArray alloc] init];
    }

    return self;
}

@end
```

Back in ListViewController.h, add an instance variable to hold an **RSSChannel** object and have the class conform to the NSXMLParserDelegate protocol.

```
// a forward declaration; we'll import the header in the .m
@class RSSChannel;

@interface ListViewController : UITableViewController <NSXMLParserDelegate>
{
    NSURLConnection *connection;
    NSMutableData *xmlData;

    RSSChannel *channel;
```

In ListViewController.m, implement an NSXMLParserDelegate method to catch the start of a channel element. Also, at the top of the file, import the header for **RSSChannel**.

```
#import "RSSChannel.h"

@implementation ListViewController

- (void)parser:(NSXMLParser *)parser
    didStartElement:(NSString *)elementName
      namespaceURI:(NSString *)namespaceURI
     qualifiedName:(NSString *)qualifiedName
        attributes:(NSDictionary *)attributeDict
```

```
{
    NSLog(@"%@ found a %@ element", self, elementName);
    if ([elementName isEqual:@"channel"]) {

        // If the parser saw a channel, create new instance, store in our ivar
        channel = [[RSSChannel alloc] init];

        // Give the channel object a pointer back to ourselves for later
        [channel setParentParserDelegate:self];

        // Set the parser's delegate to the channel object
        // There will be a warning here, ignore it for now
        [parser setDelegate:channel];
    }
}
```

Build and run the application. You should see a log message that the channel was found. If you don't see this message, double-check that the URL you typed in **fetchEntries** is correct.

Now that the channel is sometimes the parser's delegate, it needs to implement NSXMLParserDelegate methods to handle the XML. The **RSSChannel** instance will catch the metadata it cares about along with any item elements.

The channel is interested in the title and description metadata elements, and you will store those strings that the parser finds in the appropriate instance variables. When the start of one of these elements is found, an **NSMutableString** instance will be created. When the parser finds a string, that string will be concatenated to the mutable string.

In RSSChannel.h, declare that the class conforms to NSXMLParserDelegate and add an instance variable for the mutable string.

```
@interface RSSChannel : NSObject <NSXMLParserDelegate>
{
    NSMutableString *currentString;
}
```

In RSSChannel.m, implement one of the NSXMLParserDelegate methods to catch the metadata.

```
- (void)parser:(NSXMLParser *)parser
    didStartElement:(NSString *)elementName
        namespaceURI:(NSString *)namespaceURI
        qualifiedName:(NSString *)qualifiedName
            attributes:(NSDictionary *)attributeDict
{
    NSLog(@"\t%@ found a %@ element", self, elementName);

    if ([elementName isEqual:@"title"]) {
        currentString = [[NSMutableString alloc] init];
        [self setTitle:currentString];
    }
    else if ([elementName isEqual:@"description"]) {
        currentString = [[NSMutableString alloc] init];
        [self setInfoString:currentString];
    }
}
```

Note that currentString points at the same object as the appropriate instance variable – either title or infoString (Figure 25.9).

Figure 25.9   Two variables pointing at the same object

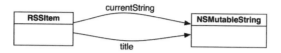

This means that when you append characters to the currentString, you are also appending them to the title or to the infoString.

In RSSChannel.m, implement the **parser:foundCharacters:** method.

```
- (void)parser:(NSXMLParser *)parser foundCharacters:(NSString *)str
{
    [currentString appendString:str];
}
```

When the parser finds the end of the channel element, the channel object will return control of the parser to the **ListViewController**. Implement this method in RSSChannel.m.

```
- (void)parser:(NSXMLParser *)parser
 didEndElement:(NSString *)elementName
  namespaceURI:(NSString *)namespaceURI
 qualifiedName:(NSString *)qName
{
    // If we were in an element that we were collecting the string for,
    // this appropriately releases our hold on it and the permanent ivar keeps
    // ownership of it. If we weren't parsing such an element, currentString
    // is nil already.
    currentString = nil;

    // If the element that ended was the channel, give up control to
    // who gave us control in the first place
    if ([elementName isEqual:@"channel"])
        [parser setDelegate:parentParserDelegate];
}
```

Let's double-check our work so far. In ListViewController.m, add the following log statement to **connectionDidFinishLoading:**.

```
- (void)connectionDidFinishLoading:(NSURLConnection *)conn
{
    NSXMLParser *parser = [[NSXMLParser alloc] initWithData:xmlData];
    [parser setDelegate:self];
    [parser parse];

    xmlData = nil;

    connection = nil;

    [[self tableView] reloadData];
    NSLog(@"%@\n %@\n %@\n", channel, [channel title], [channel infoString]);
}
```

Build and run the application. At the end of the console, you should see the log statement with valid values for the three strings. The data isn't correct yet, but there should still be three blocks of text separated by a new line.

Now we will need to write the code for the leaves of the object tree represented by the XML – the **RSSItem** instances. Create a new **NSObject** subclass. Name it **RSSItem**. In RSSItem.h, give the item instance variables for its metadata and for parsing.

```objc
@interface RSSItem : NSObject <NSXMLParserDelegate>
{
    NSMutableString *currentString;
}
@property (nonatomic, weak) id parentParserDelegate;

@property (nonatomic, strong) NSString *title;
@property (nonatomic, strong) NSString *link;


@end
```

In RSSItem.m, synthesize these properties and set up the parsing code similar to what you did for **RSSChannel**.

```objc
@implementation RSSItem

@synthesize title, link, parentParserDelegate;

- (void)parser:(NSXMLParser *)parser
    didStartElement:(NSString *)elementName
      namespaceURI:(NSString *)namespaceURI
     qualifiedName:(NSString *)qualifiedName
        attributes:(NSDictionary *)attributeDict
{
    NSLog(@"\t\t%@ found a %@ element", self, elementName);

    if ([elementName isEqual:@"title"]) {
        currentString = [[NSMutableString alloc] init];
        [self setTitle:currentString];
    }
    else if ([elementName isEqual:@"link"]) {
        currentString = [[NSMutableString alloc] init];
        [self setLink:currentString];
    }
}

- (void)parser:(NSXMLParser *)parser foundCharacters:(NSString *)str
{
    [currentString appendString:str];
}

- (void)parser:(NSXMLParser *)parser
 didEndElement:(NSString *)elementName
  namespaceURI:(NSString *)namespaceURI
 qualifiedName:(NSString *)qName
{
    currentString = nil;

    if ([elementName isEqual:@"item"])
        [parser setDelegate:parentParserDelegate];
}

@end
```

Build the application to check for syntax errors.

In RSSChannel.m, put **RSSItem** into the object tree. At the top of this file, make sure to import the header for **RSSItem**.

```
#import "RSSItem.h"

@implementation RSSChannel

- (void)parser:(NSXMLParser *)parser
    didStartElement:(NSString *)elementName
       namespaceURI:(NSString *)namespaceURI
      qualifiedName:(NSString *)qualifiedName
         attributes:(NSDictionary *)attributeDict
{
    if ([elementName isEqual:@"title"]) {
        currentString = [[NSMutableString alloc] init];
        [self setTitle:currentString];
    }
    else if ([elementName isEqual:@"description"]) {
        currentString = [[NSMutableString alloc] init];
        [self setInfoString:currentString];
    }
    else if ([elementName isEqual:@"item"]) {
        // When we find an item, create an instance of RSSItem
        RSSItem *entry = [[RSSItem alloc] init];

        // Set up its parent as ourselves so we can regain control of the parser
        [entry setParentParserDelegate:self];

        // Turn the parser to the RSSItem
        [parser setDelegate:entry];

        // Add the item to our array and release our hold on it
        [items addObject:entry];
    }
}
```

Build and run the application. You should see log statements in the console that indicate the tree is being built. The last log statement in the console should have the correct data for the channel object, which looks something like this:

```
<RSSChannel: 0x4e18f80>
forums.bignerdranch.com
Books written by Big Nerd Ranch
```

Finally, we need to connect the channel and its items to the table view. In ListViewController.m, import the header file for **RSSItem** and fill out the two data source methods you temporarily implemented earlier.

```
#import "RSSItem.h"

@implementation ListViewController

- (NSInteger)tableView:(UITableView *)tableView
 numberOfRowsInSection:(NSInteger)section
{
    return 0;
```

```
    return [[channel items] count];
}
- (UITableViewCell *)tableView:(UITableView *)tableView
        cellForRowAtIndexPath:(NSIndexPath *)indexPath
{
    return nil;

    UITableViewCell *cell = [tableView
                        dequeueReusableCellWithIdentifier:@"UITableViewCell"];
    if (cell == nil) {
        cell = [[UITableViewCell alloc] initWithStyle:UITableViewCellStyleDefault
                                    reuseIdentifier:@"UITableViewCell"];
    }
    RSSItem *item = [[channel items] objectAtIndex:[indexPath row]];
    [[cell textLabel] setText:[item title]];

    return cell;
}
```

Build and run the application. You should now see the titles of the last 20 posts in a table view. Also, take a good look at the console to see the flow of the parser and how the delegate role is passed around.

A quick tip on logging

In this application, you log a lot of data to the console. It would be easy to miss an important log statement. One way to catch important statements is to prefix the most important ones with an easily searchable token (like xxx), but that's a quick-and-dirty fix.

A more elegant and useful option is to define a preprocessor macro that you can use to categorize your log statements. For example, in Nerdfeed, you can generate a ton of log statements for checking the input and output of your web service requests. You can also generate a ton of log statements for checking the logic in the rest of the application. When you are debugging Nerdfeed, it would be helpful to separate the web service-related statements from the others so that you can turn them on or off as needed.

While there are many ways to do this, here is the simplest one:

```
#define WSLog(...) NSLog(__VA_ARGS__)
```

This statement tells the compiler, "When you come across **WSLog**, see **NSLog**." Save this statement in its own .h file and import it into your precompiled header (Nerdfeed_Prefix.pch). Then, when you want to log a web service-related statement in your code, use **WSLog** instead of **NSLog**, passing the exact same arguments. For example, in ListViewController.m, you could change the log statement in **connectionDidFinishLoading:** to the following:

```
WSLog(@"%@\n %@\n %@\n", channel, [channel title], [channel infoString]);
```

As long as **WSLog** is defined to **NSLog**, nothing will change. You will still see all of your log statements in the console. When you want to turn off the web service-related statements to concentrate on other areas, simply re-define **WSLog** to the following in its header file:

```
#define WSLog(...) do {} while(0)
```

Now any **WSLog** calls will be invisible to the compiler, so they will not appear in the console to distract you from your non-web service debugging. (Defining WSLog in this way means it will be optimized out by the compiler.)

UIWebView

In addition to its title, an **RSSItem** also keeps a link that points to the web page where the post lives. It would be neat if Nerdfeed could open up Safari and navigate to that page. It would be even neater if Nerdfeed could render that web page without having to leave Nerdfeed to open Safari. Good news – it can using the class **UIWebView**.

Instances of **UIWebView** render web content. In fact, the Safari application on your device uses a **UIWebView** to render its web content. In this part of the chapter, you will create a view controller whose view is an instance of **UIWebView**. When one of the items is selected from the table view of **RSSItems**, you will push the web view's controller onto the navigation stack and have it load the link stored in the **RSSItem**.

Create a new **NSObject** subclass and name it **WebViewController**. In WebViewController.h, add a property (but not an instance variable) and change the superclass to **UIViewController**:

```
@interface WebViewController : NSObject
@interface WebViewController : UIViewController

@property (nonatomic, readonly) UIWebView *webView;

@end
```

In WebViewController.m, override **loadView** to create an instance of **UIWebView** as the view of this view controller. Also, implement the method **webView** to return that view.

```
@implementation WebViewController

- (void)loadView
{
    // Create an instance of UIWebView as large as the screen
    CGRect screenFrame = [[UIScreen mainScreen] applicationFrame];
    UIWebView *wv = [[UIWebView alloc] initWithFrame:screenFrame];
    // Tell web view to scale web content to fit within bounds of webview
    [wv setScalesPageToFit:YES];

    [self setView:wv];
}

- (UIWebView *)webView
{
    return (UIWebView *)[self view];
}
```

In ListViewController.h, add a new property to **ListViewController**.

```
@class WebViewController;

@interface ListViewController : UITableViewController <NSXMLParserDelegate>
{
    NSURLConnection *connection;
    NSMutableData *xmlData;

    RSSChannel *channel;
}
@property (nonatomic, strong) WebViewController *webViewController;
```

```
- (void)fetchEntries;
@end
```

In `ListViewController.m`, import the header file and synthesize the property.

```
#import "WebViewController.h"

@implementation ListViewController
@synthesize webViewController;
```

In `NerdfeedAppDelegate.m`, import the header for **WebViewController**, create an instance of **WebViewController**, and set it as the webViewController of the **ListViewController**.

```
#import "WebViewController.h"

@implementation NerdfeedAppDelegate

- (BOOL)application:(UIApplication *)application
    didFinishLaunchingWithOptions:(NSDictionary *)launchOptions
{
    self.window = [[UIWindow alloc] initWithFrame:[[UIScreen mainScreen] bounds]];
    // Override point for customization after application launch.
    ListViewController *lvc =
        [[ListViewController alloc] initWithStyle:UITableViewStylePlain];

    UINavigationController *masterNav =
        [[UINavigationController alloc] initWithRootViewController:lvc];


    WebViewController *wvc = [[WebViewController alloc] init];
    [lvc setWebViewController:wvc];

    [[self window] setRootViewController:masterNav];

    self.window.backgroundColor = [UIColor whiteColor];
    [self.window makeKeyAndVisible];
    return YES;
}
```

(Note that we are instantiating the **WebViewController** in the application delegate in preparation for the next chapter where we will use a **UISplitViewController** to present view controllers on the iPad.)

When the user taps on a row in the table view, we want the **WebViewController** to be pushed onto the navigation stack and the link for the selected **RSSItem** to be loaded in its web view. To have a web view load a web page, you send it the message **loadRequest:**. The argument is an instance of **NSURLRequest** that contains the URL you wish to navigate to. In `ListViewController.m`, implement the following table view delegate method:

```
- (void)tableView:(UITableView *)tableView
            didSelectRowAtIndexPath:(NSIndexPath *)indexPath
{
    // Push the web view controller onto the navigation stack - this implicitly
    // creates the web view controller's view the first time through
    [[self navigationController] pushViewController:webViewController animated:YES];

    // Grab the selected item
    RSSItem *entry = [[channel items] objectAtIndex:[indexPath row]];
```

```
    // Construct a URL with the link string of the item
    NSURL *url = [NSURL URLWithString:[entry link]];

    // Construct a request object with that URL
    NSURLRequest *req = [NSURLRequest requestWithURL:url];

    // Load the request into the web view
    [[webViewController webView] loadRequest:req];

    // Set the title of the web view controller's navigation item
    [[webViewController navigationItem] setTitle:[entry title]];
}
```

Build and run the application. You should be able to select one of the posts, and it should take you to a new view controller that displays the web page for that post.

For the More Curious: NSXMLParser

NSXMLParser is the built-in XML parser in the iOS SDK. While there are plenty of parsers you can pick up on the Internet, adding a third party dependency is sometimes difficult. Many developers, seeing that NSXMLParser is not a tree-based parser (it doesn't create an object graph out of the box), go searching for an alternative parser. However, in this chapter, you've learned how to make NSXMLParser into a tree-based parser.

To parse simple XML, all you need are the three delegate methods used in this chapter. More complex XML has element attributes, namespaces, CDATA, and a slew of other items that need to be handled. NSXMLParser can handle these, too. The NSXMLParserDelegate protocol includes many more methods that handle nearly anything XML can throw at you. There are also arguments to the methods you have already used that can handle more complex XML. For example, in parser:didStartElement:namespaceURI:qualifiedName:attributes:, we only used the first two arguments. For the other arguments, consider the following XML:

```
<?xml version="1.0" encoding="utf-8"?>
<container version="2.0" xmlns:foo="BNR">
    <foo:item attribute1="one" attribute2="two"></item>
</container>
```

When the foo:item element is encountered by the parser, the values for the parameters to the delegate method are as follows:

- The element is "item." The namespace is ignored, and the name of the element is kept.

- The namespaceURI is "BNR." The element's name is item, and it is in the foo namespace, which has a value of "BNR."

- The qualifiedName is "foo:item."

- attributes is a dictionary that contains two keys, "attribute1" and "attribute2." Their values are "one" and "two," respectively.

One thing NSXMLParser can't do is resolve XPaths. You have to use another library to handle this. (For more information, check out the Tree-Based XML Programming Guide in the Apple documentation.)

For the More Curious: The Request Body

When **NSURLConnection** talks to a web server, it uses the HTTP protocol. This protocol says that any data you send or receive must follow the HTTP specification. The actual data transferred to the server in this chapter is shown in Figure 25.10.

Figure 25.10   HTTP Request Format

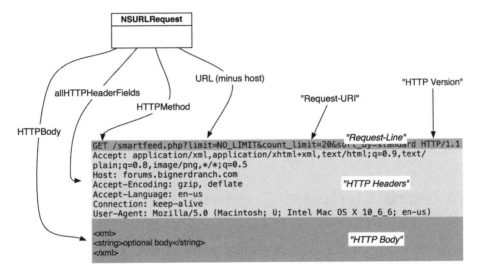

NSURLRequest has a number of methods that allow you to specify a piece of the request and then properly format it for you.

Any service request has three parts: a request-line, the HTTP headers, and the HTTP body, which is optional. The request-line (which Apple calls a status line) is the first line of the request and tells the server what the client is trying to do. In this request, the client is trying to GET the resource at smartfeed.php?limit=1_DAY&etc. (It also specifies the HTTP specification version that the data is in.)

The command GET is an HTTP method. While there are a number of supported HTTP methods, you typically only see GET and POST. The default of **NSURLRequest**, GET, indicates that the client wants something *from* the server. The thing that it wants is called the Request-URI (smartfeed.php?limit=1_DAY&etc).

In the early days of the web, the Request-URI would be the path of a file on the server. For example, the request http://www.website.com/index.html would return the file index.html, and your browser would render that file in a window. Today, we also use the Request-URI to specify a service that the server implements. For example, in this chapter, you accessed the smartfeed.php service, supplied parameters to it, and were returned an XML document. You are still GETting something, but the server is more clever in interpreting what you are asking for.

In addition to getting things from a server, you can send it information. For example, many web servers allow you to upload photos. A client application would pass the image data to the server through a service request. In this situation, you use the HTTP method POST, which indicates to the server that you are including the optional HTTP body. The body of a request is data you can include with the request – typically XML, JSON, or Base-64 encoded data.

When the request has a body, it must also have the Content-Length header. Handily enough, **NSURLRequest** will compute the size of the body and add this header for you.

```
NSURL *someURL = [NSURL URLWithString:@"http://www.photos.com/upload"];
UIImage *image = [self profilePicture];
NSData *data = UIImagePNGRepresentation(image);

NSMutableURLRequest *req =
    [NSMutableURLRequest requestWithURL:someURL
                           cachePolicy:NSURLRequestReloadIgnoringCacheData
                         timeoutInterval:90];

// This adds the HTTP body data and automatically sets the Content-Length header
[req setHTTPBody:data];

// This changes the HTTP Method in the request-line
[req setHTTPMethod:@"POST"];

// If you wanted to set the Content-Length programmatically...
[req setValue:[NSString stringWithFormat:@"%d", [data length]]
    forHTTPHeaderField:@"Content-Length"];
```

For the More Curious: Credentials

When you try to access a web service, it will sometimes respond with an *authentication challenge*, which means "Who the heck are you?" You then need to send a username and password (a *credential*) before the server will send its genuine response.

There are objects that represent these ideas. When the challenge is received, your connection delegate is sent a message that includes an instance of **NSURLAuthenticationChallenge**. The sender of that challenge conforms to the NSURLAuthenticationChallengeSender protocol. If you want to continue to get the data, you send back an instance of **NSURLCredential**, which typically looks something like this:

```
- (void)connection:(NSURLConnection *)conn
 didReceiveAuthenticationChallenge:(NSURLAuthenticationChallenge *)challenge
{
    // Have I already failed at least once?
    if ([challenge previousFailureCount] > 0) {

        // Why did I fail?
        NSError *failure = [challenge error];
        NSLog(@"Can't authenticate: %@", [error localizedDescription]);

        // Give up
        [[challenge sender] cancelAuthenticationChallenge:challenge];
        return;
    }

    // Create a credential
    NSURLCredential *newCred =
            [NSURLCredential credentialWithUser:@"sid"
                                    password:@"MomIsCool"
                                 persistence:NSURLCredentialPersistenceNone];
```

```
    // Supply the credential to the sender of the challenge
    [[challenge sender] useCredential:newCred
            forAuthenticationChallenge:challenge];
}
```

If you are dealing with a more secure and sophisticated web service, it may want a certificate (or certificates) to confirm your identity. Most, however, will just want a username and a password.

Credentials can have persistence. There are three possibilities:

- NSURLCredentialPersistenceNone says to the URL loading system, "Forget this credential as soon as you use it."

- NSURLCredentialPersistenceForSession says to the URL loading system, "Forget this credential when this application terminates."

- NSURLCredentialPersistencePermanent says to the URL loading system, "Put this credential in my keychain so that other applications can use it."

Bronze Challenge: More Data

Create a **UITableViewCell** subclass that has three labels. Parse the author and category elements into the **RSSItem** and display the title, author, and category for each row.

Silver Challenge: More UIWebView

A **UIWebView** keeps its own history. You can send the messages **goBack** and **goForward** to a web view, and it will traverse through that history. Create a **UIToolbar** instance and add it to the **WebViewController**'s view hierarchy. This toolbar should have back and forward buttons that will let the web view move through its history. Bonus: use two other properties of **UIWebView** to enable and disable the toolbar items.

26

UISplitViewController and NSRegularExpression

The iPhone and iPod touch have a limited amount of screen real estate. Given their small screen size, when presenting a drill-down interface, we use a **UINavigationController** to swap between a list of items and a detailed view for an item.

The iPad, on the other hand, has plenty of screen space to present both views using a built-in class called **UISplitViewController**. **UISplitViewController** is an iPad-only class that presents two view controllers in a master-detail relationship. The master view controller occupies a small strip on the lefthand side of the screen, and the detail view controller occupies the rest of the screen.

In this chapter, you will have Nerdfeed present its view controllers in a split view controller when running on an iPad (Figure 26.1). We will also make Nerdfeed a universal application and have it continue to use a **UINavigationController** when run on the iPhone.

Figure 26.1   Nerdfeed with UISplitViewController

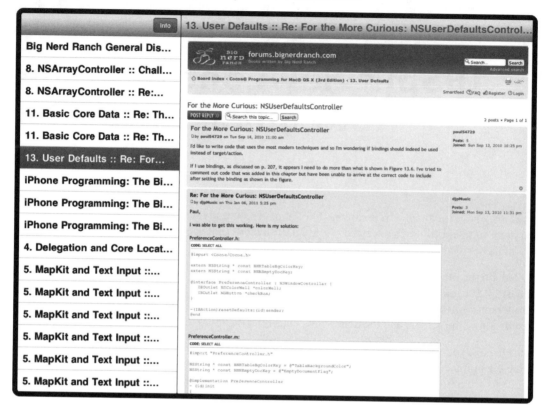

Splitting Up Nerdfeed

Creating a **UISplitViewController** is simple since you have already learned about navigation controllers and tab bar controllers. When you initialize a split view controller, you pass it an array of view controllers just like with a tab bar controller. However, a split view controller's array is limited to two view controllers: a master view controller and a detail view controller. The order of the view controllers in the array determines their roles in the split view; the first entry is the master view controller, and the second is the detail view controller.

Open Nerdfeed.xcodeproj in Xcode. Then, open NerdfeedAppDelegate.m.

In **application:didFinishLaunchingWithOptions:**, check if the device is an iPad before instantiating a **UISplitViewController**. The **UISplitViewController** class does not exist on the iPhone, and trying to create an instance of **UISplitViewController** will cause an exception to be thrown.

```
- (BOOL)application:(UIApplication *)application
    didFinishLaunchingWithOptions:(NSDictionary *)launchOptions
{
    self.window = [[UIWindow alloc] initWithFrame:[[UIScreen mainScreen] bounds]];

    ListViewController *lvc =
        [[ListViewController alloc] initWithStyle:UITableViewStylePlain];

    UINavigationController *masterNav =
        [[UINavigationController alloc] initWithRootViewController:lvc];

    WebViewController *wvc = [[WebViewController alloc] init];
    [lvc setWebViewController:wvc];

    [[self window] setRootViewController:masterNav];

    // Check to make sure we're running on the iPad.
    if ([[UIDevice currentDevice] userInterfaceIdiom] == UIUserInterfaceIdiomPad) {

        // webViewController must be in navigation controller, you'll see why later.
        UINavigationController *detailNav =
            [[UINavigationController alloc] initWithRootViewController:wvc];

        NSArray *vcs = [NSArray arrayWithObjects:masterNav, detailNav, nil];

        UISplitViewController *svc = [[UISplitViewController alloc] init];

        // Set the delegate of the split view controller to the detail VC
        // We'll need this later - ignore the warning for now
        [svc setDelegate:wvc];

        [svc setViewControllers:vcs];

        // Set the root view controller of the window to the split view controller
        [[self window] setRootViewController:svc];
    } else {
        // On non-iPad devices, go with the old version and just add the
        // single nav controller to the window
        [[self window] setRootViewController:masterNav];
    }

    self.window.backgroundColor = [UIColor whiteColor];
    [self.window makeKeyAndVisible];
    return YES;
}
```

By placing the **UISplitViewController** code within an if statement in this method, we are laying the groundwork for making Nerdfeed a universal application. Also, now you can see why we created the instance of **WebViewController** here instead of following the typical pattern of creating the detail view controller inside the implementation for the root view controller. A split view controller must have both the master and the detail view controller when it is created. The diagram for Nerdfeed's split view controller is shown in Figure 26.2.

Figure 26.2 Split view controller diagram

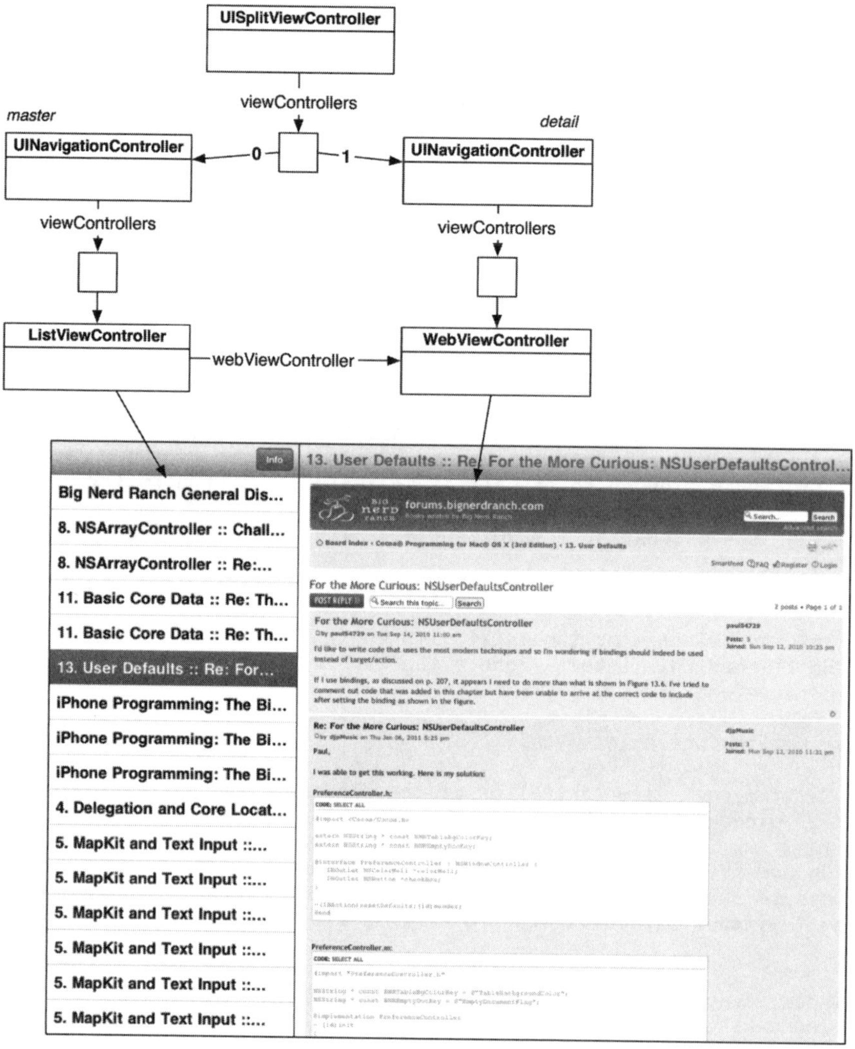

However, if you build and run right now, you won't see anything but a navigation bar on top of a blank screen. The blank screen is your web view controller. It's blank because you haven't selected a row. You haven't selected a row because the list view controller is not on screen. Why is there no list view controller? In portrait mode, a `UISplitViewController` only shows the detail view controller; there isn't enough space to show the master view controller, too. The split view controller will only display both when in landscape mode.

Unfortunately, your split view controller will not rotate to landscape mode by default. The `UISplitViewController` is a subclass of `UIViewController`, so it implements the method `shouldAutorotateToInterfaceOrientation:`. The method needs to return YES to allow the rotation and show the master view controller.

Overriding a method requires creating a new subclass, but before we do anything so drastic, let's look more closely at the implementation of **shouldAutorotateToInterfaceOrientation:** in **UISplitViewController**. It looks a bit like this:

```
- (BOOL)shouldAutorotateToInterfaceOrientation:(UIInterfaceOrientation)io
{
    if ([[self viewControllers] count] == 2) {
        UIViewController *master = [[self viewControllers] objectAtIndex:0];
        UIViewController *detail = [[self viewControllers] objectAtIndex:1];
        return [master shouldAutorotateToInterfaceOrientation:io]
            && [detail shouldAutorotateToInterfaceOrientation:io];
    }
    return NO;
}
```

This implementation asks the master and the detail view controller whether it should allow rotation. It sends the same message to both view controllers, and if both return YES, it rotates. So to get the **UISplitViewController** to allow rotation what we really need to do is modify the implementation of **shouldAutorotateToInterfaceOrientation:** in the two view controllers.

In ListViewController.m, override this method to return YES if Nerdfeed is running on the iPad:

```
- (BOOL)shouldAutorotateToInterfaceOrientation:(UIInterfaceOrientation)io
{
    if ([[UIDevice currentDevice] userInterfaceIdiom] == UIUserInterfaceIdiomPad)
        return YES;
    return io == UIInterfaceOrientationPortrait;
}
```

Do the same in WebViewController.m:

```
- (BOOL)shouldAutorotateToInterfaceOrientation:(UIInterfaceOrientation)io
{
    if ([[UIDevice currentDevice] userInterfaceIdiom] == UIUserInterfaceIdiomPad)
        return YES;
    return io == UIInterfaceOrientationPortrait;
}
```

Build and run the application. You should be able to rotate to landscape mode and, after the web service request finishes, see the list of posts on the lefthand side.

But we're not done yet. If you tap a row in the list view controller, the web view controller won't appear in the detail panel like you want. Instead, it is pushed onto the master panel and replaces the list view controller. To address this problem, when a row is tapped, we need to check if the **ListViewController** is a member of a split view controller and, if it is, take a different action.

You can send the message **splitViewController** to any **UIViewController**, and if that view controller is part of a split view controller, it will return a pointer to the split view controller (Figure 26.3). Otherwise, it returns nil. View controllers are smart: a view controller will return this pointer if it is a member of the split view controller's array or if it belongs to another controller that is a member of a split view controller's array (as is the case with both **ListViewController** and **WebViewController**).

Figure 26.3   UIViewController's splitViewController property

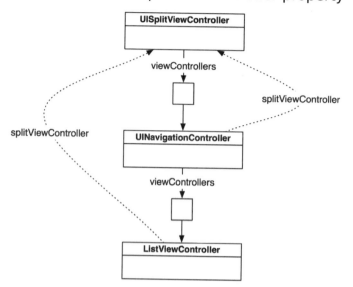

In ListViewController.m, locate the method **tableView:didSelectRowAtIndexPath:**. At the top of this method, check for a split view controller before pushing the **WebViewController** onto the navigation stack.

```
- (void)tableView:(UITableView *)tableView
    didSelectRowAtIndexPath:(NSIndexPath *)indexPath
{
    if (![self splitViewController])
        [[self navigationController] pushViewController:webViewController
                                       animated:YES];

    RSSItem *entry = [[channel items] objectAtIndex:[indexPath row]];

    NSURL *url = [NSURL URLWithString:[entry link]];
    NSURLRequest *req = [NSURLRequest requestWithURL:url];

    [[webViewController webView] loadRequest:req];

    [[webViewController navigationItem] setTitle:[entry title]];
}
```

Now, if the **ListViewController** is not in a split view controller, we assume the device is not an iPad and have it push the **WebViewController** onto the navigation controller's stack. If **ListViewController** is in a split view controller, then we leave it to the **UISplitViewController** to place the **WebViewController** on the screen.

Build and run the application again. Rotate to landscape and tap on one of the rows. The web page will now load in the detail panel.

Master-Detail Communication

In Chapter 13, we discussed different options for allowing view controllers to send messages to each other. Using instance variables is the simplest option, and that's what we've done in Nerdfeed – we gave the **ListViewController** a pointer to the **WebViewController**. In this simple application, this approach works fine. Now let's make Nerdfeed a little more complex and write a delegate protocol instead.

Right now, the detail view controller displays the **WebViewController** when a row in the master view controller is selected. In a moment, you're going to create another view controller called **ChannelViewController** that will display metadata about the RSS feed. You will also create an Info button on the **ListViewController**'s navigation bar. Then the user will be able choose what to display in the detail panel: tap a row and see a post's detail view or tap the Info button and see the metadata about the RSS feed.

But, first, let's look at the big picture. The **ListViewController** will need to send messages to two different view controllers: the **WebViewController** and the **ChannelViewController**. Instead of giving the **ListViewController** another instance variable for the **ChannelViewController**, you're going to write a protocol that both detail view controllers will conform to. Then you can generalize the message that the **ListViewController** sends the two view controllers as a method in that protocol (Figure 26.4).

Figure 26.4   Master view controller delegating to detail view controllers

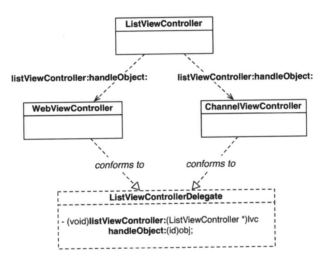

This protocol's one method will be named **listViewController:handleObject:**. The **ListViewController** will send this message to the **WebViewController** if a row in the table is tapped and to the **ChannelViewController** if the Info button is tapped.

Notice that the second label and argument type of this method are very general so that it can be used with a range of classes. When the **ListViewController** sends this message to the **WebViewController**, it will pass an **RSSItem** object. When the **ListViewController** sends this message to the **ChannelViewController**, it will pass an **RSSChannel** object.

In ListViewController.h, create the ListViewControllerDelegate protocol at the end of the file.

```
- (void)fetchEntries;
```

```
@end
```

```
// A new protocol named ListViewControllerDelegate
@protocol ListViewControllerDelegate
```

```
// Classes that conform to this protocol must implement this method:
- (void)listViewController:(ListViewController *)lvc handleObject:(id)object;
```

```
@end
```

First, let's update **WebViewController**. In WebViewController.h, declare that this class conforms to ListViewControllerDelegate.

```
// Must import this file as it is where ListViewControllerDelegate is declared
#import "ListViewController.h"
```

```
@interface WebViewController : UIViewController <ListViewControllerDelegate>
```

```
@property (nonatomic, readonly) UIWebView *webView;
```

```
@end
```

When one of the rows is tapped in the table view, the **ListViewController** will send the **listViewController:handleObject:** message to the **WebViewController**. The object passed as the argument will be the **RSSItem** that corresponds to the selected row. In WebViewController.m, implement **listViewController:handleObject:**.

```
#import "RSSItem.h"
```

```
@implementation WebViewController
```

```
- (void)listViewController:(ListViewController *)lvc handleObject:(id)object
{
    // Cast the passed object to RSSItem
    RSSItem *entry = object;

    // Make sure that we are really getting a RSSItem
    if (![entry isKindOfClass:[RSSItem class]])
        return;

    // Grab the info from the item and push it into the appropriate views
    NSURL *url = [NSURL URLWithString:[entry link]];
    NSURLRequest *req = [NSURLRequest requestWithURL:url];
    [[self webView] loadRequest:req];

    [[self navigationItem] setTitle:[entry title]];
}
```

Notice that the code creating and loading the request is the same code that we are currently running in **ListViewController**.

Next, in ListViewController.m, modify the **tableView:didSelectRowAtIndexPath:** method to send **listViewController:handleObject:** to the **WebViewController**.

```
- (void)tableView:(UITableView *)tableView
    didSelectRowAtIndexPath:(NSIndexPath *)indexPath
{
    if (![self splitViewController])
        [[self navigationController] pushViewController:webViewController
                                              animated:YES];

    RSSItem *entry = [[channel items] objectAtIndex:[indexPath row]];

    NSURL *url = [NSURL URLWithString:[entry link]];
    NSURLRequest *req = [NSURLRequest requestWithURL:url];
    [[webViewController webView] loadRequest:req];
    [[webViewController navigationItem] setTitle:[entry title]];

    [webViewController listViewController:self handleObject:entry];
}
```

Build and run the application. The behavior of the application should remain the same, but now we're sending a generalized message to the web view controller.

Now that **WebViewController** conforms to our protocol and implements the required method, let's create the **ChannelViewController** class.

Create an **NSObject** subclass and name it **ChannelViewController**. In ChannelViewController.h, change its superclass to **UITableViewController**, have it conform to the ListViewControllerDelegate protocol, and add an instance variable for the **RSSChannel** object.

```
#import "ListViewController.h"

@class RSSChannel;

@interface ChannelViewController : NSObject

@interface ChannelViewController :
    UITableViewController <ListViewControllerDelegate>
{
    RSSChannel *channel;
}

@end
```

In ChannelViewController.m, implement the data source methods to display the metadata in a table:

```
#import "RSSChannel.h"

@implementation ChannelViewController

- (NSInteger)tableView:(UITableView *)tableView
 numberOfRowsInSection:(NSInteger)section
{
    return 2;
}

- (UITableViewCell *)tableView:(UITableView *)tableView
        cellForRowAtIndexPath:(NSIndexPath *)indexPath
{
    UITableViewCell *cell =
                [tableView dequeueReusableCellWithIdentifier:@"UITableViewCell"];
```

```
        if (!cell)
            cell = [[UITableViewCell alloc] initWithStyle:UITableViewCellStyleValue2
                                    reuseIdentifier:@"UITableViewCell"];

        if ([indexPath row] == 0) {
            // Put the title of the channel in row 0
            [[cell textLabel] setText:@"Title"];
            [[cell detailTextLabel] setText:[channel title]];
        } else {
            // Put the description of the channel in row 1
            [[cell textLabel] setText:@"Info"];
            [[cell detailTextLabel] setText:[channel infoString]];
        }

        return cell;
}


- (BOOL)shouldAutorotateToInterfaceOrientation:(UIInterfaceOrientation)io
{
    if ([[UIDevice currentDevice] userInterfaceIdiom] == UIUserInterfaceIdiomPad)
        return YES;
    return io == UIInterfaceOrientationPortrait;
}
@end
```

Then implement the method from the `ListViewControllerDelegate` protocol in the same file.

```
- (void)listViewController:(ListViewController *)lvc handleObject:(id)object
{
    // Make sure the ListViewController gave us the right object
    if (![object isKindOfClass:[RSSChannel class]])
        return;

    channel = object;

    [[self tableView] reloadData];
}
```

Now you need to show this view controller and get the channel object to it. In `ListViewController.m`, add a **UIBarButtonItem** to the **ListViewController**'s navigationItem.

```
- (id)initWithStyle:(UITableViewStyle)style
{
    self = [super initWithStyle:style];

    if (self) {
        UIBarButtonItem *bbi =
            [[UIBarButtonItem alloc] initWithTitle:@"Info"
                                    style:UIBarButtonItemStyleBordered
                                    target:self
                                    action:@selector(showInfo:)];

        [[self navigationItem] setRightBarButtonItem:bbi];

        [self fetchEntries];
    }
    return self;
}
```

When this button is tapped, the detail view controller in the split view will be replaced with an instance of **ChannelViewController**. In ListViewController.m, implement the action method to create an instance of **ChannelViewController**. Then check for a split view controller and set the split view controller's viewControllers array.

```
#import "ChannelViewController.h"

@implementation ListViewController

- (void)showInfo:(id)sender
{
    // Create the channel view controller
    ChannelViewController *channelViewController = [[ChannelViewController alloc]
                            initWithStyle:UITableViewStyleGrouped];

    if ([self splitViewController]) {
        UINavigationController *nvc = [[UINavigationController alloc]
                initWithRootViewController:channelViewController];

        // Create an array with our nav controller and this new VC's nav controller
        NSArray *vcs = [NSArray arrayWithObjects:[self navigationController],
                                nvc,
                                nil];

        // Grab a pointer to the split view controller
        // and reset its view controllers array.
        [[self splitViewController] setViewControllers:vcs];

        // Make detail view controller the delegate of the split view controller
        // - ignore this warning
        [[self splitViewController] setDelegate:channelViewController];

        // If a row has been selected, deselect it so that a row
        // is not selected when viewing the info
        NSIndexPath *selectedRow = [[self tableView] indexPathForSelectedRow];
        if (selectedRow)
            [[self tableView] deselectRowAtIndexPath:selectedRow animated:YES];
    } else {
        [[self navigationController] pushViewController:channelViewController
                                animated:YES];
    }

    // Give the VC the channel object through the protocol message
    [channelViewController listViewController:self handleObject:channel];
}
```

Notice that here again you have left a non-split view controller, non-iPad option in an else clause that pushes the **ChannelViewController** onto the navigation controller's stack.

Build and run the application. After the RSS feed loads, tap the Info button. The detail view controller will display the metadata for the channel. However, if you tap on a post after you've loaded the metadata, nothing will happen – you can't get back to a web view.

This is because the navigation controller that held the web view controller was only owned by the split view controller. So when we replaced it with a navigation controller holding the channel view controller in **showInfo:**, the first navigation controller was destroyed. We have to create another navigation controller that holds the web view controller and give it to the split view controller.

In ListViewController.m, modify the **tableView:didSelectRowAtIndexPath:** to place a navigation controller with the **WebViewController** in the split view controller.

```
- (void)tableView:(UITableView *)tableView
    didSelectRowAtIndexPath:(NSIndexPath *)indexPath
{
    if (![self splitViewController])
        [[self navigationController] pushViewController:webViewController
                                  animated:YES];
    else {
        // We have to create a new navigation controller, as the old one
        // was only retained by the split view controller and is now gone
        UINavigationController *nav =
        [[UINavigationController alloc] initWithRootViewController:webViewController];

        NSArray *vcs = [NSArray arrayWithObjects:[self navigationController],
                                       nav,
                                       nil];

        [[self splitViewController] setViewControllers:vcs];

        // Make the detail view controller the delegate of the split view controller
        // - ignore this warning
        [[self splitViewController] setDelegate:webViewController];
    }

    RSSItem *entry = [[channel items] objectAtIndex:[indexPath row]];
    [webViewController listViewController:self handleObject:entry];
}
```

Build and run the application. You should be able to move back and forth between the two detail view controllers.

The **ListViewController** doesn't know how to show a post in a web view or show the info for the **RSSChannel**. So it *delegates* those behaviors to other objects. **ListViewController** does know about the ListViewControllerDelegate protocol, and it sends that protocol's message to a conforming detailed view controller to handle things it can't.

Even though the **ListViewController** never sets either of the detail view controllers as its delegate, this is still delegation. Delegation is a design pattern, not a naming convention. For another example, the table view-data source relationship is delegation, even though the variable the table view sends messages to is called dataSource.

Displaying the Master View Controller in Portrait Mode

While in portrait mode, the master view controller is missing in action. It would be nice if you could see the master view controller to select a new post from the list without having to rotate the device. **UISplitViewController** lets you do just that by supplying its delegate with a **UIBarButtonItem**. Tapping this button shows the master view controller in a **UIPopoverController** (Figure 26.5).

Figure 26.5   Master view controller in UIPopoverController

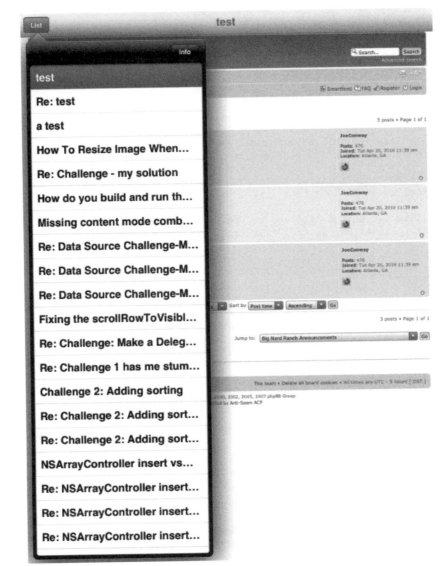

In your code, whenever a detail view controller was given to the split view controller, that detail view controller was set as the split view controller's delegate. As the delegate, the detail view controller will get a pointer to the **UIBarButtonItem** when rotating to portrait mode.

Since both **WebViewController** and **ChannelViewController** can be the delegate for a **UISplitViewController**, it's best to declare that they conform to the UISplitViewControllerDelegate protocol.

In WebViewController.h, add this declaration:

```
@interface WebViewController : UIViewController
        <ListViewControllerDelegate, UISplitViewControllerDelegate>
```

And do the same in `ChannelViewController.h`.

```
@interface ChannelViewController : UITableViewController
                <ListViewControllerDelegate, UISplitViewControllerDelegate>
```

Build and run the application. The behavior will be the same, but there won't be any warnings.

In `WebViewController.m`, implement the following delegate method to place the bar button item in the `WebViewController`'s navigation item.

```
- (void)splitViewController:(UISplitViewController *)svc
     willHideViewController:(UIViewController *)aViewController
          withBarButtonItem:(UIBarButtonItem *)barButtonItem
       forPopoverController:(UIPopoverController *)pc
{
    // If this bar button item doesn't have a title, it won't appear at all.
    [barButtonItem setTitle:@"List"];

    // Take this bar button item and put it on the left side of our nav item.
    [[self navigationItem] setLeftBarButtonItem:barButtonItem];
}
```

Notice that we explicitly set the title of the button. If the button doesn't have a title, it won't appear at all. (If the master view controller's `navigationItem` has a title, then the button will be automatically set to that title.)

Build and run the application. Rotate to portrait mode, and you will see the bar button item appear on the left of the navigation bar. Tap that button, and the master view controller's view will appear in a `UIPopoverController`.

This bar button item is why we always had you put the detail view controller inside a navigation controller. You don't have to use a navigation controller to put a view controller in a split view controller, but it makes using the bar button item much easier. (If you don't use a navigation controller, you can instantiate your own `UINavigationBar` or `UIToolbar` to hold the bar button item and add it as a subview of the `WebViewController`'s view.)

There are two small issues left to address with your List button. First, when the device is rotated back to landscape mode, the button is still there. To remove it, the delegate needs to respond to another message from the `UISplitViewController`. Implement this delegate method in `WebViewController.m`.

```
- (void)splitViewController:(UISplitViewController *)svc
     willShowViewController:(UIViewController *)aViewController
  invalidatingBarButtonItem:(UIBarButtonItem *)barButtonItem
{
    // Remove the bar button item from our navigation item
    // We'll double check that its the correct button, even though we know it is
    if (barButtonItem == [[self navigationItem] leftBarButtonItem])
        [[self navigationItem] setLeftBarButtonItem:nil];
}
```

Build and run the application. The List button will now appear and disappear as you rotate between portrait and landscape modes.

The second issue is that the `ChannelViewController` also needs to show the List button. In `ChannelViewController.m`, implement the two `UISplitViewControllerDelegate` methods.

```
- (void)splitViewController:(UISplitViewController *)svc
    willHideViewController:(UIViewController *)aViewController
        withBarButtonItem:(UIBarButtonItem *)barButtonItem
      forPopoverController:(UIPopoverController *)pc
{
    [barButtonItem setTitle:@"List"];

    [[self navigationItem] setLeftBarButtonItem:barButtonItem];
}
- (void)splitViewController:(UISplitViewController *)svc
    willShowViewController:(UIViewController *)aViewController
  invalidatingBarButtonItem:(UIBarButtonItem *)barButtonItem
{
    if (barButtonItem == [[self navigationItem] leftBarButtonItem])
        [[self navigationItem] setLeftBarButtonItem:nil];
}
```

Build and run the application. Now the List button will also appear on the navigation bar when the **ChannelViewController** is on the screen.

(There is a third issue: while in portrait mode, if you switch between the **ChannelViewController** and the **WebViewController**, you lose the bar button item. Fixing this problem is one of the challenges at the end of this chapter.)

Universalizing Nerdfeed

When first creating Nerdfeed, we chose to go with an iPad-only application. Now let's turn it into a universal application. Select the Nerdfeed project from the project navigator. In the editor area, choose the Nerdfeed target and then the Summary tab.

Figure 26.6   Universalizing Nerdfeed

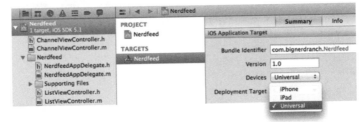

From the Devices pop-up menu, choose Universal.

Figure 26.7   Changing simulators

That's all there is to it – the application is now universal. You can test it by building and running again on one simulator and then the other.

There are two reasons the universalization process was so easy for Nerdfeed. Remembering these reasons will help you when you're writing your own applications.

- As we built Nerdfeed, we were mindful of the device differences in the classes we used. For example, knowing that a **UISplitViewController** doesn't exist on the iPhone or iPod touch, we made sure that there was an alternative interface on those devices. In general, when using an Apple-provided class, you should read the discussion in the documentation about that class. It will give you tips about the availability of the class and its methods on the different devices.

- Nerdfeed is still a relatively simple application. It is always easier to universalize an application early in development. As an application grows, its details get buried in the massive pile of code. Finding and fixing issues as you're writing code is much easier than coming back later. Details are harder to find, and there is the risk of breaking what already works.

NSRegularExpression

Currently, the table of **RSSItem**s shows each item's title, and this title is an **NSString** that consists of the name of the subforum, the title of the post, and the name of the author:

```
General Book Discussions :: BNR Books :: Reply by Everyone
```

It would be easier to browse posts if the table showed just the titles of the posts. To accomplish this, we need to parse the full item title, grab the string between the set of double colons, and set the `title` of each **RSSItem** to be just this string.

In RSSChannel.h, declare a new method that will eventually do these things.

```
@interface RSSChannel : NSObject <NSXMLParserDelegate>
{
    NSMutableString *currentString;
}
@property (nonatomic, weak) id parentParserDelegate;

@property (nonatomic, strong) NSString *title;
@property (nonatomic, strong) NSString *infoString;
@property (nonatomic, readonly, strong) NSMutableArray *items;

- (void)trimItemTitles;

@end
```

In RSSChannel.m, send this message in **parser:didEndElement:namespaceURI:qualifiedName:** when the channel gives up control of the parser.

```
- (void)parser:(NSXMLParser *)parser
 didEndElement:(NSString *)elementName
  namespaceURI:(NSString *)namespaceURI
 qualifiedName:(NSString *)qName
{
    currentString = nil;

    if ([elementName isEqual:@"channel"]) {
        [parser setDelegate:parentParserDelegate];
        [self trimItemTitles];
    }
}
```

We could loop through all item titles and write code that parses each string so that only the title of the post remains, but we can achieve the same result using a regular expression. First, let's take a closer look at regular expressions and how they work in iOS.

Regular expressions are a powerful way of searching text. When you create a regular expression, you devise a *pattern string* that represents the pattern you want to find in some other string. So, the purpose of a regular expression is to find substrings within a larger string. You apply the regular expression to the searched string, and if the pattern is found, then the searched string is said to be a *match*.

In iOS, a regular expression is represented by an instance of **NSRegularExpression**. An **NSRegularExpression** is initialized with a pattern string and can be applied to any instance of **NSString**. This is done with the **NSRegularExpression** instance method **matchesInString:options:range:**. You pass the string to be searched, and it returns an array of matches. Each match is represented by an instance of the class **NSTextCheckingResult**. (If there are no matches, then an empty array is returned.)

Every **NSTextCheckingResult** has a range property that identifies the location and length of the match in the searched string. The range property is an NSRange structure. A range has a location (the index of the character where the match begins) and a length (the number of characters in the match).

Figure 26.8 shows some examples of strings matched to the pattern string "This is a pattern" and the matched range. When a string has more than one match, there are multiple instances of **NSTextCheckingResult** in the array returned from **matchesInString:options:range:**.

Figure 26.8 Range of matched strings

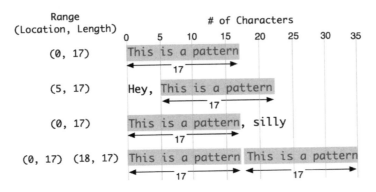

For practice with these classes, let's create an **NSRegularExpression** that looks for **RSSItem**s that contain the word Author in the title. This will get us all of the original posts; replies to posts contain the word Reply in their titles instead of Author. In RSSChannel.m, enter the following code for **trimItemTitles**.

```
- (void)trimItemTitles
{
    // Create a regular expression with the pattern: Author
    NSRegularExpression *reg =
                [[NSRegularExpression alloc] initWithPattern:@"Author"
                                                    options:0
                                                      error:nil];
```

```
    // Loop through every title of the items in channel
    for (RSSItem *i in items) {
        NSString *itemTitle = [i title];

        // Find matches in the title string. The range
        // argument specifies how much of the title to search;
        // in this case, all of it.
        NSArray *matches = [reg matchesInString:itemTitle
                                        options:0
                                          range:NSMakeRange(0, [itemTitle length])];

        // If there was a match...
        if ([matches count] > 0) {
            // Print the location of the match in the string and the string
            NSTextCheckingResult *result = [matches objectAtIndex:0];
            NSRange r = [result range];
            NSLog(@"Match at {%d, %d} for %@!", r.location, r.length, itemTitle);
        }
    }
}
```

In this code, you first create the expression and initialize it with the pattern you're seeking. Then, for each **RSSItem**, you send the **matchInString:options:range:** message to the regular expression passing the item's title as the string to search. Finally, for each title, we only expect one match, so we get the first **NSTextCheckingResult** in the matches array, get its range, and log it to the console.

Build and run the application. Check the console output after all of the items are pulled down from the server. You should see only items for original posts.

Constructing a pattern string

In the regular expression you just created, the pattern consisted solely of a literal string. That's not very powerful or flexible. But we can combine the literal strings with symbols that have special meanings to express more complex patterns. These special symbols are called *metacharacters* and *operators*.

For instance, the dot character (.) is a metacharacter that means "any character." Thus, a pattern string T.e would match The, Tie, or any other string that has a T followed by any character followed directly by an e.

Operators in a regular expression typically follow a literal character or metacharacter and modify how the character is to be matched. For instance, the asterisk (*) operator means, "See the character just before me? If you see that character, that's a match. If you see it repeated multiple times, that's a match. If you see nothing (the character occurs zero times), that's a match, too. But if you see any other character, the match fails."

Thus, if the pattern string were Bo*o, many strings would match this regular expression: Boo, Bo, Booo, Booooooo, etc. But Bio and Boot would fail.

A pattern string can contain any number of literal characters, metacharacters, and operators. Combining them gives you an enormous amount of matching power. You can see the full list of metacharacters and operators in the documentation for **NSRegularExpression**. Here are some examples of regular expressions and strings that would result in a match:

```
Pattern      Matches
- - - - - - - - - - - - - - - - - - - - - - - - - - - - - - - - - - - - - - - - - - - -
Joh?n        Jon, John
Mike*        Mike, Mik, Mikee, Mikeee, etc.
R|Bob        Rob, Bob
```

Our original problem (extracting the middle portion of the item's title) may not seem suited for regular expressions and matching at first, but we can solve it easily using the same classes.

First, we need to create a regular expression that is a wild card search that returns all item titles. Take a look at the full titles of the **RSSItem**s. They all have the same format:

```
(Subforum) :: (Title) :: (Author)
```

In trying to construct a pattern string to match this format, we can't use just a literal string as the pattern. Instead, we can use .* for our search. This combination of the . metacharacter and the * operator means "match anything, no matter how long it is." Thus, our pattern to match the title of every **RSSItem** will look like this:

```
.* :: .* :: .*
```

The first .* is the name of the subforum, the second is the post title, and the third is the author's name. These are separated by the literal string :: . (Don't forget the surrounding whitespaces!) In RSSChannel.m, change the regular expression in the **trimItemTitles** method to have this pattern.

```
NSRegularExpression *reg =
            [[NSRegularExpression alloc] initWithPattern:@"Author"
                                        options:0
                                        error:nil];

NSRegularExpression *reg =
            [[NSRegularExpression alloc] initWithPattern:@".* :: .* :: .*"
                                        options:0
                                        error:nil];
```

Build and run the application. By design, every **RSSItem**'s full title matches this pattern, so every title is printed to the console. This is a good start. Next we'll use a *capture group* to extract the title of the post (the string in the middle of the two ::) from the full title. Using a capture group in a regular expression allows you to access a specific substring of a match. Basically, when a pattern string has one or more capture groups, each **NSTextCheckingResult** that represents a match will contain an NSRange structure for each capture group in the pattern.

Capture groups are formed by putting parentheses around a term in the regular expression pattern. Thus, to get our post title, we will use the following regular expression:

```
.* :: (.*) :: .*
```

Update **trimItemTitles** in RSSChannel.m to capture the string between the double colons.

```
NSRegularExpression *reg =
            [[NSRegularExpression alloc] initWithPattern:@".* :: .* :: .*"
                                        options:0
                                        error:nil];

NSRegularExpression *reg =
            [[NSRegularExpression alloc] initWithPattern:@".* :: (.*) :: .*"
                                        options:0
                                        error:nil];
```

Now instead of having one range, each **NSTextCheckingResult** that is returned will have an array of ranges. The first range is always the range of the overall match. The next range is the first capture group, the next is the second capture group, and so on. You can get the capture group range by sending the message **rangeAtIndex:** to the **NSTextCheckingResult**. In our regular expression, there is one capture group, so the second range is the one we're looking for. You can then pass this range in **NSString**'s **substringWithRange:** method to get back an **NSString** defined by the range.

In **trimItemTitles**, pull out the range from the **NSTextCheckingResult**, get the associated string (the post title), and then set it as the item's title.

```
if ([matches count] > 0) {
    NSTextCheckingResult *result = [matches objectAtIndex:0];
    NSRange r = [result range];
    NSLog(@"Match at {%d, %d} for %@!", r.location, r.length, itemTitle);

    // One capture group, so two ranges, let's verify
    if ([result numberOfRanges] == 2) {

        // Pull out the 2nd range, which will be the capture group
        NSRange r = [result rangeAtIndex:1];

        // Set the title of the item to the string within the capture group
        [i setTitle:[itemTitle substringWithRange:r]];
    }
}
```

Build and run the application. After the connection finishes loading, reveal the master table view. The rows will now display just the titles of the posts.

You can become more comfortable with regular expressions by playing with Xcode's find interface. Hit Command-F to bring up the Find Bar. Then click on the magnifying glass icon next to the search field and select Show Find Options, as shown in Figure 26.9. Change the Style pop-up menu to Regular Expression.

Figure 26.9   Regular expression search in Xcode

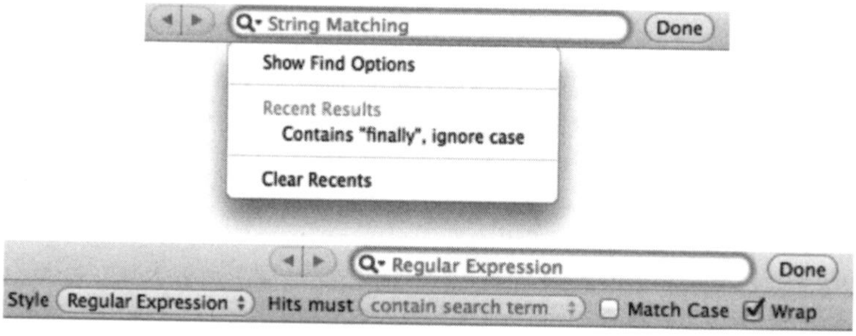

Now you can experiment with applying different regular expressions to your code files.

Regular expressions are a complex topic, and there's a lot more to them than what we've used here. Visit the documentation for **NSRegularExpression** to learn more about using regular expressions in iOS.

Bronze Challenge: Finding the Subforum

When applying the regular expression to each item's title, capture the subforum name, too. Display the subforum name in the detailTextLabel of the cell.

Silver Challenge: Swapping the Master Button

When in portrait mode, the **UIBarButtonItem** that contains a popover with the master view controller will show up on the detail view controller's navigation bar. If you switch from the **ChannelViewController** to the **WebViewController**, you won't see the bar button item anymore. Fix this so that the bar button item stays visible when switching between the two different detail view controllers in portrait mode. (The bar button item should never appear in landscape mode.)

Silver Challenge: Processing the Reply

Forum post titles start with Re: when they are a response to another post. Remove the Re: from these post titles.

Gold Challenge: Showing Threads

After handling the medium challenge, make it so posts that have a Re: in them have a pointer to their parent post. In the table, hide all child posts and show them when the disclosure indicator is tapped on the parent post. (If the parent post doesn't show up in the RSS feed, make the earliest post in the thread the parent.)

27

Blocks

In this chapter, you will learn about a C and Objective-C language feature called blocks. A *block* is a set of instructions. It is an object, but it is called like a function. Blocks provide conveniences for a programmer and performance boosts for applications. If you are familiar with other high-level languages, you may know blocks as *closures* or *anonymous functions*. This chapter will introduce blocks and their syntax. In the next chapter, you will put blocks to use in your Nerdfeed application.

Blocks and Block Syntax

In the C programming language, we separate code into functions. A function is defined as its own entity...

```
int adder(int a, int b)
{
    return a + b;
}
```

and can be called anywhere. A function can take arguments (input) and return a value (output).

In Objective-C, we separate code into classes and then further into methods that a class implements. The syntax of defining and calling a method is different than a function, but really, they are the same thing: chunks of executable code that take arguments and return single values.

```
- (int)addValue:(int)a andValue:(int)b
{
    return a + b;
}
```

The big difference between a function and a method is that a method can only be executed by an object or class: this is the conceptual difference between procedural programming and object-oriented programming.

Blocks are an interesting combination of object-oriented and procedural programming. A block, like a method or function, is a chunk of executable code that can take arguments and return a value. But a block is also an object. This odd combination gives us new design patterns that weren't easily achievable when limited to functions and objects and their methods. Like the hurdle you had to jump to first understand object-oriented programming, blocks require a similar (although less intense) leap in your understanding of programming.

Let's create a new project to learn more about blocks and their syntax. Create a new iOS Empty Application template named Blocky and configure it as shown in Figure 27.1.

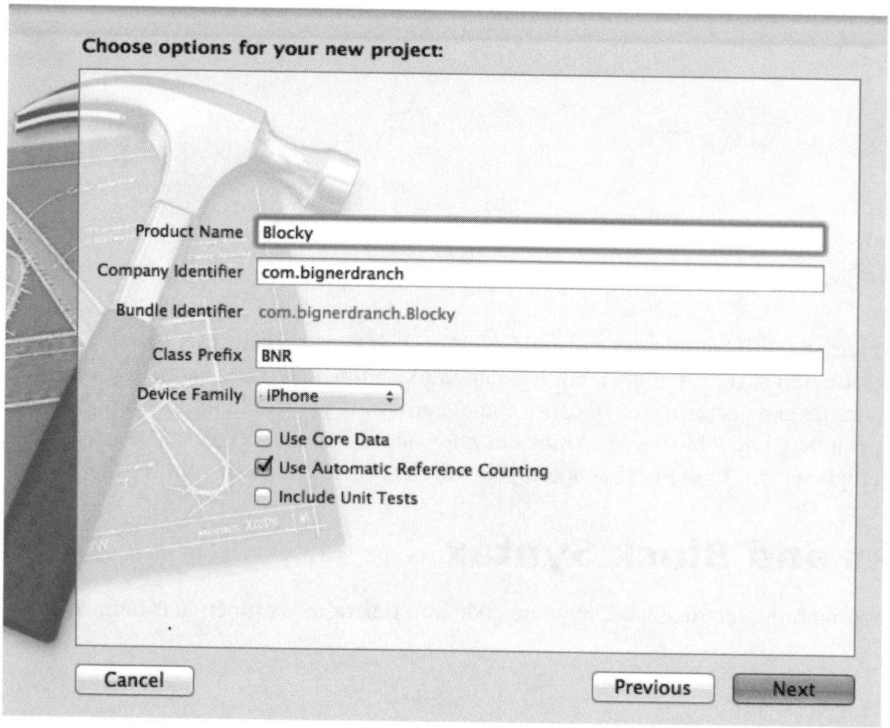

Figure 27.1   Configuring Blocky

Declaring block variables

Blocks, because they are objects, can be pointed to by variables. Think about variable declarations we've seen before:

```
NSString *string;
```

This pointer variable has a name and a type. Its name is string, and its type is **NSString ***. The type of a pointer identifies the class of the instance it will point to.

A variable that points at a block (a *block variable*) has the same two pieces: a name and a type. The type of a block variable identifies the arguments and the return value of the block it will point to. Because there are more components in a block variable's type, declaring a block variable requires a different syntax:

```
int (^adder)(int a, int, b);
```

This is what a block variable looks like. The name of this variable is adder, and it will point to a block that takes two int arguments and returns an int. The caret symbol (^) is what distinguishes the variable as a pointer to a block – just like an asterisk (*) indicates that a variable is a pointer to an object. Here are more examples of block variables that point to different types of blocks:

```
// A block variable named foo; it can point to a block that takes no arguments
// and returns no value:
void (^foo)(void);

// A block variable named jump; it can point to a block that takes one Hurdle *
```

486

```
// and returns no value:
void (^jump)(Hurdle *);

// A block variable named doubler; it can point to a block that takes one int
// and returns an int:
int (^doubler)(int);
```

Notice that the syntax is like declaring a C function except that, instead of a function name, there is a variable name prefixed with a caret and wrapped in parentheses.

In BNRAppDelegate.m, add a local block variable to **application:didFinishLaunchingWithOptions:**.

```
- (BOOL)application:(UIApplication *)application
    didFinishLaunchingWithOptions:(NSDictionary *)launchOptions
{
    self.window = [[UIWindow alloc] initWithFrame:[[UIScreen mainScreen] bounds]];
    // Override point for customization after application launch.

    int (^adder)(int, int);

    self.window.backgroundColor = [UIColor whiteColor];
    [self.window makeKeyAndVisible];
    return YES;
}
```

This declares a variable named adder that will point to a block that returns an int and takes two ints as arguments. Build the application. You should see a single warning saying that the variable adder isn't used. (If you see anything else, check your syntax and build again.)

Defining block literals

Of course, we know that a variable itself doesn't contain much information: it just stores a value. For example, the value of an int variable is a numerical value, like 5. The value of an **NSString** * variable will be an address of an instance of **NSString**.

The same holds true for a block variable. The variable stores a value, and the value will be the address of a block. A block is an object, so it needs to be allocated. To allocate a block, you specify the code that makes up the block. The syntax for creating a block looks like this:

```
^int(int x, int y) {
    return x + y;
};
```

The definition of a block is called a *block literal*. Notice the form of a block literal: a caret, the return type, and then parentheses that contain the arguments. In this case, this block takes two int arguments and returns their sum.

Typically, you create a block and immediately assign a variable to point to it. (You can also create a block and then pass it directly to a method. We'll talk more about this option later in the chapter.) In BNRAppDelegate.m, update **application:didFinishLaunchingWithOptions:** to assign adder to point to a block object.

```
- (BOOL)application:(UIApplication *)application
    didFinishLaunchingWithOptions:(NSDictionary *)launchOptions
{
    self.window = [[UIWindow alloc] initWithFrame:[[UIScreen mainScreen] bounds]];
    // Override point for customization after application launch.
```

```
int (^adder)(int, int) = ^int(int x, int y) {
    return x + y;
};

self.window.backgroundColor = [UIColor whiteColor];
[self.window makeKeyAndVisible];
return YES;
}
```

This code is just a combination of what you know: it creates a block variable named `adder` that points to a newly allocated block that returns the sum of the two arguments. Build the application to check for syntax errors. You should still only see the warning that `adder` is unused.

Here are some more examples of blocks and variables that point to them:

```
void (^foo)(void) = ^void(void) {
    NSLog(@"I'm a lonely block.");
};

void (^jump)(Hurdle *) = ^void(Hurdle *hurdle) {
    [hurdle comeCrashingDown];
};

int (^doubler)(int) = ^int(int x) {
    return x * 2;
};
```

Executing blocks

Once a block variable points to a block, you can call the variable like a C function to execute the code in the block that is pointed to. Update **application:didFinishLaunchingWithOptions:** to execute the adder block and print out its return value.

```
- (BOOL)application:(UIApplication *)application
    didFinishLaunchingWithOptions:(NSDictionary *)launchOptions
{
    self.window = [[UIWindow alloc] initWithFrame:[[UIScreen mainScreen] bounds]];
    // Override point for customization after application launch.

    int (^adder)(int, int) = ^int(int x, int y) {
        return x + y;
    };

    int sum = adder(2, 5);
    NSLog(@"%d", sum);

    self.window.backgroundColor = [UIColor whiteColor];
    [self.window makeKeyAndVisible];
    return YES;
}
```

Build and run this application. You will see the standard warning about applications not having a root view controller. Ignore this and look for the result of executing this block: 7.

More notes about blocks

There are a few things to mention here. First, notice that a block variable is not required to declare argument names. The block literal will declare the names of its arguments because it is the one that uses them. A block variable can declare the names of its arguments, but those names are irrelevant in the block itself. So, here are some legal block and block variable pairings:

```
void (^foo)(int) = ^void(int x) {
    NSLog(@"%d", x);
};

// Since the block literal calls its argument x, it doesn't matter
// what the block variable calls it.

void (^foo)(int y) = ^void(int x) {
    NSLog(@"%d", x);
};
```

This block and block variable pairing, on the other hand, would cause an error.

```
// This is a compiler error because the block calls its argument x, but it references
// the variable y, which doesn't exist

void (^foo)(int y) = ^void(int x) {
    NSLog(@"%d", y);
};
```

Furthermore, the type of a block variable must match the type of the block it points to. If not, the compiler will give you an error. Here are some examples of erroneous block and block variable pairings:

```
// This is a compiler error because the return types differ (void vs. int)
void (^block)(void) = ^int(void) {
    return 0;
};

// This is a compiler error because the argument types differ (int vs. float)
void (^block)(int) = ^void(float x) {
    NSLog(@"%f", x);
};
```

Also, notice that blocks are created inside methods (or functions). This is different than the definition of methods and functions, which occupy their own area in an implementation file. While it is possible to create a block outside of a method or function, there is rarely any reason to do so.

Finally, functions and methods can be called anywhere as long as you have imported the file that contains their declaration. A block, being an object, can only be used if you have a variable that points to it. Therefore, if you create a block in a method, any other method that wishes to execute that block must be passed a pointer to that block. You will test this behavior in the next section.

Basics of Using Blocks

Say you wanted an object that could take two numbers, add them together, and then return the result. You could probably write that pretty easily. But what if you now wanted that object to perform subtraction? Then multiplication? Division? You'd end up writing a number of methods for this object.

Instead of writing these methods, we can give this object an instance variable that points at a block. When we want to swap out the operation this object uses, we can construct a block literal that performs the appropriate operation. When the object is asked to compute the result, it executes the operation in the block.

Create a new **NSObject** subclass for Blocky and name it **BNRExecutor**. In BNRExecutor.h, add an instance variable and two methods to the **BNRExecutor** class.

```
@interface BNRExecutor : NSObject
{
    int (^equation)(int, int);
}

- (void)setEquation:(int (^)(int, int))block;
- (int)computeWithValue:(int)value1 andValue:(int)value2;

@end
```

The **setEquation:** method takes a block as an argument. Notice the syntax for declaring that a method takes a block argument. The argument has nearly the same format as a block variable. The only difference is the argument name (block) is separated from the argument's type. Instead of following the caret, the argument name comes after the parentheses that declare the argument type (just like any other method argument).

Figure 27.2   BNRExecutor and its block

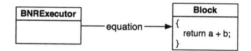

What do these methods do? Sending the message **setEquation:** to an instance of **BNRExecutor** gives it a reference to a block (Figure 27.2). Sending the message **computeWithValue:andValue:** will execute that block – passing in the two int arguments – and return the result. In BNRExecutor.m, define these two methods.

```
@implementation BNRExecutor

- (void)setEquation:(int (^)(int, int))block
{
    equation = block;
}

- (int)computeWithValue:(int)value1 andValue:(int)value2
{
    // If a block variable is executed but doesn't point at a block,
    // it will crash - return 0 if there is no block
    if (!equation)
        return 0;

    // Return value of block with value1 and value2
    return equation(value1, value2);
}
@end
```

In BNRAppDelegate.m, import BNRExecutor.h, create an instance of **BNRExecutor**, set its equation, and then have it compute a value with that equation.

```
#import "BNRAppDelegate.h"
#import "BNRExecutor.h"

@implementation BNRAppDelegate
```

```
@synthesize window = _window;

- (BOOL)application:(UIApplication *)application
    didFinishLaunchingWithOptions:(NSDictionary *)launchOptions
{
    self.window = [[UIWindow alloc] initWithFrame:[[UIScreen mainScreen] bounds]];
    // Override point for customization after application launch.

    int (^adder)(int, int) = ^int(int x, int y) {
        return x + y;
    };

    int sum = adder(2, 5);
    NSLog(@"%d", sum);

    BNRExecutor *executor = [[BNRExecutor alloc] init];
    [executor setEquation:adder];
    NSLog(@"%d", [executor computeWithValue:2 andValue:5]);


    self.window.backgroundColor = [UIColor whiteColor];
    [self.window makeKeyAndVisible];
    return YES;
}
```

Build and run the application. You will see the same output as before.

Take a look at the message **computeWithValue:andValue:**. It takes two integer arguments, which means we can pass variables of type int:

```
int a = 2;
int b = 5
int val = [executor computeWithValue:a andValue:b];
```

Or we could bypass creating the variables and just pass literal values:

```
int val = [executor computeWithValue:2 andValue:5];
```

The same can be done when passing a block to a method. Instead of allocating a block, setting a variable to point at it, and then passing that variable to a method, you can just pass a block literal as the argument. (This is what we did back in Chapter 13 when we passed a block to be executed when the modal view controller was dismissed.) In **application:didFinishLaunchingWithOptions:**, modify the code so that the variable adder is no longer used.

```
- (BOOL)application:(UIApplication *)application
    didFinishLaunchingWithOptions:(NSDictionary *)launchOptions
{
    self.window = [[UIWindow alloc] initWithFrame:[[UIScreen mainScreen] bounds]];
    // Override point for customization after application launch.

    int (^adder)(int, int) = ^int(int x, int y) {
        return x + y;
    };

    BNRExecutor *executor = [[BNRExecutor alloc] init];
    [executor setEquation:adder];
    [executor setEquation:^int(int x, int y) {
        return x + y;
    }];
```

```
    NSLog(@"%d", [executor computeWithValue:2 andValue:5]);

    self.window.backgroundColor = [UIColor whiteColor];
    [self.window makeKeyAndVisible];
    return YES;
}
```

Build and run the application. You will see the same output, but your code is much more succinct. The block is allocated and immediately passed to the **BNRExecutor**, which sets its equation instance variable to point at it. Now you can see exactly what the block does (what code it contains) right where it's called rather than having to find the definition back where the variable is declared. This makes for much less clutter in your code files.

Like any other instance variable, a block can be exposed as a property of a class. In BNRExecutor.h, declare a property for the equation block to replace the setter method. Since you will be synthesizing this property, you no longer need the instance variable explicitly declared either.

```
@interface BNRExecutor : NSObject
{
    int (^equation)(int, int);
}

@property (nonatomic, copy) int (^equation)(int, int);
- (void)setEquation:(int (^)(int, int))block;
- (int)computeWithValue:(int)value1 andValue:(int)value2;

@end
```

Synthesize this property in BNRExecutor.m and remove the previous implementation of **setEquation:**.

```
@implementation BNRExecutor

@synthesize equation;

- (void)setEquation:(int (^)(int, int))block
{
    equation = [block copy];
}
```

Build the application to check for syntax errors.

Variable Capturing

There is one special characteristic of blocks that makes them very useful: they *capture* variables.

A block, like a function, can use the arguments passed to it and can declare local variables. Modify the block in BNRAppDelegate.m's **application:didFinishLaunchingWithOptions:** so that it declares and uses a local variable.

```
[executor setEquation:^int(int x, int y) {
    int sum = x + y;
    return x + y;
    return sum;
}];
```

The variable sum is local to the block, so sum can be used inside this block. Both x and y are arguments of the block, so they, too, can be used inside this block.

A block can also use any variables that are visible within its *enclosing scope*. The enclosing scope of a block is the scope of the method in which it is defined. Thus, a block has access to all of the local variables of the method, arguments passed to the method, and instance variables that belong to the object running the method. Change **application:didFinishLaunchingWithOptions:** to declare a local variable and then use that variable in the block.

```
BNRExecutor *executor = [[BNRExecutor alloc] init];

int multiplier = 3;

[executor setEquation:^int(int x, int y) {
    int sum = x + y;
    return sum;
    return multiplier * sum;
}];
```

Build and run the application. The console will report the result of the equation as 21. When a block accesses a variable that is declared outside of it, the block is said to *capture* that variable. Thus, the value of multiplier is copied into the memory for the block (Figure 27.3). Each time the block executes, that value will be used, regardless of what happens to the original multiplier variable. (The original local variable will be destroyed as soon as **application:didFinishLaunchingWithOptions:** returns.)

Figure 27.3 Captured variables are copied into the block

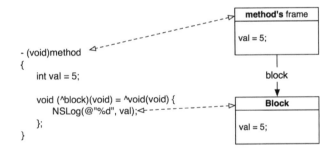

In fact, you can change the multiplier variable after the block is created, and it still won't change the multiplier within the block. When a block copies the value of a variable, it doesn't care what happens to the original variable afterwards. In BNRAppDelegate.m, change the value of multiplier after creating the block.

```
int multiplier = 3;

[executor setEquation:^int(int x, int y) {
    int sum = x + y;
    return multiplier * sum;
}];

multiplier = 100;
```

Build and run the application. Notice that the console reports the same output from the equation, even though the block is called after multiplier is changed. You don't need to do anything special to capture a variable – you simply must use it somewhere in the block.

This behavior is unique to blocks. The only way you can get values to functions is to pass them as arguments, and the only way you can get values to methods is to pass them as arguments or have them stored in an instance variable. A block can take arguments and capture variables from their enclosing scope.

This is an important point: the values of the captured variables remain the same every time the block is called, but the values of its arguments can change each time it is called. In this case, that means you can change the two values that are added together each time you call the block, but the multiplier will always remain the same.

You can capture any kind of variable, including a pointer to an object. This is useful because you can send a message to an object that you have a pointer to in the enclosing scope. Let's try this out.

In every iOS application, there is a *main operation queue*. When you add an operation to this queue, it is essentially queued up as the next event in the run loop (Figure 27.4).

Figure 27.4   NSOperationQueue

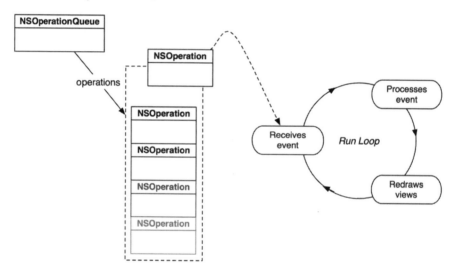

A block can be an operation, so you can add a block to the main operation queue, and it will execute on the next cycle of the run loop. A block that can be added to the operation queue must return no value and take no arguments. (You can find more information in the documentation for **NSOperationQueue**).

In BNRAppDelegate.m, edit **application:didFinishLaunchingWithOptions:** to add a block to the main operation queue that will send **computeWithValue:andValue:** to the equation when executed.

```
[executor setEquation:^int(int x, int y) {
    int sum = x + 2;
    return multiplier * (sum + y);
}];

multiplier = 100;

NSLog(@"%d", [executor computeWithValue:2 andValue:5]);
```

```
    // Get a pointer to the main operation queue and add a block to it
    [[NSOperationQueue mainQueue] addOperationWithBlock:^void(void){
        NSLog(@"%d", [executor computeWithValue:2 andValue:5]);
    }];

    self.window.backgroundColor = [UIColor whiteColor];
    [self.window makeKeyAndVisible];

    NSLog(@"About to exit method...");
    return YES;
}
```

Build and run the application. Notice the console reports it is exiting **application:didFinishLaunchingWithOptions:**, and shortly thereafter, you see the result of the executor running its equation. Using **addOperationWithBlock:** on the main queue is pretty common. Many times, you will want the run loop to finish drawing views and clearing the autorelease pool before a block is executed.

This makes sense except for one small thing: the variable, executor, is the only variable that points to the **BNRExecutor** instance. When **application:didFinishLaunchingWithOptions:** finishes, the block has yet to run, but the executor variable is destroyed – which should cause the **BNRExecutor** to also be destroyed. However, the **BNRExecutor** is clearly not destroyed because the block, which sends a message to the executor, runs without a hitch. (If **BNRExecutor** was already destroyed when the block executed, you'd get a crash.)

What, then, keeps the **BNRExecutor** alive? A block keeps a strong reference to any object it references within its scope. Thus, any time you send a message to an object or use that object in any way within the block, it will be kept around as long as the block exists. In the case of **addOperationWithBlock:**, the block is kept until it is executed, and then it is discarded. We can test this out. In BNRExecutor.m, implement **dealloc** to print out when the executor is destroyed.

```
- (void)dealloc
{
    NSLog(@"Executor is being destroyed.");
}
```

Build and run the application. Notice that the **BNRExecutor** is destroyed after the block is executed. The block held the last strong reference to it and when the block was destroyed, it lost the last reference to the object. This works because the block captures the variable that points to the **BNRExecutor** in the same way it captures any other variable. The compiler is very smart: it figures out that this is a pointer to an object and gives the block ownership of that object.

Typical Block Usage

In this chapter, our examples have been pretty trivial. In the next chapter, you will see some real world examples of blocks and see just how useful they can be. However, to whet your appetite a bit, let's talk about how blocks are typically used.

Most commonly, blocks are used as callbacks. For example, in Chapter 13 you supplied a block when dismissing a modal view controller. When the dismissal completed, the block was executed. Thus, you can think of blocks as a one-shot callback for an event to occur some time in the future. We usually call a block used in this manner a *completion block*.

Using a completion block is usually much simpler than setting up a delegate or a target-action pair. You don't have to declare or define a method or even have an object to set up the callback, you just create a block before the event and let it fire. A block, then, is an object-less callback, whereas every other callback mechanism we've used so far (delegation, target-actions, notifications) must have an object to send a message to.

Blocks are used in a lot of system APIs. For instance, **NSArray** has a method named **sortedArrayUsingComparator:**. When this message is sent, the array uses the block to compare every object it holds and returns another array that has been sorted. It looks like this:

```
NSArray *sorted = [array sortedArrayUsingComparator:
^NSComparisonResult(id obj1, id obj2) {
    if ([obj1 value] < [obj2 value])
        return NSOrderedDescending;
    else if ([obj1 value] > [obj2 value])
        return NSOrderedAscending;

    return NSOrderedSame;
}];
```

When working with a method that takes a block, you must supply a block that matches the signature declared by the method. For one thing, the compiler will give you an error if you supply a different kind of block. But also, the block has a specific signature for a reason: the method that uses it will expect it to work in a certain way. You can think of blocks used in this way as a "plug-in." **NSArray** says, "Hey, I got these objects, and I can feed them to your block to figure out which ones go where. Just give me the specifics."

There are many other ways to use blocks, like queuing up tasks (a block that calls a block that calls another block), and some objects that use blocks know how to spread the execution of them among different CPU cores. People have done some really clever things with blocks, and in the next chapter, we will show you one of those clever uses.

For the More Curious: The __block Modifier, Abbreviated Syntax, and Memory

Blocks have a few more options than we've talked about in this chapter. First, when allocating blocks we have always put the return type in the block signature:

```
^returnType(...) {

}
```

However, this isn't necessary. The compiler can figure out the return type based on the return statement in the block.

For example, these are all valid blocks and assignments:

```
int (^block)(void) = ^(void) {
    return 10;
};

NSString * (^block)(void) = ^(void) {
    return [NSString stringWithString:@"Hey"];
};
```

```
void (^block)(void) = ^(void) {
    NSLog(@"Not gonna return anything...");
};
```

Also, if a block doesn't take arguments, you don't need to include the argument list in the block literal. So, you could write a block and its assignment like this:

```
void (^block)(void) = ^{
    NSLog(@"I'm a silly block.");
};
```

The return type and empty argument list can only be omitted from the block literal. A block variable must have all of the information about the block it points to.

Earlier in this chapter, you saw how a block captured a variable by copying its value into its own memory. Subsequent changes to that variable didn't affect the block's copy. One thing we did not mention was that this captured variable cannot be changed within the block. For example, this is illegal:

```
int five = 5;
void (^block)(void) = ^{
    five = 6; // This line causes an error
};
```

Sometimes, you do want to modify a variable inside a block. A typical example is some sort of counter variable that should go up each time you execute a block. If you want this behavior, you have to specify the variable as mutable within the block by decorating it with __block:

```
__block int counter = 0;

void (^block)(void) = ^{
    counter++;
    NSLog(@"Counter now at %d", counter);
};

block(); // prints 1
block(); // prints 2
```

When a variable is decorated with __block, it actually lives in a special spot in memory: it is not a local stack variable, nor is it stored inside the block itself (Figure 27.5).

Figure 27.5   Shared Memory for __block variables

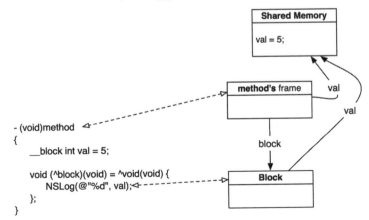

This is important because it means more than one block can modify that variable:

```
__block int counter = 0;

void (^plusOne)(void) = ^{
    counter++;
    NSLog(@"Counter now at %d", counter);
};
void (^plusTwo)(void) = ^{
    counter += 2;
    NSLog(@"Counter now at %d", counter);
};

plusOne(); // prints 1
plusTwo(); // prints 3
plusOne(); // prints 4
```

Additionally, if counter is modified after the block is defined, the value within the block is also changed:

```
__block int counter = 0;

void (^plusOne)(void) = ^{
    counter++;
    NSLog(@"Counter now at %d", counter);
};
counter = 25;

plusOne(); // prints 26
```

When capturing a pointer to an object, you can always change the properties of that object, but you cannot change what object the pointer points to. When declaring a pointer with the __block modifier, you can change the pointer to point at another object within the block:

```
NSString *string1 = @"Bar";
__block NSString *string2 = @"Bar";

void (^block)(void) = ^{
    string1 = @"Foo"; // This is ILLEGAL
    string2 = @"Foo"; // This is OK
};
```

Finally, one last tidbit of knowledge. When you allocate a block, it is created on the stack. This means that, even if you were to keep a strong reference to it, calling it later would result in a crash because the memory would be destroyed as soon as you leave the method in which it was defined.

The way around this disaster is to send the message **copy** to a block. When you copy a block, the block is moved to the heap, where storage outlasts the current stack frame. (You probably noticed that the equation property of **BNRExecutor** in this exercise had the copy attribute. That does the same thing.) If a block is already in the heap, sending it the message **copy** just adds another strong reference to it instead of making another copy of the block.

Before ARC, forgetting to copy a block was a big deal and created hard-to-find bugs when a block had a strong reference but had also been deallocated. With the advent of ARC, the compiler now knows a lot about blocks. So, even if you just assign a block to a strong variable or use a strong property, the block is copied to the heap for you if it is not already there. However, we still like to use copy for all of our block properties because it makes us feel in charge and all warm inside.

Now, you might be wondering, "If they didn't tell me that blocks are automatically copied when using a strong property, how would I ever know that?" Well, when ARC first came out there was a little chatter in the release notes about it. However, the documentation wasn't updated (and as of this writing, still isn't updated) to reflect this special block copying procedure. But the neat thing about blocks is that they are a feature of the Objective-C language, which is not owned by anyone. Thus, you can look at the source for the Objective-C language. Apple maintains their version of Objective-C and a number of other open source libraries at `http://www.opensource.apple.com`.

For the More Curious: Pros and Cons of Callback Options

A callback, as you may remember from Chapter 4, is a chunk of code that you supply in advance of an event occurring. When that event goes down, the chunk of code gets executed. In this chapter, you have seen that blocks can be used as callbacks. Other approaches to callbacks you have seen in this book are delegation, target-action pairs, and notifications. Each one has benefits and drawbacks compared to the others. This section will expand on these benefits and drawbacks so that you can pick the appropriate one for your own implementations.

First, let's note that each of these approaches to callbacks are design patterns that transcend their implementations in Cocoa Touch. For example, the target-action pair design pattern is implemented by **UIControl**, but this does not mean you have to use **UIControl** to use the design pattern. You could create your own class that kept a pointer to a target object and a SEL for the message that object would be sent when some event occurred.

A callback has two major components: the process of registering it and the code for the callback. When registering a callback using delegation, target-actions, or notifications, you register a pointer to an object. This is the object that will receive messages when events occur. Additionally, both target-actions and notifications require a SEL that will be the message that is sent to the object. Delegation, on the other hand, uses a pre-defined set of methods from a delegate protocol to regulate which messages get sent.

In these three callback design patterns, the code for the callback is in a distinct method implementation (Figure 27.6).

Figure 27.6   Callback design patterns

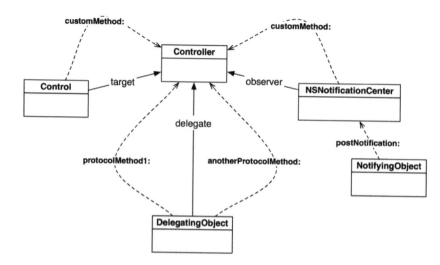

There are certain situations where one of these design patterns works better than the others.

Target-action is used when you have a close relationship between the two objects (like a view controller and one of its views) and when there are many instances that call back. For example, a single interface controlled by one controller may have many buttons. If those buttons only knew how to send one message (e.g., **buttonTapped:**), there would be mass confusion in the implementation of that method ("Uhhh... which button are you again?"). Each button having its own action message (e.g., **redButtonTapped:**) makes life easier.

Delegation is used when an object receives many events and it wants the same object to handle each of those events. You've seen many examples of delegation in this book because delegation is very common in Cocoa Touch. Delegation uses a protocol that defines all of the messages that will be sent, so you do not have control over the names of these methods, but you do not have to register them individually like with target-action pairs, either.

Notifications are used when you want multiple objects to invoke their callback for the same event and/ or when two objects are not related. Consider an application that has two view controllers in a tab bar controller. They don't have pointers to each other, unlike two view controllers in a navigation controller stack, but one of them is interested in what is going on in the other. Instead of giving them pointers to each other, which can be messy for a variety of reasons, one of view controllers can post notifications to the notification center. The other could register as an observer for that type of notification. Similarly, another view controller could come along and register for the same notification, and both observers would get updated.

Blocks are the outliers when it comes to callbacks because they are not an object-oriented approach. Blocks are useful when the callback is going to happen only once or when the callback is just a quick and simple task (like updating a progress bar).

One of the reasons blocks are better suited for this one-shot behavior is that they will take ownership of any object they reference. If a block was to stay around forever, the objects it references would also stay around forever. Of course, you can destroy the block when it is no longer needed, but what if that block is owned by an object that the block references? The object owns the block, the block owns the object, and now you can't destroy them without some extra work. Since blocks stick around for just the one event, they will own what they need until they no longer need it.

Another reason blocks are well-suited for this situation goes along with the reason why they are good for quick and simple tasks: you can define the block's code at the same point where the block is registered as a callback. This keeps your code nice and clean.

An approach to callbacks we have not discussed is subclassing. In some languages, delegation is not feasible because of the structure of the language. In these languages, classes like **CLLocationManager** would be abstract classes – ones that were meant to be subclassed. Any time you wanted to use an instance of **CLLocationManager**, you would subclass it and write the code for what happens when an event occurs in the implementation of this subclass. The subclass would probably have an instance variable for the object it was going to tell about these events, and that object would declare and define these methods. This gets complicated and ugly pretty quickly, and in Cocoa Touch, you do not see this pattern because we have better alternatives.

28

Model-View-Controller-Store

Most of the applications you've built in this book have been based on the Model-View-Controller design pattern. The exception is Homepwner, which is based on the Model-View-Controller-Store design pattern. In this chapter, we're going to look more closely at store objects, MVCS, and when MVCS is the better approach for designing an application.

This is a fairly advanced chapter. Until now, you've been leveraging the power of existing classes that are built into the iOS SDK. Here, you will write a number of classes of your own that do real work. It will be difficult, but rewarding.

The Need for Stores

Many applications (and especially mobile applications) make use of external sources of data. External sources of data include web servers, databases, the filesystem, location hardware, the camera, etc. Basically, it's anything that is not already in memory.

If your application interfaces with an external source of data, then Model-View-Controller-Store is a better approach than Model-View-Controller.

To explain why, first, let's define a term: *request logic* is code that fetches things from an external source. Examples of request logic are creating an **NSFetchRequest** in Core Data, preparing an **NSURLRequest** for **NSURLConnection**, and loading a file with **NSKeyedUnarchiver**. Request logic is typically long, complicated, and full of source-specific details.

In MVC, request logic is the responsibility of controller objects (Figure 28.1). However, this is not a good solution. Including request logic in a controller muddies up the class and makes it harder to see how the controller is managing the flow of the application and coordinating the application's model and view objects.

Figure 28.1   Standard MVC

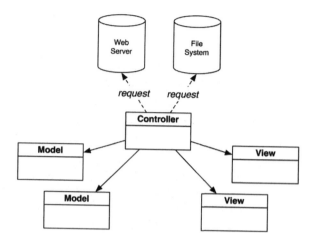

In addition, an application may interact with multiple sources of data, and a controller would have to know the intimate details of communicating with each (Figure 28.2). For example, a single controller might have to interface with the location hardware, a web server, and another iOS device all at the same time. That controller would have a painfully dense implementation file.

Figure 28.2   Messy MVC

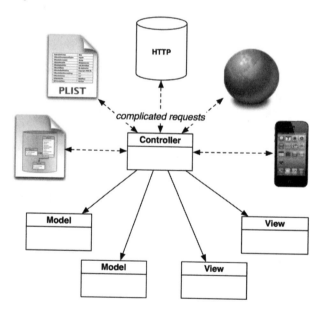

An application can have multiple controllers interfacing with an external source, too. Putting the request logic in each controller leads to redundant code. (On the other hand, if you kept the request logic in one controller, you'd end up with other controllers having unnatural dependencies on the one holding the request logic.)

Figure 28.3   Messy MVC

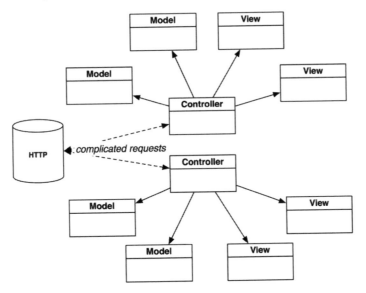

The possibility of multiple controllers interfacing with an external source leads to another complication. Often, you need keep track of the application's exchanges with an external source. For example, a web service might require you to pass authentication credentials each time you make a service call. If multiple controllers need to make calls to this web service, then each one has to know about these credentials and know how to send them to the server (Figure 28.3). Caching data is another example of a problem here. If you are caching responses from a web server, each controller needs to make decisions on when to cache, when to load from the cache, and where the cache is stored.

Model-View-Controller-Store puts request logic into a separate object, and we call this object a *store* (Figure 28.4). Using a store object minimizes redundant code and simplifies the code that fetches and saves data. Most importantly, it moves the logic for dealing with an external source into a tidy class with a clear and focused goal. This makes code easier to understand, which makes it easier to maintain and debug, as well as share with other programmers on your team.

Figure 28.4   Model-View-Controller-Store diagram

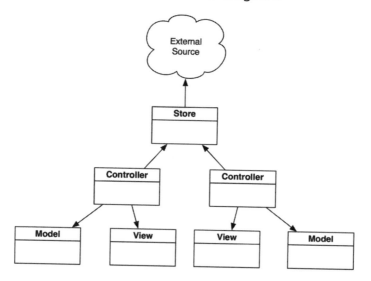

You've already seen and used MVCS in the Homepwner application. In Homepwner, you had two store objects: **BNRItemStore** and **BNRImageStore**. This freed the table view controller to focus on its work as the table view's data source instead of mucking about with fetching individual **BNRItem**s.

But what about the application you just completed, Nerdfeed? Nerdfeed has request logic for getting data from a web service, and that code is in a controller object – **ListViewController**.

Let's fix that now. In this chapter, we will add a store class to Nerdfeed and move all of the request logic out of **ListViewController**. We will also add another web service request and new features to Nerdfeed to demonstrate the benefits of MVCS.

Creating BNRFeedStore

Right now, the request logic in Nerdfeed is in a controller. Open Nerdfeed.xcodeproj and locate ListViewController.m.

ListViewController.m is a big file already, and adding new features to this class will only get more difficult as it becomes larger. However, if you look at the code in this class, you can break it into two categories. First, there is the code that deals with populating views with model objects and handles user interaction. These are the data source and delegate methods for **UITableView**, the action methods, and the methods that control the flow of the application, like **fetchEntries**.

The other code in this file is request logic – preparing an **NSURLConnection**, receiving its response, and handling the parsing of the data that returns from the server. In MVCS, a controller should not be responsible for this code, so we're going to create a store object to take over these responsibilities.

Create a new **NSObject** subclass and name it **BNRFeedStore**. This object will be the point of contact between your controllers and the server that hosts the BNR forum and RSS feed.

A store object is typically a singleton. Because **BNRFeedStore** is a singleton, all controllers access the same instance of **BNRFeedStore**, which allows us to easily cache and store information about the server in one place. In BNRFeedStore.h, declare a new method that returns the single instance of **BNRFeedStore**.

```
@interface BNRFeedStore : NSObject

+ (BNRFeedStore *)sharedStore;

@end
```

In BNRFeedStore.m, implement this method.

```
+ (BNRFeedStore *)sharedStore
{
    static BNRFeedStore *feedStore = nil;
    if (!feedStore)
        feedStore = [[BNRFeedStore alloc] init];

    return feedStore;
}
```

When Nerdfeed launches, it fetches the RSS feed. The container object for the RSS feed is an instance of **RSSChannel**, and each individual post is represented by an **RSSItem** within that channel. Remembering that a store's job is to unburden the controller, the store should make it really easy for a controller to fetch the **RSSChannel** instance.

Think back to another store you wrote – the **BNRItemStore** from Homepwner. In that application, the controller simply asked the store for all of the items, and the store loaded the right file from the filesystem and returned the instances of **BNRItem** the controller asked for. It looked like this:

```
NSArray *items = [[BNRItemStore sharedStore] allItems];
```

BNRFeedStore should make it just as easy for **ListViewController**. However, there is a problem: unlike loading from the filesystem, it takes time to make the request to a web server. **BNRFeedStore** can't just return the **RSSChannel** from a method because that would block the main thread while the request was being processed. This would prevent the UI from redrawing or accepting events and generally annoy the user:

```
// This would take a few seconds and we couldn't execute code in the mean time
RSSChannel *channel = [[BNRFeedStore sharedStore] channel];
```

Instead, the request needs to be handled asynchronously. The **ListViewController** will make the request and supply a callback for when the request finishes. The callback will have access to the **RSSChannel** so the **ListViewController** can grab the channel and reload its table view.

You have already done something like this. In Whereami, the controller made a request to an instance of **CLLocationManager** to find the current location. When the request completed, the location manager returned an instance of **CLLocation** to the controller via delegation. Believe it or not, a **CLLocationManager** is a store object, and it returned data asynchronously to the requesting controller (Figure 28.5).

Figure 28.5   Flow of Whereami

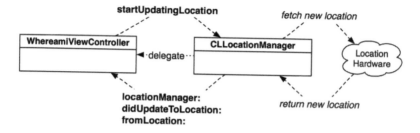

So we could use delegation to return the **RSSChannel** from the store, but here we run into another problem. **BNRFeedStore** is a singleton, so delegation won't work. Multiple controllers may want to make requests to the **BNRFeedStore** at the same time, but only one can be the delegate.

This is where blocks come in handy. **ListViewController** can make a request and supply a block to be called when the request is complete. The store will execute this block with the newly fetched **RSSChannel** as an argument. The block's code will set the channel of the **ListViewController** and reload the **UITableView**. In BNRFeedStore.h, declare a new method and forward declare **RSSChannel**.

```
@class RSSChannel;

@interface BNRFeedStore : NSObject

+ (BNRFeedStore *)sharedStore;

- (void)fetchRSSFeedWithCompletion:(void (^)(RSSChannel *obj, NSError *err))block;

@end
```

When a controller wants the RSS feed, it will send the message **fetchRSSFeedWithCompletion:** to **BNRFeedStore**. This is a very simple request for the controller, but a fairly complicated one for the **BNRFeedStore**. The controller doesn't care, though, *how* the RSS feed is fetched, only that it is fetched. The complications are the responsibility of the store object.

Take a look at the form of the block that will be called when the request finishes. It takes two arguments: a pointer to an **RSSChannel** and a pointer to an **NSError** object. If the request was a success, the **RSSChannel** will be passed as an argument, and the **NSError** will be nil. If there was a problem, an instance of **NSError** will be passed as an argument, and the **RSSChannel** will be nil.

Let's hold off on the implementation of **fetchRSSFeedWithCompletion:** for now and just implement it with an empty body in BNRFeedStore.m.

```
- (void)fetchRSSFeedWithCompletion:(void (^)(RSSChannel *obj, NSError *err))block
{
    // We'll fill this out later
}
```

Using the Store

Before you implement the details of the store, you are going to implement the code in the controller that uses **fetchRSSFeedWithCompletion:**. **ListViewController** only needs to initiate the fetch and describe what will happen in the completion block it passes as the argument.

Right now, the **ListViewController** is responsible for creating the **NSURLRequest** and the **NSURLConnection**. It also implements the delegate methods for **NSURLConnection** that accumulate the response data from the server and execute code when the request either succeeds or fails. This code needs to be moved into the store; it is request logic. You can begin by deleting the body of **fetchEntries** in ListViewController.m.

```
- (void)fetchEntries
{
    xmlData = [[NSMutableData alloc] init];

    NSURL *url = [NSURL URLWithString:@"http://forums.bignerdranch.com"
                @"/smartfeed.php?@"limit=1_DAY&sort_by=standard"
                @"&feed_type=RSS2.0&feed_style=COMPACT"];

    NSURLRequest *req = [NSURLRequest requestWithURL:url];

    connection = [[NSURLConnection alloc] initWithRequest:req
                                                 delegate:self
                                          startImmediately:YES];
}
```

Now let's re-implement **fetchEntries** to leverage the store's power. At the top of ListViewController.m, import the header for **BNRFeedStore**.

```
#import "BNRFeedStore.h"
```

Enter the new code for **fetchEntries** in ListViewController.m.

```
- (void)fetchEntries
{
    // Initiate the request...
    [[BNRFeedStore sharedStore] fetchRSSFeedWithCompletion:
    ^(RSSChannel *obj, NSError *err) {
        // When the request completes, this block will be called.

        if (!err) {
            // If everything went ok, grab the channel object, and
            // reload the table.
            channel = obj;

            [[self tableView] reloadData];
        } else {

            // If things went bad, show an alert view
            UIAlertView *av = [[UIAlertView alloc]
                                    initWithTitle:@"Error"
                                          message:[err localizedDescription]
                                         delegate:nil
                                cancelButtonTitle:@"OK"
                                otherButtonTitles:nil];
            [av show];
        }
    }];
}
```

Now, we won't be able to build and run for some time, but let's see what will happen (Figure 28.6). **ListViewController** asks **BNRFeedStore** for the RSS feed and says, "When you have the feed, do the stuff in this block." The **ListViewController** moves on with its life, and the store gets to work.

Figure 28.6   Flow of Nerdfeed with BNRFeedStore

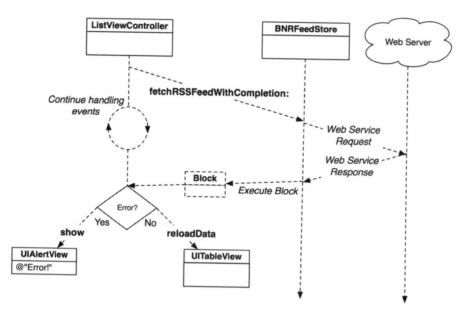

Look at the code in the block that gets executed if there is no `err`; it looks a lot like the code in **ListViewController**'s **connectionDidFinishLoading:** method. The code in the block that gets executed if there is an error looks just like the code in **connection:didFailWithError:**.

This, of course, is intentional. We are not changing what Nerdfeed does – only how it does it. **ListViewController** will no longer manage the details of the **NSURLConnection**. In MVCS, controllers don't do that kind of work, store objects do.

ListViewController now flows exceptionally well: it says, "Fetch these entries, and then do this if this happens or that if that happens." All of this code is in one place instead of strewn over a number of methods. The code is easy to read, easy to maintain, and easy to debug.

With this code in place, you can clean up **ListViewController**. In ListViewController.m, you can delete the following methods. (The bodies of the methods have been omitted to save trees.)

```
- (void)parser:(NSXMLParser *)parser
    didStartElement:(NSString *)elementName
      namespaceURI:(NSString *)namespaceURI
     qualifiedName:(NSString *)qualifiedName
        attributes:(NSDictionary *)attributeDict
{
    ...
}

- (void)connection:(NSURLConnection *)conn didReceiveData:(NSData *)data
{
    [xmlData appendData:data];
}

- (void)connectionDidFinishLoading:(NSURLConnection *)conn
{
    ...
```

```
}

- (void)connection:(NSURLConnection *)conn
  didFailWithError:(NSError *)error
{
  ...
}
```

In ListViewController.h, you can delete the instance variables connection and xmlData, as well as remove the protocol declaration for NSXMLParserDelegate.

```
@interface ListViewController : UITableViewController <NSXMLParserDelegate>
{
    NSURLConnection *connection;
    NSMutableData *xmlData;

    RSSChannel *channel;
}
```

Take a moment to scroll through ListViewController.h and ListViewController.m. These files are now very sleek and easy to follow. **ListViewController** has a primary focus now – presenting a table of **RSSItem**s. This is the purpose of store objects: let the controller focus on its job rather than the details of request logic.

Another thing to mention – in the declaration of **fetchRSSFeedWithCompletion:** in BNRFeedStore.h, you supplied the names of the arguments for the block argument. In Chapter 27, we mentioned that this wasn't necessary because the names of the arguments only matter in the block literal.

However, when you were typing **fetchRSSFeedWithCompletion:** in ListViewController.m, you probably noticed that Xcode auto-completed the block literal for you and added in the names of the arguments for the block. This was pretty handy. So when declaring a block variable as a property or as an argument to a method, it's good idea to specify the names of the arguments in the block to take advantage of auto-completion.

You can build the application to check for syntax errors, but running it won't do you much good since **fetchRSSFeedWithCompletion:** hasn't been implemented. In the next section, you will complete the store object and get Nerdfeed back up and running.

Building BNRFeedStore

The code that was removed from **ListViewController** must be replaced in **BNRFeedStore**. The **BNRFeedStore** must handle preparing the **NSURLRequest**, kicking off the **NSURLConnection**, handling the response from the server, and starting the parser. The **ListViewController** simply asks for these actions to be initiated and supplies a callback for when they are completed.

Initiating the connection

A store's job is to take a really simple request from a controller, like "fetch the RSS feed," and prepare a detailed request tailored for the external source it interacts with. In this case, the detailed request is the web service call to http://forums.bignerdranch.com. In BNRFeedStore.m, begin implementing **fetchRSSFeedWithCompletion:** by preparing this request.

```
- (void)fetchRSSFeedWithCompletion:(void (^)(RSSChannel *obj, NSError *err))block
{
    NSURL *url = [NSURL URLWithString:@"http://forums.bignerdranch.com/"
                       @"smartfeed.php?limit=1_DAY&sort_by=standard"
                       @"&feed_type=RSS2.0&feed_style=COMPACT"];

    NSURLRequest *req = [NSURLRequest requestWithURL:url];
}
```

It is important that the **NSURLRequest** is created inside the store and not in **ListViewController**. It is not **ListViewController**'s job to understand how to interact with the web server; thus, it shouldn't know about the URL or the arguments passed in that URL. In fact, the **ListViewController** shouldn't even know that the Internet exists or what an **NSURL** is. It just wants an **RSSChannel**, and by golly, it'll get one.

The store's next step is to create an **NSURLConnection** to process this **NSURLRequest**. Your first intuition would be to create the **NSURLConnection** here in **fetchRSSFeedWithCompletion:** and set the delegate of the connection as the **BNRFeedStore**. However, what happens when we add more requests to the store?

For example, the store could pull the RSS feed from another server. The store, then, would have to be the delegate for a lot of **NSURLConnections**. The **NSURLConnection** delegate methods that handle the response would become giant if-else statements to determine what data belongs to which request.

The actor design pattern

Instead of having the **BNRFeedStore** be the delegate for every **NSURLConnection**, we are going to create another class named **BNRConnection**. The sole purpose of an instance of this class will be to manage a single **NSURLConnection**.

BNRConnection instances will take the request prepared by the **BNRFeedStore**, start their own **NSURLConnection**, and then receive all of the delegate messages from that **NSURLConnection**. This object will do its work without bothering the controller or the store until it has finished. When it finishes, it will execute the completion block supplied by **ListViewController** (Figure 28.7).

Figure 28.7   BNRConnection and NSURLConnection

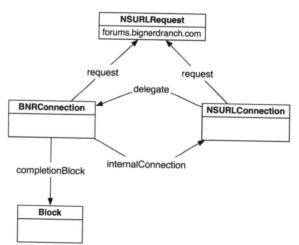

This is an example of the *actor design pattern*. An actor object is used when you have a long running task and some code that needs to be executed after it completes. This kind of object is given the information it needs to perform the task and callbacks to execute when that task is done. The actor runs on its own thread without any further input and is destroyed when it is finished (Figure 28.8).

Figure 28.8   Actor design pattern

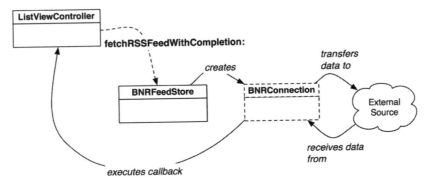

Create **BNRConnection**, the actor, as a new **NSObject** subclass. **BNRConnection** needs instance variables and properties to hold the connection, request, and callback. Modify BNRConnection.h to look like this:

```
@interface BNRConnection : NSObject
    <NSURLConnectionDelegate, NSURLConnectionDataDelegate>
{
    NSURLConnection *internalConnection;
    NSMutableData *container;
}

- (id)initWithRequest:(NSURLRequest *)req;

@property (nonatomic, copy) NSURLRequest *request;
@property (nonatomic, copy) void (^completionBlock)(id obj, NSError *err);
@property (nonatomic, strong) id <NSXMLParserDelegate> xmlRootObject;

- (void)start;

@end
```

For every request the **BNRFeedStore** makes, it will create an instance of **BNRConnection**. An instance of this class is a one-shot deal: it runs, it calls back, and then it is destroyed. The next time a request is made, another instance of **BNRConnection** will be created. The store's responsibility here is to pass on the appropriate data (the request and callback block) to the **BNRConnection** so that it can function. In other words, a store object becomes a middle man: it takes the simple demands of a controller and sends its **BNRConnection** minions off to carry out the work.

In addition to the request and callback, the store will provide an xmlRootObject to the **BNRConnection**. This object will be the object that eventually gets returned to the controller. In this case, the xmlRootObject will be an instance of **RSSChannel**. The store will create an empty **RSSChannel** and give it to the **BNRConnection**. When the connection finishes, the **BNRConnection** will parse the data from the **NSURLConnection** into the xmlRootObject before handing it to the controller.

Before we write the code for **BNRConnection**, we will finish **fetchRSSFeedWithCompletion:** in BNRFeedStore.m. First, import the appropriate files into BNRFeedStore.m.

```
#import "RSSChannel.h"
#import "BNRConnection.h"
```

In BNRFeedStore.m, add code to **fetchRSSFeedWithCompletion:** that creates an instance of **BNRConnection** and sets it up with the request, completion block and empty root object.

```
- (void)fetchRSSFeedWithCompletion:(void (^)(RSSChannel *obj, NSError *err))block
{
    NSURL *url = [NSURL URLWithString:@"http://forums.bignerdranch.com/"
                       @"smartfeed.php?limit=1_DAY&sort_by=standard"
                       @"&feed_type=RSS2.0&feed_style=COMPACT"];

    NSURLRequest *req = [NSURLRequest requestWithURL:url];

    // Create an empty channel
    RSSChannel *channel = [[RSSChannel alloc] init];

    // Create a connection "actor" object that will transfer data from the server
    BNRConnection *connection = [[BNRConnection alloc] initWithRequest:req];

    // When the connection completes, this block from the controller will be called
    [connection setCompletionBlock:block];

    // Let the empty channel parse the returning data from the web service
    [connection setXmlRootObject:channel];

    // Begin the connection
    [connection start];
}
```

We are now at the heart of the code that will transform Nerdfeed from a pedagogical example to a functional powerhouse: the code for **BNRConnection**. We've changed the code in Nerdfeed by working from the outside and moving in, allowing us to see the simplicity earned by using MVCS and then the work required for that simplicity. We are almost there.

An instance of **BNRConnection**, when started, will create an instance of **NSURLConnection**, initialize it with an **NSURLRequest**, and set itself as the delegate of that connection. In BNRConnection.m, implement the following two methods and synthesize the three properties.

```
@implementation BNRConnection
@synthesize request, completionBlock, xmlRootObject;

- (id)initWithRequest:(NSURLRequest *)req
{
    self = [super init];
    if (self) {
        [self setRequest:req];
    }
    return self;
}
```

```
- (void)start
{
    // Initialize container for data collected from NSURLConnection
    container = [[NSMutableData alloc] init];

    // Spawn connection
    internalConnection = [[NSURLConnection alloc] initWithRequest:[self request]
                                                    delegate:self
                                              startImmediately:YES];

}
```

Build the application and check for syntax errors.

There is one little hitch here. When the store creates an instance of **BNRConnection** and tells it to start, the store will no longer keep a reference to it. This technique is known as "fire and forget." However, with ARC, we know that "forgetting" about an object will destroy it. Thus, the **BNRConnection** needs to be owned by something. At the top of BNRConnection.m, add a static **NSMutableArray** variable to hold a strong reference to all active **BNRConnection**s.

```
#import "BNRConnection.h"

static NSMutableArray *sharedConnectionList = nil;

@implementation BNRConnection
@synthesize request, completionBlock, xmlRootObject;
```

(As a bonus, you can use this connection list as a way to reference connections in progress. This is especially useful for cancelling a request.)

In BNRConnection.m, update **start** to add the connection to this array so that it doesn't get destroyed when the store forgets about it.

```
- (void)start
{
    container = [[NSMutableData alloc] init];
    internalConnection = [[NSURLConnection alloc] initWithRequest:[self request]
                                                    delegate:self
                                              startImmediately:YES];

    // If this is the first connection started, create the array
    if (!sharedConnectionList)
        sharedConnectionList = [[NSMutableArray alloc] init];

    // Add the connection to the array so it doesn't get destroyed
    [sharedConnectionList addObject:self];
}
```

Handling the response

A **BNRConnection** is the delegate for the **NSURLConnection** it manages, so it needs to implement the delegate methods for **NSURLConnection** that retrieve the data and report success or failure. First, implement the data collection method in BNRConnection.m.

```
- (void)connection:(NSURLConnection *)connection didReceiveData:(NSData *)data
{
    [container appendData:data];
}
```

Figure 28.9   BNRConnection flow

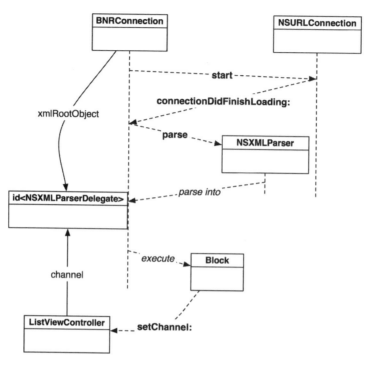

The **BNRConnection** will hold on to all of the data that returns from the web service. When that web service completes successfully, it must first parse that data into the xmlRootObject and then call the completionBlock (Figure 28.9). Finally, it needs to take itself out of the array of active connections so that it can be destroyed. Implement the following method in BNRConnection.m.

```
- (void)connectionDidFinishLoading:(NSURLConnection *)connection
{
    // If there is a "root object"
    if ([self xmlRootObject]) {

        // Create a parser with the incoming data and let the root object parse
        // its contents
        NSXMLParser *parser = [[NSXMLParser alloc] initWithData:container];
        [parser setDelegate:[self xmlRootObject]];
        [parser parse];
    }

    // Then, pass the root object to the completion block - remember,
    // this is the block that the controller supplied.
    if ([self completionBlock])
        [self completionBlock]([self xmlRootObject], nil);

    // Now, destroy this connection
    [sharedConnectionList removeObject:self];
}
```

Remember that **connectionDidFinishLoading:** is called when the connection finishes successfully; so, the root object is delivered to the completionBlock, and no **NSError** is passed. If there is a problem with the connection, the opposite needs to occur: the completion block is called without the root object, and an error object is passed instead. In BNRConnection.m, implement the method that handles the connection failing.

```
- (void)connection:(NSURLConnection *)connection
          didFailWithError:(NSError *)error
{
    // Pass the error from the connection to the completionBlock
    if ([self completionBlock])
        [self completionBlock](nil, error);

    // Destroy this connection
    [sharedConnectionList removeObject:self];
}
```

Build and run the application. After a moment, you will see the **ListViewController**'s table view populate. If there is a problem, you will see an alert view.

You be wondering why **BNRConnection**'s completionBlock takes an argument of type id instead of say, **RSSChannel**. The answer is simple: **BNRConnection** doesn't know anything about the type of its root object except that it receives NSXMLParserDelegate messages. Nor should it. This makes the **BNRConnection** usable in any situation that requires fetching XML data with **NSURLConnection**.

Now, at the end of the day, the changes we've made to Nerdfeed so far give us the exact same behavior as we had before. You might be wondering, "Why fix what ain't broke?" Well, in the rest of this chapter and the next two, you will be adding features to Nerdfeed. Using a store object is going to make implementing those features a lot easier. (Also, the **BNRConnection** class is pretty handy – you can use that in any application. In fact, that very same class is in a number of applications that are currently on the App Store.)

Another request

Now that we have **BNRConnection** and a store object, adding new requests for the store to handle is really straight-forward. Let's have the **BNRFeedStore** fetch the top songs from iTunes. First, we need to make a minor change to the **RSSChannel** and **RSSItem** classes because Apple's RSS feed uses a different element name (entry) to identify items in their RSS feed. In RSSChannel.m, modify **parser:didStartElement:namespaceURI:qualifiedName:attributes:** to create an **RSSItem** when it encounters the entry element.

```
- (void)parser:(NSXMLParser *)parser
   didStartElement:(NSString *)elementName
     namespaceURI:(NSString *)namespaceURI
    qualifiedName:(NSString *)qualifiedName
       attributes:(NSDictionary *)attributeDict
{
    if ([elementName isEqual:@"title"]) {
        currentString = [[NSMutableString alloc] init];
        [self setTitle:currentString];
    }
    else if ([elementName isEqual:@"description"]) {
        currentString = [[NSMutableString alloc] init];
        [self setInfoString:currentString];
    } else if ([elementName isEqual:@"item"]
            || [elementName isEqual:@"entry"]) {
```

```
        RSSItem *entry = [[RSSItem alloc] init];
        [entry setParentParserDelegate:self];
        [parser setDelegate:entry];
        [items addObject:entry];
    }
}
```

Then in RSSItem.m, have the **RSSItem** return control to the channel when it ends an entry element.

```
- (void)parser:(NSXMLParser *)parser
 didEndElement:(NSString *)elementName
  namespaceURI:(NSString *)namespaceURI
 qualifiedName:(NSString *)qName
{
    currentString = nil;

    if ([elementName isEqual:@"item"]
    || [elementName isEqual:@"entry"]) {
        [parser setDelegate:parentParserDelegate];
    }
}
```

Now we will add another request that a controller can ask the **BNRFeedStore** to carry out. In BNRFeedStore.h, declare a new method.

```
@interface BNRFeedStore : NSObject

+ (BNRFeedStore *)sharedStore;

- (void)fetchTopSongs:(int)count
      withCompletion:(void (^)(RSSChannel *obj, NSError *err))block;

- (void)fetchRSSFeedWithCompletion:(void (^)(RSSChannel *obj, NSError *err))block;

@end
```

The implementation of this method will be really easy now that we have the format of the store determined and the **BNRConnection** class ready to go. The two differences between **fetchTopSongs:withCompletion:** and **fetchRSSFeedWithCompletion:** are that **fetchTopSongs:withCompletion:** will take an argument supplied by the controller to determine how many songs to fetch and will access a different web service. Implement this method in BNRFeedStore.m.

```
- (void)fetchTopSongs:(int)count
      withCompletion:(void (^)(RSSChannel *obj, NSError *err))block
{
    // Prepare a request URL, including the argument from the controller
    NSString *requestString = [NSString stringWithFormat:
        @"http://itunes.apple.com/us/rss/topsongs/limit=%d/xml", count];

    NSURL *url = [NSURL URLWithString:requestString];

    // Set up the connection as normal
    NSURLRequest *req = [NSURLRequest requestWithURL:url];
    RSSChannel *channel = [[RSSChannel alloc] init];
```

```
    BNRConnection *connection = [[BNRConnection alloc] initWithRequest:req];
    [connection setCompletionBlock:block];
    [connection setXmlRootObject:channel];

    [connection start];
}
```

Now we have a store object that returns two different RSS feeds, and the controller doesn't have to know any of the details about how they are fetched. Let's give the user a way to switch between the two feeds. In `ListViewController.h`, declare a new enum for the feed types and an instance variable to hold on to the current feed type.

```
typedef enum {
    ListViewControllerRSSTypeBNR,
    ListViewControllerRSSTypeApple
} ListViewControllerRSSType;

@interface ListViewController : UITableViewController
{
    RSSChannel *channel;
    ListViewControllerRSSType rssType;
}
```

In `ListViewController.m`, add a **UISegmentedControl** to the `navigationItem` that will change the `rssType`.

```
- (id)initWithStyle:(UITableViewStyle)style
{
    self = [super initWithStyle:style];

    if (self) {
        UIBarButtonItem *bbi =
            [[UIBarButtonItem alloc] initWithTitle:@"Info"
                                             style:UIBarButtonItemStyleBordered
                                            target:self
                                            action:@selector(showInfo:)];

        [[self navigationItem] setRightBarButtonItem:bbi];

        UISegmentedControl *rssTypeControl =
                        [[UISegmentedControl alloc] initWithItems:
                            [NSArray arrayWithObjects:@"BNR", @"Apple", nil]];
        [rssTypeControl setSelectedSegmentIndex:0];
        [rssTypeControl setSegmentedControlStyle:UISegmentedControlStyleBar];
        [rssTypeControl addTarget:self
                    action:@selector(changeType:)
              forControlEvents:UIControlEventValueChanged];
        [[self navigationItem] setTitleView:rssTypeControl];

        [self fetchEntries];
    }

    return self;
}
```

Then, in `ListViewController.m`, implement **changeType:**, which will be sent to the **ListViewController** when the segmented control changes.

```
- (void)changeType:(id)sender
{
    rssType = [sender selectedSegmentIndex];
    [self fetchEntries];
}
```

Finally, modify **fetchEntries** in `ListViewController.m` to make the appropriate request to the store depending on the current `rssType`. To do this, move the completion block into a local variable, and then pass it to the right store request method. (The code that needs to be executed when either request finishes is the same.) This method will now look like this:

```
- (void)fetchEntries
{
    void (^completionBlock)(RSSChannel *obj, NSError *err) =
    ^(RSSChannel *obj, NSError *err) {
        // When the request completes, this block will be called.

        if (!err) {
            // If everything went ok, grab the channel object and
            // reload the table.
            channel = obj;
            [[self tableView] reloadData];
        } else {

            // If things went bad, show an alert view
            NSString *errorString = [NSString stringWithFormat:@"Fetch failed: %@",
                                    [err localizedDescription]];

            // Create and show an alert view with this error displayed
            UIAlertView *av = [[UIAlertView alloc] initWithTitle:@"Error"
                                                          message:errorString
                                                         delegate:nil
                                                cancelButtonTitle:@"OK"
                                                otherButtonTitles:nil];
            [av show];
        }
    };

    // Initiate the request...
    if (rssType == ListViewControllerRSSTypeBNR)
        [[BNRFeedStore sharedStore] fetchRSSFeedWithCompletion:completionBlock];
    else if (rssType == ListViewControllerRSSTypeApple)
        [[BNRFeedStore sharedStore] fetchTopSongs:10
                                   withCompletion:completionBlock];
}
```

Build and run the application. When the application launches, the BNR forums feed will load as the default. Tap the Apple item in the segmented control, and the top ten songs on iTunes will appear. Simple stuff, huh? (Tapping on a row while looking at Apple's RSS feed won't show anything in the detail view controller, but you will fix this in the next section.)

JSON Serialization

So far, Nerdfeed deals with XML data only. While XML is nice, it is becoming less popular, and a new data format called JSON (*JavaScript object notation*) is coming into favor. Like XML, JSON is a human-readable data interchange format. However, JSON is a lot more concise, so it takes up less memory and is faster to transfer across networks.

There is a class that deals with JSON in iOS called **NSJSONSerialization**. This class can take a chunk of JSON data and turn it into objects. It can also go in the other direction: take objects and turn them into JSON data. Using this class means you don't have to know with what JSON really looks like. (But, you should anyway, so be sure to read the section at the end of this chapter.)

The top songs RSS feed from Apple currently returns XML, but we can ask it to return JSON instead. Let's do this to get a chance to try out **NSJSONSerialization**. In BNRFeedStore.m, change the service URL to request JSON.

```
- (void)fetchTopSongs:(int)count
        withCompletion:(void (^)(RSSChannel *obj, NSError *err))block
{
    NSString *requestString = [NSString stringWithFormat:
        @"http://itunes.apple.com/us/rss/topsongs/limit=%d/xml", count];
    NSString *requestString = [NSString stringWithFormat:
        @"http://itunes.apple.com/us/rss/topsongs/limit=%d/json", count];

    NSURL *url = [NSURL URLWithString:requestString];
```

Of course, when this request completes, **BNRConnection** and **RSSChannel** will be pretty confused by this new type of data. Thus, we need to give **BNRConnection** the ability to determine whether the data is XML or JSON and parse it appropriately. We also need to teach **RSSChannel** and **RSSItem** how to gather their instance variables from JSON data.

First, here's how **NSJSONSerialization** works. When JSON data is received, you send the message **JSONObjectWithData:options:error:** to the class **NSJSONSerialization**. This method takes the data and returns either an **NSArray** or an **NSDictionary**. Within this dictionary or array, there will be strings, numbers, or more dictionaries and arrays.

Each dictionary returned from **NSJSONSerialization** is an instance of **NSDictionary** and represents a single object within the JSON data. For example, the channel in the feed will be represented by an **NSDictionary**. This **NSDictionary** will contain an array of **NSDictionary** instances, and each dictionary will be an individual **RSSItem**.

While having the JSON data parsed into these common data structures is really convenient, it is sometimes useful to move this data into the appropriate model objects. In Nerdfeed, the **ListViewController** knows how to present **RSSChannel** and **RSSItem**s but not **NSArray**s and **NSDictionary**s. To keep things simple, we want to transfer the data from the dictionaries and arrays into our own classes, **RSSChannel** and **RSSItem**.

To do this, we will create a new protocol. This protocol will have one method, **readFromJSONDictionary:**, that takes an **NSDictionary** as an argument. A class that conforms to this protocol will implement **readFromJSONDictionary:** to retrieve its instance variables from the dictionary. Both **RSSChannel** and **RSSItem** will conform to this protocol. Create a new file from the Objective-C protocol template (Figure 28.10).

Figure 28.10   Creating an Objective-C protocol

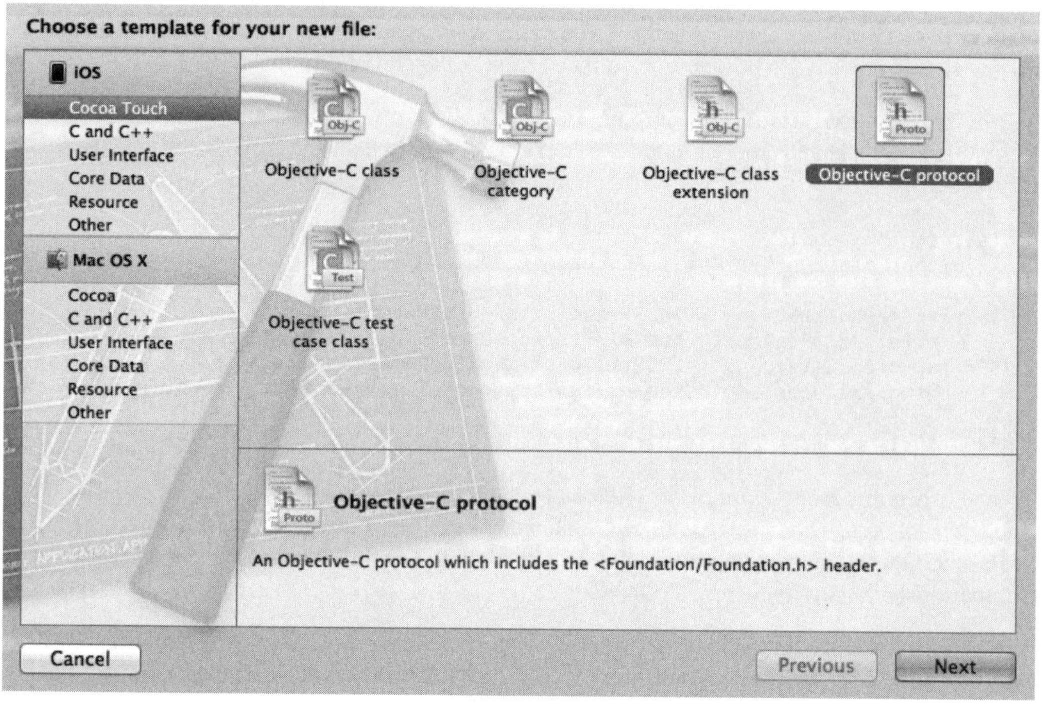

Name this protocol JSONSerializable. In JSONSerializable.h, add a method to the protocol.

```
@protocol JSONSerializable <NSObject>

- (void)readFromJSONDictionary:(NSDictionary *)d;

@end
```

In a moment, you will write the code so that both **RSSChannel** and **RSSItem** conform to this protocol. Right now, though, let's improve **BNRConnection** so that it can parse JSON data and pass the result to its root object. In BNRConnection.h, import the file JSONSerializable.h.

```
#import "JSONSerializable.h"
```

Then, add a new property to this class.

```
@property (nonatomic, strong) id <NSXMLParserDelegate> xmlRootObject;

@property (nonatomic, strong) id <JSONSerializable> jsonRootObject;

- (void)start;
```

When the **BNRFeedStore** creates a **BNRConnection**, it will either supply a jsonRootObject or an xmlRootObject to the connection, depending on the type of data it expects back from the server. When there is a jsonRootObject, the connection will parse the JSON data and hand the result off to the root object (instead of using **NSXMLParser**). In BNRConnection.m, synthesize this new property and modify the implementation of **connectionDidFinishLoading:**.

```
@synthesize jsonRootObject;

- (void)connectionDidFinishLoading:(NSURLConnection *)connection
{
    id rootObject = nil;
    if ([self xmlRootObject]) {
        NSXMLParser *parser = [[NSXMLParser alloc] initWithData:container];
        [parser setDelegate:[self xmlRootObject]];
        [parser parse];

        rootObject = [self xmlRootObject];
    } else if ([self jsonRootObject]) {
        // Turn JSON data into basic model objects
        NSDictionary *d = [NSJSONSerialization JSONObjectWithData:container
                                                          options:0
                                                            error:nil];

        // Have the root object construct itself from basic model objects
        [[self jsonRootObject] readFromJSONDictionary:d];

        rootObject = [self jsonRootObject];
    }

    if ([self completionBlock])
        [self completionBlock]([self xmlRootObject], nil);
        [self completionBlock](rootObject, nil);

    [sharedConnectionList removeObject:self];
}
```

In BNRFeedStore.m, change the method **fetchTopSongs:withCompletion:** so that it supplies a jsonRootObject to the connection instead of an xmlRootObject.

```
BNRConnection *connection = [[BNRConnection alloc] initWithRequest:req];
[connection setCompletionBlock:block];

[connection setXmlRootObject:channel];
[connection setJsonRootObject:channel];

[connection start];
```

You can build the application to check for syntax errors. You will see one warning in BNRFeedStore.m that says **RSSChannel** is incompatible with **setJsonRootObject:**. That's because **RSSChannel** doesn't yet conform to JSONSerializable.

In RSSChannel.h, import this file and declare that **RSSChannel** conforms to this protocol.

#import "JSONSerializable.h"

@interface RSSChannel : NSObject <NSXMLParserDelegate, **JSONSerializable**>

Now that **RSSChannel** and **RSSItem** conform to JSONSerializable, once the connection completes, they will pull their data from the dictionary when sent **readFromJSONDictionary:**.

The implementation of **readFromJSONDictionary:** should take values from the dictionary argument and move them into the instance variables of the **RSSChannel**. The channel needs to grab the title and all of the entries from the channel. In RSSChannel.m, implement this method to do just that.

```
- (void)readFromJSONDictionary:(NSDictionary *)d
{
    // The top-level object contains a "feed" object, which is the channel.
    NSDictionary *feed = [d objectForKey:@"feed"];

    // The feed has a title property, make this the title of our channel.
    [self setTitle:[[feed objectForKey:@"title"] objectForKey:@"label"]];

    // The feed also has an array of entries, for each one, make a new RSSItem.
    NSArray *entries = [feed objectForKey:@"entry"];
    for (NSDictionary *entry in entries) {
        RSSItem *i = [[RSSItem alloc] init];

        // Pass the entry dictionary to the item so it can grab its ivars
        [i readFromJSONDictionary:entry];

        [items addObject:i];
    }
}
```

Do the same thing in RSSItem.h.

```
#import "JSONSerializable.h"
```

```
@interface RSSItem : NSObject <NSXMLParserDelegate, JSONSerializable>
```

And in RSSItem.m, grab the title and link from the entry dictionary.

```
- (void)readFromJSONDictionary:(NSDictionary *)d
{
    [self setTitle:[[d objectForKey:@"title"] objectForKey:@"label"]];

    // Inside each entry is an array of links, each has an attribute object
    NSArray *links = [d objectForKey:@"link"];
    if ([links count] > 1) {
        NSDictionary *sampleDict = [[links objectAtIndex:1]
                                        objectForKey:@"attributes"];

        // The href of an attribute object is the URL for the sample audio file
        [self setLink:[sampleDict objectForKey:@"href"]];
    }
}
```

You can now build and run the application. Once it starts running, flip to Apple's RSS feed. Voilà! Now that the **RSSItem** is grabbing the link, you can tap an entry in the table view and listen to a sample clip. (The debugger will spit out a lot of angry nonsense about not finding functions or frameworks, but after a moment, it will shut up, and the clip will play.)

Notice that, in MVCS (and in MVC, too), model objects are responsible for constructing themselves given a stream of data. For example, **RSSChannel** conforms to both NSXMLParserDelegate and JSONSerializable – it knows how to pack and unpack itself from XML and JSON data. Also, think about **BNRItem** instances in Homepwner: they implemented the methods from NSCoding, so that they could be written to disk.

A model object, then, provides the instructions on how it is to be transferred into and out of different formats. Model objects do this so that when a store object transfers them to or from an external source, the store doesn't need to know the details of every kind of model object in an application. Instead, each model object can conform to a protocol that says, "Here are the formats I know how to be in," and the store triggers the transfer into or out of those data formats.

More on Store Objects

Let's recap what we know about stores so far. A store object handles the details of interfacing with an external source. The complicated request logic required to interact with these sources becomes the responsibility of the store so that the controller can focus on the flow of the application. We've really seen two types of stores: synchronous and asynchronous. **BNRItemStore** and **BNRImageStore** were examples of synchronous stores: their work could be finished immediately, and they could return a value from a request right away.

CLLocationManager and **BNRFeedStore** are examples of asynchronous stores: their work takes awhile to finish. With asynchronous stores, you have to supply callbacks for the controller to receive a response. Asynchronous stores are a bit more difficult to write, but we've found ways of reducing that difficulty, such as using helpers objects like **BNRConnection**.

The cool thing about asynchronous stores is that even though a lot of objects are doing a lot of work to process a request, the flow of the request and its response are in one place in the controller. This gives us the benefit of code that's easy to read and also easy to modify. As an example, let's add a **UIActivityIndicatorView** to the **ListViewController** when a request is being made. In ListViewController.m, update **fetchEntries**.

```
- (void)fetchEntries
{
    // Get ahold of the segmented control that is currently in the title view
    UIView *currentTitleView = [[self navigationItem] titleView];

    // Create a activity indicator and start it spinning in the nav bar
    UIActivityIndicatorView *aiView = [[UIActivityIndicatorView alloc]
                initWithActivityIndicatorStyle:UIActivityIndicatorViewStyleWhite];
    [[self navigationItem] setTitleView:aiView];
    [aiView startAnimating];

    void (^completionBlock)(RSSChannel *obj, NSError *err) =
    ^(RSSChannel *obj, NSError *err) {

        // When the request completes - success or failure - replace the activity
        // indicator with the segmented control
        [[self navigationItem] setTitleView:currentTitleView];


        if (!err) {
```

Build and run the application. When you change between feeds, you will see the activity indicator spin briefly while the request is processing. Also, notice how the block takes ownership of the **UISegmentedControl** that was the titleView of the navigation item so that it can put it back into the navigation item once the request has completed. Pretty neat, huh?

We've done a lot of work so far in this chapter. It may seem like overkill since we already had a working application, but as the application becomes larger in the next two chapters, the changes we've made will really pay off. Consider already how easy it was to add support for JSON data – we didn't even touch **ListViewController**! In the next chapter, we'll do a bit more work with **BNRFeedStore** and then explain some best practices and guidelines for using store objects.

Bronze Challenge: UI for Song Count

Add an interface element somewhere that allows the user to change the number of songs pulled from the top songs service.

Mega-Gold Challenge: Another Web Service

We provide our class schedule in JSON format at `http://www.bignerdranch.com/json/schedule`. Create an entirely new application to present the class schedule and details about each class using MVCS.

For the More Curious: JSON Data

JSON is a data interchange format – a way of describing data so it can be transferred to another system easily. It has a really concise and easy to understand syntax. First, let's think about why we need to transfer data. An application has some model objects that represent things – like items in an RSS feed. It would make sense that this application would want to share these items with another device.

However, let's say that other device is an Android phone (and, in our imaginary world, let's pretend this Android phone's battery is not drained dry). We can't just package up an Objective-C **RSSItem** object and send it to the Android device. We need an agreed-upon format that both systems understand. Both Java (the language Android is programmed in) and Objective-C have a concept of objects, and both platforms have the ideas of arrays, strings, and numbers. JSON reduces data down to this very pure format of objects, arrays, strings and numbers, so the two platforms can share data.

In JSON, there is a syntax for each of these types. Objects are represented by curly brackets. Inside an object can be a number of members, each of which is a string, number, array, or another object. Each member has a name. Here is an example of an object that has two members, one a string, the other a number.

```
{
    "name":"Joe Conway",
    "age":28
}
```

When this JSON object is parsed by **NSJSONSerialization**, it is turned into an **NSDictionary**. That dictionary has two key-value pairs: name which is Joe Conway and age which is 28. On another platform, this object would be represented in some other way, but on iOS, it is a dictionary because that is what makes the most sense. Additionally, all keys within the dictionary will be instances of **NSString**. The string value is also an instance of **NSString**, and the number value is an instance of **NSNumber**.

An array is described by using square brackets in JSON. It can contain objects, strings, numbers, and more arrays. Here is an example of an array that contains two objects:

```
[
    {
        "name":"Joe Conway",
        "age":28
    },
    {
        "name":"Aaron Hillegass",
        "age":87
    }
]
```

When this JSON is parsed, you will get an **NSArray** containing two **NSDictionary** instances. Each **NSDictionary** will have two key-value pairs. (One of those key-value pairs is going to get me fired...)

JSON data is really good at describing a tree of objects – that is, an object that has references to more objects, and each of those have references to more objects. This means when you deserialize JSON data, you are left with a lot of interconnected objects. (We call these interconnected objects an *object graph*.) The only real requirement of JSON – other than staying within the syntax – is that the top-level entry be either an object or an array. Thus, you will only ever get back an **NSDictionary** or **NSArray** from **NSJSONSerialization**.

29

Advanced MVCS

In this chapter, we're going to add to Nerdfeed by adding support for caching and a way to indicate to users which posts have already been read.

Caching the RSS Feed

Each time the user fetches the Apple top songs RSS feed, the **BNRFeedStore** makes a web service request to Apple's server. However, it takes time and battery power to make these requests. The data in this feed doesn't change very often, either. Therefore, it doesn't make much sense to make the resource-consuming request over and over again.

Instead, the store should save the results of the last request made. If the user tries to reload the feed within five minutes, the store won't bother making the request and will just return the saved results. This process is known as *caching*.

Generally speaking, a cache is data that has been saved in another place where it is easier to retrieve. For example, it is easier to retrieve data from the local filesystem than from a server somewhere out in Internet land. In Nerdfeed, the cache will be the **RSSChannel** and the **RSSItem**s that represent the top ten songs. We will store this cache on the filesystem, so **RSSChannel** and **RSSItem** must be able to be saved and loaded.

For saving and loading these objects, it makes sense to use archiving instead of Core Data for three reasons. First, we won't have that many records to save and load (just ten). Second, we don't have a lot of relationships between objects (just a channel containing an array of items). Third, archiving is easier to implement.

Before you can write the code to save and load the cache, **RSSChannel** and **RSSItem** have to conform to NSCoding. In RSSChannel.h, declare that this class conforms to NSCoding.

```
@interface RSSChannel : NSObject
            <NSXMLParserDelegate, JSONSerializable, NSCoding>
```

In RSSChannel.m, implement the two NSCoding methods.

```
- (void)encodeWithCoder:(NSCoder *)aCoder
{
    [aCoder encodeObject:items forKey:@"items"];
    [aCoder encodeObject:title forKey:@"title"];
    [aCoder encodeObject:infoString forKey:@"infoString"];
}
```

```
- (id)initWithCoder:(NSCoder *)aDecoder
{
    self = [super init];
    if (self) {
        items = [aDecoder decodeObjectForKey:@"items"];
        [self setInfoString:[aDecoder decodeObjectForKey:@"infoString"]];
        [self setTitle:[aDecoder decodeObjectForKey:@"title"]];
    }
    return self;
}
```

Do the same thing in RSSItem.h.

```
@interface RSSItem : NSObject
    <NSXMLParserDelegate, JSONSerializable, NSCoding>
```

And in RSSItem.m.

```
- (void)encodeWithCoder:(NSCoder *)aCoder
{
    [aCoder encodeObject:title forKey:@"title"];
    [aCoder encodeObject:link forKey:@"link"];
}
```

```
- (id)initWithCoder:(NSCoder *)aDecoder
{
    self = [super init];
    if (self) {
        [self setTitle:[aDecoder decodeObjectForKey:@"title"]];
        [self setLink:[aDecoder decodeObjectForKey:@"link"]];
    }
    return self;
}
```

Now that channels and items can be written to the filesystem and loaded back into the application, let's figure out when and how this should happen. Typically when you cache something, you use an all-or-nothing approach: a request either returns all brand-new data or all cached data. This approach makes sense for Apple's Top Songs RSS feed because the amount of total data is small. Because the data isn't updated very often, we will return cached data to the controller unless that data is more than five minutes old.

Caching is another task for the store rather than the controller. The controller doesn't have to know the details or even whether it is getting cached or new data. **ListViewController** will ask for the RSS feed, and the **BNRFeedStore** will return the cached data if it is fresh. Otherwise, it will make the request to Apple's server for fresh data (Figure 29.1).

Figure 29.1 Cache flow

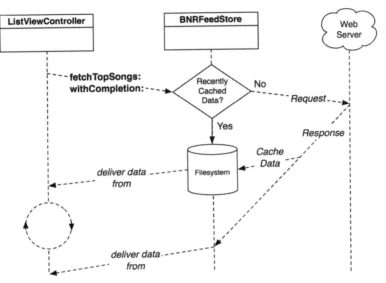

For **BNRFeedStore** to make that choice, it needs to know when the **RSSChannel** was last cached. In BNRFeedStore.h, add a new property.

```
@property (nonatomic, strong) NSDate *topSongsCacheDate;
```

We need this date to persist between runs of the application, so it needs to be stored on the filesystem. Since this is just a little bit of data, we won't create a separate file for it. Instead, we'll just put it in **NSUserDefaults**.

To do this, you have to write your own implementations of topSongsCacheDate's accessor methods instead of synthesizing the property. In BNRFeedStore.m, implement the accessor methods to access the preferences file.

```
- (void)setTopSongsCacheDate:(NSDate *)topSongsCacheDate
{
    [[NSUserDefaults standardUserDefaults] setObject:topSongsCacheDate
                                      forKey:@"topSongsCacheDate"];
}

- (NSDate *)topSongsCacheDate
{
    return [[NSUserDefaults standardUserDefaults]
                  objectForKey:@"topSongsCacheDate"];
}
```

Notice that we put this code in the store. This is because, once again, you are interacting with an external source (the preferences file on the filesystem). Additionally, this code is related to fetching the RSS feed.

From outside the store, topSongsCacheDate looks like a standard property – a set of methods that access an instance variable. That's good. The store does all of this interesting stuff while making its job look easy. Stores are kind of like Olympic athletes – you don't see the lifetime of hard work; you just see a few seconds of effortless speed.

For a store to be able to return the cached **RSSChannel**, it first needs to cache it. Every time the store fetches the top songs feed, we want it to save the channel and its items, as well as note the time they were cached. However, the way **BNRFeedStore** is set up right now, the only code that is executed when a request completes is the block supplied by **ListViewController**. This means the **BNRFeedStore** doesn't know when the request finishes, so it doesn't have a chance to cache the data. Thus, the store needs to add a callback to the **BNRConnection** that handles the request.

We already have a way to do this: the store can create its own completion block for the **BNRConnection** to execute. But alas, that spot is already reserved for the **ListViewController**'s completion block. Fortunately, you can execute a block inside another block. So we're going to have the completion block for the store run its code (which will take care of the caching) and then execute the completion block from the controller. This one-two punch of blocks will become the completionBlock for the **BNRConnection**.

In BNRFeedStore.m, update **fetchTopSongs:withCompletion:**.

```
- (void)fetchTopSongs:(int)count
        withCompletion:(void (^)(RSSChannel *obj, NSError *err))block
{
    // Construct the cache path
    NSString *cachePath =
        [NSSearchPathForDirectoriesInDomains(NSCachesDirectory,
                                             NSUserDomainMask,
                                             YES) objectAtIndex:0];
    cachePath = [cachePath stringByAppendingPathComponent:@"apple.archive"];

    NSString *requestString = [NSString stringWithFormat:
                @"http://itunes.apple.com/us/rss/topsongs/limit=%d/json", count];
    NSURL *url = [NSURL URLWithString:requestString];

    NSURLRequest *req = [NSURLRequest requestWithURL:url];
    RSSChannel *channel = [[RSSChannel alloc] init];

    BNRConnection *connection = [[BNRConnection alloc] initWithRequest:req];

    [connection setCompletionBlock:block];

    [connection setCompletionBlock:^(RSSChannel *obj, NSError *err) {
        // This is the store's completion code:
        // If everything went smoothly, save the channel to disk and set cache date
        if (!err) {
            [self setTopSongsCacheDate:[NSDate date]];
            [NSKeyedArchiver archiveRootObject:obj toFile:cachePath];
        }

        // This is the controller's completion code:
        block(obj, err);
    }];
    [connection setJsonRootObject:channel];

    [connection start];
}
```

You can build and run the application now. While Nerdfeed can't read the cache yet, it is able to archive the channel and note the date after you select the Apple feed. You can verify this by running the application on the simulator and locating the application's directory in the simulator's Application Support directory. (If you forgot how, flip back to Chapter 14 and the section called

"NSKeyedArchiver and NSKeyedUnarchiver".) You can check the preferences file in Library/ Preferences/ for the topSongsCacheDate key and look for the archive in Library/Caches/.

The store now needs to return the cached data if it is still fresh. It should do this without letting the controller know it is getting cached data – after all, the controller doesn't really care; it just wants the top ten songs. In BNRFeedStore.m, update **fetchTopSongs:withCompletion:** to do this.

```
- (void)fetchTopSongs:(int)count
       withCompletion:(void (^)(RSSChannel *obj, NSError *err))block
{
    NSString *cachePath =
        [NSSearchPathForDirectoriesInDomains(NSCachesDirectory,
                                             NSUserDomainMask,
                                             YES) objectAtIndex:0];
    cachePath = [cachePath stringByAppendingPathComponent:@"apple.archive"];

    // Make sure we have cached at least once before by checking to see
    // if this date exists!
    NSDate *tscDate = [self topSongsCacheDate];
    if (tscDate) {
        // How old is the cache?
        NSTimeInterval cacheAge = [tscDate timeIntervalSinceNow];

        if (cacheAge > -300.0) {
            // If it is less than 300 seconds (5 minutes) old, return cache
            // in completion block
            NSLog(@"Reading cache!");

            RSSChannel *cachedChannel = [NSKeyedUnarchiver
                                         unarchiveObjectWithFile:cachePath];
            if (cachedChannel) {
                // Execute the controller's completion block to reload its table
                block(cachedChannel, nil);

                // Don't need to make the request, just get out of this method
                return;
            }
        }
    }

    NSString *requestString = [NSString stringWithFormat:
            @"http://itunes.apple.com/us/rss/topsongs/limit=%d/json", count];
```

Build and run the application. Select the Apple item on the segmented control and notice the console says it is reading from the cache. The list will appear immediately, and no request will be made – you won't see the activity indicator at all when switching to the Apple feed. (You can check again in five minutes and see that the feed is indeed fetched again. Or delete the application and run it again.)

There is a slight issue here, although you can't see it. When **ListViewController** makes this request, it expects some time to pass before the request is completed – this is why it supplies a callback block to be executed when the request is finished. When the store decides to return cached data, the callback is executed immediately. This can cause an issue if the **ListViewController** has more code in **fetchEntries** after it makes the request because it expects that code to be executed before the completion block.

Let's put in a two log statements in ListViewController.m to confirm this behavior.

```
- (void)fetchEntries
{
    UIView *currentTitleView = [[self navigationItem] titleView];
    UIActivityIndicatorView *aiView = [[UIActivityIndicatorView alloc]
            initWithActivityIndicatorStyle:UIActivityIndicatorViewStyleWhite];
    [[self navigationItem] setTitleView:aiView];
    [aiView startAnimating];

    void (^completionBlock)(id obj, NSError *err) =
    ^(RSSChannel *obj, NSError *err) {
        NSLog(@"Completion block called!");

        [[self navigationItem] setTitleView:currentTitleView];

        if (!err) {
            channel = obj;
            [[self tableView] reloadData];
        } else {
            NSString *errorString = [NSString stringWithFormat:@"Fetch failed: %@",
                                    [err localizedDescription]];
            UIAlertView *av = [[UIAlertView alloc] initWithTitle:@"Error"
                                                         message:errorString
                                                        delegate:nil
                                               cancelButtonTitle:@"OK"
                                               otherButtonTitles:nil];
            [av show];
        }
    };

    if (rssType == ListViewControllerRSSTypeBNR)
        [[BNRFeedStore sharedStore] fetchRSSFeedWithCompletion:completionBlock];
    else if (rssType == ListViewControllerRSSTypeApple)
        [[BNRFeedStore sharedStore] fetchTopSongs:10
                                  withCompletion:completionBlock];

    NSLog(@"Executing code at the end of fetchEntries");
}
```

Build and run the application and tap on the Apple segment. Notice that Completion block called!
shows up in the console before the log statement at the end of **fetchEntries** when the data is cached.
If the cache is out of date and fetched again, the order of the statements is reversed. The store should
really be consistent about when it executes the callback for the request. In BNRFeedStore.m, add the
following code to **fetchTopSongs:withCompletion:**.

```
- (void)fetchTopSongs:(int)count
       withCompletion:(void (^)(RSSChannel *obj, NSError *err))block
{
    NSString *cachePath =
        [NSSearchPathForDirectoriesInDomains(NSCachesDirectory,
                                             NSUserDomainMask,
                                             YES) objectAtIndex:0];
    cachePath = [cachePath stringByAppendingPathComponent:@"apple.archive"];

    NSDate *tscDate = [self topSongsCacheDate];
    if (tscDate) {
        NSTimeInterval cacheAge = [tscDate timeIntervalSinceNow];

        if (cacheAge > -300.0) {
            NSLog(@"Reading cache!");
```

```
RSSChannel *cachedChannel = [NSKeyedUnarchiver
    unarchiveObjectWithFile:cachePath];

if (cachedChannel) {
    [[NSOperationQueue mainQueue] addOperationWithBlock:^{
        block(cachedChannel, nil);
    }];
    return;
}
    }
}
```

Now when you build and run the application, the callback is always executed after **fetchEntries** completes because the completion block is inserted as the next event in the run loop instead of being called immediately.

Advanced Caching

The caching mechanism for Apple's top songs feed is pretty simple: each time a new feed is fetched, it completely replaces the old feed in the cache. This makes sense for this particular feed – we aren't maintaining a history of top songs, just showing the current top ten.

The Big Nerd Ranch forum feed is a little different. Every time a new feed is fetched, you are getting the last day's worth of posts. If we cached this feed in the same way as Apple's feed, we wouldn't be able to maintain a history. Also, the forum feed can be pretty large since we get a lot of posts in a day, so it takes a few moments to load the feed. It would be better for the user if they could see a list of cached posts as soon as they open the application or switch back to the BNR feed. When new posts become available, they would be added to the top of the list.

Figure 29.2   Cache and update flow

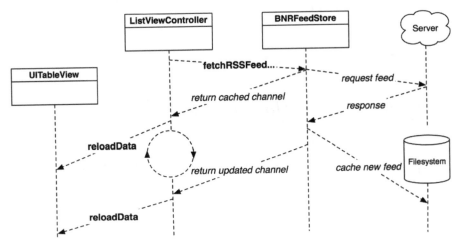

We can accomplish this task by implementing caching for the Big Nerd Ranch forum feed in a different way than we did for the Apple feed. For BNR's feed, each time a controller requests that the store fetch new items, the store will immediately return the cache and then ask the server for more items. When the items come back from the server, the store will merge the new items into its cached **RSSChannel**. Then, the store will inform the controller that the new items have been fetched so that the interface can be updated. This interaction is shown in Figure 29.2.

To pull this off, we need to do three things:

- An **RSSChannel** needs to be able to append new **RSSItem**s to its items array and, in doing so, make sure that there are no duplicates and that the items are ordered by date.

- The method **fetchRSSFeedWithCompletion:** needs to return the cached channel immediately and an updated channel when the request completes.

- The **ListViewController** needs to appropriately handle updating its views when it receives the cached channel immediately and the updated channel later.

Each of these steps requires a few small steps to achieve. We will start by teaching the **RSSChannel** to filter new items into its existing items array. First, declare a new method in RSSChannel.h.

```
- (void)addItemsFromChannel:(RSSChannel *)otherChannel;
```

When the store is asked to fetch the RSS feed, we want it to unarchive the cached channel from disk, return it, and ask the server for another **RSSChannel** instance that has the new items in it. When the request completes, the cached channel should be sent **addItemsFromChannel:** with the new channel as an argument. So we want this method to add items from the new channel to the existing channel. One little problem: because the RSS feed returns all items from the last 24 hours, if you refresh the feed more than once a day, you will get duplicates.

The channel, then, has to determine whether it already has an item before adding it to its list. To do this, instances of **RSSItem** have to be checked for equality. Every **NSObject** subclass implements a method named **isEqual:** for this purpose. In RSSItem.m, override this method to make two **RSSItem**s equivalent if they have the same link.

```
- (BOOL)isEqual:(id)object
{
    // Make sure we are comparing an RSSItem!
    if (![object isKindOfClass:[RSSItem class]])
        return NO;

    // Now only return YES if the links are equal.
    return [[self link] isEqual:[object link]];
}
```

In RSSChannel.m, begin implementing **addItemsFromChannel:** so that it adds all items from another channel if there are no duplicates.

```
- (void)addItemsFromChannel:(RSSChannel *)otherChannel
{
    for (RSSItem *i in [otherChannel items]) {

        // If self's items does not contain this item, add it
        if (![[self items] containsObject:i])
            [[self items] addObject:i];
    }
}
```

Even though you do not use **RSSItem**'s **isEqual:** method explicitly, **NSArray**'s **containsObject:** does. The **containsObject:** method sends **isEqual:** to every object within the array, and if one responds YES, then **containsObject:** also returns YES. By inverting the return value of **containsObject:**, **addItemsFromChannel:** will only add an item if it doesn't already have it.

Next, the **RSSChannel** needs to preserve the order of its items. The order of items should be dictated by when the item was posted – the newer an item is, the higher it should appear on the list. The post date of an item is available in the RSS feed, but **RSSItem** doesn't currently collect that data. Let's change that. In RSSItem.h, declare a new property to hold the post date.

```
@property (nonatomic, strong) NSDate *publicationDate;
```

In RSSItem.m, synthesize this property and have the XML parsing methods seek out the appropriate element and put it into this property.

```
@synthesize publicationDate;

- (void)parser:(NSXMLParser *)parser
  didStartElement:(NSString *)elementName
    namespaceURI:(NSString *)namespaceURI
   qualifiedName:(NSString *)qualifiedName
      attributes:(NSDictionary *)attributeDict
{
    if ([elementName isEqual:@"title"]) {
        currentString = [[NSMutableString alloc] init];
        [self setTitle:currentString];
    }
    else if ([elementName isEqual:@"link"]) {
        currentString = [[NSMutableString alloc] init];
        [self setLink:currentString];
    } else if ([elementName isEqualToString:@"pubDate"]) {
        // Create the string, but do not put it into an ivar yet
        currentString = [[NSMutableString alloc] init];
    }
}

- (void)parser:(NSXMLParser *)parser
 didEndElement:(NSString *)elementName
  namespaceURI:(NSString *)namespaceURI
 qualifiedName:(NSString *)qName
{
    // If the pubDate ends, use a date formatter to turn it into an NSDate
    if ([elementName isEqualToString:@"pubDate"]) {
        static NSDateFormatter *dateFormatter = nil;
        if (!dateFormatter) {
            dateFormatter = [[NSDateFormatter alloc] init];
            [dateFormatter setDateFormat:@"EEE, dd MMM yyyy HH:mm:ss z"];
        }
        [self setPublicationDate:[dateFormatter dateFromString:currentString]];
    }

    currentString = nil;

    if ([elementName isEqual:@"item"]
    || [elementName isEqual:@"entry"]) {
        [parser setDelegate:parentParserDelegate];
    }
}
```

(Wondering where we are pulling these crazy date formats from? The specification for the date format string is described at http://unicode.org/reports/tr35/tr35-6.html#Date_Format_Patterns. You can log the pubDate to the console to see its format.)

Of course, the publicationDate is something that needs to be cached with each **RSSItem** so that we can preserve the order of items the next time the application is run. Add code to the NSCoding methods in RSSItem.m to do this.

```
- (void)encodeWithCoder:(NSCoder *)aCoder
{
    [aCoder encodeObject:title forKey:@"title"];
    [aCoder encodeObject:link forKey:@"link"];
    [aCoder encodeObject:publicationDate forKey:@"publicationDate"];
}

- (id)initWithCoder:(NSCoder *)aDecoder
{
    self = [super init];
    if (self) {
        [self setTitle:[aDecoder decodeObjectForKey:@"title"]];
        [self setLink:[aDecoder decodeObjectForKey:@"link"]];
        [self setPublicationDate:[aDecoder decodeObjectForKey:@"publicationDate"]];
    }
    return self;
}
```

Now an **RSSItem** can be ordered amongst its peers by publication date. In RSSChannel.m, modify **addItemsFromChannel:** to reorder its items.

```
- (void)addItemsFromChannel:(RSSChannel *)otherChannel
{
    for (RSSItem *i in [otherChannel items]) {
        if (![[self items] containsObject:i])
            [[self items] addObject:i];
    }

    // Sort the array of items by publication date
    [[self items] sortUsingComparator:^NSComparisonResult(id obj1, id obj2) {
        return [[obj2 publicationDate] compare:[obj1 publicationDate]];
    }];
}
```

The method **sortUsingComparator:** is a nifty tool for sorting an **NSMutableArray**. This method takes a block that takes two object pointers as an argument and returns an NSComparisonResult. (An NSComparisonResult is a data type whose value can tell us the sorted order of two objects.) When this method executes, it compares each item in the array by passing two of them at a time as arguments to the supplied block. The block returns which of the two objects is ordered before the other as an NSComparisonResult.

The **NSDate** method **compare:** compares two **NSDate** instances and returns the one that is ordered before the other as an NSComparisonResult. The return value of **compare:** is the return value of the comparator block.

Now that a channel can update its items array when given a new channel, let's have the store take advantage of this. In BNRFeedStore.h, change the return type of **fetchRSSFeedWithCompletion:**.

~~- (void)fetchRSSFeedWithCompletion:(void (^)(RSSChannel *obj, NSError *err))block~~

```
- (RSSChannel *)fetchRSSFeedWithCompletion:
                    (void (^)(RSSChannel *obj, NSError *err))block;
```

In BNRFeedStore.m, update the completion block for **fetchRSSFeedWithCompletion:** to merge the
incoming channel with the existing channel and cache it.

```
- (void)fetchRSSFeedWithCompletion:(void (^)(RSSChannel *obj, NSError *err))block
- (RSSChannel *)fetchRSSFeedWithCompletion:
                    (void (^)(RSSChannel *obj, NSError *err))block
{
    NSURL *url = [NSURL URLWithString:@"http://forums.bignerdranch.com/"
                  @"smartfeed.php?limit=1_DAY&sort_by=standard"
                  @"&feed_type=RSS2.0&feed_style=COMPACT"];

    NSURLRequest *req = [NSURLRequest requestWithURL:url];
    RSSChannel *channel = [[RSSChannel alloc] init];
    BNRConnection *connection = [[BNRConnection alloc] initWithRequest:req];
    [connection setCompletionBlock:block];

    NSString *cachePath =
        [NSSearchPathForDirectoriesInDomains(NSCachesDirectory,
                                 NSUserDomainMask,
                                 YES) objectAtIndex:0];

    cachePath = [cachePath stringByAppendingPathComponent:@"nerd.archive"];

    // Load the cached channel
    RSSChannel *cachedChannel =
                [NSKeyedUnarchiver unarchiveObjectWithFile:cachePath];

    // If one hasn't already been cached, create a blank one to fill up
    if (!cachedChannel)
        cachedChannel = [[RSSChannel alloc] init];

    [connection setCompletionBlock:^(RSSChannel *obj, NSError *err) {
        // This is the store's callback code
        if (!err) {
            [cachedChannel addItemsFromChannel:obj];
            [NSKeyedArchiver archiveRootObject:cachedChannel
                                        toFile:cachePath];
        }

        // This is the controller's callback code
        block(cachedChannel, err);
    }];

    [connection setXmlRootObject:channel];
    [connection start];

    return cachedChannel;
}
```

Let's follow the logic of this method. When the request is made, the cached **RSSChannel** is loaded from
the filesystem. A second, empty instance of **RSSChannel** is set as the xmlRootObject of the connection.
When the service completes, the xmlRootObject will contain the new items from the server. This
channel is then merged into the existing cachedChannel (Figure 29.3). The merged channel is cached
and passed to the controller via its completion block. At the end of this method, the cached channel
(before being merged) is returned to the controller.

Figure 29.3   Merging RSSChannels

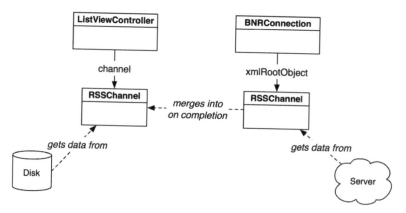

Now you can update **fetchEntries** in ListViewController.m to grab the channel from the return value of **fetchRSSFeedWithCompletion:** and update the table right away.

```
if (rssType == ListViewControllerRSSTypeBNR) {
    channel = [[BNRFeedStore sharedStore]
                  fetchRSSFeedWithCompletion:completionBlock];
    [[self tableView] reloadData];
} else if (rssType == ListViewControllerRSSTypeApple)
    [[BNRFeedStore sharedStore] fetchTopSongs:10 withCompletion:completionBlock];
```

Build and run the application and then load the BNR feed. Go to the forums and create a new post. (You can create a test post in the forum for this chapter and delete it later.) Then, switch to the Apple feed and back to the BNR feed to force a reload. You will notice that your list remains intact, and after the activity indicator finishes spinning, your post will appear at the top of the list!

Now this is all fine and dandy, but there is still a problem. Right now, the store returns an instance of **RSSChannel** to the **ListViewController** immediately. In the store's completion block, the other **RSSChannel** merges its items into the *very same* **RSSChannel** that was returned to the **ListViewController**. This is bad. A store shouldn't update values it has already given to a controller without at least informing the controller of the changes and giving the controller the decision to act on those changes. Case in point: there is no way for the **ListViewController** to know which items are new by the time its completion block is called because its channel has already been updated, so it can't indicate to the user which items are new.

To prevent this, we need a third **RSSChannel** instance (Figure 29.4). The first **RSSChannel** we use is an empty one for reading from the server, and the second is the cached one for returning to the controller immediately. The third will begin as a carbon-copy of the one returned to the **ListViewController** – the one that was in the cache. However, when the request completes, this carbon-copy will be merged with the new items, while the one the **ListViewController** has will not. The store will then give the merged channel to the **ListViewController**, and the **ListViewController** will compare it to the channel it already has. The **ListViewController** will then animate the new items into the table view, which will give the user a better idea of what just happened.

Figure 29.4 RSSChannels used by the store

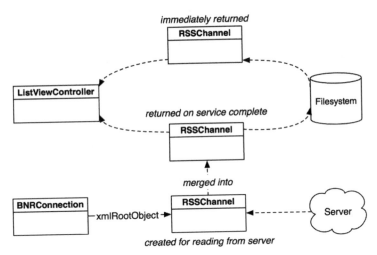

One approach to create this carbon-copy would be to load the **RSSChannel** from the filesystem twice. However, this approach is lame: there is a performance penalty for loading from the disk, and there would be two copies of each **RSSItem** in memory (Figure 29.5). While it's okay to have a few instances of **RSSChannel** (it's a pretty small object), it's not okay to have double the **RSSItem**s and suffer through loading the file twice.

Figure 29.5 Duplicate RSSItems in memory

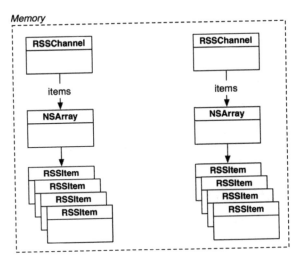

NSCopying

Fortunately, there is an easier solution. **RSSChannel** can conform to NSCopying. When a class conforms to this protocol, you can create copies of its instances by sending the message **copy** to an existing instance. Copying a channel will mean that its title, infoString, and items array are copied into a new instance of **RSSChannel**.

Now, you may be thinking, "If you copy the items array, aren't you just duplicating all of the **RSSItems** in it?" Nope. An array only keeps references to the objects that it contains, so by copying an array, you are just copying the addresses of each object into the new array, not the objects themselves (Figure 29.6).

Figure 29.6   Copying an RSSChannel

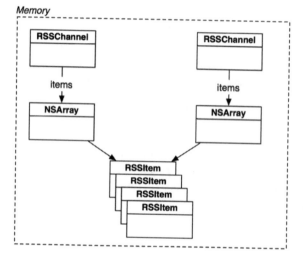

In RSSChannel.h, declare that this class conforms to NSCopying.

```
@interface RSSChannel : NSObject
    <NSXMLParserDelegate, JSONSerializable, NSCoding, NSCopying>
```

This protocol only has one method – **copyWithZone:**. When an object is sent **copy**, it really calls **copyWithZone:** and returns a new instance with the same values as the copied instance. (**copyWithZone:** is a relic like **allocWithZone:**. Zones don't matter anymore – you implement the **withZone:** methods in your classes, but send messages without the **withZone:** part.)

In RSSChannel.m, implement **copyWithZone:** to return a new instance of **RSSChannel**.

```
- (id)copyWithZone:(NSZone *)zone
{
    RSSChannel *c = [[[self class] alloc] init];

    [c setTitle:[self title]];
    [c setInfoString:[self infoString]];
    c->items = [items mutableCopy];

    return c;
}
```

This method is almost entirely straightforward. A new channel is created, and it is given the same title and infoString as the receiver. Instead of sending **alloc** to **RSSChannel**, we send it to the class of the object being copied, just in case we subclass **RSSChannel**. (Without this, a copy of a subclass would be an instance of **RSSChannel** and not the subclass.)

The curious bit about this method is how the items array is set. We know that an object's instance variables can be accessed directly within one of its methods. To access another object's instance variable, though, you must use an accessor method. However, there is no setter method for a channel's items instance variable, so the channel being copied can't change the items array of its copy. But wait! An Objective-C object is a C structure. When you have a pointer to a structure, you can access its members using the arrow (->).

There are two caveats about accessing an instance variable directly. First, the setter method doesn't get called. This causes a problem if the setter method performs some additional operations on the incoming value. So, if there is a setter method, you should use that instead.

Second, you can't access an instance variable directly whenever you please. The only reason it works here is because you are within the implementation for **RSSChannel**, and the object whose instance variables you are directly accessing is an instance of **RSSChannel**, too. It wouldn't work if, say, **ListViewController** tried to access an instance variable of the **RSSChannel** directly.

This is because instance variables of a class are *protected* from access by other objects. There are three visibility types for instance variables: protected (the default), *private*, and *public*. A protected instance variable can be accessed within the methods of the class it was declared in and all the methods of any subclasses. However, if a method from another class wants to access a protected instance variable, it must use an accessor method.

A private instance variable, on the other hand, can only be accessed within methods for the class it was declared in – not the methods of other classes or even methods of a subclass. A public instance variable can be accessed anywhere using the arrow notation. The syntax for declaring the visibility of instance variables looks like this:

```
@interface MyClass : NSObject
{
    @public
    NSObject *publicVariable;

    @private
    NSObject *privateVariable;

    @protected
    NSObject *protectedVariable;
}
```

In other languages, it is sometimes the case that you change the visibility of an instance variable to suit your needs. In Objective-C, there is rarely a reason to do this, so it's really more trivia than anything. (The one case where @private is used is when framework developers write classes that will be subclassed. This prevents the subclass from modifying a variable directly, and is typically done because the code in the setter method for that variable needs to be executed for things to work out okay. Public instance variables are generally considered a bad idea.)

Finishing the BNR feed

Now that an **RSSChannel** can be copied, you can create the third instance of **RSSChannel** for the store to use for merging the cached and new feeds. In BNRFeedStore.m, update **fetchRSSFeedWithCompletion:**.

```
    if (!cachedChannel)
        cachedChannel = [[RSSChannel alloc] init];

    RSSChannel *channelCopy = [cachedChannel copy];

    [connection setCompletionBlock:^(RSSChannel *obj, NSError *err) {
        if (!err) {
            [cachedChannel addItemsFromChannel:obj];
            [NSKeyedArchiver archiveRootObject:cachedChannel toFile:cachePath];

            [channelCopy addItemsFromChannel:obj];
            [NSKeyedArchiver archiveRootObject:channelCopy toFile:cachePath];
        }

        block(cachedChannel, err);
        block(channelCopy, err);
    }];
```

We can now update **ListViewController**. In ListViewController.m, replace the block that is passed to **fetchRSSFeedWithCompletion:** in fetchEntries.

```
    if (rssType == ListViewControllerRSSTypeBNR) {
        channel = [[BNRFeedStore sharedStore]
                    fetchRSSFeedWithCompletion:completionBlock];
        channel = [[BNRFeedStore sharedStore] fetchRSSFeedWithCompletion:
        ^(RSSChannel *obj, NSError *err) {

            // Replace the activity indicator.
            [[self navigationItem] setTitleView:currentTitleView];

            if (!err) {
                // How many items are there currently?
                int currentItemCount = [[channel items] count];

                // Set our channel to the merged one
                channel = obj;

                // How many items are there now?
                int newItemCount = [[channel items] count];

                // For each new item, insert a new row. The data source
                // will take care of the rest.
                int itemDelta = newItemCount - currentItemCount;
                if (itemDelta > 0) {
                    NSMutableArray *rows = [NSMutableArray array];
                    for (int i = 0; i < itemDelta; i++) {
                        NSIndexPath *ip = [NSIndexPath indexPathForRow:i
                                                            inSection:0];
                        [rows addObject:ip];
                    }

                    [[self tableView] insertRowsAtIndexPaths:rows
                            withRowAnimation:UITableViewRowAnimationTop];
                }
            }
        }];

        [[self tableView] reloadData];
    } else if(rssType == ListViewControllerRSSTypeApple)
        [[BNRFeedStore sharedStore] fetchTopSongs:10 withCompletion:completionBlock];
```

When the **ListViewController** makes a request, it will get back its cached copy as usual and update its table. When the request finishes, it will get the merged channel. It can count the number of items in each channel and determine how many new rows to add to the table view, animating each one in.

Build and run the application. Note the items currently in the BNR feed. Create a new post and refresh the feed. The new post will slide into the table view instead of just appearing out of nowhere. Pretty cool stuff.

Read and Unread Items

Now that you can cache both RSS feeds, let's add another useful feature: when the user selects an **RSSItem**, we want the **ListViewController** to add an indicator to the table that shows that this item has been read (Figure 29.7). Even if the user closes the application, the list of read items should persist. Nerdfeed, then, needs to store the list of read **RSSItem**s on the filesystem.

Figure 29.7   RSSItems marked as read

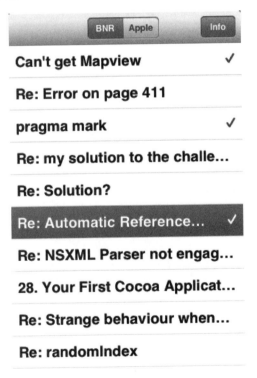

The simplest way to add this feature would be to add a hasBeenRead Boolean instance variable to **RSSItem**. When the user tapped on a row, the corresponding **RSSItem** would change its value of hasBeenRead to YES. For each row in the table, a checkmark would be displayed if the corresponding **RSSItem**'s hasBeenRead variable is YES.

In normal circumstances, this is a great approach, but our plan for Nerdfeed is more ambitious. We'd like users to be able to use Nerdfeed on all of their iOS devices, and if an RSS item is read on one device, then that item should appear as read on every device. Another feature of iOS, iCloud, will allow Nerdfeed to do this with minimal effort.

We'll get into the specifics of iCloud in the next chapter, but here's a brief introduction. iCloud allows documents to be stored in a user's iCloud account instead of in the application sandbox. These documents are then available to all of a user's devices via the cloud. When one device changes one of those documents, every other device sees those changes, so the same application on other devices can read and modify the same document.

While we could store the cached **RSSItem**s in the cloud (along with a "hasBeenRead" flag), this would be a waste of space and bandwidth. The data for the **RSSItem**s is already available on another server, so there is no reason to redundantly store it in the user's iCloud account. Instead, the only data that needs to be shared is the link of each item that has been read (Figure 29.8). (Remember, the link of an item is its URL and is what makes an item unique.)

Figure 29.8   Model diagram for read RSSItem

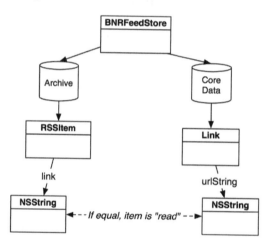

Core Data has iCloud support built in. An application can fetch and insert objects into a Core Data store in the cloud, and other devices will be informed of each change. Thus, maintaining the list of URLs with Core Data will be incredibly efficient: whenever an item is read, its URL will be inserted into the cloud. Other devices will download this small change instead of having to fetch the entire list of read items each time it changes.

In this section, we'll take care of setting up Core Data and storing its SQLite database locally. In the next chapter, we will make the necessary changes to integrate iCloud support.

First, add the CoreData framework to the Nerdfeed target.

Next, add a Core Data model file to Nerdfeed and name it Nerdfeed.xcdatamodeld (Figure 29.9).

Figure 29.9   Adding a Core Data model file

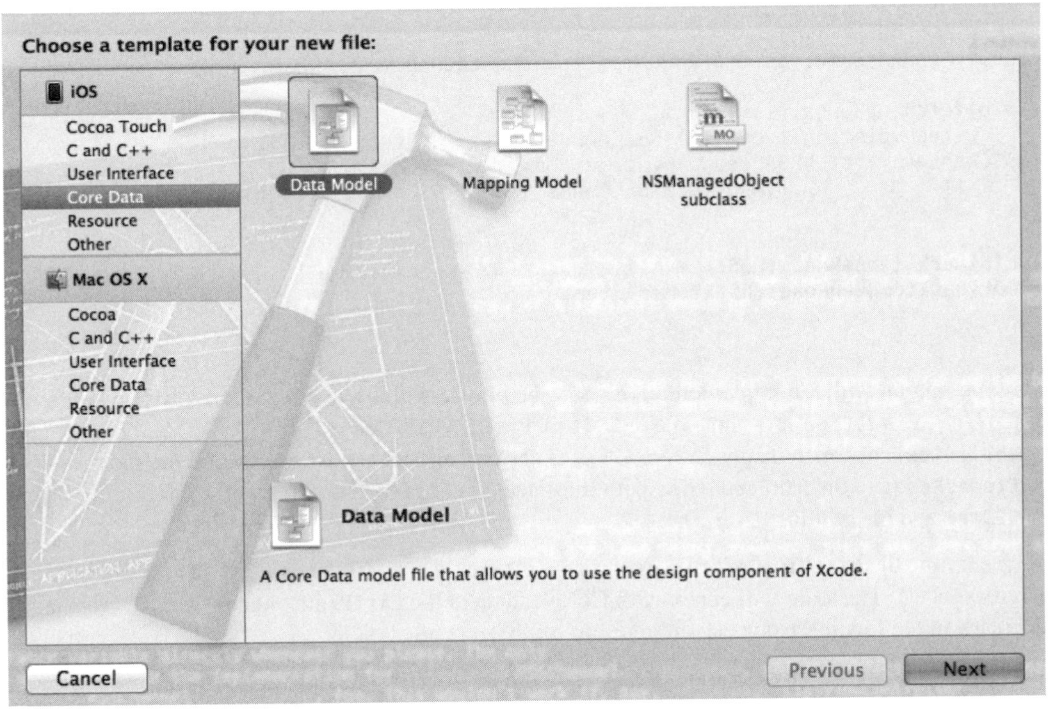

In `Nerdfeed.xcdatamodeld`, add a new entity named `Link` and then add one String attribute named `urlString` (Figure 29.10).

Figure 29.10   The link entity

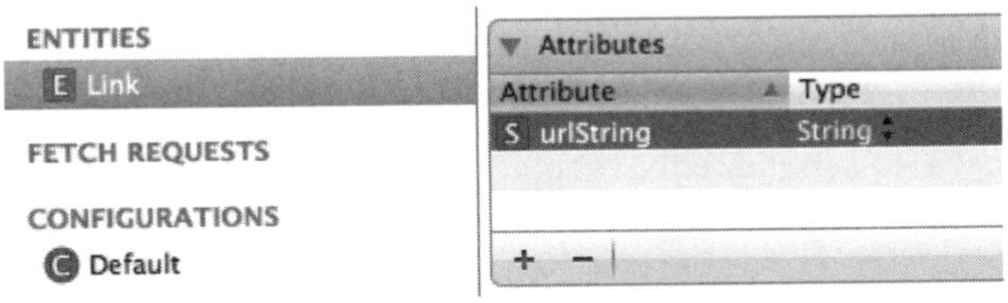

It will be **BNRFeedStore**'s job to manage interacting with Core Data (an external source of data). In `BNRFeedStore.h`, import the header for Core Data and add a forward declaration and a few new instance variables and methods.

```
#import <CoreData/CoreData.h>

@class RSSChannel;

@class RSSItem;

@interface BNRFeedStore : NSObject
{
    NSManagedObjectContext *context;
```

```
      NSManagedObjectModel *model;
}
+ (BNRFeedStore *)sharedStore;

@property (nonatomic, strong) NSDate *topSongsCacheDate;

- (void)fetchTopSongs:(int)count
        withCompletion:(void (^)(RSSChannel *obj, NSError *err))block;
- (RSSChannel *)fetchRSSFeedWithCompletion:
                      (void (^)(RSSChannel *obj, NSError *err))block;


- (void)markItemAsRead:(RSSItem *)item;
- (BOOL)hasItemBeenRead:(RSSItem *)item;

@end
```

Before moving on with the implementation, let's see how it is going to work. Currently, when the user taps on a row that corresponds to an **RSSItem**, the **ListViewController** loads that **RSSItem** into the **WebViewController** to display it. Now, the **ListViewController** will also send the message **markItemAsRead:** to the **BNRFeedStore** with the selected **RSSItem**. The store will grab the link from the **RSSItem** and insert it into Core Data.

Also, each time the **ListViewController** reloads its table, it will ask the store, "Has this item been marked as read?" The store will check with Core Data, and the **ListViewController** will place a checkmark in the row if the corresponding item has been read.

In BNRFeedStore.m, add an **init** method to create the appropriate objects for Core Data to work.

```
- (id)init
{
    self = [super init];
    if (self) {
        model = [NSManagedObjectModel mergedModelFromBundles:nil];

        NSPersistentStoreCoordinator *psc =
        [[NSPersistentStoreCoordinator alloc] initWithManagedObjectModel:model];

        NSError *error = nil;
        NSString *dbPath =
            [NSSearchPathForDirectoriesInDomains(NSDocumentDirectory,
                                    NSUserDomainMask,
                                    YES) objectAtIndex:0];
        dbPath = [dbPath stringByAppendingPathComponent:@"feed.db"];
        NSURL *dbURL = [NSURL fileURLWithPath:dbPath];

        if (![psc addPersistentStoreWithType:NSSQLiteStoreType
                              configuration:nil
                                        URL:dbURL
                                    options:nil
                                      error:&error]) {
            [NSException raise:@"Open failed"
                        format:@"Reason: %@", [error localizedDescription]];
        }

        context = [[NSManagedObjectContext alloc] init];
        [context setPersistentStoreCoordinator:psc];

        [context setUndoManager:nil];
```

```
    }
    return self;
}
```

This code – which is nearly the same as the code in Chapter 16 – sets up the context for inserting and fetching objects. This context works with the persistent store coordinator and its SQLite persistent store to save and load objects to the filesystem.

Now on to implementing the two new methods on the store. First, import RSSItem.h into BNRFeedStore.m.

```
#import "RSSItem.h"
```

Then, in BNRFeedStore.m, implement **markItemAsRead:** to insert a new **Link** entity into Core Data with the URL of the **RSSItem**'s link.

```
- (void)markItemAsRead:(RSSItem *)item
{
    // If the item is already in Core Data, no need for duplicates
    if ([self hasItemBeenRead:item])
        return;

    // Create a new Link object and insert it into the context
    NSManagedObject *obj = [NSEntityDescription
                         insertNewObjectForEntityForName:@"Link"
                                  inManagedObjectContext:context];

    // Set the Link's urlString from the RSSItem
    [obj setValue:[item link] forKey:@"urlString"];

    // immediately save the changes
    [context save:nil];
}
```

In BNRFeedStore.m, implement **hasItemBeenRead:** to return YES if the **RSSItem** passed as an argument has its link stored in Core Data.

```
- (BOOL)hasItemBeenRead:(RSSItem *)item
{
    // Create a request to fetch all Link's with the same urlString as
    // this items link
    NSFetchRequest *req = [[NSFetchRequest alloc] initWithEntityName:@"Link"];

    NSPredicate *pred = [NSPredicate predicateWithFormat:@"urlString like %@",
                          [item link]];
    [req setPredicate:pred];

    // If there is at least one Link, then this item has been read before
    NSArray *entries = [context executeFetchRequest:req error:nil];
    if ([entries count] > 0)
        return YES;

    // If Core Data has never seen this link, then it hasn't been read
    return NO;
}
```

You can build and run now, and the application will work. However, the **ListViewController** does not yet use these methods to update its user interface or tell the store when an item has been read. In

ListViewController.m, add code to the end of **tableView:didSelectRowAtIndexPath:** to mark an item as read when a row is tapped.

```
RSSItem *entry = [[channel items] objectAtIndex:[indexPath row]];

[[BNRFeedStore sharedStore] markItemAsRead:entry];

// Immediately add a checkmark to this row
[[[self tableView] cellForRowAtIndexPath:indexPath]
             setAccessoryType:UITableViewCellAccessoryCheckmark];

[webViewController listViewController:self handleObject:entry];
}
```

Then, modify **tableView:cellForRowAtIndexPath:** in ListViewController.m to put a checkmark on each row whose **RSSItem** has been read.

```
- (UITableViewCell *)tableView:(UITableView *)tableView
        cellForRowAtIndexPath:(NSIndexPath *)indexPath
{
    UITableViewCell *cell = [tableView
                      dequeueReusableCellWithIdentifier:@"UITableViewCell"];
    if (cell == nil) {
        cell = [[UITableViewCell alloc] initWithStyle:UITableViewCellStyleDefault
                                    reuseIdentifier:@"UITableViewCell"];
    }
    RSSItem *item = [[channel items] objectAtIndex:[indexPath row]];
    [[cell textLabel] setText:[item title]];

    if ([[BNRFeedStore sharedStore] hasItemBeenRead:item]) {
        [cell setAccessoryType:UITableViewCellAccessoryCheckmark];
    } else {
        [cell setAccessoryType:UITableViewCellAccessoryNone];
    }

    return cell;
}
```

Build and run the application. Select an item from the table view and note that a checkmark appears in that row. You can shut down the application and load it again – the checkmarks will still be there.

Other Benefits of Store Objects

Now that you've changed Nerdfeed to use a store and added new features involving external sources of data, let's return to the general concept of store objects and the benefits of using them.

The main selling point of store objects is that we move the burden of dealing with external sources of data away from controllers and put all the request logic in one place. This is reason enough to use MVCS, but we've found other benefits of using store objects that we'd like to share.

We can write the controller logic of an application independently of its store logic. This really carries two benefits because the controller and store logic are independent in time and in space.

When beginning a project, sometimes the external sources aren't ready for primetime, and the store logic can't be finalized until the sources are ready. For example, if the external source is a web server, the web service calls may not be able to be written until the project is nearly complete.

Using stores prevents this situation from becoming a scheduling bottleneck. A store object can expose all of its methods to controller objects so that the rest of the application knows what to expect. In addition, the store's actual implementation can provide interim fake data to controllers that make requests.

Once the external source is finalized, the store's implementation can be updated to handle the final details. The good news for the project is, at this point, only the store object must be changed; the rest of the application will work as-is.

Independent store and controller logic also means you can have programmers working independently on each. As long as the interface between them is simple and (ideally) remains unchanged, the programmers that write the store and the programmers that write the controller can work in parallel. This can speed up your project's development.

Typically, the code in a store object is more difficult to write than the code in the controller. Most developers can wire up a controller and its XIB file, but it takes experience to write a good store object. You have to know how to write flexible and robust code. (It also helps to have been through the wringer a few times and seen how things go wrong and how to fix them.) At Big Nerd Ranch, we typically have our senior-level people write store objects and our junior-level people write the controllers and user interface aspects of an application. Smart junior-level people pick up on how the store works and end up becoming senior-level people themselves.

Stores also give the application a unified point of contact with an external source. In addition to things like caching and storing user credentials for web servers that we've already seen or mentioned, there is another bonus: it is easy to test what happens when an application is "offline." Applications that do a lot of their work with a server aren't guaranteed to have Internet access. An application of this type still needs to work – at least somewhat – while offline.

Normally, it is difficult to test what an application will do when it is offline. However, with store objects and their **BNRConnection** friends, it becomes totally simple. You write debug code in **BNRConnection**'s **start** method. When debugging, this method will send the **BNRConnection** the message **connection:didFailWithError:** instead of starting up the connection. This simulates what would occur if the connection actually failed without having to turn off your device or the simulator's Internet connection over and over again.

Bronze Challenge: Pruning the Cache

The cache of **RSSItem**s for the BNR feed can get pretty big. Restrict the cache to 100 entries.

Silver Challenge: Favorites

Add an interface to mark an **RSSItem** as a favorite. Favorites should persist between runs of the application.

Gold Challenge: JSON Caching

Right now, **RSSChannel** and **RSSItem** instances are cached using the archiving data format. Make it so they can also be cached as JSON. (Hint: add another method to **JSONSerializable** for storing an object's instance variables in a dictionary.) The **BNRFeedStore** should cache the Apple feed in JSON format and load it back from that JSON format.

For the More Curious: Designing a Store Object

You have built and used a number of different store objects in this book. In this section, we will analyze these differences and give you a guide for determining how to build store objects in your own applications.

When designing a store object you must answer these questions:

- What external source(s) will it work with?

- Should it be a singleton?

- How will it deliver the results of a request?

Determining external sources

When designing a store, you must first consider what the application is trying to accomplish. How many external sources will there be and of what type? This, in turn, will help you determine how many store objects an application needs.

Should applications have one-to-one correspondences between store objects and external sources? We've seen that's not the case. For example, in Nerdfeed, the store originally worked with one source – the BNR web server. Then we added a request to the iTunes web server. Even though these are two separate requests made to two separate sources, the code for interacting with them is very similar. So, it made sense to have a single store object handle both rather than have two objects with redundant code.

On the other hand, in Homepwner, you had two store objects: the **BNRItemStore** for fetching and saving items and the **BNRImageStore** for fetching and saving images. These two stores handle different types of data and requests. So the request logic was better kept separate in two objects. The **BNRImageStore** was meant to deal with saving and loading images – it wasn't tied to the idea of a **BNRItem** or even Homepwner. Bundling it together with **BNRItemStore** would make for less tidy and reusable code.

Here are some best practices: If parts of an application's request logic can work independently of the rest, then the logic should be split across multiple stores. On the other hand, if an application's request logic contains chunks of similar code – even if it's interacting with several external sources, then it is best to keep the logic in one tidy class. Doing so makes your code easier to read, maintain, debug, and reuse when possible.

Once you have determined how many stores an application should have and what external sources they will be dealing with, then you can start designing individual stores according to what they need to accomplish. For example, in Nerdfeed, the store needs to fetch two RSS feeds. So it must know how to work with a web server in general and the BNR and iTunes web servers in particular. Another example is the **BNRImageStore** in Homepwner. That store object needed to know how access and store images in a cache on the filesystem.

Determining singleton status

The next item on the agenda is whether a store should be a singleton or instantiable. The stores you've created have all been singletons, but you used a store object that was not: a **CLLocationManager**. What's the difference? In Whereami, an instance of **CLLocationManager**s had options. It could tune how accurate it was or how often it updated a controller. If a store needs to offer these kinds of options, then it's best to allow multiple instances of it to be created.

Another thing you should consider is whether a store needs to maintain a cache of data. If it does, then it should be a singleton so that every controller can have access to the same cache. This is the reason the stores you've created have been singletons. BNRItemStore, BNRImageStore, and BNRFeedStore all maintained caches of data.

You can think of login credentials for a web service as similar to a cache. Both are "data that a store is required to maintain." It doesn't make sense to make multiple instances of a store that maintains login credentials because you would be maintaining multiple copies of the same data.

Determining how to deliver results

The final option you must consider for store objects is how they deliver their response, and the first step to answering this question is determining whether a store will be synchronous (have its results available immediately) or asynchronous (need a little time to obtain its results). The best example of a synchronous store is an object that accesses the filesystem. The code may be complicated, but the request will be processed without any delay. If you have a synchronous store, you should have it deliver its response to the controller simply by returning a value from the request method. No muss, no fuss.

With asynchronous stores, there are more choices. The two big ones are delegation and blocks. The choice between these two depends partly on the store object's singleton status. A singleton store should *not* use delegation because it would limit the store to returning data to one controller at a time. Instead, a singleton store can return its data in a block supplied by the requesting controller. A store that can be instantiated can use either delegation or blocks.

For the More Curious: Automatic Caching and Cache.db

While in Nerdfeed's sandbox, you may have noticed a file named Cache.db. This file contains data that resembles the XML and JSON returned from the RSS web services. iOS applications keep the data from web service requests here. When an HTTP request is made, the response from the server may tell the application, "This data will be good for a day, so don't bother me again in the meantime." An iOS application has built-in behavior to understand this response and to cache the data returned in the Cache.db file until it "expires."

Earlier in the chapter, when asking repeatedly for Apple's top songs feed, you may have noticed that the repeated requests returned very quickly – even before we implemented caching of our own. This was automatic caching at work. Automatic caching is especially useful for loading web pages, and it is what makes Safari run reasonably fast even on an iOS device.

So why, then, did we write our own caching mechanism for the RSS feeds? For applications that interact with web services and present data in their own views, automatic caching is not useful for two reasons. The first is that you have no control over the Cache.db file and its caching process, like what data gets saved and for how long.

The other reason is that automatic caching stores all of the data from a web service request in the format in which it was delivered. Using this cached data, then, would be a step backward for us in

Nerdfeed. For example, in retrieving the BNR form feed from the web server, we already parse a subset of XML into **RSSItem** instances from the response. So we're better off caching data in **RSSItem**s for later retrieval than using the data in Cache.db, which we'd have to figure out how to read, load, and parse again from scratch.

It doesn't usually harm anything to let an iOS application keep a cache even if you are keeping one of your own. Sometimes, though, it is a problem. This is the case when your application downloads large files, like images and PDFs. The application will not only save these big files to the filesystem, but it might also keep them in memory for a long time.

For example, if you created an application that downloads and renders PDFs, it might store those PDFs in its own cache and then render them. Rendering a PDF is really memory-intensive, and if the built-in cache is keeping another copy of the PDF file for itself, your application may run out of memory and be shut down.

Therefore, you may want to selectively cache data or just remove built-in caching altogether. To do this, you create a subclass of **NSURLCache** and override **storeCachedResponse:forRequest:**.

```
@implementation BNRURLCache
- (void)storeCachedResponse:(NSCachedURLResponse *)cachedResponse
                 forRequest:(NSURLRequest *)request
{
    // If the file isn't a pdf, store it as normal, otherwise, ignore it
    if (![[[request URL] pathExtension] isEqualToString:@"pdf"])
        [super storeCachedResponse:cachedResponse forRequest:request];
}
@end
```

If you wanted to entirely remove caching, you would override this same method and not enter any code in the body.

Then, when your application starts up, you tell **NSURLCache** that the default caching object is an instance of your subclass.

```
BNRURLCache *uc = [[BNRURLCache alloc] init];
[NSURLCache setSharedURLCache:uc];
```

30

iCloud

iCloud is a service that is available on every iOS device running iOS 5 or later. At its most basic level, iCloud is a mechanism for storing files "in the cloud," i.e. one or many remote servers. iCloud ties the stored data to a particular user in individual iCloud accounts. When you purchase an iOS device, you set that device up with your iCloud account. If you own other devices, you can associate them with your account, too. The shared data in the iCloud is available only to the user logged into the device. If another user logs into the device (which is rare), access to the original user's iCloud data is removed.

There are two big features of iOS that use iCloud – key-value storage and document storage.

Key-value storage allows an application to synchronize preferences-like data across devices. For example, an application that allowed you to read books from a bookshelf might use this feature. You could begin reading a book on your iPad. If you later opened this application on your iPhone, it would open directly to the same book right where you left off reading on your iPad. The current book and location would be the data stored in iCloud. This type of data is stored and retrieved using the class **NSUbiquitousKeyValueStore**, which works much like **NSUserDefaults**.

Document storage lets you manage individual documents across the user's devices. For example, an application might allow you to create and edit spreadsheets. You could create a spreadsheet on an iPhone and then edit it on an iPad. When you next opened the spreadsheet on the iPhone, the changes from the iPad would be there. This feature is exposed through the classes **UIDocument**, **NSFileCoordinator**, **NSMetadataQuery**, and the protocol NSFilePresenter.

Core Data leverages iCloud's document storage to synchronize a Core Data SQLite file across a number of iOS devices. In this chapter, you will synchronize the read list for Nerdfeed across all of the user's devices using Core Data's built-in iCloud behavior.

iCloud Requirements

The code you will write in this chapter is relatively straightforward, but there are some things you need to do first to be able to write that code.

- You must have a device to run Nerdfeed on; iCloud doesn't work on the simulator. In fact, you really need *two* iOS devices to realistically test if the read list has been shared correctly between devices.

- You must be an administrator or team agent in Apple's iOS Developer Program to create the provisioning profile required for iCloud use. (We'll set up this provisioning profile in a moment.)

- You must have an iCloud account set up and have iCloud enabled on your test devices. To see how to set up your iCloud account, visit http://www.apple.com/icloud/setup/. To enable iCloud on a device, go to the Settings, select iCloud, and follow the instructions.

Make sure you have met these requirements before continuing. If not, the changes you are about to make to Nerdfeed will no longer allow it to run on your device.

Ubiquity Containers

Now on to the fun stuff. So far, you know that every file that an application saves and loads is within the application's sandbox. These files are only available to the application that owns the sandbox, and they only exist on the device on which they were created. iCloud changes this situation with special directories called *ubiquity containers*.

You can think of a ubiquity container as a folder that lives on Apple's iCloud servers. An iOS device keeps a local copy of the ubiquity container on its filesystem. When an iOS device makes changes to the files in its local copy, those changes are automatically uploaded to the actual ubiquity container in the cloud. Any other device that has access to that ubiquity container then transfers the changes to its local copy (Figure 30.1).

Figure 30.1   Ubiquity containers

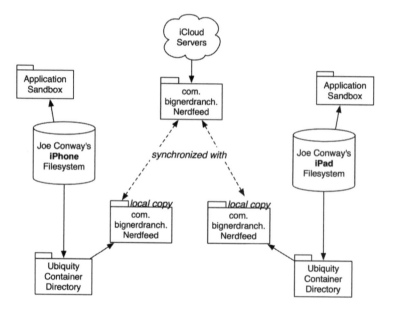

A ubiquity container has a unique identifier called a *container identifier string*. If an application knows the identifier string for a ubiquity container, then it has access to the files within it. To give an application access to the ubiquity container, you add the container identifier string to the list of *entitlements* for the application.

In the project navigator, select the Nerdfeed project and then the Summary tab for the Nerdfeed target. Find the Entitlements section and check the Enable Entitlements box on (Figure 30.2).

Figure 30.2 Turning on iCloud entitlements

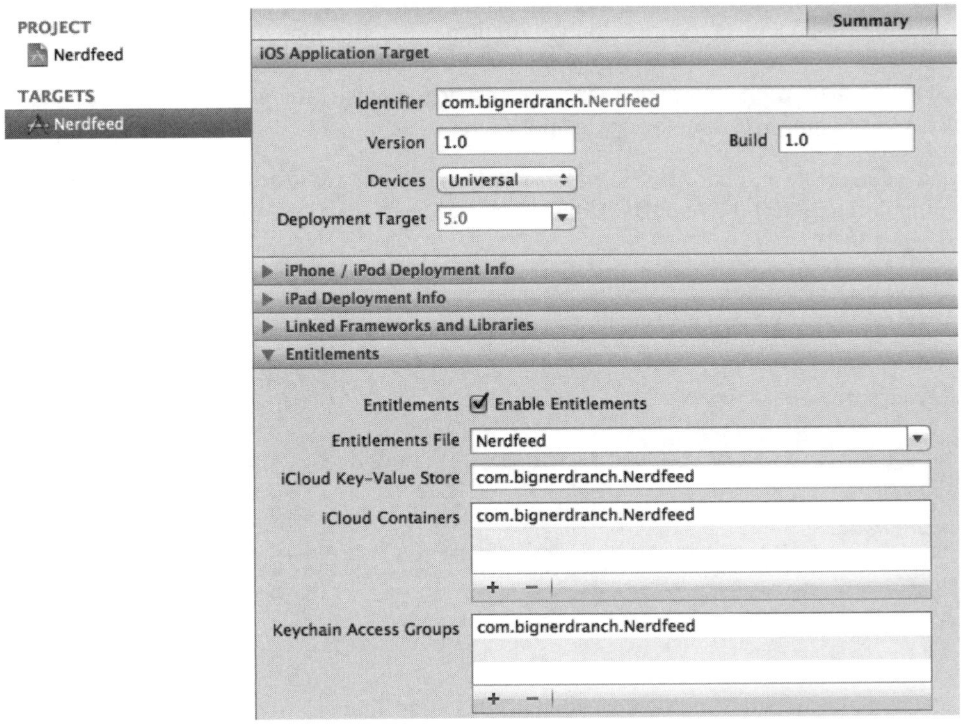

Checking this box on turns on entitlements for Nerdfeed. An entitlement is essentially permission to access a secure resource, like a ubiquity container or the device's encrypted keychain.

By default, turning on entitlements gives the application access to a ubiquity container with an identifier string that is the same as the application's bundle (as shown in the iCloud Containers table in Figure 30.2). Thus, Nerdfeed now has access to the com.bignerdranch.Nerdfeed ubiquity container in iCloud.

Giving an application access to a ubiquity container has two purposes. First, ubiquity containers allow an application to share data with other applications. This is often used for a suite of applications developed by the same company. For example, an application that created presentations could access the ubiquity container for an application that created spreadsheets, and the spreadsheet could be imported into the presentation. Better yet, because multiple devices can run the same application, the spreadsheet could even be created on a different device than the presentation.

The other purpose of ubiquity containers is to give all of the user's devices that an application runs on access to the same set of data. Thus, if a user has an iPad and an iPhone, the Nerdfeed application can access the same ubiquity container on both devices. (Remember the ubiquity container is unique to the logged in iCloud user – you can only share between devices that have the same iCloud account.)

Nerdfeed will store its Core Data information (the list of read item URLs) in the com.bignerdranch.Nerdfeed ubiquity container. When this application is run on multiple devices, the same information will be available on all of them. Then users will be able to keep track of which items they have read no matter what device they are using Nerdfeed on.

Provisioning a Ubiquity Container

Since a ubiquity container is a secure resource, Apple needs a guarantee that an application really should be allowed to access that resource. Setting up the entitlement for the ubiquity container was the first step, but there is one more: you must create a new provisioning profile and then use that entitlements-aware profile to sign the application.

Thus, we need to create another App ID and provisioning profile for Nerdfeed. Log into Apple's iOS Provisioning Portal. Select the App IDs item from the lefthand side of the portal and then click New App ID (Figure 30.3).

Figure 30.3   Creating a new App ID

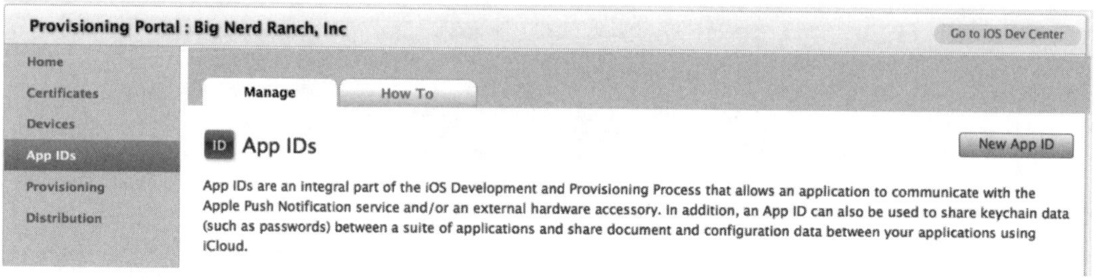

On the next screen, name the App ID Nerdfeed. Choose Use Team ID from the pop-up button. In the Bundle Identifier section, enter com.bignerdranch.Nerdfeed. Click Submit.

You will be taken back to the list of all App IDs in your profile. Locate Nerdfeed and click the Configure link next to it. On the next screen, check the box for Enable for iCloud (Figure 30.4) and click Submit.

Figure 30.4   Selecting an App ID

| U83L3WE5MK.com.bignerdran...
Nerdfeed | ⊜ Configurable for Development
⊜ Configurable for Production | ⊜ Enabled | ⊜ Enabled | ⊜ Enabled | Configure |

| ☑ **Enable for iCloud** | ⊜ Enabled |

Next, click on the Provisioning item on the lefthand side of the portal and select New Profile. Configure the profile to have the name Nerdfeed and select the Nerdfeed App ID from the pop-up button, as shown in Figure 30.5. Make sure to check the boxes for your certificate and the devices you plan to deploy to. (It doesn't hurt to add more devices and certificates than necessary.)

Figure 30.5   Nerdfeed provisioning profile

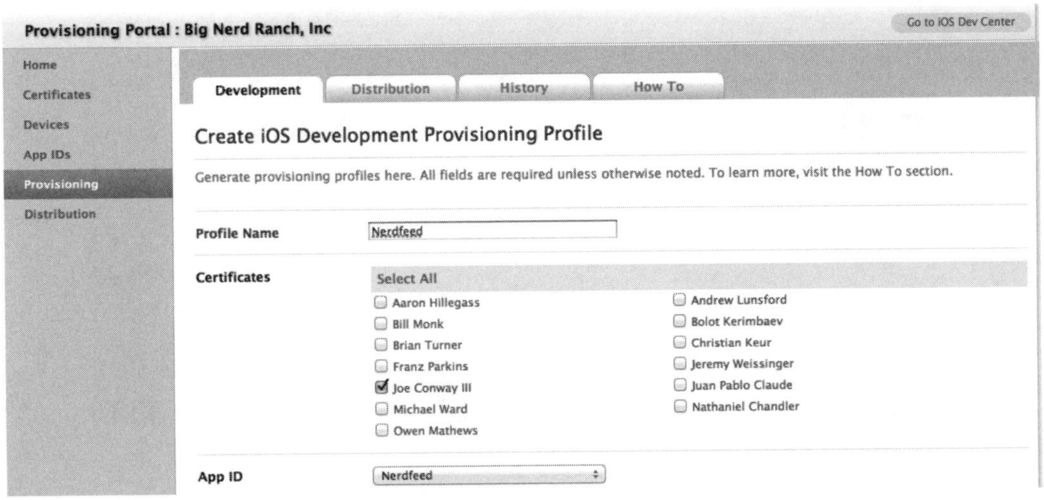

Click Done, and you will be taken back to the list of all provisioning profiles in your portal. Locate the Nerdfeed profile and click the Download button next to it. (If it says Pending next to the profile, refresh the page.)

Locate this provisioning profile in the Finder and drag its icon onto the Xcode icon. This will add the provisioning profile to the list that Xcode maintains.

Now you need to add this profile to your device. Open the Organizer window from the Window menu. Select Devices from the tab on top of the window and then Provisioning Profiles from the Library heading in the lefthand table.

With the device plugged in, drag the Nerdfeed profile from the Library in the organizer to the device in the lefthand table (Figure 30.6).

Figure 30.6   Adding a provisioning profile to a device

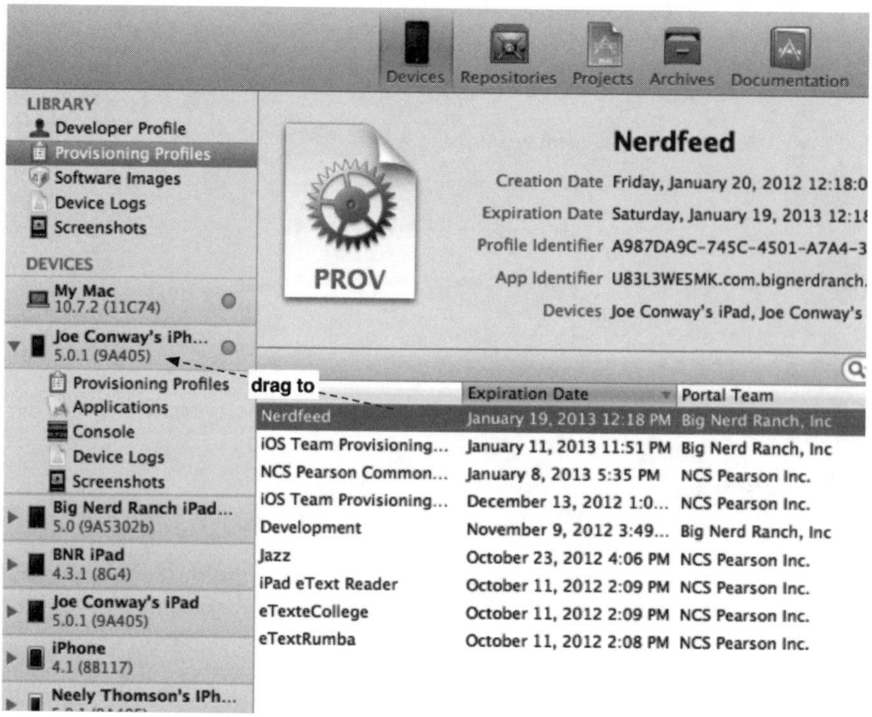

Now that this device has the new provisioning profile, it can run applications that have been signed with it. Repeat these steps for any device that you plan to run Nerdfeed on.

Time to sign your application. Select the Nerdfeed project from the project navigator and then select the Nerdfeed target. In the Build Settings tab, locate the Code Signing Identity field. Change this property to the Nerdfeed provisioning profile (Figure 30.7). The Nerdfeed application is now signed with the Nerdfeed provisioning profile.

Figure 30.7   Changing an application's provisioning profile

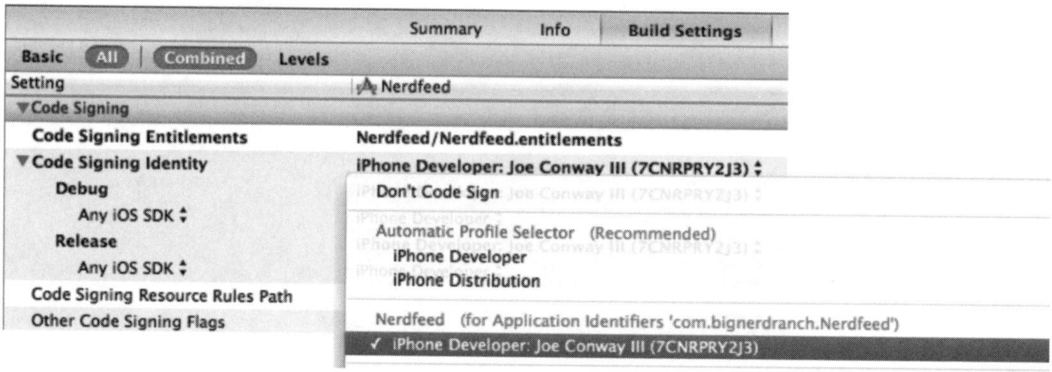

(If you cannot select the Nerdfeed provisioning profile from this list, it is because the Nerdfeed application doesn't have the bundle identifier com.bignerdranch.Nerdfeed. Make sure that the provisioning profile App ID matches the bundle identifier of Nerdfeed exactly – including case.)

Now that Nerdfeed is signed with the new provisioning profile, it can write to and read from the `com.bignerdranch.Nerdfeed` ubiquity container. Build and run the application to the device you have provisioned. The behavior of the application won't change, but when it runs, you will get confirmation that you have properly set up the ubiquity container and associated provisioning profiles correctly. Finally, we can begin writing the code.

Core Data and iCloud

So far, you know that iCloud keeps files in a ubiquity container in the cloud and that iOS devices with access to that ubiquity container pull down copies of that file and push back any edits. However, Core Data does something a little different.

Core Data is an interface to a single SQLite library file, so you might think we would store this file in the cloud. But this is a bad idea because a SQLite file can be very large and changing the data inside the file would require uploading *the whole file* to the cloud and downloading the whole thing to each device.

Instead, the SQLite file that Core Data talks to remains on the device's local filesystem, and Core Data stores a *transaction log file* in the cloud. When a change is made with Core Data, the change occurs in the local SQLite file and is noted in the transaction log file. Other devices pull the transaction log file down and use the information in it to modify their own SQLite file.

When setting up a Core Data persistent store, you can specify that it read from a transaction log stored in a ubiquity container. In BNRFeedStore.m, add the following code to **init**.

```
- (id)init
{
    self = [super init];
    if (self) {
        model = [NSManagedObjectModel mergedModelFromBundles:nil];

        NSPersistentStoreCoordinator *psc =
        [[NSPersistentStoreCoordinator alloc] initWithManagedObjectModel:model];

        // Find the location of the ubiquity container on the local filesystem
        NSFileManager *fm = [NSFileManager defaultManager];
        NSURL *ubContainer = [fm URLForUbiquityContainerIdentifier:nil];

        // Construct the dictionary that tells Core Data where the
        // transaction log should be stored
        NSMutableDictionary *options = [NSMutableDictionary dictionary];
        [options setObject:@"nerdfeed"
                    forKey:NSPersistentStoreUbiquitousContentNameKey];
        [options setObject:ubContainer
                    forKey:NSPersistentStoreUbiquitousContentURLKey];

        NSError *error = nil;
        NSString *dbPath =
            [NSSearchPathForDirectoriesInDomains(NSDocumentDirectory,
                                                 NSUserDomainMask,
                                                 YES) objectAtIndex:0];
        dbPath = [dbPath stringByAppendingPathComponent:@"feed.db"];
        NSURL *dbURL = [NSURL fileURLWithPath:dbPath];
```

```
    if (![psc addPersistentStoreWithType:NSSQLiteStoreType
                        configuration:nil
                            URL:dbURL
                        options:nil
                            error:&error]) {
        [NSException raise:@"Open failed"
                        format:@"Reason: %@", [error localizedDescription]];
    }

    // Set up the persistent store with the transaction log details
    if (![psc addPersistentStoreWithType:NSSQLiteStoreType
                        configuration:nil
                            URL:dbURL
                        options:options
                            error:&error]) {
        [NSException raise:@"Open failed"
                        format:@"Reason: %@", [error localizedDescription]];
    }

    context = [[NSManagedObjectContext alloc] init];
    [context setPersistentStoreCoordinator:psc];

    [context setUndoManager:nil];
    }
    return self;
}
```

Build the application to check for syntax errors, but don't run it quite yet.

Notice here that you created an **NSURL** instance with **URLForUbiquityContainerIdentifier:**. This method of **NSFileManager** returns the location of the ubiquity container on the device. The argument passed to this method is a container identifier string. While you could pass the container identifier string you set up in the previous section, it is easier to pass nil. Passing nil automatically constructs the container identifier using the application's bundle identifier, in our case, com.bignerdranch.Nerdfeed. (Technically, you have to pass a slightly different string. There's more about this in the section called "For the More Curious: iCloud Backups".)

Next, a dictionary is created with two key-value pairs. The first key, NSPersistentStoreUbiquitousContentNameKey, is the name of the transaction log in the ubiquity container. This name must be unique within the ubiquity container. It is used in conjunction with the NSPersistentStoreUbiquitousContentURLKey that identifies the location on the filesystem of the ubiquity container. In simple terms, it creates a transaction log file named nerdfeed in the directory that ubContainer represents. (Technically, it's a little more complicated.) This dictionary is passed as the options for **addPersistentStoreWithType:configuration:URL:options:error:**.

We have set up Core Data to store its SQLite file in the application sandbox and its transaction log in a ubiquity container. Whenever a device modifies its SQLite file with Core Data, the changes are automatically written to the transaction log in the ubiquity container and synchronized with iCloud.

However, other devices do not automatically update their SQLite file with the changes in the transaction log. To make this happen, **BNRFeedStore** needs to watch the transaction log for changes. When a change occurs, the store will merge those changes into its own version of the Core Data SQLite file.

Fortunately, this is pretty easy: whenever a change occurs, the notification NSPersistentStoreDidImportUbiquitousContentChangesNotification is posted to the

NSNotificationCenter. The store can register as an observer for this notification. In BNRFeedStore.m, modify **init** to register for this notification.

```
- (id)init
{
    self = [super init];
    if (self) {
        [[NSNotificationCenter defaultCenter]
            addObserver:self
                selector:@selector(contentChange:)
                    name:NSPersistentStoreDidImportUbiquitousContentChangesNotification
                object:nil];

        model = [NSManagedObjectModel mergedModelFromBundles:nil];
```

This notification will be posted whenever the transaction log is changed by another device. If Nerdfeed isn't running on a device when the transaction log is changed, this notification will be posted as soon as the device starts running Nerdfeed again.

When this notification is posted, Core Data needs merge the changes into its local SQLite file. To merge the changes, all we have to do is pass the **NSNotification** object that represents this notification directly to the Core Data context. In BNRFeedStore.m, implement the message sent to **BNRFeedStore** when this notification occurs.

```
- (void)contentChange:(NSNotification *)note
{
    // merge changes into context
    [context mergeChangesFromContextDidSaveNotification:note];
}
```

Nerdfeed now appropriately handles a Core Data SQLite file that lives in the cloud. But there are a few more changes we can make to get things running more smoothly.

First, when the change notification is posted, the store updates its records, but Nerdfeed's user interface is not immediately updated. A store should always notify controllers when it changes the data it returned to them, so **BNRFeedStore** will post a notification whenever it merges changes from the iCloud transaction log. In BNRFeedStore.h, declare a new string that will serve as the notification name.

```
@class RSSChannel;
@class RSSItem;

extern NSString * const BNRFeedStoreUpdateNotification;

@interface BNRFeedStore : NSObject
```

This declares a new global variable named BNRFeedStoreUpdateNotification. The const after the star (*) says that once this variable is initialized to point at an object, it cannot be changed to point at any other object. The extern says that this variable is declared in this file but will be defined elsewhere. That elsewhere is BNRFeedStore.m. In BNRFeedStore.m, define this variable.

```
#import "RSSItem.h"

NSString * const BNRFeedStoreUpdateNotification = @"BNRFeedStoreUpdateNotification";

@implementation BNRFeedStore
```

Whenever **BNRFeedStore** merges the changes in Core Data, it will post this notification. The **ListViewController** will register as an observer for this notification and update the table view when the notification is received. However, there is a small issue: **BNRFeedStore** is told to perform the merge on a background thread, so the notification will be posted and received on a background thread as well. This will sometimes cause a delay between the merge in Core Data and the updating of the table view.

Thus, we want to post the BNRFeedStoreUpdateNotification on the main thread. In BNRFeedStore.m, post this notification on the main thread in **contentChange:**.

```
- (void)contentChange:(NSNotification *)note
{
    [context mergeChangesFromContextDidSaveNotification:note];

    [[NSOperationQueue mainQueue] addOperationWithBlock:^{
        NSNotification *updateNote =
            [NSNotification notificationWithName:BNRFeedStoreUpdateNotification
                                         object:nil];
        [[NSNotificationCenter defaultCenter] postNotification:updateNote];
    }];
}
```

Now, in ListViewController.m, register as an observer of this notification in **initWithStyle:**.

```
- (id)initWithStyle:(UITableViewStyle)style
{
    self = [super initWithStyle:style];

    if (self) {
        [[NSNotificationCenter defaultCenter] addObserver:self
                                   selector:@selector(storeUpdated:)
                                       name:BNRFeedStoreUpdateNotification
                                     object:nil];
```

In ListViewController.m, implement **storeUpdated:**.

```
- (void)storeUpdated:(NSNotification *)note
{
    [[self tableView] reloadData];
}
```

You could build and run the application now, but there is one more minor change to make. Currently, the SQLite file is stored in the Documents directory of Nerdfeed's sandbox. This is okay except for one case: if another iCloud user logs in on this device, this user will have the same read list as the previous user because the SQLite file is stored in a location that is specific to the application not the iCloud user.

To make the SQLite file user-specific, we can move it into the ubiquity container but mark it so that it will not get stored in the cloud. We can tell iCloud to ignore a file or directory in a ubiquity container by suffixing it with .nosync. In BNRFeedStore.m, update **init** to create a feed.nosync directory and put the SQLite file in that directory.

```
NSMutableDictionary *options = [NSMutableDictionary dictionary];
[options setObject:@"nerdfeed" forKey:NSPersistentStoreUbiquitousContentNameKey];
[options setObject:ubContainer forKey:NSPersistentStoreUbiquitousContentURLKey];
```

```
NSError *error = nil;
NSString *dbPath =
    [NSSearchPathForDirectoriesInDomains(NSDocumentDirectory,
                                         NSUserDomainMask,
                                         YES) objectAtIndex:0];
dbPath = [dbPath stringByAppendingPathComponent:@"feed.db"];
NSURL *dbURL = [NSURL fileURLWithPath:dbPath];

// Specify a new directory and create it in the ubiquity container
NSURL *nosyncDir = [ubContainer URLByAppendingPathComponent:@"feed.nosync"];
[fm createDirectoryAtURL:nosyncDir
    withIntermediateDirectories:YES
                     attributes:nil
                          error:nil];

// Specify the new file to store Core Data's SQLite file
NSURL *dbURL = [nosyncDir URLByAppendingPathComponent:@"feed.db"];

if (![psc addPersistentStoreWithType:NSSQLiteStoreType
                       configuration:nil
                                 URL:dbURL
                             options:options
                               error:&error]) {
    [NSException raise:@"Open failed"
                format:@"Reason: %@", [error localizedDescription]];
}
```

Finally, we can test our work. Build and run Nerdfeed on a device. Click Stop in Xcode, and then build and run on another device. Restart the application on the first device, and select a row from the table view. After a few moments, you will see the checkmark appear in that row on the other device!

One thing to keep in mind when using iCloud-capable applications is that deleting an application does not delete the data from Apple's servers. Sometimes when developing an iCloud application, you will need to change the structure of your data and delete the old data structure from the cloud.

To delete an application's data from the cloud, open the Settings application on the device and select iCloud. Next, select Storage & Backup near the bottom of the next screen and then Manage Storage. You will see a screen that looks like Figure 30.8.

Figure 30.8   Managing iCloud Storage

Every iCloud-capable application on a device will appear on this screen under Documents & Data. When developing an application, its name is not yet registered with Apple's servers, so it will appear as Unknown. To delete the data associated with an application you are developing, tap the Unknown row. Then, tap the Edit button. A big Delete All button will appear – tap it to remove the data from the iCloud servers.

You only have to delete data from iCloud's storage from one device because all devices share the same data.

For the More Curious: iCloud Backups

Although not an explicit feature of iCloud, iOS supports backing up the contents of a device in the cloud. Part of the backup process synchronizes the Documents and Library/Preferences directories of each application sandbox. This is pretty neat, but you can't go hog wild. This ability to back up data in Documents/ in the cloud has led to a new requirement for applications: you can't store too much data in the Documents directory on pain of your application being rejected by the App Store.

Of course, "too much data" is frustratingly vague, but the general rule is only store in Documents/ what really needs backing up and not what can be recreated. Data that can be recreated should be stored in Library/Caches/ instead of Documents/.

However, there is a problem with this rule. The system can purge the contents Library/Caches/ when an application is running low on disk space, and it can do so without warning. Now, if an application can recreate its caches from another server, it's not a big deal if this directory gets purged – you just download the content again. However, some applications cache content for offline use. For example, an application could download web articles so that the user can read them on a plane. If the application is offline, data that gets purged can't be recreated.

If you need to store potentially large amounts offline content indefinitely, the fix is to put the data in Documents/ *and* set a special flag that prevents the file or the folder and its contents from being backed up. This protects the data from being purged and keeps the App Store happy. You set this flag like so:

```
NSArray *docsDirs = NSSearchPathForDirectoriesInDomains(NSDocumentDirectory,
                                                        NSUserDomainMask,
                                                        YES);
NSString *path = [[docsDirs objectAtIndex:0]
                        stringByAppendingPathComponent:@"somefile"];

[data writeToFile:path atomically:YES];

NSURL *url = [NSURL fileURLWithPath:path];
[url setResourceValue:[NSNumber numberWithBool:YES]
            forKey:NSURLIsExcludedFromBackupKey
             error:nil];
```

The important bit here is the key NSURLIsExcludedFromBackupKey. This key can be set on any URL (file or folder) in an application's sandbox and prevent it from being backed up. Note that this flag is not the same as the .nosync suffix, which prevents a file or folder in a ubiquity container from being synchronized in the cloud.

31
Afterword

Welcome to the end of the book! You should be very proud of all your work and all that you have learned. Now, there's good news and bad news:

- *The good news:* The stuff that leaves programmers befuddled when they come to the iOS platform is behind you now. You are an iOS developer.

- *The bad news:* You are probably not a very good iOS developer.

What to do next

It is now time to make some mistakes, read some really tedious documentation, and be humbled by the heartless experts who will ridicule your questions. Here's what we recommend:

Write apps now. If you don't immediately use what you have learned, it will fade. Exercise and extend your knowledge. Now.

Go deep. This book has consistently favored breadth over depth; any chapter could have been expanded into an entire book. Find a topic that you find interesting and really wallow in it – do some experiments, read Apple's docs on the topic, read a posting on a blog or on StackOverflow.

Connect. There is an iOS Developer Meetup in most cities, and the talks are surprisingly good. There are discussion groups online. If you are doing a project, find people to help you: designers, testers (AKA guinea pigs), and other developers.

Make mistakes and fix them. You will learn a lot the days you say, "This application has become a ball of crap! I'm going to throw it away and write it again with an architecture that makes sense." Polite programmers call this *refactoring*.

Give back. Share the knowledge. Answer a dumb question with grace. Give away some code.

Shameless plugs

You can find us both on Twitter, where we keep you informed about programming and entertained about life: @joeconwaybnr and @aaronhillegass.

Keep an eye out for future guides from Big Nerd Ranch. We also offer week-long courses for developers. And if you just need some code written, we do contract programming. For more information, visit our website at http://www.bignerdranch.com/.

It is you, dear reader, who makes our lives of writing, coding, and teaching possible. So thank you for buying our book.

Index

Symbols

#import, 55
%@ prefix, 37
.h files, 41
.m files, 41, 44
@ prefix
    creating strings with, 36
    and Objective-C keywords, 42
@autoreleasepool, 79
@class, 195
@end, 42
@implementation, 44
@interface, 42
@optional, 89
@private, 543
@property, 72
@protected, 543
@protocol, 88
@public, 543
@selector(), 235
@synthesize, 74
^, 486
_cmd, 292
__block, 497, 498
__bridge, 253, 254
__unsafe_unretained, 71
__weak, 70

A

accessor methods, 43-46, 72
    (see also properties)
accessory indicator (**UITableViewCell**), 198
action methods, 15-17
    connecting in XIB file, 242-244
    and **UIControl**, 365-366
active state, 287
actor objects, 512, 513
addAnimation:forKey:, 417
addObject:, 35, 38
addSubview:, 125, 128
alloc, 30-31, 193
Allocations instrument, 381-387
allocWithZone:, 193
analyzing (code), 379-381

angled brackets, 120
animation transactions, 406
animationDidStop:finished:, 418
animations, 411
    (see also **CALayer**, layers)
    CABasicAnimation, 412-413, 415-417, 420
    CAKeyframeAnimation, 413, 418-420
    choosing, 415
    classes of, 399, 411-414
    and data types, 413
    identity matrices in, 420
    implicit, 405-406
    key paths of, 411, 415
    keyframes in, 414-416
    keys for, 417
    reusing, 417
    timing functions of, 417-418
animationWithKeyPath:, 417
anonymous functions (see blocks)
anti-aliasing, 170
API Reference, 110-114
APIs, 399
    (see also frameworks)
    Core Animation, 399, 403, 412
    Core Foundation, 252, 253-254
App ID, 23
Apple documentation, 110-114
application bundle, 282, 296-298, 348
application delegates, 11, 170
application dock, 287
application domain, 354
application sandbox, 281-283, 296
application states, 286-288, 292-293
application:didFinishLaunchingWithOptions:, 123, 170
applicationDidBecomeActive:, 293
applicationDidEnterBackground:, 284, 288, 293
applications, 20
    (see also debugging, universal applications)
    adding frameworks to, 82
    allowing orientations, 184
    build settings for, 395-397
    building, 20, 45, 82, 97-101, 346
    cleaning, 346
    data storage, 281-282, 338
    deploying, 22-23
    directories in, 281-283

SOFTWARE

TRAINING

CONSULTING

Achieve Nerdvana

ABOUT US

BiG
nerD
ranch

THE BIG NERD STORY

Big Nerd Ranch exists to broaden the minds of our students and the businesses of our clients. Whether we are training talented individuals or developing a company's mobile strategy, our core philosophy is integral to everything we do.

The brainchild of CEO Aaron Hillegass, Big Nerd Ranch has hosted more than 2,000 students at the Ranch since its inception in 2001. Over the past ten years, we have had the opportunity to work with some of the biggest companies in the world such as Apple, Samsung, Nokia, Google, AOL, Los Alamos National Laboratory and Adobe, helping them realize their programming goals. Our team of software engineers are among the brightest in the business and it shows in our work. We have developed dozens of innovative and flexible solutions for our clients.

The Story Behind the Hat

Back in 2001, Big Nerd Ranch founder, Aaron Hillegass, showed up at WWDC (World Wide Developers Conference) to promote the Big Nerd Ranch brand. Without the money to buy an expensive booth, Aaron donned a ten-gallon cowboy hat to draw attention while passing out Big Nerd literature to prospective students and clients. A week later, we landed our first big client and the cowboy hat has been synonymous with the Big Nerd brand ever since. Already easily recognizable at 6'5, Aaron can be spotted wearing his cowboy hat at speaking engagements and conferences all over the world.

The New Ranch – Opening 2012

In the continuing effort to perfect the student experience, Big Nerd Ranch is building its own facility. Located just 20 minutes from the Atlanta airport, the new Ranch will be a monastic learning center that encompasses Aaron Hillegass' vision for technical education featuring a state-of-the-art classroom, fine dining and exercise facilities.